RINGING THE LIBERTY BELL

A Third Party Challenge for the Presidency

BY

Bert Nemcik

Lifelong Learning Network

Abridged Version 1

TABLE OF CONTENTS

Dedication

To my Mother, who gave me the love of learning, politics and the joy of challenging conventional thinking. Though she died before I finished this book, her spirit was with me all the way.

Acknowledgments

Many people contribute to a person's development and each one provides something to character development. We call these people, role models. I have many. My father taught me "if it can be done, I can do it ". He modelled for me how to continue even when doubting that the outcome will be what he wanted. My grandmother gave me a green thumb and the ability to take a seed, plant it, water it, and watch it grow and eventually harvest the fruit of my labor. Each book I write is like another seed being planted. My grandfather modelled how to enjoy life in simple ways. Every one of my teachers from Mrs. Fornear, Jefferson School Kindergarten teacher, through my last graduate classes, was an inspiration to think, analyse, propose and advocate for new ideas. My teaching mentor, Ken Eye, showed me how important it was to lead the field. My wife, Cheryl, who has been my editor and best critic, kept me from going off the deep end. My son, Ethan, who only reads something I have written when he likes it. I thank those who tolerated my outbursts of inflammatory speech, radical and conservative ideas and Imagineering. My chief of staff, Gershon Ben Franja, AKA, Gram Tashjian, who edited and gave me insight all along the way. Thanks. As I sat and watched the politicians of my life pontificate and promise and prattle, I wondered just when a real, pragmatic leader would emerge. I thank all of you for how to lead the country when there is the greatest need to do just that.

Disclaimer

This novel is fiction. Any resemblance to real people is purely coincidental. The truth is that most men and women want to be president of the United States. Yes, we want to speak "Truth to Power". We want to make a difference and every one of us is a pundit when it comes to second-guessing the President, whoever he is at the time and the cast of political characters that surround him. The protagonist in this novel is different from you and me in that his dreams press him into chasing his without fear. Our nation is the first one in the history of humankind in which the lowliest born can aspire to national leadership. Birthrights and bloodlines have no bearing. It only rests upon the individual to commit his or her life to the ideal. Perhaps this is what "We, the people" really means.

Note on Abridged Version

This abridged version of Ringing the Liberty Bell condensed the fifty chapters covering the Liberty Bell Bus Tour into one chapter. I completed this version so the book could be printed in paperback version for those readers who enjoy holding on to a physical book as opposed to reading on Kindle or some other type of electronic reader. I hope you enjoy the story. Feedback is always appreciated. You can contact me at **bnemcik@yahoo.com**

Preface

Most average Americans arise early in the morning and mechanically prepare for work. As the wheels of business and industry mesh and grind, fortunes turn, heartaches attack, toil foreshadows triumph and tribulation and agony forms a foundation for ecstasy or delusion, working men and women make it possible.

There is a consummate fear and joy in the ebb and flow of matter into money and money into matter, energy into the service of man and the energy of man's service into the service of humankind.

For many Americans the workplace has become a desert. The grinding wheels of industry are but memories of another time and place. The matter of life is consumed in speculation on the simple challenge that arises when a man cannot go to work. When he asks the question, "When am I going back to work?" Whereas, a man shall live by the sweat of his brow, what man shall live who does not sweat from his brow?

21st Century man cannot easily return to the land because it has become macadam and concrete. Small family farmers are becoming serfs of the banks. We wonder what has become of the opportunities to provide for one's own and to "earn thy keep". The "Iron Age" melted into the "Nuclear Age" and streamed into the "Information Age".

But what became of the joy of work?

The forces arrayed against common people and women are too complex for many to comprehend. Thirty million or more are unemployed or underemployed. We are squandering an entire generation's brainpower.

How many Presidents have spouted, "America's best days are ahead?"

We're told that one more deal needs to be struck, another frontier to be conquered, and another mountaintop to be blown off so we can extract the coal from beneath its surface. Money market managers maintain the end of the Great Recession is here. Corporate bank profits prove it. Prosperity is around the corner and men should not despair.

Where around the corner? What corner?

Corporate leaders wield their scepters and conduct business as usual and continue to produce goods and services for a consumer market that is like a lame man struggling to walk in a storm. Political leaders, the caretakers of the public's trust, use these times as platforms to rise or fall from power by patronizing us with conflicting messages. Clerics postulate the end of humankind is upon us, and a life of the spirit is all that matters, but they cannot see how the human spirit is starved for want of basic needs and a sense of safety and belonging.

All these forces are allayed against those who simply work. The elite respond to their critics that their leadership represents the evolution of things. In their sophistry, they minimize the simple needs of people below them in the pecking order. Theirs is an exercise in circumventing reality and promotes the acceptance of struggling against a power structure that steamrolls over the powerless.

It is into this human condition that Everyman arrives.

"When will this world see?" asks Everyman.

When the rich man can ride on his camel through the eye of the needle.

When the sun rises and does not set again.

When ocean waters lose their salinity and the people of the earth can drink it.

When the salmon of the sea return in abundance to the streams of their birth.

When the atom relinquishes its role as the Siva of mankind.

When religious people accept all faiths as part of the family of man.

When earth, air, fire and water are accepted as the four faces of God.

1. The Uprising

Some days you get the bear and some days the bear gets you. I do not remember who said that but I felt like the bear was getting me today.

If Monday morning rains forebode ominous tidings for those who must travel, then this particular deluge forecast the drowning of the natural world. Cascading drops came down upon me like marbles. An ominous, ebony cloud full of the collected humidity from a half world away dumped its acid load upon Youngstown, Ohio.

Into this downpour I waded because the drenching was part of the price I had to pay for subsistence living. Like all men and women, good or evil, I worked for my bread. As I hiked along I thought, "This rain is cleansing the earth. Maybe it would wash away the engines of industry that so rudely cast me out and told me that I am no longer needed."

What made me so aware of the rain I could not say? Somewhere in the rain, there was an answer to the big question. I felt life boiling in every part of me. I felt the anger at having to be out in the rain and not going instead to work. At times, I was an ogre to live with for the hard times caused me a lot of anguish. Even though I had the resources, skills and the common sense to overcome it, still, the times controlled me. The bear was biting my ass.

As I waded in the ankle deep rivulets that cascaded down the sidewalk and proceeded walking up South Avenue, I felt the heaviness of the water in my clothes and a greater weight bearing down upon my soul. No man should be denied the right to work, to earn a living. No man should be stripped of his pride by dumping him into an unknown marketplace beyond the open hearths.

I stopped before I went into the building and looked across the valley. The gray mists spread in layers over everything. The view was murky like the valley's future. Only the steel mill where I worked, or did until last Friday, was still standing. Seventeen plants were either now deserted or completely gone. What once was the "Steel Valley" was now more aptly called the "Valley of Despond". The lonely scene caused me to quiver inside as I realized what the paltry view meant to steel people like me. We depended upon those iron dragons for our livelihood. We were the descendants of hard working, drinking and playing people. We did not worry about the future. We lived in the present, the here and now. Tomorrow would take care of itself. Now it was quickly dying. What could we do about it? The bridge over South Avenue and crossing the Ahio River was the link to the south side of town. Resting below in the bottom of the valley was our town, slowly dying like all the rest of the valley. Malls, shopping centers and countless suburbs sucked the life out of the city and year after year more stores closed. What was left? Bars and strip clubs and pawnshops dotted the blocks. The theatres disappeared a generation ago. The Palace and the Warner were such wonders and as a child, I went there with my mother and siblings for matinees. We were enchanted with the wide screen and the sound of music. Nothing compared to those ancient places. Dolby sound did not make a cinema. Drapes opening and closing in front of a fifty foot high screen did. What could I do about it? Nothing, I knew but lament the passing of time, the end of an order. As Agatha Christie once said, "Nothing is more important in life than a happy childhood" and that I certainly had in spades.

Before me was the 2011 analogue to the soup lines of the 1930's: the State Bureau of Unemployment Services. In these hard times, it was the focal point for a large part of America's work force. The symbols had changed but the meaning remained the same." The tan colored bricks were dulled by the rain and appeared like a furnace without a fire raging inside, without scrap and ore charged, without any potential. Only the ethereal lights flickering through the windows gave anyone hope that there was any life inside. Sure, there was life within, but it was a transient kind, not based upon a man's production but the lack of it.

It was after eight but already a traffic cop was directing people to park elsewhere. My walking from a few blocks away to avoid the jam helped me to escape my own storminess. This worked for me because I felt lighter in spirit and prepared to stand in the line at one of the stations and discover whether I qualified for benefits.

Everything could be worse, I told myself, for I could have only worked nineteen and not twenty weeks and be ineligible for benefits. Playing the "what if" game was a lose-lose proposition. The mill could have shut down, or I could have been fired for some work policy violation or the state could have filed for bankruptcy. Any or all of these would plunge most people into serious financial stress. Everything seemed safe enough yet safety was relative to the world that everyman was required to face right now. Fear dominated America. It started many years ago, was exacerbated by the 911 attacks and fed by the last administration until most people felt like they were living in a war zone. In reality, we were. There was a war going on against the middle class and we were losing. I asked myself, "Is this the American dream?"

When I felt the water leaking down onto my shirt, I shrugged, turned, walked up the steps, and stood inside the unemployment office. I was late. The doors were already open and the lines were nearly to the door. As I took my place in the line that covered M-P, I saw a bunch of my chums from the mill.

"Leo, the lion, you finally made it," one elderly fellow named Fritz called out.

"Sure enough," I replied. "How you doing?"

"Can't complain, but this weather's tough on my knees. Arthritis. Damn, I sure hate the dampness. Too many years, Leo. Too many. You get the hell out of the mill before you die there like me."

"How can I die in a place that doesn't want me to work any longer than a couple months a year?" I asked.

"I hear that. I hear that. This is getting old hat. Work a few months and then go out on the dole. I hate it. Almost as much as I hate this damn weather."

Fritz was ready to retire but he had a sick wife and needed the insurance so he was working as long as he could. He wasn't old enough for Social Security and the mill retirement was not much. Like my father, he started working when he was fifteen years old lying about his age. Because he was a burly German fellow, he passed for much older. In those days there weren't any Departments of Labor to stop a "child" from getting a job. He'd worked for forty-two years giving his lifeblood to making steel. Now, like me, he was standing in line waiting for his weekly allowance from the state unemployment office. We were reduced to being beggars. None of us wanted to be there. We wanted to be at work, even in this horrible weather, making steel, feeling the heat of the molten metal burning our flesh, tasting the graphite on our parched lips and inhaling the rotten egg sulfur smell all around us. The work was exhilarating. We made steel. We took raw materials and scrap iron and rare elements and melted them together and produced steel. We made something. We were creators, Gods in our own fashion. I envied Fritz in some ways. He'd lived a full life, productive, energized, and proud to carry a lunch bucket under his arm and enter into the bowels of the dragon.

The line moved slowly forward. I shuffled along like the rest of the other unemployed, sad-faced folks who were no longer making a living wage. There was something very wrong with the picture in front of me. We'd escaped another Depression. Yes, the stock market was back above 12,000. Banks reported record profits. Corporate profits were back in the black. Yet across America thirty million men and women were standing in lines just like I was and all their creative power was going to waste. Hidden in the nooks and crannies of the society were those who were not working and tragically couldn't collect unemployment benefits. These folks didn't count. Anyone who understood numbers knew that the only way the unemployment figures were calculated by the federal government was by adding up the number of people who were getting benefits. If you weren't you didn't count. You were invisible, but you had the same dreams as we did. It was a bold-faced lie. The corporations didn't really care. I was a commodity like coal and iron and scrap metal. So I, like so many of my colleagues, played along, did as we were told, and would receive our checks. Yes, it was a heinous lie, but in the unemployment zone, it became a virtue.

The banter among some of the people was funny. Some were happy to be laid off and talked about going fishing, boating, taking a vacation or just using their "free" money to rest up and do nothing. It all sounded funny until you realized that there was an end to all of this. Yes, the government passed a bill to extend benefits. Now there was a special class of people called the "99'ers", those who had benefits that extended from the normal 26 weeks way out to a total of 99. The republicans were totally opposed to the extensions. Figures. When did republicans ever do anything for working people? But the democrats weren't much better. They were in cahoots with the republicans when the banks were deregulated. They didn't oppose it. Bill Clinton did more than mess around with an intern in the White House. He championed NAFTA and signed into law the deregulation that slowly unraveled the banking reforms that kept our economy safe from the Great Depression all the way up until 1999.

What was the sense of crying over spilt milk? This was the world as we made it. We were suckers for the "good life". We consumed too much, went into debt to buy homes, cars, boats, education and now we were going to have to pay for it all. The tragedy was that this "Empire of Consumption" was sold to people who were working. Take away the work and how do you pay for all those toys that were sitting in your garage, or worse yet, a storage garage somewhere in town where the overflow objects collected dust. The economy might look good on paper, but at the core, where the people were shuffling along, it was as sick as a pancreatic cancer patient.

I gazed around and watched the people's faces. There wasn't much happiness in them even though they appreciated the money and would take it. They really wanted to go to work and earn a living. So did I. This wasn't what I believed my adult life would be reduced to when I was growing up. I grew up thinking that I'd work beside my father in the mill and make a good living, get married, buy a house, have children and be happy. I was. Until now that is. Taking away work was like taking away air. We don't live well without either.

A woman clutching a baby under her arm asked someone in the line if he would hold her place because she had to change the child's diaper. Smiles were exchanged. That was enough. She waddled off with the wailing child.

Before I got into line I decided to go to the restroom. Already the stalls and urinals that lined the walls, made shiny and fresh over the weekend, were being heavily used. The glistening chrome and buffed porcelain and brilliantine brass presented a marked contrast to the dour faces that stood above the urinals or sat upon these marvels of modern, civilized man. This was Mudville and these were all Casey's. Their faces reflected the gloominess outside. They were kith and kin to the dark, streaking clouds that raced across the sky. They were mirrors of the distraught, the down-and-out fear-laden, men and women who knew that their checks would be forthcoming. But even more threatening than getting the checks was the realization that they would not last forever. They provided a false sense of security. These were the faces of my peers and in them I saw something of me but I didn't feel that same fear and couldn't understand the reason that my senses were telling me something different. I wasn't fearful. I was a castaway in a market place that was adrift. I wondered if I were just deluding myself because there was something rising inside that I couldn't explain. I wasn't the eternal optimist but neither did I view the world, or my life, as half-empty. Something was different. Yes, it was the realization that this was not the American dream. In the midst of urinating, a new feeling flooded out of me and it felt more like relief than just the biological one that made me stand there for a long time. In this nameless setting upon a pine-scented stage I was experiencing the overwhelming recognition of a power beyond any I had ever felt before.

Men came and left as I stood leaning against the wall transfixed, staring at them. Some returned my stare, but it didn't register at first for I was lost in thought, in feeling and in wonder. Where was the hope? Where was the dream? Who were its caretakers? Gandhi's words flowed through me like hot lead. "There go the people. I am their leader. I must follow them." I knew where they were going and I was following them.

As I climbed the steps back up to the large hall where the people were gathered, I counted them like the years of my life. I was nearly half way through my life if I lived to be 100 years old. Life was now a fifty-fifty proposition. It was clear to me now that these steps were my life. My life: zero, birth, seven, the age of reason; twelve, the onset of puberty; sixteen, legal driving age; eighteen, legal voting age and registration for the draft; twenty-one, age of legal adulthood with the permission to go into debt, drink whisky and beer and make a living; twenty-five, age of eligibility for congressional membership; thirty, age for senate membership; thirty-five, the age a citizen qualified to be president. The Cosmic Joker was having some fun at my expense, but I couldn't laugh. The moment passed and my lips felt parched and my pulse quickened and the atmosphere felt like August in February.

Three or four hundred people were standing in long lines waiting to get to the counter. Some unemployment was handled via the Internet but when you had a new claim, you had to appear in person. The process was humiliating. You stood in front of someone who had a job and were asked a number of personal questions. Fabricate any information and you would be denied benefits. You could appeal but that was a long, drawn out process and by the time you got your first check, if you did beat the case, it could be six weeks or more. Any time you had a chance to get another job, you had to take it. There were no excuses. In the mill I was making about $15.50 an hour. Not bad money. The incentive for staying was the health care plans and a defined pension plan. The work was strenuous and yet no one minded because we actually made something with our effort. Hundreds of thousands of tons of steel were shipped out via rail every year. Each ton was hand made by people. The open hearth was the soul of the mill and I was privileged to be working there. But here now were many of those same people standing in line and waiting. I could see many of the older men from the mill that probably for the very first time were coming to collect benefits. I knew them by sight and last name. We weren't chums, but we were a part of the brotherhood, the United Steel Workers of America.

In the mill, I was simply #3013. I signed my time card accordingly each day I passed through those rusted, sooty gates. Today I wondered if I'd ever do so again. Things did not look very good. The economy was still in the tanks. More and more steel was being imported from China and other countries at a far cheaper price. We just could not compete because the Chinese government was propping up their sales by imposing tariffs on our exports and keeping the price of their money artificially low. The economics were very complicated, but the outcome was simple to comprehend. If their steel was cheaper, then companies would buy Chinese and not American. Our Union's efforts to influence the government went virtually unheeded. USX didn't really care because it was slowly dismantling its entire steel subsidiary and branching out into new endeavors.

The look on the people's faces still displayed the predominant feeling: fear. Yes, we were all fearful that the end was coming. One day, USX would announce the mill was closing down permanently and we'd all be bought out and that would be it. The old timers were always talking about such a day. Every time there was a shutdown the rumors started flying. I could feel it in my gut. This time it was serious. Guys who'd never spent a minute in the lines were here. First helpers like Fritz were everywhere. We were all in the same situation. The mill was down and we were out and there wasn't anything we could do about it. A layoff was just a right jab to the face, but a veritable closure of the plant would be an upper cut to the jaw and a sure knockout.

I stood in line for the " P". How many presidents, senators or congressmen or women ever stood in an unemployment line? How many understood the harsh realities of bills not being paid, marital tensions amplified, substandard food and the host of other problems created by insufficient or no funds? Saving for a rainy day was a dream, another lie that many people couldn't believe. I wondered if either party of ideologues ever really understood what was at stake in their campaign promises. They represented the masses of working people. This was no joke. "By the people" made no sense when you looked at who was holding office. Harvard and Yale graduates were hardly the "people". Who was the last person to hold national office that was truly "of the people"? Harry Truman? Abraham Lincoln? That was a long time ago. "Of the people" wasn't like me. I was no Rockefeller nor Ford, nor Nixon nor Reagan nor Carter. Some might argue that Clinton was "of the people" but after all, he was a Rhodes Scholar and there aren't too many of them. A single mother raised Obama. But was he any different? The thoughts spun around in circles like clothes in a front-loading washer. I wanted to believe in dreams. I wanted more than a hollow life.

The lady with the baby broke my reverie. She came back and smiles were exchanged again and she stepped into the line. No one said anything. There was civility among men and women because we were all the same now: unemployed, wondering and worrying.

As I stood at the end of the line of unemployed steelworkers like me, and autoworkers, ironworkers, truck drivers, hosts and hostesses, waiters and nurses, machinists and janitors, house painters and insurance brokers, engineers and philosophers, I wondered if politicians who were voted out of office were eligible for unemployment? Two terms in Congress and the outgoing politician was eligible for full retirement. That was one hell of a deal. No wonder they spent so much to get re-elected. Stay two terms and leave with a boatload of cash coming in. No, I didn't think they'd be waiting here in line like the rest of us.

My thoughts were disrupted when a friend greeted me. His face appeared suddenly out of the sea of faces.

"Hi ya, what's up?" Caruso asked cheerfully.

I enjoyed the smile on his face and the laughter in his eyes. He was universally happy. He had eight children and I wondered with all those mouths to feed, babies to clothe and shelter, how he did it. But then again, he was an exceptional guy.

"Nothing much, Al," I replied.

"Hell of a rainstorm," he said.

"We needed it. It'll clean the air," I said wondering where my optimism was coming from all of a sudden.

"Yah and what else is new? The air is clean as heaven but the mill's shut down and we aren't going to work. I'd rather breathe the filthy air and be working."

I gave somber approval to what he said and those around us did as well.

"You're right about that. We are going to see too much of South Avenue and not enough of the blue bridge and Gate A."

"I don't mind the unemployment checks but they don't last forever. Makes a man really wonder what it's all about," Caruso said laconically.

"I wonder, too," I replied. There was a pause. Al looked so different in his street clothes. His hair was slicked back DeNiro style.

"Didya see Jolly, Bill and Denny?" he asked.

"No, are they here, too?"

"Yah. Right behind you. Some of the old guys are here, too. I'll bet this place gets jammed by noon. We've got fifteen hundred guys coming through here a week. That's a lot of folks to be on the dole. Money ain't bad, but I'd still rather be working than collecting. Something just ain't right."

There were more murmurs of approval from those around us and I had to agree. Something was just not right.

"Guys with thirty years are out now. Only maintenance is working, millwrights and motor inspectors. And a lot of 'Gold Hats'. This time it's for real, I think. They're gonna shut it down for good. I hate to think about it, but that's just the way I feel." He looked away.

"Then don't, "I said. How naïve I sounded. How cold! He couldn't afford not to think about it. After all, he had a large family and there was nothing harder than to try and raise eight kids on unemployment checks.

"Come on, man, you got to be kidding. I got eight kids, a house payment, a wife that don't work, car payments, an RV payment and other bills out the ass. Hell, I got a mess. Nobody else is going to do it for me if I don't. But what am I going to do. You can talk big because you've only got two mouths to feed. Try nine sometimes and see how it feels." He looked away again as the truth of what he said began to sink in for him and for me.

I said, "Al, there's got to be a better way."

He looked at me and beyond me. "I'd like to know what that could be. This is like a slow death. Like a cancer. Hell, I feel sick when I come here because I know it can't last. If the mill dies we all die." The words seemed prophetic, final and repulsive.

If…for years men belabored the point. If…but it never shut down completely. Rumors abounded but they were just rumors. Ever since coming to work in the mill and a long time before my tenure, men talked about it but it never happened. The rumors were like the refrain in the pop song by Billy Joel, "Allentown". Did he know something I didn't? This was not fair. No man should live in America and fear for his livelihood. Something had drastically gone wrong. Nobody liked to think about it.

People around us moved uneasily as we spoke. We did not know them, but they were like us, arrested with a fear and a complaint.

"You're a bright fellow," Al said at last. "What do you think should be done?"

I stared at him in earnest. "I'm not sure it would work, but rather than have us stand here and get money for not working, would it not make more sense if the company kept the mill working and paid us the money we would get from unemployment and when the economy turned around again, they would put us back to work at full wages. Even if we worked part-time and were in any department and not our own, we would be at least producing something and would feel a whole lot less worthless. Standing around and doing nothing isn't good for the body, mind nor soul. The entire system is outdated. We work like crazy for a while and produce mega tons of steel to meet the demand. Then there is a slow down and out the door we go. I know the Union would never agree, but they aren't doing much for us right now. We're getting eighty percent for nothing. We might as well do something for it and for ourselves."

"Now that's not a half bad idea. I'd much rather work than lay around. Get fat that's all. Yah, why not? A cut in pay and work is better than a cut in pay and no work and no future. I never thought about it that way. You ought to run for president and change this fricken' system."

"I ought to do a lot of things, but you asked for my opinion."

"Well, you couldn't do much worse that some of these clowns we've had for the past few decades. You think about it Leo and you got my vote. I know you could do it. Hey, you remember when Reagan once said that he was unemployed back in 1936 and had to collect from the government? Wasn't he a noble one? One of the biggest union busting sons of a bitch that ever held a national office. Bet you George II never had to stand in an unemployment line. He did his coke on a silver spoon no less. I wonder if Obama ever went without. Oh well, I may be dumb but I ain't stupid. The working man gets the shaft every time the economy goes south and we're way down below the border right now."

Al was a simple man but like all men everywhere he spoke the truth as he saw it. To lie was not in his nature. He gained nothing by lying and had nothing to lose by being honest. Guile was not a part of his character. Caruso withdrew into his own private space and left me alone. No one could deny the slow agonizing death from inactivity that most of us were starting to feel. There had to be a better way. But what was it? What had not been tried in this nation of experimenters and creators and designers and builders?

I spied Jolly, Bill, Denny and Skinny Jack behind me standing in the next line. Their conversation was very animated. I waited for them in my line as they moved forward.

I felt all alone in the mass of men and women and nothing feels worse than isolation in a crowd. New Yorkers must feel this way a lot, I thought to myself. Alone, yet slogging along through throngs of people. Slowly, as I got closer to the counter, my belly started to roil. I didn't know what made it do so, but the sickness wouldn't go away. Was I coming down with some kind of stomach flu? I held my guts tight and tried to endure the pain. It got worse the nearer I came to the moment of truth. Sure, I'd worked my mandatory 20 weeks this year to qualify, but what if there were some snag, some mix up, and some way that I wouldn't get my check. I didn't really want one. I preferred to go to work, but for now, I was reduced to the reality of my own condition.

Jolly, his flowing blond hair, almond eyes and hulking frame was a natural jokester. He was never serious. To him everything was okay. He carried himself loosely and yet dressed to a T. He wore expensive leather jackets and handmade shoes and always had money in his pocket. He was divorced yet he had two children and still dated his ex-wife, for fun and games. He didn't want to be a parent. His sole purpose in life was to have fun and take care of himself. He drove a Benz and we all wondered how he could afford it. He said his "mother had bread" as he put it so he did not worry about alimony. Bill was slim and had thick, black hair and robin-egg-blue eyes. His teeth were perfect and when he smiled, they glistened. He wore a light jacket that fit tightly and made him appear slimmer than he was. He always smoked nervously as if he were not supposed to do it. Marlboros. Denny appeared heavier today. He had the propensity to gain and lose weight almost daily. He was stocky, a typical Eastern European frame. His complexion was rough and stubble appeared and disappeared from his face almost as easily as fat on his waist. "Skinny" Jack earned his nickname by being the thinnest of the six Jacksons that worked with us. He displayed a perpetual smile and was not in the least self-conscious of the front teeth missing. He was a happy person, but he was not a comedian anymore. He had "found the Lord" and was now devoting his life to Jesus. It was either that or ending up burned out from drinking too much. Skinny Jack was a royal person and mixed easily with anyone of any color. He did not hide behind his blackness nor did he flaunt it. His strength lay in his capacity to help others, to love his fellow man, and in this way he had made many friends. Anyone was welcome at his home. These were my work mates. A common lot, all millrats, all cast in a similar mold but yet different as core-ten was from file steel. Each one wore on his countenance a picture of expectancy and yet each knew a separate reality. We were close because we lived together in the "iron house" and it was when we were laid off that we came together once again.

"Leo, buddy, how are you?" Jolly called to me as his line caught up to mine. He shook my hand warmly. "Are you getting any?" he added with a twinkle in his eye. It seemed all he ever thought about was sex.

"Just fine, Jolly. Hi guys," I said to the rest.

"Come to get your rat pellet?" Denny said mockingly referring to our unemployment check.

Bill was taciturn. He looked worried. He bought a new home right before the lay-off. His son just turned three months old. This time might not go like all the others. He knew it. We all knew it.

Denny interrupted saying, "You get your check once a week and then you have the whole week to screw around. Does that hurt anyone?"

No one responded to his dribble.

"Peace be to you brother," Skinny Jack said.

"And to you Jack," I replied.

"Haven't seen you much lately. When are you going to come and visit Judy and me?"

"Oh, I don't know. Sometime I suppose."

"Got plenty of time now and we got plenty of food. Family loves when you come to visit," he said.

"I appreciate the offer," I said sincerely. I always enjoyed visiting Jack and Judy and their six kids. Their place was a moveable feast.

"Denny really looked wired even though it was early in the morning. His eyes were glowing. He partied heavily whether he was working or not. He fit the mold of his uncles who also worked and partied hard. But Denny did more than drink and we all knew it. I encouraged him to take better care of himself but he listened with half an ear. He was usually too stoned to listen with both.

Jolly asked, "Are you working anywhere now?" He knew I often did construction whenever there was a lay off. The job I was thinking about probably had not crossed their minds. I smiled self-consciously and did not say anything more.

"If you get anything going let me know," he said half seriously.

"I'll do that if I do." Once I asked him if he wanted to work for me but he was into vacationing at the time.

"How's your family, Bill?" I asked.

"Just fine. Everyone's fine. It's nice to be together a lot now during the layoff. But it can't last. Sometimes I just can't handle all the off hours. I'd like to get back to work."

"Well, I hope it lasts and lasts and lasts," Denny barked. Everyone stared at him as if he was crazy, but he did not have anyone to take care of and so his reality was not like the rest of ours. He was an impatient kid and never seemed to be able to sit still. He was not married and vowed he would never tie the knot. He lived with his mother but he was never home. He had a sports car, an old jalopy for work, a speedboat for waterskiing, and a cottage at Lake Erie. His father, who also worked in the mill, died when Denny was thirteen and he still seemed to be searching. He was a pleasant person, fun to be around, never mean and nasty to others; a veritable contradiction.

A moment of silence ensued. They stared at me. "Could they read my thoughts," I wondered. I thought not, but I had to agree I was not myself today. I was a mixture of all of them for I could be jovial, serious, taciturn or loquacious. I could work and party hard. Somehow I realized just then that they fit into my plan. What the plan was I was not sure. I needed their service. Their presence would help me to set up my introduction. I thought, "I'm already beginning to use people" and it scared me. But I could not do it without asking them first. I owed them this much out of respect. All ten eyes studied me. I owed them an explanation. "How much should I say now? Just enough to let them know my predicament." Nothing in life that was worthwhile was easy. I needed to keep reminding myself of this now and in the future. The simplest part is to hatch an idea. The hard part is to sustain it and bring it to fruition. I was a majority of one planning an uprising and I sorely needed cohorts.

"Listen fellows," I said, trying to pick the right tone to capture their attention and not have them think I was joking with them. "I need your help. You may not believe what I'm going to tell you but it's the truth. I'm going to make a speech today and …"

"Make a speech," Jolly howled. "This is no auditorium, Leo. This is an unemployment office full of unhappy people who don't want to listen to any speeches. You crazy or something? People'll run you out of here and take you to the booby house," he laughed heartily as was his way.

"No, please hear me out."

"This ought to be good," Denny said with a smirk on his face.

I realized I needed to be more convincing if I were going to enlist their aid.

"I know this sounds crazy but I need your help. I've got a speech prepared. Well, not really but I've got some words to say and a declaration to make."

"So what?" Bill said. "I do too. I'm going to announce I've been to ten employers and none of them want to hire me," he laughed, nervously.

I plunged ahead. "I've got a few things to say to the people gathered here and I don't think the establishment will be prepared to listen or even let me say them."

"What kind of speech? What do you mean?" Bill asked curiously as to what I was going to say. His pale blue eyes shone brightly as he peered into mine.

"Yah, and why in here?" Denny asked.

"I've got to make an announcement and yes, I've got to make it in here," I said.

"But why in here? Why not somewhere else? That's what doesn't make sense to me," Denny said.

I collected my thoughts and my feelings. I did not wish to blurt out some foolishness. I wanted to be real with them.

Speaking softly so only they could hear me, I started to make my plea. "I'll tell you all why and listen carefully. I need to say it in here because this place represents everything that is wrong with the system, the economy, with America. Think about it. You all have common sense. We come here to get paid not to work, to sit around and pretend we are waiting for another job and lie about the fact that we are actively seeking work somewhere other than the mill. The truth is that none of us is going to look for another job. We make too much money not working to do so. There is no job in this sick economy that pays as well as the mill does, or did. Who's going to work for minimum wages when they cannot equal what we get in unemployment? But America was not founded on free lunches, but on hard work, initiative and production. We're squandering the most productive years of our lives and no amount of money is going to repay us for that. Unemployment benefits are just a token when compared with the valuable time being wasted. We are the future and it is blowing away in the wind."

They ogled me as if I were a madman. They knew as well as I did that Woodside Receiving was just over the hillside. I pressed forward not wishing to be laughed at and conditioning myself for all of that later. There was so much to say and do that I did not know where to start. I did not want to go into fine details now.

"I've thought about this every time we get laid off, but this time it's come to a head. We deserve better than what we've got. This is no way to live and yet we're forced to live this way never knowing what tomorrow will bring. I want to change some of that. There is a better way and I believe I can do something to rectify it. How far have we strayed from the ideal?"

"What could be more ideal than what we've got?" Jolly asked.

"Yah," Denny said, "a check every week and no time card to punch, no forty hours to put in. And you want to change all this? You're nuts! We've got it made."

"But how long can it last?" Bill asked. He was already thinking about what I had said. He understood.

"Yah and they all know we lie about it, too, you know. That's the fact, you know," Skinny Jack said.

"That's the truth," Al added.

"So what's the gig? Why all the mystery, Leo?" Jolly asked giving me the ball again.

"No mystery, just a plan. I'm not sure where it will take me but I've got to try it. You see, I'm not willing to let others control my destiny anymore and I think you will admit neither are you. We've let it happen for too long. We are all the same. We work hard and want to have our work mean something. As long as the money is flowing in we don't worry about it. But cut it off and push comes to shove and we have to go out and hustle our butts off to make ends meet. In the mean time, we waste our time, our talent, our creative genius. We are wards of the state. We are not really happy in this quagmire. Our culture doesn't permit us to enjoy idleness if we have not earned it. Look at what is going on all over the country right now. States are trying to bust up unions. Wisconsin, Indiana and our own state legislature are doing everything in their power to end collective bargaining. What's next? End unemployment benefits. Squeeze every working man until he bleeds. You know as well as I do we are all happier when we are going to work and earning money and spending it when we are off. This is the most valuable time in our lives and we are not being permitted to use it. If we were fifty or sixty and had twenty-five years service, then it might not be so critical."

"And what do you expect us to do?" Al asked.

"Nothing more than keeps the people from stopping me before they can hear me out."

"And how are we to do that? Beat the guards back? You're nuts, Leo. Crazy, man," Denny barked.

"Maybe I'm crazy, maybe not. All I need are a few moments to get their attention and have them listen. All you guys need to do is to tell the people to let me speak. Kind of verbally support me. No violence. Nothing like that. They don't even need to know you're with me. All I need is some time. Time, that's all."

"It's nine thirty," Skinny Jack said. "When are you going to speak?"

"Soon," I said.

I gazed at them, imploring their support. I was desperate. I needed time. They could buy it for me. Would they? I wondered what made me choose such a place and time to start this uprising. My resolve was greater than my doubts. I realized it would not be easy. I needed this forum because this was the real America.

"That's all you want from us?" Denny asked.

"Yes, that's all I'm asking for, just a few minutes and then what comes will come. Can you help me?"

"But what's the mystery?" Jolly asked more seriously now.

"No mystery, Jolly. Just a need for a forum. I have a plan that if it works I'm not sure where it will take me. I've just got to do it. I've got to," I said fervently.

"Well, I'm game to help out," Al said. "You get up and make your speech and I'll keep the goons from eating you alive for a minute or two. Easy enough. I just hope you don't turn the whole place out and we don't get our checks." He laughed nervously and scratched his right ear thinking deeply.

"How's this going to look?" Skinny Jack asked not too sure he wanted a piece of the action but respecting me enough to hear me out.

"When I get to the front of the line, I'm going to stand up on the counter and speak to the crowd. The powers that be may not appreciate it, but that's the way it's got to be." I stopped. I watched them. When the moment seemed right I said, "Haven't you ever wanted to take power into your own hands and control your own destiny? Sure, we think the money is good for now, but we all know that it will not last. The mill is going to shut down. If not this time, this week, this month, then one of these days. We don't have any freedom. There is no hope in waiting and doing nothing. I can't wait anymore. Layoffs are like an indefinite prison sentence. I'm sure you can understand. There will come a time when we won't be able to wait any longer because it will be too late. My desire is to postpone that day by making a stand now. Remember the graffiti on the wall on number four platform down at the mill. 'Why is there never enough time to do it right the first time, but always enough time to do it over again.' That's where the power is in being able to make the determination when and how we are going to act and not let others make the decision for us. We need to call the shots. We need to feel some control over our own lives. We need to feel some power."

"What you're saying sounds simple but you know it's not," Bill said.

"Yes, I realize this. What I'm saying does sound simple but it is indeed very complex, more than even I can comprehend. But I feel the power in me to do something about it and not just wait to be told I'm no longer needed. If I'm wrong, I'll admit I'm wrong and go home and hustle some odd jobs. For the moment, I believe I'm right, or at least not too much off the mark. There is no other way to overcome our fate than to take it by the horns and wrestle with it. We can wait until they tell us our services are no longer needed. I believe our services are needed right now. Your services. My service. We're young and yet we're powerless unless we act. We need to struggle to become powerful and this can be done only if we take a stand. I don't mean standing in this line waiting for our rat pellet as Denny would say. What I'm advocating is a grassroots revival of the belief in the 'Fair Trade' system where we trade our services for money. Produce or perish. Not sit and wait until it is too late to produce. We're standing here wondering if US Steel will need us again. No wonder we have no hope. We've drowned it with our apathy. We can revive it because I know it's in each one of us and all the others in here. They just need to hear it, believe it and then go and live it. I'm a simple man, a common man like all of you. I believe in the American dream. I'm sure you do. What we're living right now is the American Nightmare. It's too easy to cop out and say there's nothing we can do. The truth is there is always something we can do and therein lays the rub. There will be sacrifices along the way. I'm prepared to make those sacrifices now. Will you help me? Support me? Believe in me? That's all I ask. Nothing more. After today, if you can't believe what I'm saying I'll accept you as my friends, but please give me this chance. It won't cost you anything. What have you got to lose?"

They ogled me. I felt like some sort of freak in a side show, but I also felt relieved. It was not that they were confused, only mystified by my proposal. At least they listened to me and for that I was grateful. So this was how it was meant to be. I had not planned anything but an idea was coming to me. The mission. Couched in an uprising of the people, I was prepared to lead them forward.

There was a lot of nervous laughter for it all seemed like a lark.

"Ah well, why not? What the hell, we ain't got anything better to do and this just might be a little fun," Denny said. "Let's let them have it. They aren't doing anything for us anyway. You're right. The money's good until it runs out."

"Yes, until it runs out," Al seconded.

"Yah, till it runs out," Bill muttered.

"Yah, Leo, you give us the sign and we'll clear the air for you and you make your speech and we'll listen. We can call this Radio Free America," Skinny Jack laughed.

"I'm in Leo," Jolly said.

"I hope what you say shocks everybody just a little," Bill said.

"Nobody likes to tamper with the status quo and you know that. What's the speech about anyway?" Denny said seriously.

"The American Dream and You," I said.

I looked at them with love and affection. It would not be easy to tell them now but I wanted to shock everyone, even them. "I'd rather have you listen first. That way you can agree or disagree without any prejudgments. I hope that's okay with all of you?"

Al put his arm on my shoulder and said, "I worked for your father for many years, Leo. Well, Leo, your old man was alright by me and so are you. You just go ahead and do it and I'm with you. Time's wasting and I need to get on home."

Skinny Jack took my hand and I felt the peace emanating from him. "The Lord loves you brother. Trust in him."

"I'm ready," Bill said simply.

We moved ahead in the lines. There was a full house today, probably about four or five hundred people applying for benefits. We stopped talking. I waited and slowly moved forward toward the front and toward destiny.

When there were only two people in front of me, I could not hold back any more. I thought my stomach was going to explode. The pain was excruciating. I asked a guy in front of me to hold my spot and I dashed for the bathroom. As I entered the ancient, smelly room, I raced to the nearest stall and threw up. I stood over the bowl for a long time. My pain slowly subsided, but I had to lean against the wall to stand upright. Everything was spinning around and I could not get my bearings. Ten minutes passed and I finally was able to stagger over to the sink and wash my face and hands. I rinsed my mouth out. My lips were dry. My head was pounding. Something was going on and I could not tell just what. I stared into the mirror and what I saw scared me. I looked hollow. My skin was taut. I almost did not recognize who I was. Shaken, I slowly walked back toward the mass of humanity that seemed to have doubled in size since I exited the room so hastily.

My line was not moving. I looked for the guy who was saving my place but he'd been processed and three people didn't remember me and quite frankly didn't believe that I'd been in line.

"You want to scab, I got something for you," one hostile guy said to me.

"No problem, fellow. I was sick and asked someone to hold my spot. Hey, no sweat. I'm cool. I don't mind waiting."

Under the belligerent eyes of those around me, I shuffled to the back of the line. Now I knew I'd be there for at least a few more hours. "Getting sick was not in my best interest. Oh well," I thought. "This was the sign of the times.

As the time passed, the people grew weary and the babies being held started to cry and the rain pounded down upon the building and I wondered what was going to happen to all of us, a weird fantasy surged through me. At first, I just laughed to myself about it. "What was I suffering from?" I asked. "Did I puke out my brains in the bathroom or what?" The fantasy grew into a mild thought. Then it metastasized into a real idea. I stood transfixed and did not move forward. Someone nudged me and mindlessly I moved my feet. I did not feel them. They were disconnected from my body. I was two people: a body and a mind. The mind was in control. The body was just a hollow shell. In my fantasy, I could see someone who looked like me standing up on top of the counter top with hands gesticulating and a booming voice crying out to the gathering of the people. Everywhere in the crowd, there was shouting and catcalling and hands waving and the sea of faces look mesmerized. My breathing became rapid and intense and I couldn't stop it. Inside my chest, I could feel the thunderous beating of my heart. Bile was in my mouth and it tasted like molten sulfur. Water flowed down my cheeks. I did not know if I were crying or if the rain was leaking down from the heavens and flooding into the room. Someone nudged me again. I did not move. I was frozen in time and space. There was no yesterday and no tomorrow; only now.

"Buddy, you're next," I heard the hollow voice ringing in my ears. The noise had no effect upon me. My arms felt like lead weights. I stood with my eyes burning and incapable of focusing anywhere.

Then I snapped.

Everything happened so quickly that the body I was being carried in wasn't my own anymore.

Right now. I looked at the fellows and they raised their hands to let me know they were there for me.

Leaping up onto the counter and turning to the crowd and raising my hand high into the air, I said in a voice that I'd never heard before, "Citizens, this is not the American Dream."

The sound echoed through the great hall. I stood with my legs spread widely and my arms hoisted high into the air.

"LET ME REPEAT. CITIZENS, THIS IS NOT THE AMERICAN DREAM."

"What are you doing?" the unemployment officer hollered as I stood on top of her counter, my head a full twelve feet in the air.

For a third time, my voice ringing like a bell, I extolled, "This is not the American Dream!"

"What is this? You need to get down, get down. Get down now…Where is the security guard?"

People milled about wondering what was going on. I looked down at my conspirators and they were forming a wall of bodies to keep people from rushing me. I could feel the tension in the room, the nervous, ratty scurrying. "What's going on here?" Hey man, get the hell down." The eagle eyes of a guard pierced me from behind the wall of people standing in front of me. He rolled from his seat in the far corner of the room and came toward me but he had to pass through a maze and was delayed. I felt their eyes all over me. "Hey, buddy, get off the counter so we can sign up." "Yah, get down will ya?" "Who the hell you think you are?" "Get the frick outa here." "Check this dude out, he's gonna get himself shot." "Leave him be. It's time something was done and somebody's got to do it." "Get outa the way fella." "No." "Who the hell are you?" "Sir, would you please get down so we can get done with our business?" came the voice of officialdom but I did not respond. I became tongue-tied. Shouting poured from the gallery and the desk behind me. I was the center of attention now just as I needed to be. "Hey, you get down off there and get the hell outa here." "I been tellin' him." "What's up with this guy? He must be Looney." "Do what you gotta do, Leo." "You know this guy?" "Where's the security guard?" "Officer. Officer." Someone reached up for my leg but Jolly told him quietly to leave me be. "We got a genuine revolution here, hahahahahahaha and nobody can stop it." "Leave him be." "Where's the guard?" There was a swirling in the massive crowd as lines disintegrated and blended into one formless mass of shouting, waving and gaping humanity, but no one rushed me nor did they withdraw. They were a flock trying to decide if they should run from the wolf or gather unto the shepherd. The mayhem continued as my tongue thickened. It became steamy hot and I perspired profusely and beads of sweat streamed into my eyes until I could not see ten feet in front of me. "What are you doing up there?" "The guy's crazy!" "Check him out." "Righteous dude wants to get himself arrested." "Who gave you the right to upset this process?" "Would you please get down?" All around me sharp words cut through the air and people fused together even tighter than before. "Leo, you'd better go ahead and get on with it. We can't hold them back forever," I heard Bill shouting above the din.

"Citizens, fellow steel workers, laborers, men and women, Americans, this is not the American dream. This is an American nightmare. We're standing here like cows waiting to get milked but our bags are dry. We're here because we're just a 'human resource' that is no longer needed. Corporate leaders are shutting down the engines of industry and buying foreign made steel. They don't care if we live or die. We're not factored into the bottom line any more. We've spent our life's blood making billions for them and now we're getting the shaft. We'll collect our paltry few bucks a week. This will help to keep our mouths shut for a little while. One of these days, they will decide to make it official that the mills will never open again. We'll get a pitiful severance pay. Goodbye, Good riddance. Kiss off. We don't need you anymore. Simple. No sweat. Shut the mill down and buy foreign made steel. After all, it's cheaper and this is business, nothing personal. But Citizens, it is personal. We don't go to work every day just to make money. We go because it is who we are. We make steel. We make something. We don't push money from one pile to another. We wheel chromium and manganese and coal and sulfur in wheelbarrows to make steel. We are real people making a real product. We are the foundation of the entire industrial world that built this country. These mills, or what is left of them, were the very mills that fed the factories that built tanks and jeeps and ships during WWII. Our fathers and mothers and grandparents served in those wars so that we could have a better life. They slaved for these corporations so that one day we could be free and proud. Those days are gone. Today the liberty bell must be rung by all of us. It's time for an uprising. It's our duty to raise our collective voices and shout so loudly that anyone who is powerful hears that we are sick and tired of the games they are playing with our lives. We are the salt of the earth, the breath that industry breathes. Now we've got to speak with one voice and send the message across the land that working people are no longer willing to let those who lead us close their ears to our message."

Someone from the back of the room shouted, "Hey, asshole, get the fuck down and shut up. We don't want to listen to someone all cooked up on something."

No sooner did the voice stop than an outcry from the crowd drowned out the naysayer.

"Let him say his piece," rolled through the room. The moment hung like a guillotine over everyone.

"Citizens, you and I have one thing in common, one thread that binds us together like brothers and sisters and that is simply this. We work for a living and now we're being denied the right to work. There is no doubt that we are competing in a global market place. We can read and write even if the captains of industry don't want to accept it. We can see what is happening all over the world. We can feel the disenchantment that rolls like a malaise through our society. We're in two wars right now and we've been borrowing trillions of dollars from the Chinese to pay for those wars. Somewhere in the hallowed halls of Congress someone is pulling the strings. He or she is making decisions to allow trade with China to be easier so that we don't piss off our biggest debt holder. 'Sacrifice the steel industry' but don't upset the Chinese because they just might decide to pull in all their debt and cause our economy to experience a free fall. So we're paying the price. We're expendable. We're a dying industry anyway, aren't we? When was the last time USX invested any money in the mill? What has become of the American Dream where a man or a woman can earn a decent living, raise a family and give them a life that is a little better than what he or she had as a child?"

A rumbling arose in the crowd and security slowly pushed through the lines that were now twisted together, undefined and disorganized. I could see them coming but there was no fear in my heart.

I was possessed.

When they got closer, I heard the bellowing voice of an officer telling me to "Get down and come with me."

But before he could get close the crowd encircled him and countless voices chastised him and he wasn't able to do anything. I found my voice again.

"My fellow Americans," I roared even louder than before.

"I stand before you today, not as your enemy, nor an enemy of the system, nor as an enemy of the divine right of people to live in peace in America or anywhere upon this beautiful earth. I stand before you and ask this simple question. Is there not a better way to live? I ask you all to dig deep down into your immortal souls and answer this question. Is this all you want out of life? If you can answer this in all truth and honesty – Yes – then my words are not for you. If however, you can answer this in all truth and honesty – No – then my words are for you. I believe the vast majority of you want more than this. Most of you do not want to stand in lines like this and be paid not to work. You would rather work and never see an unemployment line as long as you live. You don't want to have to wonder what the future has in store for you."

"Amen to that brother," a voice rang out.

""Yes, Amen I say to you this morning. We deserve more. We deserve a chance to realize our dreams. How can we dream if our days are spent in fruitless searching for a job that does not exist?"

I did not pause, hesitate, nor permit those who might doubt or question me at this time a chance to respond.

"Each one of us was born and raised with a dream in his or her heart. It was not to just be wealthy or powerful or famous, but to be happy and proud and fulfilled. But now we are together as part of the vast majority of Americans who live check to check, from meal to meal, or even worse, live not knowing where the next meal will come from. We are not happy and are not proud. We have lost control of our lives. Or even worse, we've given up control of our lives to a system that would have us believe all is well and there is little or nothing that we can do to change the status quo." No pause. No hesitation.

"The power to change the system is in each and every one of us. We are not required to settle for less. We have myriad options from which to choose and to lay down and die is the very last one. Our collective strength is unbelievable. Look at what is happening in Wisconsin, Indiana and Ohio this very day. Look what happened in Tunisia and Egypt and is happening in Libya. People are standing up and being counted. They want to share in the bounty. We far outnumber the wealthy, powerful and famous. We comprise the mandate, not them. Combined, they do not produce as much as we do. Yet we get the smallest share. We are manipulated to believe that we are not important. This is our place and we need to keep quiet and just accept our lot. When the mandate of the people is truly known and established, the wealthy, powerful and famous will quake. But you see, they all know this and have not been willing to let us discover this basic truth for obvious reasons. We live in a world where the message is written 'for their eyes only.' They want our obedience. They want us to respect them for giving us a chance to work for them until we are no longer needed. This is their goal. Their systems are designed to enhance their position and destroy ours. But I say to you today, believe this can change and it will."

They were listening now. I had captured the moment.

"We will change it, if. This is the most important word. If. If we are willing to share a common task and not let those above us deter us from it. We will if we extract from our hearts a vision of how we wish our lives to be. And this is the most important if; if we are adamant about making this vision real. No one here will deny that in order to live we must work. We do not hate to work, but we are made to feel as if our labors are not appreciated by those who pay us. They never seem satisfied by our performance. We do not realize the value and necessity of our own labor. We do not cherish our own rights because we always compare ourselves with others. Without us, the system is nothing. If we withhold our labor, the industrial complex grinds to a halt. Without our power and support the complex is strangled. We possess the keys to wealth, power and fame. This is what companies do not want us to understand. This knowledge would destroy their stranglehold on us. We have too long believed we could not have more than one piece of pie, but believe me now, the pie is ours. We just need to take it."

There was soft growling in the pack, but no one wanted to stop me. I charged on. I was possessed.

"I am not advocating any overthrow of the government, of the system. Believe me I maintain our system provides the basis for all people achieving their dreams. But the problem is we are not in charge of the system. This needs to change and now. It can and must get better. I repeat it must get better. And it will. Yet we cannot delegate that responsibility to those who possess no sensibility to our plight. We, who are a part of the vast middle class, must assert ourselves and no longer be labeled the 'silent majority'. It is time we are heard. It is time we have power to control our own destiny. How can any millionaire who runs for public office understand what we need and how we feel? It is absurd to believe that a person from some upper crust family can share our true feelings and accept us as we are. The truth is that only one of our own, a native son or daughter from the rank and file, can be our spokesperson. It is our democratic right to be represented by one of our peers, not by someone who cannot understand our hopes, fears and dreams. We rarely can pick from one of our own. Elections cost millions of dollars. The deep pockets are tapped. Every candidate who digs down into those deep pockets is doomed. The candidate cannot be free to vote the true will of the people. Rarely are we afforded a sensible alternative to any of them. We are led to believe experience is necessary and no common man could lead other common men and women. Elections are held and promises are made and honored. We complain and swear not to let it happen again and then four years later forget and do exactly the same thing. It is as if we cannot see the hypocrisy in it. Or perhaps, it is that we do not wish to see it out of our own apathy. I say here today, we must see it and change it. If you do not believe it can be changed, it will not."

I paused taking a breath. They were mesmerized. The growling intensified. I could not wait any longer. It was happening at last and I believed in all that I said and the inspiration flowed through me like boiling blood.

"This land is your land. This land is my land. Our grandfathers, fathers and some of us have gone to war to protect our freedom. Ours has been a noble cause. We want to bring peace to the world. But is there peace in our own land when so many of us are sitting at home not working and wondering when the next plant closing will take away our life's work. We've won victories on the battlefields of the world, but we now must win this victory in the towns, cities and states of our own country. We can be better than we are. It is our moral duty to discern when we should go to war and when we should not. Yes, it is our moral duty to defend our nation. Freedom is the ability to be able to choose. Freedom is the opportunity to lead productive lives. Freedom is the chance to raise our families without fear of holocaust. Freedom is believing and worshipping a Higher Power. Freedom is the opportunity to maximize our potential. Freedom is voting for what we want and need. This is not some radical thinking but the design of our government embodied in our Declaration of Independence. The question is what keeps us from not taking advantage of all our freedoms. We must arise from our resting place and demand equality, justice and fraternity. These are not mysteries but necessities of life. Just as working for wages puts food on our tables, so do these ideals nurture our souls. We can never hope to be happy in life until we satisfy both our bodies and our souls. We need to work to put equality, justice and fraternity back into our system and back into our lives. We have lost them because we do not have the time to worry about some ideal when our realities are no work, little money and an insecure future. This must change and it must change now. Long ago, Henry Ford believed social unrest could be eliminated if a man were treated fairly, paid decent wages for his labors and treated with dignity and respect. Workers will always want more, but not just money: more hope, more freedom, more opportunity to fulfill dreams. This is the task at hand. We must invest ourselves in the attainment of a just and representative stake in the governing of our lives. Too often we lose sight of a better way because we believe it cannot be achieved. We can change the system by our vote. But we must all vote."

The growling grew louder when the word "vote" left my tongue and I understood but I still needed to help them to believe. This was our only hope. I could beat my gums forever but I could not do it without them. We were compatriots.

"I can tell by your reaction that the vote is no longer a cherished right of Americans. How can that be? You and I cast our votes in hope that who we elect will dutifully represent us. On a local level, the candidate is very visible and accountable to us. But on the national level, this is not necessarily so. This is not too hard to understand. Out of sight, out of mind. Politicians promise many things. How can they even remember what they've promised? Once elected, they face the reality of paying off their campaign debts by doing what their biggest financial supporters want them to do. My point is simply this. For working men and women who are the single largest voting block of all, we need fairer representation. How can a millionaire or billionaire represent us? He or she cannot. None of the people who are potential presidential candidates comes from the working class. Oh, yes, even Clinton had humble beginnings, but he quickly moved away from his roots and ascended into the 'ruling class'. They cannot visualize the American Reality of the common, blue-collar worker because none of them are one of us. A person would need to walk in our work boots for many miles in order to do that and it is nigh on to impossible to exchange social stations in life. They are who they are and we are who we are. This is not to say they are better or less than we are. They are just different."

For a moment, I studied their faces. I looked into each one of them, not glancing across them as a mass, but focusing on each pair of expectant eyes. My time had come and I hoped theirs would. What I saw gave me hope. What I felt buoyed me. What I heard muted my fears. There would be no tar and feather party. Jolly, Skinny Jack, Al, Bill and Denny and the others listened intently as did those I did not know. Whether they were in shock, I could not tell.

"Citizens, I am Leo Pollack, born in this city. I'm 47 now and of sound mind and body and am ready to stand up and be counted. We have the power to be honest above all and speak truth to power. We have the power to become truly brothers and sisters in our own land and in the world and stand together as working men and women. We have the power to create a better life for our children and their children. We have the power to stop the loss of our jobs and thereby our livelihood and recreate a new sense of stewardship in the workplace based upon pride. We have the power to correct social ills such as injustice, inequality and economic deprivation by honestly admitting they exit and then attacking them as we did the polio virus back in the 1950s. We have the power to maintain the highest standard of living in the world and still make it better for those who are not as fortunate as we are. We have the power to educate everyone who seeks to better him or herself so all can be prepared to face the global challenge. We have the power to administer to all those who are sick, not because it is lucrative to do so, but because it is the decent and moral thing to do. Now, I humbly ask you to support me with your vote as I announce to you today that I, Leo Pollack, an unemployed steel worker, a citizen of this nation who cares deeply for the people, want to be your candidate for President of the United States."

Stunned silence echoed in the room. Either, they did not believe what they were hearing, or heard what they could not believe. The bureaucrats behind the counters were no longer shouting for my removal. The officer, who was right in front of me, did not touch me. I was real because I was there in the flesh and my words were still ringing through the room. Perhaps he was fearful of reaching out to me because I was voodoo, taboo, magic, and insane or just an enigma. I dared to defy tradition. There was an eerie silence like the calm before a storm. But I was not finished.

"Now is the time to ring the liberty bell again. We the people need to speak with one voice and let it be heard all over the nation. We've listened to the democrats and their promises proved hollow. We've been massaged by the regressives and they speak with a forked tongue. Some think that the red tea party is speaking for us, working people. This is a lie. Billionaires are funding their movement. They want us to believe the government is the problem and only the free market can save America. We must repudiate their propaganda. I believe that the only thing that will save America is everybody working and producing something that contributes to the greater good. We can't continue to live on a federal credit card. We can't give tax breaks to the wealthiest Americans and bleed middle and lower income people to foot the bill. Forty-four of the founding fathers were millionaires in their own time. They created a democratic republic and thought that they would be able to mesmerize common men and women forever. They succeeded. Generations have passed and the only time that major changes in the history of our country have taken place is when common people band together and demand change. We vote for millionaires who tell us they care about us, but they don't know the first thing about work and the struggles we face every day. We hear their words and that is all they are. We know better. Our moment is now. Our uprising will sound across the nation. We are not capitalists or communists, but realists. If we are the greatest democracy in the history of the world, let us then live up to that challenge. It's happening right now across the world in Tunisia, Egypt, Libya, Bahrain, Jordan and the Mid East. It's happening in our own country right now in Wisconsin, Indiana, Ohio and New Jersey. People want their voices to be heard. Our voice must be heard. The voice of working people who want to work giving a fair day's labor for a fair day's wage. This is all we ask. We want to work and be productive and proud and free. This is the time for the uprising to begin. Stand with me. Stand up and be counted. Cast off the yoke of servitude and become a free person once and for all and share in the bounty of our land and the empire that we have created. Again, let me tell you who I am and what I want to do. My name is Leo Pollack, and I, an unemployed steel worker, a native born American citizen, a family man, of no real financial means, no specific professional accreditations, no real political affiliation although I do vote my conscience, limited religious connections, a little above average intelligence and much older than thirty-five, I am declaring today that I'm running for President of the United States. I am committed to speak for all working people, productive people, freedom loving people here and across the land and to work tirelessly to bring back justice and fairness and civility to this great land, so help me God!"

My voice died. There was silence in the room. I didn't know what to do. I stood transfixed upon the stage I'd chosen.

Then, like the rumbling of a hundred freight trains, a clapping sounded in the room and the mass of voices arose and there was pandemonium.

I jumped down from the counter top and was swarmed by the mass of people. What had happened? I wasn't fully aware of my surroundings. My eyes were flowing with tears. My heart was pounding and it was hard to breathe.

The apprehension disappeared from the peoples' faces. These hearty souls, who possessed little or no hope, little or no power, now had a chance to recoup some of it by believing in something greater than them. Though I may have bitten off more than I could chew, I knew that there was only one way to eat an elephant: one bite at a time.

There was a clapping of hands. Just two, a pair of gnarled, chapped hands clapping resolutely. To whom they belonged, I could not tell. They accepted me at face value. Then there was another pair. They shattered the silence and purged my soul of any fear I felt. Somewhere in the crowd, my words hit home. I was proud to be alive at this moment more than ever in my entire lifetime. Those first few claps like thunder forecast the coming storm. When the storm hit, I could not stand aloft any longer. The people surrounded me, clapped me on the back, congratulated, thanked and touched me deeply with an overwhelming show of affection and trust.

The voice of the people sounded.

"I heard you, brother. We heard you."

"Somebody said you were crazy, but you aren't crazy at all. You're one of us."

"I'm behind you one hundred and fifty percent."

"What do you want us to do?"

"Good speech. Great! Now win."

"You've got my vote, Leo."

"Where's your hand, man. Let me shake the hand of the next President of the United States."

I moved through the crowd on a human conveyor belt thanking them for listening to me and for their kind words but saying nothing else.

"You got guts man and you ain't a phony and you ain't no fool."

"Look out Republicans and Democrats, here comes Leo."

"Your old man would have been proud of you, Leo."

"We'll spread the word. We'll campaign for you. It's about time one of us had a chance to do it all. We're with you."

I was passed along. There were no more lines. A throng of people with bright eyes and warm smiles and open hands were milling everywhere. The words of encouragement continued to rain down upon me like a deluge.

"Steelworkers Unite. Americans Unite."

"Nobody in this place can't say you ain't looking for a job. Go get it."

"We want Leo! We want Leo! We want Leo!"

The chant arose and pandemonium echoed throughout the room.

A litany of the people continued. Tears rolled down my cheeks as people embraced me. Total strangers held me in their arms. I caught the fever.

"We want Leo. We want Leo. We want Leo."

We became a majority because we had courage. The overwhelming sense of duty to country and to my fellow man took firm root in my soul.

Still chanting "Leo, Leo, Leo" the mass of men and women became my mirror of America. I saw myself in them. They were kindred souls who would hear and have no doubt that there was a new order coming. They were not voting for me but for themselves and I hoped and believed that they would understand this intimately. The honor was not for me but for them. My energy was but a catalyst to help release the energy in them. Release their power to dream and fulfill those dreams. Perhaps now they would overcome their apathy and engage in the struggle to take back their country from the elite who treated them as merely numbers to be counted or discounted. My courage was their courage and theirs would generate courage in others. They were the source of the real power and the foundation upon which the America once promised long ago would now be founded.

An hour passed before I finally was able to sign up for unemployment and then I tried to get out of the building but the people would not let me leave.

"Are you really going to go through with it?"

"Yes. With your help," I replied.

"How are you going to finance a campaign?"

"One dollar at a time," I said.

"You know what's going to happen. Someone's going to try and buy you off."

"I'll die first before that happens. You pull the trigger," I implored.

"What makes you think you can run this country?"

"I can balance a check book and I know that there are enough smart people in this country that when there is a need for expertise, all I'll have to do is ask for help," I responded.

"You don't have a snowball's chance in hell to win?"

"If you vote for me, I'll have at least one vote. Each vote is one more that my challengers won't get," I laughed.

"Are you doing drugs?"

"Nope. Never have. Don't need them to be high. But that's a fair question and I hope that you believe me," I said.

"You got a campaign manager or a political machine to back you?"

"An hour ago, I hadn't even thought about running for President, so to answer your question, the answer is no. But what are you doing for the next year? I could use your help," I asked sincerely.

"They say that the next presidential campaign will cost a billion dollars. How are you going to raise that kind of money?"

"One dollar at a time. Three hundred million people live in this country. If everyone, man, woman and child donated one dollar to my campaign, I'd have three-hundred million dollars for the campaign. But look, I haven't really thought that far ahead. Right now I've got to just figure out what to do next," I said.

"You'd better get your head examined."

"I probably will by every pundit and journalist and psychiatrist in the country. I'm sure that Dr. Phil will have a field day with this story," I laughed.

"What qualifies you to be president of these here United States of America?"

"Like I said a while ago, I'm a native born person and I'm older than thirty-five years of age. That's all the Constitution says about qualifying to be president," I answered.

"What's your name, fellow?"

"Leo Pollack and I want to be your president."

"You ain't Polish are you?"

"Polish as they come and proud of it. My heritage is democratic. Poland was the first European country to try democracy and as you recall, it was the labor movement in Poland called Solidarity that contributed to the downfall of the Soviet Union. I come from a proud people whose land was overrun by the Mongols, the Turks, the Swedes, the Russians, the Germans, the Austrians and the Cossacks. Every time they were being invaded they dropped their plows, picked up their swords and went to war, defeated the invaders and then went back to their plows and rebuilt their country. Nothing is impossible if a man believes that it is his or her destiny to live life fully and with purpose," I intoned.

"What are you going to do right now that you've set this place on edge?"

"Go home and tell my wife that I'm looking for a new job," I chuckled. "She may be a little surprised."

"You seem pretty sure of yourself, young fellow, but you're not talking about any job. This is going to be a tough row to hoe."

"No doubt it will but nothing ventured, nothing gained. I'm up for the adventure and with your help, with your support, I'll make it," I said shaking his hand, the very first one of my infant campaign.

"If you did get elected, what would you do first?"

"Stop the bleeding of American jobs to other parts of the world. End the tax breaks for corporations who ship jobs overseas. Create an investment in America movement that would extend to every city, town, village and crossroads in America until every man and woman that wanted to work would be able to do so," I pledged.

"Pretty lofty goals to get done in eight years."

"No, four years. I'm declaring right now to all of you that I'm going to be a one term president and that's it. No waiting around killing time and trying to get re-elected. This isn't a career path for me. This is a mission, a commitment to the men and women in America who vote for me that I'm there to do the job and then get out and let someone else carry the baton for the next four years. I've always believed that no man or woman should make a career out of politics. Power corrupts and absolute power corrupts absolutely. If there is no second term the work must get done and right now. This is no popularity contest. This is a commitment to the people who may elect me that I'm not going to be hanging around waiting for the world to come to us. We're going to take the struggle to the people and the people will rise up and their voices will be heard and the country will be a nicer place to live in and that's as simple as I can make it," I said.

"What if you don't win?"

"I've already won. You're standing here listening to me, asking questions, wanting America to be better, the American Dream to be real. This election isn't about me, Leo Pollack. It's about you, American Citizen. I'm like you. My parents were born poor and worked hard and gave me a good life. My son's world isn't going to be the same as mine. The dream's dazzle has dimmed. It's time to create an uprising and take back the power from those who sell us out every chance they get. This unemployment office is just like the soup lines of the 1930s. The only difference is that we get money and not soup. The money will run out eventually and then what? We'll be living like homeless people. Jimmy Carter said it 30 years ago. There's a malaise in the country. People don't believe in their government anymore. The reason? We've been conditioned for 25 years starting with Ronald Reagan to believe that government is the problem. Well, my friends, it's not the government that is the problem but the people in government who don't represent us and do what's in the best interest of the majority of Americans."

"You've thought about this for a while, haven't you?"

"About running for President? No. I've spent my entire life watching, listening, reading, studying and hoping that just once there would be an opportunity to make a difference. I don't want to just hold a job. I want to make a difference. I want to create a movement based upon the ideals of our parents and grandparents and their parents that demands we do our best each and every day we crawl out of bed. A movement of people who respect each other's differences and cherish our similarities. I want to reward hard work with the fruit of labor and ingenuity with happiness and a sense of a job well done. There isn't anything magical or mystical about what I'm saying. It's after all, the American Dream just stated in terms that we all can understand and believe," I chanted.

"So you think you can really win?"

"What's winning? Winning the election is the final victory. Between now and the day of the general election there will be many skirmishes. In each one we move closer to the goal and that's to turn this uprising into a renaissance in America where the government of, for and by the people is finally brought to fruition. What we will have along the way is a platform for what we really need to say and that is we are no longer for sale. We are taking back our country from the corporate power elites, the billionaires who buy and sell people, the special interests whose voices are laced with hundred dollar bills. We can't fail to win if we change the course of America," I extolled.

"When are you going to start campaigning?"

"I already did. Today, tomorrow and every day until I either win or lose," I said.

"How are you going to mount a nationwide campaign without many resources?"

"I think I can do it on my unemployment checks and whatever dollar bills I collect during the campaign," I said wistfully.

"Where are you going to campaign? You don't have a plane to travel in so won't you be limited in your ability to get around?"

"As to the how, I'll figure that out by tomorrow. As to the where, I'm going to go to start with unemployment offices in every state and ask those who really understand what I'm saying to support me," I replied.

"You caused quite a stir in here today. How can we believe that you'll follow through with what you're saying? How can we believe you more than any other politician?"

"You can believe me because I'm not a politician. I'm an unemployed steel worker who's looking for a job. The new job just happens to be President of the United States. I come from little and expect little in life. I can't be bought off because I am not going to run for this office to make a career out of it. I just want to do my job and then leave office and come back here and hope that I can find another job that will feed my family and me and just be happy. That's all. There's nothing deep about it. What more can I say? You'll just have to trust that I'm a man of my word and that what I say I'm going to do, I'll do. That's my word on it," I intoned.

"You've got my vote."

"Thanks and you won't be disappointed," I replied and shook the woman's hand.

"What are you going to do now?"

"Go home. I've got a lot of planning to do," I said.

"Need a lift? You got a car?"

"A beat up old jalopy, but it still runs. Thanks for the offer," I replied.

"How will we know what to do next?"

"I haven't thought that out yet, but I'll figure it out by tomorrow," I said.

"You've got your work cut out for you. It will be an uphill battle."

"Nothing worth living for is ever easy. The time's come for a major change and not the kind of change that President Obama promised. He made his first mistake the minute he said he wasn't going to run his campaign on public funding. Once he started taking the private money, he was compromised. I won't do that. No contributions more than a $20. That's it. The rest will get sent back. Every donation will be listed by name. There won't be any PAC running my campaign. This will be the most transparent one in the history of our country."

"So if I give you money now, you'll take it?"

"No. I can't record it. Let me figure it out and then we'll start raising money. Right now I've got to make sure that what I'm saying can be done."

"Well, I'd still like to give you a buck for some coffee."

"No, let me buy you a coffee," I responded.

Everyone laughed. I shook more hands and thanked those who were gathered around me for listening and believing in a new movement of people with a mission that would never end, win or lose, as long as people believed in themselves and their own power to influence the future path of their country.

When I walked out into the rain, I was alone. The sun was peeking out in the west and the mists were rising slowly. A faint hint of a rainbow appeared and I stared at it wondering if it were a sign.

A vision is a gift. Fulfilling dreams begins with taking action. Moving from the present requires a decision. Once a yes or no is conceived, one step leads to the next and the journey begins. What the outcome will be is like rolling dice. The catalyst for every vision is human passion and the belief there is something better just ahead. If we possess the courage to seek it, we just might succeed.

2. Heritage

A man's birthplace is his heritage. Mine was steel, an amalgam of iron ore, scrap metal, sulphur, manganese, molybdenum, copper, carbon and other compounds melded together to form, when cold, a gray metal that is indistinguishable in quality from one ingot to another. Youngstown produced so much steel in the first half of the 20th Century it was nicknamed the "Steel Valley". Even Pittsburgh did not achieve the moniker. The Mahoning River was not water but a slurry of iron deposits giving it a distinctly reddish brown hue. The steel industry was the binding force for everything in the city. I was the third generation to go to the mills and was proud to be a steel worker. Even though I graduated from the State University, I shelved my degree and followed in the footsteps of my grandfather, father, mother, brother, aunts, uncles and cousins. I was the thirteenth person in my family to don the green fire retardant gear. Given my heritage, I did not have to adjust to endure the work. I was in my element: a steel worker and proud of it.

Red-brick-lined South Avenue ran north-south starting downtown and heading toward one of the suburbs. As I walked into town on the bricks, I remembered my mother telling me that my grandfather laid bricks during the Great Depression as part of the Works Project Administration or WPA. Along the way I passed Krakusky Hall where we held his funeral. He came to America in 1908 and stayed for a year but did not like being away from his Polish farm and his family. But five years later as the First World War heated up and Poland was being overrun by the Germans and the Russians, he returned to America. He worked in the mills in Chicago and then Youngstown and saved enough money to send for his wife and daughter. They arrived in America in 1919 travelling third class on a steamer. My grandfather was upset because he sent my grandmother enough money so she could travel first class, but she said it was a waste of money. She was always a frugal person and brought with her to the new country all her rural ways.

As a child, I lived in the Garden of Eden. My grandmother always raised a garden and along with it, she had apple, plum, cherry, peach, pear and plum trees in the backyard. She was a stout woman who always wore a dress and I can still remember how she rolled her nylons down whenever she went to work in the garden. Stash, my grandfather, hated to work in the garden avoiding it like a plague. But every spring, Grandma would cuss at him until he went out with a fork and turned over the rich soil covered in manure and other mulch. All summer long I ate fresh fruit and vegetables from the garden. It was a happy time. We lived with my grandparents until I was seven and my father finished building our own home.

The vast panorama spread before me was not the same town founded by John Young in 1779 and recorded in 1802 as part of the fledgling state of Ohio, 17th state in the Union. This was my town. I would always call it home no matter where I travelled or lived. I was not sure when I came to own it but I knew now that I always would. I owned it in thought if not in deed.

Once, an Olympian flame burned eternally near the Market Street Bridge and kept the city afire day and night. Now it was gone. When Republic Steel shut down, the flame went dark and the valley lost its light. When I was a little kid, I remember seeing it all the way from the north side where I lived. Unlike modern arc lamps, this natural gas inferno represented the fire that made our city what it was: a beacon for the world. We made steel. We were one of the leading producers in the universe of Core-Ten steel: a specialty grade that did not rust. Our corporate headquarters was built with it and stands even today as a symbol of what and who we were. Late at night you could see it lighting the skyline as its glow reflected off the faces of the buildings downtown. Clean, pure, natural gas from the earth burned brightly and gave us all hope. The huge pipe from which the gas flowed was still planted in the ground but now it was cracked and just a dark obelisk and a memory of things past.

I walked down Federal Street. I imagined I could feel a trembling beneath my feet. Somewhere deep inside the earth the machinations of man were still reverberating. Somewhere men were still making steel. The creaking and grotesque music produced by the production of steel filled my soul with a sense of stoic wonder. There were no plants operating now. They were gone, shut down by the captains of industry who did not want to invest in a dying complex of old plants and antiquated methods of production. My heart was heavy and I trudged along in the rain and wondered where this path was leading us. No man should ever miss the beauty of his birthplace. No man should ever feel like he cannot go home again.

White church spires and belfries and the football stadium recently completed and the Bell microwave towers stood watch on the north side to fill my eyes with the stark contrast between ancient and modern. We had come so far and yet had so far to go. I had just started myself.

Out of the old comes the new; from ashes a phoenix rises up and is born and conquers all. There was hope. There was in me a renaissance and a rebirth of wonder.

When I turned onto West Federal Street at the bottom of the hill, I sauntered on. Behind me was the impervious past and before me was the imperative future. So many men before me walked along this street, but very few walked this same path. At the square, I stopped and remembered the day when I saw Jimmy Carter standing in the center of the city and saying, "Hi, I'm Jimmy Carter and I want to be your president." In my heart, the moment lived. Was I destined to follow his footsteps? I wondered.

In 1775, Pennsylvanians from Westmoreland County poled boats up the Mahoning River to extract salt from the springs north of the city. Salt for life. Salt for war. Salt for the preservation of food. I could taste the saltiness of my own sweat as the rain washed it from my brow to my lips. I was the salt of the earth. Like LaSalle, who was credited with being the first white man to penetrate the area known as Ohio, I penetrated an area where few men dared go. I was alone. I was an unsettled man in the wilderness of his own dreams.

Central Square was an oval in reality but we persisted in calling it a square. It was redecorated, modernized, closed to traffic, ran east to west but it was still the center of our town. No subway trains rumbled through the city's bowels. We were small. Simple. Old. Dying.

Most buildings were now closed. Strouss's and McKelvey's and a host of other department stores went the way of the gooney bird. Malls and shopping centers made them obsolete. The Paramount and Warner Theatres were boarded up. I sat for a few minutes on a bench and stared in awe and wonder at just how much this town changed in the past thirty years. There was no connection with the past except through memories and they were growing dim with time. The city had matured for it was attempting to live in peace with that which it could not change. It was dependable, wobbling through this crisis unscathed, refined, rejuvenated and a little resentful. Powers beyond its boundaries attempted to humble it but it just would not submit. Living without complaint, it clung to a vital force like a magnet to iron. The cold rains of February fell upon us all and we hunkered down and knew there was something ahead but just did not know what that was. The fountain in the middle of the square was not active, but the fountain of the universe was and from its source burst an eternal hope.

I knew it was time to go when I felt the rain pouring down upon me, chilling me to the bone. Hustling along, I walked around the center of the city square.

Many years ago, all the buildings on East Federal Street were razed, and a new Post Office and the IRS building were left standing as pillars on the edge of the city. I watched the people as they scurried through the rain. They were intense, Youngstownian, Ohioans, Americans wondering during these uncertain times where America was headed. Wondering, "Who will be our next President?" I felt a chill in my spine and wondered too.

One industry dies and another is born. There is no economy like the prison industry. I stared at the supermax prison built on the east side of town and wondered, "How did we get to this state of being?" Once there were less than a half million Americans in prisons, but now, more than 2.3 million convicts were wards of the federal, state and local lockups. "Where are we heading as a society?" I heard the statistics. I wondered at how we ever hoped to reverse this descent into hell. The average convict read on a fourth grade level. Criminality correlates directly to Illiteracy. The Reverend Jesse Jackson made a concerted plea to end this madness. "Give me the fifty thousand you spend each year to house a convict and I'll spend that money on a Harvard education and end the cycle." In congress, the republicans just cut funding for "Head Start", the most

important, effective program ever created to prepare children for success in school. "Boehner is such a fool," I muttered to myself. It's madness. How can we ever hope to change what we are doing with such short-sighted thinking? I wondered how anyone could ever work in a prison. I knew I could not. I would feel like I was in prison every day. In this present economy, we were all prisoners without walls. Our fears were locking us into a mindset that kept us worried, anxious and lethargic. Sometime all this had to end or we would certainly implode as a society.

Black smoked spewed out from the smokestacks of Ohio Edison's boiler plant. Heat converted water into steam and powered turbines generating electricity to light and heat our world. There was no way to deny the contrast between light and dark. I smelled the heavy sulphur from the coal smoke and accepted it as the source of the power that ran through the lines overhead.

Casting a glance at the rusty river far below I knew everything was different and yet the same. The iron residue floated in that river like red blood cells. It never froze even on the most frigid nights. Carrying the lifeblood of the valley, the Mahoning flowed into the Shenango River, and they roared toward the Ohio and the Ohio into the Mississippi and finally, every drop poured into the Gulf of Mexico. My father once told me that he swam across the Mahoning and I believed him. But that was fifty years ago at a time when the mills were young, the water much cleaner and there were no ordinances against swimming in the river. There was a recent movement called the "Green River Ordinance" devised to return it to its former state, but it died quickly. The river was blood red for a reason. It was the main artery of the heart of our way of life and it was destined to die with us. So be it.

I turned onto Belmont Avenue and passed St. Elizabeth's Hospital. I was one of thousands of post-war babies born there nearly a half century ago. At that time, it was much smaller. Now it loomed above me with its cross-shaped architecture, the place of my birth, and my wife's and my son's. Mine was not that clear to me, but his was and, in him, the miracle of life became real to me. Somewhere in the womb of the hospital right now new life was entering this world and in its cellars, the dead were awaiting their final journey and along its corridors others were struggling to stay alive. To live: to breath, to walk, to see, to hear, to smell, to smile, to speak, to think, to feel, to touch. Life was so sweet.

Belmont Avenue continued on to become RT. 193 and went to Ashtabula and Lake Erie 60 miles north. I turned west onto Oxford Avenue toward home. Parmalee School no longer existed but a playground still was fenced in where the school once stood. It was decrepit now. Few played in it. Across from the playground, Bejak's Garage still stood but was closed to patrons. The white walls were full of graffiti and the Texaco sign was gone. George lived in Florida, or so I heard, but he might even be dead. He was a star of a man always willing to let a kid crawl down into the cellar and watch him drain the fluids that kept motors alive. He was second generation and proud to be an American, a small businessman and just too ornery to change with the times. He didn't believe in credit cards. Independence cost him his establishment because he did not compromise. He could not understand, nor perhaps did not want to, how others whom he did not know could dictate to him how much to charge for his products and his services. George made the choice to toss in his grease rag.

Stately buckeye trees lined Oxford Avenue right to our door. Each home along my path was a castle. Each owner, a lord. From the old country to the new, people journeyed to America. They were the uprooted who took root in a new land. Few young people lived here now. We were an anachronism. Suburbia stole the city's lifeblood. Ranch homes with aluminium and vinyl siding that required no upkeep like these mastodons did were their choice today. These castles were well-preserved, testimonials of old world heritage. I wondered what Oxford looked like in the early 1900's when my grandfather moved here from the old country. He was a proud man but he was chased from his home by warring nations bent on destroying one another. He had to leave his home or die. I often wondered if that was why he just sat and stared off into space smoking his cigarettes and not talking very much. In his broken English he would say to me, "This is no country. This is not my country." His opaque blue eyes reflected a lifetime of agony and travail.

The homestead passed out of our hands after grandma died and grandpa could not live alone anymore. The new owners planted grass in the garden and parked in the yard, but the dignity of the place remained. We bought it many years later before it lost all its value. An ancient porch swing hung from the rafters and provided a place for one to sit and enjoy the soft scents of the flora. Basic gloss white enamel and green trim adorned the ninety-year-old wood. Great towering trees shrouded it from a summer heat. The home, like the city, had matured. This was home. There was no place like it. I still did not own it in deed, but it was and always would be mine. I was raised in the warm surroundings and would die there for I had vowed this a long time ago. Within these walls, I experienced peace and joy, and though the outside world might be in turmoil, inside there was always a measure of equanimity. Ancient odors wafted into my nostrils from every room taking me back in time and place. I was the lord of this castle and my lady was waiting inside for me. I hoped my son would experience the joy of his youth on the same stage that I had.

I stood outside in the rain just staring at the old place. Like the city of my life and the home of my youth, I had matured and I would keep my promises, make no alibis, and offer no excuses.

3. Home Sweet Home

I marched up to the side door of the house and opened it. We never locked it. I climbed the few steps of the landing and entered the kitchen. A chill escaped my body as I stood in the billowing heat. The smell of sweet meat pie and baked potatoes filled the room. My stomach growled reminding me that I had not eaten all day long. Barbara, or "Basha" as I called her, was busy cooking. I stared at her as she bent over the ancient iron sink making a salad. Steam glazed all the windows. I took off my shoes and placed them on the rack. She did not turn around perhaps not hearing me or ignoring me. "Does she already know?" I wondered. Her strong back was facing me and I admired how lovely she looked standing there in her realm. She was my Princess. This was her domain and I respected her rule.

"Guess who?" I called out.

"Is that you, Leo?" she asked.

"None other," I replied as I padded quietly into the kitchen in stocking feet. Long ago we adopted the Japanese tradition of going with stocking feet in the home.

She turned around and we kissed. I held her back from me for a moment so I could see her face. "She knows," I told myself. A faint blush covered her cheeks and her dark eyes sparkled in the kitchen light's glow. They were smouldering embers in the fire of love.

Basha turned away and began to set the table and her hair hid her face from me again. I wrapped my arms around her and we were one for a moment.

"You took a long time to get home," she said bluntly, placing silverware down near the plates and neatly setting napkins beside each dish.

"You weren't worried about me were you?" I asked tentatively.

"No. Not at all. What kind of trouble could you get into going over to the unemployment office? So what's new?" she asked. It was a loaded question.

"Oh, I was just taking my time. I stopped off downtown and walked around for a little bit. Sat down in the square and was just studying my home town."

"And what did you see, learn?" she asked leading me along.

"We live in a beautiful city," I said courageously.

"Do we? What makes it so?" she asked.

"Yes, very beautiful."

"This is a dying city," she said. "Look around, Leo. Everything is dying. The mills, the schools, the fabric of our city is shredding around us."

"So I see it as autumn and you see it as winter. It is a mature city."

"No Leo. It is winter," she uttered strongly.

"To be followed by spring," I countered.

"Sometimes the romance of life dries up when the economics dry up. It is sad when, in some measure, beauty is lost. I guess everything has a price."

"So spring will come and the trees will turn gold and then green and we'll plant our victory garden and keep hope alive." I leaned against the sink and watched her dedication to cooking a fine meal for her family.

"I love you, Leo, because you are a dreamer and sometimes in spite of it."'

"And I love you, Basha, because you are practical and sometimes in spite of it."

Her eyes bore into me like lasers and I fathomed worry and strain. She was no common woman for she was part puritan stock and part Native American. She was a noble woman.

"Where's Janko?" I asked.

"He's in his room working on the computer. He rarely watches TV since we got that magic machine for him."

"It is a TV," I teased.

"You know what I mean," she bantered back.

John Lawrence, our only son whom we called Janko, came very late in life. Basha carried him way past term and we thought she might not be able to deliver naturally. All went well and we now had a healthy 7 year-old.

"I remember when I was seven and used to walk to my aunt's house to watch TV with her on Saturday nights. Now we can have magic boxes in every room, connect them with computers and run the entire house via the phone lines. Things have changed."

"So they have, but for the better?" she asked.

"I'm not sure. We have survived because we are better," I said, believing it to my core.

"Better than what?" she asked.

"Better than those who have lost the power to imagine a better way to live. Better than those who want to suck the lifeblood out of our people and make them slaves to the system. Better than those who accept defeat when faced with any type of adversity," I replied.

"Our parents survived the Great Depression," she added.

"And we will survive the Great Recession," I said.

"Yes they did and it left its mark on all of them as did WWII. That whole generation."

"And we survived the 1960s, 70s, 80s, 90s and Y2K. Do you realize that in 1900, a dollar was worth 100 cents? In 1930, a dollar was worth only 50 cents. By 1960, the same dollar was worth only 28 cents. By 1982, the same dollar was worth only 9 cents. Today, who knows what a dollar is worth? Times are tough but we seem to be able to adapt to them."

"That's all we can do, isn't it? Adapt?" she asked.

"No, I believe we can do more. We can come out of this gyre in better shape than we ever imagined." I wanted to tell her now but held off for some reason. I could feel it rising in me. Consuming me. Burning my soul.

"Well, you're unemployed now and hopefully that can get better.
Did you qualify?"

"Yes, I did."

"How long?" she asked.

"I guess the 99 weeks will be my run this time around," I said. "The extension will be enough to get us by and since we don't have any debt, we'll be just fine."

We were silent for a moment. She was alone with her thoughts and I with mine. I knew that she knew and yet she just would not ask me. The contemplation of money always seemed to keep us apart. I disliked this feeling but it was just our reality.

"How many times have you been laid-off now?" she asked.

"Last count, maybe ten or eleven in the past ten years," I said.

"What a strange way to live! Work for a bit and then not. Go collect money for not working and then just sit around waiting, waiting to go to work. The money is so false, so unreal, and so absurd. Nothing in this system makes any sense. Somebody ought to do something."

"Unemployment is like a common cold. It slows the body down and a person does not feel up to par, normal. But it can also be a blessing in disguise."

"How?" she asked incredulously.

"It gives a person a chance to stop and think, to sit still and contemplate what life means, what a person has accomplished, what is of utmost value, and then where one's energy should be invested. I realize it is no panacea, but it could be a lot worse."

"Yes it could. You could not qualify for unemployment and then you would have to go out and try to find another job."

"I've given that a lot of thought today," I said evasively.

"What conclusions have you come to?" she asked staring right into my heart.

"We have something special, you, me and Janko. I love to come home and be with you and the boy. Parents are working long hours and kids are just left to their own devices without guidance, without training, without love in some cases."

"I agree with that," she said. "If parents don't teach their kids what is right and honorable then who else will? The quicker we disenfranchise the family system the faster we will destroy our way of life."

We heard the pitter patter of small feet on the hardwood floor.

"Daddy! Daddy!" my son shouted as he ran into my arms and I lifted him up and twirled him around calling him my "Superboy". He laughed mightily and as I went to put him down he screamed, "More. More. More." I did it again because he loved it, this foolish special play, loved it almost as much as I did. I knew that I could not lift him forever. One day he would be a man and then he would be able to pick me up.

Finally, I put him down as my arms started to get tired. He called for "More" but I said, "We need to get ready for dinner, son."

"Ah, but can we do it again after supper?" he asked.

"Maybe we can, maybe we can."

"Let's eat, Mom. Let's eat. I want to play with Daddy some more."

Basha had already begun to lift the food from the stove. "You two boys better get washed up. We'll eat in a moment."

We both turned to go to the bathroom but as I walked out I looked back at her and winked, she smiled and we knew it was forever and not just for a season. But did she know the rest? I wondered.

When we sat down to eat, we held each other's hands, formed our "family circle" and I said, "We give thanks for our good health and this good food and our family and for the rain in the sky that waters the good earth below and for this time when we can be together, Amen."

For awhile, everything except our knives and forks and spoons were quiet. This was the time to eat, to nourish our bodies because everything else could wait for a bit. I ate heartily for I was famished because I had not eaten since this morning. We ate nothing fancy. Steak was never on our table. I never complained because a man does not live by bread and meat alone. Janko was growing fast, too fast. I knew it would not be long before he would be too big to pick up and that made me sad-happy. He would be a young man and I would be the older one.

This day, this meal was special, not because it was anything like a holiday but because we were all together and we had so much to give thanks for, each one of us. We lived a simple life with the barest essentials: food, clothing, shelter, food, family and lots of love. To complicate it would be a disservice to all. I knew it and avoided thinking much about it. Everything would change for a while. The thought whirled around inside of me. But these thoughts dissipated as I sat at this table for I had grown up eating at it. I had my first supper here as a baby and I hoped to have my last supper here as an old man. The oak and stainless steel weathered well the passage of time. Grandma had this table and it was all that I had by which to remember her. This house and this table were memories from my youth. Grandma and Grandpa were my connection to the past. She represented the power of her people. But he was its conscience. Now they were both gone and with them my connection to the Old World. But this New World with all its turmoil, its challenges, its contradictions, its overwhelming complexity loomed before me. If I were Homer, I was sure that I could write another Odyssey. My journey was going to be filled with obstacles and there would be storms and other phenomena beyond my mortal control. There would be no peace for me except at home. This one place would be my bastion. To the best of my ability I would not let the world enter these sacred walls.

Perhaps only once in a man's life does truth make itself known to him who hears it. If he fails to listen to it, then it is quickly lost. It is a fleeting shadow present for one moment and then gone forever.

"Supper okay?" Basha asked me breaking my reverie.

"Great, Mommy," Janko said. "How about you, Daddy?"

"Just fine, son." And to her, "Great meal, dear."

"You seem preoccupied," Basha said softly.

""What's pre-occ-u-pied?" Janko asked.

"I thought how best to answer his question so he would fully understand. I was proud, happy that he was an inquisitive child. "It means when you're doing one thing like eating and thinking about something else completely different."

"Oh," he said mystified.

I did not elaborate, but waited.

"So?" she said, looking intently at me.

"Well…"

"That's a deep subject," she joked. This was her way. She was not a prying person and it was because of this quality that I truly loved her.

"I know. I know. So is what I'm about to tell you," I said, stopping and waiting for a moment to gather my thoughts and feelings.

She tensed for a second and then relaxed. It was subtle, almost invisible, but after so many years of marriage we knew each other well.

Carefully, I began. "When I was at the unemployment office today I had a vision, an epiphany, and an overwhelming experience. I saw myself standing before masses of down and out people giving a speech, talking about the reasons I was the most qualified person to be the president of the United States."

"I knew it was another one of your dreams, your fertile imagination playing havoc with you."

"You going to be president, Daddy?"

"Daddy's telling us something very special, so listen carefully, Janko," she said touching him on the arm.

"You knew all along didn't you?" I asked her.

"Yes," was all she said.

"You let me sit here and eat dinner and didn't say anything?"

"Yes," was all she said again.

I felt waves of love and confusion flowing through me. "I was the leader," I continued, "and I followed my people wherever they went. It seems crazy and all, but I truly believe I am being called. It was more than an experience, a vision. It was real. You know, I never aspired to be much in life. I'm forty-seven years old now. Once I wanted to be a doctor, but I wasn't much good at chemistry. But this I can believe in. This I can do. This is not only something I can do, but want to do, need to do. I believe it's because today I saw so little hope in the peoples' faces and that just should not be. America is supposed to be a land of hope and dreams and my dream is to become the next president of the United States."

I stated it so simply it seemed too simple. There was total silence in the room.

Basha stared at me. There was an unearthly silence until Janko exclaimed, "You can do it, Daddy. Why not?" His words were an affirmation and not an interrogation. She did not speak and I knew that her common sense was reeling through that logical mind of hers. She took nothing lightly. This was her way. She was a serious, no nonsense kind of woman. Juxtaposed against my often, fickle and imaginative nature, it was our strength.

"You already knew what I was going to tell you, didn't you?"

Basha smiled wanly and said, "Yes, I already knew. We've had a number of calls asking if it were true."

"What was true?" I asked.

"Whether this was the home of Leo Pollack and were you the one who was going to run for the presidency."

"Who called?"

"WKBN News. Some radio station. I lost track," Basha said.

"I knew you knew," I replied.

"Leo, this is a small city and it's not every day that some blue collar, unemployed steel worker stands up in the unemployment office and defies logic and common sense and tells a bunch of unemployed people that he's going to run for president."

"You know it all? You know what I did?"

"They told me. I just listened. I didn't know what to say to them nor to you when you got home. Leo, what have you done?"

I hesitated for a minute and then said, matter-of-factly, "I am going to do it. This is America and all men are guaranteed the right to seek and hold office if they meet the age requirement and are native born. I'm both and I'm ready."

She knew that I was dead serious.

My declaration of candidacy was perhaps the most serious consideration in my entire life. I hoped she would realize this. Gladly, I knew she did because we knew each other very well. We were friends, lovers and soul mates.

"But there are going to be so many candidates running for president and then there is the incumbent. The odds are stacked against you even before you get started," she cried.

"As long as you believe in me then all the rest don't count, don't matter."

"I have always believed in you, Leo. You are my husband and my friend and you work hard and you take good care of Janko and me and you read and think and Oh, I don't know what I'm saying."

I hesitated for a moment and then stated, "I am ready for whatever comes with this decision. This is America and all men were guaranteed the right to seek and hold office if they met the requirements. I meet both and I'm ready."

She stared into my eyes. What she saw scared and inspired her for I was gazing back into hers with every ounce of my energy making her fully appreciate the intent of my declaration. She could see that I was resolute. Some women would have guffawed, but Basha was not that kind of person. I really did not deserve her, someone so patient, understanding and devoted to my dreams and goals.

Janko asked excitedly, "Does that mean if you win and become president that we would move to Washington and live in the White House?"

I laughed a little, more to break the tension than to make light of the matter. "It surely does. I've got a lot of work to do before we can move so just keep your toys in their box ready to travel."

"Oh, wow, the White House. We could have a good old time in that big place," he said.

"We sure could. We sure could," I exclaimed.

Sombre moments slowly passed, but she did not respond and I began to wonder. Perhaps my approach had been poor. Perhaps I should have asked her opinion first before just blurting it out. She knew all along. The moment I walked in she knew. How could she. I called a spade a spade and did not bandy any words. Perhaps it was a flaw in my character. I would not know until later. So what if it seemed absurd. Yes, the odds were against me. So what? I was no diplomat.

"You're committed to this goal?" she asked matter-of-factly.

"Yes, I am, but I need your support. It will not be easy. I am willing to make a commitment to you and Janko. I won't sell out. I won't be dishonest. Most of all, I'll try to be home for dinner every night."

"The first two I know you will. As for the last promise, hold your tongue. Once you're on the road, you're going to be gone day and night. I know you're not one to be denied. Please don't ever sell out and do everything you can to win. We will help you, Janko and me."

I laughed aloud, reached over and held her hand. I grasped my son's hand. The three of us formed our family circle and all was well.

"You are an amazing, wonderful, undeniable dreamer and if I didn't know you better I would think you were crazy."

"If you would not support me I'd give it all up as a lark and go look for a steady job tomorrow."

"Don't you get to be president for four years, Daddy," Janko said.

"Yes, son, if I get elected."

"Well, what if you don't get elected?" he asked.

"Then I get to stay on unemployment. That's not working."

"I don't mind," he said. "It's nice having you home all the time."

"And I like that, too. In order to become president, I'll have to be gone a lot of the time. You won't mind?" I asked him.

"Not if you win and we move to the White House. Then we'll have a lot of fun."

"I'll keep that in mind then and make sure that I win."

"I'm going to go back and do my homework," Janko said. "May I be excused?" he asked waiting.

"Sure, go ahead son," I replied.

He ran off leaving us alone.

Silence wrapped around us and we sat still just looking at one another. In the living room the grandfather clock struck seven. Her eyes were staring at me intently and I knew she was still feeling the effects of what was coming.

"Let me just ask one question," she said.

"Okay. Fire away."

"What makes you feel the need to be a saviour?"

"Saviour?" I asked. I was not sure how to respond. Thinking carefully, I wondered what she wanted to know. "I don't feel the need to be a saviour, but I do want to save a dream. I didn't serve my country by joining the military. I feel the need to do something. Things seem so hopeless right now. I just want to do something. It does seem a little crazy to do this. But, what the heck? Nothing ventured, nothing gained. Somebody's got to save the race."

"You're being melodramatic," she accused me.

"It's your race too."

"What race?" she asked.

"The human race. Every day we deny what's happening in the world. The leaders of our countries, not just this one, are on a collision course with catastrophe. This economic downturn is just the beginning of the real cataclysm. Food prices are going up all over the world. Look what happened in Egypt this past week. The entire mid-east is going up in flames as people realize that oppression is not the way to live. Our world is ripping apart at the seams and we Americans are sitting back and watching as if we were not a part of it, had nothing to do with it. I can't wait around and watch. I've got to do something because the time is running out."

What more could be said. She gazed at me in wonder. It was done.

Finally, she broached some practical matters. "I don't mean to be facetious," she said, "but how are you going to finance the campaign?"

I laughed and said, "You are always so practical. But I've given this some thought. As soon as I can, I'll start a web page and get people to donate. No more than twenty bucks at a time. I won't let this turn into another McCain-Obama fiasco. There are three hundred million people in the country. If each person donated just a buck, I'd have plenty to make a fight. There's a lot to think about but I've got tomorrow to start figuring out what and how. I'm going to seek as much free publicity as I can. I just don't want to be owned by anyone."

"Not even me?" she teased.

"You're the only one. You and the boy. But you know what I'm saying. I just can't let anyone buy me out. I can't be owned. I've got to qualify for public funds and to do so, I'll have to really make a good showing across the country. I'll stage some marches and get some publicity that way. I'm going to meet with the publisher of the Vindicator and get his support. I want to meet with the union leadership and get them involved. TV, radio, everything to get publicity. I want to make most of my speeches at unemployment offices across the country. Thirty million voters show up there every week. That's one heck of a voter base and it will be mine. The unemployed and disenfranchised."

"I know you, Leo. You'll worry about it. I can see you pacing the floors now and wondering why the people are just not getting behind you. It's an uphill struggle all the way."

"There are so few people who in their lives are able to fuse their vocation with their avocation."

"Since when have steelmaking and being president been so?" she asked.

"Since right now. Steel is pure when it is molten and nothing but white heat. This is the dream in its purist form. As steel is an alloy, so is the presidency, a blending of all the best minds with different skills and perspectives making something better than the individual parts. The president is the steel. The presidency is the alloy."

I stood up and started to pace the floor. The words were flowing through me like molten iron ore. I could see it all, the coming together in a new form, something never created before, a new national order with the people represented by one of their own. I sensed the power rising in me like a spring storm and it flowed through my veins, into my heart and out my mouth.

The words burst out of me like lightning strikes.

"Citizens, I am standing in front of you because I feel a profound sense of duty toward this nation. In the past three decades, greed has usurped human decency. My hope is to make an alloy of the best minds and hearts and souls and pour them into one ladle to produce the best presidency ever. I am but a catalyst to this equation. I am nothing. We are everything. This will be a presidency of the people, for the people and by the people. This will not be strictly partisan politics, but truly a representative one made up of all of us. We've drifted apart, put one agenda in front of another and lost our course. We don't accept the common good as our goal. Greed and selfishness and a personal perspective blind us to what is necessary for our nation's survival. If we are truly men and women of the Iron Age, let us proclaim it with dignity. Let us sing until our hearts burst. Let us labor until we are exhausted. Let us persevere until we succeed in repairing our nation and making the dream a reality. Then, as a people, let us celebrate and play like never before. Let's ring the liberty bell again and make it heard around the world that America is not the greatest nation in the world, but a nation among many who is willing to be the light that leads the family of man out of this perpetual darkness that has caused us to lose our way. Let us buoy all hopes with down to earth common sense. The tolling of the liberty bell is for all of us and not for just a select few. We've heard it in our sleep and when we are awake. We've studied it all our lives. It is greater than any one of us but not greater than all of us. We are a part of a greater whole. Our goal is to practice honesty above all else and be true to our own hearts. Our goal is to say no to injustice. Our goal is to support strong nuclear families not strong nuclear arsenals. Our goal is to provide full health care for every man, woman and child. Our goal is to resurrect dying cities and breathe life into them again. Our goal is to raise education and educators above the status of sports heroes and entertainers for it is the teachers who inspire children to become future steel workers, automakers, electricians, plumbers, carpenters, oh yes, and doctors, lawyers and politicians. Our goal is to make the economy work for all people not just those with influence and a politician's ear. We've got to figure out how to make a renewable economy, one that grows with realistic and sustainable metrics. Our goal is to protect the health of every person without jeopardizing the health of industries by realistically studying and proposing ways to safeguard both at the same time. Our goal is to protect freedom of speech and press and accept different and opposing points of view as the lifeblood of our system and not some sort of cancer in the body politic. For 235 years this great experiment in democratic living has taught us all it is well worth the struggle. Our freedom is not a gift but something we earn and we must continually invest in it, or we will lose it. We shall continue until our dying days to uphold the truth and beauty of that original document."

Basha was staring at me with tears in her eyes. I was not sure what she was thinking but I must have touched something inside of her. I spoke from the heart. The dream was real to me. I didn't notice that Janko had entered the room while I was pacing. He had the look of wonder on his face. I stopped pacing the floor and watched them. My heart was beating madly like a tom-tom.

I turned and wiped the moisture off the windows and stared outside at a white world. My heart chords played a tune I'd never heard before. They were staccato and somewhat discordant but not offensive to the ear. I was not sure where the sounds came from but they were in me. All my life I felt something churning in me, a calling, a challenge to do something more for the land in which I lived. This was not about power and control, status and wealth and influence. This was about service. I just wanted to stand up and be a part of the solution. The calling never had substance to it as it did now. I desperately needed their support and their love.

When she finally spoke there were even more tears in her eyes. "That was beautiful, Leo, so beautiful. So full of promise. Oh, Leo, I love you."

She arose and came into my arms. He sat in awe, not moving. I reached out to him and he came and joined us. We were three simple people in love. I felt tears but they would not flow. I wanted to cry, to scream, to shout out "Go tell it on the mountain to let my people go". I wanted to tell these two how I felt, how scared and confused and lonely I felt at that moment. I wanted to tell them that they meant more to me than anything in the world. Yet, I possessed another dream, or it possessed me and I was going to make it come true.

"I love you both very much," I said to them as we held each other and then I could not hold it any longer and wept. The tears flowed like a primordial flood. My face became sodden with all the anguish that I felt. In the deluge, a great barrier washed away. I realized they loved me for who I was and not for what I was or what I might become. All day long, I faced inner turmoil that I thought would never end. As I walked around the square, I felt some relief, but nothing like I felt now. There had been too many images dancing before me. They were demonic and elfin-like, and some made garrulous noises and others were immobile and cold as stone. Now in the safety of my own castle with the drawbridge up and the mote full, they could not reach me. My family protected me. I regained my strength. I was a man with simple wants and few needs and the love of mother and son.

Our family moment seemed to last forever. We did not want it to end. Power flowed from each of us into the other. We held each other tightly because we all intuitively knew that this connection could not last given what was coming. The power of the family union was the center of the universe, the life force of the nation. We carried within each of us a separate peace and shared it like a buoy tossed on a raging sea.

Janko, crushed in our embrace, squirmed and we released him. He walked over to the window, and peeked out and saw the snow.

"Hey Daddy, you think there's enough snow to go sledding?"

I still held Basha firmly, but I said, "Oh, maybe."

"Can we? Can we?"

"Sure, why not?" I smiled at him and her. My tears were gone now and there was joy in my heart. I felt no fear.

"Go and get dressed. We'll go out and have some fun."

"Okay," he cried and raced out of the room. His little feet banged up the steps as he raced to his room to dress.

We stared into each other's eyes. I could see wonder in hers and I wondered what she saw in mine. I found out.

"I believe in you, Leo," she said affirmatively and I felt a deep rush inside of me. "We will make this work somehow."

"I'm happy that you do because without you I couldn't undertake this mission."

"You've got it. You know you do. I could not be more proud of you. You are so special in my eyes. You've always been destined to do something more. We just never knew what it was. Maybe that's why I love you so much."

"When are you going public with this?" she asked.

"Already have," I replied.

"What? When?"

"At the unemployment office today. I flipped out. I jumped up and let the people know. I rang the bell telling them we were going on a mission together."

"This will be an interesting time as the story unfolds."

"Very, very interesting," she said.

"Yes, and we'll write the story one day at a time."

"Will they believe you?" she asked.

"We'll find out. I'm sure that most won't believe me at first, but as time unfolds and my message gets out, then there will be a rising tide of support. At least, I hope so."

"It's a noble goal," Basha said.

"Yes and a very human one. Aren't all things done honestly by men and women noble as well as human?" Before I could answer her, Janko returned dressed and ready to go.

"Let's go Daddy!"

"You've got your first follower," she said laughing aloud.

"And the best," I said.

"Let's go Daddy before the snow melts."

He pulled me from the room by the arm. He had not learned patience yet.

"See you later," I called out to her as I got my hat, coat and boots on and then he and I left her alone.

"See you," she called out to us as the door closed behind us.

We were gone, out in the new snow, sleds following us on leashes, away from the warmth of the hearth, but not too far away, never too far away, from life close to home. But it would never be as sweet or the same way ever again and all of us knew it deep down in the recesses of our spirits.

4. A Majority Is One Man with Courage

A mass of people stood before me. I was giving a speech. They booed and hissed at me until I said, "There is no hope, no hope at all unless you listen to the facts and stop killing the messenger because you don't like the message." They got a rail and some tar and feathers and were about to ride me out of town when a chorus of little angels sang about the beauty of the steel mills and fire in each man's soul. A halo appeared over the mills and there was fire in the hearths again. An airplane flew over the city dropping bombs on Central Square but it was not destroyed because the city was protected by a huge dome of core-ten steel. The square had traffic flowing in every direction: east, west, north and south. McKelvey's and Strouss's were operating and the Warner and Paramount Theatres were open. Seafood stores and poultry markets and the Park Burlesque Theatre were there. I was alone in the crowd and no one knew me because my face was as dark as coal and all the other faces were lily white. No one noticed my color. There was a brilliant sun shining. Rain was falling and a wonderful rainbow stretched from one end of the sky to the other. Somewhere off in the distance the tolling of a bell resonated across the valley and everyone stopped and looked up and listened.

Basha poked me a number of times and finally I awakened in a cold sweat and looked at her. "Answer the phone. I know it's not for me."

My mind was still foggy. The phone kept ringing. On the seventh ring, I picked it up and at that moment, my entire life changed. I answered a few questions and said "yes" more than a dozen times, and finally hung up.

"Who was that?" Basha asked.

"WKBN TV. They want to come and interview me today."

"No way?"

"Yes, you heard me. They got wind of what happened in the unemployment office and after doing some research, they are after the story."

"The die is cast, Leo," she said. "When are they coming?"

"One o'clock. They want to get the story on the 6:30 news tonight."

"Oh, and to think that yesterday you were just a statistic, another unemployed steel worker waiting in line to get your benefits. America is truly a marvellous place to live," she said.

"Can you imagine that? Less than twenty-four hours and the news is breaking. Yes, marvellous is not even close to describing the way things work in this country."

"You'd better get up and moving then. What are you going to wear?" Basha asked.

"My mill greens," I replied.

"No way. You can't be interviewed like that."

"No suits for this guy. Basha, how can I look like I'm one of the people if I'm wearing a suit and tie? No, I'll wear jeans and a blue collar shirt and that's it. People have to see an image of someone who looks like them. This is the moment of truth. I've got to stand up and let them know that I'm not like all the rest of the polished mouthpieces."

I'd better get you a clean one then," she added.

We got up and made coffee. Janko was already off to school. I hadn't heard Basha rise earlier and perform her morning routine. The time was 10 AM. I slept later than normal. My fitful sleep and the nightmare were playing on my senses. After completing my own morning rituals, I sat down at my desk and started making a list of things to do.

The phone rang again. This time it was WFMJ calling. I listened and answered their questions, and told them that WKBN was coming at 1 PM and they were more than welcome to be a part of the news conference. I could tell they did not like being one upped. I apologized but the offer was made so that we could coordinate the time I was spending. Time. Yes, so little time to get moving. Now there was no turning back. I was elated and scared to the core. What if I couldn't convince them that I was serious about what I was doing? I fully intended to make this the most important news story of the year in my town. I was committed. As Howard Zinn said many times, "It's okay if it's impossible. No fight, no fun, no results. Organize and don't count the cost."

Basha made fresh coffee. I sat and drank a cup. My stomach growled but I was not hungry. My list of things to do was growing.

The phone rang again. Al Caruso was on the line.

"Shadow, (my nickname in the mill), I heard you loud and clear last night and I want to make you an offer you can't refuse. If you're serious about this president thing, I want to offer you the use of my little RV for your campaign. I talked it over with the wife and she said do it. The machine runs fine but you'll have to clean it up a bit. You know what it's like with eight kids and a wife on a trip. Well, maybe you don't know. It's yours if you want it. No strings attached. I don't want to be secretary of state or anything. I want to stay home and enjoy the time off while it lasts."

I did not know how to respond. Silence ruled. My heart was on fire. "Al, you cannot know how much I appreciate the offer."

"Hey, win the damn race and you can make a plug for me somewhere down the line. You know, like I was the person who said, 'I was the first one to vote for Leo Pollack'. Something like that."

"You wouldn't believe what happened this morning. WKBN and WFMJ are coming to interview me today. For TV. At 1 PM. It's crazy."

"Nothing crazy about it. But hey, I'll be over in an hour and have the RV ready to go and I'll be putting up a sign in front of it saying 'Leo Pollack for President.' What do you think?"

"Fabulous. Great! How can I thank you?"

"Win you fool. That's how. See yah," and he hung up.

"Who was that?"

"Al Caruso from the mill. He said he's willing to lend me his RV as a campaign vehicle and he's bringing it over in an hour."

"Really? That's wonderful. See, there isn't anything that can stand in your way."

"I've got to get a home page up and running."

"Basha, I've got to find a place to work."

"Turn the extra room into an office and do it from there. We don't need to spend money on an office."

"Perhaps I can get the Union to give up some space."

"Now that's a great idea and I won't have to clean up after all you people."

"I'd love to work from home, but I don't think I'll be here very much."

Basha did not say anything after that declaration. I watched her as I drank my coffee and knew what she was thinking.

"I promise that I'll call you three times a day: morning, noon and night. No matter where I am, I want to hear your sexy voice and I want Janko to know that I love him."

"We know you do."

"Basha, am I crazy?"

She hesitated, then said, "No, Leo, you're a lion, a passionate man who believes in the greater good. Who cares what others think? Who cares that you've decided to chase windmills? Who cares that there isn't a big machine behind your dream pushing you forward. What did Mark Twain say? A majority is one man with courage. Go for it. Make a difference. Speak for the people and make the world know that there is still the American Dream and you're living it."

I got up and hugged her until she balked and said, "Let me go. Get to work. There will be enough time for that later."

"Later is the operative word," I said smiling at her and kissing her on the earlobe.

"Don't do that," she cried. "You know what that does to me." I did.

The phone rang again. This time it was WYFX, the local Fox News Channel. I chatted with the newsman and invited him to the party at 1 PM. No sooner did I hang up when the phone rang again and WYTV, the ABC affiliate, was on the line. We spent a few minutes talking and they said they would be over at 1PM.

"All the networks will be here at 1 PM," I relayed to Basha. She smiled wanly. "I'd better get the house cleaned."

"No. I'll meet with them on the front porch. The snow will melt in no time. That will be the place. I want them to see a real blue collar home, a place where regular folks live. Oh, Basha, this is like a dream. Am I really awake? Is this happening?"

"You opened your mouth yesterday and now you're going to have to live with the consequences of your actions."

"I need a cell phone," I said.

"Then do it. Get one for me so I can call you whenever I want to. I don't want to be disconnected from you ever."

"We won't let that happen. Never."

"I know," she said.

The time was 11 AM. I had two hours to get ready. I put on my cleanest blue shirt and jeans and work boots and then continued working on my list: internet, phone, RV cleaning, accountant, bank account, union office. On and on the list went. Who would help me with all the organizing? I plunged into darkness and could not think clearly. Multi-tasking was one of my skills but this was like trying to get my mind wrapped around the latest dumping of wiki-leaks memos.

I decided to call John Gallagher at the union and ask for his help. I needed a campaign headquarters and he was one of the few people who might be able to provide everything. I did not know him that well, but he was a fine fellow and spoke for the people. Surely he would oblige.

Dialling the number, I still felt some reservations. If I aligned myself with the union, the press would have a field day with it. So be it. I was a member of Local 1330 Steel Workers Union and proud of it. These were my roots. My grandfather and father fought to establish the steel workers union back in the 1930s and I was the beneficiary of their legacy.

"Hello, this is Leo Pollack. May I please speak to John?" I asked.

"Hold on. He's on the phone with someone right now."

"I'll wait."

A minute passed. Then another. Time hung like an obelisk dangling over my head. "Would he be willing to help?"

"Gallagher here," I heard the voice ring in my ear. He was a stalwart fellow, twenty years my senior, a lifelong organizer and not one to brook anyone or anything that stood in the way of the people getting what was due them.

"Mr. Gallagher, this is Leo Pollack calling."

"Pollack. You? Christ man, you've got my phone ringing off the hook."

"What do you mean, sir?"

"Don't sir me, Pollack. What I'm saying is that you're little speech yesterday stirred nerves all over this city. I was going to call you if you didn't call me today. I heard just a few things you said to the people at the unemployment office yesterday and I thought, 'This guy's got the moxie to do what he said he's going to do.' So I'm glad you called. How can I help you?"

I could not believe what I was hearing. I stuttered back a thank you and then launched into what I was thinking.

"No problem. We're kind of slow here right now as you must know and so we can put all our energy into doing whatever you need. Man, you've set the town on fire. One of our own running for president. We're dying here. We're going to lose the mill. It's almost certain. We've got to have a voice and tag, your it. So, what can I do for you?"

Without hesitating, I explained what I needed and I could hear him writing feverishly as I spoke. "So that's about it. I need a campaign headquarters, someplace that is above board and can't be tinged with any corruption and where people can come and volunteer and make this all happen."

"You make me believe in the future, young man," he said. "I'd almost given up hope. Really. This town's on its last legs. I know that I won't have a job in a year, but so what. I'm not important. The thing is that the people are losing all hope. I see it. I hear it. Worst of all I feel it each and every day I come into this hollow building and know that there won't be a future for this mill and this city if something drastically doesn't change. So you've got my vote, brother, and anything else you need."

"Let me invite you to the press conference I'm holding today at my house. All the TV networks will be here at 1 PM. You can mix with them and when I tell them about our plans, you can do a debriefing with them later."

"Great. I'll be there. What else do you need?"

"Nothing right now, but I just want to thank you for your support."

"Hey, you're one of us. Man, do you know what this will do for membership across the country?"

"I've thought about it and there is one thing I will need from you later in organizing my itinerary. I want to make my tour of America going from one unemployment office to the next. I want to speak to the thirty million unemployed people in every state and spread the message that we are ready to change the world as we know it. There is no stopping hard working people when the fire is lit inside of them."

"You got it right, brother. I can do that. In fact, I'll get the people here right on it and begin making calls. When can we meet to discuss the plans in more detail?"

"How about later in the day? Right now, I've got to get ready for the press."

"Do that and I'll be there. You've made my day, young fellow. By the way, you know that your father and I were good friends, don't you? He and I worked in the open hearth for years before I ran for office. So if I call you 'Little Shadow' then you won't be offended?"

"Not at all. I'd consider it an honor."

"Well, Little Shadow, let's do it."

I hung up and just stared at the phone. This was becoming surreal. I was living in a time warp and did not know what to make of it. Basha came into the room and asked me what was happening.

"I just got the complete support of John Gallagher, the president of the local. The union hall will be my campaign headquarters and he's coming over today for the press conference and then we're going to meet later to strategize how he and his people can support a blue collar campaign across the country."

"Amazing, isn't it?" Basha said. "Yesterday, you were just another unemployed American and today you're the talk of the town. Will wonders never cease?"

"Basha, right now I'm feeling a little weak. I am not sure what this all means but things are happening so fast."

"Just let the energy flow. You'll be fine, Leo. Good things come to those who work hard and play fair and tell the truth."

"I'd like to believe that. I surely would."

"Then do. I'll let you know when you're losing it. Trust me, you know I'm your best and worst critic. Right now, just let it flow and enjoy the moment. I know our lives will never be the same again, but I'm prepared for that. Let's say a prayer and make peace with our spirits and then we can move on."

We held hands and Basha said, "We go out into the world in peace, having courage, holding on to what is good, returning no person evil for evil, strengthening the fainthearted, supporting the weak, comforting the sick, honoring all people and trusting that a Higher Power takes care of us every day."

I felt inspired and ready to face the throngs of curious and possibly critical newsmen and women. I went outside for a moment to sweep the porch steps and straighten out the furniture and pick up any trash that was in the yard. The snow was melted and the sun shone brightly. Up and down the street, people were beginning to come out of their homes and take their late morning walks. I stared out across the horizon and saw the skies were azure blue. There was no telltale sign that any mills ever existed in our city. Once, the skies were a pale amber shade but no more. The world was changing and with it, so was this humble place of my birth. I could smell a faint sulphur odor, but nothing like when I was a kid and knew that the stronger the scent in the air, the hotter the day was going to be. My summers were the smells and sounds reflecting the beating heart of the industry that made the Steel Valley a dreamscape for so many men and women for almost an entire century. This sulphur scent was coming from the myriad catalytic converters attached to cars and trucks speeding along the inner belt surrounding the city. The humming of Goodyear, Firestone, Goodrich and Cooper Tires filled my ears. The beating in my heart kept pace. My face tingled as the sun beat down upon me. My vision was unfolding before me as a great panoramic vista that stretched forever. We would resurrect it again. Somehow.

My neighbor, Dan Rose, came out and said, "Hello Leo, how are you?"

"Just fine, Dan. Just enjoying a moment of peace and quiet."

"There is something in the air, but I can't put my finger on it. I'm anxious. When will spring finally come? I want to plant my garden. I've got tomatoes started in the cellar and they are crying out for sunshine and warm air. You start your tomatoes yet?"

"No, no Dan. Basha and I will have to get on the ball."

"You do that young man. There is nothing like a fresh home grown tomato to make the heart healthy and the spirit soar."

"I hear you, Dan. I'll get busy and put seeds in pots."

"Talk to you later," he said and went back inside his house. Dan was an old, Italian fellow who worked in the mill until he retired. Now he was close to eighty and still going strong. His wife was a tiny woman who was as quiet as a mouse. She worked all day in the garden in the summer and it was extremely productive. We shared in the bounty and enjoyed the fresh fruits and vegetables. In many ways, they reminded me of my grandparents who were always working outside in the warm months growing their own food. This was a throwback to the old country where eating one's own produce was a way of life and not a luxury.

Sitting still on the porch step made me appreciate just how beautiful it was outside in late February. I did not feel in the least cold but there were shivers running up and down my spine. I knew what they were. I was not afraid. No, what was causing me to shake was the anticipation of what was coming in just a few hours. I let the sun soak into me giving me energy and melting away the anxiety.

Basha came outside and sat down next to me.

"What are you thinking?" she asked, holding my hand and looking off into the distance.

"Nothing much. Just waiting and wondering what kinds of questions they'll ask me and how I'll respond. I think that it will be okay once the show begins."

"Oh, I'm sure it will be a show."

"Basha, don't make me think about it or I might get cold feet."

"Not you Leo. You come from tough stock. Think about your grandfather and what he went through early in his life. What did you grandmother go through as she waited for your grandfather to send for her? Think about the journey across the ocean in steerage with your aunt. No, you'll be fine. Tell the truth and let them know where you want to lead the country and the story will tell itself."

"You think so?" I asked looking plaintively at her.

"I know so. Trust me," she said.

"I do. Forever."

We sat still holding hands and saying nothing for a long time each lost in his and her own thoughts.

The first news truck rolled up in front of the house. Our reverie exploded and our world stood upon its head. Basha escaped inside.

Within fifteen minutes, the front of our home became a mobile communications center. On top of these trucks, Al showed up with his RV and pulled it right into the driveway. I do not know how he did it so quickly but he had a large "Pollack for President" logo painted on the side. Painted not just taped on. Al Caruso was a true believer. I hoped I would not disappoint any of them. Neighbors came outside and stared in wonder. I waved to them hoping they didn't think I was being arrested for some heinous crime. Basha came out and stood by my side. We watched as the teams set up and prepared for the news team's arrival.

"Shadow," Al said as he walked up and shook my hand. "How'd you pull all this off?"

"Al, how did you get that sign painted already?" I asked.

"Creative kids, that's how. You need an army of kids and a wife that doesn't care to ever travel in such tight quarters again. No sweat. Your campaign van is ready to rock and roll."

"I can't thank you enough," I replied smiling, wondering, "How do I deserve all this attention."

"Just win the election. That will be thanks enough," Al said.

"With support like yours how can I fail," I responded. "Stick around, my friend, I may need your help."

"Will do," Al said.

Watching the news crews set up was an amazing experience. How rapidly they could pull up, extend their cable news technology and be ready to broadcast from anywhere in the world fascinated me. I stood in the front yard and waited.

An advance crew came up and introduced themselves to me.

"You are Leo Pollack?" one young woman asked.

"Yes, in the flesh."

"We need to put some makeup on and get you ready."

"I'm ready right now," I replied.

"You won't look good without it," she said sarcastically.

"But I will look like a normal person. I don't need or want anything that alters who I am and how I look."

"Suit yourself. Jack, let's get ready." She stomped away.

The other crews were setting up cameras in the front yard. I looked around the neighborhood and could see the neighbors coming out. Dan Ross was standing on his porch. I waved to him and he shook his head. I was not sure if he knew what was going on so I walked over to the edge of the yard and told him. He smiled and said, "Only in America," and went back inside. I think he really did not believe me.

They were all there: WFMJ, WKBN, WYTV and WYFX. My world would never be the same. The moment they broadcast this news event, the entire nation would be informed. I could still back out. For a moment, I thought about doing so. If this continued, the yard would be full of people from now on. What did Obama say after he started his campaign? "No more walks to the barber shop without an entourage." Something like that. So be it. I was not backing out. There was work to do and I would get it done.

The talent rolled up in separate cars. I watched them get made up and then approach me. I was not sure if they would get what they were after but I would do my best. What did I have to lose? This was free publicity and was happening within twenty-four hours of my declaration of independence in the unemployment office.

"Mr. Pollack?" the WFMJ talent asked.

"Yes, I'm Leo Pollack."

The other newscasters let her do the talking.

"We'd like to set up right in front of your house if you don't mind."

"No problem. I was hoping that you would."

"Are you ready?" the WKBN talent asked.

"Whenever you are," I replied smiling at all of them.

"We need about a half hour because we'll do edits at the station," WYFX said.

"Oh, I'm sure you'll edit what I have to say," I replied. "But do I get any say so in what you air."

"No," WYFX. "We reserve that right."

"Just so you're 'fair and balanced' I'll agree to what you broadcast," I said chuckling trying to make light of what I heard.

"We are ready," the WYTV talent said.

"Then let's do it," I told them all.

Camera crews rolled into the yard. Lights went on. I stood in front of the porch steps. I really wanted to sit down on them and let them see me very relaxed.

"Are you sure you want to be filmed dressed the way you are right now?" the WYTV talent asked.

"Sure, why not? I am not going to wear a tie nor suit this entire campaign. I don't represent the business sector of this country. This is my 'uniform'."

"Let's get started then," WFMJ said.

I was surrounded by cameras, newscasters, grip men and flooded with lights. The yard became brightly lit even though the sun was shining and the skies were blue for once. I saw Al standing off to the side by the RV and giving me the thumbs up signal. I signed back to him.

Talents stood off to the side and did their lead in to the press conference. Amazingly they did them at the same time, but they did give each other some space so their words did not conflict. Watching it was a lesson in speed and diplomacy. I was impressed.

Then, it was my turn.

"Who wants to go first?" I asked joking with them. They did not respond in kind.

"Mr. Pollack, what makes you believe you are qualified to be President of the United States?" WFMJ asked.

"I'm older than 35 and I was born in the United States. I attended State University. I pay my taxes, work hard every day, read as much as I can, am raising a family and most importantly, I know how to tell the truth."

"You must realize that the odds are stacked against you and that third party candidates are highly unlikely to ever get elected," WYFX asked.

"Yes, everything you say is true. But these are extraordinary times. We've seen a severe erosion in American's trust in the government. Americans do not believe that either party represents them and I believe that my candidacy will provide them with an option. I am not bought and paid for by any special interest group except working people all over America who have lost their jobs and are now having to accept unemployment compensation as opposed to earning a pay check."

"You are currently a steelworker and now unemployed?" WKBN asked.

"Yes, I am a steelworker, a member of Local 1330 United Steelworkers of America and yes, I'm unemployed."

"How are you planning to finance your campaign?" WYTV asked.

"One dollar at a time. Obama demonstrated how raising small amounts of money can add up. I'll be setting up a home page for people to donate to my campaign. The finances will be totally transparent. I'm going to have my accounts open to the entire nation. One thing that concerns me is the amount of money that shows up in campaigns that can't be traced. I will not run that way. When I qualify for public funding, I'll take it. , I believe all campaigns should be publically financed and that special interest groups should be eliminated from the electoral process."

"How realistic is such a move considering that you don't even have a campaign office or any infrastructure and are going against two parties that will fight you tooth and nail all the way through the primaries if you make it that far?" WFMJ asked.

"Once the people realize I'm serious about what I'm doing. They will band together and take this campaign from a local movement to a national imperative."

"How is what you're doing different from what the Tea Party is doing?" WKBN asked.

"The Tea Party started with one man raising his concerns. Yes, but it was quickly co-opted by billionaires who dumped a pile of cash into the movement. I don't believe in what they stand for. I'm not against the government. Government is essential to insuring that civilized society continues to function responsibly and effectively. To listen to some of them, government is the problem and needs to be dismantled, or at least limited. Government of, for and by the people is what I believe in and so with that focus, I'll be able to change the belief that it is the problem."

"How are you going to compete with other campaigns that will be flush with money?" WYFX asked.

"They are flush because they are first and foremost not of the people. Most national campaigns are financed by special interests. The only special interest that I have is that working people need to be taken care of and I will do everything in my power to insure that this is the primary focus of my campaign and my presidency."

"You think you can really win?" WYTV asked.

"If I didn't, I wouldn't run for office."

"Have you ever held any elective office?" WFMJ asked.

"No."

"What then makes you think that you should be President? Don't you think that running for a lesser office might be more prudent?" WKBN asked.

"No. I only want to hold one office and that is President. Once I am elected and serve my one term, I'm out and someone else can run and do what he or she thinks needs to be done. Look, you've all heard that power corrupts and absolute power absolutely corrupts. I don't want to be doing this job for any longer than it takes to refocus this country on the American Dream."

"You must truly believe in the American Dream given what you're declaring today?" WYFX asked.

"Yes, implicitly. Do your own thing in your own time. Work hard, play hard. Get married, raise a family, own a home, go on vacation and live in such a way that you make the world a little better for your children than you had it. Pretty simple. Nothing complicated. Easy does it. This is what I believe. How about you? What do you believe in?" I asked rhetorically.

"How long have you been thinking about this wild idea of running for President?" WYTV asked.

"Since yesterday. I stood in that line at the unemployment office and looked at the faces of the people, heard their banter, felt their discontent and knew that something had to be done and that someone had to stand up and speak for them. Hey, I am a simple guy with simple needs and wants, but I truly believe there is nothing complicated about what is facing this nation right now. Our leaders don't represent us. They are disconnected from a hundred fifty million of us. Look at the people who are running for office. They are not working people. They are businessmen and politicians. I'm unemployed. Right now I'm running for the presidency so I won't be unemployed for at least four years. After my term is up, I guess I'll just have to go and look for another job."

"This is quite incredible to say the least. So what you're telling us is that because you're unemployed and looking for a job, people should just vote for you?" WFMJ asked.

"What makes me different from all the rest of the candidates, whoever they will be as time unfolds, is that I'm the only one that is truly from the middle class. I actually work for a living, pay taxes using the short form because I don't have any deductions and am as close to the people as anyone can possibly be. I didn't go to Harvard or Yale. I don't own much. I drive an old car. My house is not paid for and I still owe more than it is worth. I am not from any privileged class and most importantly, I am not in anyone's hip pocket. I can't be bought off. I stand as a representative of every working person who makes his or her living by going to work every day and doing the best possible job. How can I make it any simpler for you to understand?"

"Don't you think that many people will discount your candidacy as some kind of publicity stunt to get your 'fifteen minutes of fame'?" WKBN asked.

"If that were true, then I've more than accomplished my mission. We've been standing here for much longer than fifteen minutes. But seriously, this is no stunt. Let me be blunt. We've never really experienced the full power of the people in any presidential campaign. What we've had for most of our history is one powerful interest or another controlling the outcome. Our time is now. The people's time is today. We've seen what happens when we give our vote to one party or the other and then sit back and watch the story unfold. Promises, promises and more promises. I am not making any promises. What I'm going to say to you and every person I meet in this campaign is that we have work to do and there is very little time to reverse the unsustainable path that we are on right now. I am not simple or foolish. I realize that this country is a very complex system and there will be resistance everywhere to changes that I will promote. Nothing worthwhile is ever easy. Every problem has at least one if not a multitude of solutions. 'None of us is as smart as all of us.' You don't have a problem if you have a solution. Now, I'm ready to take this belief prime time and infuse it into the American body politic. Call me a crank or whatever you want, once people begin to believe there is truly someone who speaks for them, understands them, really knows what it means to work for a living, they will be on my side and we, the people, will for once lead this country."

"Where do you go from here?" WYFX asked.

"On the road, I plan on visiting unemployment offices to spread the message, to give hope to the people who, like me, face an uncertain future. This will be a long journey, but it's been said it's not the destination but the journey that matters. Where this will all end, I don't know. I am committed to making it as far as I can and not giving up no matter what adversity I and we, the American people, are facing. We are a nation that aspires to live in peace and harmony. Though we have not demonstrated this for nearly a generation, the time is now to reverse this destructive path and return to a constructive one."

"Your message may not be well received. How will you sell this to the American people?" WYTV asked.

"I don't need to sell anything. Most people already believe this. How many of you believe in these wars we are now fighting? What happened before we went to war in Iraq? The polls indicated that a majority of Americans did not believe in attacking that nation. Saddam Hussein was an ogre. But he was our friend back in the 1980s when we were against Iran and what it was doing. We sold him chemical weapons. Remember that picture of Rumsfeld meeting with Hussein in 1983. We were on their side because we'd been embarrassed by Iran in 1979. We were on the side of the "freedom fighters" in Afghanistan when they were in conflict with the Russians. When the Russians pulled out, we did and left the country and look what happened? A decade later we're now fighting the very same people that we armed. How many dictators and strong men have we supported and then years later had to eat crow because they turned out to be contrary to what we wanted or needed? It's time we minded our own business and stopped trying to police the world. Right now we have American service men and women in 114 countries. Read your history. The Roman Empire was in the same predicament when it started to decline. Our current leadership and that of the past 50 years continues to make the same mistake. We can't be the world's police force. We are draining our nation of blood and treasure and we're doing it on a credit card. These last two wars have cost us more than four trillion dollars, none of which we've paid for as we've fought them. It's time for a radical change in the way we manage our country's finances."

"It sounds like you've done your homework. Good ideas require that you have a platform, a party upon which to run. What are you going to call your party?" WFMJ asked.

"Party? I hadn't thought about a name for a party."

"Your view sounds very libertarian. Are you at the core, a libertarian?" WFMJ asked following up on the first question.

"No. From my point of view, I'm not a libertarian. Libertarians are committed to the belief that individuals, and not states or groups of any other kind, are primary. Libertarians believe governments are bound by essentially the same moral principles as individuals, and most existing and historical governments have acted improperly insofar as they have utilized coercion for plunder, aggression, redistribution, and other purposes beyond the protection of individual liberty. I don't believe that government is the problem. There is a need for our government to be active in our lives. It must protect us from external and internal forces that would cause the people harm. I do believe that our government is weak because the best and brightest citizens don't seek public service but opt for more lucrative careers in the private sector. My point of view is purely blue collar. We, the working people of this nation, are the majority but we are not represented. Though I may hold some ideas that are libertarian, I also believe in conservative ideas like not spending more than I earn and living within my means. The government must do the same."

"What other conservative beliefs do you hold?" WKBN asked.

"The earth is the mother of all life. Our land, water and air are being abused. When this president and the last one did little or nothing to protect the earth on which we live, the water we drink, the air we breathe, they are continuing the policies of a power structure that believes we should dominate the earth rather than live in harmony with it."

"It sounds like you believe in climate change and global warming? Science hasn't proven it yet?" WYFX asked.

"What is proven or disproven is not the issue. Look around the world and see what is happening. Polar ice caps are shrinking dramatically. Our air quality is causing kids in greater numbers to have asthma. Water quality is suspect. We are drinking ever increasing quantities of bottled water. People don't believe the water they get from their taps is safe to drink. Debate rages about genetically modified crops. We don't know yet what the effects will be but we're plunging full speed ahead to create them. I'm not against science or progress. We need to use discretion whenever we alter the natural order of things. This isn't something that we can take lightly. Remember when New York's Adirondack Lakes were dying from acid rain. We made a change in policy and over a few decades the acid rain was stopped and the lakes started to come back to life. Some may never fully recover, but we stopped killing more of them. I remember when the Cuyahoga River in Cleveland caught fire. Outrage poured across the city and the nation. We stopped the polluting and cleaned up the river. Remember the Love Canal in Buffalo? It was so polluted that it was killing the land around it. We stopped the pollution and the river started to come back to life. Government superfunds were part of the solution. But how much more effective would be a rational scientific study and policy that protected our earth from attack? We cannot rule in dominion over the earth and continue to abuse it without paying a heavy price."

"You've certainly given us more than a few sound bites," WYTV said, "but one last question."

"Shoot away," I said.

"Why you?" WYTV asked.

"Why not? I'm not tainted by any previous bad habits, bad decisions nor bad connections that would influence my judgment. Yes, I'm what one might call 'tabula rasa', a blank slate, but I'm not a blank person. In my own lifetime, I've watched our country decline from the leading producing nation in the world to one that is fast becoming purely a consumer nation. One of these days, we'll find that people are tired of consuming and want to produce something. I love working in the steel mill because every day I make steel. What a creative process. We take molten iron ore, pour it into a furnace full of scrap metal and other raw materials and cook it until the heat is ready and we tap it. We make a product that can be formed into thousands of other products and, at every step of the way, someone else gets to feel the joy that we steel workers do: making something new. I realize my own world is unsustainable. How much steel can the world consume? I don't know. I do hope we can make more while I'm still alive. Right now that seems highly unlikely because I believe my plant is going to be closed. It's an old plant but we still make some of the best steel in the world."

"My final question to you is this. What would you do with Obamacare?" WFMJ asked.

"First of all, it is not Obamacare. It is healthcare. Is it perfect? No. Is it going to be revisited? Yes, of course. It has created is the opportunity for people who could not qualify for health care to obtain it. What concerns me is the obscene amount of money the health care industry makes because people are sick. We need to control costs better by mandating across the board standard fees for procedures. When a doctor, or hospital or health care company wants to do business within our borders, they will soon learn to control costs themselves. In Japan, for instance, the average cost of an MRI costs $149. In America, the cost can vary from $1200 to as much as $3000. How can we permit this kind of system to continue and not face a meltdown? As a nation, we need to take care of the sick as part of our moral duty and not as part of a sound business decision."

"Do you advocate making all health care mandatory?" WYFX asked.

"Yes. But not the way we're doing it now. We can all contribute to it and make it universal because in numbers there is bargaining power. The latest census states we now have 307 million Americans living in this country. If we were all in one plan, bargaining with providers to give us care, we'd have some power to negotiate reasonable health care premiums. Right now, the seven largest health care providers have divided the country into sections. They form a veritable health care cartel. We've given them too much power. There is a need to take back the power and make sure that all men, women and children, old and young, rich or poor, all have affordable and exceptional health care. There are virulent critics who scream about the fact that the government is forcing us to buy health care. I've not heard one of these critics say a word about the way the auto insurance industry operates. Every person who drives a car on an American road must carry insurance. No insurance? Your registration is revoked. Get caught driving without it and you lose your license and pay a fine. Oh, yes, and by the way, part of the premium I pay is called 'uninsured motorist' coverage. What does this mean? If I get hit by someone who is uninsured, my insurance company will cover my costs. How is this any different than what is happening in the health care industry? I pay my health care premium. Embedded in it is a hidden charge to cover all those uninsured people, who may, at some time in their lives, show up at an emergency room and need care. Who pays for it? You and I do who pay health care premiums. You see, the system has already figured out how to deal with mass insurance. The more people in the insurance pool, the greater the competition for our health care dollars. Requiring everyone to have minimum health care coverage is analogous to having every driver carry liability insurance on his or her car. You want more coverage, you pay more for collision and comprehensive coverage. If you wreck your car and all you have is liability, you are responsible for fixing your own vehicle. The same would hold for the people who don't want to carry anything but minimum coverage. If they need care that is not covered, then they will have to pay for it out of their own pocket. No, it's not Obamacare that is the issue. It's the entire health care industrial complex and how it has managed to get a strangle hold on the American people."

"What are your views on education in America?" WYTV asked.

"Education is what provides the foundation for our civilization. With a high school dropout rate higher than any other industrialized nation in the world, we ought to be ashamed at our efforts to improve this essential service to our children. No Child Left Behind focused only on testing as a measure of success. We left critical thinking, problem solving, cooperative learning and a whole host of Twenty-First Century skills that need to be taught. I'm against vouchers. There is a profound need to improve our educational system from top to bottom. Let's start by adequately funding the schools. It's deplorable that some schools in America are falling apart and other ones are building monstrous athletic complexes to promote their football teams. The inequalities are horrendous. We may spend, depending upon how we cut the budget in 2012, more than $750 billion on the military and less than $40 billion on education. Where are our values? We give lip service to education. We are moving to privatize education and this is not going to solve the issue. It will only create a two or even three-tiered educational system. The wealthy will send their children to the best schools. The rest of the children will get what is left. When was the last time the Secretary of Education was a classroom teacher? I'll tell you. Never. The current secretary is a business man. He is not a teacher. There is a need to get people into office that truly understand the nature of the business and want to make every school a success. We have so much genius in this country that we need to tap. If we can send a rocket to the moon, I know we can solve the educational crisis we are facing. It requires a concerted focus on the issues and the courage to move ahead and make things work. Hear me. I didn't say better. I said work."

"My final question is on financial reform, the budget battle that is sweeping across the country and what your thoughts are about it. What would you do fix it?" WFMJ asked.

"Gee, I thought you'd never ask that question?" I said and they all laughed.

"Seriously, we're still in the most serious recession in the last seventy-five years because people are not going back to work. Cutting the discretionary spending will not solve this problem. It's another bandaid the Republican Party is attempting to use to stop the bleeding. We've cut an artery and this is serious. In the past decade, we've almost tripled our national debt by borrowing money instead of paying our bills as we go along and this is unsustainable. We financed the wars on a credit card. I'm surprised the Chinese haven't asked us to pay our bill. Yet. We lowered taxes with the intent to spur business and look what the result is. We're in the worst recession since the 1930s. The trickle down economic model just doesn't work. What does work is pay as we go. Who among you lives beyond your means? If you spend more than you make, you go into debt. If you're in debt, you have two choices: pay off your debt or continue living in debt. If you don't have enough money to pay off your debt, you have to either cut spending and put more toward your debt or you get another job, earn more money and then put that toward your debt. Wishing your debt away just won't work. Right now, what the regressive party is doing is 'wishing away the debt'. They want to cut this and that for a total of $61 billion. Nice try. It won't work. The reason is simple. This is a drop in the bucket compared to the real debt. The question is where do we get more money without borrowing? Simple. We print it and pay the debt off."

Their faces were precious. I laughed aloud.

"Just kidding. We'd be like Argentina if we did that. No, the answer is more complex than that. First, more money is needed. What did congress do last year? Yes, passed a bill to extend tax cuts. Nice move to keep the people happy, but tax cuts are not the answer. We can't borrow and spend nor can we tax and spend. We have to tax and cut spending. Yes, taxes will have to be raised and every dollar must be accounted for. Pet projects that politicians want to see passed will have to be reviewed. I believe that the American people will go along with the plan because the American people are not as naive. We all know that we can't have more services and continue to borrow to pay for them. So we will make cuts. Drastic ones. First, we'll end the wars immediately. We'll be out of Iraq and Afghanistan in 30 days, not 30 years. We'll keep our drones and other weapons off the coast and if needed will attack when and if the leaders of either country ask us for help. That's it. We're out. No more money for military personnel. No more mercenaries. No more Blackwater or Z or whatever Eric

Prince is now calling his company. No more Triple Canopy. We're done with farming out warfare to private armies. We've spent billions doing this and it cost us dearly in treasure and the hearts and minds of the people. Every item on any budget sent to me will be reviewed. Pork is out. Only the necessities will be passed along. Add pork to the package and the whole package becomes tainted and gets tossed out. We might shut the government down, but if that has to happen so be it. Stop all unnecessary spending until we get a grip on what is happening. Once we raise the taxes, I'll show the American people how much of each tax dollar is going toward paying off the debt. Just like managing our own homes, we have to use the same type of shared sacrifice to clean up our mess. There will be a gnashing of teeth everywhere but it's better to suffer now than to see a real depression five or six years from now. I'll have more to say on this later, but for now you get the gist of where I think we need to go to solve this issue that affects every American citizen, rich or poor."

There was silence. No one asked another question. They just stared at me as if I were crazy. I smiled and waited until the shock slowly settled down into their psyches. Yes, these weighted words might doom my nascent campaign, but I spoke them because no one else had the courage to do so.

"Thank you very much for your time, Mr. Pollack," WFMJ said.

The others thanked me too.

"You're welcome, I said. "I hope I didn't disappoint you."

"Not in the least and I wish you luck," WYTV said.

"Same here," WKBN said.

"We'll be watching you," WYFX added.

"I'm sure you will," I replied with a grin on my face as wide as the horizon.

As quickly as they unpacked and set up, the teams reversed their order but before the talent got back into their cars, I saw a few teams stop by and video the RV which Al delivered before they arrived and some were asking him questions. I was watching with glee knowing that Al would give them some good script to write. What a great guy! To think he already had "Leo Pollack for President" on the side of the vehicle was impressive. I needed to call his daughter and thank her directly. The group of newscasters were done with Al. They headed back to their vehicles. As they pulled away, I waved to them and sat down on the porch steps.

Al came over and sat down next to me.

"You sure stirred up a storm in this town, Leo. What a day!"

"Al, thanks for bringing the RV over. I'll take good care of it. Give me your daughter's number so I can call her and thank her personally."

"Will do. She's a great kid. I asked her if she could do it and voila, you see what you see."

"Am I crazy, Al?"

"Crazy? Man, don't talk like that. We all want to call the shots. Be the boss. You just want to be the boss of bosses. Hell, man, don't talk like that. That speech you made in the office yesterday gave us all hope. I listened to you today talking to those newscasters. You floored them. You blew them away. You gave them something to think about, Leo. They thought they were coming over to talk to some kook and what they found was the most rational person they've ever met."

"You think so?"

"I know so. Leo, my kid's school sucks. It's falling down. Yet we're spending billions to rebuild Iraq and Afghanistan. What sense does that make? None. You laid it out. Get the hell outa those countries and bring our men and women home. Fix our schools. Repair our roads and bridges. Put people back to work. Nah, you hit the nails on the head and that's all there is to it."

"I sure hope so."

"I know so. Hey, here are the keys for the RV. You need a chauffeur let me know. I ain't doing anything right now anyway."

"I sure appreciate it, Al. You're more than a friend."

"See you."

"See you."

Al sauntered off and I could tell that he enjoyed himself today. What a great friend to have. Funny, we never really spent any time together outside of work and now he offered to be my chauffeur on the campaign trail. "Would wonders never cease?"

Basha came out and sat down beside me. We held hands and did not speak. My eyes wandered away and I watched the mottled clouds above float across the skies. They were light and fluffy and reflected how I felt at that moment. I could smell Basha's sweet scent. Lavender. I loved when she wore it.

"Al sure came through in a big way, didn't he?" Basha asked looking at me.

I turned and stared into her eyes. "Yes he did. Now I don't have any excuse. I've got my name in the news and an RV to take my message on the road."

"You didn't give them any sound bites to work with. You gave them a history lesson. I hope they report it all," Basha said.

"You know they won't, but hey, they got what they wanted; a story."

"More than a story. They got history in the making."

"You think so?"

"Don't be modest with me. You know they never covered anything like this in their entire careers. They'll remember this as long as they live."

"I sure hope so," I replied.

"Now all you have to do is wait for Janko to come home and let him know that you're going to be on the road for a while."

"Do you think he'll understand what's happening?"

"What seven year old would? But he'll understand it in his own way. He should be home any minute."

We lived close enough to his school that he could walk by himself. He did not like us to walk with him. Our neighborhood was still safe enough for kids to walk to school. This was one of the main reasons we moved back into the old homestead. Besides the memories, of course.

I stared down the road and waited. Basha continued to hold my hand. We leaned against each other and did not break the spell. With what was coming, quiet times would be rare. We could see him wandering down the sidewalk. One of his little friends was with him and they were skipping as they moved toward us.

When he saw us on the porch, he started to run leaving his friend behind him. We both waved. He raced into the front yard and came up to us.

"Mommy, Daddy, what are you doing out here?"

"Waiting for you, big fellow," I said.

"Let's go swing, let's go do something."

"Janko, your father has something to tell you," Basha said.

"Can't it wait mommy?"

"It can wait," I replied. "Let's go swing."

"Leo, I think politicking is over for the day," Basha said.

"I think so too. Come on, big fellow, let's go swing.

Hand in hand we walked across the road and went down into the playground toward the swings. Basha went back into the house to get dinner ready for us.

Above us the skies cleared and the air smelled sweet for once and the sound of children's voices lifted up toward the heavens and, for a moment, all was well in the steel city.

5. My World and Welcome To It

The yellow ochre walls in the living room displayed faint cracks. They were like wrinkles in an aged face. As I lay on the couch musing, I recalled the years when the family would sit in this warm place and listen to the radio. My memories of this ancient room reflected the character of the people who had lived in this dwelling. The chairs retained a scent of tired bodies resting in them. The long, wool-covered couch was threadbare in many places but still comfortable. "Boze Dom", the Polish blessing in an oval frame, greeted everyone who entered. The cut, stained glass window in the door refracted the sunlight in the late afternoon and cast multicolored shadows in the room. These soft hues filled the soul with a kaleidoscope of feelings. The small color TV years ago replaced "His Master's Voice" RCA radio back in the late 1960's. I could still hear the sound of Grandpa's accordion as it wheezed and chortled and the "Beer Barrel Polka" reverberated from the walls as he sang the words and my mother and father danced to the tune. Whenever he got a snoot full, he would play and the sparkle in his pale, sky-blue eyes dazzled his grandchildren. Grandma never danced. She kept her hands in the soil. Her gift was the growing things she kept in the room.

I cherished the chance to recollect what had already passed and dream about what lay ahead. This quiet, painless time would pass. Already, I was no longer anonymous. My name would be on the 6 o'clock news tonight. I could lament or laugh at my foolishness, but the die was cast. I closed my eyes for a moment and so I did not hear Basha come into the room. We communicated differently now after fifteen years of connubial bliss. We shared the common bond of most people when two become one. The feeling was more powerful than the fission of atoms. We were hydrogen and oxygen bonded into water, the universal, elemental substance of all life.

She was nearby and though I did not want to exit the warmth of hearth and home, I knew it was time to move.

"Are you asleep, Leo?"

"No, just daydreaming."

"Oh," she said, not pursuing the inquiry any further respecting my dreams.

"This room is so full of memories," I said.

"I'm sure it is. You've lived here most of your life. It's a pity more of us cannot stay put in one place."

We lingered in our own separate space.

"Have you ever gone as far back in your past as you can and just remembered anything and everything you could? Feel and smell and hear and taste and touch the past as it were? I wish I had learned to play the accordion like my grandfather. Music died in me when he died. I could never understand the reason grandma didn't like him to play, but perhaps it was because he only played when he was a little drunk. Once he stopped playing, he'd just sit, sulk and smoke his Kent's and stare off into outer space."

Sometimes, my eyes might be open but they would be focused on something far, far away. Just like now, I stared off into space viewing something way off in the distance. My stomach grumbled. I believe she heard it because Basha said, "We'll eat in about an hour."

"How could you tell I was hungry?" I asked.

"I could hear you."

"What a day, Basha! Can you imagine all that has happened in just twenty-four hours?"

"Yes, it is quite amazing. Now the real challenge is finding supporters and mounting a campaign."

"I guess it's time to create a 'things to do' list and keep track of everything that is starting to build," Basha suggested.

"I hear you, Hon."

"What are you thinking?" Basha asked.

"I'm glad it's February. I feel alive during this cold month. This is the month to regenerate, make whole. In summer, we extend ourselves too much. We're here, there and everywhere. Always on the go. Even after sunset, we turn on the yard lights and continue to work. It's as if all of life is balanced between the activities of all the other months of the year and the silent dormancy of February. Somehow, I'd like to save a bit of February for June and July. Excuse me if I don't make any sense."

"I understand."

"You do?"

"I've seen you go through this cycle for fifteen years now. This year is beginning to prove to be more intense than any from the past."

"I hear you."

"How do you feel now that the cat is out of the bag?"

"Well, crazy, plain crazy. But I believe in what I'm doing so I just need to follow my bliss."

"Enjoy your bliss while it lasts."

"I know, I know. It's not for me but for them, all of them, every working man and woman whose hope is dashed because of the conditions within this nation. There will be a real struggle to regain some sort of equality."

"Then give them the chance by going all the way," Basha replied emphatically.

"I'd like to go all the way with you," I laughed.

I jumped up and went over to where she was standing and kissed her long and hard on the lips.

"Thanks," I said.

"Thanks for what?"

"Thanks for being you and being the most important person in my life," I said.

"It's the least I can do to support the one person I love more than anyone else in the world."

"Do you really?" I implored.

"Silly, do I lie?"

"No. You're the most honest person I've ever met."

"Well, then, believe it."

The phone rang. "I'll get it," I said. "Wonder who or what this can be?"

"Hello," I answered the call not identifying myself.

"Hi, is this Leo Pollack?" asked a voice.

"Yes it is. May I ask who's calling?"

"This is Bill Thomas from the Vindicator and I want to do an in-depth story about your recently announced campaign."

I was stunned. This was all happening too fast. First, the TV stations opened the door and now the Vindicator was following up. I always loved my hometown paper. The editorial board was progressive and the paper covered stories thoroughly and fairly.

"Mr. Pollack, are you there?" Bill Thomas asked again.

"Yes, I'm here."

"Then you are indeed the Leo Pollack?"

"I am, sir," I replied.

"Bill if you wish."

"Bill, I'm the Leo Pollack who did announce my candidacy for president. Yes." Making this statement aloud sounded strange to me, but it was true. So very true.

"Well, now, Mr. Pollack…"

"Leo, if you will."

"Leo, thank you. This is definitely a story and we'd like to cover it completely. Do you have the time to talk now?"

"Sure, I'm ready if you are."

"Great. We want to get this story started in tomorrow's edition," Bill said. "My first question is this. What made you decide to seek the nomination for president? Not just anyone gets up in the morning and decides to run for the most powerful elective office in the world. What is your motivation?"

"I am seeking the office because I believe it is time that we break the trend in America where only the wealthy can afford to run for office. The presidency is the ultimate elective position in the country. The campaign costs are staggering, but those who buy and sell presidential candidates don't really care. We, the people, don't get one of our own. We get whomever the wealthy people want. People who know how it feels to be on the bottom, not because they deserve to be or because they want to be, are misrepresented. The system is insensitive to their needs. I am no wealthy man. I am not beholden to anyone. I am unemployed. So I'm looking for a new job. Yes, President of the United States. If I get elected, I won't be unemployed anymore, but I'll be able to speak to the issues and hopes and dreams of every American who is just like me today."

"So you see yourself as one of these people?"

"Yes I do. I am unemployed and want to work. I work hard when I can and yet my money goes all too quickly. I live within my means, but as I continuously hear, my wife, my son and I are in debt for more than $38,000 right now as part of our share of the national debt. This is not the kind of legacy. I want to leave my son. My father left behind a world that was better than what he found. I'm going to do the best I can for my son."

"You believe you have a chance to win?" Bill asked.

"A chance? Sure. Right now it's better than ever because no one else has declared that he or she is running. The regressives have a few horses in the stable but they're being coy about their intentions. Obama will run for the democrats. This leaves the track open for anyone else who can mount a credible campaign and challenge the two major parties. I'm no Pollyanna. I know that people will wonder if I'm really serious but the truth is, I've never been more serious about anything in my life."

"What made you choose to announce your candidacy the way you did? I mean it is a little different, if not just…"

"Bizarre?"

"Well, if you want to use the word. Okay. Why didn't you come to the media with your intentions?"

"Suppose I had. How serious would you have taken my intentions? Come on now, Bill. I have more than a little common sense and know that people are always sceptical of someone who might be a true believer. No, I chose to announce my candidacy with the working people of America. I'm running to represent the blue collar, middle class, hard-working American citizens. The wealthy, the corporations, the career politicians, the lobbyists, the PAC's, the Institutes, the Better Business Bureau, every powerful organization has its own candidate. I'm not theirs. I can tell you here and now I will not be a patsy for any of the aforementioned power elites."

"What party's nomination are you seeking?"

"Neither one. They're both corrupt. Look at how difficult they make it for even a viable candidate within their own party to actually compete for the nomination. What happened to Ralph Nader in 2000? He wasn't invited to debate in any of the events in the 35 states where he finally got on the ballots. Dennis Kucinich, one of my political heroes, faced an uphill battle every step of the way. Ross Perot was the model for a third party candidacy, but he was too much of a businessman to win the hearts and minds of the people. No, I'm not in any party. I'm a citizen running for an office."

"Independent, then?"

"Yes, independent."

"As an independent candidate, what do you think your chances are?"

"My chances are hard to predict. Right now, I'm an unknown person to most Americans. Once, I get done visiting unemployment offices in every major and minor American cities, my name will be as well known as Kennedy's or Obama's or David Letterman's. The 150 or 200 million citizens who don't have anyone speaking for them and to them will listen to me. You've covered enough politics to know just how silly some of these leaders sound. 'The American people have spoken' the Republicans said after the last election. Wow! They won some seats by a negligible margin and none of the races they really wanted. But they claimed victory. They don't and never will speak for me. Their policies are anti-people. Yes, and by that I mean pro-business. I'm not against business, but I am against the unfair distribution of wealth and the policies that continue to be passed that keep working people on an endless treadmill. We are going nowhere fast. This pattern must change or our country will be facing a more serious crisis than a financial one. We may already be there: facing a crisis of the spirit."

"What do you think about the two party system?"

"As simply as I can explain it, the two party system is one of right or wrong, good or bad, rich or poor, vested interests and underestimated promises. The system doesn't need to be dismantled, but what I am saying is that it does not serve the American people in its current state of being. People need more choices and not more rhetoric."

"So you are seeking the nomination as an independent. What will you label this effort of yours?" Bill asked.

"Oh, I'm not sure. The way forward. Maybe the new way."

"Something like an outgrowth, or next generation of the New Deal?"

"Perhaps, but F.D.R. spoke to us from a lofty place. He could sympathize but he could not empathize with us. We need to feel we are powerful and in control of our own destiny. We don't need to be taken care of by anyone. We need fair treatment. With emphasis on too many government controls, we are at the mercy of the power structure."

"Then, like Reagan, you feel that big government and its controls are dangerous and unnecessary? That government is the problem?"

"No, not at all. In fact, during Reagan's presidency, he doubled the size of the government, added significantly to the national debt, raised taxes eleven times after he cut them once and broke the air traffic controllers' union leading to a demise in the union movement. He was not one of my heroes. Oh, did I mention that he underfunded mental illness treatment and thereby sent thousands of mental patients out of the wards where they were living in safety and security and many of them ended up as homeless persons. With a record like that, I don't even want you to mention my name in the same sentence with his."

"You didn't vote for him then?" Bill assumed.

"No, I did vote for him. I listened to what he said and I believed that he was really going to eliminate the national debt. But he did just the opposite. This I found intolerable. He sought the mandate of the people and then he abused it by reneging on almost all of his campaign promises."

"What kind of platform are you going to run on?"

"No promises. No lies. No trickery."

"You're serious?"

"Serious as a heart attack. Bill, the American people want to believe in their leader. But when he or she doesn't tell the truth just once, trust is eroded. Obama said he was going to close Guantanamo within one year. Two years later, it's still doing business. What's the issue? Congress blocked his plan. So what did he do? Rolled over. The prisoners are doing us no good. Set them free. Send them home. We may see them on the battle field again or we may not. What's the point? After all, we haven't stopped the 'terrorists' but inflamed them by having this symbolic place where we treat Muslims as if they were less than animals. Call them enemy combatants or whatever you want, they are political prisoners and we won't erase the stigma of what we've done as long as that place continues to exist."

"It sounds like you really don't like Obama?"

"I voted for him. I wanted to believe in him."

"How am I to interpret that?"

"A person rises to power telling people he or she is going to do one thing or another. Then, once in power, in order to keep it the person realizes changes need to be made but they are not necessarily what was promised. He gets cold feet. He wants to be re-elected more than fulfil his promises. Peoples' memories are short and as soon as they forget, the politician moves on to new and more exciting activities and nothing gets done. I'll tell the people what I'm going to do, do it and then get out."

"Does this mean you are going to seek only one term?"

"If I win, yes, I'm only going to serve for one term. Period."

"Period?"

"That's right. For two reasons. First, I believe a president or any politician should get in there and do the job in the first term. To use the time in office as a way to run for a second term and promise to do everything later is wholly dishonest. Do the job the first time and get out. Look at what we got with Nixon in the second term. How about Reagan in his second term. What about Clinton in his second term? Then there is Bush in his second term. Everyone was a major disappointment. No, one term and out. Second, term limits should be implemented across the board. No professional politicians. No one holds office more than one term. This is the only way to restore sanity and honesty to the government at all levels."

"This is not an ego trip for you? A moment to beat your tom-tom and take the presidency lightly and cast doubt on the integrity of your tenure?"

"By no means is it just that," I said vehemently.

"You're dead serious about your candidacy and what you want to do if you are elected?"

"Yes, Bill, I am."

"This has been a very enlightening and I must also say inspiring experience for me."

"I'm glad you feel that way. Inspiration is one of the feelings missing in the body politic today. Oh, we have plenty of passion, angst, disgust, disrespect, distrust, but not much inspiration. I'm not sure what causes a person to run for office and then lose the joy and enthusiasm necessary to represent all the people. What made us a great nation was our unique constitution that outlined a special form of government that became the envy of the civilized world. We built this nation upon the spirits of men and women downtrodden in other lands who came here and infused their hopes and dreams into the new land. We created a space where freedom was a given: freedom of speech, religion, and all the others. Now I'm getting older and I don't feel that spirit anymore. It is my goal to rekindle that spirit. We need to believe in something greater than ourselves. We need to embrace those who are poor, suffering, sick and disenfranchised and make them feel like the American dream is possible for them."

"What you describe are noble goals. You believe that they are practical, reasonable, and maybe even doable?" Bill asked.

"Yes. Nothing save death will stop me. I didn't serve my country in war time, so I'll serve it in peace time. However, we're hardly at peace. So many people are terrified at what is going on now. This is my real desire: to generate a climate of peace everywhere."

"How do you propose to do that? It's no easy task. Is peace really achievable? You must have a whole lot more faith than most people do."

"Faith without good works is dead. Faith is justified, fortified by good works. No, peace will not be an easy task. I truly believe to achieve peace in the world, we must be completely honest with our global neighbors."

"What do you mean by that?" Bill inquired.

"Take arms talks for one. We debate and debate and both sides hedge about what each will do or not do. Currently, we have more than 1500 nuclear weapons stockpiled. This is enough to destroy the earth a couple of times over. What's the point? Where will this lead us? No, we created this mess half a century ago and we need to clean up our own mess. Is it any wonder that non-nuclear countries want to join the nuclear powers so they can feel safe? But how safe are any of us when every nation has a nuclear arsenal? I don't feel safer because we have silos in North Dakota ready to launch at any given moment. What's the point? How safe are we with this type of cloud hanging over us?"

"But isn't your position naïve?" Bill asked.

"Naïve is a relative term. Most nations in the world know the truth. But no one will say it. Diplomats lie about what is going on. Diplomacy is just another form of lying. Look at Wiki leaks. Whether you agree or not with the leaks, they show us the duplicity that every nation, and especially America, uses to mislead its people and those with whom they hold as 'friends'. I would like to see a world where we spend money, not on nuclear weapons, but on food and schools and excellent health care and anything that is life sustaining and not life threatening."

"Leo, I'm rather amazed at the depth of thought you give each of these issues. I hear you. Don't you see? To make this happen, you will be fighting an uphill battle."

"Sure, I do. I'm up to the task. Anything that is worthwhile is never easy."

"Like running for president?" Bill asked.

"Yes, like running for president."

"What if you don't make it? I mean, what if you do not get elected?"

"My message will not die with me. It will not go away. I'm only the messenger. I'm no one special. I'm like so many Americans who read and think and know that there is a better way to do business. Once it becomes clear to all Americans that the power elite can be challenged. There will be change. There is so much dissatisfaction with the status quo. Republican or Democrat. It doesn't matter. These parties have neutralized each other. The Tea Party is an aberration, a billionaire's sad dream that found a sponsor and a platform upon which to speak platitudes. I'm prepared to challenge anyone who isn't ready to move into the 21st century with new ideas and solutions to the new problems."

"That is what your candidacy is? A challenge to the status quo?"

"Yes. More a challenge to rock-hard thinking that only wealthy people can aspire to national office. Look, I don't have $100 million in my war chest like Meg Whitman did when she tried to 'buy' the California governor's office. Mitt Romney spent $45 million of his own money to try and win the Republican Party's presidential nomination. How much good could he have done if he had spent that money on college scholarships or the health care needs of the poor? Our political campaign system is skewed."

"Changing the subject just a little. Were you born in Youngstown?"

"Yes, at St. Elizabeth's Hospital."

"Parents still living?"

"No. My father died of cancer. My mother died of a heart attack."

"You're married?"

"Yes. 15 years. One son, John Lawrence, Janko, who is seven."

"And you're unemployed at present?"

"Yes. From U.S. Steel or now as we know it: USX."

"You have no one backing you?"

"If by that you mean any political party or any organized group? No. Once my message gets out, I hope to have every unemployed American on my side and voting for me."

"Once they find out about you?"

"Yes, once they find out. It won't take long. My campaign will go viral and before you know it, every American will know who I am and what I'm proposing."

"You're pretty confident?"

"Sure. I'm on the phone with you now. Once you print this story, I'm off and running. Tonight I'll be on every local network. Tomorrow, I'll be up on the web and Facebook and twitter and a host of other sites. The movement is building. But Bill, listen to me. This is not about me: Leo Pollack. This campaign is about working people; men and women all over America who need to be represented by someone who is not only sympathetic with their plight but is also empathetic. I know what they feel, what they see, what they hear because I'm living everything they are."

"What if I refuse to print your story?"

"You won't. That's not good press. Besides, you know this story is going to fly. You know that I'm not some kook. I'm serious. You can hear it in my voice. You can feel it in my passion. You wouldn't have called if you didn't believe that one of Youngstown's own was seeking national office."

"Leo, this has been a most enlightening conversation. Yes, I will print this story. I'm excited that a native son is stepping onto the national stage and I will do everything I can to support you. This is not a matter to be taken lightly so I want you to know that I'm in your corner."

"I appreciate that Bill and I hope we can discuss this more as the campaign unfolds," I said, appreciating his support.

"We will. I can guarantee that," Bill replied.

"Last question. What does your wife think about all this? Is she supporting you in your efforts?"

"Wholeheartedly!"

"Then you'll have at least three votes: hers, yours and mine."

"I appreciate that immensely."

"Good to talk with you," Bill said.

"Thank you for your interest in my struggle. By the way, how did you get the word that I had declared my candidacy?"

"One of our unemployed newsmen was in your audience yesterday and phoned us and said that he heard your speech. He was excited and said we needed to get the scoop. He was impressed. He labelled your speech 'We've got the Power'. Is that accurate?"

"Yes it is. Could I ask if this fellow has a chance of getting his job back?"

"I'm not sure. Things are tight now. You know what the print media business is facing right now."

"Yes, I do. Things are tight everywhere. I'm sure that your colleague heard me loud and clear because I was speaking for him."

"He seemed to be pretty enthused about everything you said."

"I hope he gets his job back. People should be producing something, writing a story, making a difference, not standing in an unemployment line getting paid to not work. Production and pride in the work place are what made us a great nation, not unemployment lines and rampant despair."

"You may be right."

"I hope so. It's not a question of right and wrong. It is a matter of providing for people the opportunity to produce for themselves and others. Until we change this, there is no real hope for America to maintain world leadership."

There was a pregnant pause and then he asked, "If I could quote you on your reason for running for President what would be your basic campaign message?"

I thought about his question for a long moment. "That is a loaded question, but I would have to say without reservation, "We have the power to make the world safe, healthy and liveable for all people."

"That's it?"

"That's it," I said finally.

"I thank you ever so much for your time, Leo," Bill concluded.

"You're welcome. I'm most appreciative that you wanted to hear my thoughts and feelings and making it possible for me to reach others who have not yet heard about me and my goals."

"Goodbye, for now," Bill said.

"Goodbye," I replied.

I hung up but held the phone for a moment listening to the silence on the other end. The world, in the voice of Bill Thomas, came to me. I gripped the receiver tightly trying to hold on to the moment. I knew I was about to be exposed. There was both joy and terror in my telltale heart. There go the people. I must follow them. I sat down on the floor feeling a little dizzy. So soon. An unemployed journalist had heard my speech. He had been in the crowd. First the TV stations. Now the Vindicator. Things were moving faster than I ever imagined they could. Outside, I already had a campaign vehicle, Al's RV. Tomorrow, I would be up on the internet. Oh, and I needed to get a bank account opened. I inspired an unemployed news reporter to tell Bill Thomas what he heard and Bill phoned me. The domino effect was happening. It was just a matter of time now and soon the entire nation would know. Exposure was critical. Time was of the essence. Everything was turning at a whirlwind pace. Things would soon be widening into a gyre. This was my world and I welcomed people to it.

Basha entered the room and asked, "Who was that, Leo?" She walked over to me and massaged my neck. "Your muscles are as taut as steel cables."

"For a while, I could not speak. I did not want to break the aura of the moment. I could not turn back now. My dream was fast becoming a reality. No longer was it festering inside of me. I was unsettled to say the least. I escaped as best as I could into the world of imposed silence. I would not be able to do so in the future. The design of my days would look much different than they did now. I was becoming a public figure.

"Who was that, Leo?" she asked again.

"That was Bill Thomas from the Vindicator. He wanted to know if I were the one running for President."

"So you told him?"

"I told him a lot. But most of all, I said, I was the one."

"Then it's begun," she said with an air of finality.

"It most assuredly has. I can't turn back now."

"Do you want to?"

"No…never. It was meant to be."

"I'm proud of you, Leo. Very proud."

"I'm proud that you're proud. You make me feel so good. I couldn't do it without your support. No way. I love you for that more than you'll ever know."

"You'll at least have my vote."

"That's what he said."

"Who?"

"Bill Thomas."

"He was right."

"Oh, I've just got this feeling, Leo. A special one. You are going to go much further than you ever imagined," Basha said.

"I hope your feeling is right. I need every vote I can get."

"Leo, it's more than votes. It's a platform to generate a dialogue in America that is sadly lacking. You'll be the voice for all the people who don't get heard, who are marginalized because they don't make large contributions to political candidates and, therefore, are not represented. Trust in the power of the people to lead the way." She kissed me on the nape of the neck, and left me alone in the darkened hallway and disappeared into the kitchen.

For a long time, I sat in the dark room lost in my thoughts and turbulent feelings. The hallway was as silent as a morgue. I still felt dizzy as a rush of emotions flooded through me like a narcotic. Truth was spoken. Ears heard it. Minds absorbed it. Only the outcome was in question. She left me alone to think. This room was so full of memories. This was my home as long as I could remember. The world started for me right here as a child and now as a man I was still ensconced in my roots. I had expressed my hopes, dreams and fears to Bill. I was frightened by some of my thoughts. The joy came in the call. The fear resulted in what was coming next. Such profound contrasts formed a lump in my throat. From beginning to end, alpha and omega, we move forward. Some of us fear it. Others embrace it. I wanted to move and now I knew where I needed to go, but ennui kept me locked in place.

The closing of the door and the subsequent pitter-patter of little feet saved me from my painful reverie. He came into the hallway and saw me sitting in the dark on the floor.

"Daddy, what are you doing?" Janko, asked.

"Oh, just thinking. Come on and give me a kiss."

He came over to me and we hugged and kissed one another. He had the sweet scent of a child at play, so very sweet. "Thinking about what? Why there?" Before I could answer he asked, "Where's mommy? Mommy," he called. "Come on, Daddy, let's go find Mom. Come on." He pulled me by the hand and I arose from the floor and followed his lead out of the hallway. I was glad that he saved me. We both went to the kitchen where sweet smells rolled in waves through the air.

"Smells good, mommy," Janko said.

"She turned and bent over and hugged and kissed him. "Have fun at Mike's?" Mike lived next door and he and our son were best friends.

"Sure did. We played cowboys, then war, then we watched cartoons and then I got hungry and so I knew it was time to come home. When do we eat?"

"As soon as you and your father wash up," Basha said.

"Let's go son," I said.

"Do we have to? I washed yesterday," he protested.

"But you got dirty today, cowboy. Please wash."

"We washed up and when we returned the table was set and we sat down to share dinner.

Holding each other's hands we bowed our head and I said the grace. "Dear God, we give thanks for this good food, our good health, our family, for the sun in the sky and for the peace in our family and for all people everywhere who like us love one another."

"Let's eat," Janko said as he grabbed for the first bowl he could reach.

"Hey, not so fast, son," she said.

"But I'm hungry, mommy," he balked.

"So are we all. But a little patience please," Basha said.

I studied him. He looked somewhat like me, but not a mirror image. He was his own person and, for this, I was happy. In his impatience, he was just like me. I wondered how children always inherited the worst attributes of their parents.

"How was school today?" I asked him as I ate, being careful not to talk with my mouth full. In our family this was one etiquette practice we enforced rigidly.

"Okay."

"That's all? Okay?"

"Okay. We had fun at recess and I liked art and for lunch we had pizza and ice cream."

"Well, how was your reading class?"

"Okay."

"Is that all?" I asked.

"I didn't get any stickers today. I didn't do too well. Reading's hard."

"Maybe we need to practice some more. Are you up for that later?"

"Okay. Later."

John Lawrence, our Janko, ate heartily not speaking much. I ate in relative silence too. Basha busied herself with keeping food before us. She did not eat much herself. "Aren't you hungry?" I asked.

"Hungry? No. Excited? Yes. We all need to watch the evening news tonight," Basha said with a twinkle in her eye.

"Why, mommy?" Janko asked.

Basha looked at me for a nod. I gave it to her. "Because your father is going to be on TV tonight."

"How can daddy be on TV when he's right here?"

We both laughed. "The news stations were here today and videotaped an interview with your father. He's officially running for President."

"Really? On TV? Wow! Let's eat so we can turn on the news."

"Okay, let's do it."

A front end loader could not have shovelled food into his mouth must faster. He was excited now. Could he fully comprehend what was happening, going to happen? I wondered. "Do I?"

The phone rang and we all jumped. I felt a little queasy inside. I knew for whom the bell tolled. Before I could respond, Janko said, "I'll get it" and ran into the hallway to answer it. He hollered back, "Daddy, it's your friend, Jolly."

"Thanks son," I said and I got up to answer the phone. "I'll make it short, hon."

Jolly's voice was vibrant. "Hi, kiddo, just thought I'd give you a jingle and talk to the next President. How you doin' fellow?"

"Just fine, Jolly. Thanks a lot for helping out yesterday."

"No sweat. Least I could do. Hey man, that speech got me right in the heart. I mean, I never thought. How could you have it in you all the time and not tell any of us? I mean, man, you blew that crowd away. Really!"

"Jolly, I didn't know I had it in me either. Not until I got there and felt there was something that just had to be done."

"You mean you hatched that plan on the spot? Leo, man, that's crazy. I mean, you buy a car on the spot. You take a chick out and you get laid on the spot. But man, you don't just go out and tell people that you're running for the presidency of the United States. It's crazy. Man, but it was wild."

"In order to get on the ballot in the states with primaries, I'll have to move really fast. I may not make all of them, but I will be working on it for the next year."

"So you're serious? I mean, you're really going after the nomination?"

"Sure. Watch the news tonight. I spent the day with four TV stations and later the Vindicator. I'll be the news tonight in this old town."

"No way? Really?"

"Yes, really."

"I am making a point by running for president. A point for you and me and all the people there on South Avenue and everyone in this nation who stands in a line waiting for benefits and realizes that he is not going to work tomorrow nor the next day or maybe not for a long time. People need something to believe in and someone who will speak for them. So, I'll do just that. We've had enough of getting the short end of the stick."

"Then you are for real, man. If I'd have known, I'd really have pushed yesterday. Man, ain't this something."

"For real!" I said.

"What are you going to do now?" Jolly asked.

"First of all, I need to get a web page up and start the process rolling in cyberspace. Secondly, I need to set up a bank account for donations and make it totally transparent so that anyone can see who is contributing and where the money is going. Thirdly, I'm heading on the road. I'm going to make it to unemployment office I can within a hundred mile radius of Youngstown. Once I've made the loop, I'll figure out what to do next."

"You need any help, you call me," Jolly offered.

"Got it and thanks."

"See you later, man," Jolly said and hung up.

"Yes, see you later," I said but I did not think he heard me.

A gnawing in my belly caused me to stop and wonder, "Yes, what was next?" There were so many things to do. I needed to get to the union office tomorrow and meet with John Gallagher and set up the support network if he would consent. Yes, and the ban. Internet. So many things. My head ached. Then, I thought, "Well, tomorrow is always another day." Laughing to myself, I went back into the kitchen. I fiddled with my food growing a little apprehensive as I considered the obstacles against me.

"Who's Jolly?" Janko asked.

"Oh, he's a fellow I work with at the mill. You know who he is. You met him once."

"Does he have long blond hair and a beard and a funny laugh and a son named, Jason? Why don't they come over and visit any more?"

"Jason lives with his mom. Jolly and Kate are divorced."

"What's that mean? Divorced?"

I looked at Basha and she looked at me. The task was mine. "What it means, Janko, is that Jolly and his wife don't live together anymore." I smiled at him. "He's still his daddy but he just doesn't live in the same house. Jason lives with his mommy and sees his father every weekend."

"That doesn't sound like fun to me. I like it better with all of us together all the time. I hope it never changes."

"Neither do I son. Neither do I."

We looked at one another and reaffirmed our familial vows. We were one because we desired to be so.

My appetite came back to me. Dinner was excellent. Potato patch casserole and tossed salad and coffee cake for dessert. We finished with a flourish. I ate too much. I felt stuffed, but food always was my elixir for anxiety. Luckily, I was built like my father and had a very high metabolism.

"Fine, fine, dinner, honey," I said looking at her as she nibbled the last of her dessert.

"I like this cake, mommy," Janko said, wiping up the crumbs around his plate.

"Glad you boys liked it."

"Boys?" he exclaimed.

We laughed together: a wonderful, carefree, excited, childlike laugh.

Our division of labor was simple. If Basha cooked, I cleaned; if I cooked, she cleaned. Tonight, I washed the dishes and in this simple act of washing dishes, I experienced a measure of peace. With my hands immersed in warm water, I could feel the pressures of the outside world melting away like the grease sticking to the plates and silverware. As no man should end the day with dirty dishes, hands, thoughts or feelings, I was ending the day clean and fresh and prepared for a brand new day.

"Let me help, Daddy," Janko said pulling a chair over and climbing up to the ancient sink.

"Sure, let's do it," I replied. We finished the job together.

"What do you want to do now?" he asked me.

"It's time to watch the evening news," I replied looking at my watch.

"Can't we go for a walk outside first?"

"Maybe afterward, but now we'll watch the news."

"Okay," he said with resignation.

"We'll take a flashlight and walk afterward, okay?"

"That sounds great!" he replied and ran into the living room and turned the TV on.

Basha was sitting at the table staring out the window. "A penny for your thoughts," I said.

She gazed at me for a moment. Her eyes were glassy and she could not hide them. "Will all this change us, Leo? Will we still be the same even when you succeed?"

I dried my hands thoroughly and walked over to her, put my arms around her and kissed her on the cheek. "Even if I win the election and my salary increases tenfold and we are not living here for a while and the world knows us on sight and we can't hide in a crowd, my love for you will never change and we will return to this very house when it's all over. That is my promise to you. When we go on vacation, it will be to come home to our own 'castle'."

"Is this all an illusion or a dream, Leo?" she asked.

"I've considered that for most of the last two days since this all started. An illusion is something that you live in but can't attain. A dream is what you strive to achieve. I am living the dream. We are going to make a difference. As for change, I imagine our lives will be less private, but within these walls, we will keep the peace and maintain a measure of equanimity. When it's dinner time we'll eat together and afterward, I'll still do the dishes. As for the phone, I'm sure it will be ringing more than usual, but we'll just have to put the answering machine to work. Fair enough, lover?"

"Fair enough," she replied, turned and kissed me hard.

Just at that moment, Janko ran into the room and hollered, "Three way hug!" We hugged, kissed and laughed until it almost hurt. This was family and something I would not give up for any amount of money or success.

"Time for the news. Let's go see if daddy made the headlines today?" Basha said.

"Yah, let's go daddy," Janko hollered pulling my hand and leading me into the living room. He cuddled up against me. Even though he was now seven years old, he still liked to sit close to his mother and me. This would pass as he grew older but I hoped that we would never outgrow our affection for one another and not be afraid to display it.

Basha rested in a chair across from us and fumbled through a magazine. This was the telltale sign. I knew what it meant, but I did not comment. The butterflies were floating inside of me.

A musical interlude preceded the actual broadcast. A panoramic shot of our town depicted it as the Steel Capital of the World. How outdated. Only two of the seventeen mills in the valley were still operating near capacity. The skyline still thrilled me as I stared at the Federal Bank Building set against the evening sunset. News, weather and sports were featured, the trinity of modern mankind. Disasters and death monopolized the news. Long ago we decided not to get cable. Using a digital antenna, we got the local channels and that was enough for us. At least, these were still free. Over the years, the faces changed but the format remained the same. Commercials catered to all clientele. Broadcasting changed with the people. There was very little human interest content.

A camera panned in on a man in his early fifties.

"Good evening. These are the stories that are making headlines today. A three alarm fire on the north side in an apartment complex leaves many families tonight without a place to stay…the story unfolded and views of a burning building and fire-fighters were shown. A local boxer is trying to make a comeback. University fees are being raised for the fourth time in as many months making it a major issue for the university administration trying to balance its burgeoning budget deficits. A commercial break interrupted our concentration. We remained glued to our seats.

The broadcaster appeared again. "In a major story tonight, a local man has declared he is running for president of the United States. Leo Pollack, an unemployed steel worker says that he is throwing his hat into the ring for the highest office in the country…" The voice droned on. We watched in disbelief. The world changed in front of us forever.

"He's talking about you, daddy," Janko said enthusiastically. "Wow!"

"Looks like you've made the big time, Leo," Basha said gazing at me with glassy eyes.

"While at the unemployment office yesterday, Leo Pollack climbed up on top of the counter and made an impassioned speech ending with his declaration that he was seeking the presidency. This is an unprecedented event in the history of American politics. Pollack, a forty-seven year old man, has never held any public office. When interviewed this afternoon, Mr. Pollack summarized his political aspirations this way. My face appeared on the screen and I was stating: 'We have the power to lead the world of nations into an age where mutual concern and respect will replace selfishness. The broadcaster's face returned and I was gone. He summarized the rest of the one-hour interview. "Mr. Pollack is running a grass roots campaign. He is not seeking the nomination of the two major political parties but struggling to make it alone by sheer will and determination. Pollack, who is an unemployed steel worker, said he believes it is in his best interest to eschew partisan politics and appeal directly to the voting public from his blue collar roots as a working American. Though he is a long shot in a race that has already two republicans, including former speaker of the house, Newt Gingrich, forming exploratory committees, Pollack believes he does have a chance. He resides on Oxford Avenue on the north side in the first ward with his wife and one son. We probably have not heard the last of this maverick in our midst. In other news…"

For me, there was no other news. A cabal of feelings welled up inside of me. I possessed only a faint sense of being earthbound. Thoughts and sensations collided like protons and electrons and I was electrified by what I heard. Doubt flooded in and I pushed it away. "This was what I wanted, wasn't it?" I thought to myself. I sat still waiting for some response. Janko was strangely silent as the program continued, but he was holding me tightly. Thank God for small wonders. Basha was a portrait of confusion. Tears flooded her face and her mouth was arced in a strange smile. What more could anyone want?

"It seems like the message was well received," I offered. "He quoted me exactly. Yesterday, I was nobody, but today I'm standing on the edge of a cliff and staring at the entire nation spread out before me on an infinite horizon. It's hard to believe this is really happening."

Basha still cried but when her eyes settled upon me, I could feel both joy and sorrow. She was proud and worried. "It is unreal, unbelievable. Your dream is now fast becoming a reality and the local world knows all about it. This is no longer an illusion."

"For neither of us. My dream is our dream. We'll see it through together."

"Me too," Janko stated loudly.

We smiled at him. I said, "Yes, we're all in this together. I am a proud man and you two are what make me so."

"I just wish my parents were still alive so they could see and hear what is happening today," I quietly stated thinking about the two who gave me life and a chance to make something of it.

"Yes, that would be grand," Basha replied.

"You two are very special to me," Janko said. I think he was feeling left out.

"You are the jewel in our lives, a rare gem, one of a kind, son. You are such stuff as dreams are made of. What I'm setting out to do is make this world a better place for you. Never forget that no matter what is happening, what is being said about me and wherever I am in the country at any given time."

The phone rang. "It's starting," I said.

"Yes, and now it will never end," Basha cried.

"What won't end?" Janko asked.

"Son, there will be a lot of activity around here from now on. What you need to know is that your father is going to be busier than ever and we will have to be patient with him, with his being gone a lot of the time," Basha said to him.

"We can do it mommy. We can do it," he replied.

"Yes, I'm sure both of you will be my biggest supporters," I said.

The ringing continued. "I'd better get it."

"Hello," I said.

"William Brown, here," a strong, deep voice said with authority and power.

"Yes," I returned.

"I'm William Brown, editor in chief of the Vindicator and I'm calling in regard to a recent interview that you did with one of my journalists. When he filed this story, I was aghast. Is it true, might I ask?" he said gruffly.

"Yes it is," I said.

"You realize, Mr. Pollack, this is quite out of the ordinary and before we publish anything regarding your story, I feel compelled to contact you and hear for myself who you are and what you are up to."

"I hear you sir. I…" I began but was cut off .

"Hold on please." A faint buzz sounded and then nothing. I thought I was cut off.

His voice returned. "Sorry for the interruption."

"No problem," I said politely.

"Where was I? Oh, yes. What made you seek the candidacy and why did you announce it in such a strange way?"

"I'm not really sure. I think I made the announcement to people I thought might listen to me. I knew that in order to win any votes, I'd have to earn their acceptance first. Once I achieved that, I believed I might be able to convince others that I was a viable candidate." Listening to myself, I realized I sounded like a politician.

"Genuine soapbox performance, wouldn't you say," Brown said.

"If you say so." He was not nearly as cordial as Bill Thomas was. Though he was curious and tried to disarm me, I would not be daunted.

"Coming to the point, Mr. Pollack, I'd like to know just what you hope to gain by pursuing your plans."

I hesitated for a moment, then said, "To become the next president of the United States."

"You are serious? You really believe you have even a snowball's chance in hell to win the nomination?"

"Nomination? I'm not running as a democrat or republican. I'm running as an independent."

"No independent has ever come close to winning the office. You realize that?"

"Yes, I do. There's always a first time. Look at who's in the office today? Who ever thought when we were kids in the 1960s that an African-American would ever be president? No, there is nothing to predict what will happen. I am convinced the time is now for a completely different approach to leading our country and am committed to being the person who does it."

He was silent for a moment. I wondered what he was thinking.

"You are a strange man, Mr. Pollack. In all my years of publishing, I've never met nor heard of anyone with such audacity."

"I hope I'm not so audacious that you will not print the article that your reporter was filing. I need the press coverage."

"I'm sure you do. You'll need all the coverage you can get," Brown said.

"I'm counting on my hometown paper to start the ball rolling. You may not believe I have much of a chance to make this a competitive race, but with your help, with your support, anything is possible."

"I'll think it over and let you know by tomorrow what the Vindicator is going to do," he said. He did not say what he was going to do. I let his comment ride the silence.

He hung up curtly without a goodbye. The mystery of it all did not hit me for a moment as I stood holding the now silent receiver. Across those thin wires, the future of the nation travelled. "Will he do it?" I asked myself. There was no way to know. I would just have to wait.

Basha walked in and asked me who called. I told her. "So the story may not be published?"

"I think it will. The editor was just feeling me out. He doesn't want to get scooped by a bigger paper. What kind of business would he be running if he didn't print this story. How often in your home town does such a story appear? Maybe once in a lifetime. No, he'll publish it and we'll be moving right along without a hitch."

"It's a great chance for some publicity. I hope he prints the story."

"I do too. What an amazing day in the life of some simple folks, wouldn't you say?"

"Yes, yes indeed," Basha said with a smile on her face.

"So this is it, Basha. Life will never be the same again now that the process has begun. We'll make it through together. You and I and our son."

"Together, yes, but with you gone a lot of the time."

"It's the price we'll have to pay," I replied.

"I don't know. We have our love and that is what will keep the price within our budget."

"Our love is limitless, Leo. Limitless when it is freely given."

"Amen to that lover," I said and reached out and held her closely.

"Daddy, let's go," Janko said racing into the room. It was time for us to take our walk. "Ready to go?"

"I'm ready," I said. "We'll be back shortly."

"Bye mommy, see you later."

"I love you both," Basha said.

"Don't keep him out late," she admonished.

"No. No, I won't. Don't worry. The evening's still young."

"I won't worry but I will miss you two."

"Then come with us, mommy. Please come along."

"No, no, you two boys go ahead. There are some things men should do together and I can understand."

"See you later," I said and went to get my coat and hat. Janko followed me into the hallway. Once I was ready, we went out the back door and disappeared into the night. "This just might be the last time that I get to walk alone with him," I thought. "After tomorrow, everything will be up in the air."

We left the warmth of our home and hand in hand, giggling and laughing, entered the night world. We travelled like two companions together into the silent darkness and the peace promised beyond.

6. Solidarity

Awakening without an alarm and springing from my bed with a floor kick, I commenced to face the day without trepidation. As I performed my morning ritual, I stared at the mirror. Minor crow's feet extended laterally from my eye sockets and my forehead wore three distinct wrinkles. My hairline receded slightly and a few gray streaks decorated my thin, mouse brown hair. I noticed that my stubby hands were exceptionally clean from being idle for nearly a week. The blaze of hair on my chest curled slightly and formed a cross. I made quick order of the stubble on my cheeks and chin and slapped on some Old Spice, combed my hair and studied the effect. I was not displeased with what I saw.

There were so many things to do. As soon as I had my cup of coffee, I would tackle the most important tasks. The silence in the house added to my feeling of confidence. I felt at peace when alone for it gave me the opportunity to think without interruption. Basha would be up in about a half hour and get Janko ready for school. The night light shone like a beacon. I could find my way anywhere with its humble rays.

Drinking my coffee, I started my list. Things to do: Get the homepage set up. Fin an accountant. Go to the Union Hall and meet with John Gallagher. Set up a bank account with absolute transparency. Get the RV ready for the first road trip. "Perhaps I ought to call Al and see if he'd really be my driver?" I marked that down on the list. As the time passed, the list grew longer and longer. I was going to need help. I already knew that but someone would come along and volunteer. I had no fear. Talent was everywhere. Once the creative genius of the people was unleashed, there would be no stopping the momentum. My belief in the power of the people was absolute even if, now and then, they disappointed.

The coffee warmed quietly, and though my stomach grumbled, I did not eat because I always functioned better when slightly hungry. Just hot coffee and silence satisfied my appetite. The sun shone brilliantly as it spread through the room and buoyed my spirit instilling in me a measure of confidence. I would get everything done today. I hoped to capitalize on my reserve of unbounded energy and my common sense approach to problem solving. "You don't have a problem IF you have a solution." I lived by this motto. The only way that I could fail would be if I did not do something to move forward.

My first stop was the union hall. Located right across from the US Steel office building, I knew the way with my eyes closed. John Gallagher would already be there. This was a busy time for him because of the lay-off and the impending doom of a possible plant closing. I did not envy him his position. He would be busy for months trying to make things work for the people. I hoped he would be my most important ally. After all, I was there to support him as well as have him support me.

Fog veiled the valley. Traffic lights glowed eerily in the vaporous mist. The red lights blended with the greyness creating a dull rouge on the city's cheeks. The green lights formed a viscous mucus in its nostrils. The yellow lights transfigured fair skin into jaundice. The Mahoning River flowed like an exposed vein of coagulated blood. The open hearths were no longer pouring life into man and machine.

Everything appeared calm. No smoke floated up from the high stacks above it. Along the river wall where most open hearth employees parked, only dust and old papers remained. One car parked at the south gate indicated guards were on duty. I drove over the bridge and headed down toward the main gate. My eyes focused on the inactivity and got misty. "How can this be?" I asked myself. "Was this the final chapter in a long history of the steel valley?"

Ahead I could see the US Steel office building. There were cars parked all around it. The bosses were probably planning what to do with a plant that was not producing anything. This was a sad commentary on what was happening in America. Our shores were being flooded with cheap imported steel. In the global economy, we were losing the struggle to remain competitive.

I rolled past the building and saw ahead of me the union hall. As I turned into the parking lot, I slammed on the brakes. On the front of the building was a gigantic banner that read "Leo Pollack for President". My eyes squinted. "Was this real?" I inched forward and parked my car so that I could just stare at what was greeting me. I could not believe that the union was already in my corner. Yes, I was a member in good standing, but this was just too much. I shut the car off and headed toward the entrance.

Walking up to the front door, my heart beat wildly. What was happening? What were they thinking? What had I started?

Opening the door, I stepped inside and saw that everyone was waiting for me. I was truly the guest of honor.

"Leo, welcome," John Gallagher walked up to me and shook my hand vigorously. "You are the man of the hour and we're ready to support you in any way we can. Come on meet the team." He guided me toward a room at the back and I walked in to find a crowd of folks who clapped resoundingly as I entered.

"Hail to the chief!" they all shouted.

"See what you've started!" Gallagher said. "What do you think?"

I was speechless. I tried to smile but my face was frozen. I did not believe that they were all here just for me.

"Hey, we got it. You didn't think we'd go to bat for you. Well, my friend, you've given us new life. New meaning. New focus."

Finally, I said, "I don't know if I deserve all this."

"Deserve it? If you don't who does? Romney, Paul, Bachman, the Newt? None of those people speak for us. They don't wear blue collars. They don't know what it is like to work hard and come to find out that the company you've devoted your life to is shipping your job overseas and putting you out to pasture. No, Leo, they can't even begin to understand what is happening in America. Tell them. Tell them all. We need you now more than ever."

Judy Bream, the union public relations person, said, "Leo, it's good to meet you. I'm here to do whatever you need and there is nothing we can't do if we do it together for the people."

Carol Hawley, the union accountant, added, "I'm on your team and ready to work until we take the white house and restore honor to working class people. We can't let people like that governor in Wisconsin do the same thing to people all over this country. You say, I do it. That's the mission."

Fritz Kuhn, the union's communication manager, laughed and said, "We've already had our first assault. When the news media heard that you were coming here today, I was on the phone for an hour trying to stop them from attacking you as a flunky of the union. Leo, you've galvanized an entire city. Now it's time to go viral and galvanize the entire country. I've got some wild ideas how we can do that and give me a minute later and I'll explain them to you."

I finally smiled and said to them, "Folks, I can't tell you what this means to me. I wasn't planning on much of anything and here you've already started to work on making this dream become a reality. What can I say?"

"You can say, let's get to work," John cried laughing.

"Let's do it," I replied.

For the next hour we brainstormed about how to seriously launch the campaign. John said he would be point person on setting up the itinerary for the engagements across the country. Once he heard that I wanted to criss-cross the country by speaking to unemployed people everywhere, he said he would coordinate this with locals and make it happen. Judy offered to handle press relations and begin the process of contacting people in all the fifty states to get my name on the ballot. She asked if I realized that this was necessary and I said I did. Carol asked how I wanted to handle finances and I gave her my insights. She took copious notes. When I finished describing my ideas, she merely said, "done". I said that I wanted absolute transparency including a daily accounting of where the money was coming from, who was giving it and I wanted the press to be able to report on it anytime they wanted. I did not want any money added to the account in excess of twenty dollars. They were concerned about my limitations, but I was adamant. I did not want to be answering questions a year from now about where I was getting money to finance this campaign. Fritz said he could have a web page up and running by the end of the day. All he needed was some time with me to get my comments on key issues so he could build this into the site and expose our campaign to the country. He was ready to launch and was rubbing his hands every time he shared what his vision for a "dynamite" site would look like and I was amazed and encouraged by his enthusiasm. We drank a few pots of coffee as the time passed and before I knew it we'd laid out the entire campaign, at least on paper.

"What do you think?" John asked.

"I think you're an amazing group of people," I replied. "I knew there was some reason I was supposed to come down here today but I never expected all this."

"This is nothing," Fritz said. "Wait until you see the cyber world we create."

"There is only one thing I ask of all of you and this is non-negotiable. This campaign must represent all working people. Not just union workers. I can't be limited in the focus. Many Americans are not union supporters. We've drifted so far away from believing in collective bargaining, the rights of working people to form unions and bargain for fair and just treatment that we've got a lot of work to do to make this campaign more than just a union struggle. We've got to win the hearts and minds of working people regardless of their politics, social prejudices, religious practices, sexual orientation and on and on. If we limit our focus to just those that are already on our side, we have no chance of winning a primary let alone the election."

"I agree totally with you, Leo," John said. "We're committed to that, too. Of course, we've got our own biases and prejudices, but right now we know that this office will be closing in six months. The mill is going to shut down. The company hasn't said it yet, but it's done. We're all going to be out of work. So now the new work is to get you elected and make something happen in America that's never happened before: a true outsider steps into the most important leadership position in the free world."

"Folks, I don't mean to sound naïve or foolish or ungrateful, but how do you know I can do it?"

They looked at me and did not say a word. I wondered what their silence meant and so I asked them.

"Leo, I wasn't there two days ago when you stood up and declared that you were running for president. I was sitting in my office wondering what my next move was going to be. This mill was being shut down. My union was going to die. My life, everything that I've worked hard for over the past three decades was being destroyed right before my very eyes. I stared out the window and was feeling so down that it was like going to the funeral of all my family members who were all killed in a horrific accident. There was nothing I could think to do or say. Throughout the day, I just waited for the inevitable call from across the street and prayed it would never come. The phone did ring. I let it ring six times before I picked it up. I was dreading what the message was going to be. But you know what I heard on the end of the line? You want to hear? I was told that one of our own, a guy from the mill, namely you, Leo, stood up and said that 'This is not the American Dream'. I listened as one of the people who was in the crowd feverishly told me everything. When I hung up, my eyes were wet and my heart was light and I just knew what I had to do. So you see, it was predestined that we would believe in you. We were ready because no one has ever taken the kind of step you are taking."

"I'd like to think that I'm not that unique and special," I said. "I'm just a simple mill rat who's decided enough is enough."

"No, Leo, that's not the case anymore," Judy added. "You've galvanized the city. Look at what's happened on the news front. You've gotten coverage already and the media was rather favorable of what they saw and heard. Granted the coverage was a little sketchy, but we'll fix that in short order. We'll build a media campaign that will rival every other candidate and we'll do it on a shoestring and we'll do it with the message that the will of working people is what is supporting your campaign to change the focus of this country."

"Sounds pretty lofty," I replied.

"Well, it is," Judy said. "What we've experienced in this country in the past four years is more of the same old politics. Democrat or republican, what's the difference? Nothing. We were sold on the theme of hope and change and our hopes have been dashed and the change we've experienced is a further movement of this country toward wealth and power and there is no denying working people are in worse shape now than they were two years ago."

"What theme should we broadcast on the web page?" Fritz asked.

"I've not thought about any themes or mottos. What do you all think?" I asked.

We discussed it for a good twenty minutes and the ideas flowed like rushing water over Niagara Falls. Some were true union messages. Workers Unite. People Power. There were many we discussed, rejected, and tabled. Finally we decided upon a simple message that would make everyone sit up and listen.

"When Americans Work, Freedom Lives and Democracy Thrives."

We sat quietly for a long time looking at the theme on the whiteboard.

"I like it," Judy said. "It captures the essence of what we're trying to capture."

"I think we need to add one word," Fritz commented. He got up and put "All" in front of Americans. "Yes, All is essential."

"I agree," John replied. "Right now some of us are working and yet, the majority are not. Many of those who are working are making less than a living wage. Hundreds of thousands are underemployed. We still have millions who are not working at all. We are not healthy. The economy is in the doldrums because we're a service and not a producer society."

"Can we sell it to the people?" Judy asked. "Can we get them to believe in what we are trying to do?"

"That's my job, my new job," I said to them.

"You can do it," John offered standing up and going to the board. "This is where we will focus our energy." He drew a map of America as if he had memorized the entire interstate highway system. "From Youngstown, we head to Akron, then Massillon, Cleveland, Sandusky, Toledo, Findlay, then on to Dayton, Cincinnati and finally Columbus. Then it's into Pennsylvania and every major city in the commonwealth. Once we've established a sound blue collar base, I think it's time to head south and east and then west. This will be a long road, but I'm sure that, Leo, you can be the spokesperson for an entire nation and find the energy and the inspiration to make the people realize they have a vested interest in believing in a new national order where we, the people, can triumph over despair and hopelessness."

"You make it sound pretty easy," I said laughing. "Luckily, I have an RV and that will make the road trips a whole lot more tolerable."

"So let's get to work, what do you say?" Fritz uttered.

"We've talked enough, yes, but what else do you need from us?" John asked.

I thought for a moment. Finally, I said, "I want absolute transparency and honesty and I don't want to have to defend anything we are doing. Tell the truth every time we are asked. I don't care if it costs us votes. We can't make promises we can't keep. We can't give people false hope based upon some convoluted argument that things will get better tomorrow just because they voted for me today. This struggle will be long and hard. There will be casualties. There will be many setbacks. There will be challenges we cannot even imagine. I feel it in my bones. I know what's coming even though I can't understand what it might be. Can you all agree to these conditions? If so, great. If not, then we can't start out on this journey together."

"I agree, you've got my word on it," John said.

"I do, too," Judy cried.

"I'm in for the duration," Carol proclaimed.

"You've got my vote and my commitment," Fritz said.

"Done. Then we can begin," I said. "I feel honored to have your support and your commitment and I will not let you down. Now let's get to work and change the way America does politics," I said.

For the next three hours we labored over lists of details. We were inflamed with the spirit of the cause.

As we were finishing details, I said to the group, "I can't tell you how much I appreciate all your hard work. What more can I say?"

"Say nothing, Leo," John said for the group. "We're here to support you, your candidacy, your vision, your mission and anything else you need."

"What I need from you, Leo, is a blurb about a number of issues so that I can upload these to the website," Fritz added.

"When do you need them?" I asked.

"As soon as possible; the sooner, the better. We want to get the message out to the country right away."

"How about if I get this to you later tonight?"

"You can do it that quickly?" he asked incredulously.

"Sure, why not? You need it. I'll do it. But first I've got to meet with someone at the bank and set up an account so that any contributions can be sent directly through the site and to the bank."

"Use Mahoning Bank," John said. "We bank there and they are people friendly. Talk to Jim Kilpatrick. He'll hook you up."

"I'll do that right now. That's where I'm headed."

"As soon as you're set up let me know," Judy commented. "Then I can begin to create the type of transparency you said you wanted."

"That won't be a problem, will it?" I asked.

"Nope. In fact, I'm looking forward to it. I want to know who is really coming through for us. You leave it to me, Leo. I'll make sure there are no 'embarrassing' questions. I mean it. I never did like the way campaign financing was done and this will give me a chance to make this happen in a way that might be a model for the entire 2012 campaign season. Imagine how this will play with the other candidates who hide their money everywhere and pretend they are maintaining. I hope we can make a real difference in this one area."

"You check back in with me tonight, Leo, and I'll have the itinerary for the next week ready to go," John said.

"Sounds like you want to be my chief of staff?" I said playfully.

"Sure, why not? But I don't want to travel with you. I'll make all the arrangements for your contact persons along the way. You just got to be ready to wow the people at each stop."

"Wow? Yes, let's hope so."

"You will. If you can do for those folks out there what you did for the people on South Avenue, you'll be fine. Hey what are you going to use for a sound system?"

"I haven't considered that."

"Before you leave, we'll give you ours. It's portable and battery powered and you can charge it between stops. We had it for rallies but looks like we're not going to need it. It's powerful enough to carry a thousand yards with clarity, so use it with our blessing."

"Thanks again for everything," I said. "This entire day has reaffirmed my faith in working people and what we can do when we just make up our minds and get to it."

"We're behind you all the way, fellow," Fritz said. "Now just get those bites to me. Here's my email address. This will be faster and I can just upload them to the site."

"You'll have it before midnight."

"Great!"

"What else do you need?" Carol asked.

"Can we have a clearing house number hooked up here that will field calls and that kind of thing? I mean, I can't do much on a cell phone when I'm on the road."

"Got it. We'll have that up and running by tomorrow and it will be on the web page. Fritz will see to that. I'll get a bunch of volunteers from the union to help us man the phones. We just need to have one contact number for you so we can get updates as you move along from town to town."

"I've got to get a new phone and a plan that will cover unlimited calling. I'll give you the number later, okay?" I said.

"Sure. Sound great!"

"Then I'm out of here," I said.

We shook hands and I walked on water until I got back into my car and realized just how much was being done to make this dream a reality. "Was this really happening?" I sat still for a few minutes just to gather my thoughts. There was so much to do, but right now I had to get to the bank before it closed.

Though the sky was a mottled gray color, my eyes could only see sunshine. The brightness came from the internal light that shone with the power of a light house. "Sae la luz," I said to myself. "Be the light!" The mission was simple. Throw light on every subject that was important to working people everywhere in the country. Simple, yes. Doable? Yes. How could it not be with the support I just discovered in those four fine people?

Driving downtown, I passed over the Blue Bridge and remembered when my father- in-law built it. He was an ironworker all his life and the bridge was one of his finest structures. Every time I passed over it I could feel his spirit in the ironworks. I missed him. He was a great fellow with an unqualified positive regard for his family, his community and the country he loved deeply.

Finding a parking spot proved simple. In the middle of the afternoon, traffic was exceptionally light. Our city was dying. First plazas and then malls killed off downtown shopping. I stood on the sidewalk and gazed up and down Federal Street, and wondered what it would take to bring the city back to life again? Perhaps, we were just pissing in the wind to think it would. I walked along the sidewalk and counted more than a dozen closed stores that once housed small businesses. The windows stared at me. They looked sad. I was sad, too. Once, downtown was the hub, the epicenter of culture. Now it was a hollow shell without a future. I waved to a window and saw it waving back at me. Perhaps there was hope yet.

Mahoning Bank, founded in 1857, was the oldest banking establishment in the city and still doing business in the building constructed at the turn of the last century. The woodwork inside was old world craftsmanship at its finest. They never modernized the lobby and when I walked inside, I felt like I was passing back into another time when the country was much simpler. Though the banking services were modernized, the façade remained the same. I always enjoyed stepping into the lobby and inhaling the past.

I asked to meet with Mr. Kilpatrick, sat down and waited. Five minutes later, I walked into his office and met the man who would, I hoped, provide the kind of transparency I needed.

"Mr. Pollack, what a pleasure to meet you. My, my, my what a stir you've created in our humble little city."

"I hope it will make a difference," I said.

"A difference? I'm sure you will. More than you can even imagine," he said with a tone of absolute authority. "So how can I help you today?"

"I need to set up a special account for my campaign. By special, I mean it has to be highly transparent. I may be receiving a lot of money, but I don't want anything hidden from anyone who may be curious as to who sent the money, how I spend the money and anything else that might shed a negative light on what I'm doing."

Kilpatrick did not speak for a few moments. He stared at me intently. I wondered what he was thinking. I realized my request was probably different from most that he received. Who wants his or her finances open to anyone who makes an inquiry?

"You're serious, aren't you?"

"Yes, very much so."

"Most people want their money hidden from public scrutiny."

"Sure. But what I'm asking for is just the opposite. This will be public money and I want those who send money to my campaign to be able to see just how the money is being spent. This is not some private fund where we launder corporate contributions. I imagine most of the volume will be in small denominations less than twenty dollars. In fact, I'm going to limit contributions to this amount. You know what is prompting me to do this?"

"No, but please tell me," Kilpatrick said.

I think he knew but he just wanted to make sure that I was clear about what my goal was. "Just the other day, one of the potential candidates started a new web site to promote his exploratory campaign. The only one who has control over the site is the candidate. No one else. So, any money that is sent to him can be used by him for anything he deems necessary. Hey, he wants to go out and eat dinner with his third wife. No problem. The campaign pays for it. He travels somewhere to do a speech. He pays with other people's money. He might collect millions before he even declares he is a real candidate, but in the mean time, he spends the money any way he sees fit. If I were to operate that way, there would be a hue and cry that would unhinge the public in micro, even nano seconds. So, this is what I need and I'm hoping that you'll be able to provide."

Kilpatrick was silent again. Then he said, "We can do it. Unorthodox, yes. Necessary, yes. I agree with you, Mr. Pollack. Politics and money are a bad mix and I fully agree with you that transparency is the only way to run a campaign. You've got my support."

"Great! Judy, my accountant, will be getting with you to complete the particulars. Our webmaster, Fritz, will be interfacing with Judy and you so that we can pull this off and make sure that there are no damaging questions any time."

"I'll get to work on it right away. What else can I do to help you?"

"I need a debit card, no two, tied to this account so that when I'm on the road, I can use it and this way anyone can track what I'm doing and where I'm doing it and how much it is costing the campaign committee."

"You're really serious about this transparency issue, aren't you?"

"Serious yes. I can't be telling the people one thing and doing something else. I'm sick of that kind of business. I've watched the chicanery for the past forty years and enough is enough. No, either we do it this way or we don't do it."

"I'll get someone to set up an account before you leave and give you a blank card you can use immediately until we issue you an official one. How will that work for you?"

"Excellent."

"I'll be right back." He left the room and returned in ten minutes. "Here is your card. The pin number is ****. Pretty simple. I thought you might appreciate it."

"How did you know the year I was born?"

"Mr. Pollack, I'm a banker and my job is to know my customers. How long have you banked with us?"

I laughed forgetting that this was already my bank. "You got me, Mr. Kilpatrick."

"Call me Jim and may I call you, Leo?"

"Of course."

"I'm sure that we'll be doing a lot of business so thank you for trusting Mahoning Bank,"

"Thank you for making this painless."

"That's my job," Kilpatrick said grinning. "Here are your account and routing numbers so you're all set. Tell your people to call me day or night in case there are any problems. The last number is my cell phone. I don't want any problems with the press or 'others', so don't be afraid to call and work out anything that is not kosher."

"We will do that, most assuredly."

We shook hands. "Good luck, Leo."

"Luck is opportunity met with preparation," I replied. "I'm preparing now for that opportunity."

"We'll make sure that the opportunities are supported by us in every way possible."

We smiled at each other and I left.

When I got back outside, the sun was resting on the horizon. "Where did the day go?" I asked myself. I ambled over to my car and noticed that I had a parking ticket. I smiled and wondered just how silly this was. Free parking might bring people back to town. Ticketing a person for not putting a dime in the meter would just keep people away. I did not resent the ticket. I took the ticket and put it in my wallet. I would pay it later but not with campaign money.

As I drove west out of the downtown area, the last brilliant rays blinded me for a moment and I shielded my eyes from them. There was the real light in the universe. Now all I had to do was emulate it and be the light for the people, shine in a way that they could tell me where they thought we should go and I would lead them forward.

Driving back home took ten minutes. Belmont Avenue traffic was non-existent. When I pulled into the drive, I thought about all the things I needed to do tonight. It would be a late night.

We ate dinner together and then Janko and Basha disappeared for a while because he had homework. This gave me the opportunity to reconfigure my to-do list. I called Fritz, let him know what the account and routing numbers were and told him that I would have the talking points to him before I went to bed. Judy was not available but I sent her the numbers via email. I did not want to leave them on her answering machine. John answered when I called and he said he would email me a tentative schedule for the next week. I thanked him again for everything they were doing for me. He asked who was going to do the driving for me and I said I was not sure. He thought he might have a few volunteers who could help. I said I would let him know if I came up against a wall. We parted with some small talk about just how motivated his team was now that they were on to bigger and better things than just keeping a small union hall functioning smoothly. I laughed and said I hoped they would not get overwhelmed as the business became fast and furious. He said they would deal with that when it happened.

When Janko's bedtime came, I went up and we said his prayers and had a short question and answer period. He was curious about how I was going to go to the playground and play with all that was going on and I said that it might be hard but w would manage as best we could. He accepted this with reluctance and confusion but finally kissed me goodnight, rolled over and said, "I love you, Daddy."

"I love you too, son."

After he was settled in bed, Basha and I talked about my day and I related to her all the things we accomplished. She said that she was concerned about Janko's perception of what was going on and how he would handle not having me around most of the time.

"I don't know what to tell you, but we'll have to manage."

"I know, Leo, but he's so used to your being home. I just get worried."

"Me, too. We'll just have to do the best we can."

"I'm going to bed. You coming."

"I'd like to but I told Fritz that I'd have the main issues for my platform. He wants to have them posted on a web page by tomorrow."

"You're going to be up for a long time."

"I hope not."

"You will be. Goodnight Leo." She kissed my forehead and said, "Let them have it. Speak truth to power, my love." Basha disappeared into the dark hallway. I was alone. In the silence I gathered my thoughts knowing what I wanted to relate to the people. An hour passed and then I was ready. I went up to the room that served as a study and settled down to write.

7. Speaking Truth To Power

As I sat at my desk, I cleared my mind and slowly the outline of what I wanted to say flowed through me. I outlined the separate items that I thought people would want to know about me. My ideas must be complete enough for folks to form an informed opinion. There was no stopping the flow. I settled in for a long night of rational thinking.

"Where do I start?" I asked myself. I pondered the order in which I wanted to address the issues. "Simple," I said. "Start with A and work your way to Z."

I began.

Abortion – Right to Choose or Right to Life?

When a woman conceives she is experiencing the most profound experience in all humankind. The ability to bear new life is a sacred responsibility and is the essence of womanhood. I respect women because, unlike them, I can only contribute to the propagation of our species. Given this special power, a woman's body is sacred and only she has the right to control it. A woman possesses the right to determine what she does with her body, her reproductive power and her choice is hers and hers alone. For too many years, men have interfered with this right. Men cannot decide for any woman what she does regarding her reproductive power. If she chooses to conceive and give birth, so be it. If she conceives and decides she is not ready to raise a child and she decides to abort the fetus, so be it. When a woman is molested or raped and conceives a child, she must have the freedom to choose what to do without any interference on the part of the law or other outside powers. Her health and mental well-being are what matter. I believe in pro-choice. A woman has the right to choose what she does with her own body. I believe in pro-life. A woman's life and her child's life are her own business. I believe in pro-women. Whatever a woman decides is in her best interest is her right and responsibility.

I reread the text a few times. "Simple and to the point," I thought. "Yes, leave it alone for now."

Crime and Drugs – Legalization versus the Continuing Insanity

For more than thirty years, the "war on drugs" has been waged with billions of dollars being spent to eradicate the flow of illegal drugs from other countries into ours. We have failed miserably. As long as there is a demand for drugs, the producers will continue to provide a product for the consumers. I do not believe that drug abuse is healthy nor life sustaining. Our war on drugs has not stopped the flow of drugs. We have filled our prisons with drug abusers who need treatment. It is time to consider legalizing and controlling the production, distribution and sales of chemicals. This is a radical departure from where we are heading today. We can control this product and do so quite effectively. Research indicates that in countries where drugs are legal, there is no appreciable increase in the level of drug use. Unsafe drug use ends. Criminal activity and drug violence decreases. We are not going to end the use of mind altering drugs just because we say that it is an addiction and wrong. Yes, it is an addiction. Treat it as such by providing treatment for those who wish to receive it. For those who do not want to stop, provide them with a safe, legal way to get their narcotics.

"This one is going to be closely scrutinized and cause a lot of problems for some people to accept. Oh well, let it be."

Education – K-12 and Higher Education.

We are slowly losing our competitive edge because our public school education system is not meeting the needs of our children. Our educational model is antiquated. Look at our school system. We start school in the fall and end in late spring. This model is based upon the agrarian society we were more than a hundred years ago. Students do not need the summer off to work on family farms. If only three percent of our population still lives on a farm, we are truly operating in the past. Consider changing the school year from a nine-month schedule to year-round. Schools operate for six weeks and then there is a week break. Another six weeks of education and then another break. Planning to take an extended break in July for a month and two weeks around the Christmas holiday and we have a system that significantly improves the quantity of education. We work year-round except for scheduled vacations. Students will adjust to whatever we do.

Another outcome is that school buildings do not sit idle for months. They get used as they should be: learning centers that never really shut down. How else do we improve the quantity of education? We continue to educate grade school students from 8-3 PM. This fits their biological patterns. For high school students, we start the school day later and end it later. Research indicates that teenage students tend to do better when school starts and ends later in the day. Minnesota schools are already doing this with remarkable results.

Now let us address the quality of education. In every school where teachers are paid well, leaders create a rich learning environment and parents are involved in their children's educational development. This is a three-pronged attack on the issue of quality. First, teachers need to be paid well and treated with respect. Wisconsin is cutting the education budget by $900 million dollars. Yes, the state may be in financial trouble, but the answer to saving the state is not to undermine the next generation's future by going after education. Educators did not create the economic recession. Most teachers make a decent wage. There are few teachers making six figure salaries. We find no complaint when our sports heroes, who are nothing more than entertainers, make millions of dollars for hitting or shooting or carrying a ball on some kind of playing field. When teachers ask for a 2-3% raise, the citizenry goes crazy. We pay billions of dollars for sports paraphernalia, but when a small tax hike for schools is on the ballot, it generally gets voted down. We spend more per year on new television sets and other high tech gadgets than we do on education. We spend ten times more money on our military than we do on education. We spend four times as much on agriculture than we do on education. What does that tell us?

We do not really value education because we do not finance it adequately. Head Start is one of the most successful programs ever designed to help children get ready for their education experience. What do we do with Head Start every year? We underfund it. I believe in reform and the need to make education the number one focus in this nation and not something that is considered a "necessary evil".

Lastly, public education is the great equalizer in this country. Public education created the middle class. Giving parents vouchers, starting more charter and private schools is not the answer to improving our public education system. We can improve education by putting people in control of the department of education that truly comprehend the issues and have the knowledge and skills necessary to implement a renaissance in American education.

"That about does it for now." I read the section again and knew there was a lot more that I wanted to say about education, but for now I left it alone.

Embryonic Stem Cell Research

Recent advances in stem cell research give us some hope that this innovative approach to eliminating disease in humans must be pursued. Stem cells are the basis of human life. There is the ethical dilemma that persists. If we destroy a stem cell, do we destroy life? Yes, we do, but not life as we know it in the form of a child. It is still just a cell. What makes this research important and essential is that stem cells are the source of initial life and from them we may be able to produce the greatest benefits for humans. This is not a religious question but a scientific one. Yes, science has not demonstrated that it can make this type of research produce extraordinary results. However, the research has been stifled by the moral question that has limited its scope. If we give scientists permission to proceed and monitor and evaluate just what we are getting from the research, we can assess if we should continue. Let us focus stem cell research on five major medical issues that we believe can be solved via this method and continue until we prove or disprove that it is feasible. In pursuing this research we are not attempting to become "gods". We are using our God-given talents to solve medical problems and provide a higher quality of life for people who suffer from debilitating illnesses like Parkinson's, Diabetes and Alzheimer's to name just a few. Anyone who has ever had a family member suffer from one of these diseases knows how the quality of life was affected.

"Boy, this one will alienate a lot of people who believe in pro-life. We just can't sit idly by and let this potential curative research go untapped. Moral issues aside, we owe it to the people who suffer to give them some hope."

Energy Independence.

"Drill baby drill is one step in the movement toward energy independence. We begin to address this problem by first of all conserving energy. Take light bulbs. There was a move to eliminate incandescent bulbs in favor of high energy ones by 2011. The Republicans blocked this change. They stopped the use of paper products in the congress and replaced them with Styrofoam, a petrochemical product that does not disintegrate for a thousand years in landfills. We must conserve in every way possible and it begins with our eliminating any products that are not recyclable and made of non-renewable resources. For a few years, we have received energy credits for making our homes more energy efficient. One way to make a home more energy efficient is simply to make it smaller. Offering major tax cuts for building smaller, energy efficient homes would be a great incentive to make people change their lifestyles. We need to research more energy efficient solar energy resources. The sun produces so much energy that if we could capture what it sends to the earth in one hour, we could power our entire globe. These are the facts. Automobiles consume about twenty percent of our energy use and here we need to make radical shifts away from the current types of vehicles we are now driving. Any vehicle that is energy inefficient would be phased out. SUVs are the prime example. The use of automatic transmissions would end. Manual transmissions use less gas. If we engineer a car with eight manual speeds, we could increase mileage. Even, even in rather large vehicles, this would be one way to improve auto efficiency. Railroads are underutilized. Warren Buffet understood this fact and that was the reason he invested five billion in the rail systems. He knows what is coming. Follow the money. If we moved fifty percent of our products via railroads as opposed to trailer trucks, we would save significant amounts of energy and money.. The average food product we consume is trucked more than 1400 miles. The cost of food is high, not because of production, but because of packaging and transportation. Wind, solar, geothermal, bio fuels have not been given the support necessary to move them from alternative energy sources to primary ones. Nuclear power is an option, but given what is happening in Japan today, we need to design safe production methods. We have not solved how to discard spent fuel rods safely. No state wants to store them. We know that this is a carbon free source of electricity, but we have not done enough to make this form of energy safely. If we were to design smaller bomb and storm proof plants that were all the same design, produced in areas where they will not affect human health, and monitor and evaluate them effectively, we might safely use these plants to help eliminate dirty coal burning plants. We cannot continue to burn dirty coal because it is cheaper. Until we can make a complete shift to renewable energy sources, we can use what we have right now with conservation being emphasized at every level from production to consumption. We are not "addicted" to oil, but we certainly "dependent" upon it. We can end this dependence by rational, long term all inclusive conservation and conversion policies.

"I'm not sure how this will be received by the energy companies and those who don't want to change, but I guess it's pay now or pay later." I thought about that maxim and wondered just how I would be able to convince people to change their attitudes. This would be an uphill fight.

The Environment.

Mother Earth is all that we have to sustain human life. If we continue to abuse our mother we will die. We cannot continue to pollute water sources and hope to have clean drinking water. We cannot let those who do not respect our earth to make policies that directly impact its destruction. Sustainability is essential. We know there is a finite amount of natural resources that we can hope to use. Our current rate of consumption is unsustainable. Every species that lives deserves the right to continue to live. When we let any "endangered species" disappear, we move closer and closer to mankind become the final "endangered species". One way to protect the earth is to make a concerted world wide effort to slow down population growth. With fewer mouths to feed, there will be less demand on the earth to provide for them. Birth control is not a religious nor moral issue. It is a matter of life and death for our planet. Scientists are predicting that a population above 8 billion is not sustainable. In 2009, the US defence department produced a report that indicated that future wars will be fought over food and water supplies and not because of terrorism or religion. Global climate change will cause masses of people to emigrate to places where there are adequate food and water resources available. It may be an inconvenient truth that the earth's climate is changing. The majority of the world's climate scientists believe in climate change. Businesses that destroy land and water sources must be seriously fined or eliminated. This may be a painful change to our lifestyles. However, even worse is the catastrophic effects we may experience if we do not change. Our earth is precious. We must revere it as we do life itself.

"Boy, what will happen when the regressives get their minds wrapped around this point of view? I thought about the Native Americans and how simply they lived and how we slowly eliminated them as we invoked "manifest destiny" and stole their lands. Once millions of buffalo lived in this country. We killed the majority of them and replaced this highly adaptable animal with our cattle.

Guantanamo Bay.

Shut it down now. Send the prisoners back to their respective countries. If the countries do not want their own people, drop them off on their shores or at their borders and let them fend for themselves. We are spending millions of dollars to house 140 prisoners that someone determined are the most evil men on the face of the earth. The world is watching and judging us. We are guilty of bringing them to our prison and then holding them without due process for years. What have we become? Guantanamo is our own gulag. Yes, let us not pretend that we are noble in our design. We are all losers in this fiasco. We lose because we are operating illegal prisons. We have created a term to label these men: enemy combatants. What does this mean? We can pretend we are doing this to be safe from terrorism. It is time to end this saga.

I got up and went to the bathroom. After washing my face, I looked at my watch and realized that it was nearing midnight. "The first of many long nights I'm sure I'm going to have."

Gun Control.

The supreme court ruled that individuals have the right to keep and bear arms. Guns don't kill people. People kill people. However, there is some reason to reconsider the sale of automatic weapons and extended clips that turn a semi-automatic pistol into a veritable killing machine. The majority of Americans who own and use firearms are law-abiding citizens. They do not kill people. Therefore, to punish them by making it harder to keep and bear arms is unfair. For those who break the law using a firearm, there must be severe accountability. This is what separates freedom from responsibility and

accountability. What is the solution to end the amount of gun violence in the country? First, we need to educate anyone who wants to own a firearm in the safe use and storage of a lethal weapon. Registering a new firearm provides some control over keeping firearms out of the hands of those who should not own them. This is not a fool proof system. It is too easy to purchase a firearm from just about anyone who wants to buy one. Once a person owns a firearm, he or she is responsible for what happens with the use of that gun. This is a serious issue and there is a need to accept sole responsibility for its use, storage and safety. There is a movement to pass legislation called the "Castle Doctrine". This gives people the right to use lethal force to protect themselves when they are out and away from their homes. This is a serious step toward permitting people to carry firearms, and use them any time they feel threatened by others wherever they are. This is a serious extension of the "right to keep and bear arms" and must be reconsidered. It is not rational for people to be able to own and use assault weapons. Once they are for sale on the open market they become available to criminal elements. There is no way to control those who choose to use firearms for illegal use, but we can stiffen the penalties. This may need to be a non-negotiable criminal offense.

I thought about the number of issues facing this nation and wondered if I were really up to the task of solving them. I figured that I as well as anyone could offer my views. Granted there were a lot of people who had similar ideas, but nothing ventured, nothing gained. Let it all hang out. I was having some fun even though it was getting very late and I still wanted to get this done tonight.

Health Care.

The health care bill passed along strictly party lines. The Republicans were adamant in their opposition to it and have vowed to disassemble it piece by piece. Yet this bill provides health care for millions of children and this is a major step forward to insuring all Americans. No longer can a person be denied health care coverage because of an existing condition. It is true the bill mandates that all people purchase health care by 2014. The argument against this provision is that it is taking away our freedom. The federal government cannot do this because it is unconstitutional. This is just not true. Consider auto insurance. If we want to drive a car in any state in the nation, we must buy auto insurance. If we do not buy it, we cannot drive. Simple. Oh, but in each of our policies there is a premium we pay called "uninsured motorist coverage". This charge covers each of us against the person who slips through the cracks in any state and does not have coverage. We are paying for those who violate the law. We do not think much about it until it happens to us. Then we are really glad we have the coverage. The same principle applies to health care. We are already paying for those who are uninsured. Yes, those people who do not have health care just show up at the emergency ward and the hospital team must take care of them. We pay for it in hidden premiums. It is the same system but the health insurance companies do not let us know that we are subsidizing those without health care. When 307 million people are covered and the risk is spread across this vast group, we can negotiate lower premiums because there will be greater competition.

The government can stipulate just how much it will pay for any prescribed Medicare procedure. For instance, in Japan an MRI for a knee averages about $149.00. In the US the cost varies from $1500 to $2600 depending upon where you live in the country. If this sounds amazing, it is. Given this disparity, we need to get this under control. Once the Medicare system sets standard fees and enforces them, then other health care providers will follow suit. Controlling costs is the first step to solving the health care crisis.

We eliminate the excessive profits that health care companies make. They are sucking the life blood from our economy and many people's savings with their greed. How much profit is enough? Revoking their for profit status will be a start. The top seven healthcare corporations in the nation each made an average of $5 billion in profits in the past year. A lot of this money that is going into CEO pockets and this needs to stop.

We need to make a national prevention program a part of everyone's life. Incentives for staying healthy need to be implemented. For people who lose weight and keep it off, their insurance costs go down. Those who smoke and quit pay less. Those who do not smoke pay even less. Every incentive to get people to live healthy lifestyles needs to be invoked.

We need to improve the American food supply. Processed food is not food. Sugar, fat and starch are the predominant fillers in most of our food. We are eating ourselves to death. Michelle Obama has already started this movement and I give her credit for beginning the process. We need to take it one step further and make it mandatory that food products cannot contain 20% salt and 30 % fat and 15% sugar and call it "food". This will not be an easy fix. Lobbyists will fight this every step of the way.

"That's a mouthful. Now what? I need to get a cup of coffee." I went down and fixed one and then came back up to the study and went back to work.

HIV-AIDS.

With all the other issues facing America and the world, HIV-AIDS has disappeared from the radar screen but this deadly disease is still rampant. The previous president made a concerted effort to end the epidemic in Africa, but we still are not devoting enough research to find a cure for it. This will not be an easy struggle because it has become an ideological struggle as well as a medical one. However, a person contracting AIDS is not the issue. Finding a cure benefits every person who may be faced with a positive test. It is time to get to work and never stop until a cure is found.

I went right on to the next issue.

Immigration.

"Give us your tired, your poor, your huddled masses yearning to breathe free, the wretched refuse of your teeming shore, send these your homeless, tempest-tossed to me, I lift my lamp beside the golden door"…is engraved on the base of the Statue of Liberty. We built this country on immigrant labor. My grandparents were immigrants. They came to America seeking a better life. They found it. When it is convenient, we import immigrant labor. When we are finished using them, we want them to go back home. It is ironic that immigration became an issue when the economy went into recession. All of a sudden immigrants were stealing jobs from Americans. But let us be honest. What jobs do many immigrants do? Immigrants fill low paying jobs like meat processing and manual labor. Most of us could not live on $5.00 an hour. Do they complain? No. They are the new slaves of the 21st century. They are replacing the slaves we finally freed in the last century. People sneak into America to work and make a better life for their families. For them, this is the American Dream and we want to deny it to them because we are selfish and greedy and unwilling to share in our bounty. It is time for a change. We need to create a pathway to citizenship and stop denying that there is a problem with our immigration policy. The time to accept people no matter how they got here is now. We are a democracy. We are the light upon the hill, a beacon for the world and as long as we are shining people will see it and come.

My eyes were burning. I needed something. I ran to the bathroom and washed my face, went downstairs and made another cup of coffee. Back at the desk, I continued my work.

Lesbians, Gays, Bisexuals and Transvestites.

Our social war over accepting those who adopt a different sexual preference than heterosexuality continues to divide this nation. Ironically, where conservatives claim that granting gays and lesbians the right to marry will destroy traditional family values and erode marriage as an institution, the converse is true. Massachusetts was the first state to recognize same sex marriages in the United States. At the same time, it is the state with the lowest divorce rate in the country. If same sex marriage were going to adversely affect "traditional family values and marriage as an institution" it would seem logical and reasonable that Massachusetts would be the state to first experience a decay. The facts are indisputable. One of the states that is totally against same sex marriage, Texas, has one of the highest rates of divorce in the country. If social policy is based on fact, not fiction, then how should we choose? When people love one another, the feeling is not dependent upon their gender. The love experience is something that cannot be explained by pure gender alone. Therefore, let the law read that anyone who wants to marry may feel free to do so with all the responsibilities and joys associated with it.

Evolution versus Intelligent Design (Creationism).

There is no way to prove whether evolution or intelligent design is the true story of how the universe was created. Science promotes evolution. Religion presents intelligent design or creationism. One is founded upon the slow, biological changes that a species undergoes over millions of years. The other is depicted as being driven by an unseen but omnipotent being. The scientific method guides thought related to the former; faith leads to the latter. The question is does it really matter? How can this one argument divide a land so intensely? There is enough factual information to discount the notion that the earth was created in "six days". Millions of years of fossil history discount it. Facts are not enough to convince the faithful. So let them believe what they will. Their beliefs are not going to stop the earth from evolving. There is no need to make one belief or another the predominant one. Beliefs are beliefs. This nation, secular or religious, is still one of religious freedom but not a theocracy. Christianity is just one of the many faiths practiced in America. Therefore, let all faiths be honored, not just one. The Higher Power accepts all believers however they come to him, or her.

The Budget and the Economy.

I stared at the words and sat there numb and silent. We were in the worst recession in the last seventy-five years. The wealthy were fat and happy. Working people were struggling. There were no easy answers.

The Budget and the Economy.

Government is not the problem. It is the solution. We cannot let greed consume this nation. Unfair trade is not a free market economy. Currently, thousands of corporations are getting huge tax cuts while working people are paying the price for these cuts. We need to level the playing field. More than a million people have lost their homes and the number is increasing. Yes, many people might have purchased homes they could not afford. Immediately stop all foreclosures. Make banks refinance every loan and create a payment schedule that makes it possible for people to keep their homes. They may never pay them off. This is just a fact of life. It is better that they keep their homes even if they never own them than to let them lose them and become a part of the homeless masses that are a part of the growing tide. Wherever inequity exists, the government must stop it. Monopolies are killing our economy. Microsoft is not just a company. It is a monopoly and must be broken up immediately. When 95% of all computers in the country run on one operating system this is a monopoly. When seven to ten banks control 90% of the flow of money in the country, this is a monopoly. The notion that a company or bank is "too big to fail" means that it must be broken up into smaller parts and competition not collaboration, be the order of business.

The Republican party took a pledge not to raise taxes. This is unrealistic and unsustainable. We cannot spend more than we take into our coffers. Immediately, the Bush Tax Cuts are ended. Pre-2003 tax percentages will be reinstituted. The presidential commission on economic reform presented its report, "The Moment of Truth" we will adopt the recommendations in it. We must plan for Social Security reform by raising the age of retirement to 70 years of age by 2045. Immediately, we will raise the social security cap from $106,000 to $500,000. There is no need to wait on this recommendation. With the extra amount coming into the social security trust fund, it will begin to grow. We will stop raiding the trust fund by letting the money flow into the general operating fund and placing "IOU's" into the box.

We will not finance any wars on a government "credit card". If we can't pay for it, we will not do it. We will eliminate government contractors like Triple Canopy and Blackwater. Any weapon system that is not "mission critical" will be ended. We are not going to sacrifice our future by living in fear. Terrorism will not go away, but we are not going to fight wars wherever there are a few "jihadists" living in the mountains. There are ways to deal with them. This constant war spending is killing our economy. We will commit to bringing back a industry to America by immediately ending any tax break or benefit that any company thinks it can use to export jobs to other countries. For instance, I-phones are made in China and sold in America. Immediately, there will be a tariff on any product that is owned by an American company but not produced in this country. Global trade is only global if we let companies in America make products in other countries and sell them here. If it is to be an American product it is American made. Any product not made in America will be taxed to the same amount it would cost if it were made right no these shores. We will create parity by taking care of our own. There is nothing magical or mysterious about this policy. We've been faced with years of unfair trade created by the legions of greedy businesses. Banks will no longer be the engines of our economy. People will. People who are working and producing goods and services that our own people want will be the new order. If all you do is play with money, you will have to go and find a real job. Banks will no longer be permitted to be anything but banks. They will not speculate. They will not sell derivatives. They will not be in the mortgage backed securities market. They will bank your money and lend it to others and make a fair but not obscene profit. We will enact a true American Service Corps. There is enough work in this country to last a hundred years. Just look at our bridges, roads, parks, sidewalks, ponds, lakes, rivers and streams. We will create a land that is the envy of the world because it will be a clean, safe and peaceful one in which all can live out the American Dream.

Labor will be honored, not disrespected. Every man and woman who works will earn a living wage. No longer will the captains of industry make billions of dollars on the "slave labor" of a labor force that is subject to their whim and fancy. Workers will be respected. Labor Day will mean something as a holiday.

"That will go over big," I laughed aloud. "Too bad, the current president doesn't stand up and protect working people from the gubernatorial attacks taking place right now in Wisconsin, Ohio, Indiana, Michigan, Maine, Pennsylvania, Kentucky, Texas and who knows what state next. There is enough frustration in this land today to inflame the entire country. I believe it is time to light the spark and make it burn. After all, when a prairie fire burns it kills all the harmful insects. Perhaps it's time to let the earth burn a little and get rid of the parasites."

Trade and the Global Economy.

We consume 25% of the world's resources yet we make up only 5% of the world's population. Our greed is voracious. This is unsustainable. We need to change our lifestyle and our vision for the future. We are setting standards of selfishness, not self-sufficiency and service to our fellow man or woman. How can we live in a land where homelessness exists and do nothing about it. The global community sees our land and hates the way we waste things. We are at once, the envy of the world, and cursed for our wantonness. Sharing in the common bounty of the world's resources means we need to stop being so enchanted with "toys and baubles". There are some who will say, "I work hard for my toys. Why are you penalizing me?" We are not penalizing anyone. We are merely saying, "We are no longer going to be a profligate nation flaunting our wealth in the face of world poverty, hunger and depravation." G-20 nations meet and these leaders decide how best to distribute the world's wealth among the richest nations. Yet, the poorest nations are not included in the dialogue. How can we survive when we are living on a bounty that is restricted from the masses? We cannot live in a world where mass starvation exists while at the same time others are eating filet mignon and caviar and drinking 100 year old vintage wines. Sharing my wealth means that I care about the world in which I live. This is the global economy at its finest. A landscape where hunger is eliminated, homelessness does not exist and people are healthy and happy and can participate in arts, entertainment and education.

I sat still and digested this segment. There was so much more to say, but for now, this was enough. I would have more to say, I knew, but the global economy and a vision for the future would evolve just as I would over a period of time.

National Security.

Our safety is dependent upon the safety of all nations. If one of our brother or sister nations is in jeopardy, we all are facing it." Ask not for whom the bell tolls, it tolls for thee," wrote John Donne. Look at what is happening in Japan today. Nuclear power was chosen as the primary source of energy in that ancient land even though it was the only nation to ever face the ravages of nuclear destruction. They committed to the good use of nuclear energy. Now they are facing the consequences of their choice. Arabs and Israelis must come to a table and face each other as people and not as enemies. The mistake we have made for too many years is that we do not talk with one another. Enemies avoid sitting down at the table and talking with one another. Let me say this again. We must sit down at the table and talk with one another. As Native Americans taught us, we must learn to "bury the hatchet" meaning lay down our arms and accept that we are not alone in this world. So today, what do we do? We bomb Libya! What an asinine way to make peace. The presidents need to sit down at the table and talk. Talk until they are blue in the face. But talk. Talk. Talk some more. Talk until there is mutual understanding.

Foreign Policy.

We lead by example. However, our example leaves much to be desired. We say we are a democracy, of, for and by the people. What we see in our nation is a government of, for and by corporations. All over the world, nations watch us and wonder what we are doing. We go from Ira   q, to Afghanistan, and just yesterday, to Libya. We are functioning as the "police department" of the world. This is unsustainable. There is no way we can continue to spread our military throughout the world and expect to be able to secure our nation. We are reluctant to talk with our enemies. Our policy is based upon gunboat diplomacy, not mutual respect. The ongoing Arab-Israeli Conflict is one example. Not once did the last or the current president meet with both sides, face to face, and work through all barriers and come to a collaborative solution. One secretary of state may not be enough to do the job effectively. We may want to select the person most connected with a particular nation and engage his or her services in working with other nations. Since we became the sole super power, our foreign policy has disintegrated. We are the "ugly Americans". We have created an aura of omnipotent military power, omniscient answers to all problems and omnivorous consumption of natural resources. We are envied and despised because we do not listen and hear what other nations are telling us. We give money to dictators to keep their friendship and support and let democracies struggle to survive.

The time for a major shift in our foreign policy is now. We need to embrace all people as our neighbors. We must relinquish our imperialistic tendencies and embrace the "united nations" as we move into this 21st Century. Going it alone whenever we undertake any kind of foreign policy initiative is foolish and counterproductive. During the last presidential campaign, every candidate made it clear that he would not talk with dictators without pre-conditions. Anyone who said he would meet with Iran's president was chastised as cheapening the presidency. Yet, how do enemies ever become friends if they do not sit down and talk with one another. Our world is rapidly shrinking and we need to become better neighbors. We can only do this if we are not chronic antagonists.

"We have so much work to do to resurrect sound American foreign policy. Right now, our war planes are making policy and we'll be paying for this maneuver for a long time to come." I sat back and thought about the ramifications that bombing Libya would have on our presence in Northern Africa and I was not encouraged.

Religion.

America was founded by Puritans who fled England so they could practice their religion without persecution. As waves of immigrants arrived, we have found ourselves facing a plethora of new faiths, new beliefs and new moral and ethical challenges. Let us accept that God is God. There is no one faith system that is better or worse than any other. If we accept this premise, religious tolerance will continue to be the norm. We are seeing is a movement toward Christian Fundamentalism and a growing intolerance for other belief systems. Islam, Buddhism and a host of religions are emerging to challenge the fundamentalists. What is needed is acceptance and not attacks upon other faiths. There is no "proof" that one faith is truer than another. Every faith system has, at one time or another, attempted to make it the predominant one in society. None has ever succeeded. Now, more than ever, we need to practice tolerance and patience with our brothers and sisters of all faiths.

Not wanting to slow down, I moved right along to the last topic.

War.

War is hell. In the history of mankind, wars have succeeded in achieving one thing; they have reduced the human population. Every war begins with noble intent and generally ends with significant death of innocent bystanders. The last administration used the euphemism " collateral damage" to describe the killing of innocent civilians. In the end, whether they were innocent or guilty, they were dead. Due to our human nature, some cynics conclude that war is inevitable. We humans are struggling to survive and only the fittest will make it. This contention leaves us with no option but to fight to the end of one war only to begin another one. The only way to end warfare is to stop fighting. Taking a hint from the first step of AA, we must admit we are powerless over our violent human nature and that our lives have become unmanageable. We can quit fighting. We can seek peace. We can be more noble than the animals. We do not need to kill others to feed ourselves. After all, we are not cannibals. What is the purpose of most wars? Religious dominance. Economic expansion. We could go on and on assessing what causes war, but in the end, after every war is ended, there is a sense of meaninglessness. What was the sense of it all? What did we achieve? Some might argue that there are just wars and there are unjust wars. What is the difference when in the end innocent people die? The time for making war is over. It is too easy to make war. How much more exciting will it be to make peace at long last? From the very first time one man coveted what another man owned, our conflicts have resulted in death. It is time to call a moratorium on warfare. Take swords and beat them into plowshares. Though the most violent civilizations have seemed invincible for a long time, they have declined and fallen. Is America to follow this self-destructive path?

I was done. Checking my watch, I read 2 AM. Time to go to bed. I saved the file, attached it to an email message to Fritz, sent it, and then logged off. I could barely move my fingers. They felt like solid lead. My knuckles were twitching. I got up and went to the bathroom, brushed my teeth, , washed my face, went to the bedroom, dropped my clothes where I stood, crawled under the warm covers and snuggled up against Basha. She squirmed toward me and I leaned over and kissed her on the forehead and said, "Goodnight sweet princess." She didn't answer, but her warm body next to mine said volumes. As I fell asleep, I could feel the cancer inside of me draining away and I felt light and airy. My mind was resting. Everything that poured out of me tonight was the accumulation of years of frustration and now it was gone. My spirit soared. My eyes grew heavy and my heart beat dropped to forty and I drifted off into a deep, peaceful and well-deserved slumber.

8. Reap The Whirlwind

Everything started to happen all at once and I was overwhelmed with the amount of attention. John Gallagher called and informed me that the web page was up, money was starting to flow in, union halls were contacted all over the state and he had a preliminary itinerary for me. I was speechless. When he asked if I heard what he said, all I could do was thank him. He told me that Fritz was excited about the information I sent him. Everything was posted on our web page. He described the need to take advantage of the discontent that people were feeling right now with the concerted attack against working people all over the Buckeye State by Governor Kasich. I was well aware of the current state of affairs that working Ohioans were experiencing. Lastly, he said that the money would keep on flowing and he believed that in no time there would be plenty of cash to fund the campaign. I wondered about this Pollyannaish assessment, but soon found out.

"Nothing you do or say from now on will go unnoticed," John said. "You've become phenomena."

"Really?" I asked incredulously.

"Leo, think about it. When was the last time that some regular guy like you ran for president? I'll tell you. Never. Who's running? Trump? Palin? Romney? You heard that Governor Hailey Barbour dropped out before he even started to run. They don't represent anyone but the money people. Who can take them seriously?"

"I fancy that someone probably is saying the same thing about me," I responded thinking about the level of competition that was already out there and I was just getting started.

"Leo, don't sweat the small stuff. Really. Man, we are going to make a race out of this campaign and that's all there is to it, you hear?" John said emphatically. He sure was in my corner.

"I hear you, John. It's just that all this seems so unreal."

"It is. Believe me. We were sitting around the hall just a week ago lamenting the condition of things and what we were going to do and all of a sudden, you walk into our lives. You get what I mean. You've breathed new life into all of us. Now just go and do your thing. We haven't gotten the kind of support that we hoped Obama would give us so you're our best hope for fairness in the treatment of working people. Can't trust a Harvard graduate, that's my opinion. You just do what you can do and make us proud."

"I'll do my best," I said.

"We know you will. I'll have Fritz send you all the particulars regarding the offices around the state and you can make plans and let us know when and where you will be and we'll make the calls and do all the set up work for you. Just let us know."

"I'll do that. Now I have to get my RV road ready."

"You tell us if you need anything. Okay?"

"You said there was already money showing up. Can you tell me what operating cash I have?"

"Take a guess."

"I have no idea," I said truthfully.

"As of this minute, you've got $1133.00. Can you believe that?" Gallagher asked.

For a moment, I was dumbfounded. Truly, I was reaping the whirlwind.

"You've got to be kidding," I said.

"Nope. Just keep receipts and we'll do the books whenever you give us the paper. You know what you said about total transparency. We'll hold you to it."

"I will. John, this is becoming surreal."

"In some ways, Leo, I can understand your feelings, but just go for the ride. Don't sweat it. I read what you wrote and sent to Fritz. I can't say that most politicians out there will be happy with what you're promoting, but it's not for them anyway. It's for the people and they will listen. Go and get them, Leo. Be the Lion that we need to lead the way out of this mess we call America, 2011."

"I'll do that," I promised.

"Later," Gallagher said and hung up abruptly.

I sat still and reflected on how much was already happening. What was I going to do next? Road trip. He had the itinerary all ready for me. I checked the email and sure enough, there it was: Akron, Cleveland, Toledo, Findlay, Dayton, Cincinnati, Columbus and finally Canton, the home of Hoover sweepers and the NFL Football Hall of Fame.

Now what was I supposed to do. I needed someone to go with me. I could not drive alone and do all this work by myself.

The phone rang and my political angel helped me out again. It was Al and he said that if I needed some help with the RV and perhaps a driver he was available. I told him that he was needed and right now. Al listened to what I had just learned with interest. He said he would get back to me in a half hour and tell me if he could do what I was asking. I thanked him and hung up.

Basha came into the room and asked me what was happening. When I told her, she sat down and tears welled up in her eyes. I knew what she was feeling because I was sharing them.

"When are you leaving?" she asked.

"Al is calling me back in a half hour," I replied. "This will determine when I leave."

"I knew this was coming, but I'm excited for you, for America."

"I couldn't do this without your love and support," I said, reaching out and holding her hands in mine. We stared into each other's eyes for a long moment and a smile twinkled in hers. I knew I had her unqualified positive support.

"I love you with all my heart," Basha said caressing my face and kissing my cheek. Her hands were so smooth, soft and yet strong like steel.

"I know you do and that's what makes all this possible."

We did not speak for quite a while letting the silent moments flow between us like a gentle stream meandering along through a forest.

The phone rang. I answered it. Listening, I grew nervous and excited all at once. "I'll be ready," I replied. I smiled broadly.

"Who was that?" Basha asked but intuitively knew.

"Al. He said everything was a go. His wife told him to do all he could to get me elected and so he's coming over and we're going to get the RV ready for our first road trip."

"Don't leave before Janko can say goodbye," she implored her tears flowing like a cloudburst.

I kissed them away tasting their saltiness and caressing her smooth cheeks.

"I won't."

"I'll leave you alone now so you can get ready. When is Al coming?"

"Soon. He's a swell fellow. I hope he stays with me throughout this process. I feel his spirit, his passion."

"He seems like a good soul," Basha said. "Take good care of him." She left me alone.

I studied the itinerary and was amazed at the detail. Fritz and John Gallagher were highly organized people. I was glad to have them in my camp. As I sat there thinking about what their support meant to me, I wondered how soon it would be before I would be attacked by the press, other candidates and the right wing media. When I heard how much money was already in the campaign coffers, I realized that there were people who really believed that I could succeed.

When the doorbell rang, I got up and went to greet Al.

"Shadow, how the hell are you," Al said shaking my hand as I walked out to meet him on the porch. He called me by my mill nickname. I was pleased. Sometimes I was called "Little Shadow" because, in truth, my father was the original "Shadow". I felt especially close to him at that moment.

"I'm doing fine, Al, and I cannot tell you how much it means to me that you're going to be a part of this first road trip."

"Hey, I wouldn't miss this for the world. I want to be a part of American History. You know, my great grandfather was the 'Great Caruso'."

"No, I didn't know that," I replied.

"I didn't either, but it sure sounds good, huh?" he said guffawing.

"So what's the plan?" I asked.

"That's what I wanted to ask you?" Al responded.

"I have an itinerary made up and so a road trip is the order. All I need is a driver, someone to come along, keep me company and help out with crowd control."

"I'm your man, Shadow. Let's get the rig ready to go. I'm game."

"Are you really sure you want to go through with this? I mean, you're going to be away from home for a few days. What does the missus have to say about this?"

"Shadow, we're on the same page. She told me to do what I want to do. She would rather have me out of the house doing something than hanging around all day driving her nuts. Hey, we understand each other. Besides, you need someone to keep the buggy on the road and I'm your man."

"Okay. I'll take what you're saying at face value. So let's get to work."

"Let's do it."

"We've got to be in Akron by 4 PM. Can we make it?"

"Done. I mean it. Lead the way, Leo, lead the way."

We went out to the driveway where the "Leo Pollack for President" mobile was parked. Al took about 30 minutes to show me every feature on the rig. He was very proud of it and especially the beautiful sign his daughter painted on the side. We checked the tires, oil, fluids, turned on the refrigerator and checked out the heater to make sure that it worked. Propane tanks were full. We needed gas. I told Al we had a credit card and about $1000 in the kitty to make this first run. All we had to do was keep track of the receipts so we could justify our expenses.

"Where did the $1000 come from?" Al asked curiously.

"Money's already being donated. Actually we have $1130.00 so far. Can you imagine that?"

"Sure. People believe in what you're doing. Leo, accept it. Americans are hungry for a real leader. We've had enough of those phony mothers who really don't give a damn who we are and what we have to deal with day in and out."

"Let's get to work," I said and we did. An hour later, we were ready to leave. Al and I went back into the house to tell Basha goodbye and wait for Janko to come home from school. He arrived a half hour later and I had a chance to tell him know how much I loved him and that I would be back home the next day.

"Will I see you on TV tonight?" he asked curiously.

"I sure hope so," I replied. "But if you don't, it's only because we may not get that city's channels. I'll be thinking about you wherever I am."

"I know you will because I'll be thinking about you and saying a prayer that you are okay and that people know that you're my father and you tell the truth."

"Out of the mouth of babes," Al said, smiling proudly as if Janko were his own son. He gave Janko a Dutch rub and my son grabbed his hand and tried to get him to stop. Al's hand was like a vice and there was not much he could do but I could tell that he loved the attention. Al was good with children. After all, he had eight of his own so he had a lot of practice.

I kissed Basha goodbye. She said nothing. Her strong arms around my neck told me everything I needed to know.

Al and I left five minutes later. The whirlwind was at our backs. We were headed to Akron, Ohio, the "Rubber City", the birthplace of big rubber and AA. We were Don Quixote and Sancho Panza chasing windmills. We represented the voice of the silent majority that never had a spokesperson. We raced toward destiny and loved every minute of it because there was so much at stake and we did not want to let fate or destiny control our world any longer.

9. Bouncing Around the Rubber City

Interstate 80 became 76 just west of town where the Ohio Turnpike split and went north toward Cleveland. We passed the turnpike and headed west toward the Rubber City. The skies were overcast, as usual, with only a hint of sunshine peaking out now and then. During WWII, Ravenna Arsenal was built to store munitions because the Defense Department determined that this area was one of the cloudiest places in the United States and enemy bombers would have a hard time attacking it due to the visibility. The war was long over but the overcast conditions remained to this day.

Though it was just fifty or so miles to Akron, the trip seemed to be lasting for hours.

"How are we doing on time?" I asked Al.

"Great! We have plenty of time to get there. You got the directions?"

"I have what John gave me. Downtown. Hope it's easy to find."

"We'll be okay. This is it, Leo. We are going big time now. You ready?"

I hesitated for a few moments. Then I said, "I'm ready. What's not to be ready for, I mean, this is what a man lives his entire life to do. Make a difference. Stand up and be counted. Test his metal against other men. But you know, Al, this isn't about me. It's about the people. All the people who don't have a voice. Look at the mess we're in. Look at Wisconsin and Michigan and Indiana and our own state. These Republican governors are beating up on working people and the government isn't doing anything about it. Obama should have come out and said something. Remember during the campaign when workers' rights were being attacked and he said give him a call and he'd put on his organizer's shoes and come and march with the people? Where was he? How come he didn't come out and march? No, he was afraid if he took a stand, he'd lose votes. He's taking the safe route to re-election. There is no safe way to lead this country. That's all there is too it."

"I agree. Damn, Leo, we're on the way and there's no stopping us now."

"Let's hope not," I replied.

We rode along in silence for a few minutes, and were awakened from our reverie when we heard a loud blast from an 18-wheeler right beside us. Al looked over and said, "Hey, check that out!"

The trucker was flashing his lights off and on and pulled ahead of us and was leading the way for us into the city traffic on the outskirts of Akron.

"Fancy that," Al said. "The word is out. Leo Pollack is coming to town."

My stomach started jumping up and down like a kid on a trampoline. I felt a little queasy.

"You think?" I asked hesitantly.

"What else could it be," he said. "We're in for a rollicking good time in the rubber city. I can hardly wait."

We followed the truck right into the city, passing the aging rubber manufacturing plants along the way. Firestone, Goodyear, Goodrich and others once made this the center of tire manufacturing in the United States. Goodyear and Firestone still had their main offices in town. Goodrich was somewhere else. Tires were made all over the world and that was the dilemma. Good paying jobs were cast to the winds, or at least to the countries that had significantly lower labor costs and, perhaps, what was more important, simpler or even non-existent environmental and working regulations that let companies do just about anything they wanted to do without having to face stiff fines from the governments where they were doing business.

"What's the address?" Al asked.

I got the papers out and started to give him directions. Traffic increased as we converged on the I-76 and I-77 split.

"We go north here, Al," I said.

"Good. I'm in the right lane."

Heading into downtown Akron, we cruised along in three lanes of speeding vehicles. I was glad that Al was driving. He was right at home behind the wheel of this thirty-eight foot RV.

We were heading right downtown and I was doing my best not to get too excited. As I stared out at the city, I wondered how many hopes and dreams were dashed over the years as this rubber city rose and fell as the leading producer of tires in the world.

Harvey Firestone invented the process of vulcanizing rubber when he accidentally spilled some sulphur into a batch of rubber he was working with in his laboratory. Although modern chemistry is much more sophisticated now, this simple discovery changed the entire industry and established this city as the center of tire manufacturing. The skyline was new. The neighborhoods were old. The contrast could not be more pronounced as we drove on the inner belt and headed toward our rendezvous with destiny. This was not my hometown. This was the real playing field. This was the Big Time. I could feel the energy building and my heart pounding in my throat.

I think Al could, too, because he said, "Leo, we're going to wow them today. Trust me, brother. It's a no brainer."

I was sure glad he was my pilot on this maiden voyage of the Leo Pollack for President Express.

"The office is on Main Street," I relayed to Al. "We get off at the next exit."

"Roger that," he uttered and turned on his signal. The huge RV slowly moved into the right lane and even though it slowed down, my heart beat even faster. My bpm's were near red line.

Up ahead, I could see the building because there was already a crowd of people waiting in front of the place.

"I guess we're not going to sneak into this one," I murmured.

"That's not the plan. We're going to make a big splash, Leo. Check it out will ya'," he said as he slowed the vehicle down and pulled to the side of the road where a police officer was waving us over.

I got up, slicked my hair back into place, unruffled my clothes and when Al opened the side door of the RV, I walked down and was greeted by a throng of people. I was awestruck.

"Welcome to Akron," a voice said, a hand reached out and a face smiled at me. "I'm Jerry Sanchez, local president of the services union. We're glad you're here, Leo and we're ready."

I smiled at him and shook his hand vigorously.

My eyes were glazed. There were so many people gathered around us I did not know what to make of it all.

"We've gotten permission for you to speak from the other side of the parking lot. What can we do to help get you set up?"

My mind drew multiple blanks. "I've just got to stop for a moment and take this all in," I said. What I really needed to do was go to the bathroom. My kidneys were screaming loudly. I leaned over and whispered this in his ear and he laughed and led me into a side door toward a bathroom. Once inside, my body slowed down and my brain started to work again.

"All I need, Jerry, is the electric bull horn and something to stand on."

"Real soap box stuff, huh?" he said smiling broadly. "Well we can get you something that will work." He led me back outside and then I became fully aware of just how large the crowd was.

The parking lot was full of people, not cars. Jerry got the police to move the traffic around the building and park elsewhere. I had a view of a lot a hundred feet by a hundred feet with nothing but people's faces staring at me. For a moment, I was overwhelmed, and then, I realized this was the way it was going to be from now on.

Inside, I thought to myself, "Man up, Leo. This is the chance of a lifetime. Don't blow it by being a wimp."

Al was coming over with our equipment. Jerry led me over to a makeshift stage that he and his crew had set up near the side entrance to the "Akron Works" office. I stood quietly by while everyone around me rushed into motion.

"Mr. Pollack, a word with you," I heard someone talking to me.

I looked up. A young fellow was staring at me. "Sean Hammill from the Beacon Journal. Just one question before you start."

"Sure," I said, smiling now, feeling the energy starting to flow and my fears subsiding.

"Why you?"

I laughed and clapped him on the arm. "Why me? Why not? Who else is more qualified to speak to the needs of working people in America than some person in America who actually works for a living? I'm no millionaire and never will be. I go to work every day, or at least I used to until I was laid off, did my eight hours, came home and hoped that my efforts would help make a better life for me and my family. Now all that is changed. Working people are under attack all over this country. You see it in your own town. Where are the jobs? Companies want us to buy their products but if we are not working, what are we going to use to pay for those items? Why me? Because I know what it means to work for a living and that is the basis of this entire campaign. We are n longer willing to give our vote to someone from the privileged class, a Romney, Perry, Huntsman, Paul or anyone else who pretends to speak for us but can't even understand the first thing about what it means to struggle with the tasks of daily living. Hope that makes sense to you," I finished.

"More sense than most people I interview," he replied. "Thank you, sir, and good luck."

We shook hands and he stepped into the crowd.

"We're about ready to begin," Jerry said, pulling me aside over near a platform his team had set up. "John called me and said you'd draw a large crowd so we were trying to be proactive. I hope this works for you."

I smiled and said, "Jerry, given what we're attempting to do, this is fabulous. Let's get this show on the road."+

Al, thanks for being here, my brother," I said to him and gave him a hug. "Wow'em Leo," he barked into my ear.

Jerry led me up onto the platform, took the bullhorn placed on a chair behind him and called out to the crowd, "Ladies and gentlemen, let me have your attention." The crowd continued to mill about and to my ears, the noise was deafening. Even when it became quiet, there was still a sound reverberating in my eardrums. Again, it was the sound of my own heart beating madly inside my brain.

"Ladies and gentlemen. Today we have gathered to be a part of history. Yes, we are going to make history today. We, the working people of America are going to elect a president who will come from our own ranks."

Screaming and clapping erupted and reverberated against the walls of the buildings.

"We are going to take back our country from the moneyed interests, the lobbyists who camp out in Washington and buy votes, the corporations who hide behind superpacs and spend millions of dollars trying to influence us to vote for this millionaire or that one."

Another explosion of sound filled the crisp morning air.

"Today, we have with us a true believer, a man who is ready to run the gauntlet for us all the way to the White House, a man who, like you and me, works for a living like many of us here today. He is not working, not because he doesn't want to work, but because companies like his are slowly moving production elsewhere. It's time for this to come to a halt and so, without further delay, let me introduce to you, the next president of the United States, Leo Pollack, the People's Candidate."

Spontaneously, people started chanting my name. I stared out in front of me and all I could see was a vast gathering of people just like me. There were no suits and ties. There was no bunting. There was simply a gathering of the people who represented the essence of America – working class people who slaved for a wage that was slowly, irrevocably being withdrawn from them leaving nothing in its place.

I waved to the crowd and this encouraged them to continue to roar. This was different for me now. In the office in my hometown, I was at ease. Now, out here, I was in a new world and was not sure just what to do and when to do it. My heart was still racing and my mind was flowing with ideas.

How long the roar lasted I do not know, but finally, I found my voice and picking up the bull horn said, "America belongs to the working people who made great sacrifices with mind and body to build this nation into the envy of the world."

Excited voices punctuated my comments.

"We are rapidly being disenfranchised by corporations who care nothing about our fate and measure their success using only the bottom line of their profit and loss columns. Since it costs money to pay us to work, they are forever trying to find ways to cut labor costs and still produce their products. We have become irrelevant in this discussion, in their business equation."

The applause was loud and raucous.

"When they can cut costs by moving production overseas, they do it in a heartbeat leaving behind dying cities and confused and dazed workers. Enough is enough. We are not going to stand for it any longer."

Cheers arose and made it hard to continue.

"Workers of the world unite was the union movement's cry nearly a century ago. We made great strides in the middle of the last century. We have fallen on rough times and there is no doubt that we have a lot of work to do to make up for our serious losses."

The voices of the people continued to ring out with cries of, yes sir.

"Once it was merely a blue collar issue. Once it was just those of us who are working in industry that faced this dilemma. But no more. No, the battle is being waged in the white collar world as well. There are as many skilled, professional people being attacked as there are people like you and me. Look at our own state and the assault on teachers, police, firemen and other public employees who are facing this governor's constant attack on their rights, their future."

Cries of "Amen" burst out.

"This movement of ours is the universal plea of all people for the right to have a decent job making a decent wage so that they and their families can lead a decent life. No, we are not asking for anything more than decent treatment by those who manipulate the government to give us our fair share. There is no reason why a corporation that is haemorrhaging money and losing market shares like General Motors was should be paying its CEO millions of dollars in salary and bonuses. There is no reason that banks that are borrowing money from the Federal Reserve for one quarter of one percent should be lending money to us to buy a car or truck at ten percent interest. The entire economic system is turned upside down and has been getting worse and worse for the past three decades. We've seen our real income decline and yet corporate profits and CEO and others' earnings continue to climb. There is class warfare taking place right now, as Warren Buffet said, and his class is winning. We are losing because we are foolish enough to continue to vote for those people who pretend to be supportive of us, but are really just wolves in sheep's clothing."

The crowd erupted into a loud chant: "We want more…We want more…"

"Standing in the unemployment line made me think about what I was doing, what was happening to me. I was going to be paid not to work. I was going to get money for not producing anything and was supposed to go home and be content with my lot in life. Something in my soul cried out to me and said, 'No, this is wrong. This is an abomination. This is not the American Dream.' My mind was filled with tyranny. My heart was about to break. So I stood up and said, 'Enough is enough'. We can make a difference. We can take back this country from the democrats and the republicans because, I'm sure that you've noticed, neither party has truly represented us very well for the past thirty years."

The people went nuts and that made me realize that this was not just a crowd but a genuine mob of angry men and women who, like me, did not want to be paid not to work. They wanted to work in the worst kind of way but not be cheated out of their fair share of the pot.

"My fellow Americans and working people of this nation, we are not asking for anything but the right to work, the ability to pay our bills, to make a good living for our families and to be able to retire some day and enjoy our children, grandchildren and some free time before we die. This is all the American dream really is. Nothing fancy, elaborate. We don't need ten thousand square foot homes and vacations to the Bahamas every few months to be happy. We believe that with the sweat of our brows we can make enough money to be well off – IF we are given the opportunity to do so. Herein is the rub. The system is stacked against us. We have leaders and presidents who are really looking out for the big corporations and not the working people. It is as obvious as the sun rising in the morning and setting every night. We don't count. We don't matter. Except once every four years. Yes, when it comes time to elect a new president, or senator or congressman or woman, we matter. These moneyed leaders want our vote. This time around we are wiser and are not willing to sell out. Our time has come. This is the end of business as it used to be. No more."

The crowd started stomping its feet and the sound on the hard pavement, echoed loudly up and down the street.

"You ask, 'Why you? Why you, Leo Pollack?' I simply answer this question like this. I say, I am ready to be your president because I can't be bought off. I won't take a dollar from any lobbyist, any corporation, any man, woman or child who expects me to govern in such a way that they, whoever they are, receive favored treatment. What is the government of, for and by the people than a government of We, the people? You and I. We count. We are more than a percent of some poll. We begin to believe that this is true and work and fight for what we believe. Imagine for a moment, 160 million workers who vote for the candidate that best represents their economic interest. Imagine these Americans donating just five dollars a person to a national campaign. This would add up to millions of dollars. We'd be ready to take on any party. We'd be ready to kick their butts up and down the red and blue states. We'd be a force to be reckoned with and they'd be cringing in their corporate suites, their congressional and senatorial offices. I don't know about you, but I've had enough of the same old, same old. It's time for a drastic change, and that's what this is all about. When you vote for me, you vote for yourself."

The applause was deafening.

"Exploitation of the working people anywhere in the world is not okay with me. I can't influence the other countries of the world to change their policies, but I do know and believe, we can change the way we do business in our own country. Anything less than that is uncivilized. We are all aware of the issues that arise when we send jobs to Sri Lanka or Bangladesh and don't monitor what is going on in those places. Children are exploited but that's not all of it. The inequality we experience here is just magnified in those countries. As we seek to make a fair and equitable market system work in America, the ripple effect will be felt all over the world."

Loud clapping erupted.

"Now it is time to rise to the occasion and make a difference. You might notice that I don't have a teleprompter in front of me. No, and I don't have any speech writers either. I am giving this to you straight from the heart. There is nothing that needs to be filtered for one audience or another. Wherever I go, you will hear the same message and that is we, who work for a living, demand that we be treated fairly, justly and equitably. We will not accept anything less than that anymore. We demand our rights and we, the people are ringing the liberty bell to let all those who are opposed to us know that the campaign is on and we are not stopping until we take the White House back from those who never really represented us in the first place."

Chants of "Leo-Leo" began to fill the air.

"My fellow Americans, I am not anyone or anything special. I am like you, a working person who's been treated poorly. Like you, I want to work, not be placed in the unemployment lines and made to beg for my living. We will change all of this. We will do it or die in our tracks as we struggle to change the world one working person at a time."

The chants continued.

"I ask for your vote. I ask for you to donate a dollar or two to the campaign. I ask that you get out and promote what we stand for to your friends and family. I ask that you do not give in to the lies and deceit that will follow our movement wherever we go. We know this task will not be easy. Already, we are facing challenges and these will continue from now until we succeed in overcoming the forces that would keep us in our place. So I ask you, I implore you to continue to stand with me and face opposition with the truth: working people made this country what it is. Working people demand their fair share. We want nothing more and nothing less. I thank you for letting me be your candidate and hope that my message rings loudly and clearly in your hearts and souls and that you will stand beside me and carry this message to every nook and cranny of America."

Another roar resounded and with it, I stepped off the stage and into the crowd. At that moment, I feared nothing. If my life ended right then, I would feel as if I had lived more in those five minutes than most people live in a lifetime. The will of the people carried me into their arms. I was patted, slapped, hugged and touched by their collective embrace. There was no escaping the bodies. How long I moved through the crowd escaped my sense of time. The closeness of it all made me feel so warm that I thought I might pass out, but then what became real for me was the heat, the open-hearth heat, of the people, of those who truly loved America and Americans. I was being forged in their smithy and loved it.

When the press slowly began to dissipate, Jerry came over and asked, "Can we get you something to eat, Leo. You must be tired and hungry."

"I just ate and drank with the people. I'm fine. What a moment in time."

"You can say that again. You really laid it out for them. I just hope they don't give in to despair. We have a long way to go, but we can do it, I'm sure of that," he finished, leading me back toward the RV.

"What do you want to do?" Al asked. "I think we're supposed to be in Massillon in about an hour or so. We'd better get moving."

"I almost forgot," I said to Al. "Jerry, I can't thank you enough for making this all happen. I hope we didn't disappoint you in any way."

"Leo, today we made history in Akron. Firestone might have invented vulcanized rubber here, but we've reinvented American politics. Thanks for being willing to risk everything and be our leader."

"I just hope you feel that way a year from now when the rubber really is streaking along the road."

"I'm sure I will, Leo, because I know you can't be bought and that is what really matters to people like me here in Akron and I'm sure all over the land."

"Then, organize and we'll be in touch," I said shaking his hand and crawling up into the RV.

"Will do and now, get going and wow'em in Massillon."

Al climbed aboard, revved up the RV and slowly we rolled down the narrow street, but not without a plethora of horns honking and hands waving as we passed through the dispersing crowds of American working people who were returning to their homes with a new sense of dignity and self-worth and hope for the future.

10. An Afternoon in Hoover Country

Interstate 77 ran north and south from Cleveland all the way through Ohio and into West Virginia and down to Interstate 81 in southern Virginia. The casual traveler can see many interesting things along the way. In east-central Ohio, the Native American Indian mounds are just off the freeway. These were built prior to the revolutionary war and remind us that another people lived here well before we ever set foot upon this hallowed ground. Through West Virginia, the landscape changes dramatically and the highlands erupt like a bad dose of acne on a person's face. There is no flat place in the Mountaineer State. Native West Virginians joke that if West Virginia were ironed flat, its land mass would be greater than that of Texas. All along this magnificent highway, the traveler is immersed in the industrial heartland of America. Coal is mined, shipped and used to power most of the eastern United States with electricity. The method may be dirty, but it works and is cheap. This is the main reason it is so hard to switch from coal to more renewable sources of energy. Railroads still work their magic land moving millions of tons of raw coal from the hollows north and south to major metropolitan areas for energy production. We used a significant amount of coal too in the process of making iron ore in blast furnaces. Given its ubiquitous usage, replacing it with solar panels and wind turbines and other forms of renewable resources was proving to be extremely difficult because none of these were cost effective. The issue of energy was one that needed major consideration in our national planning but was constantly being kicked down the road like an empty tin can. Neither party wanted to take it on because it affected the economy and so many people directly.

"What do you think about energy independence, Al?" I asked as we were speeding south on I-77.

"Me? Oh, I don't know. We need to get cheaper gas, that's for sure. This $3.40 gallon stuff is killing me. I can hardly get out and enjoy this RV right now because I just can't afford it being laid off."

"We've got the cost of the gas covered for now," I reminded him.

"Yes, I know, but this is different. I mean for, you know, fun and things."

"This isn't fun?" I chided him.

"Leo, come on man. Sure, this is fun. But you're not my old lady and the kids. We're on a mission. This isn't a fun trip to the lake and camping out and fishing and sitting by the fire and eating S-mores and singing songs and all that stuff."

"Okay, so what do you think about the energy thing?"

"I think we all need to make some sacrifices. That's it. There's no doubt that we're in trouble. We can't continue to burn coal and gas and use electricity as if it were an endless supply. Eventually it's going to run out and then we'll be in a world of hurt. That's my opinion."

"Then what do we do?" I asked.

"I don't know. You're the president. You figure it out. What do we do Mr. President?"

I laughed aloud and sat quietly for a moment.

"There is no easy answer to this one, but there is an answer. Let's take the auto industry. For the past twenty years, cars have been getting bigger and more powerful all at the same time that gas has become more and more expensive. The major manufacturers are not doing much to make cars and trucks more efficient. We had that scare back in 1974 during the oil embargo and for a time, we started to drive smaller vehicles. As soon as gas got cheaper, we went right back to the bigger vehicles. I truly believe that we could build cars that get 50 miles to the gallon and these don't have to be hybrid cars. What is needed are better transmissions and smaller engines that are geared differently and use the fuel to move a vehicle down the road more efficiently, not faster. My God, Al, how fast do we need to go? Think about this. My old Ford Focus could do 124 miles per hour out on the open road. That's an insane speed and totally illegal, but it could go that fast. It had a 2-liter engine. So I had all that power and that speed and didn't need it. Yet, the car did get an average of 40 miles per gallon. If I had a six-speed transmission in it instead of a five speed, I think I could have gotten 45-50 miles per gallon. That would be how much more than what we are getting in this vehicle?"

Al guffawed. "Leo, we're lucky to get 5-6 miles per gallon in this buggy."

"There you go. I'll bet there is a way to make this RV get 10 miles per gallon though and the only reason the company didn't do it is because there was no demand to do it. The government has a responsibility to lead the way when it comes to energy independence and curtailing consumption."

"To listen to these Republicans, you'd think that the government was the problem with everything in this country and not the solution," Al added.

"Ironic isn't it that every one of the guys and the one gal who are running for president are dead set against the federal government doing anything for the people. You'd think that they'd be in favor of government being active and effective. But no, they are constantly knocking it like it was the worst thing in the world. I just don't get it."

"That's just it, Leo. They want in so they can change it to suit their needs. They don't like government meddling in their businesses and their personal lives. They don't want to pay more taxes. They don't want their companies to be regulated. They will get into office and change these things to suit themselves. You know that as well as I do," Al concluded.

"Sure, Al, I do, but it just seems so disingenuous, so dishonest, and so downright hypocritical. The government is designed to take care of the needs of all the people who live within its jurisdiction. There are so many needs. Just look at that bridge out there." We stared at the rusting beams of a bridge overpass as we went under it.

"A good sandblasting and a few coats of paint would make that bridge look like new. Yes, it would cost money to do it. But an ounce of prevention is worth a pound of cure. We'll let it rot until the bridge is unsafe and then we'll tear it down and replace it. Makes no sense."

"Tell me about it. But this is the American way," Al reluctantly stated.

"Then we've got to change 'The American Way' and make it more practical," I responded.

"That's the very reason we're on our way to Massillon and Canton, to make things more practical," Al reminded me and slapped me on the shoulder.

"I hear you, pal," I said and lapsed into my own reverie.

What was the solution? Was I pipe dreaming? What could I offer this country to truly make a difference? The questions rolled around inside my head like marbles in a tin can. The light went on.

What stopped the government from truly making a difference was the leaders were not wholly free to do what was in the best interest of most of the people. Most leaders were beholding to one or another special interest group and they could not get past that. If they wanted to get re-elected, they needed to raise money. The people who gave them the money expected that their special needs or requests would be met. There were a few leaders who stood above the rest for pure independence. They did not seem to care if their legislation brought home "the pork" for their constituents. However, these were few and far between and they usually were not in congress for a long period of time. I did not have to worry about this issue. When I was elected, I would be free to do what was best for the people, not for GE and Bank of America and Goldman-Sachs and any other fortune 500 company that slipped mounds of cash into campaign coffers either directly through contributions to the campaign or through special superpacs.

As we entered the outskirts of Canton, I started recalling all the city's attributes: home of Timken Roller Bearing, Hoover Sweepers, Diebold, Shearer Foods, the National Football League Hall of Fame, and so much more. Sadly, Hoover sold out and was no longer producing sweepers in the North Canton plant. The National Football League considered Canton the city of its birth; hence, the organization placed its hall of fame in the city. Each year, the football season begins with an exhibition game at the local field. The William McKinley Presidential Library and Museum is located within this adopted city of the former president. Canton was once a rich and thriving city, but like many others in the "rust belt" had seen better days.

"Where do we go first?" Al asked.

"John set us up first to be in Massillon so we need to find US 30 and head west. Massillon is just west of Canton."

"The Lincoln Highway it is," Al responded.

The Lincoln Highway was one of the first transcontinental highways. It was conceived as a memorial to Abraham Lincoln, and was formally dedicated in 1913. We headed west on this old road that really needed to be resurfaced in a bad way.

"Massillon was once the home of one of the largest mental hospitals in the state," I said to Al.

"What happened to it?"

"Ronald Reagan," I replied.

"What do you mean?"

"When Reagan was president, he cut federal spending for mental hospitals to such an extent that, all across the country, these types of institutions were closed due to a lack of funding. There are some people who believe that the increase in homelessness is a direct result of his austere policy toward the mentally ill."

"How come people revere him so much? All I remember from when he was president was he beat up the air traffic controller's union and after that, unions have been on a steady decline."

"You're right, Al. That was one of his major accomplishments and he did it well. The sad part is that it did nothing to make the skies any safer. He promoted that 'trickle down economy' model and we've seen a thirty year decline in our incomes as a result."

"The only thing that trickled down to the working stiff were a few crumbs left over after the rich people picked over the spread laid out on the table," Al retorted.

"Ironically, Reagan cut taxes one time and did so in such a big way that his own cabinet told him that he'd gone too far. So, for the rest of his term in office, he raised taxes eleven times. By the time he left office in 1989, he'd raised federal revenues by more than $100 billion above any of the taxes he had cut."

"So much for tax cutting, Mr. Reagan," Al said haughtily.

"He was the first president to express disgust when he heard that a bus driver was paying more in taxes than some millionaires were. He called this unfair and he said he was determined to fix such an injustice."

"Did he?"

"Not really. He gave it lip service. He got embroiled in the Iran-Contra Affair and then in the savings and loan scandal and his term ended and we were left holding the bag. Who knows what the truth was. We'll never know. He got senile all of a sudden and that was the end of it."

"Sounds like that Mafiosi who faked senility and escaped justice for many years," Al added.

"Who was that?"

"Some guy on 'Law and Order'. Saw it on TV."

"Ah, then it was just a story?"

"Well, yes, it was, but who knows? Maybe they wrote it after they watched Reagan pull that stunt," Al said laughing aloud.

"We need to get into the right lane up ahead and head down into town."

Just as Al pulled over into the right hand lane, we heard a sustained honking and stared out the side window and saw someone in a red pickup truck waving at us with his middle finger. We looked at each other and then at the fellow beside us. He was persistent. He drove along side for more than a quarter mile and then spontaneously cut us off and sped down the highway.

"Gee, I guess someone is not happy about our coming to town," Al stated. "Wonder what his problem was?"

"Who knows, but I'm sure that the more we travel, the more we'll pick up disrespectful comments and behavior like a ship does barnacles. I guess we'd better get used to it."

"He doesn't even know what we're about! He's just ignorant."

"The world is full of ignorance and that is what makes it possible for politicians to bamboozle so many people so much of the time."

"Leo, you get stupid along the way, I guarantee that I'll knock you upside the head. That's a promise," Al said vehemently.

"Al, I expect you to, and in fact, demand that you do it. We've got too much to do to go brain dead along the way."

"You got it, pal," Al said. "Now what's that address."'

I gave it to him and we started looking for Albrecht Avenue.

Driving through city traffic in an RV is truly an adventure and I was glad that Al was behind the wheel and not me. He negotiated a number of one-way streets with aplomb as he directed our campaign mobile to the site of our next encounter with the public.

The crowds were already gathered. I could see a large bunting draped across the front of the building reading "Leo Pollack for President".

"I guess this is it," I said, pointing at the sign.

"Much better greeting than what we got on the road back there," Al remarked as he pulled the RV to the side of the road in a spot being held for us by a police officer. I was amazed at how organized things were. John and his colleagues were on the ball.

As I got out of the vehicle, I was greeted by a man in a Carhart jacket, jeans and a broad smile on his face. "Bill Sloan, here. Welcome, Leo."

I shook his hand and said, "Hope we didn't keep anyone waiting."

A loud cheer erupted as we walked toward the parking lot outside the unemployment office. My eyes were smarting from the cold air and though blurry from the wind, I estimated there were at least 200 people gathered.

"Good turnout," I said.

"We'd have 1000 people, but it's late in the day and most of those who sign up here are already gone. You'll find this crowd is very enthusiastic. They've been gathering for the past hour."

"Really?"

"Sure have. Leo, you don't know what you've done for this town, and these people."

"But I haven't done anything yet."

"You've given them hope. That's what. Real hope. Not that phony Obama kind of hope. No, they believe that there is a chance that someone will actually, once and for all, speak for them."

"I sure hope they realize what a battle we are in for as this campaign continues to unfold."

"Hey, we're not naïve. We all know what you're up against. Just give it to them and they will go out and make the waves and do what is necessary to get this campaign really moving forward."

We'd reached the front steps of the building. From what I could see, this would be the venue for today. I stood aside and let Bill get things rolling. While I stood there, a little fellow came walking up to me and said, "Are you really going to be our next president?"

I smiled and shook his hand and said, "I sure hope so, young man."

"If you are, will you make my teacher stop giving me so much home work?"

I did not know how to respond to that inquiry.

His mother reached over and led him away. "Come on, Joshua, Mr. Pollack must have a lot more on his mind than you and your homework."

Before I could respond, she whisked him away. I think she was a little embarrassed by his boldness. What should I tell teachers about homework? I was not sure.

As I walked toward the steps, a number of people reached out and asked to shake my hand. I was not used to the attention, but I thought I had better start get accustomed to it was only going to amplify as time went on.

I could see that Bill was getting ready to introduce me so I smiled and stood off to the side and paid attention to what he was saying.

"Today we're honored to host this campaign rally for what we hope will be the first presidency of a man of our own. Someone who, like you and me, works for a living. Someone who, like you and me, knows what it is like to be unemployed. Someone, like you and me, who stands for working people through and through. Someone, like you and me, who isn't afraid to stand up and be counted when what he sees around him pisses him off. Someone, like you and me, who knows what it is like to be asked to take money, not for working but for not working. Someone, like you and me, who wants to see America become a full employment economy once again. Ladies and gentlemen, I want you to meet our next president of the United States, Leo Pollack."

A roar rose from the crowd, and even though there were less people in this one than back in Akron, they were much louder. I could feel their energy vibrating through my body. I took the steps and waved to all of them and the shouting and clapping continued. Later, Al told me they went on for a full two minutes. To me, it seemed like an eternity.

Finally, I was able to speak.

"Thank you, my fellow Americans, my blue collar brothers and sisters, for such a resounding welcome."

Another roar went up from the crowd.

"My message is simple. America belongs to working men and women and not to banks, financial advisors, lobbyists, and those who do not produce anything. What we do is what has made America great. Making Timken Roller Bearings for cars and trucks and tanks and jet airplanes is what made America great. Making Hoover Sweepers right here in the Canton-Massillon area is what made America great. Where is Hoover today? We all know. Some financial advisor told the board of directors that more money could be made by manufacturing sweepers in China or Korea or somewhere else and so the plant was closed, jobs were lost, and we no longer make them here in our own country. To make this story even more disgusting is that, because of the tax code, Hoover could write off on its taxes, all the costs of moving production to China or wherever. Yes, they got a break for shipping our jobs offshore because our leaders are too weak or unwilling to take a stand and stop this kind of madness."

The crowd erupted into loud booing that made the air vibrant with their energy.

"We do live in a global economy and we do need to learn how to compete in it. However, we must be able to compete fairly. There is nothing fair about what I described to you just now. We lost our jobs, but Hoover did not lose its company. In fact, it increased its bottom line, the executives got bonuses and people on the other side of the world got low paying jobs. Fair trade is what we are about, not free trade. What republicans and democrats call free trade means trade without any regulations to stop unfair labor and trade practices by our trading partners. No, we need fair trade that protects us as well as workers on the other side of the world. The irony is that most of those workers who now make the sweepers can't afford to buy one for them. The unfairness is not just in the trading but in the sharing of the wealth."

Applause rang out across the crowd. I stopped to catch my breath.

"We've watched as people across the country have realized just how inadequately the bounty is divided. One percent of the American population has more accumulated wealth than that of the other ninety-nine percent. This inequity is not something I'm making up. It is a fact. The republicans say that when we mention facts like these we are promoting class warfare. No, we are not. In fact, as Warren Buffet, the second richest man in America says, 'We are already engaged in class warfare and my side is winning.' We, my working friends, have been losing ever since the 1970's when wages were frozen as unions were slowly and inevitably strangled by businesses and then in a big way, by Ronald Reagan in his assault on working people."

Booing erupted. I waited until it died down.

"Look around the Midwest today. In Ohio, Indiana, Michigan and Wisconsin, the recently elected GOP governors have all used their power to stop the collective bargaining rights of working people. The attack is so concentrated that it is affecting more than 20 million people. Right now, we Ohioans are planning to reject Senate Bill 5 through referendum, but look at what is happening. Even though thousands of teachers, police, firemen and other working people marched on the state house in Columbus, Kasich and his cronies defied all the people and passed the bill anyway. Now it will take a referendum to reject their overstepping their boundaries and stomping on working people's rights."

A chant rose "No on Issue 2...No on Issue 2...No on Issue 2".

"These are the facts. I don't need to paint the picture for you because you already know it. You're living it. You and I are in the same boat. It's called not being able to work because our industries are dying and there is no one speaking up and saying enough is enough."

"Stop the Bleeding," was heard from one corner of the parking lot.

"What we are ready to do is stop the bleeding. Yes. We're hemorrhaging jobs like a stuck pig. Since 2001, when the former president took office, Ohio alone lost more than three million manufacturing jobs. People, do you realize what this actually means? Ohio's population is 11.5 million. Three million jobs is one fourth of our population. One in four people who worked in Ohio was in some form of manufacturing and these jobs are now gone. Those are rough numbers but you get the picture. You know what this means. A guy or gal earning twenty or thirty dollars an hour is now, not working, or has a new job making half as much or perhaps less than that. While the top one percent's net worth expanded exponentially, the middle fifty percent's income nose dived. The median income in America today is, get this, $24,400. Imagine that! No, it's hard to imagine how so many people can even live on that amount, but this is the median income. Clearly, 50 percent of all Americans live on less than that amount per year. It's time to do something about this inequality and that time is right now."

The people clapped resoundingly and I listened for an opening so I could continue.

"The tax code is skewed to protect wealthy corporations and people and this is the first thing I will do as president. There is nothing that makes me hotter than to see corporations like General Electric not paying its fair share of taxes. Last year, GE did not pay any income tax at all. Last year, GE actually got an income tax credit of somewhere around $275 million. Last year, GE was the largest job creator in the country, but there is one problem with that statistic. They created 200,000 of those jobs overseas, not here in America. Last year, GE had 945 lawyers working on their tax return and when they were finished, the document was 24,500 pages long. Who in the hell could even read something that size let alone interpret it and find where GE was cheating the government, and in turn, all of us. And if that is not enough to smoke you a little, what did Obama do? He appointed Jeff Immelt, GE's CEO, to head his commission on job creation. Now how does that grab you? This guy, whose company created nearly a quarter of a million new jobs overseas, is going to be in charge of creating jobs here in America? I don't think so. What we have here is the slickest shell game I've ever seen and I don't know about you, my friends, but I'm sick of it. Sick to death of such kinds of hypocrisy."

Chants of "Obama must go" rang out.

"Our president hasn't gone far enough to protect working people. He pays lip service to us. As for the other party, they are anti-labor, we all know that, and there is no way we can tolerate their leadership. We must band together and make our movement so powerful that we cannot be denied."

"Leo...Leo...Leo"...erupted.

"I pledge to you to make the dignity of work our primary platform. I will demand that America takes care of its own working people. There is no future in expanding business all over the world if the people in our own country cannot afford to live a decent lifestyle. Enough is enough. But I need your help. I don't need a million dollars or even twenty dollars from you. What I need, first and foremost, is your vote. Secondly, we will need money, but if every working person gave just a dollar, we'd have 160 million to work with. If everyone gave a five, we'd have more than enough money to fight the battle and win this race. Already, we've heard that Obama is planning on raising a billion dollars. Well, Mr. President, working people are going to put their money elsewhere. The republicans don't need our money because corporations will fund them nicely. This is a call to arms. I need your vote, a few bucks and then, you to get out and support this movement. Talk to your friends, your family, your work mates, anyone who will listen, and especially those who do not want to listen, and get them on the bus with us. Together, we can win. Together, we can make a difference. Together, we can change America and make it, once again, a decent place to work and live. Together, we the people can ring the liberty bell and make such a noise that all over this country people will hear the tolling and come to our aid. Thank you for listening, for being here and for wanting to be involved."

I stepped down from the steps into the crowd and began to shake hands and accept pats on the back and the kind words of those gathered to hear the word of a new kind of revolution. As the time flowed along, I moved among the people and felt the heat of the massed bodies, the smell, the sounds and sight of powerful men and women engaged in the change process. I was elated and scared. What had I started? How was this all going to end? How could I ever know?

When the crowd finally started to disengage, I met Bill near the steps.

"Something else, huh?" he said to me.

"Bill, you sure got them fired up. I never experienced anything like this."

"Leo, neither have they. This is the power of the people to make a difference. They want to believe in something, a future, anything but what is going down right now. They're sick and tired of the same old, same old. You give them real hope, not this canned stuff they've heard most of their lives. 'America's greatest days are ahead of her.' Yah, right. Tell that to the guy who just lost his job after 26 years on the assembly line. Tell him that the future is going to be rosier. It's a lie. Bush and Obama and all those candidates running for the GOP nomination are lying to us. They don't get it. They don't realize just how close we are to a real revolution. Your being here today is the first step in that process. I'm blessed to be alive now and be a part of this movement. Thanks for being here and giving me hope, Leo. Thanks."

I did not know what to say, except, "You're welcome."

"Looks like there are some folks that would like to ask you some questions.

I turned around and saw three television crews setting up behind me.

"Your fan club awaits you," Bill said. "Go get'em Leo."

"Al, are we good?" I asked him as I got ready to be assaulted once again.

"Leo, my time is yours. Wow'em brother."

For the next hour I answered questions and hoped that they heard me loudly and clearly. I pulled no punches. I did not give Obama or anyone in the GOP any benefit of the doubt. This was a third party movement. Yes. This was a working class revolution to take over this country from moneyed interests. Yes. This was being financed by donations of less than twenty dollars. Yes. This was not going to end until the election was over and the people would decide which one of three candidates for president won by a majority of votes. Yes. This was for real. Yes. Yes. Yes. I thanked them for their time and hoped they would vote for me as their next president. I was not sure if I won any of them over to our side, but they were interested in what I had to say.

"Leo thanks for being here," Bill said as I returned to where he and Al were standing smoking cigarettes.

"Bill, the pleasures been all mine. Thanks for your hard work and getting this so well organized."

"Where you heading to now?" he asked.

"We were supposed to try and do another gig in Canton but it's already 5 pm and the office is probably closed. I just hope the people were not there waiting for us to come in at the last minute."

"Gotcha covered. I called my friends over there and they let everyone know what was going on. No sweat. You didn't disappoint. Many of those who had planned to be in Canton, just scooted over here and caught your speech. This is a lot to expect of one man."

"No, two men. Al and I are a team," I said, and put my arm around my one and only roady.

"Yes, we're a team, but I'm the one who's got to get this guy all around this country safely and securely," Al added.

"Fellows, I suggest you get on the road and be safe. We'll be in touch. I've already set up the entire team here to start to get out the vote and get signatures to get you on the primary ballot and the ballot in November. This will be a major undertaking but we will get it done. Trust me."

"I believe you will," I said, shook his hand and then Al and I piled into the RV and headed toward the highway and home.

"What a day!" I said as Al wheeled the RV back onto I-77 and headed north toward Akron.

"You said it. What great crowds and what a great message. Leo, I didn't think you had it in you, but you sure wowed them."

"Al, what I have in me is a lot of poison. I have a cancer that gnaws at me. It is the cancer of disgust, of antipathy, of resentment, of despair. It eats at me like a dog chewing on a bone. I can't get away from it. I look around and see this country changing so fast and not for the better. Yes, we have so much more now, so much more goods but so little of it is being produced by us. We are on the receiving end of this economy and not on the giving end. We are not making for each other the things we want and need. This is what is so disheartening and something we are going to change."

"Then let's do it."

"Right on, but now, let's head on home and take care of what really is important because you and I both know, this movement is just going to pick up more and more momentum and a home cooked meal will be a real luxury a month from now."

"I hear you, my brother, but I'm in this with you all the way to the glorious end."

"I know it and for that all I can say is thank you from the bottom of my heart."

"Accepted."

"Now let's roll."

"Hammer down, north bound, on to Youngstown…"

Above us, the sky was inky black, but now and then, brief splotches of moonlight filtered down to the earth and lit our way as we plunged through the eventide heading home to the warmth of family.

11. Rest Stop for a Tired Candidate

The "Leo Pollack for President" express pulled into the driveway long after dark. We were both feeling road weariness.

"I've had enough fun for one day," Al chirped. "Man, it's good to be back home."

"You're not there yet, my friend."

"You know what I mean, Leo."

"Take my car. Leave the RV here," I offered.

"Sounds good to me. See you in the morning."

"You bet. We'll make another day of it," I replied as we shook hands.

Al drove off as soon as he got his stuff into my car. I waved goodbye to him

Basha and Janko were waiting for me in the living room. We hugged each other, lingering for a long time holding on to one another. I sat down on the floor with Janko and asked him about his day. He did not have much to say and immediately started asking me many questions.

"Where were you all day, Daddy?"

"I was in Akron and Massillon doing some speaking engagements."

"Were there a lot of people there with you?"

"Yes, there were. A whole lot and they were very friendly."

"How far away is Massillon?"

"It's about 70 miles from here."

"I wish I could go with you, Daddy. I could help out."

"I'm sure you could, Janko, but you have to go to school and that is far more important than what I am doing."

"Being president is important. Mommy says that the president is the most important man in the entire country."

"In some ways, he is, but what is important for you right now is to be a good student, learn as much as you can and when the time is right, you can travel with me. After all, school will be out soon, and then it will be summer time and you will be free to go to work for me."

"Do you mean that, Daddy?"

"I mean it from the bottom of my heart."

"Gosh, Mommy, did you hear that? I'm going to work with Daddy when summer time comes. I can hardly wait."

Basha rolled her eyes at me. I knew I was digging myself into a deep, bottomless pit so I closed my mouth and said no more.

Janko got up and said he was going to do his homework, gave his mother and me a hug and left the room.

Finally, alone, Basha and I could talk. She moved over onto the floor with me. We tucked pillows under our heads, she nestled down into the nook of my armpit and we just stared at the ceiling for a long time without saying anything. The silence felt heavenly. I wondered if I was talked out after only one day on the campaign trail.

"How did it go today?" she began.

"What an amazing day!" I replied. "The crowd in Akron was large and loud and we were well received, but in Massillon, it was even better. I can't tell you what a feeling it is to stand in front of a group of people who just want to believe in their government and want the best for everyone, themselves and their fellow citizens."

"No problems at all?"

"Not really. Well, we had one guy flash us the bird on the way to the Massillon gig, but that was a minor thing. I'm sure we'll see more of that as time rolls on. Basha, the people are hungry for something and that is the truth. They are feeling left out of the banquet. They worked hard, believed in the system and it let them down. They don't want to feel hopeless. There is a need to provide for them the opportunity to feel the joy of being productive once again. This movement is not only about jobs as the politicians are crying, but about the honor of work. Enjoying work is something altogether different and that is what is missing right now. The more we move away from actually producing something, the less people feel connected to their work. I hope that throughout this movement, we can begin to recapture that feeling which is sadly missing for so many people."

"How is it your responsibility to accomplish this for them?"

"It's not. I am only the catalyst for the process. I mean it. Someone needs to stand up and set the record straight. Working people don't envy rich people. They don't want a piece of their big pie. What they want is simply an opportunity to earn their fair share. Fair share. That's it. How fair is it that someone works long hours and abuses his or her body in the process and then when the tally is made, he is not making enough to adequately take care of his family let alone have anything extra for some needed fun and relaxation? We have been blessed in the mill. We have good benefits. Look at what Walmart employees face. Most don't get benefits and those that do pay through the nose for them. They are kept on part time status for years and maybe never will get the chance to move to full time. Even though the Supreme Court threw out the class action lawsuit against them, the million women who were discriminated against are not some figment of the imagination. Where there is smoke there is fire."

"There are so many issues to deal with and all at the same time."

"Yes there are, but there is a common theme that runs through all of them. People can either be 'kind-spirited' or 'mean-spirited'. We can either follow the principle of 'I am my brother's keeper' or we can deny it and let people fend for themselves. Many of the republicans I listen to are just mean spirited. They really don't care what happens to most people. Their theme is 'let everyone fend for himself'. What about the person born with a congenital disease? How does he or she fend for himself or herself? This is the reality for so many people. What about the person not blessed with native intelligence? What about the physically handicapped individual who can't work? Do we just let all these people die? This is what is at the core of this entire struggle. Are we a nation of caretakers and caregivers or are we just takers who let those fall that cannot take care of them?"

"The more people we have in the country, the more complex the problems become. No wonder there is such disagreement on what to do."

"I agree there is a lot of disagreement, and most of it comes from a difference in ideology. I've read Ayn Rand. She applauded greed as being good. She believed that, in the world, survival of the fittest was the way of all flesh. Yes, that is true to some extent. What separates civilized people from the primitive world is the ability to demonstrate empathy for our fellow man and woman. We are not a pack of wolves running around hunting for our next meal, although, at times, it sure appears to be so. No, as civilized people we have a duty to look out for each other and make the whole better by cherishing and nurturing all the separate parts. What makes diversity special is that every different person brings his or her best to the table and what we have is a genuine smorgasbord where everyone enjoys the bounty."

"Oh, Leo, do you realize just how naïve you sound. I don't disagree, but you are sure paddling your canoe against the current."

"Not a canoe, Basha, a veritable barge."

"What will happen next?"

"I'm sure that any moment the phone will start ringing since the 'Leo-mobile' is parked out in front of the house."

"How did Al get home?"

"He took the car."

"What if we need to go somewhere?"

"Where are we going this time of night?"

"Who knows? Maybe out dancing!"

We both laughed. I wrapped my arms around her and kissed her long and hard and then we just lay still and enjoyed the moment.

"I love you, Leo, but this is going to get very, very complicated and very, very soon."

"I know, and I believe we'll make the best of it."

"I'll do my best to give you all the rope you need."

"When I get to the end of your rope, I'll tie a knot and hang on for dear life, sweetheart."

Janko ran back into the room, spied us both lying on the floor, scooted down between us and nestled in closely. None of us said a word. We did not want to break the spell of magic time.

The phone rang. The spell was broken. I got up to answer it leaving Janko and Basha cuddled together.

"Leo, you sure made a splash out west," John said. "Ready for some more action?"

"How are you? And yes, why not?"

"We need to meet and make some long range plans."

"Sure. When?"

"How's tomorrow?"

"That'll work for me."

"Make it 10 am. That'll give me time to line up all our ducks."

"Okay. How is the fundraising going? Al and I are going to need some money soon. We burned a lot of fuel on the trip."

"Great! In less than a week, we've gotten more than ten thousand in donations and the money keeps flowing in every day. It's amazing really."

"It sure is. Who would ever have thought that some movement as grass roots as this could really catch on?"

"Leo, it's you, man. People want someone who is like them to be their leader. They don't want some buzzilionaire telling them what to do. They know what they want and need. The politics as usual is dead and buried. The republicans kind of know it and the democrats are going to soon figure it out. They've banked on the people's vote for years now and have continued to blow on their promises. Now it's time to make them all pay. Anyway, I'm preaching to the choir. You already understand this better than I do. Hey, so it's 10 am, right?"

"See you then."

"See you." John hung up.

I felt arms around me as I stood making notes on the counter.

"Who was that?"

"John from the union hall. I have a meeting with him and the crew at 10 am tomorrow morning to do some long range planning."

"I'm getting Janko ready for bed. Do you want to help?"

"Sure, let's go."

The three of us went upstairs. I needed a shower, so Janko and I jumped into the water and got squeaky clean together. We brushed our teeth, dressed in our pajamas and headed toward his bedroom. Basha was already there waiting for us.

"What are we going to read tonight?" I asked.

"Can you read from the poem book?"

"Sure, why not," I replied and pulled the Shel Silverstein poetry book off the shelf. "Let's see. How about…"

"True Story…True Story!" Janko cried.

"True Story it is."

I licked my lips, cleared my throat, wrapped my arm around my son, and read:

'This morning I jumped on my horse
And went out for a ride.
And some wild outlaws chased me
And they shot me in the side.
So I crawled into a wildcat's cave
To find a place to hide,
But some pirates found me sleeping there,
And soon they had me tied
To a pole and built a fire
Under me – I almost cried
Till a mermaid came and cut me loose
And begged to be my bride,
So I said I'd come back Wednesday
But I must admit I lied.
Then I ran into a jungle swamp
But I forgot my guide
And I stepped into some quicksand,
And no matter how I tried
I couldn't get out, until I met
A water snake named Clyde,
Who pulled me to some cannibals
Who planned to have me fried.
But an eagle came and swooped me up
And through the air we flied,

But he dropped me in a boiling lake
A thousand miles wide.
And you'll never guess what I did then –"

Before I could read the last line, Janko blurted out, "I died."

We all laughed. I am not sure how many times I have read the poem to him but he always says the last line before I can read it. Given how many times I have read this poem to him, I really think that he could recite it by heart now.

"Another one, please Daddy. Please."

"This one is my favorite, son."

"Read it. Read it."

He knew which one was coming.

"Invitation. If you are a dreamer, come in. If you are a dreamer, a wisher, a liar, a hope-er, a pray-er, a magic bean buyer...If you're a pretender, come sit by my fire for we have some flax-golden tales to spin. Come in ! Come in!"

"I like that one too, Daddy."

"So do I," Basha said. "Now, let's say our prayers and get to sleep."

"Okay." Janko led and we followed him. "Now I lay me down to sleep, I pray the Lord my soul to keep, guard me through this long, dark night and wake me with the morning light, amen."

Kisses and more kisses were given and received.

"Good night son," I said.

"Good night, Daddy. Good night, Mommy. Sleep tight."

We left him alone in his room and quietly went back downstairs. Luckily, he was not afraid of the dark. Tough kid. I was afraid of the dark when I was his age.

"Are you hungry?" Basha asked.

"You know, come to think of it, I'm famished."

"What did you eat today?"

"I don't think Al or I ate anything all day long."

"Leo, you're going to waste away to nothing if you keep going like this."

"But at least no one will be able to call me 'one of those fat politicians'."

"That's not funny. Some people just have a hard time losing weight."

"Sure they do and especially when they're eating five meals a day at fund raising receptions."

Basha ignored me and just went ahead and made my favorite, tomato soup and toasted cheese sandwiches. We ate in relative silence. I just enjoyed the quiet.

"Thanks for making dinner," I said.

"You're welcome. It wasn't much."

"To me, it was heavenly."

"Where are we heading, Leo?"

"What do you mean?"

"You know what I mean."

"Seriously?"

"Seriously. Yes. Where are we heading?

"I think we'll never know until next spring. Either this dream will face reality and end or the reality will be that a dream can become real. Either way, we can make a difference and that's all that really matters."

"What about us?"

"You mean, you and me?"

"Yes, you and me and Janko."

"We are family. Nothing will ever change that and the only thing that will be different for a while is I will be on the road. But hey, as soon as school is out, you two can come along for the ride. Al won't mind. We have plenty of space in the 'Leo-mobile'. What do you think about that?"

"I think I'd hate it. Being on the road every day does not make me happy. I don't know, Leo. I just don't know."

"You're not getting cold feet, are you? I mean, I'll stop right now if I don't have your vote and I mean that, Basha."

She looked intently into my eyes. A pregnant moment passed.

"Leo, you have my vote."

"Let's go to bed. We need our rest, don't you think?" I asked.

"Sure, if you really want to get some rest."

Into the dark and wonderful silence, we went upstairs side-by-side holding hands.

12. When America Works, Democracy Thrives

The morning came too soon. Janko, Basha and I shared breakfast and then I walked my son out to the corner and off he went to school. One of the real joys of living in the city was that our son could walk to and from school and we really did not have to worry about him. Four blocks was not too far for him to stray. I remembered when I used to walk to school. What a joy! The very first day, I left home alone and ambled all the way to Jefferson Elementary by myself. The sense of freedom, of self-importance, of pride that I felt was overwhelming.

"What's your schedule for today?' Basha asked me.

"Union hall. We have a planning meeting."

"When will the long road trips start?"

"Oh, I imagine soon enough."

"You looking forward to them?"

"Yes and no. Mixed emotions. On the one hand, I want to make a difference. On the other hand, I know that I won't be home every night. We'll be living in the RV. I don't mind the lack of accommodations, but I do mind not seeing you and Janko."

"Last night was lovely. That is what I'll miss."

We hugged each other for a long time, and then I kissed her eyes and left. I didn't want to drive the RV but I was sure that Al would meet me down at the hall with my car, so I got in, started the machine, let it warm up, tried to get used to driving a bus-sized vehicle, and headed downtown.

Surprisingly, driving the Leo-Mobile was not tough. I was glad I did not need a CDL license to get behind the wheel. As I slid down Griffith Street, I thought to myself, "What a magical mystery tour I was beginning."

The air was heavy and there was a hint of sulfur in it. I remember the scent well, because the sulfur smell meant summer vacation. There were a few months to go before school would be out, but right now, where had all the time gone?

Crossing the Blue Bridge, I thought about my father-in-law again. The bridge was one of his last projects and he said it was one heck of a challenge. Below the bridge was the entrance to the mill, the lifeblood of this community. Everything in the city revolved around this island of industrial production. Now it was silent.

Steel Street was brick. Built by workers during the WPA, Works Project Administration, fifty years later the surface was still in fine shape. I headed past the mill and turned into the union hall parking lot. I sat still for a few minutes and just gathered my thoughts. Staring out the window, I gazed at the mill sitting idle across the street. A few guys, mainly skilled tradesmen like millwrights and electricians, were working to keep the plant operational. We deserved better. This was such a waste of people power. The pounding in my head was the refrain playing over and over again: This is not the American Dream.

Gathering my thoughts and emotions, I took one long, deep breath, got out of the RV and headed into the Union Hall.

The crew was already there working on a number of different things. I waved to them all as I went over to the coffee counter and poured myself a cup. One thing about the hall, they brewed the best cup of java in the valley.

John Gallagher came over to see me. "Great to have you home, Leo. We got a report from Bill and Jerry over in Summit County. You really wowed them. They're on board 110%. Bill said he wanted to spearhead gathering signatures to get you on the primary ballot and then on the November slate as well."

"I can't thank you enough for making this all happen."

"Leo. I'm just a center. You're the quarterback."

"Thanks for making me feel so important, but I don't know?"

"You're not getting cold feet are you? Come on, Leo, this is a team effort. We're just in the first few steps of an ultra marathon, a long race covering a thousand miles and we just have to keep plugging along one step at a time."

"I know, I know. It's hard to fathom all that has happened so far."

"When it gets ugly, then you'll really feel it. Right now, we're on a honeymoon. Everything is coming our way. We're not feeling the hate yet, the discontent, and the fear that will arise once you start to make some real impact in the election numbers."

"You think that is going to happen?"

"Count on it. But hey, let's enjoy the lull while it lasts. Come on, let's get the rest of the team together and do some work."

As we were walking over to the conference room, Al came in and I waved to him. He went right to the coffee counter. Smart guy. He knew what was up. When he came over to the room, I said, "Good to see you, road warrior. Get any sleep last night?"

Al smiled. "Old lady wouldn't leave me alone and the kids, Oh…La…La… they pestered me all night long about where I'd been, what was I doing, when was I going to take them along in the RV and on and on. I was glad to get out of there today. But all in all, it was good to be home again. I miss my gang. How about you?"

"Great night. Went too fast. RV drove nicely over here. I kind of enjoyed it."

"You can't have my job and I don't want yours."

"We'll just keep it the way it is. I'll drive. You make speeches. Deal?"

"Deal."

John called everyone together. Fritz, Carol and Judy came into the room, said hello to Al and me and then we got down to business.

"What a great day to be alive," John said to open the meeting. "Leo and Al are back from their first road trip and from all indications, everything went well, the crowds were great and Leo filled the people with hope. Is there anything you'd like to add, Leo?"

"Someone flipped us the bird on our way to Massillon, but other than that, we were well received in Akron and Massillon. I had a chance to press the flesh and meet the press. Al's a great road warrior. Overall, for our first venture out beyond home plate, we are well on our way to first base. Thank all of you for making this work so well."

"Great! Great! Al, you want to add anything?"

"Leo's being modest. He made the people stand up and take notice. He churned the cream and made it into butter. I was proud to be there and hear his speeches, both of them, and watch the people become engaged with a belief in their future."

"That's what we want to hear. Really! Great!" John continued. "Now, let's report out what we're working on and figure out where we're headed and what we need from each other. How does that sound to you all?"

"Let's do it."

"Fritz, why don't you start?"

"Okay. Home page is up and running. We've interfaced with every union hall in the country. We're up on Facebook and Twitter and are having a lot of activity on both sites. I know that this is going to become a burden but we're going to need someone to start monitoring the blog and some of the other email communication. I would have to be on this twenty-four hours a day and that's impossible. We need to keep up with this because, through this media, we will continue to raise the money we'll need to finance this entire operation. Money is flowing in pretty well. No bugs thus far. We haven't been attacked, hacked or cracked yet. I'm using every firewall protocol I can to keep us safe, but we may need more expertise if we face any outside interference. Other than that, we're right on track."

"Great! Great!" John almost shouted. His enthusiasm was contagious.

Fritz asked me if I had any questions and I said, "Only one. How do you do it? Most of the things you were talking about are way over my head. But I'm sure glad that I'm on your team. You're going to have to show me how to get email on the smart phone you gave me."

"Me too," Al added. "If you can't show me then get me a dumb phone, one that I can understand." Everybody laughed but we, Al and I, were probably the two most technologically challenged folks in the room.

"I can do that," Fritz replied. "Just give me a half hour and I'll get you up to speed. There's no need to know it all, but at least, you'll be able to do the basics."

"All I want to know is how you turn it on, answer a call, make a call and turn it off," Al said. "Keep it simple. I don't want to surf the web and I don't text and I don't Facebook and I don't 'like' things that are too complicated."

"Okay, Al, we can do that," Fritz replied. "Nothing complicated. Got it."

"Let's move on, shall we?" John said. "Carol, give us the latest on the money front. How are we doing?"

Carol sat up, cleared her throat, pushed her dress sleeves back, swept the strands of long black hair streaming down over her face to the side and said, "We are doing amazingly well financially. Since two weeks ago, we have $63,567.22 in the kitty. How about that? Just since yesterday, we took in more than $20,000 and that is the single biggest jump since we started this campaign."

"How much did you say?" I asked wondering if I heard her correctly.

"$63,567.22. You heard me correctly. Yes, it's a lot of money, Leo. We're really starting to build a war chest. How does that grab you?"

"Amazing. Now, I've got to ask. How is the money coming in and by that I mean, are we getting a lot of small donations, less than twenty dollars?"

"Yup. Any donation that is above twenty dollars we have kindly sent back to the person or persons and that's that," she said emphatically.

"I'm glad to hear that because if that changes, I'm done. I don't want any piles of cash somehow just stacked up inside the doorway."

"Buddy Roemer is presenting the same argument in his campaign. You all know who he is, don't you?" John asked.

We all did, but he was just making sure because Roemer was not even polling one percent in any national poll. I was pleased that some other candidate was also thinking the same way I was. Actually, I knew that Roemer was taking a lot of positions that were analogous to mine, but he was still a republican running in a republican field and his past performance was interesting, to say the least.

"Carol, anything else?"

"One concern that I have and it is not a minor one. As long as we are handling the money for Leo's campaign, the public is going to begin to see us as running the campaign and there will be a price we will pay for this somewhere down the line. I don't mind doing what we are doing and know that we are not doing anything illegal, immoral or unethical, but Leo might lose some of his influence if we are seen as in control and not him."

"What do you think we should do?" John asked.

"Nothing right now," I replied to the group. "Carol, I hear your concerns and they are right on. No matter what we do, there will be people who will say this or that. The judgments will come at us from the right and the left. Oh yes, some on the left will see this campaign as messing with Obama and that's okay. We are not doing this to make friends but to change the status quo, the politics of big money and special interest influence controlling the message. If it becomes a serious issue later, we can figure out something. Right now, I think we're just fine."

"If we all agree with Leo's position, well, then, let's move on. Anything else, Carol?"

"Hmm. I was thinking that we ought to be putting this money to work for us. We could place the money in a short term CD that would earn some interest. I don't mean we are going to make a lot of money. We might make a few dollars to help with the bottom line. We're going to need lots of cash down the way and this may help."

"How much of the funds do you want to put away?" I asked.

"Oh, I think no more than ten percent," Carol responded checking her figures.

"Do it. Just keep this open and above board. Folks, let me respond to this issue of money. We've restricted contributions to twenty dollars or less. We are making available to the public every donation and donor's name. We are not going to spend a lot of cash on big parties and entertaining fat cats. We will not spend money we do not have. When the campaign is over, no matter how it ends, any money that is left over will be donated to the charity of our choice. Mine would be the Salvation Army, but we can give it to any charity we so choose."

"I like that idea," Carol responded. "Now I do have one more thing." She got up and walked around the table and handed a credit card to me and one to Al. "Now you guys can go in style. Just keep the receipts so I can make sure that we have double entry capabilities in case we get audited."

"Which we will!" John blurted out. "Heed Carol's words. We're a union and we are not everyone's favorite party."

"Will do," Al said. "I'll make sure that Leo spends his money wisely. But Carol, can I get a nicer picture on my card? This one's kind of dull," he said winking at the rest of us. She almost bit into the jibe, but then laughed along with us.

"Now, let's move on to Judy."

"We are gearing up to make a concerted effort to use every possible media to spread the word about our campaign. I've contacted every union hall in the country and asked for their assistance. The national office is supporting this effort by interfacing with the leaders of the other major unions. Now our union leaders are being asked to interface with their local better business bureaus in their towns to form coalitions. Yes, you heard me right. We are working hard to build relationships with those who we might believe are antagonistic toward our movement. Secondly, we've gone after the youth vote in a big way. I put out feelers to every college campus in the country via the SEIU and, we can be on every campus throughout the next year. This will help us make connections with young people and hopefully, we'll tap into their boundless energy."

"Sounds like a great plan," I replied.

"Now, we've sought to balance the message, so we've gone after the seniors as well. Using the service unions, we are pressing our message in the AARP world, in every nursing home, assisted living environment, at every senior citizen's gathering, on and on. We think by bookending the voting population we can make some significant inroads across the spectrum of voters and make sure that we cover as much of the landscape as possible."

"All I can say is thank you," I said.

"Genius! Pure genius! Judy," John said.

"Oh, it's just what I thought up along with Fritz and Carol when we were eating our lunch the other day and it just came to all of us."

"I'm impressed beyond words," I said.

"Hey, Leo, what do you think we do here all day long, suck on coffee and eat donuts?" John offered.

"I'm so proud to be on this team," I said.

"What else, Judy?"

"Oh, we're pushing the theme of this campaign: When America Works, Freedom Lives and Democracy Thrives. We have been de-emphasizing the creation of jobs and focusing on the 'dignity of work'. What we want people to realize is the importance of dignified work, doing something they can be proud of every time they go to their place of business or industry."

"Boy, that sure would leave out financial services for me," I said. "That is something I could never do. I just can't fathom sitting around all day long buying and selling money or futures trading. We've drifted so far away from actually producing something that now we're just stuck in an economic system that is incapable of taking care of it."

"So that's why you're running for president and not spending your time being a day trader," John said. "Now that we've covered the spectrum of our activities, we need to stop and consider the bigger picture. Let's make this open forum. No holds barred. Let the ideas just flow."

Everyone was silent for a period of time.

"Pregnant pause," Fritz joked. "I have a notion." He got up and took the marker and drew a circle on the white board and said, "Let's mind map this campaign. You say it and I'll draw it up here on the board."

We started. We had fun. Our brainstorming, captured in a mind map, made all of us sit up and take a more active part in the process. Within 20 minutes, we had the entire board filled with ideas. The list was comprehensive and made us stop and wonder just how we were going to do all the things we listed.

"Amazing, wouldn't you say?" John remarked as he stood in front of the white board and started to read off the topic areas. "Here we go." John read the following:

- Go to Bentonville, Arkansas where Walmart is located and get the CEO to support the campaign, raise salaries, give free medical care, two weeks paid vacation and, whenever possible, only sell American made products.

- Ask Obama to run with Leo as Vice President.

- Promote a movement where Christians, Muslims and Jews agree to form one religion and end the strife among them.

- Visit every county in the United States and meet the people.

- Collect enough signatures to be on the ballot in all 50 states.

- Get an endorsement from the Pope.

- Figure out a way to immediately reduce unemployment down to less than 1%.

- Build broad bi-partisan support for universal health care that works for all people

- Conduct a campaign that inspires voters to participate in unprecedented levels.

"Wow! What a list," John said as we finished our work. The white board was filled with Fritz's scribbling. "We've got some monumental work ahead of us."

"Nothing we can't get done if we keep at it," Fritz said enthusiastically.

"What may be needed is additional support. Volunteers are fine, but we may need some full time people on board to get this work done in an efficient and timely manner," Judy added.

"What will it cost?" John asked. "Do we have the money?"

"I'll check on it and see what we can do," Carol responded, pulling out her calculator, cell phone and some other papers and getting right on it.

"What else do we need?" John continued.

"I don't know," Al said, "But now that we have credit cards we're good to go. I really was strapped for cash."

"Yes, for sure. Thanks Carol," I added.

"Here's what else we can do. The travel issue is going to become the most important one of all. Leo, you and Al can't continue to do things the way you are. I mean, you'll be spending hundreds of hours on the road just going from here to there. We've got to solve this right now or else there will be no way to travel the land effectively," John stated bluntly.

"I disagree," I said, "and here's why. The people will see us pull up in a used RV and get out and there won't be an army of people inside with us. We won't have one of those fancy Sarah Palin RVs decorated like a circus wagon. We will have one simple sign on the side and that's it. I think the old RV is part of our message. We aren't the establishment crew. We are working stiffs and we know what it is like to be down and out. Hell, both of us are unemployed right now. This is the real message we're communicating and we don't even have to say it."

"I agree with Leo," Judy said. "This older machine makes our job easier."

"I think it might be prudent to get some work done on the buggy to make sure that it is really road worthy," Fritz said.

"Do it then. Can you make that happen, Al?" John asked.

"I'll do it today. We're not scheduled to be back on the road until when?"

"What's the schedule, Judy?" John asked.

Judy scanned her laptop and said, "Tomorrow 10 am, Cleveland. 4 pm, Columbus. 8 pm, Cincinnati. The Three C Circuit. I know that's a lot of travel for one day but all the halls asked to try and get this done as soon as possible. They want their people to get a chance to meet Leo right now so they can generate support and mobilize their volunteers to get out and start working for the campaign. Is that okay, Leo?"

"We can do it, can't we Al?"

"No sweat. I'm heading out to get our buggy serviced. Be back in a while."

We continued to strategize trying to figure out what we needed and where to get it. After two more hours, we were finished. My head was spinning like a top. My eyes were full of sand. I could have used a nap right then, but there was so much work to do.

Judy asked me, "You need any help with messaging, Leo?"

"No, not really."

"What are you doing for your speeches? I mean, are you writing them as you go to each town or what?"

"Actually, I haven't written anything down at all."

"Really?"

"Nope."

"That's amazing, but there's a concern here. You'll need to start giving me something to work with so I can get out the message using what you're doing on the road and coordinate it with TV, radio, newspaper, magazine, Facebook and Twitter."

"I hadn't thought of that," I responded. "How do you want to do this?"

"If you will text me some of your thoughts, even in bullet form, I can use that to make the necessary connections. This will help immensely."

"Done."

"You sure that you'll have the time to do this?"

"Why not? When we're hauling butt across the highway, I can sit there and send things to you on the phone."

"Great. That's all I really need from you right now," she said and went back to her work.

"We're in good shape financially right now, Carol said.

"I'm glad to hear that. Carol, are we really doing things on the up and up? This is something that concerns me more than anything else. We can't be like the other candidates. We've got to be above reproach at all times. This is more important than winning the election. If we can't do it with honesty and integrity, then it's not worth doing."

"I hear you, Leo, and yes, we're doing things with as much transparency as we can. I mean, the money we're raising is not a lot but anyone who wants to see who's donated can go on our web page and look at the names and figures. No other campaign is doing that. In fact, in this age of superpacs, we're the only one that is not using some surrogate to speak for us."

"Let's not do that. No superpacs. I mean it. I don't need some superpacs doing it for me."

"You know, they may come along anyway even if you don't invite them."

"Then I'll denounce them as not speaking for me. These other clowns can do whatever they want. I just don't care to have that kind of ugliness a part of what we are trying to do."

"I hear you, agree with you and appreciate your firm stand on this. I respect what you're saying and will do everything I can to insure that we stand firm against anything that smacks of hypocrisy," she said emphatically.

"Thanks, Carol. You're top notch."

She went back to work and I wandered over to the coffee counter and poured another cup of rich, black, strong java. John soon joined me.

"Leo, what are you thinking?"

"I don't know, John. So much has happened so quickly. I'm kind of amazed at all that we've done in such a short time. I can't even remember when this all started. It's like we've always been running for president and that's the work that we do."

"I hear you, pal. I hear you. Right now, we just have to keep the momentum going and our eyes on the prize. I know this must be hard on your family, but it will work out. Good things come to those who wait, and plan ahead."

"Basha and I talked about this last night. She is behind me one hundred percent. Janko is in his own way. Things will get tough as the year unfolds. I'll be gone a lot and that will make it difficult for her and the boy."

"They should travel with you, Leo. You've got the RV."

"Sure, but that seems unfair to Al. He's leaving his kids back at home and he has eight of them. I only have one son. No, I don't like that idea. Oh well, we'll just have to endure. After all, no one said this was going to be easy."

"Leo, do you feel safe out there? I mean, that finger-waving fool is just the beginning of what might become a lot of ugliness. When we really start impacting these other campaigns, there will be more unpleasantries with which to deal. If you ever feel the need, we can get some security for you, and if need be, the family."

"I sure hope it doesn't come to that but I'm not naïve, John. Thanks for thinking about my safety and that of my family's."

"Hey, that's what I'm here for, my friend. After all, I'd probably be closing down this office if it weren't for you. Now we've got something to really do and that makes everything worth it."

"You really think this is the end for the mill?"

"I do. Just look at the way the company is acting. They haven't spent a dime on this shop since the 1970's when they installed the scrubbers to clean the air. Now we're competing with China, Japan, Germany and Korea and we're losing the battle. We just can't produce steel as cheaply as these countries do and that's a tragedy. Something is wrong with our business model."

"You mean this unfair capitalism where companies can move to wherever production costs are cheaper and just shut down their old industrial sites without even thinking about the impact of their decisions? I hear you and that is something that will change when I get into office. The global economy is here to stay, but the unfair global trade practices won't be tolerated. China won't be dumping steel into our economy and we won't be borrowing more and more money from them. We will find the balance no matter what it takes."

"Let's hope so. Hey, Al's back already. That guy is worth his weight in gold."

Al strolled into the lobby smiling broadly as if he had just won the lottery.

"Done. We're good for a million miles. I got the buggy taken care of and it didn't cost us an arm and a leg. I told them what we were doing and the guys at Martin's Garage pulled me right inside and went to town on the vehicle. Changed all the fluids, rotated the tires, checked brakes, lights, everything and did it all at cost. This machine never ran so good since I've owned it."

"Great. I'm glad to hear that because tomorrow, Al, you and Leo are doing the Three C Circuit."

"What's that?"

"Cleveland at 10 am, Columbus at 4 pm, and Cincinnati at 8 pm."

"Looks like an all-nighter then, because we won't be able to roll back home without driving well into the night."

"I don't mind, if you don't," I said.

"No, man, this is what we do now. This is our job. Nope. What time do we leave in the morning?"

"If we're on the road by seven we'll have plenty of time to be in Cleveland by ten."

"Okay. Then I'll pick you up at 7 am."

"Done."

"See you down the road," Al said, handing me my keys and taking off.

"Anything else we need to do today?" I asked John.

"No, unless you can think of something, I think we're finished for now."

"John, am I crazy? Is this whole idea just a hair brained scheme or what?"

John put his hand on my shoulder and looked me dead in the eye. He smiled and said, "If I thought it were crazy, I'd have said so the first time I called you. I wouldn't have offered our services if I had any doubt about what we were doing and what we hoped to accomplish. No. Forget any notion that you are crazy. Hell, man, just because your father wasn't a governor or you didn't go to Harvard or Yale doesn't mean you're not qualified to be president. We've been fed this line of pious baloney that only those who are privileged can really lead that we've come to believe it. Look at the trouble we're in today. Yes, Obama made some changes. Yes, he did get health care passed. Yes, he did finally get the minimum wage raised. He hasn't done much else. The reason is simple. He, like the republicans, is too cozy with big business and big banks, big money, and he can't make independent decisions. Frankly, I like the guy, but that's too bad. We need new leadership and we don't need Republicans. They made the mess with two wars and all that borrowing. Now we're just trying to dig our way out and there are many people who are suffering because of their ineptitude. We need you, Leo. You and a million more like you to stand up and take this nation in another direction. When America Works, Democracy Thrives. Now take that to the bank. See you when you get back."

"Okay. I got you, John. Thanks for the pep talk."

"Hey, that's my job. Go home and get some rest. You're going to need it for tomorrow."

We shook hands and I said goodbye to the team and walked out to my car. The sky was mottled, a speck of sunshine was poking through one filmy cloud. Across the valley, the sound of traffic filtered up into the air from the I-11 inner belt. I looked down into the Mahoning River and saw blue green water flowing past. The air smelled fresh, almost scented with a hint of jasmine or something exotic. I leaned against the hood of my car and stared off into the open spaces where the new vision was hiding. What would tomorrow bring? How would this all end? I had some doubts but who would not. After all, what we were doing was something no one ever tried to do in our nation's history. Whether we would succeed or not was not the concern. Would we be able to sustain the effort until all possible opportunities to take the White House were beyond reason? How would we know that until after the November election a little more than a year from now? No, this was something that was beyond the norm. We were in unchartered waters and only belief in the human spirit could keep us moving forward. I was so blessed to be on such a great team. I did not feel like their leader but more like a follower. I was being tugged along by them. They were inside, right now, working for me, to help get me elected to the highest office in the United States. Just that thought amazed me beyond comprehension. I felt a chill race through my body and realized it was sprinkling. "Figures," I thought to myself. "Cold, damp, dreary, November in my soul. This weather is what makes me doubtful. Shake it off, Leo. It could be worse. You could be a man without vision and going home depressed because you are laid off and there is not much hope of finding a new job." Now I knew, in some small way, just how Don Quixote must have felt when he first donned his armor and went in search of adventure. I was getting all that I could handle.

Starting my car, I drove slowly out of the parking lot and headed home, back across the blue bridge, across my hometown, toward the one place where I knew that I was safe and it would be warm.

13. A Mysterious Stranger

How nice it was to drive home in my own car. I made a note to remind myself to give Al a big hug the next time we got into the Leo-mobile because he was driving and I was not required to get behind the wheel. The skies were mottled gray and dusk was descending over the valley. I stared at the Mahoning Bank Building as I drove over the blue bridge and headed toward the north side. In the darkness, its aura filled the valley with some class. Crossing over Division Street, I headed past the small church school where Janko went. The building was quiet, the playground empty, but during the day the little people's world made this a perpetual motion zone. The arc lights lit the empty spaces and a quiet glow filtered out into the surroundings creating an eerie presence. Pulling into the driveway, I studied the lights. Janko was in his room. Basha must be cooking, but strange. The dining room light was on.

When I entered the house, I found Basha preparing dinner. There were four places set at the table.

"I'm home," I announced brightly.

"I can see and hear," she replied and I could immediately tell that there was a strong force in the family energy field.

"What's up?" I asked intuitively.

"We have a guest." This was all that she said.

"And," I continued.

"And, you didn't tell me that anyone was coming."

"I didn't know anyone was coming."

"Strange. He says he knows you?"

"He?"

"He's in the dining room. I'm getting dinner ready. Janko is studying. We'll eat in thirty minutes." She did not say any more.

I walked into the dining room and found a middle-aged man sitting at the table, studying a computer screen. He was an average sized person, wore a light jacket, khaki slacks, and his hair was salt and pepper much like mine. His glasses were hanging down low on his nose indicating he did not have to wear them except for reading. He looked up and smiled.

"Hi, I'm Leo Pollack," I said reaching out to shake his hand.

"I'm Graham Tashjan. It's a pleasure to finally meet you," he said reaching out and shaking my hand.

I walked around the table and sat down.

"So, how can I be of service to you?" I asked not sure how to approach him.

"Easy. Let me go to work for you," he said quietly, emphatically and with an intense stare.

"You want to go to work for me? I am an unemployed steel worker. I don't run a business. I don't own anything but this house, and in reality, the bank owns it and I just pay them to live in it," I said trying to make light of his request.

"I want to work for your campaign is what I really mean."

"You want to work for my campaign?" I said repeating his comment.

"Yes." He did not elaborate.

"Graham, you said?"

"Yes, Graham, like the cracker. You can call me Gram for short. It's easier to spell."

"Gram, you want to work for me, work on my campaign. Do you realize that this is a shoestring affair? We have no one working for us. We are just in the infancy of this movement and all we've done so far is raise a few thousand dollars, make a few speeches, and travel to a few towns. That's it. Nothing big. We're probably not going to last more than a few months."

"I think you're heading to the White House, Leo, and I want to go along for the ride. This is the Chinese year of the Dragon."

"What does that mean to me?"

"You are the Dragon coming to slay the imposters who want to steal your fire."

"What? Are you serious?"

"Hey, we can say or do anything we want as long as it works. Look at Romney running around calling himself a 'job creator' when in fact, as a corporate raider, he destroyed far more jobs than he ever created."

"Graham," I started.

"Gram, call me gram. I'm just a small part of the bigger scheme of things. One gram, plus one gram, plus one more gram and before you know it you have a kilogram. This is the way of all movements. One person, plus another person and soon, you add a batch of people up and you have an unqualified mob. Get it. We're creating a movement and you're the leader. No, you've already created the movement and you don't realize it yet because more people, like me, haven't shown up at your doorstep. You'll get used to it," Gram said smiling broadly.

"Who the heck are you, really?"

"Like you, my grandparents were from eastern Europe. Mine were from Lithuania. So I'm part Polish. I was raised part Catholic, part Jewish and my distant relatives came from Turkey and Lebanon so I have some that are Christian and others that are, get this, Muslim."

"Where are you from? I mean, where do you live?"

"Currently, in Colorado. Originally, I was from Pennsylvania. I was in the Air Force. Now I'm retired. Ready to work for you. NO, you don't need to pay me. I get enough money to live on and that's all I need. I'm self-sufficient, extremely computer literate, can fly any airplane that has an engine and have a clean driving and flying record. I've never spent a day in jail, don't get high but feel high all the time because I just love life, have a son who's out in the world making his own way, a daughter who's a peach, an ex-wife who leaves me alone, and no parents that are still alive except in my mortal memory. I love to read, hike and solve problems. I love a challenge, am physically fit, don't need much to eat, don't smoke nor drink too much, and last of all, don't have too many bad habits like picking my nose or toes, laughing too loudly at bad jokes, nor wearing clothes that don't fit my style or me. What else would you like to know?" He sat staring at me with a strange grin on his face.

"Gram, are you for real?"

"Squeeze my arm and you tell me."

"I just don't know what to make of all this."

"What's to make of it? I mean here I am ready to go to work for free to get you elected to the presidency of the United States. That's all there is to it."

"Do you work for the CIA, the FBI, the current White House, or the Republican Party?"

He laughed heartily. "Sure, I can stand some vetting. Go for it. I'm immune to the challenges. I'm an honorably discharged Air Force pilot, a graduate of the Air Force Academy and now a humble citizen who believes this country is just screwed up enough to warrant a new type of leader and that happens to be you. Yes, you, Leo Pollack, a blue collar guy who's unemployed and has the balls to stand up and say to the American People, 'Hey, I'm running for president because I know how it feels to not have a job and be low man on the totem pole this economic system right now.' That's it. Nothing more. Nothing less."

"So you're a pilot? Do you have a plane?"

"Nope. Can't afford one. But if we rent one, I can fly you anywhere in the country you'd like to go. I mean it. I am a good pilot. I stopped logging hours over 10,000. What was the use? I flew a lot."

"Gram, you must understand my wariness. I mean, I'm a simple guy. People don't normally show up at my door and say they want to go to work for me."

"Sure, Leo, I fully understand what you must be feeling. That's okay. I should have called first, but I thought you might reject me as a crank caller and not give me a chance. I took the risk of just showing up here and was greeted by your lovely wife and son. Ready, willing and able to get the job done: namely, get you elected. So what do we do first?"

"First, we call the police and find out if you are really who you say you are or just someone who's on some kind of power trip."

"You're not serious are you," Gram asked wide-eyed and imploring.

"No. If I thought you were a lunatic, I'd have kicked you out of here a long time ago."

"What makes you think that I'm not, that I'm just who I say that I am."

I laughed at him and said, "I can tell by the way a man ties his shoes whether or not he is who he says he is."

Gram looked at me quizzically.

"Marine style or overhand. Perhaps in the Air Force you called it 'Air Force Style', I don't know."

"What are you talking about?"

"Do you tie your bow with an overhand knot or a square knot?"

"Square knot. Is there any other way to tie your shoes?" Gram asked me now.

"Show me how you do it," I directed him.

Gram untied and then tied his shoes. "See, that's it."

"No civilian ties his shoes that way. You're genuine."

"I hear they do it that way in the Ohio State Prison," Gram said chuckling.   "No they don't. They use Velcro. Shoestrings can be used to commit suicide, garret another inmate or guard and to castrate your roommate when he's sleeping."

"Yikes, I didn't know all of that."

"Perhaps that was too much information for you," I said, watching his reaction.

"No, but I like knowing trivia like that. Heck, you never know when you might need to use it."

"Okay. Now who are you and what do you really want? I already have life insurance and it's enough to bury me if I die. I don't want any probiotics because I get all that I need sucking in the 'precious metals' from the air in the steel mill. I am satisfied with the car I'm driving so I don't need a new one. I don't have money for a plane so I really can't afford having a pilot on retainer. Having said all this, what are you up to and give it to me straight."

"I am up to the task of getting you elected to the highest office in the land. That's all. What makes it so hard for you to believe that this is my only design?"

"Let's reverse rolls. You're at home. Some guy shows up and wants to go to work for you. You've never met the guy before. He tells you he came all the way across the country to help you. What would you think? Be honest."

"I see your point. So, here's my driver's license, my credit cards, my birth certificate, and my discharge papers. Oh, and my passport, too. I don't leave home without it. I never know when I might be assigned to do a mission overseas. You know CIA and all."

"Okay. Okay. I'm starting to get the picture, Gram, but I swear, this entire process has really been an adventure."

"What made you use the unemployment office venue as the place to launch your campaign?"

"Venue? Hmm. I like that word. What happened was simply this. I was standing in the line like all the rest of the people and it just hit me like a brick. This was not the American dream. Who wants to be paid for not working? Where is the pride, the honor, the nobility in that? That's how it started. Now the road is laid out before us and it's going to be a very long one. So you still want to come along and make a difference.

"Yes."

"That's it?"

"Yes."

"Well, then, let's go in and get some dinner. You're hired."

"That's it?"

"Yes.

"That's it?"

"Yes."

I introduced "Uncle Gram to Janko and Basha. The boy liked the idea that he now had a new uncle. Basha asked Gram what he was going to do for a place to live and he said he was not sure. She offered him the guest bedroom. Of course, he refused to accept her hospitality but she said it was non-negotiable.

"If you're working for Leo, you're family. That's all there is to it. What are you going to do anyway?" She asked.

"Oh, I thought I'd be Leo's chief of staff. You don't have one right now do you, Leo?" he asked.

"No. No, I don't. You think I need a 'chief of staff'?" I asked him in a joking manner.

"Sure, why not. Every candidate, politician, leader, President, has a chief of staff. I'm good at organizing things, computer savvy, know how to influence people when necessary, and if I have to, I can bust a knee cap too," he said winking at Basha and me.

"What does bust a knee cap mean, Uncle Gram?" Janko asked.

"It means that if someone makes trouble for your father, I can take care of the problem by busting a knee cap moving as fast as I can to solve it."

"I'm glad you're working for my Daddy because he needs a lot of help."

"He sure does," Gram said.

"Will you say grace for us?" I asked our newest family member.

"I'm kind of an ecumenical prayer person so I hope you don't mind," Gram said.

"Not at all. We're pleased that you're here and a part of us now," Basha said. "Please lead us in prayer."

"Dear God, we give thanks for this good food, our good health, for being together to share this meal, for having friendship and for possessing the strength to undertake this special path to lead America out of this wilderness and back into the light, Amen."

"Very nice. Very nice," I said. "Now let's eat and no political talk. Hear me?"

Family. A man, a woman, and children. A man, a woman and no children. A man and another man and no children. A man and another man and children. Women and children. The world is made up of families and there is no substitute for being a part of one regardless of how it is structured. There is no such thing as a dysfunctional family. Every family functions in its own unique way. Some families are healthier than others. Some are more nurturing. All families, when filled with love, meet the requirement for being a nurturing environment that makes children grow into healthy adults. Without affection, a family is hollow ground; with it, it is a hallowed place to live and grow.

We sat in the living room for hours just talking. Gram told us about his childhood in Pennsylvania, how he grew up and was accepted into the Air Force Academy. He told us how he learned to fly, what it was like to be as free as a bird, and how he wished sometimes that he did not ever have to come back down to the earth because aloft he felt so free. Janko asked him many questions and he was patient and answered all of them with a sense of wonder and awe.

Basha took Janko at 9 pm and put him to bed. I went up to help. We read the usual stories. I tucked him in. We prayed and then I returned back to the living room.

Gram was reading.

"You ready for bed?" I asked.

"No. Not unless you are."

"Yes. We're on the road tomorrow."

"Where are we going?"

"Three C's. Cleveland at 10 am. Columbus at 4 pm. Cincinnati at 8 pm."

"Wow! Nothing like making a day of it. Who made these reservations?"

"Judy Bream, our local PR person. She coordinates all the travel with John, the union president and other local leaders."

"Then I guess we ought to get some sleep. I'm ready to go."

"Gram, I'm glad you've decided to be a part of this movement. I don't know where we're heading but there won't be a dull moment. You can count on that."

"How are we going to travel? Bus or car?"

"RV. Al will be over in the am. Al's one of my work pals. He has donated his RV for the campaign and he's the main driver."

"He won't mind that I'm coming along now for the ride."

"No, as long as you earn your keep."

"I'll do my best. You can count on that."

"I am counting on that and much more."

"I'll try not to disappoint."

"We'll soon find out what you learned in that Air Force Academy."

"More than you will ever know. Trust me," Gram responded.

"Gram, thanks for volunteering to help. When I first got home, seeing you put me on guard. I'm not normally a suspicious person, but you're showing up all of a sudden, out of nowhere, just seemed strange to me. You were a genuine 'mysterious stranger'."

"I hope to change all of that in short order," Gram said. "I read about you, heard one of your speeches on TV, read more on the internet, and decided that this movement was something I just had to be a part of and so I left home and now I'm back home again. In your home. Thanks for making me feel so welcome."

"No problem, Uncle Gram. Now let's get some sleep. I'll show you your room and the bathroom."

Once I got Gram settled, I checked in on Janko, kissed him goodnight, and then silently padded into my own room. I disrobed and crawled into the warm spot next to Basha, kissed her on the back of the neck, wrapped my arms around her and slowly drifted off to sleep nestled in the safest and quietest place any man will ever find: beside his friend, lover and wife.

14. Adventure Along the 3-C Highway

Many years ago before the Eisenhower Interstate Highway System was conceived and people got used to driving on four-lanes, each state had a series of United State highways that carried the nation's traffic. One of the most famous in Ohio was US 42 running from Cleveland all the way south to Columbus and ending in Cincinnati. Travelers were challenged to drive the entire distance through countless small towns and villages and not fall asleep along the way. Strongsville, Brunswick, Lodi, Ashland, Mansfield, Mount Gilead, Delaware, Plain City, London, Xenia, Waynesville, Pisgah and Mount Holly were just a few of the romantic places that this famous highway carried the traveler to along its path. When the interstate highway system was proposed and started, many of these federal highways were swept aside by the new construction. Now, Interstate-71 assumed the role of the former 3-C highway and carried travelers across the state in less than half the time. Before the trip from Cleveland-Columbus-Cincinnati would take at least all day. Now the driving time was reduced to less than six hours. The romance was gone, but time was saved and that made all the difference to most people navigating the state's highways. As a college student many years ago, I used the interstate system to get back and forth to school quickly and efficiently. Hitchhiking was still in vogue and I used my educated thumb to travel free from my home in Youngstown to Columbus. I enjoyed the adventure at that time, and today, as we prepared to navigate this famous highway again, I was especially excited. It was 60 miles from Youngstown to Cleveland. From Cleveland to Columbus, the distance was 142 miles. From Columbus to Cincinnati, the distance is 111 miles. The distance alone would make for a long day even if we were just driving from one city to the next. However, we would be stopping in each city and there would be a program. I knew that this was the real beginning of my campaign because I was stepping outside the comfort zone of cities I already knew. The crowds would be made up of total strangers. Now I would discover if my message would resonate with those who were not just like me. Columbus was not an industrial town and Cincinnati was the beginning of the southland. Our adventure would require that our message be honed for those who might be skeptical about a blue-collar candidate being qualified to hold the highest office in the land. This did not frighten me. What was the worst thing that could happen along the way? I could be heckled. I could face a crowd that did not want to be challenged to think differently about the future. I could stand before a gathering of the people and they would continue to be led to vote against their own interests. This phenomenon confused me no end. This was the essential theme in the book, what is wrong with Kansas? When were people going to wake up and realize people who did not care one iota about their future were manipulating them?

Gram was already up and helping Basha in the kitchen when I came downstairs. Janko was eating his breakfast.

"Sleepy head, Daddy," Janko chanted when I came into the room.

"You got me, pal," I replied. "Morning all. You sleep well?"

"Like I was in my very first day of heaven," Gram intoned.

"Good deal," I commented, kissing Basha on the back of the neck. I poured a cup of coffee and sat next to Janko. "Al should be here any minute."

"When will you be back?" Basha asked.

"Late, if at all. We aren't done in Cincinnati until about 10 pm. It's at least a 5 hour drive back home."

"Better pack some extra clothes. You, too, Gram. Nice that you could come and stay for a night," Basha said smiling broadly letting him know that he was welcome back.

"When I was in the Air Force, I was used to long deployments, horrible sleeping arrangements and drafty places so I've had a lot of training for this kind of sortie."

"I'm sure you did, but you were much younger then," she said.

"Are you implying I'm an old man now and can't take it?" he asked feigning offense.

"Yes and no," she countered not giving him an inch.

"Okay. I just want you to know that I'm just middle-aged and not an old man yet."

"Uncle Gram, do you have a dog?" Janko asked.

"No, but I wish I did. I just travel too much to ever take care of one."

"I want a dog."

"I'm sure you do," he commented. "So what is the problem?"

"Mom and Daddy want me to be ten first so I can take care of the dog all on my own."

"Hmm. I see. You're almost there."

"Almost, but not quite."

I was happy when I heard knocking on the door and got up to let Al in.

Al was his usual jovial self. He spied Gram, immediately went to him, and shook his hand, "I'm Al. Leo's main driver, companion and body guard. Who are you?"

"Graham Tashjan, Gram for short. I'm Leo's new 'Chief of Staff'."

"Really? Leo, you didn't tell me we were expanding so soon."

"I didn't know it until Gram showed up here last night and said he wanted to go to work for me. I told him I couldn't pay him anything and he said that would be fine. He didn't need the money but he did want to work for us and support the movement. I accused him of being a spy for the democrats or republicans and he showed me his credentials and made a compelling argument for being a member of our team so I hired him."

"Any friend of Leo's is a friend of mine. Welcome to the team," Al said pumping Gram's hand briskly.

"Thanks, Al, and it's good to meet you. I hear we've got a great campaign mobile and we are going on our longest run thus far in this effort."

"You betcha, and we need to get going," Al encouraged us.

"Let's do it," I responded. Hugs and kisses were exchanged. Basha, Janko, and I were quiet for a moment.

"See you when I see you," I said to both of them.

Al, Gram and I left quickly.

Gram liked the Leo-mobile and quickly found a comfortable spot to settle into as we headed toward Cleveland on I-80, the Ohio Turnpike. We could pick up an outer belt and this would take us right downtown to the unemployment office where we were meeting the people of Cleveland.

"Ready for your morning workout?" Gram asked me.

"What do you mean?"

"Everyday I'm going to shoot questions at you and let you answer them spontaneously and then we'll analyze just how well you answered them. Al will be the audience and give you feedback on what he heard and what it made him think and feel. How does that sound to the two of you?"

"Great idea! I like it. Let's get to work."

"Shoot, Gram. We've got plenty of time to 'warm up'," I said.

"Okay. Mr. Pollack, as president, what would you do to win the war on drugs?"

I laughed aloud and said, "I can tell that this is going to be a lot of fun."

"I hope so, but take this seriously because you know this is coming and every word that you say will be played and replayed and thrown up in your face and distilled and fermented and you'll be made to swallow every last drop of the brew that is made by your own words. So, what's your answer?"

"We have fought this 'War on Drugs' and failed to make any significant headway in stopping the flow of drugs into our country, ending addiction or slowing down criminal activity related to narcotics sales. More than a million men and women are in prison for the sale of marijuana alone. We are punishing them for selling an herb that grows naturally in much of the world. Legalize marijuana, end the taboo on its use, stop making people feel like sinners when they smoke it and eliminate the extensive cost of this entire enterprise by the DEA. For those who do use drugs and want to stop, want treatment, we'll provide counseling and other services to assist them in ending their addiction."

"Nice. Nice," Gram said. "Now, what do you think, Al?"

"I think that most people who can think on their own will get it. However, those republicans will accuse Leo of being soft on crime. They won't see the real problem as waging a losing battle, but being tolerant of criminal activity and just making it easier for criminals to do their business."

"Interesting way to look at it," Gram concluded. "So how do you answer this question and address Al's 'American Values Candidate' concerns?"

I took a deep breath and said, "There will be some among you that believe what I am saying is going to make this country less safe, more prone to criminal activity and that we, or I should say I, I am soft on crime. Nothing could be further from the truth. I believe that criminals should face the consequences for their actions. If you steal a car, you ought to be responsible for cleaning up your mess. If you assault someone, then you should be held accountable. However, smoking marijuana is not a crime against society. The behavior does not warrant a prison term. Just like smoking, a Camel cigarette does not land someone in the county jail. What reasonable person would expect that smoking some marijuana should prompt law enforcement to jail a person for such behavior? We've been following this practice for more than forty years and nothing has changed. Marijuana smoking has not gone away. Marijuana growing is not slowing down. The prison population continues to grow as a result and we spend billions of dollars foolishly trying to end the behavior. We are losing the war. We are unwilling to consider major changes in our policies and attitudes. This is what is insane: continuing to do the same thing over and over again and expecting different results."

"Al?" Gram asked.

"Much more thorough answer. Now I have to think about all that we've done for these forty years and unless I'm a fool and a closet conservative, have to admit that we are acting in a foolish way given how we fight this war."

"My same sentiments," Gram added. "Now, Leo, file this away for later. Legalize marijuana. No 'Sin tax'. Yes, it's not a sin to smoke pot. It's certainly better than alcohol because most people under the influence of marijuana do not become violent like many do when intoxicated. Do not tax pot. Let people cultivate it as they do in Colorado, California and a number of other western states. Since this started in California, law enforcement officials have grudgingly admitted that street crime related to marijuana sales is way down. They don't like this because a lot of their operating money comes from busting dealers. They get to keep a portion of the money for police business."

"Got it. Hey, this is fun. I like having a 'Chief of Staff'. What do you think, Al?"

"Anything that sharpens your game, the better we'll be. Let's do some more."

We spent the next hour going at it. Gram would ask the question, I'd answer and Al would provide feedback. We were working out like athletes before a game. Gram was certainly worth his weight in gold.

"Where did you learn to do this kind of stuff?" I asked him.

"I told you I went to the Air Force Academy. We were always challenged to think about our mission well in advance of what we were setting out to do. The mental preparation was far more challenging than the actual flying. This is no different. Take a heading and see if you can follow it to the ultimate end. Whether it is marijuana or taxes or anything else, you've got to be on your toes, Leo. You know what's coming? There are trip wires, booby traps, mines, roadside bombs and IEDs everywhere along the political trail. You just need to know how to protect yourself so that you don't get 'taken out.'"

I was truly amazed at his depth of knowledge and expertise and finally said, "You know what Gram. I'm sure proud to have you as a mentor. Perhaps you ought to be the one running for office."

He laughed so hard that tears came to his eyes and he finally blurted out, "I don't have the cajones to stand in front of a large crowd and ask them to vote for me to be their president. No, I'm the pilot. I am the navigator. I'm the strategist. I'm the special ops planner, but I'm not the front man. No, Leo, you're the one who has to get out there, win friends, and influence people. I'm not that kind of guy. If I were, I'd have been the one running for office and you'd be my special ops man. No, we're all where we're supposed to be. Trust me. I know what I'm talking about when it comes to this."

"If you say so," I responded. "But I've learned a lot this morning already."

"We're coming into downtown Cleveland. ETA ten minutes," Al said.

Cleveland, Ohio, home of the baseball Indians and football Browns and now the rock and roll hall of fame. Miles of lakefront spread before us as we drove across the elevated highway along the lakeshore boulevard. I was not paying attention but somehow we had attracted an escort of police cars. I looked in the mirrors and could see them coming in behind us and others lining up in front.

"What do you make of the escort?" I asked the guys.

"Maybe they want to make sure to get a good spot for your speech," Al offered.

"Don't know but I'd say the word is out that a rabble rouser is coming to town and they are just making sure they have enough security on hand to insure nothing goes awry," Gram added.

"I thought they were just coming out to greet us. You know, kind of welcome wagon action."

"I doubt that," Gram said. "Police don't like change. They are your arch conservatives dressed in liberal blue."

"We'll have to just make our way with or without them. No sweat. We're just a block away. Last night, I had the kids Google the site for me," Al said.

We drove down to the unemployment office complex. Given that this was a major metropolitan city, there was a huge parking lot. It was filled with cars, people, banners, and the ubiquitous black and white police cars.

"I see we have company here," I commented pointing at the black and whites.

"They will make this fun. Let them be here to keep the peace. No heckling now. This is a good sign. Trust me," Gram said, "Anytime you make an attempt to change the system, the power elite will react and go into protect mode. Like I said before, the police are here because someone tipped them off that a political neophyte was coming to town to upset the status quo."

Al drove into the parking lot where a policeman was directing him and slowly eased to a stop.

"Made it in plenty of time," Al said, leaning back and flexing his shoulders and hands. "I feel good. How about you, Leo? You ready?"

"Hey, we had our warm-up with Gram. Now let the games begin."

"What do I do?" Gram asked.

"Let's find the local union president and see what the arrangements are."

While Al secured the vehicle, Gram and I sought Jesse Sepulveda. I started asking questions of some people who were working around an impromptu stage when a middle-aged woman came up and said, "Leo Pollack. Welcome to Cleveland." She reached out and I shook her hand. "I'm Jesse Sepulveda."

"Good to meet you, Jesse. I was looking for a…"

"Guy? Happens all the time. It's okay. We're good to go. We've got a little stage here. Sound system is donated but works fine. How do you want to do this?"

"Gram, what do you think? By the way, Jesse, this is Gram, my chief of staff."

"Good to meet you, Gram."

"Same here," Gram said checking out Jesse. I watched with a smile on my face. Gram could read my lips. He did not say anything.

"Jesse, you make the introduction, and I'll do the rest."

"Okay, Leo. First, though, some reporters want to ask you a few questions. Do you mind?"

"Free press. No, I love it."

Jesse led me over to the reporters who were gathered behind the stage. Gram tagged along curious about what they would ask me. I was pleased that we had done a warm-up on the way here.

"Folks, you have ten minutes with Leo and then it is show time," Jesse barked, leaving Gram and me alone with the reporters.

Most of their questions were low level, softball questions. "What made you want to run for president?" "What makes you think you're qualified to be president?" "How are you going to finance your campaign?" "How long do you think you can be on the road before the novelty wears out and the reality sets in that this is a big country and you can't drive everywhere in America and meet all those people you need to meet to make your case?" "How is your family dealing with your being gone so much of the time?" "Given that a union hall is your campaign headquarters, don't you think that you'll be pegged as 'labor's candidate' and this will limit your political reach?" "How will you know when you absolutely don't have a chance to win?"

I fielded all the questions with a smile on my face and joy in my heart. I did not try to elaborate on every answer. I kept the responses simple, direct and honest. Before I knew it, Jesse was back and it was time for the big show.

"Come on Leo, we've got a big stage waiting for you."

Jesse and I stepped up onto the stage. The crowd was huge. I could not see where it ended. The entire parking lot was filled with people. I saw banners in the background and signs up that read "Leo for President". What made people believe so easily? I was amazed that there were people who had not even met me yet and they were already promoting my candidacy.

"Here goes," Jesse said and reached for the microphone.

"Cleveland. Wake Up! A new star is born. There is a candidate entering this year's presidential race that is capturing the hearts and minds of working people wherever he goes because he's one of us. Leo Pollack is an unemployed steel worker. He knows what it means to work hard for a living. He also knows what it is like to be told that his services are no longer needed. He is our candidate because he works for a living and was not born into wealth and influence. My fellow Americans, with great pleasure, I give you Leo Pollack, the people's candidate for president of the United States."

The roar was deafening. I walked to the center of the stage, raised my hand, and waved to the gathering. They did not stop applauding, shouting and chanting for a full three minutes. I know. I timed them. I was amazed, exhilarated, confused and invigorated all at the same time.

Finally, I was able to speak.

"My fellow Americans, working people of this great land, listen. The time has come to change the story line, the American script. My name is Leo Pollack and I'm running for president, your candidate because I am like you, a working person, or at least I was until a few weeks ago. Now I'm unemployed and don't know what the future holds for me or you."

"For too many years, we've been giving our votes to politicians who promise us the world before the election and then feed us the leftovers after the election is over. They play us for patsies. They believe we are too simple to catch on. Yes, it's taken us many years to do so. At our core, we are hard working, decent, trusting people. We've been taken advantage of because we want to believe that, at heart, people are just like us, hard working, decent and trusting. The facts indicate that this is not true."

"This current batch of republican candidates wants to strip Medicare of its security, privatize social security, and give bigger tax breaks to corporations and millionaires and continue to cut funding for education, social welfare programs and the environmental protection agency. I am opposed to anything that harms the social welfare network that has provided a safety net for low and middle-income people for the past half century. Paul Ryan speaks for the wealthy and well-heeled, not for the hard working people who do the lion's share of making this country great."

"The median income in America today is $26,433. Stop and think about this number. I'm not a numbers person, but you've got to understand this number and see just how screwed up this economy is. Fifty percent of the people in this country make less than $26,433. Yes, fathom that. More than 155 million make less than this median income. I don't know about you, but this is just unacceptable. How can anyone raise a family on such a small amount of money? The fact is you can't without making severe sacrifices."

"Working people have gained no ground in the past three decades. In fact, actual earning power and sharing in the profits of doubling our productivity during this period has not panned out. We are making less now than we were thirty years ago. Yet, as a nation, we working people have doubled our input of goods and services. Yes, corporate profits are up even though we are in the middle of a recession. On the other hand, wages are frozen and the attack on working people is being waged at every turn in the road."

"You all know these facts. You are living them. So let me stop with the facts and go right to some solutions."

"First and foremost, we need to start a movement that is very simple. It's called 'Americans Supporting Americans'. What we are going to do is buy American to support our working brothers and sisters across this great land. If we can't buy American, we just won't buy if we can do without the product or service. We need to stop the bleeding of American jobs to countries around the world. This is not a selfish movement, but one undertaken to change the way we do business. I don't mean big business, but our business, our buying and selling products and services, day in and out, as we go about living our lives. If the tent I want to buy is not made in America, I don't buy it. I write to the company that if they make it here in America, I will buy it."

"The inequality of opportunity is killing this nation. Even wealthy people will eventually realize this, but by then it will be too late. One thing we had to admire about Henry Ford was that he realized, quite simply, that by paying his employees a decent wage, each employee could then buy the very product that he or she was producing. This is not the case today. Unless you can deduct from your taxes the cost of a new truck, who can afford a $45,000 Ford F-150 or 250? No one. We are living in economic warp times."

"Get rid of your cell phones. They are not made in America. They are the symbol of this economy gone awry. Many people claim that Steve Jobs is a real genius. He's the face of Apple. He made the company grow beyond comprehension. There is just one problem with Steve Jobs and what he did. Apple does not and never did make one product in the United States of America. Every smart phone, I-pod or I-pad is made overseas. Yet, you and I have seen people sleeping out on a street corner waiting for the chance to go inside a store and buy an I-pad that costs $500 to $800 dollars. Apple is undermining the very nature of our economy by sending billions of dollars overseas to have these products made. Isn't it ironic that this fellow has the name 'Jobs' too?"

"Take your credit cards and cut them up and stop using them unless they are from a credit union, a monetary entity that looks out for working people and does not pray on them. Being in debt means we are enslaved to the system. Being out of debt, we are free to choose where we place our money and how we spend it."

"My fellow Americans, I am asking for you to stand up and be counted. I am asking for you to get involved. I am asking you to get out the vote and be a part of the solution and not the problem. I am asking you to Buy American, vote your pocket book, support your local union and stores. I am asking you to go to our web page and donate a dollar or five or ten and help us to make a difference in America, in Cleveland, in your home, in your life."

"Lastly, I am asking you to vote for me. I am your candidate. I am not bought and paid for by any company, organization, union, Pac or superpacs. I am a blue-collar guy who works for a living, has a home that I do not own, a car that is almost paid for, a wife and a kid and no pets. I haven't taken a vacation for more than three years because I can't afford one. What I can do is speak for you, lead this country toward fairness and justice and this I believe is all that anyone of us can expect in life."

"Thank you for being here today and organize and enjoy the fight."

"Thank you. Thank you. Thank you."

A roar erupted and the echo banged off the walls of the nearby buildings and back and forth throughout the neighborhood. I stepped down into the crowd and began shaking hands, signing autographs, smiling, laughing and living in the moment. If it were not for Gram reminding me that we had another engagement 140 miles away in a few hours, I would have continued "pressing the flesh" for the rest of the day.

"Now that was a crowd," Al said as we drove away from the gathering. "Leo, did you ever think things would get like this. Man, we were in the thick of it."

"No, Al, not this quickly. I was impressed to say the least."

"You know what I was thinking?" Gram added. "These people are hungry for the truth. They are ravenous for the facts. They want to believe in something greater than themselves and that is what you are providing them: something to believe in. This is not that hollow 'Change you can believe in'. No, this is real change. This is the kind of stuff that dreams are made of and they want every bit they can get."

We drove along basking in the sunlight of success. I was pleased with our work thus far, and was looking forward to the next gathering in Columbus, our state capital. However, this was going to be what I would consider "enemy territory". Our new governor, John Kasich, was on a rampage attacking the rights of working people and using his republican majority to ram Senate Bill 5 down the throats of public employees. This bill ended collective bargaining rights for state employees like teachers, firefighters, police and other state and municipal workers. The outrage sparked massive demonstrations in the capital and the people were mobilizing to get a petition signed so that an amendment could be made to repeal the bill. Thus far, they were doing a fantastic job gathering signatures and making this a national referendum on workers' rights. Public employees were the last bastion of the middle class with any power to stop the onslaught of conservative policies eroding their bargaining ability. The vote would not come until October so there would be a lot of time for the governor to build support for his position and for the people to rally voters to reject his anti-middle-class stance. I was concerned that we might be walking right into a mess in Columbus and then it dawned on me that I was the person who was really "making a mess" of the politics as usual. The two party system was denying people a real democratic voice. Now I was standing up and saying to anyone who would listen, "We are the people. We are the government. We can make a change and it is not something that a lot of money will buy. No, we will do it a dollar or five at a time."

Rain started to splatter on the windshield. I was sitting in the back seat. Gram was riding shotgun and Al was the wheelman.

"Here we go. I guess we're going to get a little bit of real rain coming down on our parade today," Al said.

"Good. This will show how genuine the people are who will come out and stand in the bad weather to hear Leo talk and they will see just how real we are standing there with them and not letting a little bit of moisture affect our message. This is perfect. I'm psyched," Gram yelped.

"One way or another, there are going to be days when we have to deal with whatever shows up and this may be one of them. Columbus is ground zero for the fight for workers' rights in the state of Ohio. Since Senate Bill 5 was passed by the republican dominated congress and signed into law by Governor Kasich, people have been protesting almost continuously. In the next year, this will be a battleground state for every seat from the state house to the presidency. If the people win and overturn the bill via the referendum going onto the ballot next fall, this will bode well for any progressive cause and candidate that is on the ballot the following year. So there is a lot riding on this movement and Ohioans are not sitting around taking it on the chin but fighting back and letting America know they are not happy with these republican attempts to erode the people's rights."

"Good, then we should have a rollicking good time in the capital city," Gram said. "I've never been to Columbus so I don't know anything about it."

"I went to school there for four years. It is a meeting place of the south and north. West Virginians moved north to the city to find better paying jobs. Columbus, being the capital and the home of one of the largest universities in the country, attracts all kinds of people from all over the world. The Ohio State University has the largest population of Jewish students of any school in the country."

"Really?" Gram asked.

"When I was there a full ten percent of the students were Jewish. Hey, it was a good school and very reasonably priced for a four year bachelor degree education."

"I got my degree for free but if I had known that when I was younger, I might have considered a different path," Gram said.

"Businesses and industries settled in Columbus to be near the seat of power. Verizon has its headquarters west of town. Nationwide Insurance is a main fixture on the near north side. I can't tell you all the rest but this is one of the few northern rust belt cities that actually grew in the last decade as documented by the 2010 census."

"What I like about Columbus," Al added, "is that it is an easy town to drive through. The roads are great. The directions are clear and traffic generally isn't that bad   because they spend a lot of money expanding the roads to fit the ever expanding traffic needs of the place."

"Money is everywhere, that is true," Gram added. "Where there is a political seat of power, there will be money."

"We're almost at the outer belt," Al said. "The office is downtown so we'll just roll in on I-71 and get off on the Main Street Exit."

"Right on," Gram said. "Columbus here we come."

Ten minutes later, Al activated his turn signal, we exited the highway and dropped down on East Main Street and headed two blocks to the State Office of Unemployment Compensation Services.

This time we did not need a police escort to get to the place. The traffic was congested. We crawled along at a turtle's pace as we moved toward the building and parking lot. Rain was coming down hard. I got out my rain gear. Luckily, Basha reminded me that I should carry it. What a good woman!

"Will you look at this," Al cried, as he wheeled the long RV through the traffic. We were moving into a vast parking lot and there had to be at least a 1000 people standing in the area. Signs, posters, banners and people were everywhere. We could hear music playing. Cops were surrounding the four sides of the gathering. Already, we could hear the cheering as the Leo-Mobile pulled into a slot reserved for it near the side of the building. I was a little intimidated by the entire panorama.

"My Oh My, look at what you've gotten us into," Gram cracked.

"Leo, this has got to be the biggest crowd yet," Al cried. "Just look at all these people. We're in for a real good time here."

"I sure hope so," I said, and then exercising my voice, "Mi...Mi...Mi...Mi...Mi..."

"You sound silly," Gram said. "Do this instead." He led me in an Om chant and helped to center me. It only lasted a minute or so but I was calm and relaxed and my voice felt strong.

"Thanks," I said to him.

"No problem. It's what I do best. Now go out there and give them the speech of their lives."

I jumped out of the RV and met a throng of people waiting to shake my hand, slap me on the back and shout my name so many times that I thought I would go deaf if it continued for too long. There was no escaping the throngs. Truthfully, I did not want to because this was kind of unique and special to me. I admit I did enjoy the attention. I just hoped that these people would feel the same way a year from now when it was time to vote.

Some official looking people came my way. I lost track of Gram and Al. The crowds were so large there was no way we could stick together unless we held hands like kindergarten kids. I waited for the group approaching me from besides the office building.

"Leo Pollack?" I heard someone ask.

"Sir," I responded.

"Great to have you here. I'm Sam Delaney and these are my committee. Boy we are surely glad that you are here. We heard that there was a possibility that you might not make it and we nearly panicked."

"I'm here and we did not ever consider not showing up. What made you think that I might not be appearing for the event? I'm curious."

"We got a call from someone in Cleveland, don't know exactly who, he didn't identify himself. He just said you were busy and might not make it. We couldn't call you because we didn't have your cell number. I did talk to John Gallagher in Youngstown and he said that as far as he knew you were on your way with your crew and would be here at 4 pm. So we are excited that you are here."

"I just wonder who would call ahead and tell you that I was not coming. That concerns me. I mean, there is no one who speaks for me other than the few folks at the hall and they would call me if they needed to change anything. Interesting."

"We're just glad you're here. Anyway, we've got a few minutes before you're up on stage. Can we get you anything? Coffee? A pop? Anything?"

"No, not really. Al, my partner and driver, has us pretty hooked up in the RV. We don't even have to stop at a rest area to use the johns. All in all, we're quite well taken care of for a shoestring outfit."

"This is a tough time in Columbus. I'm surprised that you were able to get into town without having to deal with the police or anything."

"Because?" I asked.

"Because you and our illustrious governor are on opposite sides of the political spectrum."

"What does that matter?" I asked wondering what difference this made at this time.

"You are already on this governor's radar screen. Believe me. These politicians are like Herod dealing with the Three Wise Men. When the king hears that there is some new power in town, he wants to know, not because he wants to embrace the person but to perhaps stop him from expanding his sphere of influence."

"This is amazing!" I replied wiping the sweat off my brow. For some reason, I was starting to get very warm.

"What will matter now is that you are able to continue doing your thing. You don't know, Leo, how many small people are excited that one of their own is taking on the status quo and creating big waves."

"There are no small people. We're all equal. That's what folks need to really understand and believe. I'm no more nor less than anyone else is. We've listened for too many years to the lies that only certain people are qualified to govern. The skill set needed to govern is a practical understanding of how to identify what is the problem, how to gather problem solvers together to work on it, and to solve it in a timely manner. You don't need to go to Harvard or Yale to learn how to do that. Heck, I learned how to do it right in elementary school when the teacher said to us, 'Here is a problem for you to solve' and gave us the simple steps to problem solving."

"Leo, I just wanted to forewarn you, that's all. I'm sure that you've got a handle on what is happening."

"No, not as much as I'd like. Sam, thanks for the heads up and giving me something to think about as I get ready to share my message with the folks gathered here."

"Do you need anything? I mean anything?" Sam asked.

"No, I'm good to go. Let's get the show on the road."

Gram wandered up just as Sam headed to the makeshift stage.

"Quite a crowd," he said loudly to me over the din of people's voices and the chanting and other noise.

"Sure is. Sam told me that he was worried we were not going to show up today. He said he got an anonymous call today saying we weren't going to make it. What do you think of that?"

Gram squirreled his face up and did not respond right away. Then he said, "I think there is a force in the world that is just beginning to realize that you are someone to be reckoned with and it won't be long before many strange and not so wonderful things will begin to happen to you and this campaign. Let me do some digging. I think I can find the underlying cause of this. Who was it that took the call?"

I pointed to Sam and said, "He took the call. His name is Sam Delaney. He's the local president of the SEIU."

"Good. I'll catch him while you're on stage. Go give it to them, Leo."

"Thanks," I replied and walked up toward where Sam was addressing the crowd.

"Ohioans, welcome to the moment we have all been waiting for since we were born. Yes, in our lifetime, now and then, someone comes along that stands above all the rest of us and, like a beacon, lights the pathway for us to follow. Today, my fellow unemployed, we have the honor and privilege to welcome to Columbus, another unemployed American who just happens to be using his checks to apply for the most important job in the country, the presidency. My friends give a hearty Columbus welcome to Leo Pollack, unemployed American and the next president of the United States."

As the crowd went wild with cheers, clapping, whistling and chanting, I waved to everyone and listened with astonishment. In all my life, I would never get used to such noise, to such adulation. Indeed, I was humbled.

Finally, the sound diminished slightly, and I said, "Thank you, my fellow Americans for such a hearty Columbus welcome. Thank you from the bottom of my heart."

"I am not selfish enough to believe that you applaud me because you think I am in some way any better than any of you. Remember this. I am unemployed right now just like many of you are, and like 15 million other Americans all across this great and depressed land of ours."

"I am Leo Pollack, an unemployed steel worker, and I am asking you to vote for me for president of the United States."

A loud chant erupted: Leo…Leo…Leo…

When they calmed down again, I continued.

"This is what I believe. We do not want to be unemployed. We want to work and earn a living and be proud that we contribute to the greater good of this country, our communities, and most of all, our families. This is a tragedy that we are not able to be productive. What makes it a tragedy is that it is wholly preventable. Yes, we did not do anything to justify our being laid off from our jobs. In the past decade, American workers have increased productivity in the workplace by more than two hundred percent, but at the same time, our take home pay from this increased productivity has risen by a mere 3.4 percent after taking into consideration inflation. Something is seriously wrong with this situation and that is we are not represented in the board rooms where the big decisions are being made."

"Ohio was once a lead producer of steel in the world. Today, we produce less than one percent of the world's steel. What happened? We know what happened. Companies lobbied for tax breaks to make it possible for them to write off any expenses incurred when they moved their production operations to other countries. Ohio has lost more than 300,000 manufacturing jobs in the past decade. How can we believe what our governor says? We are not going to bring these jobs back as long as there is an incentive for companies to shut down local plants and move them anywhere they can get a tax break or can cut their labor costs in half."

"Our current governor is committed to destroying the right of working people to organize and negotiate for their rights. He claims that collective bargaining is what is destroying jobs. It is all a lie. He and his policies, and lobbyists and CEOs and boards that think more about the bottom line than they do about how their decisions affect the lives of people are what caused the critical mass that is our current economic meltdown."

"We who work for a living have nothing else to share but our labor, our minds, bodies and spirits to make a company successful. What is wrong with asking for our fair share? What is so wrong with asking to be counted in the decision making process? No, we are not asking for anything that we are not due. We do not get multi-million dollar bonuses when we produce more goods and services. Most of us don't even get bonuses. In fact, most of us have to negotiate for a simple ten, twenty, or thirty cent per hour raise. Even when we ask for it, the company gives us the sad story about how it's unable to spend more on labor because it's not making enough money to justify the raises."

"At the very same time that we are being denied increased salaries and benefits, corporate heads are making record bonuses. This is what really grates on our nerves. Share the bounty. Share the bounty. Share the bounty with those who actually created it."

The crowd went nuts. I could not stop the chanting that erupted for more than a minute.

"What does it benefit a man to gain the entire world and lose his soul?

"There is a moral dilemma that America is facing and that is the conflict between the power of corporate executives and the workers. How much is enough? I ask the question again. How much is enough? When corporate leaders make 435 times what the lowest paid employee in the corporation makes, there is something wrong. If I made $50,000 last year, the average CEO would have made 435 times that much or $2,175,000. Now that is a lot of cash no matter how you stack it. The question is again, how much is enough? No, we can't all make that kind of money. The corollary to that question is how can that man or woman make that much money? What makes him or her worth that much? What goods and services are produced that justify such a grand salary?"

"This is not a call to class warfare. No, not at all. This is a call to simply demand a fair share of the bounty. This is as simple as I can make it. We do not envy those who are wealthy. We do want everyone to have a fair chance to succeed. We want to be treated fairly. We want to be accepted as being integral to any company's success."

"I applaud those of you who have demonstrated against this governor and his cronies in the senate and house who have insulted and assaulted Ohio working people. Unless we take this issue to the streets, the authorities will continue to disrespect us as we strive to be treated fairly. We don't have to apologize for our demands. We are Americans and we don't beg. We do demand that, as we strive to protect our striving for life and liberty and the pursuit of happiness, that we are not maligned for our efforts."

"Enough said. I am Leo Pollack. I'm running to be your president. I know what it means to live from paycheck to paycheck. I don't have a million dollars in assets. I am, like many of you, unemployed. I am, like many of you, unhappy that I am being paid to not work when all I want to do is go to work, be productive and enjoy the bounty of my labor."

"I am Leo Pollack and I want to be your president. I ask for your vote, not for me but for every working person who believes that no politician alive speaks for the common man or woman. I ask for your support. Go to our web page **www.ringingthelibertybell.org** and make a donation. However, don't give me a lot of money. I want a dollar, five, ten or twenty from you. No more. I don't want any corporate money in the coffers. I want this to be the money from the people, for the people, to make a difference in the way we govern this great country of ours."

"I am Leo Pollack and I will not give up until the final vote is cast and I either win or lead the new revolution in America where the working person is being led by a working person and not someone born with a silver spoon in his mouth. I will work until every person who wants to work can find a job and be productive. I will work hard until there is justice for all. I will work until I draw my last breath to bring America into the twenty-first century leading the way toward an all-inclusive society that does not discriminate against anyone for beliefs, gender, religion, health status, sexual orientation or past history."

"I am Leo Pollack and I hope you will vote for me. Thanks for listening and now let's get to work."

As I did in Cleveland, I stepped down into the crowd and was swamped by hands, faces, and bodies and disappeared into the mass of beings. What a thrill to be among the people who believe in the power of the people. The Ezra Pound haiku kept rolling through my brain: "The faces of the people, petals on a wet black bough". These people were not wet and not black but shining, brilliant, engaging and wanting their world to be respected. I was happy to be alive and hoped that this moment would last a lifetime. I knew that it could not but I could always hope.

The time passed swiftly as I moved along meeting people, listening to their fears, concerns, hopes, joys and sorrows. I just listened. What else could I do in a crowd of hundreds of people?

When Sam Delaney grabbed my arm and rescued me from the crowd and my desire to go on and on, I followed him to the side of the stage and listened to what he had to say.

"Leo. The call was made from somewhere in Columbus. We're tracking it down now. This guy, Gram, that you have working for you is amazing. Where did he come from?"

"He didn't tell you?"

"No."

"He graduated from the Air Force Academy. He flew big birds for Uncle Sam. But who knows what else he did. I just met him yesterday. He showed up at my house and said he wanted to go to work for me so I hired him."

"Amazing. What a wild story."

"You tell me. I am finding out more and more as the day unfolds."

"He got right on the case. I'm sure that before you get too far down the road, he'll have an answer for you."

"Well, we shall see."

The crowds continued to mill around and even as I moved toward the RV, I was asked repeatedly for my autograph, to stop and take a picture, to listen to a new idea about something related to this or that, and a host of other things. I know the people did not realize we were on a tight schedule. We had a few hours to get to Cincinnati but we did not want to make it a last minute ordeal.

I shook hands with Sam Delaney and thanked him for his hard work in making this event happen with such flawless precision.

"The pleasure was mine."

"Leo, we will meet again. In the mean time, we are going to raise money, get your name on the ballot and make waves that will cause this current administration to get seasick."

"Power to working people," I replied.

"And to those who want to work and are being denied that opportunity because the business world is so skewed. Keep the spirit alive, Leo. Don't let us down."

Spontaneously, we hugged one another. I normally am a hugging person, but I did not expect him to hug me. I grew up in a very affectionate family. My grandmother, mother, aunts, uncles and cousins were all huggers and kissers. We were not afraid of touching. I sometimes missed that in the current social environment. I was happy that Sam felt close enough to me to reach out and touch someone; namely, me.

Gram and Al finally grabbed me and led me to the RV. I did not resist. I stepped inside and then realized that it was not raining anymore. I laughed and sat down in my chair behind Al and just sunk down into the plush cushion. My body felt drained as if someone had pulled the energy plug and let out all the juice that generated the electricity that was driving me. I heard the roar of the engine as Al fired up the Leo-mobile. The door closed with a shush and soon, I could feel the vibrations flowing up through the floor, through my seat and into my body. I was elated that we were moving and heading down the highway toward our final rendezvous of the day. I did not fully comprehend the significance of the moment, the last hour, the earlier part of the day and this entire experience.

There was so much happening that I just needed to sit still and let the world pass by in front of me.

We drove south out of Columbus on Interstate 71. I gazed at the Ohio landscape outside. Farmland so rich and productive stretched as far as I could see. The northeast corner of the state was once devoted to manufacturing. The rest of the state was a farmscape and what I saw did not disappoint me.

Al and Gram were making small talk. I barely listened to them, but, every now and then, I caught a word or two. I did not let on that I was eavesdropping, but what difference would it make anyway.

"So the call came in about 11 am this morning you say?"

"Yup. Just about the time we were finishing in Cleveland."

"No one knows who made it?"

"Nope. The local president listened to the message and then the caller hung up before he could ask any more questions."

"What do you make of it?"

"Dirty tricks are not new. We will see more of it."

"Who do you think made the call?"

"I'll be able to tell you more when I get to a computer that has high speed internet access."

"What would it take to get it on board the Leo mobile?"

"A dish would do it. We could hook up any time we're stationary and be able to connect."

"Let's do it."

"Let's do it."

"How about a sandwich?" Al said.

"Okay, now I heard that," I answered him. "Hold on while I get my legs back under me and I'll make you one. How about you, Gram?"

"No thanks. I don't eat and think at the same time."

As I made Al a sandwich, I asked Gram what he thought would be the next type of dirty tricks we might see?"

Gram laughed loudly and asked, "How tight a sphincter do you have, Leo?"

"What?"

"Yes, the forces that are arrayed against a real time third party candidate are beyond your comprehension."

"What do you mean? What kinds of things can they do?"

"Can and will!" Gram said. "Oh, don't be surprised when it happens, my friends. This is a high stakes poker game and we, my friends, have a very small stack of chips, just enough to get into the game."

"But we're in," Al said.

"Yes, we're in and that's the rub. We're just in but we're not able to call any bets just yet."

"So what are they going to do, Gram?" I asked.

"You have a cell phone, don't you?"

"Yes, I do."

"Don't ever let it out of your possession or someone will be loading all kinds of new numbers on it and making calls to a whole lot of unsavory characters and that will lead to inquiries by the press. When they find all kinds of unquestionable calls on your phone, goodbye presidential campaign."

"No way," I said incredulously. "My phone is not even connected to the internet."

"Someone will magically connect it."

"How is that possible?"

"How did someone find out who was in charge of our gig here in Columbus today and make a call to him and set you up for something that could have crushed many of your hopes for this campaign."

"These guys are going to start playing hardball, Leo. They don't care what they have to do to stop you or anyone from entering their elite stage. The candidates know that any third party candidate will affect them."

"From what you're saying, this means that Obama won't be happy either."

"You got it my friend. He will be more affected by your candidacy because you will steal more votes from him because you are far more progressive than he is. Oh, it will not be pretty. Trust me."

"I like this guy," Al said. "Gram, where did you come from?"

"Colorado. The Rocky Mountain State."

"No, man, I mean, are you some kind of political operative."

"Or are you a spy like I asked last night?" I added.

Gram laughed heartily, slapped his knees a number of times and then said, "You guys crack me up. You actually thought that you could get into this campaign and not face some dirt, some nastiness, and some downright disgusting behavior on the part of the competition. Look Leo, Al, this is just the beginning of a long slog toward the prize we all want to win and that is our man, Leo, as president. To get to that goal, we will have to tramp through some real horse manure that will repulse and amuse you day in and out. Welcome to the world of big time politics."

"You sound like you've been through this before," Al said.

"I have. I was in the military for 22 years and was a part of the campaign to change the 'Don't Ask, Don't Tell' policy. I can tell you some hair-raising stories about what people will do to protect their turf. Yes, and that was just about gays and lesbians serving in the military. Hardly all the marbles that a presidency is about at any time. So get it now my friends. We are in for a real roller coaster ride. Quite frankly, I'm looking forward to it. What else do we have to do today but have some fun!" he said finishing his commentary and humming a tune that we all knew to be the "Air Force Fight Song". Gram was a true believer.

"I'm glad you're on our team," Al said.

" Me too," I chimed in. "

The sun peaked through some heavy clouds and light burst upon the flat southern Ohio landscape and the rays filtered into the front window and spread throughout the interior and we sat and were mesmerized by the color display. The vista we witnessed looked exactly like the "Great Seal of Ohio" with a radiant sun shining on the western horizon across fields of waving grain. This time of the year, most of the plant life along the highway was winter wheat and it was green and not amber colored. The world looked a whole lot brighter when you captured it now at its greatest beauty. Nothing else mattered for the moment.

"Wow!" Al muttered.

We did not say much. We just waited and eventually every bit of light faded away and we were left shrouded in the darkness of the late spring evening. I finished making Al's sandwich and took it to him.

"Thanks, Leo. Now let me taste it to see if I want to continue these extended road trips." He crunched into the ham, cheese, tomato, onion and pickle on Schwebel's rye bread toasted.

"Now that's a sandwich."

"Not bad for a Pollack, huh?"

"Funny guy," Al sputtered, taking the sandwich and holding it with one hand while he drove with the other.

"Need some help?" I asked him. "I didn't know you could multi-task?"

"Boy, this fellow sure has gotten uppity since this whole campaign started, you know, Gram. I may just have to knock him down a peg or two."

"How far to Cincinnati?" Gram asked.

"About 50 miles or so," Al said.

"I've never been there. Tell me about the town."

"They call it the 'Queen City' because it is right on the Ohio River and was once the jumping off point for points west before St. Louis became the focal point of western adventure. It is a combination of northern industrial might and southern charm and hospitality because the bridge linking Ohio to Kentucky conveniently connects north and south. Once upon a time, Jerry Springer was its mayor."

"No way," Gram exclaimed.

"True. He still shoots his show from here. The Cincinnati Reds are the baseball team and the Bengals are the NFL franchise."

"Reds, like in rednecks?" Gram asked.

"Some might think that. This is one of the more conservative cities in the state, even more so than Columbus is. John Boehner's district is just outside the city. He is a symptom of the problem with Ohio. You probably are not aware of his roots in this area, but yes, Ohio claims him for its native son."

"So we might have a tougher audience here than anywhere else?" Gram inquired earnestly. I watched as he started jotting down notes on a clipboard that he produced from his daypack.

"We might. Who knows? One never knows about a Buckeye. There is a strong, or there was, manufacturing base here, but the recession has cut it right to the quick. In one of the recent budget battles, Boehner lost a fight with his own party when they cut spending for some military equipment that was being manufactured in his own district. He took a solid hit from this vote. He played if off, but he was hurt by it because he was not able to deliver the pork to his own constituents even though he is the speaker of the House."

"Amazing. So this is southern Ohio. A mixing of the north and south to produce a confused, cautious and conservative electorate," Gram said with a flourish.

"You got it. We're going into the heart of the beast," I concluded.

"What's your message?"

"Fairness and justice for all. It is time that working people are united against special interests and the power elite. Speak truth to power. Don't let those with money and message divide us based upon some social issues like abortion, religious differences, military spending and other issues that confuse the people and distract us from the real ones of work, education, equal opportunity, fair taxes."

"Stick to the equal opportunity and fair taxes theme. It sounds to me like education is not the main issue down here. Just a hunch."

"You really think so?" I asked.

"My assessment, but who knows. We may miss it completely. If this place is more conservative than up north, then you want to play to the issues that affect all people and work and fairness are the ones that will engage most people. What time are we on?"

"8 pm."

"My that's awfully late. Any reason this was set up this way?"

"We just couldn't make it across the state any sooner. Besides, this is going through Judy Bream, our PR person and John Gallagher, the union president."

"When can I meet them?"

"When we get back home, possibly tomorrow."

"I want to make sure that what they are setting in motion is realistic. Logistics on any mission is more important than the mission itself. If we error in the planning, the mission is almost doomed to failure."

"Hope you can resolve it. These long days will soon catch up with all of us."

"Go and get some sleep in the back, Leo, if you're tired. I can drive without someone in the back seat giving directions," Al half joked with me.

"I'm good to go, Al, but thanks. I think we might want to spell you on the way home."

"We might just camp out tonight depending upon what time we finish this gig," Al responded. "You already know that, Leo."

"Yah, I do, but was just hoping. Before we get to Cincinnati I'm going to call home."

"You do that. Give Basha my love."

I dialed our number. This was my first call from out on the campaign trail. When she answered, I felt a little homesick. We chatted for a few minutes and then she said that someone else wanted to say hello. Janko got on the phone, told me about his day at school and what he did when he got home. He said he did the dishes for his mother without even being asked and that he was going to make sure that mom was okay while I was gone. I thanked him for being the man in the house for me. He got off and Basha and I said our goodbyes. I felt a lump in my stomach. How long had it been since I was away from my family for even one night? I could not remember.

"Everything okay at home?" Al asked breaking my reverie.

"Just fine. The little guy is taking his role seriously. He told me he's looking after his mother since I'm not there to do my job."

"I like that kid," Al said. "He's got his priorities."

"Who is our contact person in Cincinnati and where are we heading?" Gram asked focusing on the business at hand.

I got out my phone and looked through my log. "A guy named Seth Rogan is the contact and we're going to be meeting at the unemployment office on the south side of town just off I-71 before you cross over into Kentucky."

"Office will be closed for business, I'm sure. Hope these guys got permits to use the space."

"Never thought of that but hopefully, John and this Seth discussed the issue when the event date and time were set."

"We shall see," Gram said ambivalently. He did not say any more.

Quietly, I pondered the issue. Being the trusting kind of person I was, it never crossed my mind to ask these kinds of questions. Having Gram aboard, I surely could see his value. He was a critical thinker, a skeptic, not cynical but curious about the logistics of everything. He would be a real asset as the campaign expanded beyond the local venues in the Buckeye State.

Ahead of us, we could see the outskirts of the city looming into view. Where we were once riding through rural Ohio in the semi-darkness, the dull orange glow of myriad lights now filled the sky. We plunged into the northern suburbs and immediately were immersed in heavy traffic. Al was totally focused on the task at hand. His sandwich sat unfinished on the console. Both hands gripped the wheel intensely.

As we plunged further into the evening traffic toward the center of the city, I noticed more and more cars and trucks flicking their lights on and off at us as they drove past. At first, I didn't get the gist of what was happening. Then, I finally caught on.

"Hey, are you guys getting the lights flashing on and off?" I asked.

"Sure, I've been watching it for the past ten minutes. You must be asleep back there," Al, chided me.

"Looks like a firefly garden," Gram offered. "Kind of neat. They are acknowledging that you are coming and they are lighting the way."

"You think that's what is going on?" I asked.

"I believe so, Leo. What else can it be? We haven't seen a state copper since we hit the main lights."

"Amazing. Just amazing!"

"Hey, buddy, we are advertizing who we are. Remember that we're in this RV with your name plastered all over the outside. The only thing we don't have is a flickering neon light with your name shining in one of the windows."

"Now that might not be a bad idea," Gram cracked. "We would be visible 24/7. Put the web site on a screen flashing across the bottom so people would know where to go to donate. I can see a million possibilities."

"Gram, you are one wild and crazy dude," Al said. "We are blessed to have you on the team."

"The feeling is mutual," Gram replied. "You drive this buggy like it's a compact car. I feel very safe riding with you. I just hope I never have to drive it."

"You flew big birds in the Air Force but you're afraid to drive an RV out on the highway? You're an enigma, Gram," I added to the conversation.

"Flying a plane at 30,000 feet above the earth using radar and all kinds of sophisticated navigation equipment is a whole lot safer than driving an RV on I-71 in Cincinnati Ohio at 7 pm in the evening. Trust me. I felt quite different behind the sticks at altitude than I do staring out into this sea of imbecile drivers weaving and bobbing back and forth across four lanes of traffic as if this were some sort of bumper car track."

We watched as the cars careened here and there in front of us. Gram did have a point, but we had no choice. This was all that we knew. Our perspective was simply earthbound. I wondered what it would be like to fly at that altitude through the clouds relying only on instruments. Then it donned on me. This campaign was just like that. We did not know where we were truly heading. We were flying blindly using only our instruments: the human mind, body and spirit.

"We're getting off at the next to the last exit before the Ohio-Kentucky Bridge," Al said. "I know this one because it is right near the ballpark. Believe it or not, I once saw a game here back when Rose and the boys were winning lots of ball games."

"Too bad Rose couldn't control him. What a fool he was. He blew an entire career betting on his own team," Gram stated emphatically.

"Gambling was his addiction. He paid a severe price for it. Prison time and still not elected into the hall of fame," Al said.

"Hall of Shame," Gram replied. "We'll never know how many of those guys in Cooperstown were gamblers, drunks, dopers and who knows what else. We make too much of sports. Sports are the pabulum the media feeds us adults to keep us well fed and happy. As long as the NFL, NBA, MLB and NHL are functioning, the adults will be quiet and satisfied with their lot in life. Look what is happening right now with the NFL lockout. People are already getting depressed about this upcoming season. Will we have it or won't we. Who really cares? If the entire NFL season just went away, Americans would adapt. In fact, we might even get outside and play football ourselves. Who wants to watch a bunch of testosterone filled guys bang into each other repeatedly, get into stupid fights, complain about bad referee calls and in the end make a pile of money for playing a game? I could care less if they ever played another game in my lifetime," Gram concluded.

"My, I guess you're just a little concerned about the overemphasis of sports in this country," Al chided. "Didn't know it meant that much to you."

"Al, if we kept things in perspective, I might enjoy it a bit. Look at the lunacy of it all. People spend $100 on a team jacket that doesn't keep them warm and that goes toward paying someone's salary that adds up to more in one weekend than some people will make in their entire lifetime. What the hell! Favre was making a million bucks a game last season with the Vikings. At the same time, Minnesota was cutting its budget for education and other social services. No, I don't give a damn about sports because, like I said, its adult pabulum and I ate enough of it when I was a kid to last me a lifetime."

"What do we do to end this overemphasis on sports and sports programming?" I asked. "I don't disagree with you, Gram, but what do we do?"

"I don't know. I wish I had a simple answer like just pulling the plug and going for a hike. I don't know. For me, I just don't watch TV. That's the end of it but I know that many people would probably crack up if they didn't have their television set on most of the time. We're conditioned to being entertained."

"You've said a mouthful, "Al commented. "But now I know that as long as we're in the Leo-mobile, we won't have to fight for the remote with you." He laughed contagiously and we joined in.

"You mean there is a TV in this RV?" Gram asked.

"Wide Screen. Back of that panel behind you. Good reception, too, when I remotely raise the digital antenna. Now what do you think about those crackers, Gram?"

"I'm traveling with Chevy Chase and company. Time warp. National Lampoon's Vacation. Yikes," Gram chortled. "Let me get outa here."

We started laughing so hard that we nearly missed our exit. Al whizzed over two lanes, pissing off quite a few drivers, and down off the highway we skidded to a stop at the bottom.

"Now that was some wheeling," I commented, releasing the death grip that I had on the armrests of my seat.

"Sorry, fellows, but I got a little distracted back there with all the goofing around," Al apologized.

"Don't let it happen again, or we might not let you drive this RV on our next outing," Gram piped up.

"Ah, now that would be downright mean and nasty," Al retorted. "I said it won't happen again."

He took over and headed down two blocks to a major intersection. "The office should be three blocks west of here." He turned right and we looked ahead. Sure enough. In front of us there was a three-story building with a huge parking lot next to it. We could see traffic, people, news teams, and police everywhere. This was going to be one heck of an evening's entertainment in the Queen City.

"My God, will you look at the crowd," Al cried out as he slowly weaved his way through the traffic and pulled to a stop where a police officer was directing traffic. "Get this. Curb service from our boys in blue."

"Don't get too excited," Gram replied. "Look at how many boys in blue are gathered around the place. Something tells me we are in for some trouble."

We got out and immediately were approached by a police officer, a Sergeant Mike Kowalsky.

"Who's Leo Pollack?"

I stepped forward and identified myself.

"I'm going to have to arrest you for illegally hosting a public event in the city of Cincinnati without having a public gathering permit. We were notified just this evening about this event and are here to enforce the law." He gritted at me the entire time he was making me aware of the violations.

Almost immediately, a guy who looked official and harried stepped forward and said, "Hi everyone, I'm Seth Rogon, and I can explain all of this."

"Hi Seth, I'm Leo Pollack. This officer says we're illegally hosting a public event. What is going on?"

"I already told you what is going on, buddy," the Sergeant stated. "You don't have a permit to host a public gathering here in this city."

"Officer, that is not exactly true. We do not have a permit to host a public event in this city if we had broadcast the event as a public gathering and let people know the time and place when such an event was going to take place. An impromptu event can happen anytime, anywhere and that's just what is happening here."

I watched the officer's face and I could tell he was not buying it.

"Look, Mr. Rogon, who are you and what makes you think that I am slow enough to believe that this is not a planned, organized and hosted event?"

"Officer, I am not implying that you are slow or that we are trying to dodge the law, but that is the truth."

"Truth or not, Pollack, you're breaking the law. You're under arrest. You're going to have to come with me." He stepped forward ready to put his hands on me when Gram spoke up.

"Officer, my name is Graham Tashjan and I'm Mr. Pollack's attorney. Can you please point out to me what city statute my client, Mr. Pollack, is violating so I can interpret whether or not my client, Mr. Pollack, candidate for president of the United States, is actually doing anything wrong."

I looked at Gram. He looked at me. Al and I looked at each other and then back at Gram. We did not utter a word.

"What do you mean, the statute? I'm telling you he's in violation of the law."

"Show me," Gram said emphatically. "Otherwise, I may pursue filing charges for false arrest if in fact you cannot show me the statute."

"I don't have it with me," Kowalsky said.

"Then I'd suggest you go and get it. In the mean time, you are violating my client's, Mr. Pollack's, civil liberties by stopping him from meeting with some of his friends here in the great Queen City of Cincinnati. I'm sure that you would not want this type of harassment reported to all the media gathered over there who are eager to meet Mr. Pollack, candidate for president of the United States and a guest of Mr. Rogon's here in this city."

Kowalsky started to back down. You could see the fight going out of him.

"Sergeant Kowalsky, as an officer of the law just like yourself, I too would not permit anyone to knowingly and willfully break the law, but as I said before, unless I can read the city ordnance and interpret it for my client, you do not have the right nor the authority to restrict my client, Mr. Leo Pollack, candidate for president of the United States, from meeting with some of his friends in this fair city. Am I making myself perfectly clear?" Gram concluded.

"I'm going to check with downtown. We're not finished with this issue just yet, you hear?" Kowalsky said in a threatening manner.

"I did not think that we were, but you go ahead and check with 'downtown' and we'll just go and visit with our friends. When you get confirmation that what I am saying is valid you and I will quietly conclude this matter. In the mean time, my client, Mr. Leo Pollack, and his friend, Seth Rogon and others are going to get a chance to say hello to one another without being harassed."

To us, Gram said, "I'll join you fellows shortly. Al, would you mind making sure that the vehicle is parked legally and there isn't anything we are doing that might be a violation of 'city ordinances' so that we do not wear out our welcome in the Queen City?"

"No problem, Gram, will do." Al hustled off to secure the RV.

Seth and I quickly left Gram and the Sergeant and moved over to where the press was gathered. Immediately the press corps wanted to know what was going on between us and the police.

"My dear friends," Seth said raising his hands in an assuring way to keep them from being concerned about the intervention of a moment ago. "Cincinnati's finest men in blue were just making sure that Mr. Pollack, candidate for president of the United States, was welcomed by safety forces and that he did not fear coming out this late at night into a crowd of people he did not know."

I listened to Seth's comments and wondered where he got this line of BS.

They asked him a few questions and he answered them. I kept my mouth shut but smiled the entire time. My turn would come. I was sure of that, but I did not want to overplay my hand just yet. Out of the corner of my eye, I could see Gram discussing with Kowalsky what needed to be done. I was hoping that he was not going to get himself arrested.

Was he an attorney? This fact just zapped me between the ears. He lapsed so easily into the role that I did not even consider that he might be making it all up. Would he be that brazen? Would he actually lie to the cops in a large city like this hoping that his credentials would not be checked? Or was it just a case of his feeling compelled to playact being an attorney today to help out his fellow man; namely me.

"Leo, it's about time. I'm sorry that happened. There was a screw up with the permitting process. We didn't get it in on time, but we were assured by the precinct chairperson that we could use the parking lot without any concern because we were not charging any money and we were not broadcasting that a public meeting was being held."

"How did all these people know that I was coming tonight at this time to this place?"

"I'm sure you have heard of twitter, flash mobs, and those kinds of things. Well, that's the essence of tonight. We're using all the media to make things happen. Kind of spontaneous stuff, but highly effective and much cheaper than paying the radio stations to make announcements that most people never hear."

"Amazing" was all that I could say.

"Let's get to the mics so we can start. I'd rather get this thing going before any trouble happens. How about you?"

"You mean like my getting arrested for not having permits to congregate?"

"Something like that," Seth said, hustling me over to the people who were helping him set things up.

I stood aside and watched the people. What would I say tonight? I did not want to incite anyone to riot but this whole affair was starting to get under my skin. Being arrested was the last thing I thought about as we were driving down to this city. What was going on? How did the police figure this all out and who gave the word to arrest me? Were these some more types of dirty tricks that Gram mentioned? Was I really that naïve?

Seth called me over and asked, "Are you ready?"

"Yes, let'er rip, my friend."

Seth took the microphone, and without any fanfare, said, "Friends of labor and working people everywhere and especially those who live in the Queen City, we are privileged to have one of our friends back in town tonight and he wants to share a few words with all of us as he embarks on the journey of a lifetime seeking the presidency of the United States. My friends, our friend and the next president of the United States, Leo Pollack."

A loud and raucous shouting erupted as I took the stage, accepted the microphone from Seth and stood before the people. I let the noise continue for a few minutes feeling the energy pouring out from them and into me, and trying to capture the moment in my heart and soul and let it inspire me.

I began.

"My friends, thank you for such a fine welcome to the Queen City. I'm Leo Pollack, you already know, and yes, it is true, my friends, I'm running for president of the United States and I want your vote."

"When America works, Freedom Lives and Democracy Thrives."

"Right now, Americans are not working up to their capacity. More than fifteen million of our friends are unemployed. Look around you. How many of you are in this predicament. Raise your hands."

The majority of people in the crowd raised a hand.

"Like me, you men and women are facing an uncertain future. We are being paid to not work because some company has decided to eliminate our jobs or cut back because the economy is in such bad shape that people are not buying the products we make. Or, what is even worse, our companies are moving our jobs off shore because they do not want to pay a living wage to their neighbors and friends."

"Let me ask this rhetorical question. Do the captains of industry, those big decision makers who move factories to other countries, care how the workers who are displaced by such a decision are going to make a decent living and actually buy the very same products they used to make? I don't get it. How much profit is enough? How much money can anyone actually spend in his or her lifetime?"

"You've all heard of the republican, Mitt Romney, who is trying to be that party's candidate. He made his money buying and selling companies. Yes, he would buy a company and make it better and then sell it and make a profit. It didn't matter to him, if, in the process of doing the buying and selling, people lost their jobs and as a result, lost their homes, their cars, their sense of security and their hope for the future."

"No, what mattered most to him and many other business people like him is the bottom line. Some estimate that he is worth $250 million. Now that is quite a nest egg. He owns four homes. Rumor has it that he is tearing down his San Diego home that is some 4,000 square feet in size and building a 12,000 square foot new one. He told the press that the old home just did not meet his needs. What kinds of needs does he have? He doesn't have any kids at home anymore."

"Greed is not a virtue. I'm sorry folks, Ayn Rand and all her true believers got it very wrong. It is because we live in a civilized society that we must look out for one another. Wait, did I say that correctly? Did I actually espouse what some might call the Golden Rule: Do unto others, as you would have them do unto you? Is this not what we claim to be as a Christian nation? 'Under God'? Did not Jesus speak to this repeatedly. Feed the hungry. Clothe the naked. Care for the sick. Yes, I believe he did but what are we doing?"

"Let's just look at one issue that affects all of us. Eventually, no matter if you are rich or poor, you and I are going to get sick and need health care. This is not a privilege, or a right, but a human need. We have a new health care program. The republicans call it Obamacare. The Democrats call it health care. I call it not enough and too expensive. We did not go far enough. We stopped short of insuring all people regardless of their current health, their financial status, their employment history, their race, creed, color or sexual orientation. We were cowards. We were fearful of being called socialists. My friends, we are a socialized network of people, families, villages, town, cities, states, and a nation. We are a social body with a stake in being safe, secure and happy. Being healthy is a major part of achieving this goal. Everyone needs to be insured and we all need to share in caring for our fellow man, woman and child."

The crowd erupted into loud applause and some chanting. I let it rumble through the night air.

"Ever since hospitals were permitted to become for profit entities under Richard Nixon, we have seen the cost of health care skyrocket out of control. Again, I ask the question, how much is enough? Some of the CEOs for these health care conglomerates are making in excess of eight figures. Yes, that's more than $10 million a year. There have to be many people paying premiums to those companies to justify those kinds of salaries. How do they do it? By denying services, that's how! All those stories by John Grisham, the lawyer turned novelist, about the way insurance companies do business are based on facts, not fiction. He is telling us the truth. We just don't always get it."

"Being unemployed is the worst feeling in the world. Yes, for a few minutes, the money rolls in and we think, 'How cool is this?' We aren't working and we are being paid to stay at home with the wife and kids. The feeling lasts for only a moment because, deep down inside, we really don't want to be at home and doing nothing productive. We want to be working, earning our living, being productive and making a difference in the world."

"The republicans don't get it. Obama doesn't get it. We, the people get it. The lack of fairness, the lack of opportunity, the lack of justice is not a condition that we created but one that was dumped on us by those who would rather have us be slaves than proud working people. This entire "Right to Work" movement is a sham, a lie and a crime. It does not mean that we have any more rights. It means we have no rights. These republicans have mastered the new double-speak. The Clean Air Act that weakens the EPA's ability to enforce clean air laws. The Healthy Forests Initiative that gave the National Forest permission to log our forests with abandon selling trees to private companies so they could make a lot of money from our federal resources. This Right to Work initiative, which means an employer can fire you any time he wants because you are not protected by a union, erodes any protection a worker ever had. The phrase sounds good like it is protecting workers. In fact, it is making the work place less secure for workers and more secure for employers. You are at the mercy of the company. Good luck with that."

"I am Leo Pollack, an unemployed steel worker, and your candidate for president of the United States. I want your vote. I need your support. I want to lead this country back to a place and time where work is honored, family life is protected, industries thrive because companies are not moving our productive capacity overseas and our government is not a flunky of wealthy corporations that can buy and sell senators, congressmen and yes, even presidents."

"Citizens United created a tornado of money being blown into 2012 campaigns. We have only begun to see and hear how this Supreme Court decision has made it possible for millionaires and billionaires to buy and sell elections. I know in my heart of hearts that we working people are either going to have to band together and fight this plague we are facing or we will be consumed by it and devoured by the ravenous appetite of corporations that want to control everything: our minds, bodies and spirits."

"We, the people, not the government, not corporations, not the churches nor any other organizations, must work together and make a difference, push back against this virulent assault on working people and stop the march toward wage slavery that is killing this country."

"I am standing in front of you now, but I want to really stand beside you, and all of us march forward into a future where we all share in the dream that once was our hope: to live in a better world than our parents did and to leave a better one for our children and grandchildren."

"Stand up and be counted. Stand up and be a part of the solution and not the problem. Stand up with me and let the corporations and the politicians they have in their pockets know that a new day is dawning. Stand up and raise your voice in protest and let leaders know that it is their privilege to serve and they are not special but work for us. Stand up and let those who rape our land know that we are not going to let them continue to kill our Mother, earth. Stand up and be a voice for change. Stand up and be part of a movement of working men and women who, when collectively speaking can tell congress that the time for playing games is over and we mean business when we say we've had enough of this dishonesty, duplicity, despondency and deadlock. We want action and we are going to vote out those who are not serving us, with integrity."

"I am Leo Pollack and I ask for your support and I pledge to you to speak for you because I am one of you. I am a blue-collar guy and proud of it. Thank you for being here tonight, and thank the police officers standing anywhere near you for letting all of us 'friends' gather here and chat for a little while."

Though I was drained, I flowed into the crowd to meet as many 'friends' as I could before all my energy was gone. Time stood still. The cares of the day were flooded by the emotion of people embracing the possibility of something new. I resurrected in them faith, hope and a bit of charity.

When Al and Gram started tugging me toward the Leo-mobile and back to reality, I finally let myself go. Slumping down into the back seat, I was finished. Al started the RV and slowly eased out of the traffic jam that was this memorable night in the Queen City. I did not say a word until we were moving along without starting and stopping so that my conversation would not distract Al from his task.

"We're on our way home?" I asked.

"Yes, we are and a welcome time this will be," Al replied. "We made a splash in this town, Leo. Trust me. You should have been on the sidelines listening to your speech, hearing, and feeling the reaction to your words by those standing near me. How cool! The world looks a lot brighter tonight for them because you were here and touched their hearts."

"What an amazing day!" Gram continued the thought process. "I had to detain the police but I caught almost every word and the people were tuned in like nothing I've ever seen. I enjoyed every minute of this day. Leo, Al, thanks for letting me come along for the ride."

"Speaking of coming along, how did you finally resolve the problems with the police? I can't thank you enough for stepping up and feigning a law degree to dispel their charges. But, by the by, are you really a lawyer?"

Gram laughed and said, "I don't lie, Leo. I am a lawyer. I went to law school if that's what being a lawyer means. I don't practice the law because I can't stand the hypocrisy of it. I do have a law degree but I do not have a license permitting me to practice law in front of the courts. So, technically, I am a lawyer, but I am not a licensed lawyer who can stand for you in a court of law."

"What else do we need to know about you?"

"I once played Santa Claus in a class play in high school."

"And what else? Seriously," Al asked.

"I did not play basketball in the NBA because I turned down the contract with the New Jersey Nets because they would not honor my request to let me not play on Saturdays, Sundays and holidays. I told them I was willing to forego 30% of my salary but they would not agree to my demands."

"Yah, Yah, we hear all that. You're being a mystery man, now, Gram," Al said.

"Okay, I can't think of anything else. Right now, that is. I'm not trying to be a mystery man. I just never mentioned the fact that I had a law education because there was no need to do so. When the cops got contrary, it was time to open my mouth and put my education to work."

"We sure were glad to hear you put that sergeant in his place," Al said. "He was tongue tied after you got done brow beating him. What a show!"

"All I did was give him a little dose of the law. He was way out of line. I knew he didn't have a warrant to arrest you. He was sent there to harass you and nothing else. In fact, he might have decided to do it of his own volition. He struck me as being a little right of right."

"So how did it end?" I asked.

"He couldn't produce the ordinance. He didn't have a warrant signed by a judge. He didn't have a leg to stand on. When he finally acquiesced, he and I talked baseball. He was happy to share all that he knew about the Redskins. I listened but didn't hear much."

"Redlegs, not redskins," Al corrected.

"Like I said, I really don't like baseball. Who are the Redskins?" Gram asked.

"The Washington Redskins, D.C.'s NFL football team," Al added.

"Oh, I didn't realize they had a team. Are they any good?"

"Not much but the D.C. crowd loves them," Al replied.

"Okay. Facts filed away."

"What do you guys want to do?" I asked the team.

"Anything anyone wants to do. Just don't ask me to drive," Gram offered.

"I'd like to head on home," Al added. "I like sleeping in my own bed."

"So consensus is to head all the way back to Y-town? All those in favor say Aye."

"Aye," all three of us voted.

"Unanimous. Let's get going."

"Hammer down, north bound, see you on the rebound," Al barked and the RV lugged forward.

We headed north in the deep darkness toward home, loved ones and a place where protests and loud noises were just something a person dreamed about on a restless spring night, happy to be alive, surrounded by loving friends and living in a land where anything is possible.

15. Assembling a Grassroots Campaign

Awakening to the ringing of the phone made me painfully aware of just how much work was ahead of us. John Gallagher wanted another meeting as soon as we could assemble the team. I agreed to 11 am and told him about Graham Tashjan. He was excited to meet this new "Chief of Staff". I hung up. A moment later, the ringing chirped again and this time it was Cleveland's "Morning Show" with an offer to appear on the program the next day. I replied I would love to be on the show, but I would have to get back to the producer after I checked the schedule. Before I could shave, the phone was calling me again and I discovered that the Vindicator was writing an editorial and needed some facts about the campaign, my current work status and a number of other bits and pieces of information. I put my shaver down, took notes, and said I would call them back by 10 am. The editorial writer encouraged me to return his call with all the information needed as soon as possible. I thanked him for his interest, his support, and promised I would do what he was asking. I closed the bathroom door and hid the phone under a towel so I would not have to listen to it while I sat on the throne. "Some time must remain sacred," I told myself. I could hear it ringing even under the protective cover of a thick, white Cannon bath towel. This was a message from Seth Rogon concerning the police and some leftover issues regarding their wanting to fine the union for violating the city ordinance. Gram could handle this one. I exited the bathroom, slipped down the stairs to the kitchen, and found that Gram had already made coffee and was sitting in the living room reading.

"Hi Ho," I called. "Thanks for making coffee. Basha will appreciate the effort."

"No sweat. I am an early riser but not necessarily an early eater. Drink first. Maybe eat."

"First things first. Thanks for all you did yesterday."

"You're welcome."

"Now, with that said, Seth Rogon from the Cincinnati gig yesterday needs your help. He called and said the city still wants to fine us. Would you mind giving him a call and see what you can do to cover this?"

"Got it. I'll give him a ring after 9 am. What else do we have going on?"

"Meeting at 11 at the union hall to organize things. This is going to be a busy day."

"Leo, this is going to be a busy year. Get used to it."

"I am, Gram. Oh, how quickly these past few weeks have gone."

Basha got up and we drank coffee together, made small talk, got Janko out of bed and ready for school. I walked him down the block, kissed him goodbye and returned home. Along the way, the phone rang three more times. I was starting to think I needed a secretary. "Wait a minute," I thought. "I have a chief of staff. I should be letting him take all these calls." I made a note to talk to Gram about the possibilities.

When I got back to the house, I sat down on the porch steps and stared off into space. The sulfur scent usually assaulting my nostrils was gone. The mill was not in full production. Millwrights were maintaining it for the time being, but the plant was shut down and there was no plan to open it again.

The mottled clouds floated across the morning skies leaving me with a sense of wonder. How did clouds form, store billions of gallons of water, and not fall to the earth because they were so heavy? Somehow, just this one mystery, was more important than solving some of the nation's other pressing problems. Climate change was a political hot potato. The republicans were rejecting the science. Obama was not rejecting it but was not adequately addressing it via the EPA and other governmental agencies. Overall, we were at a standstill.

Now where did I fit into this scheme? Staring at those clouds, I knew humans were affecting the world. Since I was a little kid, the weather patterns were changing dramatically. We were getting more rain and less snow. Winters were warmer than in the past. Radical weather was the norm and not the aberration. Yes, we were affecting the earth's atmosphere and needed to do something about it. What to do was the issue. We could not move from a fossil fuel based economy in one generation, but we could head in that direction by promoting alternative energy resources. The oil, gas and coal lobbies would buck and kick all the way to the bank as we moved away from them as primary sources of energy. We needed to move. This was a simple fact. The complexity was in the fine details. How did we move away from coal as the primary fuel for our power plants? What other fuel would we move toward as we shifted to more renewable resources? Nuclear power was a consideration but after the tsunami in Japan and the meltdown of the Fukajima Power Plant, worldwide concerns were high. Westinghouse's new AP 1000 nuclear reactor featuring modular design construction eliminated one of the problems with these types of energy sources. By making the plants the same, costs could be reduced, planning simplified and security enhanced.

The issue of where to dump the waste still was being batted back and forth across the country. Yucca Mountain in Nevada was still being considered, but the Nevadans were not too keen on the idea even though it would be a boon to their economy. Yes, the mottled clouds were symbolic of the murkiness of just this one issue facing America and I knew that this one would be a major issue I would need to be more prepared to address. I did not want to go inside but a chill spread across my body and I realized that I was sitting outside in just a long sleeved shirt and no jacket. I headed inside and found Gram still reading and Basha preparing a light breakfast for us. I sat down at the kitchen table and watched her elegant movement as she continued her labor of love.

"You were up awfully early even though you got in awfully late. Couldn't sleep?"

"I just woke up wide awake. I didn't need to rest anymore."

"Janko was happy to have you walk with him. I could tell. He misses you when you are not here to tuck him in, read and pray with him."

"I miss it, too. What can I say?"

"Nothing. I know. This is not going to get any better."

"You're still supporting the effort, aren't you?

"Leo, I support you. I love you. I realize that this is something you have to do. I don't know what else to say. Would I rather not have you gone so much? Yes. Would I want you to stop doing what you need to do? No. I am betwixt and between the selfish desire to not share you with others and the patriotic will to have you make a difference in the world. So what do we do? I don't know. I take it one day at a time. This is the only way to live in this kind of controlled chaos."

"I don't want us to draw apart," I stated emphatically, got up and hugged her closely. She clung to me like a magnet.

"We are one," I said.

"One and only," she added.

We ate breakfast, egg tortillas, listening to "Morning Edition" on NPR and chatting quietly. I told her about all the calls I had this morning. She said, "It is time for you to have a secretary or someone to filter all this phone traffic."

"You want the job?"

Basha slapped the back of my head "Gibb's style" and said, "I have a son to raise, a house to care for and a husband to support who is running for the presidency of the United States. I think I might need a secretary myself."

Once we were finished, I went in to talk with Gram.

"Sleep well," I asked.

"Like a baby. Thanks for letting me move in like a relative. I didn't really expect this kind of treatment."

"The room was available. Besides, we are not going to be living here very much. Al called today and said he needed to get the RV ready for long-term road trips. I agreed with him."

"Will there be room enough for three?"

"He says it will sleep six. I imagine it will be very tight."

"You're not considering motels at all?"

"Oh, of course, but this method of travel is convenient and extremely mobile and efficient."

"How are finances?" Gram asked.

"You know, that is what amazes me. We are in excellent condition. I can't recall what the exact amount is, but it is in excess of $10,000. Maybe it is much more than that. We got credit cards. We'll get you one. I'm excited that we are not going to be in debt for any of this campaigning."

"Not until you start trying to buy TV, radio and other campaign ads. This is what will cost big bucks."

"Perhaps we can continue to get as much free press as we can. Cleveland Today called and wants me to appear on their show tomorrow. I said yes."

"Good move. That's the best kind of exposure. Many women watch those kinds of shows. Women talk and spread the word. 'Hey, did you see that Leo Pollack this morning? He's an unemployed steel worker and he's running for president. Yah. What do you make of that? I think it's great. About time one of our own is running for office.' That's the way it goes and we get maximum exposure."

"We'll have to do some warm-up exercises before the show tomorrow," I said.

"Yes, we can do that. It will be fun."

"Please call Seth Rogon and let me know how it goes."

"Will do."

"We'll leave for the Union Hall at 10:30 am."

"I'll be ready."

"What are you reading?"

"A book called 'See You Down the Trail'."

"What's it about?"

"One man's thru-hike on the Appalachian Trail."

"Are you a hiker?"

"I fancy myself to be, but nothing like a thru-hiker."

"How many miles is the AT?"

"Last year the official mileage was 2181 miles."

"That sure is a long way to hike."

"You can say that again. I admire people who take the long way home."

"There was a song by that title."

"I remember, but can't for the life of me recall who sang it."

"Super Tramp. It was the final song on their fourth album in 1979 called 'Breakfast in America'. It reached tenth on the hit charts that year."

"How do you remember such trivia?" Gram asked.

"I don't know. I don't even like music that much, but I do like that song."

"Strange isn't it how we remember some things and can't remember others and there is no rhyme nor reason to it."

"I agree. I'll get back with you shortly. Right now, I have to call the Vindicator. They had some requests for information for some editorials they are writing."

"When do you want me to start filtering your calls?" Gram asked.

"I thought you'd never ask. Anytime you're ready, but perhaps we need to figure out the logistics of how, when and who gets what?"

"I agree. Let's do it after the meetings today. We can keep it as simple and efficient as possible."

"I'm off to call the Vindicator. How long does it take to thru-hike the AT?"

"Depends on the hiker. Most take six months to do it. Some have done it in as little as three months."

"Someday I'd like to do that. Six months of nothing to do but hike every day. Wow! I could dig that," I exclaimed as I left the room, went back outside, but this time with a jacket and hat on, called the Vindicator and spent 20 minutes on the phone answering questions posed by the editorial staff. They were curious about the way we were organizing our efforts to raise money. I gave them Carol Hawley's name and number and said contact her directly. I told them she was handling all of our finances. I encouraged them to check out our on-line donation information with a full access to the database so anyone could see who was supporting our campaign. They were not aware that they had this kind of access. We ended our conversation with an agreement to talk at least once a week as the campaign continued to expand.

When I came back in, Gram was making notes on a clipboard and talking on his cell phone. From what I could eavesdrop, he and Seth Rogon were strategizing on how best to deal with the city fathers in the Queen City. I left him alone and went in to get another cup of coffee. Basha was upstairs doing some housework. I sat at the kitchen table and drank alone. How peaceful it was. No phones ringing. No people asking me questions. No chaos and confusion. I could always stop now and protect this peace and quiet. I could, but I knew that I would not.

At ten fifteen, I found Gram just where I left him an hour earlier and said it was about time to get ready to head down to the hall. He relayed to me that Seth and he solved the Queen City dilemma.

"They wanted to cite us for the event. I said to him that they needed to send us a citation via the mail and then we could challenge it and request a hearing and this would extend the amount of time we would have to build a case for not having to pay the fine."

"How much is the fine?"

"I don't think you want to know."

"Gram, how much is the fine?"

"Ten thousand dollars."

"What? You've got to be kidding me?"

"I wish I were."

"This is crazy."

"They won't get it. I'll make them an offer they can't refuse."

I eyed him closely. He eyed me back. "Yes, we can beat this. Trust me, I'm a business man."

"You're mixing two movies together: the Godfather and Beverly Hills Cop."

"You know your movies, too. Great. We'll beat them."

"Let's go. We've got a lot of nuts and bolts to work on to keep this campaign going and this morning will be very important in achieving that result."

"Let me get my laptop and we can get out of here."

"I'm going to let Basha know that we're leaving."

We met at the front door, headed to the car, drove down to the Union Hall. Along the way, Gram asked me to relate to him the history of my home town and how I saw its de-evolution as the steel industry was slowly and irrevocably moved to places like China, Taiwan and other Pacific Rim countries.

When we entered the union hall parking lot, Gram said, "Thanks for sharing your history. It makes me understand you and your city more and how I might be better able to support you in this campaign."

"I'm sure we'll share a whole lot more with one another in the next year or so, if you stick around all that time."

"Count on it. I'm in this for the duration."

John Gallagher interrupted our conversation. "Hey, you must be Gram. Welcome to campaign headquarters. Make yourself at home. Coffee on the counter. Phones, copiers, anything you need. Just go for it."

"Thanks," Gram said, quizzically, "but you don't even know me."

John slapped him on the shoulder and continued. "If Leo hired you as his chief of staff that's all I need to know. He tells me you were Air Force Academy. We're honored to have you with us."

"I hope I earn my keep," Gram replied.

"Given what you pulled off down in Cincinnati, you already have."

"Leo didn't tell you the rest of the story. The city wants to fine us $10,000. I'm delaying their action with some motions. Hopefully we can settle later on with a no contest and no fine and perhaps some "community service" like having Leo come back to Cincinnati and do some speaking engagements there to bring in tourist money."

"Leo, I like this guy. I like the way you think, Gram. Whatever you think best. We have lawyers, too, if you need more firepower."

"I'll keep that in mind."

"So what's on tap for today?" I asked.

"Plenty. Come on over to the conference table and I'll fill you in. Before we do that, let me show you something."

We followed John into the back of the hall where we held meetings. As we passed through the office space, we could hear noises. Opening the door to the large room, we now knew why. Tables and chairs were set up. Phone lines were running everywhere. At least twenty people were sitting on card table chairs and talking on phones. My first impression was the union was running a large telemarketing business. The Union was. They were marketing me. Leo Pollack for President.

"Folks, look who's here," John said to the people working at the tables. When they looked up, someone shouted, "The Man is Here".

People started chanting my name and after a few choruses, I stopped them and said, "I just want to thank you from the bottom of my heart for your willingness to help in this real grassroots campaign. We are making history, my friends, and when this campaign ends and we, the people, are finally leading this country, we will make new American history. So thank you. Thank you one and all."

"Okay, folks. That's it. Now back to work." Everyone laughed and the chatter and focus went from me back to the phones and other projects people were focused on at their tables.

"Let's check out what's happening here," John said.

As we walked around the tables and I shook hands with the volunteers individually, John explained that the mission was to spread the campaign across the country based upon dividing the country into sections.

"We divided the country into sections based upon voting histories. New England, Mid-Atlantic, Southeast, Deep South, Mid-West, Northern Plains, Central Plains, Texas, Rocky Mountain States, Pacific Northwest, California, Hawaii and Alaska. We are contacting every labor organization, public employees union, volunteer organization, any group of people leaning forward and not connected with the Republicans and Democrats. We already have picked leaders in each state capital to make it easier to coordinate activities that relate to getting your name on the ballot. This is mission critical. Unless we can get you on the ballot in all 50 states, you can't win. We need to gather registered voter's names and get them listed with the state."

"Sounds pretty comprehensive to me. How are we doing so far?"

"We need to get the rules down first. This is the first task. Fifty states. Fifty different sets of rules to get on the presidential ballot. What a cluster! But hey, that's what we're good at: dealing with clusters, right? Anyway, we're doing Ohio first and foremost because we want to absolutely be on our home state ballot."

"I would hope so."

"Raising money is second. We are doing extraordinarily well right now. You know how much we've raised in the last 24 hours?"

"Hmm. I have no idea, but let me guess. $30,000?"

John snickered as if he got the last cookie out of the jar. "How about $165,700."

"NO WAY?"

"Yes, we are really starting to make a dent in the money raising ceiling. Leo, we're right now hovering close to $300,000 and you have spent only about $600.00 and we've spent about $5000 putting out a few radio and newspaper ads. We are running way under budget."

"This is beyond my comprehension. It just can't be. It's not possible."

"Then call this 'Mission Possible'."

"John, I can't thank you enough for all your hard work."

"Leo, the pleasure is mine. Quite frankly, there is a selfish reason for doing this. Unless we stop this relentless attack on working people, we won't be able to protect ourselves any longer and will become simply wage slaves and have absolutely no control over our lives. So, it's for all of us and not just you, Leo. However, we hope that when you are president, working people will finally have a voice speaking for the government. Period. This is our hope, our prayer, our charge."

"I hear you, my friend."

We walked around the room for the next hour or two seeing and hearing what each volunteer was doing to support the campaign and move our cause forward. I was astonished at how many people were working for me, to make it possible for my candidacy to actually take root and grow. Phone banks were being created. Politicians who were potential allies were being courted. Ads for television, radio, magazines and other media outlets were in production. At each stop, John introduced me to the volunteer, let each person explain what he or she was doing and asked me if I had any questions. The depth of the organization is what really amazed me. After all, we were only in existence for a very short time. John was like Santa Claus in his workshop with all his elves working feverishly.

"What do you think?" John asked as we stood in the back of the room watching the team perform.

"John, you're a magic man. How did you do all this? It's simply amazing!"

"Leo, you are the catalyst for all of this activity. You made the decision to stand up in the middle of the unemployment office and ask them to believe in you, support you in your bid to become the president of the United States. What I'm doing is small potatoes. Believe me. I could not do what you're doing. You're the man on the firing line. Now, I've got a few things to get done and I believe Judy wants a minute of your time."

"Okay. I'll go and see her now."

John skipped off to take care of some issues. I went and found Judy in a small cubby hole office talking on the telephone. I stood outside the door where she could see me. She held up one finger to indicate she would soon be finished. I watched the people at work while I waited and considered just how complicated it was to make a run for office and especially for one as grandiose as the presidency. The fact of the matter was I did not really know what it took to get on the ballot in one state let alone all 50 of them. John had the system working on the problem. I was encouraged and believed he would succeed in getting it done.

"Come on in, Leo," Judy said waking me from my infatuation with the beehive of activity.

"John said you wanted to see me about something."

"Yes. He told me today that you hired a chief of staff. His name is Gram? Where is he? I'd like to meet him."

"He's here somewhere. Guy a little older than me. Salt and pepper hair. Bright eyes. He showed up at my house the other day and said he wanted to work for me. He's a graduate of the Air Force Academy. He flew planes for twenty years. He's an avowed progressive and get this, a lawyer on top of all this."

"No way?"

"Yup. While we were in Cincinnati, he intervened when the police wanted to arrest me for illegally congregating in the parking lot of the unemployment office."

"I want to meet this man."

"Be right back." I exited and searched for Gram. He was talking with one of the volunteers who was making a database of donors and was showing her how to manipulate the software to create simple but useful reports.

"Gram, you got a minute?" I asked.

"You bet. Jamey and I were just doing a database. Hope that helps."

"Thanks Gram, it sure does," she said. "Leo, this guy is a keeper."

"You're building quite a fan club, Gram. I'm glad that you're finding so many applications for your wide range of talents."

"It's the reason I came east. I knew there would be a golden opportunity for me to show off for the girls," he said with a wolfish grin on his face.

"Well, I don't want to rain on your parade right now, but Judy Bream, the PR person, wants to meet you."

"Let's go," he said and followed me to Judy's office.

"Judy, this is Gram. Gram, Judy."

Introductions done, Judy asked, "So what are your goals? What do you think we need to do first? I'm here to serve in any capacity I can."

Gram looked at her, at me, and then said, "Judy, you and I both know that PR is about appearances. This is just the way it is. So, what we need to do right now, given that you asked and I'm sure that you understand the need to do so, we must vet Leo right now. Agreed?"

Judy looked at him, then at me and said, "I agree. Do you understand what Gram is referring to, Leo?"

"I really don't." I did not. "Vet me? You know who I am. You know where I live. What else do you need to know?"

"Leo, the campaign can die quickly if major parties start to realize that you really are a threat to them and they begin to dig into your past. What we need to know, what vetting means in the context of what we are asking you is simply this: what skeletons do you have in your closet?"

"Leo, the other day when you asked me about dirty tricks and other such things, well, we need to know what we are working with before something comes up that we can't account for because you have not told us. Hey, friend, this is as hard for me as it must be for you. I just met you a few days ago. Leo, I believe in you, what you're trying to do, and I don't want to see that undermined by some dirt that comes up months from now."

I looked at her. I stared at Gram. I thought about what they were asking me and realized that it was just as uncomfortable for them as it was for me to sit here and listen and then to divulge my deep, dark secrets. This was part of assembling a do it yourself campaign.

"Where do I begin? How far back do you want me to go?" I asked.

"Frankly, Gram, we won't know until you tell us what there is to know. Then we can say that is enough or is there more," Judy said clarifying what she was looking for and what I needed to do to avoid creating some dirt for dirty tricksters.

"I've got to think for a minute," I replied.

"We've got time. There is no rush," Judy said.

"You want a coffee?" Gram asked.

"I could use one. I'm kind of dry."

Gram got up and left the room. I think he felt about as uncomfortable as I did.

"Gram seems like a good guy," Judy said. "I'm glad that he came to us. You can tell he's got a sharp mind and wit."

"I agree. Everything about this campaign is good."

Gram came back with the coffee fixed just how I liked it.

"Thanks, Gram." I took a long swig and then started. "When I was a kid, I mean a teenager; I was arrested for breaking and entering. I was trying to steal guns from a house. I faced juvenile charges, was placed on probation for a year and did not get locked up."

"How old were you?" Judy asked for clarification.

"Thirteen or fourteen, I think."

"Okay. Thanks," she said.

"Anything else?" Gram asked.

I did not hesitate. "Six months later, I was arrested again for breaking into railroad cars. Railway police got me. The FBI was called in because there was an issue with interstate transportation of stolen goods. What I really did was break into a railway car and look inside it and as I was doing that, a guy with a gun came running down the pathway to the car and arrested me. Thieves were targeting the railroad and the primary targets were cars on sidings full of food. The one I broke into was stacked from floor to ceiling with cases of Campbell's Soup. I wasn't going to steal anything. I just wanted to see what was inside, but by the time I opened the door and had a peek, it was too late. I was busted."

"What was the disposition the second time you went to court?" Gram asked.

"I got probation for another full year and a stern warning from the judge that if he saw me one more time, he would lock me up for at least two years."

"What did you do?"

"Kept my nose clean. I didn't get arrested ever again."

"No arrests as an adult?"

"Nope. I did get two speeding tickets a few years ago. Recently, my record is clean."

"Any extra-marital affairs?" Gram asked bluntly.

"I knew you would ask that one. No, I'm clean in that department."

"Ever smoke dope, or get in trouble with drugs and alcohol including prescription drugs?" Judy asked.

"I smoked dope a few times when I was in school. Since then, I've been clean. Yes, I did inhale. I got a good buzz, thank you. Booze. Few times I've gotten sloppy drunk. No DUIs. Basha is my designated driver. I've never abused any prescription drugs. I haven't ever had a prescription other than penicillin and other antibiotics."

"Clean as a whistle, right?" Gram asked again.

"As clean as I can be right now," I reiterated. "No, getting high was not something I enjoyed doing. I'm high all the time just being alive. That's not my world."

"Cheat on your taxes?" Judy continued.

"Not that I'm aware of but I've always worked for someone. I pay the payroll tax. How could I cheat? Well, I guess I could but no, I never have."

"You have any money invested in the stock market, bonds, and futures?" Gram asked.

"No, never had enough liquid cash to buy anything more than food, clothing and take care of the shelter thingy."

"You father any children out of wedlock?" Judy asked.

"No. One child is my claim to fatherhood I'm proud to say."

"You ever stalked, harassed or chased a woman who did not want you around her?" Gram asked.

"Never. I respect women."

"Ever fantasize about little boys or girls, surf the web, watch or view kiddy porn?" Judy asked.

"Never. This is one of the areas that makes me squeamish. I just don't get that kind of thing."

"Have you ever hired a prostitute or gone to a whore house?" Gram asked.

"No. Never paid for sex. Too cheap."

"Do you gamble, have a gambling problem or been tapped out because you owed money to bookies or any other betting establishment?" Judy continued the intense inquiry.

"No. Again, I'm too cheap to spend money gambling. I mean it. There is no way that I'd risk losing my paycheck on a pony or some game. I don't even get into the football pool down at the mill."

"Is Jon your real son?" Gram asked.

"Yes. No doubt about that."

"Do you have any children that were put out for adoption?" Judy asked.

"No. Not at all."

"Ever take a bribe, bribe someone, or know that bribes were being made and you did not do anything about it? Gram asked.

"No. never."

"What, if anything else, do we need to know that might be information that could compromise you, this campaign, your family or anything related to this union and the people who are engaged in the Leo Pollack for President Campaign?" Judy asked.

"Folks, I have been totally honest. I can't think of anything that anyone can use to spread dirt on this campaign. That's it. I'm clean. I don't have skeletons in my closet and no, I am not gay. Not that it matters, but there are no skeletons like that in my closet."

Judy looked at Gram. He looked at her. "Can you think of anything else?" Judy asked. "No," Gram declared. Judy looked at me. I looked at her. We both looked at Gram. Everyone was silent for a moment.

"Okay," I said. "Now it's my turn. Judy, have your ever taken bribes, gambled beyond your capacity to pay back your bookies, smoked so much dope that your hair got curly or drank so much rot gut whiskey that, if any of these facts come out, we'd think you were a cool hippy chick?"

She gawked at me. Gram at her. Then we all burst into resounding laughter.

"Gotcha," I cried out. "Now what's next?"

"I've got to get up and move around," Gram said. "I feel like I just flew across the Atlantic in an open cockpit plane." He left the room.

"What do you think?" I asked Judy. "How are they going to come at us and how will they do it?"

"I don't know, Leo. This is a strange political year. There are so many republicans running right now we won't know which one we'll have to compete with during the general election. Obama is going to run again. Either side will be worried that you will siphon away votes, but I believe Obama will be more concerned because you will be way left of where he is hunkered down in the middle. So the attacks might come from both sides. We are not just upsetting the status quo. We are blowing it up. When Ross Perot ran as a third party candidate, he was right of the right and on top of that a billionaire and part of the power elite. We are truly running a grassroots campaign and we don't have much money, no superpacs lining up to help us and nothing more than the power of the people to carry us forward."

"Wow! That's a heap of reality to swallow."

"We'll be fine. Just make sure that, if anything surfaces that might be used as dirt against you, you let us know before it gets out so we can manage the damage. Okay?"

"Sure. Got it."

Gram came back smiling. "This operation is amazing. How many people are actually working in here day in and out?"

"Oh, I'd say more than thirty," Judy exclaimed proudly. "These are just the volunteers who are here today. We have just as many who are not here right now. We are mobilizing as fast as we can to keep this office running 24 hours a day."

"Are you kidding me? You mean around the clock? Seriously?"

"Yes, what makes that so surprising to you? Hey, we're steel workers, Leo. We don't stop working just because the sun sets. This is what will make the difference. We are true believers and we've got somebody who is very real to believe in, our candidate, Leo Pollack."

"I'm proud to be a part of this fine group of people," I responded. "Now, I've got to move. What else do you need from me, Judy?"'

"Nothing. You're off the hot seat now. Thanks for being so open and honest with me."

"And with me, too," Gram said. "I feel a whole lot closer to you now."

"So this is what it takes to assemble a campaign from the roots up? I must say, I never thought what I was doing when I got up on that countertop and declared I wanted to be the next president of the United States. Well, bring it on, my friends. What else can happen now? I just went to confession. Now, let's go commune with the people out there and make a difference."

We wandered around for another hour or two, sharing anecdotes, telling jokes, recalling days gone past on the job making steel, remembering old friends, hearing about kids, grandkids and other life and death issues. Before we knew it, the day drifted past us, twilight descended and I asked Gram if he'd had enough fun for one day.

"Do tell, I think I have had enough," Gram responded.

"Where's Al been all day?"

"I don't know but he's been in and out throughout the day."

We found Al in the parking lot working inside the RV. He was cleaning the bathroom. When we came inside, he was mumbling a string of expletives.

"Women, children and priests on board," Gram joked.

"Close your ears. We don't filter anything on this bus but the motor oil," Al barked.

"What's happening?"

"Plugged toilet and defective storage tank valve. I got it fixed now but if I smell like caca, then you know why. We can't go on the road again unless we can use the toilet and trust that it will flush and that we can empty the tanks when we are done."

"So it's fixed?" I asked.

"Like new. Boy, what a day. Now, let's get the heck out of here. I've got a hot date with the children's momma and I don't want to be late."

"You should have said something sooner, Al," I chastised him.

"We're done. But I need to leave this RV at your place. You've got to take me home and then you can park the Leo-mobile in front of your home. When we're going on the road, I'll drive over to your place and leave my car in front of the house."

"What's wrong with leaving it at your place? I don't mind."

"My wife minds. My neighbors mind. My kids mind. I get nothing but grief. Molly, that's my wife, Gram, gets a dozen calls a day from people thinking that Leo Pollack is living in my house. The kids get teased at school. The neighbors say they don't want the extra traffic coming up and down the road trying to get a 'peep' as they call it, of the presidential candidate. No, you got to take and keep it, Leo, or I'm going to lose my head and happy family along with it."

"Okay, brother, I got it. I'd like to get home early tonight, too. You know tomorrow we're on the road to Cleveland. Cleveland Today is having me on. We have to be there at 7 am. Can we do it?"

"Leo, we can do anything we put our minds to, so yes, we can."

"Let's roll."

"Ah, Leo, what about your car?" Gram asked.

"Duh! Thanks pal. Would you mind driving it home?"

"Nope. See you there."

"Do you remember the way?" I asked.

"Leo, I was a pilot. Navigation was my world. I could drive back to your house blindfolded. Really," he said sarcastically.

"Good. Then how about your driving the RV to Al's and dropping him off and I'll drive the car home?"

"I don't have a CDL license," Gram said defending his position.

"You don't need one," Al said.

"See you at home," Gram said, grabbed my keys, ran to the car, started it and drove off.

"I guess he didn't want to drive the RV," Al concluded.

We chatted about nothing in particular as we drove across town. Along the way, we got lots of honks, flashing lights, a few gestures and now and then a thumbs up. I made it without any problems.

"See, you don't need me to be your driver. You can wheel this rig right fine," Al said as we stopped in front of his split-level home on the east side of town. He lived in a neighborhood that was upscale thirty years ago, but had seen better days.

"No, Al, I need you because you and I are partners so don't get any funny ideas about quitting and leaving me in the lurch."

"Goodnight, and thanks again Al for being you."

"Ah shucks, Leo, I didn't know that you cared," Al guffawed. "See you at 6 am."

Before I could complain about the time, he ran off.

As I drove across town, the city lights flickered bravely illuminating the skyline and broadcasting to the world that there was hope again in this steel town where so many people's dreams were riding on the shoulders of one of its native sons.

16. Cleveland Today

Cleveland's skyline at daybreak impressed all of us as we rolled into the downtown area well before the major rush hour traffic started. We drove around until we found the parking lot for WKYC-TV, the local NBC affiliate that was producing the morning show that I was invited to attend. The Cleveland tower was diminished in the high rises that surrounded it. On the northern horizon, Lake Erie, the second smallest of the Great Lakes, spread off into the distance as far as the eye could see producing a flat, blue canvas to reflect the beauty of the morning.

"We made it without having to face any of the nasty traffic," Al said, pulling the RV off the freeway and on to a side street that led to the TV station. "We are early. What are we going to do?"

"Make some coffee and drink it," Gram said casually. "But first, Leo. What do you own that was made in America? This is the morning warm-up."

I thought for a moment. We were fully stopped and in the parking lot before I could respond accurately and honestly. "My car was made in America. My home. Some of the furniture in the house. Most of the food was produced in America. But you know, Gram that is about it. Sad to say, isn't it?"

"It is what it is," Gram replied. "Now how do we change this?"

"Like we discussed yesterday, if it isn't made in the United States, unless we absolutely need it, we will not buy the product. This will force us to buy American and promote jobs in our own country."

"Okay, we're on the war path now," Gram cried out. "One simple idea that makes us face our own reality. We can't blame others if we are the ones who are consuming mostly foreign made goods."

"But what will happen to those other countries when they realize we are not buying their goods? They will stop buying ours, won't they?" Al asked.

"I don't know. We haven't done this yet. It will take about three to six months to affect the markets but the Chinese, Japanese, Koreans, Indians, and Europeans will get the picture eventually. When they do, we'll see what happens."

"What if they do the same thing? What if they stop buying our goods?"

"We win," Gram said. "If we are producing our own goods and buying our own goods, what do we care what other countries do? We win. We make good on our promise to bring jobs back to America. I love it."

"I love it, too," Al said. "Maybe we can bring back our steel jobs from China and Japan."

"We will," I said to him. "We just have to get a handle on the tax code that promotes sending jobs overseas and rewards the companies that do it."

"If you get a chance to push that point, do it. We have to hammer home how these companies are the problem, not the solution."

"Got it. I realize we're in for a real fight so we might as well load both barrels and blast away," I said.

Al stopped the Leo-mobile and we got out and stretched our legs. The skies were clear, crisp and cool. This was a wonderful morning to be in Cleveland. This was a city that was slowly rising up again to become a healthy, vibrant community.

"You know fellows, I'm happy just to be alive today," I said to them as we watched the city come to life.

"Me too," Al seconded.

"Ditto that," Gram added.

"Now, we've got the opportunity to reach a million people today. I am amazed at how far we've come in just six weeks. There is something magical about how, with just a few ideas and a lot of guts, we moved so far, so fast."

"It's you, Leo," Al said. "You give us hope. This is what the movement is all about. You represent the future, the way things can be, not the way they are."

"I'd like to believe that," I said.

"Believe it. When I heard what you were proposing to do, I sold all my earthly goods that were not needed anymore, gave away the rest of my stuff, got on a plane and flew to your home. Here I am today. What does that tell you?"

"You're crazy?" I played with him.

"Right. As crazy as a lunatic who's on the grass," Gram said.

"Pink Floyd. You can't fool me," I laughed at him. "But really, Gram. Think about it. You come across the country having never met me and want to go to work for me. How crazy is that?"

"No crazier than a person who seeks employment with a company that he thinks is the one that he will enjoy working at for the majority of his life. Look, there is nothing crazy about making a decision to follow your bliss," Gram said.

"I'm glad that you decided to come along for this ride and so we're going to be the three musketeers until we decide that we need to go our own ways."

"Amen. I'm up for that," Al said.

"All for one and one for all," I exclaimed.

We high fived one another and then walked over to the entrance to the TV station.

WKYC-TV, Cleveland's NBC affiliate, was the only one to invite us to be on air.   Once inside, we asked for the morning show host. The receptionist politely asked us to have a seat and wait for a moment. I sat down and looked around station and it reminded me of when I was a little kid and went on the "Dusty Roads Show".

Dusty was a grizzled old fellow who hosted an afternoon movie program. He had guests on every day. One of his favorite things to do was to have a quick draw contest against a contestant from the audience. I hoped to get picked and challenge Dusty, but another kid won the draw and was "dusted" by the host. Now it was years later and the memory was still as vivid as if it were yesterday. What an amazing device the human memory is!

The receptionist came up to us and said, "Mr. Pollack, please come with me. We need to get you into the prep room pronto. I'll come back in a few minutes and take your friends to the off stage viewing booth, okay?"

We agreed. What else could we do?

I was led to a small room where a woman was waiting for me. Sitting down, she introduced herself as Maggie and said, "I will try to make this as painless as possible, Mr. Pollack, but we need to make you look good for the camera."

"Maggie, I've never been on camera before so whatever you do will be fine to me. Thank you for being so kind."

"Oh, my, this is my job. I don't mind," she said.

"Maggie, if you do your job with joy and enthusiasm then you're my kind of person."

"I feel privileged to meet you, Mr. Pollack."

"Please, call me Leo. You and I have more in common than you think, but in fact, you're working and I'm not. This makes us different in that very unique way."

"What a strange time we live in, don't you think, Leo?"

"I sure do. This is what we are prepared to deal with because until we put Americans to work producing the kinds of goods and services that we all want and need, we will be in this endless loop of losing the best and the brightest of this generation and the next one as well."

"My children asked me to do something today and I feel kind of funny doing it, but if you wouldn't mind, Leo, could I have your autograph?"

I smiled broadly. "What an honor! Why sure, you can have as many autographs as you want, and please tell your children that I'm truly humbled by their request."

I signed a small pad that Maggie gave me. "This feels so strange. I'm not used to anyone asking me for my autograph."

"Leo, you don't know how much you've affected this city. When people came out the other day to hear you speak, there was a significant change in the way they viewed politics in this city, the state and nationally. Even the kids were wondering what was going on and my kid's teacher was one that prompted them to think about what it meant for a person like you without a whole lot of money and no real political affiliation to be actually running for president. You see, what she was teaching them was that anyone could run for president. Yes, you were teaching them to live beyond their limitations. I was so excited when I heard you were coming to the station today. I told my kids that I was probably going to get a chance to meet you. They would not let me come to work today unless I got your autograph."

I smiled and signed the pad. "Again, I am honored to be able to give you this."

"The honor is all mine, Leo," Maggie said.

She finished my makeup and I stared into the mirror wondering if I would ever feel the same again. Maggie made me look ten years younger.

"Maggie, you're a magician. Where did all my wrinkles go?"

"Leo, we can make you look old or young, but you're easy. You're a handsome man and you don't really have bad wrinkles."

We were done. Maggie took me out to the set and turned me over to the director, James Downs.

"Welcome to KYC TV," he said. "Thank you for being on time and we hope that you get as much out of our show as we are hoping to get from your being here at our invitation. What questions do you have for me?"

"None, really. Thanks for inviting me. I realize you're taking a risk letting me come on and covering my campaign. But hey, I guess that you're doing what's good for your station and I'm doing what's good for my campaign."

"You got it," he said. "We both win. But I'm curious, Mr. Pollack, what made you think that you could really run for president? I'm sure that you get asked this all the time but I'm curious to know, just as a citizen and not as a television producer, what makes you want to run."

"This is America. We are taught from the time we are born that anyone can be president. Now I'm challenging that belief. We are going to find out if that statement has any merit. Above and beyond the esoteric answer I just gave you, we need someone to speak for the 160 million working people who are subject to paying the payroll tax."

"I hope you succeed in your efforts, but this is going to be a long way home," he offered.

"Yes, I know it will be, but hey, good things come to those who wait, work hard and sometimes have a hell of a lot of luck."

We walked over to the set. I stood and watched as the morning news program wrapped up and the set was changed for the morning show with Holly Strano.

This was America. This was how movements were won and lost. I was aware that this would become a standard scene for me as the campaign unfolded, but this time it would be unique. I was being invited to speak to the people of Cleveland and beyond about my candidacy, my beliefs, my goals, aspirations and vision. I was psyched.

"We're about six minutes to show time. You look good. I hope your face doesn't crack before we get you on set," James said, laughing at his own joke. I did not realize that sometimes made-up people actually do crack before they go on set and have to be redone.

I waited patiently until I was finally brought on stage. Holly was scurrying about but had enough time to say hello to me as I sat down in an easy chair on the set. A guy checked my hair, smoothed out my collar and asked if I had a tie. "No, I don't wear them," I told him. He just stared at me and continued primping me.

"Two minutes," I heard. The fellow left me alone.

Holly sat down next to me. "Good to meet you, Mr. Pollack," she said reaching over and shaking my hand.

"My pleasure as well," I replied.

"We have 15 minutes. I'll try to keep things moving along. Be brief in your answers. We don't have much time. You understand. Any questions?"

"No. Thank you for inviting me to be on your show."

"You're big news, Mr. Pollack. You will make this week's show. Now, we're ready. Remember. Answer the question. That's it."

I admitted she was all business. The moment of truth was upon us.

We got the key from James Downs that we had 15 seconds. I could feel the sweat under my armpits. Strange.

"Good Morning, Cleveland. It's Holly. Welcome to the show. We have a special guest today, one making big news in northeastern Ohio. Mr. Leo Pollack, an unemployed steel worker, was in town this week speaking to a crowd of unemployed Clevelanders as a candidate for the presidency of the United States. Mr. Pollack, from Youngstown, Ohio, is with us today. Welcome, Mr. Pollack, to Cleveland and the morning show."

"It's great to be with you, Holly," I responded. I did not know if the camera were on me but I just tried to be as natural as I could be given the heat of the bright lights blasting down upon me and the camera's red light glowing brightly and my own wonder at the entire process.

"Mr. Pollack, it must be said that your candidacy has raised a lot of questions because you've never run or held any political office, and still, you believe you are qualified. What makes you believe that you are qualified?"

"First of all, thank you for inviting me to be on your show today, Holly. I appreciate the opportunity to state my case for being the next president of the United States. To answer your question directly, first of all, I am at least thirty-five years of age and secondly, I was born in the United States of America."

"That's it?" I mean, you believe that is enough to be our next president?"

"Yes. There is nothing in the constitution that demands that I went to Harvard or Yale, that I was a congressman or senator or governor, or that I was a businessman who made millions running a company or companies and now wants the final prize of a public life, a high political office. No, I am qualified to be president because I meet the requirements. I am a man who knows what it means to go to work every day, and feel the joy of making a living by the sweat of my brow. I can look a man in the face and tell the truth. I pay my fair share of taxes and go home each night, kiss my wife and child, eat dinner with them, share time at home and sleep peacefully because I don't have a belly full of guilt about anything I've done throughout the day."

"Thank you," Holly said. "The economy is a major issue that affects all of us and especially people who have lost their jobs like you have, Mr. Pollack. What would you do to improve the economy, to make jobs a priority and bring unemployment down from the current 9.5 % to something like full employment?"

"Buy American. This is the answer. I believe that we must support our fellow Americans by buying only American. If you're going to buy something not made in America, don't purchase it unless it's absolutely essential. Buy American. When companies realize that 150 million working people are not buying Chinese, Japanese, Korean, Bangladesh or any other products because they are not made by Americans, they will slowly but surely begin to make products at home in America."

"You really think that this will work?" Holly asked as a follow up question.

"Yes. What do we have to lose? We're losing jobs so fast we can't even count them in the hundreds of thousands. Ohio lost 300,000 jobs in the past decade. I won't buy a sweeper that is not made in the USA. Hoover is just one example of a company that left our country and killed jobs. Enough. Buy American or don't buy anything at all."

"Sounds like a pretty simple solution," Holly said.

"You don't need a degree in economics from MIT or Harvard or Yale to realize that if you buy something made by a neighbor, you might actually be stimulating the economy right in your own neighborhood."

"Let's turn to another subject. Paul Ryan, a congressman from Wisconsin, put forth what he believe to be a solution to the Social Security, Medicare and Medicaid financial dilemma. His plan would provide vouchers for seniors to go out on the open market and purchase their own health care. What are your thoughts about this Ryan Plan?"

"Mr. Ryan is a true believer in Ayn Rand's philosophy based upon one virtue: greed. His plan is hopelessly flawed. Senior citizens would not be able to purchase insurance with vouchers. His plan estimated that a senior citizen would be given $15,000 a year to purchase insurance on the open market. Sounds good. Sounds like a lot of money until you go and do the math. If I were 65 and in excellent health and went out on the open market to buy insurance, I'd discover that a Blue Cross/ Blue Shield plan would cost me $1400 a month in premiums. Multiplying that by 12, you get $14,800 in premiums for the year. Yes, you could get insurance and it would cost almost every nickel of the vouchers you would get under the Ryan plan. However, this is the fine print. The policy would be, get this, a $10,000 deductible plan. Yes, you'd be responsible for the first $10,000 and then the company would finally begin to pay for your care. Oh, and if that isn't enough to make you sick to your stomach, this plan would be available to you IF the company actually were willing to insure you. The current plan that congress passed has embedded into it guaranteed insurability. Under the Ryan plan, most companies could simply deny senior citizens the opportunity to buy insurance. There is no guarantee in his plan that seniors would be able to buy insurance. They might have vouchers, but if a company won't insure them, they are SOL."

"SOL?" Holly asked.

"This is a family show. I can't say what that is but I think you know what it means."

"What is your answer to the health care dilemma?"

"Medicare works. The way it is being managed is the problem. We have more than 100 million people on Medicare and Medicaid but we do not let these programs negotiate drug deals with the drug companies. This mismanagement is leading to higher costs and needs to be changed. Secondly, Medicare can be made solvent if we would fund it adequately. When we do this, we have the healthy people and the sick people all paying premiums. This makes the system better not worse. Yes, everyone needs to carry insurance, but I don't believe it should be through private companies. All hospitals should be non-profit corporations. No one should make money from human misery. No one. This is immoral. When hospitals were non-profit entities, health care costs grew 2-3 percent a year and that was it. Once they were privatized, the costs grew exponentially. This needs to stop. As president, I'd fight for this type of system."

"So what you're saying is you believe in universal health care?" Holly asked.

"Yes. We live in a social system called a country. Ours is the United States of America. We are connected to one another and need to solve this problem together and not as opponents, democrats and republicans."

"The economy is dominating conversations, but what has taken a back seat to it is the issue of illegal immigration. How would you resolve this ongoing social and legal issue in a way that makes sense and still protects our country?"

"Many plans have already been proposed. Former president Bush and John McCain and Ted Kennedy proposed a plan to create a pathway to citizenship. Not Amnesty. A pathway that means everyone acknowledge that there are millions of illegal immigrants in this country and they need to be accounted for and accountable for being here illegally. What difference does it make now how they got here? They need to register that they are here. They need to be held accountable for their illegal behavior and that may mean they pay a fine. Once they've done this, they can apply for citizenship when they are eligible, they become a citizen. In the mean time, no, they don't get the benefits of true citizenship."

"So you are willing to have another round of amnesty?"

"No. They must be held accountable. Somehow, in some way. Just to say, okay, they're here. No problem. Fine. We aren't going to do anything to them. Wrong. What we are going to do is make sure they pay their dues and they do something to clean up their mess; namely, they face the consequences for coming to this country illegally."

"Taxes, tax cuts, tax increases, every candidate is talking about taxes and what he or she would do to fix the tax system in this country. What would you do to make our tax system fair and equitable?"

"First of all, a flat tax is not the answer. A flat tax benefits wealthy people. A progressive tax is the only fair way to go. We must, however, have everyone pay his fair share of taxes even if it is a very small amount. Okay. If you make from 0 to $10,000, you would pay 1% income tax. If you make up to $20,000, you would pay 2% in income taxes. You get my drift. $30,000, 3%. $70,000, 7%. Now when you get up to $270,000 you would be paying 27%. If you make $1,340,000, you would pay 100% on money up to the first million, and then after that, the tax would be progressive going backwards. If you make a lot of money, you pay more in taxes. If you make a lot of money, you probably consume more of the commons like roads, police and fire protection and other infrastructure 'held in common' than someone who makes $20,000 a year. Notice I didn't mention any tax write offs. There are none. Everyone pays a payroll tax. There are no annuities and dividends. Everyone gets paid a wage and that is it. Bonuses are out as a way to hide wages. Non-market acquisition of stocks is out. Everyone is treated the same."

"Mr. Pollack, you are not a wealthy man. You are not someone who came from a ruling party family. You are a blue collar, unemployed steel worker. How are you going to finance your campaign?"

"Oh, Holly, this is such a great question. When I first conceived this idea, I did not think about the money issue. I knew that I would not let my campaign be financed by corporate high rollers and billionaires who want to get their own way and buy me as 'their candidate'. No. This campaign had to be financed by the people for the people. I have said that I will not take any contributions larger than $20.00. To date, we've raised more than $167,000 and the amount is growing by the minute. We have total transparency. If you want to find out who gave money to my campaign and how much, you can go on line or contact the bank and find out. There is no superpac money and I won't accept any."

"There is a significant difference between $167,000 and millions of dollars. How are you going to make up the difference?"

"Holly, we have raised that amount of money in less than a month. I believe that we will begin to raise dollars exponentially as the message gets out and we campaign across the country and people begin to believe there is a candidate who speaks for them, the fund raising will grow."

"What if you are elected, what would be the first thing you would do as President?"

I smiled and did not speak for a moment. This was one of the most important moments in the interview and I did not want to blow it. Finally, I said, "I would take the oath of office, walk down to the White House and get to work. No parties. No frills and thrills. I'd ask that everyone who wanted to party with the president, take that money and do some good with it. We can't be celebrating anything as long as there are people unemployed, people losing their homes through foreclosures, people who are hungry, sick and do not have the money to provide for their basic needs. We have so many needs to take care of that there won't be time for idleness."

"Lastly, why you, Leo Pollack?"

"We Americans are blessed with the most extraordinary country ever created in the history of mankind. What makes it so special is that the leader of this nation is not someone who has been born into the office, has been granted it by his or her father, or has been able to buy the office. I will be the first president in almost a century that comes from the masses and not from any political elite. I am not a lawyer, have never run for any office, have no baggage from past political campaigns, am not a corporate raider or business man with a record antagonistic to working people. I expect the best from other people and I have faith and hope in the goodness of Americans and in their inherent desire to fulfill their dreams in pursuit of life, liberty and happiness."

"Thank you for being here today, Mr. Pollack, and good luck in your campaign."

"You're welcome," I said.

We sat still until we heard the cut signal and then Holly quickly shook my hand and thanked me again, got up and raced from the set.

I drifted off the stage and past the cameras and out beyond the production set to where Al and Gram were standing talking to James Downs.

"Nice job, Leo. You will make a hit here in Cleveland. There are no candidates on the right side that can stand on the same stage as you," Downs said.

"Thanks for the compliment," I replied. "There is a lot of work to do before we can even the playing field with the Democrats as well as the Republicans."

"A third party campaign is very tough in this two-party country," Gram said. "This will require a lot of grassroots organizing that is underway and will continue for more than a year to break down the barriers set up against anyone challenging the status quo."

"We have high hopes that Leo will be that man," Al added.

"What else can we do for you?" Downs asked.

"Can we get a copy of today's show? I mean a DVD or something like that so we can use it later?"

"Sure. Already got it ready for you. We figured you might want a copy for the campaign and any ads you might want to make later. If you need any help with production or anything of that nature, you just give me a call and we'll go to work on it. We're with you all the way."

"Mr. Downs, I can't thank you enough for making this possible today," I said.

"We need change we can believe in and you're much more believable than the last person who spouted that phrase. He disappointed all of us by not going far enough to make the plight of working people better. Now it is your turn. You've got to go all the way and make a real difference. I mean it, Leo. This is the time. This is your challenge."

We shook hands and then got ready to leave. I wanted to thank Holly again, but she was nowhere to be seen. The next show was already running and we watched as the broadcaster presented the latest news and weather. We exited into the clear morning air.

"Breakfast on me," Al said. "What are you in the mood for on this lovely spring morning?"

"How about eggs and coffee?" Gram replied.

"Leo, you?"

"Coffee will do. I'm not really hungry."

"You will be boy, you will be when that adrenalin that is pouring through your veins finally wears off," Al chortled.

We climbed into the Leo-mobile and Al went to work fixing breakfast.

"I thought we were going out for breakfast?" Gram asked. "What's up with this?"

"We're practicing frugality," Al said. "This government needs a dose of it."

We ate quietly. For some reason we did not have the urge to chatter much at all. Eventually, we decided to get back on the road and head on home.

Al said, "What's the agenda for the rest of the day?"

"I think it's time we get out of this RV and go for a hike. My legs need a work out. How about you, Gram?"

"I'd like that. Let's head on back to the homestead and then get the boy and find a nice park and amble about," Gram said.

"Done."

We drove back toward home chatting about the morning, wondering what would come of it, planning on making the rest of the day as normal as possible, knowing that there were not going to be many more days like this one where the sun, moon and stars were aligned in such a way that we were cradled in a heavenly place rarely known to humankind.

17. Warp Speed Ahead

Everything in our campaign moved forward at warp speed. There was barely time to breath. We chased every rainbow. We solicited every possible person, place or thing that could support our effort to ring the liberty bell. We fought to crush the belief in America that corporations were people. We promoted the platform that wealthy individuals were not more qualified to be president than those with less financial resources. We broadcast the idea that 160 million working people's voices and votes were more powerful than a gob of superpacs permitted by the Supreme Court decision in Citizens United to spend obscene amounts of money to get a candidate elected. We shouted out that this type of system could not continue deluding citizens into believing that this form of democracy is what the founding fathers had envisioned for us.

At first, our movement oozed across the landscape like lukewarm molasses, but as our efforts warmed to the task, we were spreading into every political nook and cranny of the nation. What we promoted was sweet to middle class working people's ears. We believed that it was time again for all who produced the wealth to share in its bounty. This was not a socialist campaign to demand a redistribution of wealth and deny capitalists their earnings, but to not accept less than what a person deserved.

Women came on board in droves because they realized this was their time to rise and shine. For too many years they were treated like second class citizens. After all, one hundred and forty-six years passed before women were permitted to vote. As recently as 2010, the Supreme Court still would not uphold a decision that women should be paid the same as men when performing the same duties. The fire was lit in the minds, hearts and wombs of the women who believed there was a better way to govern. I almost wished that I were a woman so I could intimately understand, feel and appreciate what it felt like to be kept in subservience to others. I knew that, no matter what, I would have a partner, a vice presidential candidate, that would be a woman.

Fund raising was blowing the doors off the conventional wisdom that there needed to be major backers for any campaign to succeed. We had no one donating more than twenty dollars, and we were gaining rapidly on the million-dollar mark and would soon pass it. The number of people donating to the campaign was in the millions already. People believed what they were hearing. We did not measure our success just in money, but in the spreading of the grass seed across the nation that sprouted everywhere.

Our goal was to be on every ballot in every state in the country. We were already on seven states and the tally was improving daily. This was a difficult task and there was no doubt that some of the states, mainly below the Mason-Dixon Line, would prove difficult to organize. We would not be denied. Courageous people, often risking their own safety, went out beyond the sidewalks to gather signatures and make it possible for the people's voice to be heard in places where that puny sound was almost extinct. The other national campaigns were still denying that we had any legitimacy. They viewed our efforts much like major corporations watched small unions organize and believed they could crush us at any time.

The president's party was concerned because we were bringing to the political table a new perspective on the issues and this would hurt him the most. The push back, we knew, would come from his party as much as from the right, far right and the regressives who wanted to take us back to the dark ages of Ronald Reagan whom they still held up as their savior. We knew better. We read our history. We realized just when the decline and fall of the middle class began. Oh, his sweet tongue decried the power of government to make life better. Oh, his radio voice said that we should look to business to solve the nation's ills. He was crowned the tax cut president, but during his reign, he raised taxes eleven times and left office having taken in a net $100 billion more than he cut. The savings and loan scandal erupted during his tenure in office and it cost all of us billions of dollars to clean up the mess. Yes, they were praising his legacy. Let them. They would soon find out that the people were not foolish enough to believe he was any kind of savior for anyone but the wealthiest Americans who benefited from the many decisions he made.

In the last thirty years, the median income in America has remained almost the same and earning power for working people has risen about eighteen percent, while the wealthy have seen a two-hundred and seventy-five percent increase in their net worth. This does not represent a healthy and successful American distribution of wealth. A healthy middle class is one metric that indicates a healthy economy. Trickle-down economics is an abject failure and we are telling every person we met to just do the math, stop and consider just how little growth he or she has experienced in the past few decades and judge for him or herself whom to believe.

We pressed the issue about the median income every chance we got. In the richest country in the world, how was it possible that half the people, a 153.5 million people, made less than $26,400 a year? How was it possible in this country that 1 percent of the people possessed an accumulated net worth more than the 153.5 million who were living on poverty level wages? Were these Americans lazy, ignorant, unskilled, and stupid or something else that kept them from succeeding like all the rest? Or, perhaps more insidiously, were the rules stacked against them? We were flooding the darkness with the facts. We would not stop until every American who wanted to know the truth was fully informed and could make a political decision as to who really spoke for and to them.

We believed in a fair, not free, trade system. We knew that free trade was a code for unregulated trade. Where unregulated trade existed, the working people were under the thumb of corporations that cared little for their health and well-being. Working people ceased to be "personnel" and became "human resources", something that could be amortized like a piece of machinery when the time came to invest in new "human resources". The concept of downsizing achieved a whole new level of meaning. When a company found that its profits were not meeting expectation, a "downsizing" could be manufactured, human resources let go and the company's profits would go up. In the process, the corporate leadership, because of the ingenious way it helped spur increased earnings, would take massive bonuses as rewards. There was no way to control the redistribution of wealth because the practice was legal according to most corporation's charters and by-laws.

Across the land, the hue and cry to level the playing field was being broadcast. The conflict with the other newly formed grass roots organization, the tea party, became intense. Funded by silent billionaires who got surrogates to mouth piece for them a hatred of government regulation, democratic ideals and working people's rights, this struggle started to take on monumental proportions. For a while, the people on both sides were kept at cross purposes. Working people who were manipulated by the tea party elite, eventually realized that unfettered corporations, and unregulated capitalism were not the answers and they started to reject the tea party platform. Liberty would not be achieved by destroying the government, leaving almost all decisions up to states and letting corporations be the guiding force in the body politic. No, there was a need for a social system that connected everyone to everything and that was the government: of, for and by the people.

The difference we were promoting was that we, the people, were ringing the liberty bell again and asking all to participate in the process. Voting was just the final step in being a citizen. Activism was the beginning. Stepping out of one's comfort zone was the first demonstration that the country, if it were worth saving, demanded. This was not a spectator sport. We needed to get up from our couches, shut off the television, put on our work clothes and come out into the public and get to work. What the work was each person had to decide for him or herself. There was plenty to do. Volunteer to do something to make the country better became the charge to everyone. We asked each person to give a dollar and a few minutes of his or her time to talk to someone about the movement and to spread the word that we were taking back our country from the power elite who did not want us to succeed. We decried the type of absentee ownership that corporations had become where wealth was distributed upward and the risk downward.

We promoted a main street form of capitalism. Support your Neighbor by buying something made in America. If it is not made here, do not buy it. Go without. Keep the money at home. Even though we were being told that the economic crisis was over and things were getting better, fifteen to twenty million unemployed people did not see, hear nor feel the improvement. Wall Street banks and brokerage firms were "better" but not working class people.

We preached that the difference between capitalism and communism was indistinguishable because, in both systems, the creation of concentrated wealth was the same and people in the top one percent shared very little in common with the bottom ninety-nine percent.

Adam Smith, we stated, presented the true form of capitalism and that included: first, honest dealings between employer and employee; second, equitable distribution of wealth; and third, investments kept within one's own borders. Every tenet of capitalism under his system was violated in the current American bastardized version. As we now experience it, capitalism and the common good are mutually exclusive. We hammered home the argument again and again that a free market was code for an unregulated market and would not let the corporate message continue to drown out the need for people, places and things to be protected from unfettered greed.

We promoted the idea of a decentralized banking system where banks returned to the neighborhoods and people could go in and deal with their banker like a neighbor and friend. The size of banks needed downsized more than the work forces of most companies.

The attacks from the opposition became a daily occurrence. The FOX channel became the mouthpiece for corporate warriors who saw the Liberty Bell movement as a communist conspiracy to overtake the greatest country in the world. Regressive radio show hosts called our movement the greatest threat to America since 911. We were called terrorists because we did not believe in America and did not love her and did not want to see her succeed. We stood our ground, but the assaults and insults increased exponentially as the summer arrived. The hot days warmed the spirit of rebellion and the power elite realized that we were not going away, not now, not tomorrow or ever.

The world was changing and that meant the Republicans were going to have to listen or else. The "or else" is what scared the living daylights out of them. For more than thirty years they had almost completely dominated the message. They had massaged people into believing that everything was fine, that the problems we were facing could be solved if we just gave them a little bit more time, and if we did not get too concerned about what was actually happening in the work and market place. We were told that our national debt was the real problem and we needed to cut spending. Yes, if we just did that all would be well. However, when newly elected governors in states like Wisconsin, Michigan, Indiana, Minnesota, Ohio, Pennsylvania and others started cutting budgets, what was targeted was education, police, fire, teachers, public employees and their unions. Corporations were left alone to continue doing business as usual.

Every day we saw the people's agitation increasing and we continued to promote it. We supported it. We encouraged people to take back their own country. Yes, 160 million working people who paid payroll taxes were much more powerful than a few elite corporate and political leaders who wanted us to shut up and go away. We would not be stifled.

The summer heat inflamed the hearts, minds and spirits of the masses of people facing foreclosures on their homes, continuing unemployment and underemployment. In minority communities where these conditions were amplified two or three times, the crescendo of discontent gained momentum.

In August, the Republicans held their first of many debates and an Iowa "straw poll" that gave rise to the roller coaster ride their party began. Michelle Bachman won the poll and it boosted her to front runner status. She climbed aboard the roller coaster in the front seat and raced down the cascading rail and crashed a few weeks later when her personal life and political views started to scare the electorate. This began a series of leaders and followers that made the people wonder who could satisfy an unhappy conservative group of people. Mitt Romney continued to maintain about a quarter of the people in his camp but he could not break away from a pack of conservatives, neo-conservatives and a libertarian who wanted to overtake his front-runner status. His wealth and name kept him consistently hovering at the top until the debates started in earnest.

The discontent erupted with the "Occupy Wall Street" movement. OWS descended upon New York like a deluge. People did not know what to make of it. First, the government just saw it as a bunch of discontented college kids who wanted something. When no demands were made, when no organization emerged claiming that it spoke for the OWS, confusion set in among those who hoped they could divide and conquer those who were occupying their city. No one could explain the phenomenon. True, at the core were young college graduates who were unemployed and could not use their degrees to achieve gainful employment. They questioned the American Dream. As a result, they were in serious debt having borrowed thousands of dollars to pay for their education.

At the time of the first OWS outpouring in Zuccotti Park in New York City on September 17th, the news media covered the story from this point of view and estimated that college loan debt was at least, if not greater, than credit card debt in America. Getting a good job after graduating was proving elusive and the debt was smothering the hopes and dreams of these newly graduated young adults. Something was amiss in the economic system when this kind of situation was permitted to fester. They stepped out of their classrooms and onto the streets and said, "We want more." The Republican candidates chastised these protesters, called them "mobs" and did everything they could to make them disappear. Nothing worked. The movement continued to berate the unfairness of the system that preached to them to get a good education and the world would be theirs. They earned their degrees and they incurred mountains of debt and all they had to show for it was the debt. The dream was smoke and mirrors.

The president did not support their efforts. He appointed the CEO of General Electric Corporation, Jeffrey Immelt, to head his Council on Jobs. As the CEO of GE, he did create about 200,000 new jobs the year before, but they were all overseas. GE was moving most of its manufacturing capacity off shore. The appointment did nothing to change the way Washington was doing business.

Neither Democrats nor Republicans could come to any type of agreement on what needed to be done. Their political impasse was so rancorous that even the most die-hard conservative started to complain that this do-nothing congress was getting to be too much. The students wanted some relief. They wanted something to be done to protect their future. We encouraged their continued protests. We believed in their inherent desire to live and work in a fair and just society. We promoted the idea of contracted free universities where students could matriculate and earn degrees and then serve the country for a number of years in their chosen field to pay back the cost of their degrees. We acknowledged that the price of an education did not often balance out what a graduate might earn after he or she completed his education. How long would it take for a teacher to pay back $100,000 of college debt while working as a teacher, and especially, in states where education budgets were being slashed by the newly elected and short-sighted conservative governors? With the cold weather coming and the city fathers being concerned that they were losing control of their message, the movement was attacked by authorities and it seemed to be dying. What happened was the protesters simply went indoors, got on their computers, fired up their smart phones and the challenge to the system continued.

We eventually had to return to Cincinnati to face charges for our illegal gathering. Gram did not inform the judge that he was a lawyer without a license to practice law in the state of Ohio. The judge never asked so he did not lie to him. He did tell him that he was legal counsel for me. Gram explained that he had been researching the municipal code for permits in Cincinnati and could not find any ordinance that restricted assembly in parking lots. There was one for assembly in an auditorium but our gathering did not meet that standard. There was one for assembly in public parks but our gathering did not meet that standard. We did not meet in a public street so that ordinance was not in question. Our confusion, Gram concluded, was that our assembly did not appear to violate any ordinance in Cincinnati's code. Therefore, what were we being charged with by the authorities? The judge clearly was discomfited and in the end, he dropped all charges based upon the lack of a clear-cut violation of any city ordinance. The press had a field day with the hearing. Leaving court, we were asked what we thought of the whole proceeding and Gram simply said, "Justice works most of the time." I was asked what were my thoughts and feelings and I said, "America is a land where every voice must be heard and this was just one example of how the system was not going to stop the voice of the people from being heard."

Road trips increased dramatically. We logged thousands of miles. We spread out across the land and Al, Gram and I and an entourage of well wishers, roadies and "Leo-heads" went from Ohio, into Indiana, Michigan, Pennsylvania, New York, Illinois, and south into Kentucky and Tennessee and West Virginia and Virginia, North and South Carolina and up into New England carrying the same message, "Wake up America. The Liberty Bell of Freedom is ringing. Middle class people are uniting and taking back America from the corporations, lobbyists, career politicians, neo-conservatives and will not quit until America is again a land of the free and the home of the brave." We knew we would need to be brave more than anything else, if we were going to get our message out across the landmass of the country.

We noticed that the crowds became increasingly agitated when the police showed up and circled the gathering. We quickly diffused any conflicts by publically thanking the police and other security services for their willingness to insure our safety and security at no cost to our campaign and welcomed them to join our movement and be represented by us in the name of democratic freedom, truth and the American way. Most of the time, this confused them. This served to keep all our people focused on the message and not the overwhelming show of force that they presented. In the end, we tried to get everyone to hold hands and sing "Kum by Yah" but it only worked some of the time. We passed out cards with our major "talking points". We did not care if the opposition stole our ideas or saw our game card. We wanted them to see everything because we wanted to win over their supporters as quickly as possible. Our campaign buttons simply read "Leo Pollack – When America works, Freedom lives and Democracy thrives".

The speed at which we traveled was not measured in miles per hour but in people per minute. How many people were we winning over minute by minute, hour by hour, day by day was measured in the number of folks who joined our movement, sent in a one, five, ten or twenty dollar pledge, volunteered to knock on doors, made phone calls, signed petitions and gathered signatures.

We laughed when we watched the pundits and other politicians complain that we were not doing things according to standard practices. We must be cheating. We must be getting support from some progressive billionaires like George Soros or someone else. We guffawed when we were accused of taking foreign money. We laughed and threw our books open to the public for review. Mr. Kilpatrick at Mahoning National Bank was one of the most popular bankers in the entire country. He was a household fixture. Given that we were using his bank for our campaign and everything consistently appeared to be on the up and up, business grew exponentially. We were elated, because Mahoning was not a "corporate bank". This local bank had offices around the county and that was it. We were proud to make a difference in its business and encouraged everyone who wanted to be treated like a real person to bank with Mahoning. In just a few months, Mahoning National Bank's assets passed a billion dollars. What a phenomenon.

Our campaign was spending about $10,000 a day to finance our continual effort to get out our message and to fight the misinformation that was being posted by the other campaigns. We took every lie seriously. When we were accused of being communists, we invoked our right to protest as guaranteed in the First Amendment. We asked our supporters to let us know how many of them had served the United States in the armed services, taught in a public school, worked in some government service or worked for some non-profit agency, organization or corporation serving the people of this or some other country. The statistics were staggering. Thirty-six percent of our supporters were veterans, fifty-two percent were teachers, social workers, community agency personnel, and a whopping sixty-eight percent worked for non-profit agencies or corporations doing work here and abroad. We were exuberant when we reported these facts to the national media and shut off the rumor valve. Fact-check and Politico caught on to the maneuver and wanted to make sure that we were not lying. They gave us thumbs up. No "liar-liar pants on fire" rating like many of the other campaigns got for their embellishing the truth. We were telling it like it is. We did not need to nor want to lie to the American public. As a nation, we were still reeling from so many lies told for so many years that we hoped that with a few years of honest politics, we might recover and become healthy once again.

The most serious physical attack came one night when our RV was torched right in front of my home. Though it was a total loss, luckily, no one was hurt. The entire campaign was in shock. Clearly, I needed to have greater security and so a friend from work, "Big Jack" Robinson came on board as my constant body guard and head of the security detail that protected anyone and anything that was connected with the campaign. This was a strange time for us because we did not believe that anyone would attack us in this way, but we were wrong. The national media covered it briefly, but because the Republican primary campaign was in the limelight due to nine candidates still vying for its nomination, our story was relegated to the back page of newspapers, to the second and third stories on the internet and only local coverage on the television. We did not decry this injustice. We knew there were forces that were not going to take our candidacy lightly without fighting back. We just had to tune into the realities of what we were facing and what was at stake.

Given the amount of power and money the government wielded, whoever was in control of the government was able to literally buy and sell the bodies and souls of people. This was what we wanted to end. This was what many forces allied against us did not want to happen. We knew that and did not care. Like the OWS people, we were willing to brave the cold and the entrenched security forces of the local, state and federal government to bring our cause to the front and lead by example. We could stand on our own and face the future with grit and determination making a difference just because we were not willing to sell out at any cost.

When the RV was burned and we realized that we needed a new one, Al went out and found the ideal machine to carry us safely across the land. People from a local painting company donated their time and effort and decorated it with such a splash of color that we were amazed at its beauty. This was not just a campaign vehicle; it was a work of art. The entire Constitution was printed on the side of the machine. The Bill of Rights was listed on the front. A giant Liberty bell adorned the back. Somewhere in this patriotic fresco, my name was listed and our web site and phone number and other details. We were excited, proud and happy to be a part of something greater than ourselves. The message would roll down the highway every time the Liberty Bell Bus was fired up and pulled away from the front of my home.

Sitting inside at night, as I was able to do about once every two weeks now, I marveled at just how far we had come in such a short time period. Back when the snows of February stuck to the ground, we opened a Pandora's box and found a new world order and this was not one that neo-cons, conservatives and even moderates would easily digest. There was a need to improve the plight of working people in America. Enough was enough. We wanted more. We wanted justice and fairness in the regulations that insured that all who came to the economic table would have a chance to benefit from their hard work, honesty, and perseverance.

Thus, as the days slowly ebbed from the year, we stood our ground. We made the light of the future shine for all to see. Whenever we held it above us, we led the way. We tramped a large, faithful, energized, committed, intelligent, righteous, fearless body politic into the 2012 election year with bells ringing and eyes ablaze staring at the prize.

Through it all, whenever I was at home, Basha, Janko and I shared dinner, read before bedtime, prayed with one another and snuggled together at the end of each day keeping each other warm, safe and secure.

18. Hawkeye Headwinds and Headaches

Most New Year's holidays, we would be lying around the house watching multiple college bowl games, eating pork and sauerkraut, and celebrating a new year. Everything changed now. There was not one bowl game on the television on the holiday. The major bowl games were being played before or on January 2. The Bowl Championship Series game between LSU and Alabama was scheduled for January 9, a week later. LSU beat Alabama during the regular season and was 12-0. Alabama lost one game to LSU. This rematch raised a host of questions again on how the NCAA championship was determined. Advocates for a playoff system were beating the drum again for change. The NCAA and its college president members, who were really CEO's of major educational corporations, were not in favor of creating anything new that would cut into their lucrative contracts with television and especially ESPN-ABC, the network that was broadcasting 27 of the 33 bowl games. In the end, the CEOs won and the season came to an anti-climax when Alabama laid a hurt on LSU. So now, the national champion was 12-1. The losing team, LSU was 12-1. Each team beat the other. Who was the champion?

If this were not enough to make college football face itself, the child abuse scandal at Penn State University burst during the football season, Eventually, the President of the University, two other high ranking officials, and revered long-time football coach, Joe Paterno were fired. Nothing seemed sacred anymore. What the college bowl season revealed even to the casual observer was the consumption of the sport by big businesses. Corporations sponsored every bowl game. Just like in politics, there was a need to "own" the game. What was frightening was the American populace was not screaming bloody murder about the decline and fall of the amateur athletic system in the country. We were fed such a steady dose of entertainment that we were now almost numb beyond recognition. There seemed no end in sight. What did it really matter? This was sports and not something to get all upset about in the first place. Right? Wrong! The sports climate was just the canary singing in the mine. The death of a way of life was slowly filling the body politic of America like a cancer. We would see the beginning of it with the first campaign mega-spending by superpacs in the Iowa caucuses.

Our strategy session, held during the holidays between Christmas and New Year's Day, prompted us to reconsider our plan for Iowa. There was not much hope to make a play in the Hawkeye state. We did not have enough of a team on the ground so we would have to sit this one out, but not without making our presence known as best as we could. The demographics of Iowa were interesting. Almost centrally located in the United States, Iowa was almost ninety percent Caucasian. The influx of minorities into the state was a result of the meat packing industry and low paying jobs that attracted them. One kosher meatpacking establishment was raided, four hundred employees arrested and the owner charged with violating immigration laws. He eventually lost the company, but the issue remained. Cheap labor was inviting people to immigrate to Iowa. Arguments for and against immigration laws and enforcement surfaced every time one of these episodes made Americans aware just how extensive the problem truly was. Most of the employees working in the plant were illegal workers. The company fostered this practice. They even schooled their workers on how to answer questions if they were picked up by immigration officers. Social security cards were doctored to make them look like legal workers. This was Iowa. This was mainstream America and this was not an isolated incident. Across the land, wherever there was any opportunity to bypass immigration laws, companies were doing so.

Into this maelstrom, we descended on January 2nd to spread our message across the state and see what would happen. We were in for a series of shocks. The mainstream media gave us a cool welcome. We expected that because we were interlopers and they were not sure yet how to take our upstart campaign. If and when I became a viable candidate, they would have to take our platform, our message, seriously. We were not in the position, like Ross Perot, to funnel millions of dollars into the coffers of media outlets to broadcast our message.

What we did was much simpler. We divided the state into sections and decided how best to use our time wisely to get our message into the dialogue. We entered on Interstate 80 in the Quad Cities area and made Davenport our first stop.

Our venue was the same as always, an unemployment office and our message was simple: Education.

"What is wrong with American education is not the question. What is right with it could be a better way to address the issue. We are constantly making our schools the scapegoat for the ills of our society. Teachers have become the whipping boys and girls for our unwillingness and inability to change with the times. We have not made a major shift in education policies and procedures for a century. No we have not. 'No Child Left Behind' did not address anything but some nebulous outcomes standardized tests produced. There is no real measure for critical or creative thinking that any test can measure. What we need to do is focus on three parts of the education equation. First, reduce class sizes to less than 15 students in any class. Yes, we would incur more cost. What is the rub? Do we want an educated population or do we want to continue doing what we've done for the last 50 years and expect different results? Secondly, teacher training must be ongoing. Just because a teacher goes to college and gets a degree to teach does not mean that he or she is a teacher. The individual has just met the minimum requirements to enter the classroom. We need a system of ongoing training and development like the trades provide their apprentices. Every new teacher would have a teaching mentor. This might be another teacher, the vice principal, the principal or perhaps a college professor who comes into the classroom, videotapes the teacher weekly and then gives him or her feedback on the process. The third, and perhaps most radical of changes that must be made, involves the entire school scheduling system. Our current educational schedule is based upon an agrarian society where children were let out of school for the summer to work on the farms with their parents. We have not been an agrarian society for almost half a century. Yet, we still take our kids out of school for the summer time. They doddle away three months of their lives, and then we immerse them back into the routine in the fall. We need to change the schedule dramatically and this is the formula. Six weeks of intense learning and then a week off. School goes year around with one month off in July for vacation. Holidays like Christmas to New Years are left alone as a natural break in the school cycle. However, there is no more summer off. If you look at the time students spend in school actually learning, the 180-day school year is inadequate for teaching our children how to function in this complex, modern, highly technical world. In 1950, a student could graduate and enter the work force with a basic math background and marginal writing skills. This is not adequate for today's world. American children are being left behind. We fall short internationally in our performance and a significant part of the problem can be attributed to our antiquated scheduling practice. Teachers, parents and most of all, students, may not like it, but they will have to adjust. This is the 21st century. New times and new needs demand that we provide new solutions to keep up with the changes."

After the speech, I fielded questions from the local media. They were most curious as to what I hoped to achieve by coming to Iowa even though I could not participate in the caucuses. I simply told them, "We have a message to present and that is more important than anything. We'll be back for the general election later and that is all that matters. Iowans are savvy people. They know what a dog and pony show is and they will be able to decide who will be the best leader to take us forward in 2013."

Next stop. Iowa City. Topic. Ethanol subsidies.

"Please don't boo me off the stage before you hear me out, but we need to end the subsidies for ethanol production. Yes, Iowa gets a significant kick back from these government monies, but in the end, it is hurting the business climate. The longer anyone remains on any type of subsidy, the worse it is for the economy and for the individual as well. Let's take unemployment compensation and parallel it with ethanol subsidies. Right now I'm getting unemployment compensation. I'm being paid not to work. At first, it feels okay. Nice to get easy money. But as time moves along, I feel the lethargy starting to settle in. I am not as sharp as when I am working. My edge is dull. I am not being productive. The longer I don't work, the worse it is because I continue to lose my productive edge. Working and being productive are the only answers to ending this dilemma. I believe the parallels are the same with the ethanol subsidy. The longer a business is propped up by the government or any other external entity, the less productive and self-sustaining it will be. Iowa corn farmers have enjoyed the benefits and financial rewards of the ethanol additives industry growing dramatically. Now it is time for the industry to stand on its own two feet. The same must be done with the oil, gas and coal industries. It is madness to be paying oil and gas companies subsidies for drilling. Each year they produce record profits and yet, taxpayers, you and I, are sending money to them for taking the risk to drill a new well. I don't know about you, my friends, but there is a better way to spend our money than to give billions to Exxon-Mobil, a company that made almost $50 billion in net profit last year. Where subsidies can make a difference and spawn new energy sources, we need to give them the kind of support that will insure that we continue to lead the world in innovation. However, the moment an industry can stand on its own, and then it needs to be left to do so. This is only natural and we should not mess with the natural selection of business. Some will make it over time. Some will fold up and cease doing business. This is the way things should be. We have too much corporate welfare."

The second audience was more hostile to my comments. I could feel the cold air flowing from the crowd, and when the reporters had a chance to talk to me afterward, the attacks were thinly veiled. "Look," I said. "Everyone has their favorite cash cow. I am unemployed. Do you think I want unemployment compensation to go away? No. But I also know that this is not a healthy way to live. This demoralizes the spirit of a working man and woman. Unemployment compensation is just an insurance to keep people like me from ending up in the poor house because my company, for better or worse, has decided that they don't need my services today, or tomorrow, or for the near future. I know what is up and so do you. Let's not insult one another. Okay? We know that these kinds of policies exist and we don't want to change anything that takes away something that makes our lives easier. I would be in real trouble right now if there were no unemployment compensation coming into my household. It will run out shortly. Then I'll have to get a real job. Hey, I'm hoping by then to be employed by the federal government as President. I won't need any more UC to get by then. You get my drift."

The reporters laughed but we left one another as antagonists.

Next stop: Cedar Rapids, Iowa. Topic: National Defense and Military Spending.

"Our last president got us into a war we did not need. He left office and we were still mired in that unnecessary war. This president finally has pulled us out of Iraq, but he did not go far enough. We do not need 16,000 mercenaries in Iraq to protect our embassy and other assets. This is not financially responsible. We do not have military personnel in Iraq, but we are not saving any money by paying military contractors many times more than an average soldier makes to do the very same work. This is absurd. Iraq is a sovereign nation again. It has its own elected leaders. We may not like the way that they conduct their affairs. But you know one thing that amazes me. In their very first election, women, yes women, in a Muslim country, were permitted to vote. It took America 146 years for us to permit women to vote. You see, my fellow Americans, our history is not as democratic as we might like to believe. Now on to Afghanistan. We are now in our tenth year fighting in that land. 2014 is marked as an end date. What difference does it make if we leave now or leave two or three years from now? We have not done anything to eradicate opium production. This crop is still being produced openly. What have we actually changed in that country for the better? Yes, we have eliminated the Taliban from power, but as we speak, the US is negotiating with the Taliban covertly to engage it in power sharing with the current unpopular government of Karzai. So we are not winning the 'hearts and minds' of the people. Is this what the war was really about? We got bin Laden. Thank you Mr. President. You did your job as commander in chief. No doubt about that. Now, let's declare 'Mission Accomplished' like Bush did on the aircraft carrier and come home. This year we're going to spend $752 billion on defense. We spend more on defense than all the other nations combined. This may be a slight exaggeration but not by much. We cannot continue to sustain this type of spending indefinitely. We cannot continue being the police force for the world either. Something has to give and I believe we have reached a saturation point. No more wars for a while. We've tapped our military strength to the core. Our men and women are noble, brave and enduring, but they have a limit. What is really tragic is some of the soldiers recently brought out of Iraq in a big show of success by the president have already received orders to get ready to deploy to Afghanistan. They are getting no real break. They might have done three tours in Iraq and now they will do the same in Afghanistan. Enough is enough. If we continue doing what we are doing, we will face the same fate as the Roman Empire did. As overextended as it was, the world started closing in on it and eventually it declined in power because it could not sustain such pressure. We are in the same dire predicament. Unless we know our history, we are condemned to repeat it. I don't want to repeat it. I want America to remain a world power by protecting herself from being so overextended that eventually she erodes."

The press was downright brutal in its attacks, but I stood my ground. I was accused of being Un-American. I snapped back, "What makes me Un-American? That I want our military to be safe, at home, and ready when we need it? What purpose do we serve being in even a half of the 114 countries in the world where our forces are currently deployed? I don't get it. Just because we are not fighting some war somewhere, does not mean we are not keeping America safe. Let's change the paradigm. Perhaps we might be safe because we will have a fresh military not bogged down in a war. Every 'enemy' that we can think of has been watching us and knows that we can't go after them because we are already, or were until just a few weeks ago, in two theatres at once. Now we are only in Afghanistan. Once we exit there, we will be back to full strength. We will be able to move anywhere in the world again. We will be more powerful than we are now."

I did not convince many of them that what I was saying was the truth. They were still functioning in a cold war paradigm. This was the heartland. The military was all powerful. No one criticized it. I was being a heretic by even broaching the topic. So be it. I may not get their vote, but they would at least know what they were voting for or against when they cast their ballot in November.

Next stop: Ames, Iowa. Topic: College Education and Financial Debt.

"Once, a college education was considered the most important step in insuring a successful future. As an average, a college graduate makes more money in a lifetime than a high school graduate does. Choice of careers is more flexible when one possesses a degree. What has been changing is the cost of this education. Now, we might want to question if paying for a college degree is worth the expense. What if, after investing $100,000, one can't get a job? Today, many college graduates are unemployed or under-employed meaning they are working in some field other than their own and not utilizing the degree they earned. What we have is a huge brain drain taking place. I am an unemployed steel worker. My talents, my skills and abilities are being wasted. A college graduate who is not working is wasting his or her talents, too. This is a tragedy. We cannot continue to waste brainpower without eventually hurting the world that we live in. Granted, there are many college grads that have degrees that cannot and will not earn for them, in the short term, what the degree cost. This is something that we really need to address. In the mean time, we need to figure out how to best utilize the talent, the knowledge, skills and abilities that we have created with each college graduating class. We reward MBAs but we do not reward teachers, nurses, and other human services workers. This needs to change drastically. Fully 43 percent of our GDP last year was produced by financial services, banking and money management types of activities. This means that counting money can earn more for a person than making a car, or caring for an elderly patient in a nursing home, or building a cabinet to be installed in a home. Having a choice between a banker and an auto mechanic, I opt for the mechanic. At least he can keep my motor running. The banker just takes my money and smiles and then when I want a loan, he says that my credit score is too low or I don't have enough collateral to qualify for one. Nice try. We are finished with such wasted effort. The time is ripe for a major revision in the way we do college education. We are killing our best and brightest minds with numbing debt. There is no reason we need to do this. Stanford University, one of our premier universities, offered a course on artificial intelligence on line for free. The two instructors emailed their idea out to one of their friends. One hour later, more than 100 people were signing up for the course. A week later, there were over 100,000 students registered. No one got credit for the course because they did not pay the fee but the response was amazing. What is the point? We can change the way education is being offered and consequently, how it is being paid for and this will save students a lot of debt and universities a lot of expenses. Two professors, teaching a class on line to 10,000 students paying a nominal fee of $100.00 will make more money than if they do it the traditional way. On top of all that, the learning will spread around the country faster and cheaper. The traditional college education system is dying. The sooner we realize it, bury it, and erect the new system the better off we will be and students won't be in as much debt as they are now."

Given that this was a college town, my message met with greater acceptance, but there were naysayers here, too. What do we do with all the brick and motor universities that we have built? "Keep them. Make them into factories. Who knows what the possibilities are. We just can't continue to do business as usual and not face the whirlwind."

As we drove on to Des Moines, the largest city in the state and the next one on our agenda, Gram asked, "How are you holding up?"

"Fine. Fine. Little tired. But hey, this wasn't going to be a sprint to the finish. The real work is just beginning. Up until now, we've been coasting downhill. Now we're going to have to do some tough climbing back up the slope."

"Tough crowds. Kind of interesting though when you stand back and hear the concerns. No one really wants to change. Few, if any, are even prepared to take on the process. We all have to do it and yet we don't want to and generally come bucking and kicking like a bronco to the corral."

"You can say that again," Al admitted. "Look at me. I used to be driving a 30' rig that I knew well and could wheel it anywhere I wanted. Now look at what I am driving. 43' and more than a handful. Life is just too tough. I have to change but I don't want to." He said with a loud laugh at the end negating how tough it was to drive our new bus. We really liked it. We could sleep six comfortably and had a full kitchen, bath and living room in which to work on campaign stuff while we moved along. We had a built in dish so Al could watch shows when he was not driving. All in all, the fire turned out to be a boon for us. We never did find out who sabotaged us by burning our machine. Strange how the police could find no leads at all. Gram always maintained it was a professional job, kind of a Watergate Ph.D. crew that came in and did it and then flew out of the country. I really did not care because no one got hurt.

Next stop: Des Moines. Topic: Climate Change.

"You may wonder what would prompt a candidate like me to come and talk about climate change in a state where many people do not believe the science and do not accept that we are dramatically altering our climate. What would it take for you to conclude that we are doing harm to the world we live in? Consider this. Remember last summer when you came out into this parking lot and felt the heat billowing up in your face and you could hardly wait to get into your car, start it and turn on the air conditioning. The heat sink that was this parking lot was storing hundreds of thousands of BTUs, like a body stores fat, and later in the evening, when the sun set, the heat in the asphalt or concrete seeped back into the environment. The city never really cools off much because everywhere we have created these heat sinks to store the sun's radiant heat. At the same time we are storing heat in the asphalt and concrete parking lots, buildings, highways, all types of structures, we are also producing BTUs when we operate our cars and trucks. We are sending this heat up into the atmosphere. It goes up and is reflected back down again because of the cloud cover. Where does the heat go then? Heat is absorbed by the buildings, asphalt, concrete and other structures and stored and later seeps out into the environment. To say that humankind does not alter the environment is foolish because, by these simple examples, we can see and, most importantly, feel just how we do impact our world. Now, if you take an open space and walk through it and there is nothing being done to alter that space except your passing through it, chances of it feeling any different are pretty slim. Now take that same open space and have a hundred cars an hour drive through it, what do you suppose will happen? How about a 1000 cars? How about 50,000 cars? How many cars are speeding around Des Moines on any given day? I'd venture a guess and say it is far in excess of 50,000. Where does all that heat go? You guessed it. Into the environment and into the structures around this city. The roads, buildings, bridges. They all absorb some of that heat. Now evening comes and the heat seeps out slowly all night long. What once were cool evenings now are not much cooler than daytime temperatures. But you all know these facts. We can reverse this process and someday, unless we do, we may irrevocably damage the atmosphere of our mother ship, the one and only earth we have. I for one would like to live a long time breathing clean air. After all, we are made up of just a few elements: water, carbon, a few rare metals. Mostly water and carbon though. About 50 cents worth of chemicals. Not much when you think about it. The balance is the thing. This is what makes it all work. We are 78 percent water. Hmmm. Wouldn't it be nice if that 78 percent were pure H20? Get my drift. What's the solution? First, stop denying that we are affecting the climate in which we live. Secondly, figure out what we need to do to slowly restore some balance into the atmosphere by altering our behavior. We don't need to eliminate all automobiles from the face of the earth tomorrow, but we could simply drive smaller and smaller ones until we have decreased the carbon footprint of cars by a hundred percent. We could create more mass transit systems and eliminate the individual automobile when commuting to work. What if there were a high speed rail system crisscrossing this city and making it possible to get to work from anywhere around town in twenty minutes or less and no parking worries? Would you go for that? I would. This freeway traffic coming into Des Moines was treacherous, and I wasn't even driving. I was watching my partner and friend, Al, wheel through it all. Amazing. Enough of this. We have a chance now to make a difference. Let us not waste time being ostriches and burying our heads in the sand."

The Des Moines Register reporter attacked my science. I listened to his arguments and then finally said, "Are you asking me a question?" He was dumbfounded. I then said, "We can't debate an issue if there is no way for either you to accept my idea or for me to accept your idea. I can listen and learn from you. Are you willing to listen and learn from me?" He stopped his attack but did not ask me any more questions. The crowd was friendly enough and a few of the people asked me for my autograph. I enjoyed bantering with them. "What will you do next year when this becomes really valuable? Put it up for sale on eBay?"

I lost track of time. The sun was setting and we were heading toward Sioux City, the northwestern corner of Iowa and a conservative strong hold. I was not sure what would happen but I knew that there was a need to take the message into every corner of America. So off we went and arrived there about 8 pm. What amazed me was there were so many people waiting for us in the parking lot. The organizer, Jeff Blaine, said that some of the national candidates were in town so this was part of the reason for the interest. Nine republicans, one independent. The odds were not in my favor, but I hoped they were willing to hear my simple message and not discount what I had to tell them.

Next stop: Sioux City. Topic: Social Security, Medicare and Medicaid.

"If I hear the word 'Obamacare' one more time in my life, I'm going to scream out loud and tell people to stop swearing at me. What is wrong with making sure that every person who wants and needs health insurance can get it? Think about it for a moment. You wake up one day. You've been a generally healthy person. Now, you can't breathe. You're rushed to the hospital in an ambulance. Cha-ching. You are diagnosed with lung cancer. The doctor wants to operate immediately. You say yes. Cha-ching. After he cuts out the cancer, you face weeks of chemotherapy and radiation treatments. Cha-ching. Finally, you lose your hair and then it grows back. You make it for five years and you are glad to be alive. You are not in debt because you have good insurance. You only had to pay the deductible and that was nothing compared to the $250,000 the actual treatments would have cost you if you had been uninsured. This story would have been completely different if you had not had insurance. You would be facing a massive amount of debt and you probably would never, in your lifetime, pay it off. Prior to the Patient Protection and Affordable Care Act, if you had a pre-existing health condition, you were SOL. You all know what that means. Yes, and you'd be liable for all your expenses. You might get marginal treatment because hospitals must provide you with care but they don't have to give you the bells and whistles treatment package. This act made it possible for more than twenty million Americans to now qualify for insurance. Folks, it is a fine act but it did not go far enough. We are paying way too much money for the level of care that we are getting."

"This is the dilemma. The health insurance industrial complex has a monopoly and is not about to willingly change the way they are doing business. We need a pool of all American people participating so we can bargain for care from a place of strength, not weakness. We are facing a generation of 80 million people who are aging and we must be able to take care of them effectively and efficiently and economically. We cannot do this if we permit the health care industrial complex to continue to hold us hostage. How do we break this strangle hold they have on our health care system? First, we set standard rates for all procedures for every place in the country. Oh, but some will say, you can't do that. It's not fair. Hey, when you buy a new car, you pay the same delivery charge in California as you do in Massachusetts even if the car you are buying came from an assembly plant in the little town right next to the dealership where you are buying the car. You don't grip about that standard practice. You don't even think about it. But when we mention such standardization for health care delivery of services, Americans are foolish enough to believe the propaganda the health care industrial complex has been feeding us for so many years. Yes, it's fair to set a standard, reasonable charge for a procedure. Why should an MRI in one city cost $1500 and in the next city, the same MRI costs $2500? This makes no sense, but this is what jacks the price of health care up and up and up. In Japan, the government sets the rate. The insurance companies provide the services. The people get the care that they need. Oh, but now you might argue that we are comparing apples to oranges. Our health care system is far better than Japan's or any other country in the world? Says who? Our health care system lobbyists, that's who. We actually rate about 29th for quality of care in the world market. First is France. Yes, you remember France."

"The health care system needs an overhaul. The plan Obama pushed through took us only so far. We need to go all the way and make our health care system work for all people. We need to provide for preventive as well as remedial care. Think about this fact. Three percent of the people who have diabetes account for approximately twenty percent of the health care dollars spent. If these people received preventive care, these dollar amounts could be reduced dramatically. Yet, the current law does not provide for the preventive care. Medicare and Medicaid have worked for so many years, but now, all of a sudden, they are in trouble. What caused this sudden crisis? Let's simply look at the system and follow the money. Yes, you guessed it. Hospital organizations and insurance companies are making vast profits on our human misery and are complaining that they are not the problem. Who is causing the increase in fees for service? Who is charging a $1.00 for an aspirin when you are flat on your back in a hospital bed? Folks, it's time to get a grip on what is happening and reign in the hospital industrial complex and make it work for all people."

"Let me finish with this simple fix for Social Security. The federal government must stops taking money from the fund and using it for general operating costs. Second, the current cap gets moved immediately from $106,000 a year to $500,000. This will insure the investment of needed capital to keep it solvent in perpetuity. Third, as the president's commission recommended but was rejected by its own conservative members, social security retirement age needs to be moved up from 67 to 70 years of age by 2045. Fourth, wealthy people will get less from the pot than those who are less well off. Fifth and finally, social security is a safety net. It is not something that will work for all people all of the time People still need to do retirement planning on their own and make sure that they save enough during their active, productive years to insure they will have ample funds to see them through their later years. That's it. We can make it better. There is nothing unsolvable about anything if we are willing to make the tough decisions and most of all, tell the truth to the American people. Anything less than the truth is insulting."

I stepped away from the microphone really feeling the energy drain. The questions still came at me and I could feel the tension rising inside me. I repeatedly heard the word that was so disrespectful. Were these people pure idiots? Did they not realize how conditioned they were to believe lies and deceit? One reporter barked at me that my criticism of the American health system was without merit. "You're entitled to your opinion. Where does merit come into this? Where is the merit in letting 50 million people go without insurance? Where is the merit in watching people slowly die of diabetic consequences because they cannot afford insurance and medication? You tell me where the merit is, my friend, and I'll listen. But I'm pretty sure that you don't know where the merit in that type of system is because you know what, there isn't any and to criticize me for wanting to make it better just prolongs the agony for many Americans." He was taken aback by my tone of voice and my assault on him. For a moment, the next few questions were softballs and I answered them with alacrity. Then, the final one that pushed me over the edge came from a rotund individual who said as much as asked, "You don't have a chance changing the health care system any more than you do becoming our next president, so what's your angle?" I stared at him. People could feel the energy passing from me into him. They could see the fire in my eyes and then, I let him have it. "Fellow, it is people like you that keep us stuck in the status quo. You're an example of what is worst with the regressive party, that grand old party that wants to take us back to yesterday when everyone was a farmer and lived off the fat of the land, when the law was measured out at the end of a six-gun and creatures like John Wayne roamed the earth. We will change the system in spite of people like you. NO, we will change the system to spite people like you. How does that sound? Yes, the status quo does no one any good. I just hope that when your day comes and they are wheeling you down the hallway to go into surgery, your premiums are all paid up and your insurance company does not find some way to disclaim the procedure you are having to save your life because it was a pre-existing condition resulting from being too foolish to believe in a better way of life for one and all."

I walked away from the crowd. Gram rescued me by taking further questions and then followed me back into the Leo-mobile and shut the door.

"You nearly blew it out there, Leo. You fool. You can't fricking loose your cool like that, you got it? There will be bear baiters like him everywhere from now on. You ought to be glad that you made it this far today without having to face more bull crap like he was handing you. Yes, he was an asshole, so what? You don't treat him like one. He is a potential vote. You answer his question, challenge his thinking, hope he listens, thank him for listening even if he wasn't and then move on. Leave the crap to the republicans, to guys like Gingrich and Romney and Santorum and Paul to throw around. This campaign has to be clean and pure and natural. No more of that kind of crap or I'm outa here. I didn't come along for this ride to listen to politics as usual. You want to cuss someone out, take it out on me. I've got big shoulders and big ears and I'll still vote for you no matter what you say, but I won't stick with you if you disrespect the voters no matter what they say or do. Got it?"

Chastised completely, all I said was, "Got it."

Gram looked over at Al and said, "Al, let's you and I go out now and break that guy's knee caps for dissing our brother?"

"Let's do it." Al jumped up like he was going out with Gram who was already heading for the door.

They looked back at me. I was google-eyed.

They burst out laughing, slapping each other on the back, giving each other high fives and having a good joke on my behalf.

"Psych," Gram barked at me. "We gotcha."

Al jumped back into the driver's seat and said, "Let's roll. Hammer down...I don't know where we're bound but let's get out of this here town."

We drove for an hour and eventually pulled over into a well-lit roadside rest area where I made dinner. We ate, sat and analyzed the day.

"Oh, by the by," Gram said while we were drinking a glass of beer, "a guy I graduated from the Air Force Academy with called me today and asked if we had any use for his Learjet. He said it's just sitting in the hanger. I could fly us around, he said, and that would lend an air of legitimacy to the campaign."

"What did you tell him?" Al's eyes lit up as he rubbed his hands together.

"I told him, 'no thanks'. Such a donation would be more than twenty dollars and would violate our campaign pledge to not accept anything of value greater than twenty dollars."

"You've got to be kidding me?" Al asked.

"No, I'm not. What would you have me do?"

"You did what was necessary," I pledged. "However, it would have been nice to drive down to the airport and fly back home tonight. Shucks. Principles. Love or leave them."

"Hey, what would we do with the Leo-mobile, this Liberty Bell Bus?" Al asked.

"Why drive it back home," Gram exclaimed. "We couldn't leave it out here parked until we come back in the fall."

Al drove on. I wondered just how unreal it would be to have our own jet airplane with Gram flying us around the country. "You weren't making that offer up, were you?" I finally asked a half hour later.

"Nope. Guy made a fortune in computer network sales and service. Genius. Nice guy. Couldn't fly a plane though. Was afraid of heights."

"What did he do in the Air Force?"

"Chase women and program computers, but not in that order. Forget that stuff about women don't like geeks. He was one Cassanova. The babes he bedded. Oo-la-la," Gram uttered.

We finally got tired and crawled into our luxury berths aboard Leo One and said good night.

As I drifted off to sleep, I could hear the whining of wheels on the freeway and I recalled so many wonderful hours spent hitchhiking across America being serenaded by the orchestral sounds made by Goodrich, Firestone, Bridgestone and Goodyear.

19. Live Free or Keep On Trying

We barely caught our breath at home and then headed back out on the road to New Hampshire for the first primary of the campaign. John Gallagher called and gave me the lowdown on how we were doing with getting on the ballot. Conditions were tight and we could not qualify. This did not deter us because we were going anyway and would make our case with the people in our own form of "town hall meetings". From what our people were telling us, the other campaigns did not like our using public gathering places to hold events and especially unemployment offices that focused so much attention on the economic plight of so many Americans. We did not consider changing anything. Gram pointed out in one of our planning meetings that the more they complained to the press and the public at large, the more we needed to continue just what we were doing. We were beginning to erode support by engaging independent voters who did not like any of the Republican candidates and who were upset with and questioning the performance of President Obama.

The New Hampshire Primary was proving to be a major test for Mitt Romney. He won the Iowa Caucuses by 8 votes. Santorum came in second. Paul was third and Perry a distant fourth. Perry went home to Texas to decide what he was going to do. His campaign was faltering badly, but he still had buckets of cash to spend so he was going to focus on South Carolina. Paul was unabashedly in the race to the end. He did not care where he finished. He knew he could not beat Romney in the former governor's home state. Romney owned a home in New Hampshire and lived there part of the year. He owned three mansions around the country. Newt Gingrich was incensed that Romney attacked him so bitterly in Iowa and was making New Hampshire a referendum on superpac's money being used to run negative campaigns. He was upset because he could not afford to run the same kind of ads. Romney was sure of winning the state. We entered this political climate with high hopes that we might begin to interject an entirely new conversation into the political discourse.

Our game plan was simple. Go to as many places as we could in the next week, meet with as many people as possible and present our case for changing the political climate in Washington. This was going to be a tall order in New Hampshire because, in general, it was a rather conservative political environment. On our way to the Granite State, we studied the maps and tried to figure out how to cover it most efficiently. Gram's navigation skills aided us immensely in breaking down our journey into manageable units. Along the way, we ogled the spectacular scenery as we passed through gaps and over bridges fording wild looking rivers.

"What do you think our chances are to make headway in this place?" Al asked as we motored along enjoying the quiet moments before we had to disembark and get to work.

"Tough, to say the least," I responded. "This is still a republican stronghold and we won't get many votes from these folks, but we need to be here to offer the voters an alternative to either party. Right now the stage is set for a Romney win, but that is on their side of the fence. President Obama did not come close to winning New Hampshire so he won't take its electoral votes. We might not either, but who knows. The people are pretty rugged folks and anything is possible. One thing that we have going for us in New Hampshire is that anybody can vote for any party. The primary is wide open. Independents can cross over and vote either Republican or Democrat."

"I think we should keep hitting hard on the issues we know are working for us and that will open the door to some fantastic results even here in this conservative bastion," Gram countered. "If we leave next week with some percentage of write in votes on the books, think what that will do to boost our campaign. We can go to South Carolina with some real momentum."

"Wouldn't that be cool?" Al cackled. "Leo getting a higher percentage of write in votes than say, Rick Perry or one of those other conservative pups."

"We'll find out in less than a week. That's not much time, but we can make the best of it. After all, what else do we have to do?" I countered as I made notes on a clip board that I started to carry all the time now for remembering things I wanted to cover in speeches along the way.

"What do we know about Nashua, our first stop?" Al asked.

"Let's see," I responded and fired up our mobile internet system. "Nashua is the closest major city in New Hampshire to Massachusetts so there is some influence with that state. Once upon a time, the textile industry dominated the city, but with its demise, Nashua lost some of its luster. In terms of population, at 85,000, it is the second largest city in the state. An economic revival of sorts is taking place because it has been swept up in Boston's growth. Ironically, twice Nashua has been rated as one of the best places to live in the United States by Money magazine."

"Hey, if we like it here, let's move," Al chuckled. "We would fit right in this town with so many dying industries."

"Nothing to joke about," Gram remarked as he listened to the facts. "Too many cities across this country are dying just like this one. There is no reason we let these industries get away except for one thing: companies benefited by moving their factories overseas and now we are seeing the East turn into that 'rustbelt' that is so depressing."

"So we are heading into a depressed city with nearly a hundred thousand people and probably a lot of unemployment," Gram concluded. "What is the message?"

"Buy American," I spouted out. "This plays right into our platform about bringing back factories from off shore. Malden Mills, the maker of Polartec, is over the line in Massachusetts. When the plant burned down and the workers feared that the owner would move it off shore, he met with them right after the tragedy, told them they would continue to receive full paychecks until the plant was running again and they were going to remain right where they were. Imagine that? Taking care of your employees. Think about company loyalty at that plant. When I heard that story, I wondered just how some capitalists justified moving their plants away from the place where they first started. I'm sure that Malden paid a heavy price for keeping his plant where he did. I imagine he lost a lot of money, but something was more important to him than that. These are the kinds of people that I admire most. He did not worry about his own misfortune, but the fortunes of his people," I concluded.

"Think about this now," Gram continued. "What if Steve Jobs and Apple manufactured their I phones, I pads, I pods, Macs and any other products right here in America? Sales for the I phone last quarter topped 37 million. All of them were made in China. To my knowledge, none of Apple's products have ever been made in the USA."

"I wouldn't own one," I piped up.

"My kids all want I phones," Al said. "I told them to get a job and earn enough money to buy their own."

"Cold blooded dictator," Gram joked.

"I don't have the kind of cash it takes to put eight kids on cell phones. No way. I don't even have one myself, and I'm going to get phones for them? Do you think I'm nuts?"

"What do you tell them when they say that all their friends have phones?"

"I say great, go and use your friends' phones. You don't need a cell phone. We have a house phone and it works just fine," Al defended himself.

"What if they need to call home from school for something, or they are out and need your help?"

"Listen, I made it all these years without a cell phone and I'm still alive. I think they'll be just fine. Really. You guys take the cake. You think I should get phones for my kids?"

"Nope," Gram said. "We're just trying to make you feel like the heel you are. Meany. Meany," Gram continued calling Al names.

"Oh, I get it. Make me the butt of your jokes because I can't do anything about it like come over there and bust you up side of the head because I'm driving and you two are just having a good old time at my expense."

"You got it," Gram said. "But we love you just the same, Al."

We arrived in Nashua early in the morning and met with the local union president at a coffee shop. Jason Witt was a young fellow but full of energy. He was excited that we were in town and said he hoped we could really influence some of the people to join our movement because he was having a hard time organizing due to the chronic unemployment.

"We're in tough times here, and there does not seem to be any end in sight," he lamented. "We need to bring back the industries that made this town great once upon a time. So let's get to work, shall we?"

We were not going to be doing any major rallies in Nashua. Most of our campaign was going to be the traditional town hall style. Jason had arranged for us to gather at a small auditorium near the local high school. Gram immediately asked if we had permission to use the hall. Jason assured us that we did.

When we got there, the crowd was already gathering and we entered and moved through the mass of people shaking hands, telling people who we were and what we hoped to achieve by coming to this famous working class city.

A few minutes later, Jason called everyone to attention, introduced me to the people, and said, "Fire away, Leo is here to answer any and all your questions. I hope you are ready for a new political point of view and can support our own candidate in the next election for president of the United States. Leo," Jason concluded and turned the stage over to me."

A tepid round of applause greeted me as I took the microphone from him and said, "Good morning, my fellow Americans. Thank you for being here to listen to what I have to say and hopefully come to believe in the ideas that we are promoting, namely, that when America works, freedom lives and democracy thrives."

I studied the crowd and did not see any strong emotion in any of the faces that were staring intently at me. I continued. "We believe the American dream is threatened because the corporate structure in this country right now is slowly eroding any hope that lower and middle class people have of rising up and enjoying the bounty that is available for one and all if a person can find gainful employment. Nashua is a prime example of just what happens when corporations place profits over people. This once proud and productive manufacturing center is now facing slow decay because of the policies of the last four presidents. Yes, I am including President Obama in the mix. It is now time to reverse directions and make American workers a priority in the national conversation. Republicans and Democrats have done little to reverse the direction in which we are heading. I believe we can do better. I believe we can make our industries thrive once again. This will take effort, sacrifice and a commitment by all of us to band together and support one another by buying American. I could say a whole lot more now, but let me answer your questions."

Hands shot up in the room. A portable microphone was passed through the crowd to the center aisle.

"We've heard everything before. We've heard this song and dance about 'buy American' but what do you do when you go to a store and all the products that you look at are made in China, Taiwan, Sri Lanka, Korea or Israel? Hell, I can't even buy good tools any more that are made right here in the USA. What am I to do?"

"Thank you for bringing up this issue. I, like you, and I'm sure many of the people in this room, have had this same experience. We want something but it's not made here in America any more. Camping gear is a good example. Once upon a time, Kelty and a host of other brands were the standard of excellence in camping and backpacking. Slowly, but surely, these companies moved their manufacturing base off shore, mostly to China. Now there are few companies still producing products in the USA. The challenge is to find those that are and support them and them only. Don't buy something if it is not made here. This is where shared sacrifice comes in. This means sometimes we are just going to have to do without something we thought we wanted. The second part of the challenge is to call, write or email these companies and tell them that you would like to purchase their products but since none of them are made in the USA, you will not buy them until they start to manufacture their goods right here at home. This may take years, but remember Gandhi. He changed the entire culture in India when he encouraged Indians to use homespun and stop buying cotton products made in England and sent to India. The British were incensed but this was the beginning of the end for the British Empire in India."

"What makes you think you can ever win this race? You don't have a big name, very little money and the two major parties will do everything they can to rub your nose into the dirt. How can you win against odds like that?"

I smiled and said, "I agree wholly with your concern. Yes, how can I win against those odds? The Republicans and Democrats are so entrenched in our body politic that any third party cannot get a real foothold in the process. Yes, we've had a few try but they have failed miserably after one election cycle. I agree it will be difficult. However, the journey of a thousand miles begins with the first step. I am here today talking to you because already, people across America are waking up to the fact they do not have any voice in government. There is too much money talking. Lower and middle class people are barely represented in the political discourse. Look at what happened in Iowa with the Republicans. Romney's superpac beat up on Gingrich and he was almost annihilated. Gingrich is fighting back now because a billionaire from Las Vegas gave $5 million to Gingrich's superpacs to counterattack Romney. This is what we are up against. We can and will prevail in the end because as Gingrich aptly observed, 'People power always trumps money power.' One hundred and sixty million working people are a whole lot more powerful than the one percent of Americans who control a lot of money but can only vote once just like all the rest of us. Well, that is unless they buy your vote." People laughed. "No seriously," I continued. "The cost of each vote for Romney in the Iowa Caucuses was something like $147.00. Santorum spent the least at only $9.00 a vote."

Someone burst out, "How much are you spending?"

"Good question. Gram, do we have this number?" I asked.

"Not right now but we can work on it. We haven't really gotten any votes yet since we could not be in the Iowa Caucuses. We can now be counted as a write-in candidate here in New Hampshire and that is what we are counting on. No pun intended."

"There you go. This is the real beginning of our campaign. We can make a difference. It will just take time, effort and a willingness to challenge ourselves to believe that we can and will speak with a louder voice if we stand together and not let the billionaires control the message."

"I don't believe in unions. I don't like them. I don't want this country to become a socialist country. Sounds to me like what you're presenting is some socialist idea like we're getting from Obama."

"Not at all. What I am advocating is Fair Trade Capitalism, not fixed trade or false trade. Look, the corporations have fixed the rules on how we do business in this country. How is it possible for GE to create 200,000 new jobs in other parts of the world and eliminate thousands of jobs here in America? We already know the answer. They played the tax break game that the Congress over the years has failed to address. Just this year, Senator Bernie Sanders proposed an amendment to stop the tax breaks that corporations get for moving a factory out of the country. The amendment went nowhere. The Republicans wouldn't even let it come up for a vote. Why? We know the answer to that one. So many senators are beholding to corporations for donations they cannot make a decision that will kill off the golden goose that keeps them in power. We are devolving into a modified fascist type of state here in America with a heavy dose of social conservatism, anti-people policies and a thwarting of personal liberties and freedoms. We've been conditioned to fear that which is different, not to embrace it. We are judged to be Anti-American if we question our country, its leaders, policies and political activities. The threat that someone who opposes this government could be sent to Guantanamo as a 'terrorist' for challenging the system scares the bejesus out of most people. Yet, the most recent military spending bill includes a provision that permits the president to arrest American citizens and treat them like 'enemy combatants'. We have so much work to do, my friends. We just have to keep plugging away and not let our government get too far out of our reach."

"Brighter guys than us haven't been able to solve this economic crisis. What makes you think you can?"

"I can't solve it alone. We can solve it together. This is the difference. If I buy an American car instead of a foreign one, then my neighbor who builds the car makes some money. If he uses steel to build my car and I'm the one making the steel and his company buys steel from my company to make the car, I make money. This is the essence of fair trade as I see it. Free trade is when the corporations are free to do anything they want to make a buck including moving a plant from one country to the next anytime there is a better deal on the table from another country. Do you realize that Nike, the shoe company, doesn't own any plants at all? They own just the brand name. They move their production from one country to the next as the labor market dictates. Nike was making shoes in Cambodia paying workers $2.00 a day. When it got a better deal from Vietnam, Nike moved its manufacturing base to that country because it only had to pay workers $1.65 a day. Even though the shoes were still selling for more than a hundred dollars in the USA, Nike was cutting costs whenever possible to maximize its profits and minimize its costs."

"I don't like unions and I don't like people like you who think you have all the answers and come up here asking for us to support your communist ideas. Why don't you go back to where you came from and leave us alone. We don't need anyone with your kind of un-American ideas."

I smiled at the fellow who leveled the attack at me and then looked over to where Gram was standing. I could see his slight wink.

"Sir, I am not sure what makes you think I am a communist or that what I am saying is un-American. I believe in America and Americans. I have always believed in the honor of hard work. I am a steel worker, sir. I make a living by the sweat of my brow. I work in an American company on American soil and wish that I could go to work today producing steel and doing so right in my own home town. I cannot because the economic climate in this country, and quite frankly, in this world, is rather shabby right now. What I am advocating is not communism, but a solution for changing the way we do business so that lower and middle class working people share in the bounty of their labors." I stopped and waited to see if the fellow wanted to respond. He did not.

"Next question," I said opening the floor to more inquiry. I noticed that Gram gave me a thumbs up. I passed the test.

"Mr. Pollack, did you go to college and what did you study?"

I thought to myself, "Finally a softball question." "I went to The Ohio State University and studied history and social studies."

"What made you go to work in a steel mill if I may ask? Why didn't you go and use your degree for something else?

"When I graduated, I taught school for a year and then, when they were hiring people at the mill, decided that I wanted to go and work like my father had for forty years before he retired and eventually died from cancer. I wanted to experience the world that he lived in for four decades. I knew there was something missing in my own education, and I went there to get it. You might call working in the mill my Yale College or my Harvard." The people laughed at this not realizing fully where the quote was from and what point I was trying to make.

"We hear about crime all over the country. Murders, rapes, robberies and we wonder what makes people think that by keeping guns out of the hands of law-abiding people that we will be safer. Guns don't kill people. People kill people. What are your thoughts on gun control and gun ownership?"

"Though I don't own any guns, I believe that people do have the right to keep and bear arms. I don't know if the cities would be any safer with people packing heat as the saying goes. Who knows? They may be. I am not one to deny someone else his or her rights just because I don't necessarily believe that toting a sidearm will make me any safer. Even if I was carrying a gun and someone assaulted me, I don't know if I would want to shoot him. I would probably want to kick his butt and pronto, but to shoot him, I think not. We do live in a very violent country. Among industrialized nations, we have more murders per capita than any other. I am not sure what the cause is, but taking guns away from citizens will not stop people from killing people, that is for sure."

I drank some water. My mouth was dry. My eyes were unfocused and I needed a moment's break. "Excuse me," I said, "Can I run to the bathroom quickly and come right back? I won't be gone long."

Applause rang throughout the hall. I left and came back in less than two minutes. Relieved, I thanked everyone profusely.

"Next question," I said, re-engaging with the crowd.

"In this state, we don't like the federal government telling us what to do. We don't want Obamacare. We don't want anyone telling us we have to buy insurance. We just want to be left alone. I can't afford the damn stuff anyway."

"Sir, if you get sick what are you going to do?"

"You asking me, sonny," The elderly questioner replied.

"Yes. What are you going to do?"

"Well, go to the doctors and get some medicine and hopefully get well."

"How are you going to pay for it?" I continued the dialogue.

"Why, like I always have, with cash money."

"But what if you find out you need open heart surgery? You have clogged arteries and the only way to keep you alive is triple bypass surgery."

"Well, I guess I'll just go ahead and die, cause I can't afford that kind of operation," he replied and people uneasily laughed at his levity.

"No, you would get the surgery. The hospital would do it because you are a citizen, it is not elective surgery, and yes, you might have to pay the rest of your life for the service, but you would live. Consider this. We all pay for your surgery. Anyone who pays health care premiums pays for the uninsured person's health care. Hospitals and insurance companies are not charitable organizations. They are about as mercenary as any corporations can be. They just divide the cost among all their policy holders and that is the end of it. I don't think the health care plan went far enough. We still have pockets of people who are not going to be insured. We are also going to have people who are not going to receive preventive care because not enough of those kinds of procedures were included in the health care reforms just passed. Sir, health care is not a luxury. It is a human need. We may not 'need' it for 75 years but then when we are 75 years and two months old, we discover we have cancer and need serious medical attention. Without health care, we would just die. There is no need for this type of doomsday scenario. When we spread the risk across every person in the country, we can negotiate much cheaper health care premiums than we can if we have small pools of people."

"I just don't like the idea," the fellow concluded.

"You don't have to like it and you don't have to participate, but in the end you will probably need health care and we'll still take care of you even though you didn't pay your fair share."

"Too many times, people running for office make their ideas sound really good but if you got to be president you're going to have to work with congress and you won't have anyone in either house on your side. In fact, you might not be able to get anything done because both the republicans and the democrats are going to be pissed off that you're the president and not one of their own. How are you going to be able to work in such a climate as that where both sides don't like you or what you've done to their candidate?"

"I hope your prediction comes true and that I am the president. I wouldn't be running for the office if I didn't think I could win. I realize that a divided government may be hard to manage, but I would like for all of us to consider that this might actually be the best of all worlds. I won't be beholding to any corporations or wealthy people so I won't have to make decisions that satisfy them. I won't be a republican or democrat so I don't have to do anything to satisfy them. I can stand alone and take the middle ground and promote what is best for all people. You see, my friends, I believe that there are just as many conservative people as there are liberal people who want this country to flourish and for all people to realize the American dream. I don't think we are that divided. What and who is divided are the politicians and those who want our country to remain in turmoil so they can exploit the confusion for their own interests. I will be able to work with both sides of the aisle because I don't have to stand on one side or the other to find support. I can find it anywhere it is."

"You really believe you can work with both sides? You must be a real dreamer."

"Yes, I really think so because there is no other way to effectively govern. This government by antagonism has gone too far. This government by name calling is unproductive. Civility is essential no matter what way you are leaning politically."

I think I answered his question because he sat down and smiled at me and I smiled back.

"Our national debt is way out of control. What are you going to do to stop raising it every few months because the politicians just don't get it? We can't keep borrowing Peter to pay Paul."

"I agree. We owe $15 trillion dollars to a host of debtors. We need to do a number of things and do them well. First, we will end all Bush era tax cuts. Yes, we will all have to pay more. Just by ending those tax cuts, the Office of Management and Budget or OMB said we would be able to remove about $4.2 trillion of the national debt in the next decade. Second, we need to spend our money more wisely. Duplication in government services needs to cease yesterday. No, joking aside, there are more departments in the government than there are holes in Swiss cheese and that's the problem. The holes are more productive."

People laughed and I was amazed that I actually told a joke.

"Now, we are going to raise the taxes on capital gains, dividend earnings and a number of other hedge fund type, skip paying taxes kinds of loopholes that we all know exist and don't benefit anyone but the wealthy people. Folks, even if you were one of the 1% who makes in excess of $10 million a year, what would you do with all that money? You couldn't spend it all. Think about this. Even if you bought a new Mercedes Benz that cost $100,000 every day, you would only spend $3.5 million of your $10 million. What the heck would you do with 365 brand new Mercedes Benz autos anyway? You see what I'm driving at? Wealthy people really can't spend the money they earn. They just have it. What is even more amazing is that they don't invest it in starting new businesses as we might think. Sure, some do, but most hoard their money. They sit on it. Right now, it is estimated that there are $2 trillion dollars of net worth sitting on the economic sidelines because people and companies that are wealthy don't want to take any risks. What are they risking? They might lose half of their net worth. Oh, so they might go from two billion down to one billion or from ten million down to five? Once we get people paying their fair share and we stop borrowing money to pay off the debt and instead use the money that we have coming into the treasury, we will see the beginning of the debt declining."

"You really think so?" a follow-up question was asked.

"I have to believe so. What we are doing right now is just not working. We can't continue to cut taxes, cut spending and expect to pay off this debt. And by God, we are not going to pay off the debt by putting the burden on the backs of working people. This is not going to happen or there will be a revolt in this land. 160 million working people have paid dearly for the folly of so many ill-intentioned financial services people."

"What are your thoughts about energy independence and things like the Keystone pipeline?"

"My friends, it is a myth to believe we can ever be totally energy independent. We are interconnected with the entire world for resources that help us to power our civilization. What we can do is minimize some of our dependence and especially that which comes from nations that do not like us. What makes me laugh is that people still like our money. They like dollars and as long as they like dollars more than they like Euros or yen or other currencies, we will be able to sustain our lifestyle. Yes, we will pay more for finite resources like gas and oil, but we will not be destitute. As for the pipeline, I agree it should be built. I do not agree it should be built over the aquifer in Nebraska as planned. We cannot risk the possibility of contaminating safe fresh water resources. Secondly, we can consider shipping the oil to refineries in other parts of the country. My campaign committee studied this issue carefully. Do you realize that more than 30% of the refining capacity in this country is located in Texas and Louisiana? Now, we ship all those barrels of crude down there across the breadbasket of America. It is refined into gasoline, heating oil and other products. Then what? We truck it back across the country and distribute it. To think that this oil will stay in America alone is foolhardy. The oil will be sold on the world market. We will make money in the transportation of it, but we will not keep it totally in America. So, we've got to figure out how to use less fossil fuels, develop more alternative energy sources and find the balance between the two as we move slowly and irrevocably away from the one source and toward the other."

"So would you approve the building of the Keystone XL pipeline?"

"No. Not until we insure that we can do it safely," I replied and then continued. "The pipeline can and will be built. However, we don't need to rush to do something that can be an environmental disaster if we do not do it safely."

"Most New Englanders heat their homes with oil. What would you do to ease the pain of high oil costs?"

"What can I do? What can any president do to lower the cost of energy? These are perplexing questions. What I can do is to encourage conservation, insulation and downsizing."

"Downsizing? What do you mean by that, sir?"

My eyes lit up. I loved talking about small versus grandiose. "What I mean is make your home smaller. Downsize it. Shut the second floor down if you have one and live on the first floor. Drop ceilings in your home if you still live in one with ten footers. If they are eight feet high, lower them to six and a half feet. We don't live in the upper cubic space in any of our rooms. We live from the floor to the area about six and a half feet from the floor. Heat only that amount of air. Sounds crazy, but imagine if you stopped heating 25% of your house. You might not lower your heating bill by the same percentage but you would reduce it by at least a percentage of that amount and that means money in your pocket."

"What do you think about the Afghanistan war and what, if anything, would you do differently to either win the war or get the hell out of there?"

"Our military people work miracles wherever they go. We sent them into Iraq to take out Saddam Hussein and they did. Then, for years, they kept the peace even though this was not their primary mission. Now we've finally pulled out of that country. Amen. Let's stay out of there forever. Now as for Afghanistan, we have missed the mission. We pushed the Taliban out. We got a new government elected. Now we're bumbling along in a country that has been in armed conflict for more than a quarter century and is sick to death of foreign troops traipsing up and down its roads. We cannot do much more there so let's just gracefully exit and allow the chosen leaders to lead. If the Taliban, terrorists, or el Qaeda begin using the country as a staging ground again, we tell the world and ask the Afghan government to stop the organization or we will come in and take out this threat to world-wide peace."

The crowd was starting to get restless. Long ago, I lost track of the time. I looked over at Gram but he was studying the crowd and I could not catch his eye for any signals. I did not want to look at my watch and give the crowd some sense that I was anxious about the time. I did take a few more swallows of water. Luckily, Jason had enough water for me to continue to keep my throat wet.

"What do you make of this sewer of negative advertising that these candidates are flooding each other with? I'm sick of it. I can't stand it. What are you going to do? Add to it, too?"

"You won't see our campaign doing anything like this. First of all, we don't have the money to do so. Secondly, we wouldn't waste the money to portray our opponents as bad guys. Hear me today; believe me tomorrow. I won't waste my time attacking the other guys. I think they are all Americans. Ask me what I think of President Obama. I like him. He's an American. Ask me what I think of Newt Gingrich. He's an American. They are different from me. I've always lived from paycheck to paycheck. This is the norm for Americans. There isn't a candidate in either party that can actually say 'I understand that lifestyle, that condition of life.' So this is something that sets me apart from the others. I don't need to run ads to tell you that. I'll tell you directly, myself. This is who I am."

Finally, Jason Witt came to my rescue.

"Friends and neighbors. I think we've had a great opportunity to meet and understand our candidate and my next President, Leo Pollack, so let's give him a great round of applause like only New Hampshire folks can and wish him well in his campaign to fundamentally change America in the next four years."

The crowd applauded loudly and there was a marked difference from the earlier tepid endorsement of my being in their neighborhood.

I made no closing remarks and actually I did not want to do so. The question and answer session was enough. "Don't beat a dead horse". Once Jason shook hands with me I stepped off the stage and spent the next hour moving through the crowd, answering more questions, listening to the concerns of the people, posing for photographs with constituents, signing autographs, drinking more water and all the time, wanting to run to the bathroom again and again. I was sure that I was permanently doing damage to my kidneys by holding my bag for so long.

A pattern was quickly emerging as I ended each of my presentations. People would flock to me. They would want to see, hear and feel if I were for real. Some would want to ask more questions. Some would thank me for speaking for them. Still others would just stand aside and listen, not say a word, smile at times, or just stare as if I were some kind of novelty item. Women would get close, sometimes too close, and I would feel uncomfortable. Men's handshakes would vary in intensity. Some of the guys actually hurt mine when they gripped and stroked up and down. Those who wanted pictures of me taken with them seemed to be vain and I did not know how to respond except to submit to their requests. The time stopped. I was held in suspended animation. The people did not sense what was happening to me. They did not ask me when was the last time I ate, or drank or went to the bathroom. They did not inquire about my family, wife, children or anything that was personal. No, instead, they were trying to grasp who was this strange being in their midst who was asking them to trust that he could and would speak for them, and would represent them on the national stage. They would stare long and hard and form their opinions and then, once ossified, would stick with them until the election was over. Try as another candidate might, once the voter's mind was made up, nothing could change it, least of all facts and figures. Day after day, for an entire week that dragged along like a heavy weight upon a hiker's leg, we traveled up and down and across New Hampshire holding town hall meetings in Manchester, Portsmouth, Dover, Rochester, Concord, Laconte, Keen, Lebanon, Hanover, Plymouth, North Woodstock, Littleton, Gorham and Conway. So many towns and cities in so few days and in each one, the message was the same: When America works, Freedom lives and Democracy thrives.

We did not know if our efforts would make a difference. We could not be on the ballot as a party. In reality, we were not a party, but a movement, a loosely connected group of idealists making our way into the battle called the presidential race of 2012. We did not know what the outcome would be, but there was no fear that we would fail because we already knew we were making a difference by just being there and providing people with a third point of view and another choice.

When Gram, Al and I exited New Hampshire at the end of primary day, we could not predict what would happen. We drove back home to rest for a day before heading to South Carolina. We met the challenge. We gave it our all. We would just have to wait and see if the seed we had sown would produce fruit.

What happened next was shocking.

20. Big Time but Not Big Shots

When my phone rang, I snapped to attention. I thought I had shut it off before I went to bed so the ringing shocked me back to reality. I looked around and wondered where I was. The Liberty Bell bus cradled me from the elements. Yes, we were still on the road home from New Hampshire after spending a week immersed in town hall meetings. Rubbing my eyes, I stared at the glass screen. The name and number were familiar. What was he calling for at this time of the morning? What time was it anyway? Ahead of us, the lights were still on. Al must not have felt tired tonight because he was still driving. Strange. Everything was strange now. Who lives in a bus and travels all night long when he has a bed, a home, and a beautiful wife to cuddle with instead?

"Morning, John, what's up?" I answered the phone moving my mouth away from it while I cleared the thickness in my throat.

"You awake?"

"No, not really. I'm dreaming, right?"

"You will think you are when I tell you what just happened."

I shrugged off my torpor. "What?"

"You ready?" John challenged me.

"Sure. Shoot."

"We took 4.5 % of the vote in New Hampshire. Leo, our campaign has hit the big time. We are in the game. Do you hear me?"

I sat stunned for a minute, maybe two. Who knows? Maybe three or four.

"Leo, we came in ahead of Perry and were not too far behind Paul and that is without having you on the ballot. These were all write in votes. This is phenomenal. This is unheard of and now we're being inundated with requests for interviews, scheduling appearances, all kinds of things. The center is buzzing like a factory floor. Volunteers are pumped beyond comprehension. Our fund raising went up 200% in the last day. The moment the news broke, I was on the phone for two straight hours. I haven't slept all night long. Hey, how're you doing?"

"Fine now that I'm almost awake. I'm not dreaming am I, John?"

"Nope. This is for real. Where are you now?"

"Al, where are we?" I called out to one of the three musketeers.

"Who wants to know?"

"Your backseat driver," I replied.

"Somewhere near Ithaca, New York on the Southern Tier Expressway heading westbound."

"We're in central New York," I told John.

"Good. Good. You'll be home in about six hours. Are you coming in to the center today?"

"Sure. What else would I do but come in, but I'd like to see Basha and the boy."

"I know, I know. See them first and then come on in. We've got to capture the wave when it's rolling into the shore. Do you realize what this means? Do you understand that we've made it to the big show, the big time? This is wild, man."

"It was just a matter of time," I chipped in and rubbed my eyes again just to make sure that I was not really dreaming.

"We've got an ad campaign ready to roll this week in South Carolina and the money to put it on the air waves. Leo, you'll like it, but we need to get you to voice in your support. No Bull. This ad will capture people's attention and is not a lot of hype. They want you on the Today show in New York, too. What do you make of that?"

"Sounds great to me, John. This was a long week. We did so many town hall meetings that I lost count. My throat feels like it was rasped with a hack saw."

"How's your team holding up?"

"Al's a real trooper. He won't let anyone drive. We don't argue with him. He is tireless. Gram's insight is phenomenal and he is a great navigator. We make a good team. I do the cooking when we are moving, but most of the time, we get to eat on the trail. People are always offering us a lot of food. I've got to watch so I don't gain weight."

"Sounds like with the schedule you're keeping, you will lose instead of gain. Well, phone me when you get back to town. See ya," John said and hung up.

I leaned back and just stared out the front window and watched as the gray goose of dawn winged its solitary way across the landscape. The big time. We were on the national stage. This was the break we were all hoping for, waiting for, and now it was thrust upon us. Now what we needed to do was avoid becoming big shots. This would be the challenge. As I let this new reality flow through me, I could feel a sense of power bubbling up like a geyser inside of me. Soon, it would erupt. People wanted to interview me. The Today Show? How cool and yet how unreal. Everything about this experience contained a significant amount of unreality to it. Who was this Leo Pollack anyway? How can some unemployed steel worker really believe he can be the president of the United States? This thought rolled inside my brain like a marble on a pinball machine. I kept banging into the bumpers and up and down the board. I bounced feeling the ebb and flow of the campaign pushing me from one side to the other without any real sense of control. "Perhaps this is what all candidates feel," I said to myself. "I can't be that unique." Sure, when anyone contemplates being the leader of the entire country, there must be some sense of unreality about it. After all, this is not just any job. This is becoming the leader of the free world. The president is in charge of the most powerful country in the history of humankind. Now, the question was, how does a person not let the pressure, the responsibility, the status of it all get to him? I shrugged my shoulders and felt a cold chill flow down through me. The mission was clear. Be yourself. Change nothing but your underwear and socks and step up to the microphone wherever you are and tell the truth. Keep looking toward the future. Leave the other candidates do what they are going to do. They are Americans, too. They want the country to be the best it can be. They want people to go to work. This last thought stopped me in my thoughts. I wondered if some of them really did. Their plans were based upon already failed policies. I could do nothing about them. I would have to continue pushing our agenda. This was what we would do. Let them do what they were going to do. In the end, there would be three choices. I wanted our choices to make the most sense so that all working folks would find fulfillment in what we were proposing. The future need not be a fearful adventure. America was not staring into the abyss as some of the other candidates were stating. The battle lines were quickly being drawn. The Republicans wanted the government out of the way, less taxes, less spending and let people determine their own fate. President Obama was trying to navigate the middle ground. He was being too tenuous. I liked the guy. I voted for him. He disappointed a lot of people because he did not push hard enough to move America forward and heal the pain of so much economic chicanery. In the past three years, almost no Wall Street Bankers, nor financial services CEOs faced criminal charges for the clear fraud perpetrated upon the country by that entire industry. No wonder unfair lending practices were at the core of the housing meltdown. If you could rip off a million or two in selling subprime loans to unwitting buyers, scoot with the money and not face any charges, what would stop you from doing it? Other than the fact that it was illegal, unethical and immoral? Most crime is deterred because the criminal wants to "abort the crisis" and in this context, this means "not get caught". However, if the fear of being caught is reduced to less than a 1% chance, how many would take that chance? Since 2004, a lot of people have thought the risk was worth it. Now we are reaping the outcome of an entire sector of our economy that failed or chose to ignore the illegal, immoral and unethical nature of its acts. My mind kept coming back to John's call and what it all meant and what amazed me most was that we were on the road in the middle of rural New York state when we heard the news, not in some hotel lobby, pressing the flesh, and celebrating our "victory". We were really lowbrow. I was proud of that and would not change it for anything.

With that thought percolating through me, I got up, made coffee, and started to cook some egg tortillas for the crew.

When Al smelled the coffee brewing, he said, "Finally, I thought I was working for a slave master."

"Hush up! Drive on and keep your mouth shut."

"Yes, master. However, listen to this. I'm the one with the CDL. The old days are over. You can't drive anymore. This isn't the Leo-mobile. This is the Liberty Bell Bus and I'm the main man. So just you watch how you treat me or I might go on strike."

"Watch that kind of trash talking," Gram said waking up and sitting on the side of the couch where he crashed last night. "We don't need anyone coming at us and alleging we're unaware of racial stereotypes. Newt might like the message that he's using calling Obama the 'food stamp' president, but our campaign has to be above that kind of trash."

"Got it. Thanks Gram," I said wholeheartedly.

"What we do in this bus will eventually leak out somehow. I'm sure that one of us won't be the source, but who knows, we might be bugged already."

"What?" Al asked incredulously. "Who would want to bug this bus?"

"Who wouldn't? By the by, did I hear a phone ringing earlier?"

"Sure did," I said to him biting my tongue wanting to blurt out the good news.

"So who was it? You're being awfully mysterious, Leo."

"Gallagher called," Al chimed in. "I don't know what he was talking to Leo about but I could tell it was from home."

"So?" Gram asked.

"Let's turn on the morning news and see what's happening in the world," I replied.

Two minutes later, reports from the New Hampshire Primary were on the screen and then, magically, miraculously, my picture and the story of our 4.5 % performance n first primary of the 2012 Presidential Campaign made the headlines. Gram and I watched in awe. Al, still driving, turned his mirror so that he could see behind him and multi-tasked. When it got too much for him, he pulled over on the berm, flicked on the four-ways, and sat with us watching the big screen TV.

Flicking across the channels on the remote, the story was on all the major network and cable news programs. Our eyes were crazy glued to the images. Nothing could distract us. Nothing that is until we were awakened by red, blue, and white flashing lights flickering through the bus windows. Al got up quickly, opened the door and went outside. We looked out and watched as he waited for a New York State Police Officer to exit his vehicle.

"What are we doing wrong?" I wondered.

"Hosting a celebration party on the side of a New York Interstate," Gram responded. "We might be parked illegally."

"We have four ways on!"

"We'll find out. Al looks like he's doing fine. What's this? The officer is walking around to the other side of the bus. Hey, get ready, Leo. Meet another voter."

Sure enough. The officer wanted to meet me and I stepped out on the side of the highway and talked for a few minutes with Officer Myron Daily. He was just going off duty when he drove past, saw the Liberty Bell Bus and decided to be the first to congratulate us on our win in New Hampshire. I replied that I did not consider it much of a win. He said, "Mr. Pollack, for working people without a voice and a battery of lobbyists in Washington fighting for us, it is a win. Besides, we're the people that across the nation are being attacked day in and out by the regressive governors who think that all public employees are selfish, ignorant and don't care about America." He shook my hand, thanked me for running, said he was going to vote for me in the New York primary and in the general election, and finally asked us not to park too long on this stretch of the highway because it was not safe. He drove off with his siren wailing and we waved at him standing there by the side of the road like thunderstruck schoolboys.

"Now what?" Al asked.

"Now what, what?" Gram chuckled. "We go on home. There's nothing we can do standing here by the side of the highway in central New York state except get stopped again by a less accommodating and perhaps Republican state copper."

We rolled west on the Southern Tier Expressway drinking pot after pot of fresh coffee, talking as fast and as loud as we could about everything that was happening and wondering what surprises we would discover when we got home. All along the way, drivers passing the Liberty Bell Bus honked, flashed their lights, turned on four ways, waved and pointed at us. We were just beginning to feel the "Big Time" and it was amazing.

Driving into the Buckeye on Interstate 90 was always a thrill for me. I loved the old sign that used to say: Ohio – Heart of it All. When viewing its outline, it did resemble a heart. I was not sure what made the state adopt a new catch phrase, but I liked that one. We headed down I-11 toward home. I suggested that we go straight to the hall to check in before we dispersed for home. Gram said he was home meaning the bus was it. I smiled and said, "I'm talking about home home." Al said he didn't mind. Marie was not ready for him yet anyway. She was not sure where he was because he had not called her today.

Pulling into the parking lot of the union hall, we noticed that there was a new banner on the side of the building. It read: Temporary National Headquarters of Leo Pollack – next President of the United States. Al was impressed. He laid on the air horn for a full minute and in no time, people came streaming out of the building. We held a grand reunion in the parking lot. There were hugs and kisses, laughing, catcalling, teasing and joking flowing through the crowd. Someone watching from the sidelines would have thought that we were having a love fest. Indeed, we were.

Finally, someone broke the magic spell and said it was time to get back to work and we all headed inside. John was elated that we were home safely. He called an impromptu "cabinet" meeting of the team and we all huddled up in the conference room.

Everyone was in an extraordinary mood. Our energy was infectious. Laughter filled the air. We did not get right down to business because we just wanted to enjoy the moment. Every person in the room was working doubles every day and loving it and now the fruit of our labor was showing.

Finally, John grounded us in reality. "Okay, team, we've got many miles to go before we sleep. Leo. Your thoughts."

I stood up, walked around the room and hugged everyone. "All I can say is that I am a part of the best team that any man could play on and thank you all for making this dream become a reality. We did it. We've made the national stage and the light is on us now. Wow! What a rush!"

Everyone clapped, hooted and hollered.

"John," I said, "When you called me the next day after I stood up and started this unbelievable journey, I could feel your enthusiasm and unqualified belief that we could do this. You made the difference in me. All of you, each and every one of you makes me feel proud to be standing among you and experiencing what joy there is in working toward a goal that will profoundly change America, politics, the way we do business and most of all, our own perception of ourselves as powerful people in our own simple way. No one could ask for more. If I died right now, I'd be in heaven."

"Man, don't talk like that," Fritz cried out. "We don't want any bad mojo in this room."

"Leo," Carol added. "You can't die now. What are we going to do with the $3.4 million dollars the campaign has raised?"

"No way, Carol?" I exclaimed.

"Yes, and the money is flowing in faster than I ever imagined it would. We were at only $3.13 yesterday and today, we've gone up that much. People are buying into our message and we are poised to reach $5 million by the time we get into South Carolina."

"Which brings me to the next item on the agenda that does not really exist, but it sounds good, and that is, South Carolina? We have less than a week to get down there and start running ads and doing appearances. When do you want to leave?   "Tomorrow, John, we can't waste time, can we."

"I thought you might want to spend a day at home with the wife and kid," he responded.

"I would love to do that, but we are pressed for time. We've got to get down there and on the stump."

"Well, first, you've got an engagement in New York. They want you on the Today show, remember?"

"Hey, you didn't tell us anything about that," Gram and Al both attacked me.

"I forgot to," I defended myself.

"How could you forget something that cool?" Al asked.

"Al, I just did."

"I think you should do it as soon as possible," Gram said. "Strategically, the iron is hot now. Pick it up and brand yourself as the only candidate who truly speaks for working people."

"I hear you, Gram. What about tomorrow?" I asked the group.

"Figured you wouldn't waste any time. We got two tickets for you and Gram to go to New York tonight. Arriving at 10 pm. Cab downtown to a hotel. Show tomorrow morning. Back here by 4 pm tomorrow afternoon. Rushed affair but there is so much to do like you said."

"Gram, you ready to hit the Big Apple?" I asked my chief of staff.

"Let's do it?"

"What about me? You don't need your lowly bus driver now so I can't go along for the ride and not have to drive?"

John walked over and handed three tickets to Al. "No Al, you can drive on this one. You've got to get these guys to the airport and only you can do it."

We all harassed him because of his surliness when he thought he was not being included in our travel plans.

"On a more serious note, we've been hacked. Fritz, you want to let the team know what's happening."

"Sure, John. Last night we experienced a major shutdown on our network, an outage on the home page, and an attack on our on line donation protocols. Carol believes we did not lose anything but someone wanted to put a damper on our party today. I am backtracking and doing all that I can to isolate the source of the attack, but folks, this is not something we need right now. I can only believe it will get worse as we become more successful. John's authorized some money to beef up our system and I'm getting some of my geek buddies to come in and give me a hand to stabilize things."

"Was what happened criminal in nature?" Gram asked.

"Not overtly but any time someone hacks into a site and messes with financial transaction protocols, there is an element of criminality to it. The hard part is to catch the person or persons and then prosecute them, Fritz added.

"We'll lose out on that end. By the time we track them down, we'll be another month into the campaign," Gram lamented.

"I am hoping that Fritz's reinforcements will shore up the network and we'll be safe. In the mean time, Carol is in close communication with Kilpatrick at the bank and things are safe there. He is aware of what is going on and is taking steps to insure that his assets and ours are safe. We may shift our procedure to a larger system using the bank's own site to collect donations in a safer manner. We're just not sure yet what we are going to do," John concluded. "Nothing ventured, nothing gained. Hey folks, it could be worse. We could have been robbed by hackers and trying to mount a campaign without any money. This whole episode just reinforces how high the stakes are in this election."

"I still think its Democrats that are playing the dirty tricks," Gram said. "They have the most to lose."

"We don't know now and let's not even bring that up except in this room. We don't want to antagonize them any more than we already have by mounting a campaign that will unseat their sitting president."

We all listened to him and pondered what he was saying.

"Now, Judy, what about the ad campaign?"

"We've taken on the monumental task of creating 30 second ads that can be run in multiple markets for a minimal amount of money. Some are for TV and most are for radio. We've modified the theme somewhat from 'When Americans Work, Freedom Lives and Democracy Thrives' to, for South Carolina at least, 'Buy American and Put an American Back to Work'. The economy in South Carolina is in worse shape than many places in the country and unemployment is way above the national average. North and South Carolina saw a major industrial meltdown in the last two decades as we all know and so we want to play up this angle. Leo, all I'll need from you is ten minutes to get you staring into the camera and saying, 'I'm Leo Pollack, Candidate for President, and I approve this message.' That's it. We can roll with it starting in a day. I've got a number of contracts ready to go and all I need is the tape. Can you do it today before you leave?" she asked.

"We'll do it right after this meeting," I said.

"Great. Then I can get on to the production team, send it out to the media and have it playing by tomorrow night across South Carolina."

"Amazing," I said. "Thanks, Judy. You're a peach."

"I can help you with anything you might need," Gram offered to Judy.

"I'd like that, Gram. We can talk after the meeting."

No one in the room said a word, but we were all aware that these two were forming some sort of liaison.

Before anyone started to say something about them, John focused us on security issues again. "Big Jack is on to something and it relates to the hacking into our site and other breaches of our security. Jack, you want to give us an update?"

Big Jack stood up. He was a tall man, at least six feet five inches in height. He was muscular, agile and he had a glare, not a stare. Unless you knew him, you would think that he could knock you down just by looking at you if he wanted to do so. Jack and I worked together in the mill for six years. At first, he did not trust me. It took nearly a year before he would talk to me at all. We would work all day long on a job and he would not say anything. I would make small talk and he would listen but he would not respond in any way. Finally, one day, he broke the ice and glared at me. "I don't like people who tell lies." That was all he said. I did not respond to his statement. I tried to remember if I ever lied to him in the past. I could not remember anything that he might have interpreted as a "lie". Day after day, we worked side by side doing all sorts of manual labor. He never talked unless

I asked him something specifically related to what we were doing right at that moment. When break times came, I would sit down, drink some coffee and eat a snack, but often, Big Jack would disappear and not return until the break time passed. I never asked him where he went or why he did not take his break right where we were. More than a year after Big Jack and I started to work together, an incident occurred that changed our relationship.

I was the kind of person who always helped others do their work. I believed that what went around came around: Do a good turn today and someday a good turn would come my way. Skinny Jack, a second helper and a fellow who was a preacher outside of work, was having a hard time doing his job because he got overheated and probably got a dose of heat exhaustion. None of the third helpers would come to his aid. Most of them were white guys and Skinny Jack was African-American. I realized that Skinny needed help and I jumped right in and helped him get his job done including digging out his heat when it was time for the furnace to tap. He was appreciative and thanked me repeatedly. I said, "Jack, pass it along." After this incident, Skinny Jack and I were very close, but some of the other third helpers or "slaggers" as they were called, resented my helping him. I assumed it was because he was African-American and I was white and they did not like that at all. I really did not care, but I could feel the cold shoulder whenever I was around them. Big Jack had observed all this and from that time on, he began to talk to me whenever we were assigned to work together.

Our break out day came when we were forced to work inside a furnace that was being torn down using a jackhammer to break apart the bricks forming the floor of the furnace. We were at it for a solid seven and a half hours. I never let up. I held my own even though I was almost half the size Jack was and my arms were garter snakes compared to his pythons. That day, when we took our breaks, Jack sat with me and we talked. He told me about playing college football at Youngstown State. He reflected upon the day when the old coach called him a "boy" and Jack called him on that and said he owed him an apology. The coach, a grizzled old character who would eventually die before he retired, called Jack "uppity". Jack told the coach that he would not play for someone who was a racist. The coach told him to leave the field. Jack filled the coach's ear with some expletives, left the field and never played football again. He did not graduate from college because he lost his scholarship. Since then, he worked odd jobs until he got hired in the mill and here he was and probably would be for the rest of his life.

Big Jack was an intense person. He was street smart, strong as two normal men, intuitive, fast on his feet like a sprinter, and devoted to his wife and son. Like me, he had only one child, a boy that he doted on. Of course, he called him "Little Jack".

Now we were again working together but in entirely different circumstances. I was elated that Big Jack wanted to be a part of the campaign. I wanted to have him in my life. Since we took such a long time bonding, we were like brothers.

"We're being watched all the time. Leo, your house is under constant monitoring. I need to get inside this week and make sure that your phone is not tapped and there are no other bugs inside as well. Al, before you drive away today, let me get into the Liberty Bell Bus and scan it for devices. This seems like fantasy, but there is a strong indication that the other sides will not stop at just watching us from a distance as this campaign unfolds. Mr. President, I have guys monitoring your home 24/7 and will continue to do so as long as you are just a candidate and not living in the White House."

"Jack, I'm not the president yet and you don't need to call me sir," I said to him.

"Sir, you are, sir, or Mr. President to me. I didn't come to work for you because you are a loser. I knew long ago that you were not a liar and I told you that I don't like people who lie. We have to make sure that you are protected. Until the government commits to providing you with Secret Service protection, you are in my care. Period. Now, when we leave for South Carolina, I'll be with you. We'll have a lead and a follow car and I'll be driving one of them. This will be our standard pattern. At least four men will be on duty at all times. We will keep you safe, sir. The future belongs to us and we are not going to let it get away by letting something happen to you or yours."

I sat mute, feeling very safe, cared for, protected by a man who once did not even talk to me for more than a year.

"Jack, I am honored to be on the team with you."

Big Jack barely smiled. We sat quietly for a few minutes. No one broke the silence.

"Welcome to the real world," John finally said breaking the negative spell that was cast over us. "We just have to be constantly vigilant. Don't leave your cell phones lying around. Be aware of what you put in your email messages. Shred any documents that you do not want someone to get their hands on. I don't want to put us into a scare mode of operation, but just let's be careful, shall we? Now, what's left? Al, how's the bus?"

Al took the opportunity to extol the pure joy of driving such a classy vehicle. "To bad no one of you have a CDL because you'd love to drive this sweet ride."

"I have one," Gram said.

Al glared at him. "You haven't offered to drive one mile since you came on board. Hey, I know you can fly a plane but can you drive a bus?"

"I said I have a CDL. I didn't say that I wanted to use it. You do a fine job, Al. You are smooth and should have been a pilot. So no, I don't want to drive the bus, but yes, I do have a CDL."

Al calmed down quickly. He really had a short fuse, but he was getting used to the way that Gram teased, and once he realized just how much Gram had led him, he smiled and said, "You got me again, sucker. Stay awake. This day is not over, not by a long shot."

Gram feigned sleeping in the meeting. We all laughed.

"Carol, what's the latest total?"

Carol pulled out her cell phone and pushed a few buttons and then she said, "We started the day at $3.4 and now we are at $3.76. How about that?"

"Amazing, simply unbelievably beyond words," was all that I could say.

"Leo, you reached the people and they want to be a part of this movement. What's so surprising?" John asked.

"Oh, I don't know. That kind of money is just beyond my comprehension."

"Remember it tomorrow when you're on the Today Show. They may ask how we're doing with fund raising and you can tell them we're making remarkable headway and want even more people to join us."

"I'll do that," I replied.

"Fritz," John asked. "Is there any way that we can get some kind of digital marquis set up in this building that would record in real time the money we are raising?"

"I don't see why not," Fritz said.

"Coordinate that with Carol. I think it will make all the volunteers really get excited. I want this up in public so that anyone who comes to visit us will see just what we are doing and everything is above board."

"We can make this happen," Judy concluded.

"Great. We are just beginning to hit on all eight cylinders," John concluded.

"What time do we have to be at the airport, Al?" I asked.

"Three PM. I'll come and get you about 2:30. Big Jack, are you going?" Al asked.

Big Jack held up his airplane ticket, but he did not smile.

"Folks, we've made the big time, but now we've got to be really cool and not get big heads. We're not big shots but real people who can really affect the course of history in America if we work together and continue to tell the truth, focus on the prize and don't let our guard down because as we have heard, there are forces out there that are not happy about our upstart campaign. Let's go out there and make a difference."

We broke up. I thanked each person individually for his or her hard work. Al, Gram, Big Jack and I finished the logistics for our trip. We walked outside and stood chatting with one another. We did not want this day to end, but it was only half over and we had a lot more to do. I checked my watch. Twelve thirty pm. I would have less than two hours at home with Basha and I would not even get to see Janko. I decided to stop by his school, surprise him, then go home, and spend an hour or so with Basha.

As we drove out of the parking lot, I stared at the huge new banner that read, "Temporary National Headquarters…" I had to look away. Tears welled up in my eyes and I leaned back in the seat and marveled at how far we had come in such a short period of time and wondered just how far we would go in the next ten months.

The skies exploded, the rains came down and we rolled across town through a deluge, but I did not care because I was going home for at least an hour and that was better than not going home at all.

21. The Today Show

While sitting in the airport terminal, I read in The Nation that in the last presidential election, people in the red states that voted for John McCain had higher rates of divorce and spent more money on internet pornography than the people in the blue states that voted for Barack Obama. On the surface, such facts did not mean much. Divorce rates were higher in Georgia than in Pennsylvania. More people in Florida paid to view porn than those in New York. What struck me the most about these facts was that family values issues were a platform in the Republican Party. How many times did Sarah Palin rail about family values while she was on the campaign trail making it sound like only Republicans loved and respected their kinfolk? Now we had another way to view their world and it was a little shocking.

I looked around the airport terminal and saw folks scurrying here and there. I wondered what all the busyness was about and began studying some of the actors on this reality stage. Businessmen were no longer obvious. Many men did not wear suits when traveling. Businesswomen were more apt to be dressed nicely than their male counterparts were. They were still paying their dues as they "arrived" in a men's world. More packs were on people's backs now than luggage being dragged behind on wheels indicating a shift toward carrying one's own load. Dress hats were missing. Ball caps appeared the new standard. What overwhelmed me more than anything else was the dullness of peoples' dress. Black, blue, brown and gray were the dominant colors. Gone were flashy reds, yellows, and chartreuse. Rarely did I view a shirt that stood out from the masses, a sweater that caught my eye, a pair of pants with a design in them that made me think that the person possessed a little daring in his soul. Our world was becoming colorless. Like Communist China, our people were slowly losing their individuality. What happened? Where were the free spirits of the 1960s who sported tie-dyed clothing and bandannas and scarves and brilliantly colored jewelry? I searched for just one such soul but after ten minutes gave up. The species was gone. I made a mental note to start wearing brighter clothing. Red shirts instead of blue. White pants instead of black. Do anything to raise the peacock factor in the body politic.

To pass the time, Gram and Al were engaged in some sort of orienteering game that he, Gram, had created. His flyboy years were gone but he still loved to pretend that everywhere he went he was on some sort of mission. Since he was our main man on the road, Al fell right into the activity just like any schoolboy would who saw some way to be distracted from the boredom of waiting. Gram called it "Vectoring in a Bubble" and was intense in his pursuit of perfection. He was intense about most things and that was a quality he brought to our team that made him special.

Big Jack was here and there. If you were looking for him, you would have a hard time finding him in the crowd even though he was six feet five inches tall and dark as Hades. He amazed me in his chameleon-like ability to move about without being obvious. If I did not know his life story, I would bet he had been a Navy seal or something like that, an operative in the CIA, an undercover cop in a big city. I felt very safe with him on my side. I did not like to admit it, but the last meeting demonstrated to us all the need for enhanced security. In many ways, I was pissed off that protection was necessary in the United States of America. After all, what was I doing wrong? What kind of people were out there that did not want to see a third party candidate rise up from the ranks of the American citizenry? Whoever they were, Big Jack was not going to let them spoil our fun, derail our mission. I did not know who else in the airport was also on our team. I asked him before we went through security, "Who else is on our side?" He just stared at me and did not answer. His eyes were blank dark orbs set in an ebony visage. I did not pursue it. They were somewhere. Only he knew who they were and they were even less visible than he was. We had not spoken since disembarking from the car we brought to the small airport. At once, he left us and moved right into surveillance mode.

We boarded and our flight was quick and easy. New York was just an hour away by commuter plane and so we were crawling out of the cramped aluminum tube in no time. We quickly found a cab, gave the driver the address and piled out in front of our hotel in New York City.

After registering and checking out our rooms, we decided to take a walk around town. Big Jack did not like this idea, but he could not override our veto.

"Jack," Al cried, "I've never been in the Big Apple. Come on, man. Lighten up. We've got to walk around a little bit, see the big skyscrapers, ground zero and all the hookers walking up and down the streets."

"In what order of preference?" Gram asked.

"Funny guy," Al barked back at him.

Big Jack did not respond. We knew what he thought. We went anyway. He was our shadow, our back, our invisible shield against harm.

New York streets are unlike any other streets in the country. The franticness of the moving people is unique. Other big cities have their activity. New York's is almost frenetic. We could not walk side by side down any sidewalk we chose. Even at 6 pm in the evening, the crowds were still thick like flies swarming a piece of dung. We were hungry and found a little place to eat. Italian. Simple. No big deal. The food was good but we were shocked when we saw the bill. Nothing was cheap in this city. Big Jack encouraged us to return to the hotel and get some rest. Al and Gram decided to mosey about town a little bit. Big Jack escorted me back to our room. He was staying with me.

"So here we are, Jack. New York. What an adventure."

"Sir, we are on the right path. We just need to watch and be careful."

"You really think there are folks watching us here in town tonight?"

"I know it."

"How do you know it?"

"Two people on the commuter plane that flew in with us are in the hotel. They have rooms. One is a floor above. One is on this floor."

"Are you kidding me?"

"No sir."

"Who are they?"

"I don't know, but they won't be bothering us tonight, or tomorrow."

"What do you mean by that, Jack?"

"I'd rather not say, sir."

"Jack?"

"Yes sir?"

"We've got to be on the up and up all the time. I mean it."

"Yes sir."

"So what do you mean, they won't be bothering us."

"They won't be bothering us is what I mean."

"Jack?"

"Sir?"

"You are not going to elaborate?"

"No sir."

I did not know what else to say. Taking a warm shower helped me to relax. The exchange with Big Jack filled me with mixed emotions. I realized he was doing everything he could to protect me but I did not want him to begin doing things that might be interpreted, or in fact be, illegal and unwarranted. His inscrutable nature was something that unnerved me when we worked together, but now it was more pronounced than I remembered. I concluded that I would rather have Big Jack on my side than have him against me.

While I read quietly lying in bed, I wondered how the family was and so I called Basha. She was just putting Janko to bed. We talked for a while and then I signed off, telling both of them I loved them dearly. Janko and I said his prayers over the phone before I hung up. Some things we just had to keep as normal as possible.

I did not remember falling asleep. I remembered waking up and staring at the light that was still on. Big Jack was not in the room. I wondered where he was prowling at this time of the morning. The clock read 3:33 am. I stared at it for a long time. There was something symbolic about that number. What was it? I would not learn the meaning of 333 for many months to come.

Gram, Al and I packed and were down eating breakfast when Big Jack slipped down at our table and reported that we were doing well this morning. None of us asked what he meant by that. We had to get moving. We were on in less than two hours and the studio told us that we needed to be there by 7 am.

The cab whisked us from the hotel to the studio. In less than ten minutes we were in front of Rockefeller Center where the show's broadcast facilities were located. What an impressive building. We piled out, Al and Gram took charge of our gear, and I went inside to find the set managers.

Inside the lobby, I was met by a host who immediately recognized me, called me by name, and ushered me back behind the scenes. I was amazed that she knew me, but then again, I was here to do the Today Show. These people were not amateurs.

Makeup was the next step. I sat down in a chair where directed and the woman applied my false face. She was not friendly and did not talk to me so I did not say much to her. Perhaps what unnerved her was that Big Jack kept checking in on me. When she asked me who he was, I responded, "My brother. He's very protective and always wants me to look my best whenever I'm going on camera." She applied the cosmetics very meticulously. I enjoyed the moment.

It was time. An usher came to get me. I thanked the woman for making me look so handsome. She said, "Honey, I didn't have to do anything to make you look good." I gave her a hug and told her that today, I was here to represent her and 150 million more people like her who deserved to have a voice in American politics. She was taken aback by my words. Her cool crust quivered slightly.

A television set is an amazing place. It's the collection of high tech machinery which picks up the sound and picture in one place, converts it into energy, sends the information along through wires and space and is decoded in the distance by a television set. What genius! What a team effort it takes to make the world a little better place in which to live. Everything about the process fascinated me. I was a grown man, but at that moment, I was back again in Dusty Roads studio. This time I was not packing a gun, but a whole lot of ideas that I hoped would shoot the daylights out of the old myths, lies and deception that plagued our nation today.

I was met by the set director, Phil Jones. He was polite and efficient. "We'll be going on in just ten minutes. You will have three minutes prep time with Mr. Lauer and then we'll be ready to broadcast. Any questions?"

"None that I can think of," I responded but wishing Gram was here so that he could help me out. I did not know where Big Jack was but I was sure his presence was being felt somewhere in the building.

Matt Lauer could not come and meet me. I saw him sitting on the stage talking to the current guest. I was not sure what they were discussing. I tried to remain calm, but this was not Cleveland Today. This was "Today", the fourth longest running American television series and first broadcast in 1952. Dave Garraway was its first host and the program continued to evolve for the past 60 years. Now it was my turn to experience the show, to have my 15 minutes of fame as Andy Warhol said we were entitled to expect in this lifetime. Deep down inside, I was hoping for a whole lot more than just 15 minutes, but not for me. What I was hoping for was that our movement would live on long after my fifteen minutes were up and that more and more people would emerge from the nooks and crannies of working America to assume leadership roles in every part of our local, state and national government. Ronald Reagan was dead wrong. Government is not the problem. The problem is the people in the government who do not do their best every day to make the world a better place in which to live.

"It's time, Mr. Pollack," Phil Jones said to me and waved his hand sideways for me to follow him. As I stepped from the shadows onto the brilliantly lit stage, I could feel the heat pressing down upon my skin. Luckily I was a steel worker and this was nothing compared to what it felt like when you stuck your nose over the edge of the chute when molten steel was pouring out of the tap hole and draining into the ladle. That was real heat; close to 3000 degrees.

Matt Lauer stood up and shook my hand as I walked up to him.

"Welcome Mr. Pollack. We're excited about having you here today. Please have a seat." Matt Lauer was all business. I knew that time was of the essence so I just listened and prepared myself for whatever was about to happen.

"We will start out with my brief introduction of you and then the format will be simple question and answer. Please try to keep your answers short. You know, less than a half minute or so. I know that might be hard, but we want to make sure that we cover as much ground as we can in the thirteen and a half minutes we will have for your segment."

"You mean I don't get my full fifteen minutes of fame?" I asked.

Lauer laughed and said, "No, no, but we'll give you an IOU. Something tells me that you are not going to get shortchanged on your fifteen minutes, Mr. Pollack."

The floor director gave us the sign. Lights on the cameras started flashing. I could see the red beam brightly. Now I was psyched. This was the moment when we really were going "national" and I so wanted to do my very best.

"Five, four, three, two, one," Phil Jones counted as he flashed the last three numbers with his fingers. We were now live across America.

"Welcome back. This morning we are privileged to be the first national program to host Leo Pollack, an unemployed steel worker who is mounting a third party campaign for the presidency of the United States. Just this week, Mr. Pollack received 4.5 percent of the vote in the New Hampshire primary through write in votes astounding the political press and pundits everywhere across the country. His is a populist movement, and he is here today to share some of his ideas with us. Thank you for taking the time to be with us, Mr. Pollack."

"You're very welcome," I replied and smiled as brightly as I could.

"To call your candidacy unconventional truly minimizes what is taking place. You are an unemployed steel worker who has never held office in your life, never run for any elected position, are skipping all the preliminary steps and seeking the highest office in the land. What makes you believe you are qualified to be President?"

Right from the start, I could expect no softball questions. So be it. "What qualifies me is the Constitution of the United States. I am at least 35 years of age and a native-born citizen of this country. There are no other requirements that are listed that I am aware of that would disqualify me. Running an equity trading company or being a former senator, congressman or governor are not more important positions than being a working person who gets up every day and goes out into the world and produces a product. We are all equal before the voters of this nation. What may make me more qualified than any of the current republican candidates and the President, too, is that I actually am a person who can speak to working class people because I am truly one of them."

"Your announcement that you were seeking the highest office in the land was made in an unemployment office in your home town. Since then, almost all of your campaign stops have been the same venue: places where people who are unemployed gather. What is your point? What are you trying to achieve?"

"These are the people who really need the leaders of our country to shine light on them. They are not just statistics. They are not just the 'fourteen point two million' unemployed. They are mothers and fathers, brothers and sisters, yes grandmothers and grandfathers who through no fault of their own are not able to work. There is no one I've ever met who was unemployed and getting unemployment compensation and maybe food stamps that was happy with his or her lot. Like me, they would rather be working. What is wrong with our society, our economic system, when it does not provide for the working people who want to be productive and contribute to the society in which they live?"

"Mr. Pollack, what is wrong with that society?"

I took a deep breath. "What is wrong is we let global competition trump taking care of our brothers and sisters right next door. My mother used to say, 'Charity begins at home'. She's dead now but I remember that principle of hers and live it every day. We are running around the world making other countries safe for democracy while our own people are struggling to make ends meet. Yes, we are still the richest nation in the world by far, but the relative gains that working people have made in the past thirty years are rapidly being eroded by this inequity in our economic system. This erosion of the working people's healthy standard of living needs to be reversed."

"When America works, freedom lives and democracy thrives. When you buy American, you are putting an American to work. I have nothing against the workers in other countries, but I do have something for American workers. We have moved so many manufacturing jobs off shore that it is time to stop it, reverse the process, and bring them back. Don't buy anything if one of your neighbors does not make it. I mean an American neighbor. Buy a GM car because your neighbor makes it. Yes, there are parts made overseas that are put into that machine. Demand that GM makes its parts here in the US. After all, we still own 24% of the company. We can tell the leadership what to do. This is the way we begin to take care of each other."

"Yes, Mr. Pollack, but we live in a global economy. We can't just turn our backs on other nations and expect them not to react in much the same way, can we?"

"No, they won't like it. They will react to it. We cannot continue to live on the credit card economy. We need to pay our bills. This will require sacrifice and not just from rich people paying more money in taxes."

"What are you advocating, Mr. Pollack?"

"End all the Bush tax cuts for all people. Close every loophole that corporations use to hide their money off shore. We lose hundreds of billions of dollars every year because of legal but unethical tax provisions that permit a company like GE to pay no taxes to the federal government. I paid more than that company did and I only worked for three months last year. Where is the fairness in a system like that?"

A red light started flashing. "In a moment, we will return to our interview with Mr. Leo Pollack, the working person's candidate for president."

Cut. The camera lights stopped glaring at me with their red, beady eye.

"I must say, Mr. Pollack, your ideas are rather radical wouldn't you say?" Lauer asked me while we waited. "You realize that we are not going to reverse the process we've started and that we will become even more globally competitive."

"I disagree. Look around you now. Across the country, young people are protesting because they are sick and tired of the lies and deceit that this fake capitalist economy has spawned upon them. They are bright, intuitive, well read and perceptive and informed about the truth. We are letting this democracy get away from us by selling out to the wealthiest people who believe they can buy anything they want like a seat in the house or senate or even the presidency of the United States."

"You really believe that?" Lauer asked with eyes popped wide open as if I had said the F word in front of him on national television.

"Yes, just look around you and see where we are. Only a blind man would miss the decay in the trust that people feel for the leaders of our country. Congress's approval rating is about thirteen percent. The president's goes up and down like a yoyo. The republican candidates as a whole are polling way below the president. Few people seem excited about this election because the choices are limited. I offer an alternative. I am the voice of the people. I am able to speak for working people because I am a working person. You won't find any silver spoon in my house."

The red light was flickering again. The countdown began. We went back on air.

"We are here today, talking to Mr. Leo Pollack, candidate for president of the United States as a third party nominee. Mr. Pollack, what is the name of your party?"

I laughed and said, "We have no real name. We are the people's party, the working people's party, the ninety-nine percent party, the green party, the unemployed American's party. You can call it what you want. We are the Alternative Party. We are outside the mainstream of Yes and No, of everything that keeps us running on the treadmill of politics as usual. Perhaps before this is all over, we will have a name. Who knows?"

"Your campaign bus has a liberty bell on the side of it. Are you, not, in fact, the Liberty Bell Party?"

"Ringing the Liberty Bell is what we are doing. We want everyone to share in the bounty not just those who can spend millions to get their 'boy' or 'girl' elected. We can't be bought. We won't quit until the race is over and we have either won or lost, but not until then."

"So what if you don't win? What will you do then?" Lauer asked and I could feel that he was ending this.

"Hopefully, I'll go back to work in the mill. I wouldn't be here today if it weren't for my company laying me off and giving me the opportunity to think about how I could use my time away from my day job to make a difference in this country."

"Mr. Pollack, this has been an enlightening few minutes and I want to wish you well in your campaign and hope that Americans are ready to hear your message and vote for you if so inclined."

"Thank you for having me on your program. Let me close with this statement. We are committed to do what is in the best interest of all Americans who work for a living, play by the rules, pay their fair share of taxes, care for their families, respect the law, and who want to no longer live in fear of losing their vision of the American dream."

"Thank you Mr. Pollack. We'll be right back," Lauer concluded and the red lights went blank. We were finished.

I stood up to stretch my legs. My armpits were soaked. Lauer said, "I never get used to it."

"What an adventure," I commented.

"I must say, Mr. Pollack…"

"Leo," I corrected him.

"I must say, Leo, that this has been one of the most unique experiences of my broadcast journalism career. You are about the most down to earth national leader I have ever met."

I slapped him on the arm and said, "Thanks for the promotion, but I wasn't aware that I was already a national leader. Before that title will be mine, I have a lot of work to do.

"You don't realize it do you?" he asked seriously. "You already are. You have my vote so what does that tell you?" He shook my hand and said, "Now, I've got to get back on the set. Good luck and call me if you need anything." He walked away and I exited the set.

Phil Jones came over to escort me out. "We appreciate your coming at such a short notice."

"I appreciate your giving me the opportunity to step out on the national stage. We both win here."

"I would say that we do. Good luck in your campaign," he said, shaking my hand and then returned to his set.

I exited the stage set doors and returned to the lobby where Gram and Al met me. I did not see Big Jack.

"You wowed them, Leo," Al said rushing up to me and giving me a big bear hug.

Gram was a little bit more subdued. "You really laid it on them with the buy American campaign. Good job. Hope we get a lot of traction with that statement and what it means to working people all across the country."

"We shall see. How did my voice sound? Did I sound nervous or anything? Wow! How unreal. The Today Show. Fellows, we sure have come a long way since this all started."

"Yes, and we have a long way to go before we are finished."

"Four years and counting!" Al chanted. "I am getting used to this kind of excitement," he said. "Better than watching the Browns beat the Steelers!"

"We're in Giants country now," Gram said.

Big Jack walked in from outside. He looked at the three of us and did not say anything. His eyes were bright, cheerless and vigilant. He was waiting. There was no emergency. We were okay.

"What time does our flight leave?" I asked Al.

"Three hours from now. Why?"

"Do you think we have enough time to go see the Statue of Liberty, fellows?"

We all agreed we did have enough time. Big Jack opened the door and we went out, caught two cabs because Jack wanted to ride behind us, and headed to Liberty Island and the most sacred of all American icons.

As we rode the ferry out to the island, we stood gazing in awe at her magnificence. Regardless of what country a person was from, the statue inspired a profound reverence for freedom and liberty for all people. As Americans, we were privileged to possess her. I could not help but feel tears rolling down my cold cheeks as we stood beneath her. The outstretched arm holding the light for the world to see was just what we hoped to do. We wanted to "Sae la luz", be the light for the people who were living in the darkness of despair and hopelessness.

Our time on the island was brief, but our resolve was fixed firmly within our minds, bodies and souls. We would not forget where we came from in our journey. We headed forward into uncharted lands where we could exclaim "There be dragons" or likewise, "There go the people leading the way; we must follow them."

22. Palmetto Politics

The long road south to the land of palmetto politics provided us with ample time to plan strategies on how best to cover the entire state in a week. We were not on the ballot. We did not care. New Hampshire showed us that it did not matter. We were after exposure and focusing on independent voters who were disgusted with the republican field of candidates and disappointed in the president for not making the changes in which we could believe. Not much had changed. Yes, the president did have foreign affairs successes like getting bin Laden and pulling out the troops from Iraq. On the former issue, it only took ten years to get the most wanted terrorist in the world. On the second issue, Iraq already signed a "status of forces agreement" in 2008 with former President Bush that stipulated at the end of 2011 all American military forces must leave Iraq. Even though the troops were being pulled, some of those exiting were being told that their next deployment would be to Afghanistan. They were not getting much of a reprieve. The American war machine continued to press on spending money, occupying foreign lands and creating ill will around the world.

The national news was disheartening. Every moment of the day, there was something that made me wonder if there were any way we could solve so many problems that were affecting so many Americans at the same time. The economy was at the top of the pyramid. Affecting ninety-eight percent of the people, there was a palpable malaise that gripped the citizenry. What do we do? Those who had work were fearful that they might be next to lose their employment. Those who were unemployed faced an uncertain future, too. Will I ever work again? Public service employees were being attacked in Wisconsin, Indiana, Michigan, Pennsylvania and Maine. In Ohio, the people were fighting back. In Michigan, the Governor, Rick Snyder, and his republican senate and house, created an "emergency manager" system to deal with towns, cities and school systems in his state. If a city was in financial distress, Snyder now had the authority to send in an "emergency manager" to run the entity. Forget about duly elected officials doing their jobs with the support of the state government. This was essentially political "martial law" and the governor did not see any problem with it. City managers were running at least five cities in Michigan. Detroit was the largest metropolitan area under consideration. The OWS movement polarized many people in the country. It prompted intense dialogue on the left and violent attacks on the right. Gravitating from Wall Street, the movement was now moving into the home foreclosure front and calling itself "Occupy Real Estate". Activists were showing up at homes where people were preparing for eviction and supporting the homeowners by camping on their property and opposing law enforcement.

What could we do?

Congress was constipated. They could not pass a bill without experiencing severe intestinal pain. The ideologues on the right were rapidly devolving from mean-spirited to downright pit bull ugly. There did not seem to be any end to the hostility that arose every time the president tried to get something done. One side opened its mouth and the other side responded. The world of bipartisan politics was shredded in the mission to keep power by one side or the other. Mitch McConnell and Harry Reid were squaring off on every decision. They were two paper tigers but their effect was crippling the government. The republicans controlled the house, and the democrats, the senate, and squeezed in between, were the people, the ninety-nine percent who did not have millions of dollars to lobby for them. Matt Lauer's question was a fair one. How would I work with these two parties? I contemplated this issue a lot. There might be even more reluctance on their part to collaborate, compromise, or at the very minimum, discuss the issues with one another because they would be smarting over losing the presidency. In this scenario, the real tragedy was that Obama could not get the republicans to stop their mission to make him a one-term president. These two bodies of congress were more tragic than a man and woman in an abusive marriage.

In some small measure, I felt sorry for the president. He tried for more than three years to be a bi-partisan leader. He compromised heavily on last summer's fight over raising the debt ceiling. Every political analyst knew that the "committee" appointed by the house and senate to resolve the budget deficit impasse was bound to fail. Given that there was an even number of republicans and democrats on the committee, there was no way to break a tie. Even before the committee held its first meeting, Senator John Cornyn, Texas, stated emphatically, that if defense-spending cuts were considered he would veto anything the committee considered. By this declaration, he was already condemning the committee to failure. They reached their deadline hopelessly deadlocked and disbanded. The president stayed out of the scuffle. I would have handled it very differently.

As president, I would have engaged the two sides in making concessions, compromises, and collaborating doing what was best for the American people. When they made an agreement that worked for the people, I would let them take full credit for getting it done. If they failed to do so, I would point out just how each one of them did not work hard enough to make the process succeed. The need for active leadership was becoming painfully clear.

"What do we know about South Carolina?" I asked as we crossed the border into the "Palmetto State".

"Our message won't be as well received down here below the Mason-Dixon Line," Gram said. "We are entering into a whole new political world."

"There are working people here just like there are up north," Al offered. "We will be meeting these kinds of people most of the time."

"Yes, we will, Al, but many of these folks have been convinced that unions are bad, the government hates them, and the Bible is the only book we should all read and use as our guide through life," Gram concluded. "They don't vote with their pocket book or wallet. They vote with their heart and soul. It's harder to convince them to do what is in their economic self-interest."

"We'll just have to get that done," Al retorted.

"What concerns me most of all, "I said, "is the disparity that exists here like in all the southern states. There are two economies; one white, one black. Now, there is a third one emerging and that one is brown. The latest immigration law passed in Alabama is really creating a hardship for immigrants. Did you see where the head of the new Mercedes-Benz plant was stopped and checked for his papers because there was some fear that he was an illegal immigrant? The governor had to apologize right away to him and make a statement to the press encouraging people not to take this incident as any indictment of his state. When I hear him speaking in the news, I get flashbacks to Governor George Wallace almost a lifetime ago. It's unnerving."

"The Dixiecrats that eventually became the Reagan democrats are not ready to swing to our side. They are still fighting the civil war in their own hearts and minds and once this next generation is dead and buried, perhaps, the south will emerge as a wonderful, enlightened place to work and live," Gram concluded.

"You are not too keen on the south, are you?" I asked.

"I served for years in the military, remember. Many of our bases were down here. I saw the best and the worst of this landscape. The best was wonderful. The worst was downright ugly. I really didn't like living down here. Too many times, I felt like I was a target, too. Somehow, my one-quarter Jewishness must have flashed on my back and I became a target for those who were still hiding their white sheets in the secret closet in their house. No, this is not my favorite place to visit, to say the least."

"We've got to make the best of it. If we are going to win, we need to spread our wings and fly all over this southland. From here, you realize we are off to Florida."

"Florida is like New York, Ohio, Pennsylvania, Indiana and Michigan lumped into one state. Add a little spicy Cuban mix to the pot and what you have is Florida. This state is full of immigrants and emigrants. Who is a native Floridian? One who lies about it," Gram cracked the joke and laughed to himself. "I am less concerned about the 'Sunshine state' than I am about South Carolina. This is where the civil war started and in some ways, I think they are still smarting over their loss. You realize they still fly the confederate flag over the state capital."

"Not right over it," I commented.

"No, but right in front of the main building. They are sore losers and now they want to influence the presidential campaign process by being the third state, the second primary state, in the selection process. Granted this state is more heterogeneous than New Hampshire or Iowa are, it still lacks a well-defined cross section of the country. The Christian conservative element is still extremely vocal and influential. We will face some of it when we start moving around in the major areas that we'll have to cover."

"Where to first?" I asked.

"We might as well start where we enter and hit Spartanburg and head southeast across the state like we initially discussed. This is going to be a long week, I can tell you," Gram added. Spartanburg is not large, about 50,000 people if that. The major business in town is Milliken, a world-wide textile and chemical manufacturing company. BMW makes the series 3 vehicle outside of town. They've been around since 1996.The next major employer in town is Walmart. Natch. After Walmart, Wofford College is the other large employer. It's not a very progressive city, but it is trying to enter into the 21st century as best as it can."

"What are the taboo topics?" I asked.

"Race. Unions. Federal Government. Gay marriage. You take your pick. The people will not shine to you if you start with some sort of liberal agenda," Gram said.

"Stick to the economy and I will be safe. Then, the economy is the simplest and most straightforward approach," I said.

"I'd agree," Gram replied. "There are a lot of people down here who have lost their jobs as a result of the recession, the NAFTA trade agreement and a host of other economic policy decisions that have been fought over in the last two decades. Leo, you'll have to excuse my negativity, but I've seen some downright ugly things down here and they are still part of my visceral reaction to heading into the south land when I hoped I'd never have to come back here again."

"You can opt out and go home," I offered him.

"What kind of chief of staff would I be if I did that? No, I'll get over it. I just want you and Al, and Big Jack, if he were here now, to know how I think and feel about this part of our country."

"I wonder where he is." I asked aloud.

"I can't say for sure but there is a vehicle that has been following us for a long time and so I think he is in a chase car," Al said.

"I just hope he doesn't get pulled over and harassed because he's driving an out of state vehicle and his complexion is a little tawny," Gram said. "Damn, there I go again. I'll get better," he apologized.

As we crossed into South Carolina, a wave of humid air greeted us. The weather was so different from up north. We left the cold behind and now, like snowbirds, were landing in a land where people were walking around in tee shirts and shorts. In my entire life, I had never traveled out of the snow during this time of year and so it was an awesome scene that greeted me as I stared at the people who were outside in what was to me summer clothing. Whether the people would be friendly or not, I was going to make the best of the balmy weather.

A number of times as we drove toward Spartanburg, we were greeted with honks and other signs that indicated our entry into this political climate would be received with mixed views. So be it. No one said this was going to be a "walk in the park". We drove on with high hopes and an appreciation for the challenges that lay ahead.

Our campaign would be just about the same down here as it was in the other states. Our connections had us lined up to talk to people at unemployment offices. We were doing a few town hall meetings but they would not be in "town halls" but union halls, the few left in the south. The people's antagonism toward organizing was hard to fathom. The working people were under attack from every direction. Companies lobbied to get South Carolina to be a "right to work" state that meant working people had no rights. The people were suspicious of union organizers and so they did not want to band together and bargain for their rights. The agrarian influence was still very strong in their thinking. All in all, the Palmetto state was a tough political row to hoe. We would have our work cut out for us in the next week.

We exited the interstate and followed our GPS device to the address we were given by the head of the local services union.

Spartanburg was a renaissance city, a blend of the old south and the new wave of modernization that was leading it forward into the twenty-first century bucking and kicking like a small boat on a turbulent sea.

When we pulled up in front of the address we were given, there was a small gathering in front of the building but nothing like we were used to seeing up north. This was the first sign that things were not going to be "business as usual".

Exiting the Liberty Bell Bus, I was met by Jody Wates, a slim, attractive woman possibly in her late forties, who welcomed me with the loveliest drawl, "Mr. Pollack, nice to have you here in our fair city."

"It's good to be here in a warm place in the middle of winter. I've never been south in my life at this time of year."

"I hope it isn't too warm for you, Mr. Pollack."

"Leo, please," I said.

"Thank you and I was saying I hope it isn't too warm for you, Leo. We've faced a lot of opposition to your coming into town and campaigning in our city. I'm sure you must know that a movement like yours is not something that the folks down here are too keen on because your message isn't one that many want to hear. This bible thumping is louder than native drummers at a powwow. You wouldn't believe what kind of hog wash they've been spreading about your being here today."

"I can only imagine," I replied.

"Leo, I don't think you really can, to tell you the truth," she said.

I introduced her to Gram and Al and then asked what the plan was.

"We have to take our program indoors because we couldn't get a permit to meet out here in this public parking lot. Against code, I was told. Against change, I concluded. We made arrangements to use the elementary school across the street. It's small inside but as you can see our crowd is small."

"Any press?"

"I think we'll have some. They aren't going to roll the cameras just yet. You're campaign hasn't hit the big time down here. We're a few decades behind, y'all know that."

"I believe we can change that," I offered.

"I sure hope so. I sure do. Now let's get on over to the school and get to work."

We followed her. In less than fifteen minutes, we were inside, set up and ready to meet our first southern brothers and sisters curious enough to come in and listen to what I had to say. Just before I took the stage, I saw Big Jack enter the room, talk to Gram quietly, look my way, give me the thumbs up sign and then go back out. I was relieved. I had the utmost confidence that if Big Jack indicated all was well, we were in good shape.

I began with a flourish.

"Good morning, citizens of this fine, warm state of South Carolina. I've never been out of the Snow Belt in January so coming here is like getting a belated Christmas present. I will be wearing shorts before this road trip is over and that is something I've never done in my lifetime. I just hope the paparazzi don't get a picture of my spindly white legs."

The people laughed at my lame joke and I felt a little bit better. For some reason, the words were not flowing easily today. I cinched up my mind, got myself into the mood and pressed on.

"When America works, Democracy thrives. Yes, we're in the throes of the worst recession since the great depression. Some people have called this 'The Great Recession'. Millions of people like me are unemployed and are not sure if we will ever go back to work for the companies we once worked for and that provided us with the opportunity to take care of families and contribute to our nation."

"We did not bring this condition down upon ourselves. No, it was a man made crisis. Whether we want to admit it or not, we have been living way beyond our means and now we are being called to pay up. We financed two wars on borrowed money. We bought homes, cars and trucks on borrowed money. We refinanced our paid off homes so that we could buy more things on this borrowed money. Our government borrowed money to give all of us tax breaks. Now we are facing the lender. We borrowed this money from ourselves."

"When I got a tax break years ago, I liked it. I won't deny that it was nice to take a few more dollars home with me every pay. I knew that this was not something that could last but while it did, I didn't complain. What I was taking home though, was pennies to what wealthier people were carting off to the bank. My five percent tax cut on my fifty thousand dollar a year earnings was worth about $2500 a year. Not bad. The four percent tax cut that a person making a million dollars a year got was $40,000 a year. Even though the millionaire's tax cut was four percent and mine five percent, his or her actual tax cut was 25 times more than mine. Now, I ask you, how can that be fair? How can we say that everyone is paying his or her fair share?"

"There are some of the candidates campaigning this year who are saying that anyone who challenges the tax cuts and wants everyone to pay their fair share is promoting 'class warfare'. I reject that notion. We are not promoting anything but the goal to have a fair tax system for all people."

"I believe we need to rescind the Bush tax cuts and return to the old rates for the next year. While we are doing that, we must revise the tax code. This plea for a flat tax is ludicrous. Doing the simple math, anyone who pays taxes will realize that the more money you make the less tax you will pay."

"One former candidate was promoting a flat twenty percent tax rate. Two others were pushing for fifteen percent. The last one was down to nine percent, but he's dropped out of the race. What is the reality of these kinds of rates? Let's take my $50,000 as an example. At twenty percent, I'd pay $10,000 a year. This is more than I pay now. At fifteen percent, I'd be paying just about what I pay now or about $7500. At nine percent, I'd pay a lot less. Now let's apply the same math to the person earning a million dollars. At twenty percent, the millionaire's tax liability would drop from $350,000 to $200,000. Now, applying the fifteen percent rate, the same person's taxes would drop from $350,000, at the 35 % rate, to $150,000, at the 15% rate, an even larger drop. Finally, applying the nine percent rate, the same person earning a million dollars a year would pay, not $350,000, but $90,000 a year. Obviously, the more money you make the more you would love a flat tax. This is not true for the working, middle class individual. We will pay more, and if not more, we will not see any real change in our taxes."

"Now, where do you think the money will come from to finance our government, to pay for schools, the Food and Drug Administration, Homeland Security, and all the other agencies? There will be cuts. The major programs that will face the hatchet are the three most important programs that elderly people depend on as their safety net and they are Social Security, Medicare and Medicaid. You have already seen and heard about the Ryan Budget. This was a direct assault on these three social safety net programs. For the moment, they are still being protected. How long do you think this will last?"

"I believe we need to protect them for eternity, insure that the programs take care of seniors who are dependent upon them now and do what it takes to make sure that our children and grandchildren can have their own safety net in the future."

"How do we do this?"

"First, we end this payroll tax break that the president promoted and the democrats and republicans supported. All it is doing is draining future funds from the social security trust."

"Second, we revoke the Bush tax cuts and begin to pay our fair share again for the next year. Economists figure that this one action alone will cut $4.5 trillion from the national debt over the next decade."

"Third, we implement the Simpson-Boles Plan to revamp social security, Medicare and Medicaid. Their plan is austere but it will work. Yes, younger people will have to work longer but they are living longer and can save money in 401-K plans for a much longer period insuring they have sufficient funds for their later years."

"Fourth, we change the tax code to a simple progressive tax. Anyone making $10,000 or less pays zero tax. How could anyone live on such a small amount anyway? If you make $20,000 or less, you pay 1 % or $200.00. No deductions. If you make $30,000 or less, you pay 3% or $300.00. If you make $75,000 you would pay 7.5 %. If you made $450,000, you would pay 45%, still no deductions. If you made $900,000, you would pay 50% up to $500,000 and then a decreasing amount until you got to $1 million. After $1 million, taxes would be a flat 50%. Therefore, the more you make the more you pay. There will be no tax loopholes that let wealthy individuals pay little or no taxes."

"Corporate rates would be the same. How can GE pay no taxes? This is absurd. They paid no taxes. Do you hear what I am saying? I paid at least ten percent. I don't know what you paid, but this just cannot be the way we dig ourselves out of this hole we call the recession."

"These numbers are boring as anything. I admit that to you now. I am sharing them with you for one reason only; that is to stop the lie that cutting taxes further or making the Bush tax cuts permanent will save the economy. If these tax cuts were so wonderful, then why are we in this recession? These tax cuts have been in effect since 2003. Shouldn't we have seen by now an economy that is booming for everyone? The fact is, my fellow Americans, these tax cuts, like these two wars were financed by using the federal government's credit card. This is unsustainable. We all know that so let's stop lying about the facts."

"Work is the answer. Work. We need to create work for our own people. When America works, democracy thrives. Immediately, we will institute a "Buy American" program. The government, you and I, every American must begin to buy American. We cannot continue to buy goods and services produced overseas. We will bring work back to our shores with our buying American movement. Just recently, the Keen Shoe Company built a new plant in Portland, Oregon. They are making shoes in the US. This is one example of a company who is way ahead of the curve. We cannot continue to send our industries offshore and expect that our economy will improve."

"Tax breaks for any company exporting jobs will end and penalties will be the new norm. Yes, go ahead and shut down a textile plant here in South Carolina and try and move it offshore. You will face the full power of the justice department and the IRS as you attempt to close your doors. By the time we get done with you, you will be asking where should you build your second plant in South Carolina?"

"Folks, what I'm talking about is not rocket science. This is basic mathematics and business practices. What we as citizens need to do is demand that our government and its leaders do what is best for most Americans. I can speak to you with a straight face and say I fully comprehend your plight. I am just like you. I am an unemployed American steel worker who has watched our economy go down the tubes because both democrats and republicans have been dishonest with us about it and have not done what is in the interest of all working people. Now we must hold them accountable for their waywardness, their lack of concerted action to protect American industries and American workers."

"I am Leo Pollack, an unemployed steel worker, coming into your home state this week to ask for your support. Please vote for me for president. Please vote for me knowing that I can lead this country back toward a place where working people have a real leader that understands and will work tirelessly to change the decay we all feel in our lives. Please vote for me so that together, we can insure that there is still an American dream for us, our children and grandchildren. Please vote for me so that we can end the constipation in our Congress. Please vote for me so that I can go to Washington, serve one term, do what is best for working people all over this land and then go home again, having done my best to insure that we all can share in the bounty of this great nation."

A loud applause erupted and I just waved to everyone and let it take its course.

Finally, I said, "I need your vote next Saturday. Write my name in on whatever column you need to. I don't care. Democrat or Republican. It doesn't matter. This will just convince those who manage the status quo that there is a movement among the people to rewrite history and make the world sit up and take notice that peaceful revolution is still possible in America."

"We are counting on South Carolinians to raise their collective voices and shout out to this nation that we want to restore the dream. We want to believe that we can and will be counted in this movement that rekindles the American spirit of working hard, playing hard and enjoying life to the fullest. We need your help, your prayers, your voices and yes, too, your ones, fives, tens and twenties. Please support us in this effort. Thank you all, thank you South Carolina."

Applause exploded this time and like many times before, I stepped down off the stage and into the crowd. Hands touched mine. Shoulders rubbed shoulders. We, Americans, were saying hello.

The day was still young when we finished with this first event. Jody asked us what we were doing for dinner and we said that we were unsure. She recommended a few local restaurants and we thanked her for her hospitality.

"I'd take you along myself, but I've got a family of my own and they're waiting for me to come home and fix their dinner for them. My husband works second shift so we split our days taking care of the kids. I'm sure that you fellows know what that is all about so welcome to my world."

"Jody, thank you for getting us off on the right foot here in South Carolina."

"I hope the rest of your journey across the state is as productive and safe. Goodbye, gotta run." She sprinted off toward the other parking lot.

"What do we do now?" I asked.

"Where's Big Jack?" Al asked.

"He was just here a moment ago," Gram said.

"We can't move until he tells us that he is ready," I said.

"Let me call him. In the mean time, let's make some coffee and decide what we are going to do," Gram said.

Gram called Big Jack. I made the coffee. Al checked the vehicle to make sure that everything was okay.

Gram's conversation was mostly listening and little talking. When he hung up we just stared at him, waiting.

"So, here is what we know, according to Big Jack," Gram offered. "Since we crossed into South Carolina we've been monitored by unmarked state police cars. They were at the event today, too, but did not come inside that he could tell. However, the police might have sent someone in with a wire and taped the presentation. Big Jack says to get out of town and he will reconnect with us somewhere outside the city. You get that, Al."

"Got it. We're heading out now." He started the bus and slowly wheeled out to the freeway leading to Greenville."

"So much for dinner at any of the places that Jodi suggested."

"Let's be glad that we have someone watching our back," Gram said.

"I'm hungry. Let me get into the kitchen and whip up some gumbo."

"Oh, Oh, Al, you know what's coming!" Gram moaned.

"Sure do. Mac and cheese and tuna fish. Sheesh…what a diet we have to live on. Makes me feel like I'm on a diet."

"What are you guys crying about? I don't see either of you standing up and slaving over this hot stove." They waved at me with their special finger.

"How disrespectful. Wait until I am officially the leader of the free world. I'll make you pay for your disrespect."

"Yah, sure. You'll make us eat the same gruel for breakfast and not just for dinner," Gram joked.

"What's wrong with macaroni, cheese and tuna fish?" I asked.

"Everything. This is a non-food item. You're unbelievable, Leo. You take the cake. There is no one who would believe that you eat this kind of stuff. We could be eating steak and eggs, but no. What are we eating?" Gram asked.

"Mac and cheese," Al said. "This is too much. I didn't sign on for this kind of abuse. You with me on this?" Al asked Gram.

"I've got your back, Jack," Gram said. "We don't have to put up with this. We can tell the people at the next stop that we're enslaved by this crazy Polack who is pretending to be a presidential candidate."

"We can show them how many belt holes we've had to pull up to keep our pants from falling down as we lose extraordinary weight because we are being starved to death," Al said.

"Come on fellows. You'd think I was some sort of slave monger."

"You are!" Al cried out.

"You are!" Gram cried out, too.

"Okay. Okay. What do you want to eat?" I asked.

"I don't know about you, Al, but I would really like some pasta tonight."

"Me too. How about mac and cheese?"

"That would be great. Leo, Al and I want mac and cheese and tuna fish, if you have it," Gram stated.

I slapped both of them up the side of their heads.

"My friends!"

We headed southwest toward Greenville hoping that we could find a good place to stop for the night that would not need any special security.

Fate and destiny are not twins, but they are distant relatives.

What lay ahead was something that would make the past seem like child's play and the future, a lesson in shock and awe.

I did not resist the movement forward. I embraced it like I did every challenge in my short, blessed life.

Now the Liberty Bus rolled along the highway. We moved along at what felt like lightning speed even though it was only 57 miles per hour. Al was paranoid. He did not want to speed because he was sure that those state police were waiting to pounce on us if we made just one mistake. Gram assured him that the speed limit was 65 miles per hour over and over again, but Al did not want to take any chances. Gram sat back and hushed up. I did not comment. I was not driving. What could I say? I would be no better than a back seat, or in our case, back hallway, or out of the kitchen driver. I made the mac and cheese and tuna fish. When it was ready, I let my team mates know but they said we would eat when we got off the freeway. We drove on and on as if the road would never end and finally, found a safe enough place to pull off the highway. We just wanted to eat a meal. Nothing special. Nothing complicated. This was what made this campaign so special. We were not going into some five-star restaurant dropping $500.00 and smiling as we burped our way on to the next venue. No, we were living what we preached and that was what made all the difference.

Bring on the macaroni, cheese and tuna fish. We knew how our bread was buttered.

23. Pollack's March to the Sea

The march to the sea became our total focus. We would end our campaign in Charleston, South Carolina, but we had a long way to go before we could call it quits for this state. Every day, we watched, listened and learned how the "big boys" played the game. We vowed to avoid almost everything they were doing lest we become too much like them. Campaign political ads polluted the radio, TV and internet. Every political junkie was getting his or her fix given that the twenty-four hour news cycle was maxing out campaign coverage. The republican primary devolved into dirty mudslinging. The minute the New Hampshire Primary was over, the major campaigns headed to South Carolina and went at it.

Jon Huntsman dropped out. He rallied in New Hampshire where he finished third. He said this result was "his ticket to ride". However, South Carolina did not treat him very well. Some pundits believed it was because his father, a billionaire, would not fund his superpacs and make him competitive. Whatever the reason, he was gone.

Rick Perry quit. His campaign was "on the ropes". His numbers in New Hampshire were abysmal. He could not compete anywhere but Texas and maybe not even there. His campaign, flush with money, was low on focus. His consistent gaffs in the debates made him a laughing stock on the campaign trail. Perry made "Oops" a new campaign slogan.

Newt Gingrich vowed to be competitive in the Palmetto state. Now he could because billionaire Sheldon Adelson, a Las Vegas casino operator, plopped down $5 million in Newt's superpac, Winning the Future. This financial boost was what Newt needed to begin his attacks on Mitt. He did, with a vengeance. The sad and befuddled Newt Gingrich, who in Iowa wanted to run a clean campaign and vowed that he would, cut loose on Mitt and was taking no prisoners. He was letting out every ounce of misguided frustration he accumulated in Iowa and New Hampshire when he was stymied by a lack of money to fire back at his number one rival. The attacks were downright ugly. He did not care. He was Newt Gingrich and he was the "most interesting man in the world" or so he wanted us all to believe.

At every campaign stop, these two warriors traded barbed shots. Now and then, they focused on the president, but Obama was not the real object of their ire. Mitt did not appear to dislike Newt as much as the latter appeared to dislike the former. In the two South Carolina Debates, Newt called Romney a liar to his face a number of times.

Another major development occurred that threatened to derail Newt's campaign. His second wife, Marianne, broke silence and said that she was going public about her life with him just before he divorced her. She said that Newt came to her in the late 1990's, told her that he was having an affair with Callista, asked her, Marianne, if they could have an "open marriage" and said that Callista did not mind sharing him with her. Marianne said she would not agree to an open marriage. Newt divorced her and then married Callista Bisek, a congressional aide and a woman twenty-two years younger than him. In the debate held after this story broke, John King, the moderator, asked Newt about the allegations and asked if he would like to comment on it. Newt took this opportunity to rail against the moderator, the elite New York media, Washington, D.C., Obama and the world in general, and was supported by the crowd that heckled anyone who disagreed with anything that he said that night. Newt was able to deflect this damaging information and turn it into a win for him.

At the same time, Newt was pressing Mitt to release his taxes so that everyone could see just how much money he paid to the federal government in taxes, how much he made and what his net worth was. Mitt was reluctant to do so and this became a bone of contention throughout the South Carolina campaign. In both debates, Mitt had to fight off allegations that he was one of the one percent and that he was hiding something.

Santorum was endorsed by almost every notable religious right organization or person and this, he hoped would make it possible for him to cut into the lead of the frontrunners. He just could not get any traction. He tried hard to win the support of the tea party people but they would not warm up to him. He made his strongest case for being the only real "conservative" on the stage, but his arguments did not energize the people.

Ron Paul continued to make slow and steady movement toward the perimeter. Everyone said he had no chance to win the nomination but he was not giving up. He said he was going all the way to the convention. He was amassing some delegates and that was fine with him. His organization was much better than Santorum's and though he did not have anywhere near the cash on hand that Romney had, he was actually raising decent amounts of money. He did not, like Romney and Gingrich, have any billionaire backers running superpacs for him.

We wallowed in this political climate as we made our way toward Charleston.

Basha and I talked on the phone a few times a day. Whenever I was not being asked a question or facing some other internal or external task, I would give her a call just to tell her that I loved and missed her. In the evenings, Janko and I would share what we had done that day. He did not like my being gone so much and asked me when it would end. I told him not for a while yet and he said that would be okay if when it was over we could just be together every day. I guaranteed him that we would make that happen.

We were heading into our third week of campaigning without much of a rest. The guys were in good spirits. Luckily, our team was small so we could check in with one another and make sure that we were not rubbing each other the wrong way. Gram was content to navigate for Al. Al was content to drive and have Gram navigate for him. Big Jack was everywhere and nowhere. We still did not know how many other people were working with him. He did not tell us. I asked John Gallagher the last day we were at home who was on Jack's team and he would not comment. All he said was "Leave things up to Jack. He's on the job. He knows best." Where Big Jack got this sort of specialized training, I would never find out, but I did feel safe. What was there to fear anyhow?

Greenville was the new south. The economy was formerly based largely on textile manufacturing, and the city was long known as "The Textile Capital of the World." In the last few decades, favorable wages and tax benefits lured foreign companies to invest heavily in the area. The city is the North American headquarters for Hubbell Lighting, Michelin and BMW. The International Center for Automotive Research was created establishing CUICAR as the new model for automotive research. The Center for Emerging Technologies in mobility and energy was opened in 2011, hosting a number of companies in leading edge R&D and the headquarters for Sage Automotive. When the former Donaldson Air Force Base closed, the land became the South Carolina Technology and Aviation Center, and home to the Lockheed Martin Aircraft and Logistics Center, as well as 3M and Honeywell. Caterpillar Inc. located a diesel engine manufacturing plant and engineering operations nearby. General Electric Company built a gas turbine and wind energy manufacturing factory. O'Neal, Inc. a project planning, design and construction firm located its headquarters in Greenville.

Greenville was less hospitable than Spartanburg. We made our presence known. The venue was a church recreation hall. The crowd came and went and there was not much else to say. I talked to John Gallagher and reported what we experienced here and he said his team had a hard time getting someone to commit to organizing something for us. I told him that this was a major issue if we were going to be able to compete across the south. He agreed wholeheartedly and said he would get some people right on it. We agreed that we were truly flying blind by just showing up in the state without much fanfare. Granted, we had our small victory in New Hampshire to build on, but we also spent more time in New Hampshire and it was a much smaller state than South Carolina with a completely different demographic.

We managed to exit the city without incident. I did have a minor run in with a local reporter from the Greenville News, the leading daily paper in the city. He asked me what business I had coming down to the south and trying to dump my liberal Yankee ideas on real Americans like him and his readers who knew better than to believe what people like me had to say. He was not even polite in his attack. I did not remember seeing him in the sparse crowd to which I had spoken, but that was really not the issue for the moment. Reflecting back to my "Gram" moment, I smiled at the man and asked his name, what paper he worked for, how long had he been a print journalist, where he went to college, what did he major in, did he like the Clemson Tigers or the South Carolina Gamecocks and what lake had the best largemouth bass fishing in the state? By the time he answered all my questions, I simply said, "Well, it's been great to meet you and thanks for taking the time to come over and visit with me a spell. I hope we'll see you again when we are back down in the Palmetto State for the general election." I shook his hand with gusto and then jumped onto the Liberty Bell Bus and made my getaway.

Gram said, "Nice work."

"That's it?" I responded.

"You want more than that?"

"It would be nice," I continued.

"You played him like an eight pound bass on a two pound test line. Good job, Leo. I couldn't have worked him better myself. You're learning, Boy!"

We all laughed as we made our getaway.

Big Jack checked in regularly throughout the day. He spoke mainly to Gram, not me. They had conspired to keep anything away from me that might cause me to lose focus. I could hear Gram talking in code. He and Jack thought they were slick, but I knew that the state police were still tagging along with us. I wanted to go out and meet these silent tails but that probably would have been foolish. Whenever we were driving along, stopped at some roadside rest area or fueling, I would try and scope out who was following us. I did not have any luck. In fact, I could not even find Big Jack most of the time and I even knew what he was driving. His team remained invisible. I began to wonder if he were the only one. I did not ask him, John or Gram. I figured they would not tell me anyway.

As we headed into Columbia, South Carolina, we were enchanted by the modern and elegant appeal of the city skyline. Many of the designs were the work of prominent architect, Alfred Built Millet. One of Columbia's most interesting geographical features is its "fall line" which is a boundary between an upland region and a coastal plain across which rivers from the upland region drop to the plain as falls or rapids. Columbia grew up at the fall line of the Congaree River that is formed by the convergence of the Broad and Saluda Rivers. The Congaree is the farthest inland point of river navigation. The energy of falling water also powered Columbia's early textile. The city has capitalized on this location that includes three rivers by christening itself "The Columbia Riverbanks Region". Columbia is located roughly halfway between the Atlantic Ocean and the Blue Ridge Mountains. The city, largest in the state, was one of the first to end Jim Crow practices in the 1950s.

Given its legendary place in Civil War history, the feelings I experienced as we headed into this bastion of the old south were mixed. Every time I thought about racism and the tragic amount of blood and treasure that were spent fighting the civil war, my heart ached.

What was wrong with people? When would there ever be peace in the world? Even now, in this election, the republican candidates were attacking each other as if they were truly enemies. This did not make any sense. Surely, they knew that the statements they were making now would be used against them by the Obama campaign during the general election. This strategy was as old as American politics. Who knew when negative campaigning started?

The outcome of all this viciousness ultimately led to the American people not respecting their leaders. Who can have much respect for someone who is called, repeatedly, a liar? The hypocrisy of it all was that when the primary campaign was over and one candidate was selected by the party, the other candidates, who just weeks or months ago were slinging gobs of mud at the winner, would rally around "their" candidate and let bygones be bygones.

The entire process was laden with deceit. There was no way that Mitt and Newt would patch up their relationship after the way they were going at it for the past month. Ron Paul was more diplomatic than the others. He often judged they were wrong and stated his position demonstrating the fallacy in their points of view and the accuracy of his. For some reason, they did not practice his form of diplomacy. Perhaps that was the reason he was consistently finishing fourth and they were exchanging the lead every other day or so.

I vowed not to fall into the trap of judging the other candidates. My position needed to be clean and pure. I was making a case to be president because my ideas were better than theirs were. Their ideas were the issue, not the candidate. Did it matter if Newt had three wives? Not really. Did it matter than Mitt was an extremely wealthy man who paid very little taxes? Not really. Did it matter that Rick Santorum was a senator who was very successful in getting earmarks for his state while he was serving? Not really.

What mattered was today. What was each candidate offering America and Americans today that would make the country better? This was the crux of the campaign, and the only thing that mattered to me was how well I could communicate my vision to the people who came to meet me. If I had to resort to attack ads to make my case, I would end the campaign in a heartbeat. If one superpac came out and started blasting away at another candidate and doing so in my name, law or no law, I would publically denounce the activity. Nothing would get me to change this no matter how many more votes we could garner by doing otherwise. If nothing else, our campaign would set a new standard for the entire presidential campaign process.

I applauded what was happening in Massachusetts. Senator Scott Brown who won the seat after Ted Kennedy died, and his challenger, Elizabeth Warren, the architect of the president's consumer protection bureau and law professor, committed to not allowing superpac's money enter into their campaign. If any superpacs spent money attacking the other person, that person had to donate an equal amount of money to the charity of his or her challenger's choice. What a novel idea.

With this kind of thinking bubbling over in my mind, we descended upon Columbia prepared to meet the next group of would be supporters with a strong belief that every day we were picking up support.

When we drove down into Columbia city center and found the address we were given for our next stop, I was enchanted with the beauty of the place. Though it was January, flowers were still blooming, the air was relatively mild, and a sweet gum scent flowed in the air.

James Buchanan, a stolid, intense looking man, met us as we exited the Liberty Bus.

"Gentlemen, welcome to the new south," he said, shaking our hands. "You must be Leo Pollack?" he asked looking at me directly. His eyes were laser beams burning a hole right through me.

"I am sir. Good to meet you."

"We are meeting right across the street from the state capital. We managed to inveigle the city fathers to host our event in the interest of showing off to the world that South Carolina is no longer a backward state. Whether or not it is, we will not discuss here and now. We will, indeed, take advantage of their willingness to be open minded."

"Sounds wonderful to me," I said.

"We are excited to have you here, Mr. Pollack. As you probably know by now, as you've made your march across the state, we're inundated with negativity and this is starting to make everyone a little weary. I hope your message today will make Carolinians see there is some hope."

"I'll do my best, sir," I said.

"I'm sure you will." He said no more, but led us to where a crowd of more than 500 people was gathered. This was going to be a formidable group to work. I felt my lips getting dry and the sweat start to pour down my back. I knew my body was getting ready. Now, all I had to do was get my mind in synch with it.

Gram walked with me to the side of the makeshift stage. "You ready, Leo?"

"As ready as I can be," I said to him wiping some sweat from my brow.

"I've never seen you sweat before like this."

"I was not in the heart of Dixie before like I am now," I replied.

"We're not in the heart of Dixie yet. Wait until we get to Mississippi. Then you'll be in the heart of it all."

"When we get there, I'll deal with it."

"You ready?" James Buchanan asked.

"Yes sir," I replied getting myself psyched up and ready to live in the moment. I was not sure what I was going to say. I did not use Teleprompters. They were too artificial. I wanted whatever came out of my mouth to be a product of my mind and heart.

"Stick it," Gram said. "Don't be bashful, but avoid religion, marriage, gay and lesbian issues and let's see, yes, politics. That should do it."

"Right. I'll talk about the NASA space program."

"Hey, Newt wants to put a colony on the moon. Can you top that?"

"Nope. He wants to star in a new Star Wars," I said.

"Yah, he's the new Darth Vader," Gram chuckled.

We heard James Buchanan booming voice calling all Carolinians.

"South Carolinians, welcome to this special event, this special time when we get to meet, for the first time in the modern history of this nation, a candidate for president who is not someone from the privileged class, someone who works for a living, someone who is right now unemployed and looking for a job. The one he wants is the presidency of the United States. He needs your support to get it. He's here today to apply for that job so let's give him a warm and hearty South Carolina welcome!"

There was a loud explosion of applause. I skipped up to stage center, took the microphone from James, thanked him for the warm and kind introduction and said, "Hello South Carolinian working people, thank you for being here today and thank you for being willing to listen to the future."

I walked to the front of the stage and got as close as I could to the people gathered there.

"When America works, democracy thrives. We are still in the Great Recession. We know that because we all know people that are not working. We all know people whose homes are being foreclosed upon or are already gone. We know that the American dream is slowly eroding and there is no one on the national stage who is speaking to it. How can a man worth hundreds of millions of dollars truly comprehend what it is like to try and make it from paycheck to paycheck?"

"No, Americans, we are being squeezed from the top by the privileged who have bought and sold politicians, policies, laws, statutes and are still not done shopping to expand their influence. They are in control of our country in a way that we have never seen before. They will not go away. They will not give in to what we want and that is simply to share in the bounty."

"Who among us wants to live off the government nipple? Who among us does not want to go to work, contribute to the greater good, take care of his or her family, experience the joy of living as a productive member of the community? Who among us wants to shirk his or her responsibility that involves making sacrifices so that the world in which we live will become healthier, happier and more holistic?"

"Now I am here to ask for your support. I am asking you to consider voting for me to become your next president. I want to be your president. Your voice. Your eyes, ears, heart, and soul right there in the White House. This will not be an easy task, but with your help, we can accomplish this goal."

Some voices roared in affirmation.

"What I believe is that when all Americans are working, we are a healthier nation. Right now, we are not healthy. At the core, we are sick and that is because the system is stacked against working people."

"We can and will create more jobs by promoting the practice: Buy American – Put your Neighbor Back to Work."

"We can do this together. We can raise our voices and cry out for change. We can be the America that we have always dreamed about when we stand up and demand to share in the bounty of this land. We are the ones who work for it and create much of it."

"We are not envious about them having more than we have. We are not asking a privileged person to give us anything from his or her larder. No. We are demanding that when our votes are counted that our voices are heard. It is not okay to take our vote and then forget about us for the next four years. Enough is enough."

"I am Leo Pollack, an unemployed steel worker who is running for president of the United States, and I want your vote. I hope that what I've shared with you puts some fire in your soul, makes you want to get involved and support a movement of working people to return our government back to the people, a government that is truly of, for and by the people. We, the people."

"Thank you, Carolinians. Thank you."

Down into the crowd I plunged and spent another hour meeting people, listening to their stories, moving with the ebb and flow of the crowd that was really engaged with me, my message and the chance to make history.

The crowd was mixed. White, black and brown people were in attendance. I did not worry that we would miss any of the minorities. I hoped they could feel that I was in their world with them. I was not some "privileged" cat who just was on an ego trip.

Eventually, James Buchanan rescued me from the people. "Leo, there is someone you must meet. He will be an instrumental person in your future down here below the Mason-Dixon Line. Folks, Leo and I need to adjourn," James said to the people who were around me. They slowly moved away as he led me to a meeting off to the side.

"Leo, meet Richard Johnson, the working director of the Southern Christian Leadership Council."

I looked into Richard's eyes and saw an intensity that amazed me. His eyes were coal black, but brilliant. Shining. Focused. He was a medium built fellow, wearing jeans, a blue sweatshirt and a ball cap with NASCAR embroidered on it. He smiled softly.

"We're watching your movement, Leo, and we want to help. We believe that what you are bringing to this campaign and to this country is a new voice, one that will make America finally embrace the Sermon on the Mount and practice the beatitudes. Poor people, the working poor, middle class people all need a spokesperson. We want to do whatever we can to get you elected. Am I being clear?"

"Clear as sunshine," I said.

"What do you need from us?"

"Help us plan our southern strategy. Work with John Gallagher up north, get on the same page, and figure out what we need so we can engage the system county by county across the south. That's what I need from you."

"Done," Richard, said. "We can do that."

"Now what do you need from me?" I asked Richard studying him carefully for any nonverbal communication cues."

He did not hesitate. "Remain true to your initial message. Do not sell out. The minute you change your focus, we'll cut you loose like dead fish on a stringer. We want to believe that there can be a person who rises up from the working ranks of our country to lead us into the Promised Land. Oh yes, this is a symbolic journey, Leo, and we want to be a part of it and we want you to be the leader of it."

We just stared at each other. Spontaneously, we hugged each other. I saw moisture in his eyes and I could feel that same emotion welling up inside of me as well.

"We can do this," I said.

"We can do this," he said.

I looked around and saw my colleagues off to side. I called to them, "Gram, Al, meet Richard Johnson, our newest team member. We've got someone who is going to take on creating a southern strategy to carry us through the entire campaign."

They came over and introduced themselves to Richard. We made small talk for a few minutes. Gram and Richard exchanged cell phone numbers. We invited Richard to come join us for some coffee in the bus, but he said he had to get to work.

"We're on for the entire ride," Richard said. "Leo, don't disappoint us. We need your voice. We need a leader to guide this wayward flock back to the safety of the American ideal. With that, I'm going to take my leave. Thank you for being here and good luck down the road in Charleston. I've got my people ready to assist you in that rebel stronghold," he concluded shaking my hand again.

"Richard, will wonders never cease?" I said.

"No, but prayers are answered. You are the answer to many working people's prayers. Amen, I'm off, peace, my brother," he said and left us quickly disappearing into the crowd.

"Can you believe that?" I asked the people. "We just have to keep on moving forward and good things will continue to happen."

"Mr. Pollack, you've captured the imagination of a lot of people who want to believe in this country, this political system, and make a difference with their vote. You are the person who can deliver that promise. Please do," James Buchanan concluded.

"James, this has been a memorable day, and I'm sure that there will be many more to come with wonderful people like you and Richard paving the way for us."

"It's my pleasure to serve, sir," he offered.

"Now, I think we need to get moving. Team, are we ready?"

"Always," Al replied.

"Gram, what do we have to do before we leave town?" I asked.

"Stop at a food store and get a few groceries," he said.

"Good. Where is the nearest Food Lion?" I asked James. He directed us to the store.

We said goodbye, climbed aboard the bus and Al drove us to the store. While Gram went in and shopped, I stood outside and talked to shoppers who were curious about the Liberty Bell Bus, my campaign and me. I laughed and joked with a few dozen people enjoying the moment, out of the limelight but still pressing our message home to every person that asked a question, made a comment, wondered what we believed was actually possible in this 2012 campaign year.

Gram came back with a few bags of groceries. He and Al took the food aboard. I said goodbye to the people, encouraged them to support the movement, and climbed into the bus. Al fired up the engine and we slowly motored down the frontage road. As he wheeled back onto the interstate, I settled down to cook dinner for the fellows. Gram did not cook. Al could not cook. I was nominated and elected to do the chore.

"What a day," I said as I cut onions into small chunks for a salad. "We got a major gift in Richard Johnson, wouldn't you say so?"

"He may be the answer to the entire southeastern seaboard states," Gram replied. "We are making some real headway now, Leo. Amazing, huh?"

"Beyond amazing, fricking unbelievable," Al chortled. "We are like whiz kids. We go out and just do it. We are unstoppable."

"Don't get carried away now," I admonished my friends. We've got a few more stops to make on this march to the sea and then there is the actual primary on Saturday. What happens on that day will be what matters most."

"Don't rain on our parade," Gram said. "We just want to be happy and carefree for a few minutes. You are such a 'grad grind', Leo. Lighten up, will you?"

"Do you want to eat?" I asked.

"Sure," they replied.

"Then hush up and let me cook."

Gram talked to Big Jack. I could hear the conversation a bit. Jack was right behind us and preparing to come aboard when we stopped to eat. Al began looking for a place to pull over. Ten miles ahead, we found a rest area and rolled to a stop.

Big Jack climbed aboard and told us what he was monitoring and it was not pleasant. There was a movement afoot to keep us out of Charleston. He got the word from his crew that was already on the ground in that city. Word was passed along through law enforcement and he got it through his network.

"What does this mean?" I asked Jack.

"We need to be alert. We need some intervention. I've talked to John and he is mobilizing his people from up there. What about this guy you were talking to at the event? What's his angle?"

"You saw him?"

"I see everything, Leo. This gives me the edge in keeping you safe on the campaign trail."

"When I become president, there is only one job that you can have."

"What's that?" Jack asked.

"Homeland Security," I said.

"Shucks," he jived, "I really wanted to be the Secretary of Agriculture so I could go and smell all that bull pucky out west and make farmers' lives miserable by telling them they can't use chemical sprays on our food anymore and cannot plant genetically modified seeds."

"What?" I asked incredulously.

"You heard me. Secretary of Agriculture. Yes. Chief Bull Semen Salesman," he blurted out and then laughed so heartily that the bus shook.

"Let's eat and then we can call Richard Johnson and get him on the task," Gram said.

"Done," Big Jack said.

"Food," Al said.

First, we said grace, giving thanks for the blessings of the day and then we ate lustily enjoying the food, the companionship and the moment.

We finished our meal. Gram and Jack went to work on the mission ahead. Al got a shower. I called home, had a wonderful chat with Basha, said prayers with Janko as he got ready for bed, blew her a long distance kiss and said goodnight.

As the evening ended, we basked in the glow of a job well done. The time slowly ebbed away until we all grew tired enough to finally close our eyes and drifted off to sleep listening to the crying of the tires spinning on the asphalt surface of the highway just outside our window.

24. Another Civil War of Sorts

When we realized that Charleston was not going to be a simple stop on the campaign trail, we decided to put all our heads together and figure out some strategy. Conference call was becoming the norm now and not the exception. Gram suggested that we contact the entire team every day so that we were always on the same page and not doing anything that could appear to be at cross purposes. The system was very simple. We set up a connection with a cell phone, patched it into a unit that gave us conference calling capabilities with a microphone pick up we could all talk into and then we just dialed the main number at the hall and we were on.

Today we wanted Richard Johnson in on the conversation. He was quite the find. James Buchanan was definitely right on when he said he had someone we would definitely want to meet. Richard was a true blue community organizer in the ilk of the current president. However, before anyone could include him in anything we were about to do, Big Jack said he wanted to vet this "new guy" as he called him. Jack went to work. I did not know exactly how he was going to vet Richard, but Gram assured me that he had checked out Jack's vetting process and he believed it rivaled even the Air Force's methodology.

"How about the FBI's or the CIAs?" I asked Gram.

"Don't know. Never had the chance to be vetted by them," he replied.

"How many times have you been vetted?"

"Don't know. Sometimes you just don't know when you're being vetted."

"You think Richard will pass the Big Jack test?"

"If he doesn't, Jack might make Richard disappear," Gram said seriously.

"Seriously?" I asked, wondering if he were serious.

"Jack doesn't mess around, I'm telling you. I know. When he got done with me we had a talk and he explained to me just what the stakes were and that he did not like having to deal with the 'bad guys' as he called them who might want to mess up the campaign."

"What did he tell you that he did to them?" I asked again.

"Leo, if I told you, I'd have to kill you so let's leave it at that," he replied with a grin on his face.

"Ah, man, you're just pulling my leg," I cried out at him.

"I may be pulling your leg, but don't let Jack ever be the one pulling your leg, legs arms, or anything else. You'll get a whole lot bigger, longer, painfully, I'm sure if he does."

I did not know what to make of anything he was saying. All I could think was that I was glad that these guys were working for me and not against me.

Our conference call included John Gallagher, Judy, Carol, Fritz, Richard Johnson, a fellow named Fred Childs from Charleston, Gram, Al, Big Jack, and me.

John was one organized fellow. He had an agenda to us within seconds of the call coming through nicely set up by Fritz, our main techno geek.

"Let's get quick reports from all. One minute manager stuff. No more. Carol?"

"Finances are looking good. We just topped $4 million. Way to go Leo. The southland is opening up. Donations from Greenville, Columbia and Spartanburg are pouring in."

"Excellent. Excellent," John said. "Judy?"

"Our message is getting out. We bought $100,000 worth of radio ads in South Carolina. Thirty-second spots. This was our first endeavor so we shall see how it works."

"Which ad did you run?" I asked, interrupting her.

"The one about work and strengthening democracy and ending with your encouraging all working people to vote their economic interest and join you on your mission to shake up Washington by ending the millionaires' and billionaires' strangle hold on our political system."

"Great! I'm excited to hear that. I hope we can pick it up on the radio when we get to Charleston," I said."

"You'll like it, Leo," she replied. "We kept it simple, clear and precise. No doubt what side we are on. We kept it positive. We did not attack the president or any of the other clowns that are running. Oh, but this past week, with all the crap that came out on Gingrich and Romney, we could have a field day."

"Leave them alone. They don't count," I said. "Folks, we just can't fall into that trap. For once, we have to do this clean, pure and natural. I mean it."

"We got it, Leo," John said, "and I'm speaking for everyone. You along with us, Richard on that?"

"Yes sir," he responded. "I would not be here if that were not the case."

"Great. Fritz?"

"No more security threats on the web. We've tightened up everything as much as we can. Thanks Jack for the heads up about you know what?"

"No problem," Jack responded.

"What?" I asked.

"Need to know basis," Jack said and did not elaborate. I dropped the subject.

"Richard, so what's the rub in Charleston? Are we fighting another civil war of sorts?" John asked.

"This is the bastion of the old south. The other cities have grown up. They are much more progressive than even most northern cities. Charleston remains a hold out. There is an element down here that will not give in to seeing the world in a new light. Anyway, we could not get a permit to do a gig anywhere around the unemployment office, or downtown near it. Fred and I spent the last day trying to line up something but we are facing opposition at every turn."

"Fred, welcome to the team and tell us what you think," John said inviting his input.

"Hi Ya'll. Now this old town is just pushing us around because it can't stand the heat coming out of the kitchen. Leo, you raised the temperature quite a few degrees in the last week. My cracker brothers and sisters just don't want to face the push to listen and hear the message coming at them. Seems they like the old ways best. They can't handle new people and new ideas any more than an old hound dog wants to stop chasing deer even though he's been getting thumped by his master every time he does it. We don't have a venue. This is the bottom line and that's the rub."

"So what do we do, team?" John said. "If we can't legally host a gathering, we're in a pinch. The primary is Saturday. It's now Thursday. What is the answer?"

"Seems to me that we go rogue," Richard said. "Perhaps it's time to expose this entire state for what it is: a backward leaning place hostile to working people."

"I agree with you that this is a backward leaning state," Gram added, "but rubbing it in their faces by defying the authorities and hosting an event without having some legal protection is just asking for trouble. We do have to come back here in the fall for the general election campaign and we don't want to be on the authority's back side."

"So what do we do?" Richard said. "What do you think, Fred?"

"Good to be a part of your team, Leo. Thanks for having me along for the ride."

"No problem. What do you think, Fred?" I asked.

"I was asking my wife today what she thought and she said, ' honey child, when you can't get the master to let you do what you want, you just gotta go and do what he wants. So have a picnic in the park. Invite all your family and friends and hope they all come. Then you can play games, throw Frisbees around and if the spirit moves you, well, then you can even listen to your favorite cousin from up north tell the family what's happening in his world as he, believe it or not, sets out to run for a new job called president of the United States."

"Hot damn," John barked out. "Now that's one hell of a smart woman. You give that wife of yours a hug for me, Fred. I mean it."

"Will do," Fred said.

"What do you think, folks?" John asked all of us.

"Sounds like a really cool plan," I said. "Southern Fried Chicken outside at a barbecue is just the ticket."

"Oh you won't be eating much, Leo. This crowd will flash form and you're going to be pressing the flesh the entire time. We'll eat a little but you've got to get these people tuned in to what you're doing."

"I got it, John. Everyone gets to party but me. I got it."

"Leo, you're the man," Gram said. "We realize that you'd like to play around like the rest of us while we're at the park, but you've got to be about business. Just accept responsibility for what you've started," he concluded, winking at the rest of the guys around the table. Jack did not wink, but Al thought this rather humorous.

"Fred, what park are you thinking we should use?" John asked.

"Though Battery Park would be a wonderful venue and symbolic of the battle we are engaged in, I think that Waterfront Park would suit our purposes much better. We can picnic there without too much headache and then we can use the large grassy area near the water fountain for the 'gathering' and the message."

"What do you think, team?"

"Sounds good to me," I said. "But how soon can we get this organized?"

"We just needed a place," Richard said, "and permission to proceed. Fred and I didn't want to just go ahead and do this without alerting the team and making sure you all agreed."

"Jack, any problems with this plan?" John asked.

"Not right now. I'm already working on the security. Sea is to the east. Large open areas but no grassy knolls from which to launch an attack," he said.

We all looked at him. For once, just this once, he said, "Psyche!" in his booming voice. Everyone laughed. We were happy that we could joke with one another, at least now and then.

"Okay. We've had our fun now. Let's see. It's 9:15 am. How much time do you need to organize things, Fred, Richard?"

There was some small talk on their end. "We can be ready by 4 pm," Richard said.

"Leo, how about your fellows?"

"Can you get us there by 4 pm?" I asked.

"Leo, we're almost in Charleston now. We have plenty of time."

"Okay. It's a go. Gram, legal issues? You ready?"

"Always," Gram said.

"Jack?"

"Ditto!" Jack replied.

"Leo, check in with us at day's end. We'll need a report. Fred, you and Richard try and get the press down to the park too, but keep it low profile. We don't need any entangling alliances with the local gendarmes."

"Got it, John," Fred replied.

"Thanks everyone. Let's do it."

We let out a sigh of relief. We were on. I was the one who was really "on". They would be partying while I would be working my tongue off. No wonder I was losing weight.

"Anyone hungry?" I asked.

"No, not I," Gram said. "I'm saving my appetite for the picnic. How about you, Al?" he asked, knowing that he and Al would be pigging out while I was doing my thing.

"Oh, I'm good, Leo. Thanks. I'm like Gram. I'm saving my appetite for that good southern fried chicken I know that will be everywhere."

"Yah, I got your backs, too," I said and sat down at the table and ate a bowl of cereal while Al jumped back behind the wheel and pointed the bus toward Charleston. Gram assumed his navigator's seat. Jack left us there and disappeared into the traffic in his car.

While Gram and Al piloted the bus toward Charleston, I relaxed on the couch, stared out the window and watched the South Carolina landscape swiftly float past. The issue we faced today was not something we could not overcome with just some simple planning What concerned me was we were skirting the law in order to be able meet the people who wanted to hear me. I wondered what would happen the next time we were in this state and one of three candidates for president and a serious threat to the republicans and the democrats. The negative campaigning flooding the airwaves was just the beginning of the onslaught that would eventually be directed at me, too. What would they say? What would they attack? Luckily, I never worked for an equity firm and destroyed whole companies in a mad rush to build capital from the bones of a picked over company. I was not divorced and remarried three times. I had not switched religions. I was definitely not a flip flopper on major issues. I had no track record of being a pork barrel leader in the senate. I did not have a voting record that was anti-government through and through and I was much younger than 76 years of age. The anticipation that there would be negative ads thrown at the campaign and me was something that I just had to prepare myself for mentally and emotionally. When the first one came, I would watch it repeatedly until the message was not something that frightened me, upset me or caused me to want to lash out and attack the attackers. After all, this was national politics: the Big Show. If I could not take the heat, then I needed to get out of the kitchen. I wondered who would be more vicious: democrats or republicans. I would soon find out.

South Carolina's history in the Union was unique. The passion felt by its citizens was intense and there was no doubt that the citizens were anxious to go to war with the north. As soon as Abraham Lincoln was elected president, South Carolina's legislature voted to secede from the union. The attack on Fort Sumter was just a ploy to get the North to begin the war. For years after the war, South Carolina languished economically. Those days were long gone in terms of calendar years, but embedded deep into the spirit of the people was a pride that still fomented rebellion. I sat and pondered just how I might tap into that spirit and reverse the flow of energy that was anti-government and labor. This was not going to be an easy task, but to it, I was committed.

As the leader of the "A-Team", the television series that I watched when I was a much younger man, used to say, "I love it when a plan comes together."

Our plan evolved and we were in Waterfront Park at 4 pm. How many people were actually there, we could only estimate. Everywhere I looked, I could see people: men, women and children laughing, talking, moving around, cooking, listening to music, tossing footballs and Frisbees, playing with dogs and toddlers. The aroma was overwhelming. No one would go home hungry tonight. The sky blessed us with its blueness. Soft zephyrs floating across the land from the ocean cooled us. The rich, green carpet of grass covered our vast living room. The moment was electric. Everywhere I saw the joy of people in communion with one another. This gathering was taking place near the very spot where once brother shot brother; where death's odor filled the air. I wandered through the crowds, shaking hands, listening to jokes, hearing tales of woe and heroism and simple graciousness. I saw fear in the eyes of some of the people and revolution in the eyes of others. The hands touching me were rough and used to a hard life. Now and then, soft hands would meet mine and I would wonder just how these escaped the rigors of a difficult life. Some of the people thanked me for being there and taking on their cause. Some wondered if I was daft thinking I could compete against the political machines mowing down the competition across the state. I autographed a number of people's books for them even though I was not the author. I signed pictures of me taken from the papers in the other cities. Watching some of the elderly men and women take my hand in theirs and tell me to make sure that they were not forgotten brought tears to my eyes. How could I forget these venerable saints, these grandmothers and grandfathers who were attacked by the right from the likes of Congressman Paul Ryan who wanted to give all seniors "vouchers" and let them go onto the open market and buy their own health insurance; thereby, ending Medicare as we know it. I assured them that our commitment to these programs was going to make them better and not eliminate them. Each one who held my hand seemed to not want to let go as if I were, in some way, an anchorage for their lives in a storm tossed national experience. I did not eat at all. Though everyone offered me food, I was committed to listening, seeing, touching and feeling the stories. I did not want to be numbed by the ingestion of heavy foods no matter how good they smelled and most assuredly tasted. The afternoon light flowed softly from the heavens. Everyone's face was bathed in a gentle glow that made them all appear angelic. Perhaps it was this view that made my heart feels heavy, burdened, laden with a sense of profound grief. There was no reason for this to be happening to these people. They did not make the policies that hurt them.

How the message got out that I was going to say a few words, I do not know. I just realized that, all of a sudden, gathered around me was a vast crowd of eyes staring intently at me. I could feel their heat, their intensity, their loving embrace and I just could not disappoint.

"What a wonderful afternoon to be alive, American and together like this in a city park, enjoying family, friends and food."

"Thank you all for coming to the party."

Loud applause echoed through the park.

"My name is Leo Pollack. I'm an unemployed steel worker, a simple man, married with a wife and one son, and I am running to be, with your help, the next president of the United States."

I heard calls of "Leo"…"Leo"…flow through the crowd.

"I claim no genius. I am a worker who has not yet, like I am sure many of you have not, realized the American dream."

"What makes it so elusive? This dream? This thing we are supposed to all want to achieve? Let me tell you what it is for me and see if this fits for you as well. The dream is that you and your family are happy, healthy and hopeful. Happiness must be defined by each one of us for ourselves. Healthy is pretty self-explanatory. But hopeful is the elusive point of this wonderful triangle. We are hopeful when we know we can go to work every day and make a decent living and go home at night knowing that we did our best to care for those whom we love. When this hope is gone, the dream becomes less achievable."

"Now here is the rub. In the past three decades, many of us have seen our lifestyle eroding and we have been unable to stop it. The reason is simple. There is no one in Washington who speaks our language and can relate to the reality of our lives."

"I don't believe that any of the current candidates or the current president can 'relate to our pain' as former President Clinton claimed he could. I don't think he could either. Perhaps when he was a kid, but somehow, he forgets where he came from and that made all the difference."

"My friends, and I hope I can call you that from today forward, you must realize that this candidacy is not for me, not for Leo Pollack to achieve fame and glory, but for the people, you as well as me, to once again have someone working for you in the White House."

"This is no easy task. This will not be a cake walk to use a cliché. We will have to band together, pass the word among our friends, neighbors, work mates, and anyone who will listen and especially those who will not that there is a movement in America today to take back our government and make it work for us as it was designed to do."

"The tea party wants to eliminate the government, get rid of this and that, and that is all well and good if we believe in what they believe. However, we live in a social network that is based upon mutual respect, shared responsibility and a focus on the future. What keeps all this in some semblance of order is the government. No, government is not the problem; the people in the government are."

Loud, raucous cheers erupted when I said this last sentence.

"Leadership is something that makes all the difference. We can sit back and say to ourselves 'ain't it awful'. The people in Washington just don't care. My friends, we have to make them care. We have to vote out the scallywags who are not doing their jobs. We need to challenge those who are working at a less than acceptable pace. We have to encourage them to listen to what we are saying. When they don't listen, we send them a clear message: your services are no longer needed."

"We were told we could not gather here today. We were not told any real reason why this was the case. We are not slow. We know there is a great fear that if 160 million working people said tomorrow that we are not going to do one more minute of work until we are treated fairly by every one of the corporations that pretend to care about us, this country's leaders would quake in their boots. Working people are the most powerful force on the face of the earth. American working people once led the world in their willingness to stand together and confront the unfair, disrespectful and unacceptable manner in which corporations acted toward their employees. We've grown soft in the last few decades. We've lost our way. We've given up our mojo."

"Join me now in the quest for a new American order where work is sacred, corporations cherish their employees, policies protect people and not hurt them, the government advocates for and not against working folks and the dream of a better tomorrow for our children is within sight."

"Come, ring the liberty bell with me. Let everyone see the faces of working people across the country banded together, speaking in one voice, saying loudly, proudly and simply, 'When America works, Democracy thrives.'"

"Join me in this campaign for our future. Join me by donating a dollar or two, but no more than twenty, and stand up and be counted for changing the way we do business in America."

"Join me in buying American so that when I buy a product made by my neighbor who works in a factory in Indiana or Ohio or South Carolina, I am putting my neighbor to work. If I can't buy an American made product produced by my neighbor somewhere in the United States, I just don't buy anything."

"Join me in buying and eating food produced by American farmers."

"Join me in driving American made cars in plants where workers are paid at least a living wage."

"Join me in raising one voice and shouting out across the hills and dales, across rivers and to the mountain tops that we are finished with accepting the status quo."

"I am Leo Pollack, an unemployed steel worker, and I want your vote, your support so that I can be your next president and speak for you as your leader. Please join me in this journey.

"Thank you for being here, listening, and wanting to make America a land where working people can and will achieve the American dream."

"Nuf said," I said to myself and walked back into the crowd that I had flowed through for a number of hours and met the people all over again. This time, I was a different person in their eyes, hearts and minds. I was one of them and yet, one who wanted to risk it all to achieve a goal that no working man who lived from paycheck to paycheck had accomplished for more than a century and a half.

"If I died right now, I would have lived a wonderful life and would have no regrets except that I did not see my family one last time," was what I kept thinking as I shook hands, talked, laughed and responded to the crowd of well wishers, new believers, and people just like me who wanted a simple but better life. We did not envy the wealthy. We did not want mansions or castles. We did not need buckets of money. We needed to be respected. We needed to be appreciated for our contribution to the economy in which we worked, spent our money and hopefully, shared in its bounty. The time flowed so swiftly that before I knew what was happening, darkness was settling down upon us and the people started to clean up and disband.

My colleagues finally wandered over and slapped me on the back and said, "So have you had enough fun for one day?"

"Never. As long as I live, I'll never get used to being with the people and feeling their energy, their joy and enthusiasm and wanting to insure that they will always feel the power to make a difference in their own lives. What a rush!"

"Don't get too carried away, because I think we're about to be visited by one of Charleston's finest and I'm talking about you know who and what they are about."

I turned around and sure enough, a half-dozen blue uniformed officers were heading our way. I stood still, smiling, wondering what to say and do.

"Let me do the talking," Gram said. "We don't need a night in jail."

"If I let you do the talking, that may just be where we end up," I replied.

"Where is Jack when you need him?" Al asked.

"Don't worry. We'll be fine. I see Richard over there and he's amassing a crew to come to our aid," Gram said.

"A crew? That looks like a gang to me," Al said.

"Gang, crew, what difference does it make as long as these yokels don't start to think they can intimidate us," Gram said.

"They're doing a good job of it so far," Al retorted.

The lead officer came up to us and said, "Howdy fellas, what's happening' here?"

"Just having a big picnic, that's about all, officer," Gram replied.

"Well, appears to me that you're doing a whole lot more than that. Appears to me that you're holding' what I'd call an illegal political rally. Appears to me that you're doing something to incite these fine people to break the law and that is not okay in our town."

"What makes you think that we're holding' a political rally," Gram asked.

"Well, smart aleck, we was standing' over there and listening' to your friend here talk that stuff that makes folks get uneasy and want to riot," he complained.

"So what did he say that was so upsetting to you, officer that it made you want to go and riot?"

The fellow scratched his head and then responded, "Now, I didn't say it made me want to get up and go and riot. No sir. I said it sounded like what he was saying was making others get up and go out and riot, question their government, and the like."

"Did any of these people do that? Did they get up and go and do anything that, from your point of view, was illegal or was like rioting?"

"Well, no not really, but that is what I was hearing," he said.

"What else did you hear?" Gram asked.

"I heard that people were encouraged to band together and make their voices heard and that sounded like the people were again being incited."

"Hmm. What happened when they heard this?" Gram asked.

"Well, nothing happened," he said.

"Then what's the problem?"

"The problem is that political rallies like this one without a permit are illegal. That is the problem."

"Who said this was a political rally? Look around you, officer. Everywhere you look, there are people packing up their picnic supplies and getting ready to go home. They all look like they were having a wintertime picnic and that's about it. I am looking now at groups of people, laughing, talking, packing up, sharing leftovers and getting ready to go home. Looks and sounds pretty peaceful to me," Gram concluded.

"Now see here, fellow. We heard what we heard and that's all there is to it," he remonstrated. "You fellers from up north can't come down here and just make a mockery of our laws. That's not the way it works."

"If we made a mockery of your laws, which ones were we mocking? Picnicking in the park? Talking to friends? Telling jokes? Well, which ones?"

The officer was tongue tied. He did not know what to say. Gram hushed up and let him stew for a minute or two.

"Officer, sir, we were just about ready to pack up our own picnic stuff and head on out of here, but if there is something else you'd like to share with us, well, please do. We know you're a busy man and don't want to waste your time. We're all ears. Please let us know what you want us to do?"

The silence was oppressive. I knew that all we needed to do now was hush up and we would walk away from here unscathed.

More silence.

Every bone in my body told me that this cop wanted to arrest me and the rest of the crew in the worst way but he was not sure just what to do right now. Gram's arguments were swaying him back and forth like sea oats in an offshore breeze. He did not want to make a mistake and look bad, but he knew that we were doing more than what Gram said we were. I noticed that Richard kept his distance. I wondered where Big Jack was. Where was he when you needed him most of all. Perhaps he did not see this as any threat. Who knew what Jack thought anyway? He kept his own counsel. We stood there waiting, wondering, and did not want to break the spell. The next one who spoke would surely lose. I kept mum. I knew my place. I smiled and waited.

"You fellows are a right smart bunch of Yankees and I can tell that if I say you can go that you will do so and not come back and that will be it. Am I making myself clear?" he said, waving his hand toward the freeway a few blocks away.

"I believe, officer, you are making yourself perfectly clear, and we thank you for your clarity, for your willingness to listen to reason and for your hospitality. With your permission, we'll just finish picking up the few articles we have right here, carried our trash to the bus and be on our way."

"You do that, you hear," he said and moseyed away with the officers in tow spreading out through the waning crowd but always keeping a watchful eye on us.

"Let's get out of here pronto," Gram said.

"You don't have to tell me twice," Al seconded. "Let me get that bus revved up while you two fellows clean up the rest of our stuff."

"Wait a minute," I balked. "I would really like to know what he meant by 'am I making myself clear'. From what it sounded like to me, he was threatening us and I don't like being threatened by some hick cop in Charleston, South Carolina," I finished.

They both looked at me like I was crazy.

Before they could say a word, I busted out laughing, and ran toward the bus, "Last one in has to pick up all the trash" and disappeared inside.

"Why you son of a..." Gram hollered and picked up the rest of the gear and trash and headed, along with Al, back to the bus and our forced exit from Charleston.

Just as Al was firing up the motor, Jack slipped into the side door and settled down on the couch next to Gram and me.

"Nice you could show up," I chided him.

"You surprised I didn't show up when you were being hounded by that cracker cop?" Jack said. "Lord knows, this is the south and some things don't change much, Leo. I still know my place, even if you think that I am speaking in tongues."

"You really believe that he would have acted differently if you had showed up and come to my defense?"

"I think this is the heart of Dixie and what is happening right here today is just a symptom of the depths of distrust that still exist."

"What about the picnic, the people, the rest of the day?" I asked.

"Leo, there is good and bad and indifferent everywhere. You just got to find it in the hearts and minds of the people. Now that we've had our moment in the sunny south, let's get the hell out of here before he comes back, sees we are still here and decides that he wants to make an example of us."

"Out of here," Al shouted. He shifted into drive and slowly we moved away from the parking lot and headed toward the freeway.

"You really wanted to argue with that cop, didn't you?" Gram asked.

"Sure did," I responded.

"Thanks for keeping your jib shut," he replied.

"You're welcome," I said.

"Now, with that in mind, you really were afraid to say anything because the last thing you wanted to do was go to jail today. Tell me the truth."

"You're right," I said.

"Al, Jack, you owe me a buck," Gram barked at the two of them.

"Leo, you're so willy-nilly," Al fired back.

"What kind of bet did you two make?" I asked.

"I bet these two that you would do something that would almost get us arrested today and that I would have to sweet talk the cops out of doing it. They said that you would probably spout off to some cop and that would be it. I bet them that I could keep you quiet somehow and get the cops to leave us free men."

"Well, well, well, now aren't you a cool customer," I said to him applauding his efforts. "The funny thing is I bet these guys that you would try and make a bet with them that I would get us arrested today because you were feeling a little queasy about coming into this bastion of the south. So now how do you like this turn of events?"

Gram did not say anything.

"Everyone is even, now, I catcalled to all of them.

"What are we going to eat tonight?" I asked.

"Whatever you make," Gram said.

"Let me out, Al, I've got work to do," Big Jack said.

"No you don't. You eat what we eat," Al said.

"Someone's got to drive my car and I don't want to leave it there for our local yokels to ticket and then tow away for illegally parking."

Al turned the bus toward the end of the parking lot and stopped. Jack waved to us, got out and was gone.

"So what will it be fellows?" I asked.

"Do you suppose, Leo, we could have tuna fish along with our cheese and mac? How does that sound?"

"Doable, now leave me alone while I cook. Go on up there and keep Al company."

Gram left me alone in the kitchen. I surprised them. I make Albacore instead of tuna fish, mac and cheese. When it was ready, Al pulled off the freeway, found a safe spot for us to rest for a moment, and we ate together.

"Now was that so bad?" I asked.

"Leo, nothing you cook is hard to swallow," Gram said, "but a little variety does add spice to life."

"I'll take that into advisement."

"Where to now fellows? Al asked. "The night is young."

"We've got one more stop to make," I said.

"Where's that?" Gram asked.

"Darlington," I replied.

"What's there?"

"Darlington International Speedway," I said.

"What?" he cried. "A speedway?"

"Yup. Always wanted to see it."

"What a waste of time," he judged.

"No. We have to meet the NASCAR crowd some time. Tomorrow is as good as any," I said. "Once they realize we are not scary people, we will be really making a dent in the red states."

"Is he serious?" Gram asked Al.

"I don't know," he said. "Let's just say he must know what he's doing because we're considering the destination."

"What did I get myself into?" Gram asked no one directly.

"The adventure of a lifetime," Al said driving on into the nighttime that was totally wrapped around us as we headed northeast toward that fabled race city.

I called home, chatted with Basha and Janko, and then cleaned up after the crew. Dishes away, I sat back down on the couch and watched the last republican debate. Gram joined me and we laughed and cajoled one another as the four aces went at one another.

We rested peacefully that night nestled below the bright lights of a Walmart Superstore half way to Darlington, South Carolina, wondering what tomorrow would bring and how much of an impact we would have on our southern brothers and sisters who were listening to our message and would be voting on Saturday night.

25. NASCAR Nation Goes for Pollack

Darlington is a small city in Darlington County in the northeastern part of the state of South Carolina. It is a center for tobacco farming. Darlington, named for the Revolutionary War hero, Colonel Darlington, is famous for its Darlington Oak and Spanish moss. Darlington County was named thus by an Act in March 1785. Darlington is best known for Darlington Raceway, a speedway that is home to an annual NASCAR Southern 500 race. Darlington is also the site of the National Motorsports Press Association (NMPA) Hall of Fame.

What made me want to go to Darlington had more to do with the home of NASCAR racing than anything related to the campaign. I wanted to see the racetrack, the famous Darlington track where so many great races were held. There was something to be learned in that hallowed racing milieu.

Gram and Al were perplexed. They were not into the mission. Jack didn't say anything but I felt his tenseness.

"Trust me, brothers," I said. "This is a good move."

"This is crazy," Gram said. "Who gives a damn about racing?"

"I like my cars, trucks and other toys, but NASCAR is fake," Al cried out.

"Let me say this simply. NASCAR is America. If we can win over the hearts and minds of the NASCAR Nation, we are on our way to winning the presidency," I claimed. "Think about it. Once, the south was solidly democratic. Now, it hovers between the Republican Party and the tea party. What does that tell you? The south shifted because the message they were hearing was acceptable to them. They did not want to believe in the government and the democrats who were feeding the welfare state ushered in by President Johnson. They shifted thirty years ago and have not returned. Now we have a chance to change this by changing the message."

"So what are you going to sell them?" Gram asked.

"America. What else? The American Flag. American cars. You get my drift? You hear the theme? You realize that this is our time."

"You really believe this?" Gram said. "What am I doing here then? I thought I was your chief of staff, and here I am arguing with you instead of supporting your decisions."

"Hey, it's okay to challenge my thinking," I said. "I expect that. However, in this situation, I think I know what we need to do. Think about a Sunday race. What do you see? Flags flying. America on parade. Raceway chaplains praying over the drivers and America. The Star Spangled Banner being sung. The skies bursting with the sound of Air Force fighters flying over the track. This is America down home. These are the people who want to celebrate America when they see many things that are hard to celebrate. So we go to Darlington and meet the people."

"Let's go," Al said.

"I hear you, Leo," Gram echoed. "Lead the way."

With their support, I called in to John Gallagher and told him what we were doing. He did not hesitate to give me his withholds. I reiterated my arguments to him and finally, reluctantly, he said, "Go ahead and get it done," mimicking Larry the Cable Guy.

I was not Larry, but I was committed to getting it done.

We arrived in Darlington about noon the next day and I said, "Let's go to the track and then find a restaurant and stop and meet the people."

"Got it," Al replied and off we went.

The Darlington International Speedway was an awesome structure and I wished they were racing today. The famous turn four has ended many races for careless drivers. We got out of the Liberty Bus, walked around the place and felt the magic of one of the oldest racing venues in the country.

There were no race teams on the track today so I decided to go looking for the next closest thing.

"Al, let's find a local eatery nearby and we'll make our stand. You fellows game?" I challenged them.

"I don't know about this," Gram uttered reluctantly. "Have you cleared this with Big Jack?"

"I haven't seen him today. He's hovering somewhere nearby. Since we had nothing planned for this morning, I think he's doing other things. Who knows? He doesn't tell us much, does he? I'm calling the shots. Let's go." I started toward a side street leading away from the track.

Al jumped back into the Liberty Bell bus and followed me as I headed down the side street.

Five minutes later, I spied the ideal place to test my notion. In front of me was the "Raceway Cafe". Painted in a black and white checkered flag pattern on the outside, the exterior represented a gigantic winner's symbol. The roof was flat. The parking lot was half full. The odor of fried foods cooking wafted out from the side windows. Most of the vehicles parked outside were muscle cars and big trucks. This was not a Volvo or BMW driving school.

"This is it," I said aloud, but no one heard me.

"Gram, are you with me?" He did not hear what I said. He was hiding in the bus. I think he was truly intimidated by the stage we, or at least, I was about to enter.

I stepped up to the doorway, took a deep breath and went inside the establishment. The aroma of bacon and eggs flooded my nostrils. Taking a seat at the counter, I sat down and watched the waitresses scurry like red ants in the sunshine. This was one busy place. I was pleased that I would be able to test my case in this type of southern venue. I could feel the eyes on me from every corner of the room. They must have seen the Liberty Bus pull up in front. They had to see me walking around outside. They did not miss anything. I did not want them to, so I waited until there was a relative silence in the room. "Mother Mary comfort me," I said to myself. Then, I stood up and started the show.

I looked around and most people were not watching me. They were minding their own business, talking to the people at their table, eating their food, but out of the corner of their eyes wondering what I was doing there. I realized it would be a mistake to open my mouth right now. The timing was not right. I decided instead to walk around and meet the people, table by table, and forget the speechmaking. The themes I wanted to share with them were simple.

Taking my cup of coffee with me, I wandered to the first table past the doorway and introduced myself to four middle aged fellows all wearing ball caps and sweatshirts and clearly looked like construction workers but without any place to go on this January morning. I told them what brought me to South Carolina, what I believed were the essential issues of this presidential election year and hoped they would support me in my effort. I used a NASCAR analogy. I maintained that the gridlock in Washington was like a race team that was having an internal feud. The engine shop could not get it together with the body shop. The race day pit crew was not synchronizing with the driver and the crew chief. The president was the team owner. He was responsible for maintaining the smooth flow of the entire enterprise. Unless he stepped in when needed to insure a winning combination, the team would enter a car on race day, but they would not have any chance of winning. NASCAR was like the federal government. Without a strong federal regulatory body, there would be rampant cheating and no way to have a fair race. We needed regulation to keep the competitors in check. Leave the banks up to their own devices and we would have an ongoing recession like we were having right now. No, regulation was necessary, not something to be avoided and railed against, but used to level the playing field. The men sitting at the table thanked me for making my plea, for simplifying the process and explaining it in terms that made sense to them.

At another table, I shared my view of the commons: the roads, the safety systems, the airlines, and the interstate commerce and how important it was for us to have someone who understood the way these variables worked and how to make them interact even more efficiently.

Moving through the dining room, I met "salt of the earth" Americans who were curious about the country, the direction we were headed and what could I do to make sure that their kids were safe, that terrorists were not going to invade us and that we would respect the life of unborn children. To each, I implored tolerance, forbearance and patience. No one had all the answers. Likewise, no one was completely wrong on any one issue. Abortion was not just a matter of choice. The choice to conceive a child was often done in haste, or at least, in passion. Now that the seed was sown, was it logical that a fifteen year old give birth? Was it conceivable that the child be carried to term? What was the answer? I asked as many questions as I received.

Some of the patrons were a little standoffish. Who was this Yankee coming into their neighborhood and boldly asking for their vote? Whenever I sensed some resistance, I simply said, "I don't blame you for being leery about some Yankee coming into your neighborhood and asking for your vote. There is a difference between the rest of the candidates and me. I am like you. I work for a living. I wasn't born into a rich family. I didn't write a bunch of books and run around the country promoting them so I could make money from them. I am not a doctor, a lawyer, historian or any other type of professional person. No, I'm a working stiff, just like you. I pay the payroll tax just like you. I work for a corporation that decided my services after fifteen years were no longer needed. I watch the economy fall into the pits and the banks still make record profits and the gas and oil companies still bank billions and wonder, what the hell? I am not some simpleton who thinks that the problems we face in our country are going to be easy to fix, but I do know that the politicians, big moneyed interests and those already in government have had their day. Now it is our turn. With your support, I can go to Washington and begin the process of moving us toward a more just and fair society."

The moments swiftly passed. Some families asked me to sit down with them so I did. Breaking bread with them was the most intimate activity. Sharing food was more important than ideas, but they flowed too. Integrity was a theme that ran through every conversation. What made people say one thing and then go to Washington and do something else? I replied, "I don't know. I can only tell you what I am going to do. Those who seek the presidency and need to raise millions of dollars to run their campaigns find many people who want to have their voices heard so they donate buckets of money to the campaign. Currently, one candidate has received $10 million from a billionaire couple who want their point of view pursued. They are symptomatic of what is wrong with the current crop of candidates. The president is raising hundreds of millions so he can be re-elected. His big donors are going to influence his decision-making. This vicious circle needs to be broken. The time has come to reverse this process. You and I know that folks like us don't really have a voice in this or any government because we don't contribute mega-bucks to any campaign. We vote. This is our only bit of power. However, if 160 million working people vote as a block, vote for a candidate that speaks for them, they can hope that the nation will move in a direction that supports their dreams and not those of corporate America."

The dining hall buzzed with conversation. I moved relentlessly and patiently on from one table to the next, listening, laughing, telling stories from the campaign trail, asking them for their opinions and listening to what they had to say. "You know Mr. Pollack," the man said, "we work harder now than we ever did and each time we come up for a raise the company says times are tight and there isn't any extra cash to spread around. Yet we see the bosses get big bonuses and drive big cars and trucks and act as if we are too stupid to see what is going on. When we ask for our fair share, they quickly remind us that if we don't like it we can just move right along. I don't believe in unions, but I surely don't believe that a worker's gotta be treated like he was nothing more than a slave. You agree?"

More than ever, I agreed with the need for fairness, justice and sharing the bounty of production. "Ain't that socialism?" one woman asked.

"Socialism is spreading wealth among people in some legal, defined way that makes everyone get his or her share," I replied. "In our system, we all work toward a common goal. We might be building cars or fabricating a piece of machinery. Each person who contributes to the production of the product ought to share in the financial outcome. How is it fair for one person to barely make a living wage and another, an executive, to earn 300-400 times as much for doing nothing but making production decisions? Folks, our economic institutions are backwards. Those who actually do the work are making so much less than those who sit in corner offices and make the 'big decisions'. This inequity started when corporations assumed global status. To reverse this trend, we need to reward those who do the work and not just those who make decisions. A shared, democratic way of running a corporation is necessary, and in time, it will become the new way of doing business. We have miles to go before this type of institution becomes the standard."

Some raised concerns that we would not be able to compete with the major parties because I would not have enough money. I agreed that money was an issue, but as the former speaker of the house believed, "people power trumps money power." "Whether or not we can succeed is not the issue. Raising our collective voices and sending out a clear message that what we want is our fair share and to be treated with dignity and respect is what mattered. Unless we received this kind of treatment, we might as well consider ourselves, 'wage slaves'."

One of the children said to me, "You don't look like a president." I asked him, "How should a president look?" He thought about it for a moment and then said, "Older and with a beard. You aren't old enough to be the president." I thanked him for the compliment.

At each table, folks offered food to me, but all I did was continue to swill down black coffee. Once or twice, I excused myself and went to the bathroom. I stared in the mirror. "Yes, you don't look old enough to be the president." I chuckled and went back to the people.

"What are you going to do about jobs?" I was asked repeatedly. "Buy American," was my standard response.

"Whenever you buy something made by an American in America, you put your neighbor to work. If it is not made in America, don't buy it."

People were concerned that prices would go up if we started buying things made here. I responded with this simple argument.

"Folks, prices will not go up if we are making products here again and there is competition on our own soil. Right now, there is no internal competition. Therefore, prices are artificially lower. What irritates me is this one fact. Companies like Nike make shoes overseas at a pittance. The last time the company made the news, they shifted all their production from Vietnam to Cambodia because in one country they had to pay a worker, $2.00 a day. In the other one, they only had to pay $1.65 a day. So they moved. The price of the shoes did not come down. Americans were still paying, on average, $100.00 or more for a pair of Nikes. Phil Knight said that Americans were not interested in making shoes. The reality is that he never once considered building a factory in the United States. I wouldn't wear Nike shoes even if they were given them to me because they are not made in America. Redwings are. I own a pair and wear them proudly. You see, we contributed to this mess, too. We are suckers for cheap goods. Yes, things might cost more for a time, but once production is being done here and there is competition among companies, the prices will slowly level out again."

One grandmother said that I looked awfully thin and that I needed to put some meat on my bones. "I appreciate your concern for my health, Ma'am." I said. "I have to admit my cooking is not the best in the world." She asked me if we actually lived in that bus outside and I said, "Yes, whenever we are on the road. Yes, I do most of the cooking. My team doesn't like to cook." Grandma said I needed to get me a good woman and I told her that I had the best woman in the world but she was home taking care of our son and could not travel now because he was in school. "Well, get this campaign over pronto, and take the little woman and your child and settle down. This life is no good for a family man." "Yes Ma'am," I replied respectfully.

"The problem with this country," an elderly gentleman said, "is that the young people don't know their place. They are easily misled. They don't stand on their own two feet. They get things too easily. They don't work as hard as we used to and that's the problem. They don't respect work and they expect things to be handed to them without much struggle." I asked him, "What do you think we need to do to fix this?" He said, "I don't know. That's your business. I'm just telling you what I think, that's all." I thanked him for his concern and said that I would have to think about this issue because I was not sure if there was an easy answer to the problem. "You do that, sonny," he said. "If and when you solve it, this will be a better nation." Walking away from that table, I knew that I dodged a bullet. There was no easy answer to solving the generation gap.

One young couple asked about home foreclosures and the issue facing so many people who had homes that were "under water". They believed the government had turned a "blind eye" to their plight. I asked them if they tried to refinance and they said yes, but the process was not simple. In fact, it was almost painful because of the application and then the long waiting period to get a simple yes or no. They thought that Ron Paul's ideas about doing away with the Federal Reserve Bank had some merit. They wanted to know what I thought. I said, "The Federal Reserve, for better or worse, is our form of central banking and can and will respond to the needs of the system if the president tells them to do so. For instance, one of the things the president can do is tell the Fed to lend money only to banks that are renegotiating home loans. Right now, interest rates for the big banks are .25%. This is essentially an interest free loan. Now, these same banks turn around and lend this money out to smaller banks at 2 or 3 %. The smaller banks use the money to make loans at higher rates. Currently, the lowest home mortgage interest rate is hovering around 4 %. This means that the big banks are making 2% on a loan to a smaller bank. The small bank is making 1% on the loan to the homeowner. Given that the Federal Reserve is lending the banks money at the .25 % we could force banks to lend money at no more than 3% and the banks would still make money. I would change this by executive order. No more lending money to banks that won't refinance home loans. Period. We need to stop the bleeding in America."

They liked this idea, but another person at the table said, "That sounds good today but how can you get a bank to lend money at a cheaper rate when they are quite happy to keep the original loan and not change a darn thing. Heck, if I gave you a $1000 bucks at ten percent, I wouldn't want you to come back to me a year later and ask me to cut your interest rate to five percent. How do you deal with the greedy bastards who know they have the home owner over a barrel and want to keep on dunking his head under water?"

"There is nothing to say they will. Cut off their supply line to readily available cash and they will come along bucking and kicking like everyone else who does not want to change what they are doing in order to make America's economy solvent again. Look, folks, there is no easy answer to this problem. We are all going to have to make sacrifices. Most of all, we must learn to live within our means. This is something that we have not done for a generation," I said finishing with some gusto.

"Easy to say, hard to do," a middle-aged woman said. "We got so down and out when we both lost our jobs that we used credit cards to make ends meet. Now we're digging out of a deep, deep hole. We may never get out. It's horrible to see just how little progress we make each month in our attempt to rid ourselves of the debt."

"I can only sympathize with you because I don't have that kind of debt. What I don't have is many frills in my house or parked in my driveway. I have a ten-year-old car. No other vehicles. No other toys. No motorcycles. No ATVs. No boats. No nothing. However, no debt either. I try to live within my means and as president, I will make the country live within its own means."

"So you're into cutting the entitlements?" a man asked. "What are we going to do about the cost of social security, Medicare and Medicaid?"

"Last year, this president set up a commission to study this problem. They produced a very valuable plan to solve this dilemma. They titled it, 'The Moment of Truth'. The plan is radical and yet doable. The committee that created the plan could not come to consensus and vote to implement it. Sadly, the conflict broke down upon party lines and that ended the possibility of its implementation. I believe it is the core plan, and I would do all in my power to get it passed into law. Now, what it does is make everyone sacrifice a little bit. The wealthy and the not so wealthy all have a stake in the success of these important social safety nets. Unless we can come to consensus and stop this war between the parties, America cannot get well."

"What will you do to get the two parties to go along with anything that you're trying to do? This president hasn't been able to do it. The last one couldn't. Maybe Clinton did a little, but he made a mess of things, too. He brags about his leaving us with such a surplus but we all know that the government was using Social Security trust money to make up any shortcomings in the general operating fund. So what will you do differently, Mr. Pollack?" asked a grizzled fellow who looked like he was one meal away from the poor house or becoming homeless.

I laughed and said simply, "They won't get along ever. By the very design, a two party system is determined to be antagonistic toward one another except in the gravest matters like war and peace. What I have going for me is that I am not connected with any of the members of either party. I can be the negotiator, the power broker, the person who stands in the middle and says, let's get this job done. The second reason I think I'll have an advantage is because I'm only going to run for one term. As soon as President Obama was elected, he was already thinking about his second term and so he made decisions that reflected that desire on his part. The minute he was elected, the republicans made it very clear that they were going to make him a one-term president. Has he done poorly? Not really. He's done the best he can with people on one side who said they were going to undermine his success and people on the other side, his side mind you, who said he needed to do more. He can't win for love or money. This is because he wants to run again. I don't plan to be president for more than one term. Get in, do the job, get out. End of story."

"You mean that, young fellow," he asked.

"I mean it. I don't want to be a career politician. I think that is unhealthy for the person and for the country. One term and out for all elected officials at all levels of government," I almost shouted and immediately there was a rousing round of applause.

Someone shouted, "Leo…Leo…Leo…" and others joined in the calling. I raised my hand and quieted the crowd.

"Thank you for welcoming me here in NASCAR nation," I said, and the crowd went wild. "One thing I love about NASCAR and its fans is the loyalty they show to the sport. Now what we need to do is take that same loyalty and reinvest it into the nation. We need to become politically active and demand that our leaders stop underperforming. How much money do we waste in the interminable gridlock that affects all Americans? I won't stand for it. I'll take my case to the American people each time the congress fails to do its duty. There are real issues facing us that can make or break our society, our way of life. We must band together and solve them, or less than a generation from now we will be both financially and morally bankrupt and this country will be beyond repair. I don't believe it needs to come to this. I believe we can work together and make a real change in this country. What makes me believe this is that you are letting me share this vision with you today. Yes, a Yankee is standing in King Richard's Court, and you haven't tarred and feathered me yet. I believe we can all work together. I don't believe in red and blue states. I believe, yes, like this current president, in the United States. However, what he has failed to realize is that his party is keeping him from succeeding and the other party is determined to defeat him at all costs. One of the costs is the future for American workers. All this will end when I am elected president. I ask that you vote for me in this primary. Write my name in anywhere. Put it in the side column. Make your voice, your choice known. Together we can make a difference. Together we can change America and make it once again a country of, for and most importantly, by the people."

Cheers broke out and the people stood up and gave me a standing ovation. Well-wishers mobbed me. I felt the power of the people flowing into me as I made my way toward the door thanking everyone for their southern hospitality. How long it took me to exit, I have no idea. Out in the parking lot, I was still listening to the people tell me their stories, ask me more questions, fill my mind to the brim with new and more perplexing problems. Through it all, I kept my composure knowing that these race car fans, these people who lived and breathed NASCAR, were what made America great just like every other group of patriotic Americans did in their own way. What divided the congress divided the people. There was no one that I met today that did not want to have a good job, raise a healthy family, live in a pleasant home, feel safe in his or her neighborhood, expect to see his or her children grow up and be better off than he or she was. They wanted the American Dream and that was as simple as it gets.

I asked some of the folks if they would walk over to the track with me and tell me some of Darlington's history. Five or six of the fellows said they would and off we went. I left Gram and Al at the bus.

We went over to the track and slipped through the open gate and stood near the start finish line and I heard story after story of the famous racers who made history racing on this famous oval. King Richard Petty was a local hero and a winner here. The locals were happy that I wanted to know about the "Old Girl's" history. They did not believe that someone like me might really be interested in stock car racing. I told them this was how we can come together. We needed to learn about and appreciate all aspects of our American culture.

Darlington is still known as the track "too tough to tame". One of the fellows told me that it is still remembered as the original super speedway and as one of the pillars of the NASCAR establishment. "There is no other sporting facility more steeped in history and tradition than Darlington which has aged gracefully over the years but has retained its feisty charm", he said.

Dale Earnhardt, seven times NASCAR Champion, another race fan said, was in love with the track. "You never forget your first love," Earnhardt said. "Whether it's your high school sweetheart, a faithful hunting dog, or a fickle race track in South Carolina with a contrary disposition. If you happen to be a race car driver, there's no victory so sweet, so memorable, as whipping Darlington Raceway."

Some of NASCAR's most historic moments have unfolded at the track "Too Tough to Tame". A third South Carolinian, said, "In 1985, Bill Elliot recorded wins in three of NASCAR's crown jewel races winning the season opening Daytona 500 at Daytona International Speedway, the Winston 500 at Talladega Superspeedway, and Southern 500 at Darlington Race and was awarded the first ever Winston Million. We don't have the Winston Cup anymore. Now it's the Sprint Cup. I know why they changed it but I still like the old name. Kind of Southern, you know. Winston Cup. Winston cigarettes. Cigarettes. Tobacco. What we grow here. They're all tied together. Oh well, things change. We've got to change with the times," he sadly concluded.

"The closest finish in NASCAR history also calls Darlington Race home. In an epic battle on March 16, 2003, Ricky Craven recorded his second career NASCAR Sprint Cup Series victory. He beat Kurt Busch by two-thousands of a second. It was an amazing race and I was there to watch it. This old track makes you a believer in the sport. When they're driving at nearly 185 mph, these corners jump right out at you and want to suck you into them. I love sitting on turn four and watch the drivers spank their cars off the wall," he chuckled.

These men were proud to share with me the stories and I was happy to listen to them. I thanked them for taking the time to give me a history lesson and they said they were glad to spend a few minutes with the next president of the United States. We found common ground and that made all the difference.

Gram and Al met me back at the bus.

Well?" I asked.

"Amazing grace," Gram said. "I never thought we'd be a hit here."

"You made them sit up and take notice," Al said. "They were eating out of your hand before you left."

"I'd rather think we were feeding each other. These folks are the salt of the earth and unless we win their hearts and minds, we cannot succeed. What a wonderful day. What an amazing group of people. You know, fellows, we are too quick to judge. I was somewhat fearful about going in there, but now I know we have to greet all Americans with the same message. We are the 160 million and we need to stick together."

"What are we going to do now?" Al said. "It's the middle of the afternoon and we don't have any other plans for today."

"I think we head back to Columbia, meet with Richard Johnson and make plans for Florida, wait for the returns on Saturday and then head south to Florida on Sunday," Gram offered.

"No way we can get back home for just one day?" I asked.

He stared at me as if I was crazy. "Leo?"

"Okay. Okay. But you can't blame me for asking. I miss my family."

"The road is just beginning to straighten out," Gram said.

"You ready to roll, Al?" I asked.

"Let's do it," he called to us.

We climbed aboard and Al slowly eased out of the parking lot. The diminishing gathering of new converts saluted us as we drove away. What an exciting day! What a way to make a million new friends. Deep in my heart, I wished that the Darlington Firecracker 500 were today because I would not be leaving town.

As we drove past the outside of the great raceway, I marveled at just how unique and special America was that it could devote so much talent, money and creative effort to something as insignificant as stock car racing. It was the acceptance of such a dichotomy that made this great nation we call the United States of America.

26. A Much Needed Holiday

We wanted to head home to Ohio, but Florida was a week away. We knew that there was only one thing to do. Head to the "Sunshine State" and continue our sideshow. Basha and Janko were upset that I was not going to be able to come home. We talked for an hour. I could tell she was holding back the tears. He was not. I was half-way in between the tears and something else.

Al said everything was fine at his homestead. In fact, he said, "I think my sweetie likes it when I'm gone. She doesn't have to cook for me." He minimized being away from home, but I knew better. He was a family man through and through so this was a major sacrifice for him.

Gram was the only one of us who did not care. "Hey, there is no one to go home to each night so what the heck. Let's go south to the sunshine state."

Wanting to have some fun with him and test his mettle, I asked, "Hey Gram, what about you and Judy? I thought there might be something brewing. You are going to stay away now avoiding her completely?"

There was silence for a few minutes. Gram finally responded. "Leo, I am a man who has maximum self-control. Sure, I'd like to have a relationship with a good woman. What normal guy wouldn't? However, there is something more important. What is important now is focusing on restoring the American Dream. That means getting Leo Pollack elected. If he does not get elected, he motivates people to restore the American dream and planting their own 'Tree of Life'. As we circle the country, we need to have restoring the American Dream as our 'Tree of Life'. This is the symbol of our goal. It inflames us. It keeps our passion alive to persevere when the trail gets difficult. Kind of like climbing Springer Mountain can be a "Tree of Life" for south bound thru-hikers on the Appalachian Trail. If getting out of the rain, the mud, the pain, the hunger, the loneliness, the asking 'Does it really matter?', the asking 'Does anyone really care?', 'Do I still care?', never becomes the hiker's new 'Tree of Life' then the hiker will fail. Restoring the American Dream is my 'Tree of Life' until it is full-grown. A romp in the sack with Judy would chop down that tree."

I sat still for a few minutes before I responded to him. "Pretty deep, my friend," I said. "I didn't realize just how committed you were to this cause."

"I didn't come all the way across the country to watch you lose. No, my friend, I am here to make this happen. That's it."

"Me too," Al chimed in. "Gram doesn't have time for the ladies. He's got to keep navigating. Now, regarding navigation, what are we going to do? It's Friday night and we are still not out of this state. North or south?"

"South," Gram and I said at the same time.

"So be it," Al replied, turned the Liberty Bus south on I-95, and headed toward Florida. We found a quiet rest area south of Darlington, pulled off the highway, and prepared to settle in for the night.

Big Jack showed up as soon as the bus was stopped. He came right in and sat down. His huge bulk was an imposing force in our midst.

"What's up, Jack?" I asked breaking the silence.

"We've lost our tail for now. I don't know why. They just disappeared after we left Darlington. Strange place. You were doing something dangerous going into that place, Leo. Wish you'd let me know what you're doing in advance."

"Spur of the moment decision, Jack. Sorry,"

"Don't be sorry, be safe," Jack said.

"What do you want me to do now?" I asked.

"Nothing, Leo. Call me in the future. Let me know what is happening. We are in the heart of the south. You lucked out in this last stop. Good moves."

"All's well that ends well," Gram said.

"Now, are we safe out here on the freeway?" Al asked.

"Very. My people are all around us."

I looked out the window. "Where?"

"Leo? Really?" he said.

"What do we do tomorrow?" I asked.

"I think we convene a conference call. Check in with everyone. Make sure we have a game plan. What do you think?"

"Agreed," I said.

"Sounds good to me," Al agreed.

"We are heading into the most populous state in the south and fifth in the nation. This means we have to be as strategic as possible. We will be a sideshow in the state just like here but we're going to gain momentum after tomorrow night," Gram concluded.

"Because," I asked.

"Because we're going to get a percentage of the vote in the primary and that will keep our momentum going. Trust me. We are going to get blowback from the results that will give us a real push in the sunshine state."

"I think we should get some sleep," Al said. "This has been one long day."

"I agree," Gram said. "Tomorrow is always another day."

"Jack, how about you?" I asked.

"I'm out of here," he said and left.

"Strange guy," Gram said.

"Strange guy? Whom are you talking about? Yourself?" I joked with him.

"Ha. Ha. Funny guy."

We slept like well-fed babies. Dawn broke but we did not rise. We were tired. Sleep was a balm massaging our tired bodies, minds and spirits.

Entering the Sunshine State, we drove south toward Jacksonville. Outside the outer belt, we pulled over and set up the conference calling technology. For nearly an hour, the Ohio team, Richard Johnson, Big Jack from somewhere, and the road team strategized about how to approach Florida. We had ten days, one weekend and that was it. John was encouraged that we were going to do well in South Carolina. Judy said the messages were being prepared for Florida. She said that we bought ads in Florida on TV and radio. The expense was significantly higher. Carol reported that fund raising was blowing the doors off the bank. We were up to 8.3 million dollars and the money was growing exponentially. We were all amazed at the amount. We finally decided that the itinerary would be Jacksonville, Orlando, Miami, Key West, Tampa-St. Petersburg, Tallahassee, and Pensacola and then we would decide what to do next. The speed at which primaries and caucuses were happening made the travel schedule intense. After Florida, the next primaries and caucuses were Nevada, Minnesota, Missouri and Colorado. I shook my head when I thought about the amount of driving Al was going to be doing. I could see the look on his face and he was concerned. We would talk about this matter later on when we were alone. We decided that, if possible, we would find some place to relax today and just watch the results come in from South Carolina. John suggested we find a lake and do some fishing. I asked what we were going to do with the Liberty Bus. Could we really hope to disappear? John said that I had a good point. Jack said he could make the bus disappear if we needed to do that. We did not ask him how he would, but it was an amazing offer. Two hours passed and then the conference call was finished. I thanked everyone for his or her hard work and pledged to keep up the pace as long as we were headed in the right direction.

"Wow!" Gram said. "More than eight million. Man that is a lot of cash."

"You can say that again," Al seconded. "Yes, and we all have credit cards tied to that account."

We looked at him.

"Just kidding, fellows."

"Sure, Al. Leo, I think we need to put a call in to the card company and see if there are any strange charges on it," Gram said.

"You mean like adult books stores and things like that?" I responded.

"Oh, that and much more," Gram continued the jibe.

"Gram, Leo, I'm clean as a virgin," Al cried out.

"Yikes," Gram said. "Al's invoked the 'V' word. Now we know that we have to check the account."

Al looked frustrated. Gram and I backed off.

"We're done, Al. We're just playing, man, you know that," Gram said.

"How do I know that? You guys get so serious when you play," he said.

"Okay. Okay, but we're done," I seconded. "What are we going to do?"

"I think we take a holiday," I said.

"What? Are you serious? With all that we have to do, you think we can afford a day off?" Gram exclaimed.

"Sure, I do. We can't work seven days a week and not face some kind of chronic fatigue. Come on, fellow. Lighten up. Let's enjoy ourselves today."

"I wouldn't mind getting out from behind this wheel," Al said.

"See, two of us vote for a day off. Jack's not here. We'll call him and get his vote. What is your decision, Gram?"

He realized he was outnumbered. What could he do? He knew that Big Jack would do whatever I was going to do.

"I don't like it but I'll go along with the flow."

"Where to now?" Al said. I just want to get out of this vehicle.

"Head for the ocean. It's only about 30 miles from here. We can play on the beach. How does that sound to you guys?" I asked.

"Let's do it. I'll just use this time to make some notes," Gram said.

"Forward, onward, outward," Al cried. "I'm going to the Atlantic Ocean. I can hardly wait. Wish I had my bathing suit."

"Al, it's January," I remarked.

"January in Florida, not Ohio, Leo. Don't you know anything about geography? Down here, it is warm in the wintertime. At least, warm enough for a fat Italian guy to get into the water." I knew he was serious.

Gram was writing on his clipboard. Al was concentrating on the roadway. My phone rang and I answered it. John was on the phone and had some questions for me, some ideas he wanted to share and some new information from Judy and Carol.

When the blast shattered the side windows, I ducked to the floor, Gram rolled off his seat and Al swiftly banked the bus on the side of the road.

We were all in shock. I looked up and saw a pickup truck racing away and a black car speeding after it. Jack!

"You guys okay?" I heard Al asking as he stopped the bus completely in a safe place beside the highway.

"What?" Gram gasped. "Okay? No. Damn man, someone just shot at us."

"What? Shots?" I exclaimed.

"Better than a bomb!" Al said trying to make light of what just had happened.

We looked at the shattered window on the driver's side of the bus. There was glass strewn everywhere on the small couch under it and on the floor. We got up, opened the door, and walked outside. Already, a number of trucks and cars were stopped around us staring at the damage on the side of the vehicle.

Gram had enough sense to call 911.

Al walked around the bus to see if there was any other damage.

I stood there and just stared at the damage.

"What the hell," I said.

"We were damn lucky," Gram said. "It must have been a shotgun and not a rifle."

"Is this really happening to us?" I asked aloud.

"Look. This is real," Gram said.

"I'm just glad no one got hurt," Al said.

We heard the sirens. A few seconds later, the world went topsy-turvy. This was going to be some holiday.

Jack pulled up a few minutes later. He and Gram talked. He jumped back into his car and drove away.

"What was that all about?" I asked Gram.

"Jack has a lead on the shooters."

"Shooters?" I asked.

"There were a few guys in the truck. Jack wouldn't elaborate but he thinks these three locals were just patsies."

"What the heck is going on? This sounds crazy to me," I cried out.

"Any act of violence is crazy but someone is threatened by what you're doing and they are going to try to put the fear of God into you. Who knows what else we'll face in the days, weeks and months to come."

"Gram, I just had a rush. Hold on." I called home to talk to Basha. I tried to be cool, but she was on to me in a few minutes. We talked for ten minutes. I felt better, but I was not sure if she did.

"Everything okay at home?" Gram asked.

"She says it is."

"Don't worry, she's covered."

"What do you mean?" I asked staring at Gram.

"Jack said not to tell you, but he has had security around your home ever since he came on the job.

"What?"

"Yes. He said that he wasn't taking any chances."

"This is crazy," I hollered.

"Hush up, Leo," Gram said. "People might hear you acting like a sissy. Chill out. Your family is safe. So are you. Safer than most folks, that is. Now what we need to do is figure out how to get this bus fixed and get the heck out of the middle of the freeway."

"I need to talk to John."

"Already done. He's aware."

"How did you do all that while I was standing here?"

"Leo, you're slow, my man. This is the reason I am your chief of staff, my friend. What good would I be if I didn't take care of you?"

Al came over and said that we could roll any time. He was finished with the police. Gram and Al kept them away from me. I do not know how they accomplished that feat, but I was exempt from investigation. I think they wanted me to keep my head screwed on right. Deep down inside, I was pissed off. It is one thing to come at a guy and threaten him face to face. It is a very different, cowardly act to do a drive by shooting, then run off, and hide in some rat hole. What did these guys hope to accomplish? Did they really think that I would go home now because someone had taken a pot shot at the team and me? Now that I knew Basha and Janko were being watched, I said to myself, "Bring it on, fools. I've got nothing to lose."

I crawled back up into the bus. Al and Gram followed. We sat inside and did not talk. The evening was coming. The sun glowed faintly as it settled on the western horizon.

"What a day!" I uttered as I slumped down into my chair behind the newly plastic covered window. "You did a great job fixing this window, Al."

"Thanks, but I'd rather not have to have done that. What makes people so crazy? What causes them to want to hurt someone they don't even know? What's wrong with people anyway?" Al asked in general not expecting anyone to answer his questions.

"I'll tell you," Gram said, "the world is made up of responsible people who realize they live in community with others, and another group that doesn't respect others and denies the need to live in community. They are selfish to a fault. They don't give a damn about anybody but themselves. They use and abuse others as if they were expendable. What these people believe is that they are not their brother's and sister's keeper. We will meet many of them before this campaign is over. This violent behavior is just one way in which the second group seeks to achieve social dominance."

"We have to do something to change this country. This kind of mean spirited behavior is ugly."

"Leo, this was more than mean-spirited," Gram said.

"You can say that again," Al added speaking over his shoulder as he drove the bus out of the city and back onto the interstate. "We need to get to the south side of town and see if we can get this window fixed on Monday. There is a huge RV dealer down there and we should be able to get what we need at that dealership."

"We'll do what we have to do," I said.

"Hey, let's turn on the TV and see what's happening with the South Carolina primary returns."

"You know who's going to win this one," I said.

"No, who?" Gram asked.

"Gingrich," I said.

"You think so?" Gram said.

"Yes. He's come on strong these past two weeks because he got money from his own billionaires, Sheldon Adelson and his wife. Together, they each gave him $10 million. He had the money to go after Romney with negative ads and it is going to pay off."

"Remember when he was in Iowa complaining about Romney's negative ads? He was whining like a baby. He came out with a vengeance this past week. Yes, he is pissed at Romney and has tried to take him out just like Romney did to him in Iowa."

"Let's find a place to stop, eat some dinner, and watch the show," Al said. "I've had enough fun for one day."

The best we could do was a Walmart parking lot. The lights were extremely bright. Truckers were already lining up for the night. We pulled in and found a nice spot off to the side of the lot where there was less light and almost no noise.

As I was cooking, I blurted out, "I just can't believe that we're sitting here tonight with a hole in the side of our bus. Damn. What a way to express yourself! Cowards."

"I hope Jack succeeds in tracking down the culprits," Gram said.

"I kind of hope he doesn't," I said.

"What?" Gram uttered.

"If Jack finds the guys, they may not be healthy for very long. I sure would not want to see him get into any trouble. He's a true believer. I know the guy. I worked with him for a long time. He's one intense fellow. Trust me."

"Hey, are you going to cook something or what?" Al asked me when he finally secured the bus for the night.

"I'll get on it right away, Boss Man," I said with a quiver in my voice, went into the kitchen, and got to work. While I prepared our evening meal, we watched the results come in. At 8 pm Eastern Standard Time, the major networks projected that Newt Gingrich was the winner with 41%, Mitt Romney was second with 28%, Rick Santorum was third with 17% and Ron Paul, fourth with 13 % and Leo Pollack, 2%.

We stared at each other and then you could hear the bus bounce up and down as we yelled and slapped each other on the back and hugged one another. We had done it again. We were right in there and we were not even on the ballot. We were being written in on the Republican ballot right in the face of these conservative candidates who were so anti-worker that it made me sick to my stomach.

"We did it again!" Al shouted.

"We made it to five percent!" Gram said.

"We are in the hunt!" I added.

After fifteen minutes of celebration, we settled down and watched the rest of the coverage.

"What did I tell you," I said from behind the stove as the percentages were read repeatedly as the coverage continued.

"You called it, Leo," Gram said. "I wasn't sure that the Newt had it in him. I guess South Carolinians have forgiven him his sins. He did make a concerted effort to tell people that he had 'made mistakes' and that he 'asked for God's forgiveness' and now was ready to move on in his life."

"Easy as pie," Al said. "Reminds me of the Godfather, part 3. Michael Corleone had his brother killed and many others, but he confessed his sins to the Cardinal and died in peace, an old man sitting in a chair out in sunlit Sicily. That's the beauty of being a Catholic. You can confess your sins and go to heaven bypassing purgatory and, of course, avoiding hell altogether."

As we ate the stew, bread and butter and fruit cocktail, we listened to the network news coverage on MSNBC, our favorite channel. Having a dish connected to the bus was a real plus. We could not believe that the fortunes of the Newt had changed so much since Iowa.

"Newt is out for bear now. He attacked Romney repeatedly for being a person who was a 'Massachusetts Moderate'. He's one vindictive fellow who speaks in polar terms. There is no gray with Newt. When he calls Obama the 'food stamp' president, he makes it sound like no other president ever had people on foods stamps while he was in office. Actually, more people were on foods stamps when George Bush was president than now with Obama. This is going to be a long drawn out primary season for the republicans."

"We will have a lot to think about as our campaign unfolds," I said.

"These guys are ripping each other to shreds. This is unbelievable. I have never seen such smear campaigns in my lifetime," Gram said.

"Citizens United truly has affected the entire election process. The Supreme Court screwed the pooch when they voted to uphold 'corporations are people and have the right to free speech' principle. We are going to have a hard time competing with these superpacs that have unlimited money to run negative ads and not be held accountable for their messages. Look what has happened in just these three events to date. This decision is making it possible for people with a lot of money to truly buy a nomination and perhaps a presidency."

"We'll have to deny them that reality," Al said. "I hate the way we play politics, Leo. I know that there is a need to let the other candidate know that you disagree with him because of his views, but these guys have gone over the edge."

We rolled past midnight and into Sunday morning still talking politics, wondering where Jack was, hoping he was safe and deciding it was time to get some sleep.

"Some holiday, huh?" I said to Gram and Al as we got into our beds.

"Could have been worse," Al said. "We're okay and no one got hurt."

"I could sleep for a month," Gram said.

"Let's do it," I said.

"Sure and let Newt and Mitt get a jump on us in Florida," Al said.

"We're already here," I said.

"Leo, do you realize that we now have arrived. We are a part of this national presidential campaign. We are on the roll. We need to continue this in Florida, a much more diverse state."

"I agree," I said. "What a day. We were going to take a holiday. We got attacked along the roadway. We end the day having once again gained momentum in a state where we did not expect anything. I'm just amazed at the entire process."

"Let's get some sleep," Al said. "We have a long day ahead of us tomorrow."

"I agree," Gram said. "Enough fun for one day."

"Fellows, thanks again for making all this possible. You are the real salt of the earth. No man could ask to play on a better team. I'm honored to be in this with you two," I said.

"Don't forget about the 160 million working people out there that we are speaking for and to and with," Gram said.

"Amen to that," Al commented.

"Goodnight, my friends, here in this bus, and all over the United States of America."

We rested peacefully knowing that our efforts were making a difference and soon, our message would begin to affect the overall temperament of the campaigns. The negative nature of the messages from the other candidates was slowly eroding any semblance of confidence the American people had in their representatives. The wind whipped the plastic window Al had constructed and reminded us of the reality of the day's events. We were safe now, but the world outside our secure bus was beginning to crash in upon us. We would not be deterred. We would not give in to the pressure. We would not only endure, we would prevail.

27. Sunshine State Sideshows

We could not get the bus fixed until Monday, but that did not stop us from heading into Jacksonville and campaigning. We had a tentative plan to park the Liberty Bus at the largest mall in the area and just meet people. Richard Johnson was working on connections in the rest of the state but he was not able to provide us much support in Jacksonville. We were not too keen about doing cold campaigning. However, we did not have much choice. The primary was just nine days away. We knew we would be a sideshow in Florida, but we did not care. We were making forward progress and that was what mattered most of all.

Yesterday's events created a surreal feeling in me. I wondered just how far someone would go to stop what we were trying to do. How serious was the threat? The entire world was compressed into the daily challenges mounting a third party presidential campaign. I wondered if I should have considered a run for congress or the senate first. I was not sure that this path was the right one. Given what happened, my friends, Gram and Al, could have been seriously hurt or killed. The last consideration was something that did not register. Was that really a possibility? There were so many things floating around inside my head I thought my brain would float away with the flotsam. Big Jack's assurance that my family was safe reassured me. How strange was it that they would need to be watched? The world was topsy-turvy and that was something that I never planned for when I started this journey. Beyond the personal threats, I wondered what it was like for people to be facing this kind of situation day after day. How could any person wait and watch for someone to come after him or her? I was sure that President Obama wondered if he would make it through his first campaign without anyone getting a shot at him. These past three years were not kind to the president and I was sure that he was under even more intense scrutiny by the Secret Service. I wanted to believe that he would be safe. There was no reason to go after him. How could someone hate another person so much that he would actually try to harm him? I wish that I could stand face to face with the coward who shot the windows out of the side of the bus. I would love to ask what motivated him to want to harm me or anyone else.

We found the mall that Richard Johnson told us was probably the best place to set up for the day without having to procure a permit to congregate. I was wondering what we would do to make our setup attractive, but Gram and Al knew what to do. Before I knew it, they had the awning out, two tables set up, chairs around the area, and boxes of bumper stickers, buttons, leaflets, and other campaign materials that I did not even know existed.

"Where did all this come from?" I asked my team members who were hustling around like hyperactive kids.

"Where do you think?" Gram asked. "We got the materials a while back. We did not want to wait until the last minute to get 'er done!" he said with gusto.

"I'm impressed," I said. "Look at these bumper stickers. 'Leo Pollack – President 2012.' How cool is that? One question."

"Shoot," Gram said.

"Where is the name of my vice president? You know that's kind of tradition. Obama-Biden, Bush-Cheney, Kerry-Edwards, Gore-Lieberman."

"We didn't think that far ahead," Gram said sheepishly. "What we have is what you get. Like it or lump it, pal. We are not miracle workers."

"Right. We're not miracle workers. We're just a couple of good old fellows who want to be able to go to work every day, come home, spend time with the kids, eat a good meal, watch a little TV, and feel like life is worth living today, tomorrow and forever," Al said.

"I got it," I said. "What do you want me to do?"

"Get some cookies and soda ready," Al said.

"Now where am I going to get cookies and soda?"

"Check under the bus. Open up that long door and see what you find," Al chortled. He and Gram continued to decorate the outside of the house. I did as I was told and found a huge cooler filled with ice, sodas, and a number of boxes of chocolate chip cookies, plates and napkins galore.

"You guys are starting to make me wonder," I commented to them.

"What is so wonderful about us?" Gram laughed at me as he started spreading out the materials across the tables.

Before I could answer his question, our first "interested bystander" came by and that was the beginning of one of the busiest days in my life. From that moment, there was a steady stream of people asking questions, taking materials, looking inside the bus, wanting my autograph, making indictments against all politicians so that I could not keep track of what was happening a few feet away from me. The people's faces enchanted me. Old and young, white, black and brown, tall and short, all types of people came by to see what I had to offer them. I tried to be as gracious as I could, even though some of the people were less than kind in their judgment of what I was doing and what I believed. What was more informative was the number of people who were truly curious about what I was doing and how I was running a third party campaign. Many asked what it was like to stand up every day and talk and talk and talk. I laughed and said that it was no worse than standing up all day long and shoveling coal into a furnace as I did at the mill where I worked until I was laid off. What they could not grasp was where I was going to get enough money to continue to mount a realistic campaign. I said that the money was coming in one dollar at a time, and to date, we have raised more than 4 million dollars. No way, they exclaimed. I said this was the current amount. They were amazed. If 100 million people donate $1.00, that is 100 million dollars. There are 160 million working men and women in America. I encouraged everyone who stopped by to consider donating a dollar or two. I would appreciate any amount but I told all that they could not donate more than $20.00. I did not want to explain to the people later on in the campaign that I was taking buckets of money from lobbyists and special interest groups. Time was suspended. The longer we hosted the party, the more party goers showed up, shared a little bit of themselves with us and then moved on, but not before taking with them information, posters, buttons, and perhaps, a new perspective. For some reason, I kept looking at the people and wondering if any of them were the culprit who shot out our window yesterday. This was not healthy. I needed to face the world with a stronger face. Gram decided to make some hotdogs. I do not know where he got the grill. I think he might have procured it from someone in the parking lot. He started to cook food. The aroma slowly wafted across the lot. Even more people came to the spot where we were enjoying the moment in the heat of the day. We continued to hold our own. We were answering questions and promoting our agenda with every word. I liked the ebb and flow of the crowd. I enjoyed the bantering. The elderly people found me to be too young to be president. The younger people wondered if I were old enough. I cajoled all of them and said I was old enough to know better and not old enough to know it all. The sound of their voices continued to filter through my brain cells and filled me with the complexity of the body politic. I did not believe for one moment that I could empathize with the majority of those surrounding me, but I was sure that I could with at least some of them and this is what made our campaign so different. They said as much. This was a different way to spread the word. My caution flags were cast to the wind. Gram was feeding the masses. Al was entertaining the old timers who found his "bus" to be a curiosity piece. I was the third person in this three-ring circus, this Sunshine State Sideshow that made everything I ever did in my life insignificant.

Big Jack came strolling over to the "Big Top", pulled me aside, and asked, "Leo, what the hell are you doing?" His stare was really a laser glare.

I stared at him and realized what his stare was about and then I said, "Oh, Jack, man, I'm sorry. I didn't call you and let you know what we were going to so. Ah, man, I screwed up again."

"You sure did. Luckily, I was hip to the fact that you guys didn't come out on the route as planned and I doubled back as fast as I could. I wasn't taking any chances."

"What did you find out about who did the shooting?" I asked Jack.

"You don't want to know," Jack replied looking away from me.

"What do you mean, I don't want to know. What's the big deal?"

"Leo, we're not going to solve this one. We just need to be careful from now on because that shot is not going to be the last we see. There is an element out there in this world that does not want the working man, and namely, you, Leo Pollack, to make it past first base in this campaign baseball game."

"Jack, you're being cryptic," I said. "What is up?"

"I can't say. I don't want you to be concerned."

"You think I won't be even more concerned because you're not telling me what is really going on? Come on, Jack, what kind of pie are you baking?"

"Baking a pie? What the…" Jack uttered.

"I'm just making a point. You are always doing something to take care of me. You're 'baking the pie'. Me. Forget it, Jack."

"Leo, this world is moving too fast for us. I mean it. Sometimes I think we bit off more than we can chew."

"I hope you're not getting cold feet, Jack. I'm counting on you to take care of business."

"Leo, the fact is there is no way to tell exactly who did what. The boys and I tracked down all leads. We could not make heads nor tails out of what was going down, but what we do know is they are going to try again. That's all there is to it. Now you understand the reason I want you to tell me what you're doing. Okay?" Jack pleaded.

"Okay, I got it, Jack. No more lone ranger stuff. I'll call you and keep you in the loop. Now, you've got to tell me something."

"What's that?"

"How many men do you have on our team?"

"Men?"

"Yes." I thought for a moment. "No, men and women," I said.

"Less than a dozen, more than a half dozen," Jack said.

"Where are they now?"

"Around."

"You won't tell me anything more?"

"No, that's the end of it."

"You've got my word on it. I will not move without letting you know."

"Done. Now I need to fade away," Jack said.

"Right, you're going to fade away in this crowd," I said but I was distracted and when I turned around, he was actually gone. I could not see him anywhere, but I could feel his black eyes burning on my back.

"Mr. Pollack," I heard a voice calling. I turned around again and this time, a quite attractive woman with a cameraman in tow was staring at me. "I'm Angie Dewine. KDDC TV. We would like to have a few minutes of your time." She smiled so broadly that it was hard to ignore her, not that I would.

"Miss Dewine, I'd be happy to oblige you. There is nothing like a little free press coverage to make my day."

"Please call me Angie," she said. "I have been following your campaign since you first stood up on the counter top and said you were running for office."

"Amazing," I said. "This can't be true."

"Mr. Pollack, you are the biggest news story in the country and today, you're right in my neighborhood. I want to make the most of this time. Can we get started?"

"Yes, by all means, but please call me Leo. Mister makes me sound like an old geek."

"Got it, Leo," Angie said. "Fellows, let's set up right here and we'll be ready to go."

I enjoyed my newest 15 minutes of fame. Angie treated me as if I were royalty. Every question was softball. I did not have to think. I made the most of the moment. We enjoyed our time together. When we were finished, she thanked me for being the only candidate in her short life that she actually wanted to meet and for whom she would actually vote.

"You've made a lot of Americans hopeful. You are the change that we can believe in," she concluded and then rushed off with her crew. I just stood there watching her pack up and leave. When she waved from the window of the television van, I waved back. I was star struck. Crazy me. What was going on?

Gram walked up to me and said, "Now that was fortuitous. Free press never hurts and we're in the sunshine state where you can pay a million dollars an advertisement. So, what was her name?"

"I knew you'd notice her. Angie Dewine."

"Now that is a wonderful name. You didn't think about inviting me over to meet her?"

"Gram, you're hot and cold. What's up with you today?"

"I don't know, Leo. Perhaps it was that blast from last night. I awoke to the reality of life and its relative shortness."

"We'll make it one way or another," I said trying to assure Gram that everything was in our control.

"I don't have anyone in my life that would even care if something happens to me and that is one of the things that bothers me. No one cares."

"Wrong," I said emphatically.

"Who cares?"

"I do. Al cares. Jack cares. Hell, we all care. Stop feeling sorry for yourself, Gram. I mean it. None of us is ever really alone. We need to remember that and not let the fear get inside of us."

"It's hard, Leo. You don't know what it means to lose your family and then have to start all over again."

"No, I don't know what it is like and would hate to learn about it. Right now, we need to focus on the present and the future, not the past. We can do it. You, Al, Jack, John, Judy, Fritz, Richard, Carol and I and God knows how many other people that are a part of this movement we don't know but who are right here with us in spirit if not body."

"Speaking of that notion," Gram said, "Check out this email that just came through from Richard Johnson. I was just about to give it to you when this brief thought of depression descended upon me. What a strange bag of feelings to have in a short time period. This is something else. I had to read it more than once to make sure that I was actually seeing it for what it was."

Gram handed me a printed copy of an email message. I stared at it for a moment and then let out a loud whoop.

My exclamation shocked Al. "What the hell's going on back there?" He asked.

"Listen to this Al. You won't believe it.

I read the email from Richard Johnson.

From: Richard Johnson To: John Gallagher CC: Gram T

I got this email from a well-known journalist. She wanted to confirm her facts before publishing it in the paper.

Mr. Gallagher,

I examined the record of the donations to your campaign. So far, you have raised $8.23 million and the number is going up rapidly. Incredibly, the average donation is only $2.03. That means 4.1 million people who will vote for you. Many of these donations represent families. So it is closer to 6.25 million. In the last general election, 131,304,731 voters voted for president. You will need about 45 million votes to win and you are already 15% there considering there will be only three candidates. This is after visiting only OH, IA, NH, SC and FL. This is just 10% of the states. We would like your permission to put a logo of the number of people "Ringing the Liberty Bell" each day on the front page of our paper. We would also have to give equal space to the other candidates. That will work in your favor because it will put you in the same arena as the current President and other hopefuls.
Say hi to Jack for me,
Sincerely,
Jennifer Williamson
New York Times

"What do you make of this?" I asked them.

"Best thing that's happened to us since we started," Gram said. "We will have national attention in the form of a daily counter on the front page of the New York Times. Fricking Amazing!" Al uttered in disbelief.

"We've certainly hit the big time. I'm flabbergasted."

"Call Richard right now and make sure," I directed Gram.

Gram did. Two minutes later he reported, "Everything is on the up and up. We're going to be on the front page of the New York Times every day now until the end of this campaign. This Williamson is an up and coming reporter and what she is doing for us is making our campaign national news with a daily focus unparalleled anytime in past campaigns."

"Is it true that we've raised more than $8 million?" Al asked.

"Hold on," Gram said. He called Carol and five minutes later reported, "She said we're over $8.3 million dollars right now. Somehow this Williamson was hip to what we had in the coffers."

"Sure, easy enough. When Kirkpatrick and I talked about total transparency, he made it possible for anyone to be able to monitor our donations at any time. Anyone who donates money is listed on our home page and Kirkpatrick said it's in real time."

We just sat there for a few moments trying to digest what we had just learned. There was so much at stake. We wondered how these people were ahead of the game and taking this campaign to the next level. I started to giggle and soon, all three of us were doing the same. Our giggles became guffaws, then laughs, finally deep belly rolling rumblings that made the bus start to rock. Slapping each other's hands, we stood up and said to one another, "Bring it on, America. We're ready!"

The facts were amazing. If what Williamson said was true, we were much further ahead in our campaign than the other candidates were because we had amassed a greater "base" than they had. In the greater scheme, all that mattered were votes. The candidate with the most popular votes in a state won the Electoral College votes for that state. Everything was a matter of numbers and I was now in command of them. We were winning in the numbers game by raising less money but from more people. This was the essence of what Williamson was communicating to us. The impossible was fast becoming the possible. If we were able to get $138 million from the same amount of people, we would win. We would get 100% of the vote. This was impossible, of course, but was it? If this movement continued to expand, we would be in command of more than 100 million votes. People power would defeat money power. We did not need a billionaire pulling the strings of our campaign. We would defeat the billionaires with our votes alone. Let them buy all the attack ads they wanted. The people would know what to believe. The people were savvier than the elites thought. We would win because the power of the people would take us over the top. The race would be over. We would have won. We would be in the White House in January 2013. If we could just hold on, the future would be ours. Working Americans would be in charge of this country. We would insure that transparency and integrity would make all Americans believe in their government again. How tragic it was that the current congress commanded less than a ten percent approval rating. We would change that immediately. We would focus on restoring the meaning and intent of government as the Constitution originally commanded. This must be a government of, for and by the people with the emphasis on the last phrase: BY THE PEOPLE.

"Now what's next?" Al asked, breaking the spell that hovered over us.

"Gram, call Jack and tell him we're heading to St. Augustine and we'll be there in about two hours. Let him know what's happened with the Times and how much money we've collected. He wants to know everything so let him have it."

"Will do," Gram said.

"Al, we're down with the time."

"Sure are, Leo."

"I'll make a nice lunch while you're driving. We can eat, talk and be ready for the next stop. I'm trying to digest all that has happened in the last ten minutes."

Gram and I ate our sandwiches at the table. Al ate while driving. We were ecstatic about the possibilities. Now we needed to insure that we held up our end.

"Jack's aware of our itinerary," Gram said. "Now we've got to take advantage of everything that has happened today. This story gets more amazing than even I could have imagined," Gram finished.

"Gram, when I think about our efforts thus far, nothing surprises me. This has been one magical mystery tour. Now let's prepare to have some fun in St. Augustine."

"Right on, Leo, let's make tracks and see what's down the road," Gram cried out.

"Al, roll on, brother," I said.

"Back to the Future," Al said.

The bus rolled down the highway south toward St. Augustine and the next stop on our tour.

We laughed, joked and teased one another as we headed toward our destiny mixing in a twist of fate for good measure.

28. Immigration, Medication and Confrontation

St. Augustine is the oldest inhabited city in the United States. Ponce de Leon first explored the environs and claimed the land for the Spanish crown. Prior to the founding of St. Augustine in 1565, several earlier attempts at European colonization in Florida were made by both Spain and France but all failed. Once established, the Spanish influence in the area continued for more than a century.

The Spanish influence was evident in the names of the streets and the architecture. We drove into town and looked for the small mall that Richard Johnson said was the best place to meet and greet the people. He was not going to be there, but he forwarded the contact person's name and phone number to us.

This pattern of moving into a city, setting up our sideshow, doing our performance and then moving on was working quite well for us. The cost was minimal, the contact was local and we were getting significant press as time unfolded. We did not mind the constant movement. Gram was a great navigator. Al never complained about the driving. I did not mind cooking for them between venues. Jack was always hovering over us like a dark, brooding guardian angel.

Jorge Manos greeted us when we got to the Spanish mission area on the south side of town. We pulled into the vast parking area and were immediately greeted by a throng of people. I was overwhelmed with the numbers. This was becoming the norm now, but still, for a simple guy like me, a crowd assembled to hear me speak was something that continued to amaze me.

Florida's themes were simple. What are you going to do about immigration reform? What are you going to do about social security, Medicare and Medicaid reform? What are you going to do to spur the economy and get Americans back to work? The social issues that the Republicans were focused upon gained little traction in the world where I was speaking. People did not really care about tax reform and birth control and the pro-choice and pro-life conflict. What they wanted to know was simple. Will my sister be deported? How can I get decent health care?

In the last election, McCain and Obama avoided the issue of immigration. Originally, McCain was for comprehensive reform, but the right wing of his party was not listening to his message. He wanted the nomination so he changed his tune and the people heard what he said and liked it. "We need to first secure the borders," he preached. Obama wanted reform. He said he would enact it. The people cheered and elected him. Three years later, there was no reform, but he did achieve a higher deportation rate than George W. Bush. Yes, Obama promoted the "Dream Act" but it got no traction in a congress that was determined to deny him a second term. The impasse was palpable. Everyone in Washington could feel the constant tension between what the President wanted to do and what the reluctant republicans would let him do. Into this foray, I dipped my foot first, got slightly wet, and then, feeling the need to make a difference plunged in to the chest.

"Immigration is what made America a nation of high performance people. Only one group of folks did not come here from another land. Native Americans paid a dear price for being indigent. We still have not reconciled with this noble people regarding the way they were treated by the earliest settlers. What we have is a nation of immigrants who came here to live a better life. Yes, some came through the Ellis Island portal. Many entered without permission. We know this. We need to fix the break in the dam and we need to do something to insure that all Americans and immigrants are accounted for, protected and held accountable. Stronger borders can only stop the weak, feeble and not too highly motivated souls who want to enter America. The rest will get in. Once here, how do we insure that they are law-abiding people? How do we get them to contribute to the society in which they have chosen to live? How do we know who they are and what they are doing? I maintain that comprehensive reform must include an immediate path to citizenship. This five-year number tossed about by some politicians makes no sense to me. People need closure. They need to know that their futures are not in doubt. All immigrants will have to register with the local office of the Immigration and Naturalization Service. This way they can get their case on the docket to be processed. They will need to pay their dues. When we find people who refuse to cooperate, we will deport them. When we find people that are illegal immigrants and have committed crimes, we will try them just as if they were citizens. We cannot let people, no matter their place of origin, function outside the law. The projected twelve million immigrants now in this country will continue to serve the greater good and be even more productive if we make a concerted effort to bring them into the American family with dignity, respect, simple accountability and citizenship."

The people appreciated the perspective that I was framing for those who were hiding in the shadows afraid to declare who they are and wanting only to belong.

Our movement through the "Sunshine State" was an exercise in long days, long nights and little sleep. We did not stop moving. The miles piled up rapidly. Al did not complain about the traffic, the heat, the congestion or the chronic hassles with local police who did not want us to be creating any more problems than they already had with the Republican Party simultaneously flooding the state with its candidates and their surrogates. We were an upstart movement, an "Occupy Florida" fringe element and they did not like it.

Gram was phenomenal in dispelling their constant complaints. The right to assembly was on his tongue half the time. He smiled broadly and gave it to them with both barrels. He was finesse personified. What a treat it was to watch him flummox the local gendarmerie. His smooth tongue made them feel like they were bumbling idiots. Only once, were we almost arrested and that was because Al decided to give his unwanted opinion when he was accused of parking illegally. Gram saved his butt and we were able to move along without too much concern. Big Jack was always nearby and making us aware of what to watch out for, where to go, what to do and not do.

Daytona Beach was the home of the "Great American Race". We were a month away from the event, but I wanted to see the track, so Al rolled past the area and we ogled the mighty complex. The timing was not right, but I was happy to see where the race would be run.

What makes senior citizens so special is that they are never too old to contribute to the greater good of our society. Many volunteer organizations function smoothly because they have a core of senior people who, now freed from the daily grind of making a living, donate their time and money to charitable works. This is what was making the New America a vibrant and healthy society. Once upon a time, a sixty-year-old person was considered elderly. Now, sixty had become the new forty, and eighty-year-old men and women were still driving, volunteering, dancing, hugging and kissing, getting remarried and living life fully. Modern medicine contributed to the longevity, but the positive mental attitude on the part of these seniors was what made the change possible. Their major concern was the constant attack by many ultra-conservatives like Congressman Paul Ryan on Medicare. The Ryan Plan would give vouchers to seniors who could then go out on the open market and purchase their own health care insurance. Even if they had the money, would the insurance companies sell them a policy? In theory, his plan would make the government less responsible for the senior population. In reality, it would cast an entire segment of our society out into the cold to fend for itself. The plan did not make it past second base, but the conservative element in the party was persistent with reforming the current Medicare system. Yes, it was bloated. Yes, it was costing us billions of dollars to operate. Yes, all this was true, but the real reforms that needed to be made were not being discussed. Seniors needed to hear that there was not a plan to cast them out into the fields and fend for themselves. We needed to respect them, their contributions, their lifelong citizenship and care for them with dignity and respect as they entered into those years when health care was an essential component of living out their last years without fear. We had a duty to our elders to do everything we could do to insure they were not facing the grim reaper without having all of us at their side taking care of them.

In Daytona Beach, we were to meet in a huge parking lot adjacent to the racetrack, and thousands of interested people were gathered there when the Liberty Bell Bus rolled to a stop. We could see the people were anxious and the police were, too. Blue shirts were everywhere. The organizers, Julio Martinez and Julie Sykes, came to meet us, ushered us to the staging area, gave us some pointers on what we needed to do and not do, framed the time for our gathering and then said, "Let's do it."

I was happy to be alive and well and in the shadows of the famous racetrack and with its history, wanted to make sure that my message did not disappoint.

"Health care is not a privilege. Health care is a human need. At some time in his or her life, every person is going to have to see a doctor and receive medical care. The catastrophic health events that some people face should not be the reason they live like paupers the rest of their lives. More than fifty percent of all people who file for bankruptcy do so because they suffered from a major health issue that they could not afford. This is unacceptable. What society can call it civilized if it lets the sick people suffer? Comfort the sick was one of Christ's teachings. I do believe that in all great religions, caring for those who cannot care for themselves is the standard. What this means is we are not going to solve the Medicare problem by instituting a voucher system."

The crowd erupted into a loud chant and I waited until they calmed down again.

"We can accept the reality that all people, as part of this nation, can be included in the Medicare system and not frozen out of it. The lobbying by for profit hospitals, for profit health insurance companies, for profit pharmaceutical companies is so intense that the truth is hard to get. Medicare can and should be saved. Medicare serves more people than all the other insurance carriers combined. Medicare's favorability rating is higher than any private insurer system, and Medicare costs less to administer than any private plan. Where we are falling short is that within Medicare, we have siphoned off billions of dollars in the fiasco set up by the former president with the Medicare Part D plan. Instead of making it a standard practice to negotiate for drugs for all participants as a block, the bill expressly forbade the government to do so. This was pure politics and lobbying that created this mess. This needs to be changed. This one aspect of the Medicare program costs taxpayers the most money. Once this is fixed, we will see an appreciable decline in the doomsday preachers who say that Medicare will be broke by 2026. If this date is fact, then let us do what it takes to fix the system. Giving seniors vouchers is not the answer. Giving seniors more choice only adds to the confusion. Simplifying the system, making it more efficient, removing paper from the billing and other cost cutting measures can save billions of dollars insuring that the program can sustain itself for a hundred years. Every time you hear a politician say that it is unsustainable, you are hearing a doomsday prophet trying to dismantle the program. He or she is not a problem solver, but a worthless critic and these folks need to be told to get out of the way while we go to work saving something that insures seniors' decent health care. What do we do first? We stop talking as if the system is beyond salvage. This causes elderly people more grief. They don't need it. We younger people must respect their need for continuity, safety and security. We must not expect them to try to navigate a complex highway of Medicare policies, but simplify it so that even a first grader can understand it. Failing to do so, we will be only a second-class country and that, my friends is unacceptable to me, and I am sure, to you as well. Join with me in this campaign to fortify this system so that all people can look forward to enjoying their senior years with a profound sense of security because Medicare is solvent and works for everyone who needs it."

Gram and Al had to rescue me from the crowds. The people who mobbed me were well aware of the attack on the very program that kept them healthy and happy. I gave them hope that the future was not dire. We could solve this problem if we chose to do so. It would require a concerted effort on the part of all the people, with a stake in the system, to work diligently to find solutions that kept costs down, services up and minimized fraud, waste and duplication of effort.

Day and night we moved along the I-95 corridor and headed down the peninsula stopping wherever there was a planned venue and meeting the people, sharing our ideas with them, hearing their concerns, answering their questions and asking them for their input. This last strategy made them feel connected to the movement and was integral to making them a part of it. I could not count the number of times that a person would shake my hand and say, "Mr. Pollack, I donated five bucks to your campaign. I'd like to give more but that is all I could afford. However, as you said, every dollar is a vote. You have mine, sir. Go get'em and make sure that you speak for working people when you're sitting in that White House that the people built." Kind words like these gave me faith and hope that our work was not in vain. We would overcome any obstacles if we just remembered who were fighting for and what the goal was. We needed to keep our eye on the prize.

Outside of town, we ran into a roadblock of sorts. We could not gather where we had been told the next meeting was to take place. For some reason, the local authorities reneged on the permit that would give us permission to meet with more than three thousand people in a mall parking lot. The mall owners did not want the distraction stating it would adversely affect business. We called Richard Johnson in on the case and he was able to resolve the issue in an hour or so. In the mean time, after alerting Big Jack to what I was planning to do, I went out into the crowd, wandered around meeting the people, seeing and listening to their stories and engaging them in meaningful dialogue. I noticed that there was a cadre of the press corps following me including television crews and their reporters. They were not asking me questions but were recording my responses.

"Do you believe that corporations are people?"

"No," I said. "A corporation is a legal entity that was designed to make it easier to do business and harder to regulate. There is no such thing as a breathing, bleeding corporation and anyone who believes this is trying to give life to a zombie." People laughed when I labeled the corporation with this term. In my heart, I believed it.

"What are your thoughts about putting kids to work in their schools doing janitorial duties to teach them job skills?"

"I believe janitors ought to be doing janitor work and children should be doing the work of learning and not cleaning toilets. It is a misrepresentation of our society to even hint that the working poor do not have a good work ethic. How many single moms hold down two jobs so that their children have a good home, food, clothes and are able to get an education because they, these working moms, know how to make sacrifices for their children?"

"What do you think about forcing religious organizations to provide birth control for their employees?"

"When are we going to let women manage their own bodies and stay the heck out of their biological business? Who am I as a man to tell a woman what to do with her body? My friends, we are so hung up with sexuality that we cannot see the forest for the trees. Let women decide what they need and what they want. Men, let's stay out of this issue. However, to answer your question, I think that if a company provides health care to its employees, and contraception is part of the health care package, then they need to provide it. What are we going to start doing? Decide on every aspect of health care based upon belief system that is not related to the health and well-being of the employee who is seeking the service. I think not. This may not make me popular with the religious right and the Catholics who are still advocating that people have large families, but this is a foolish position. We have too many people on the face of the earth right now to adequately sustain the population. Even China realized this a generation ago. Let's face it. We are competing for dwindling resources as the population increases. The one sure way to control the population is contraception. 'Just Say No' to sex does not work. I'm sorry to break the news to you folks, but those are the facts."

"What do you think about the complaints that government is too big and needs to be cut down in size, that government is the problem, not the solution?"

"First of all, the person who uttered that statement was the president who oversaw a major expansion of the government during his tenure. He was also the one who cut taxes once and then raised taxes eleven times afterward to make sure there was enough money to run the expanded government that he created. He was also the president who said, there is something wrong when a bus driver is paying a higher percent of income tax than a millionaire is. Oh, yes, this president was also the one who broke up the air traffic controllers union and made it harder for working people to organize. He was the president who indirectly authorized the sale of drugs for weapons in what became known as the 'Iran-Contra Affair'. Big government is not the problem. Government leadership is the problem. If that president were to appear today and want to run for the republican presidential nomination, he would be laughed off the stage. I believe in government of, for and by the people. It's part of our Declaration of Independence and our Constitution. Government is not an evil entity, but a necessity of life for those of us who want to live in a civilized world where we each don't need to go out and build the road to get to the food store, or form our own police force to protect our homes."

"What do you think of this current crop of Republican presidential candidates?"

"I believe they are all good American men who want to do the best for the country. I do not agree with most of what they want to do and that is the reason I am running for president."

"How do you think President Obama has done as president?"

"I think President Obama has done the best job he can do thus far since he was elected. What I think he has not done is make this economy work for all people and not just those who are and were already well off. He is a great American and I admire him, but I think I can do a better job representing the 160 million working people in this country."

"What are you going to do if you don't win?"

"Go home and look for another job. What else can I do?"

"How realistic do you think it is for a person like you to run for this office as a third party candidate and have any real chance of winning the race?"

"Let's see. If I don't run, I'd be 100 percent sure, I would not win. Since I am running, I have a fifty-fifty chance of winning. With three people running, I need to get only 34 percent of the vote and that would insure that I win the presidency. I think that my odds are good."

"If you do win the race, what is the first thing you'll do after you take the oath of office?"

"Go back to the White House and get to work. There is no time to party. We have a nation of people trying to make ends meet. The last thing they want to see is the new president dressed in a tuxedo going to fancy balls where millions of dollars are being spent. No, the work starts on day one and on the last day of my presidency, when I give the keys to the next leader, I can say, I did it my way."

"You said you'd only run for one term. What if you win and don't get everything done that you want to do? What will you do then?"

"As I said, one term and out. I mean it folks. I don't want to be a career politician. Hey, it's nice work. You get to meet many people and travel around and do exciting things, but that is not what the job really involves. It demands that you work to better the lot of the majority of the people who live in this society and that is something that cannot always be done by consensus. Too many career politicians are concerned with re-election and not serving the people. I say to you vote them out. You won't have to vote me out because I will leave without making a fuss. One term and out. Remember this. Shoot me if I don't live up to my commitment."

An hour passed and still there was no resolution to the issue of congregating in the mall parking lot. We continued to move through the crowd answering questions, holding babies, shaking hands, autographing books and tee shirts, hats and memorabilia and feeling the power of the people who wanted nothing more than to believe in their elected leader. I felt so blessed to be walking upon this ground with the American citizens who, like me, wanted to believe in something greater than themselves.

"We can't resolve the issue," Gram finally reported to me. "I've been in discussion with the local police and the city leaders and this is a no go."

"What do we do with this crowd?" I asked.

"Leo, if I knew I'd tell you, but this does not look good."

"If we just pull up and leave, there might be some serious trouble," I responded.

"Tell me about it."

"Okay. You have to get me a loudspeaker and I need to say something to the crowd. We can't just let this go. It will get out of hand in a minute. I feel the energy. Right now, it is positive. Give it a minute, tell them this is over, tell them to disperse, and there will be hell to pay."

"Let me get the bullhorn," Gram said and left.

Working my way back toward the bus, I could sense tension beginning to rise in the masses. They could see there was something about to happen. Those who could overhear Gram and my conversation passed the message through the crowd. I could tell that they were not happy. I did not want a riot breaking out and so I carefully moved forward toward the bus still talking to people and encouraging them to take responsibility for their country, their future and their lives.

Gram handed me the bullhorn. I had not used it since we were in Akron. How nice it felt. The simplicity of the instrument made me smile. This was the way of my forebears, the first real working stiffs who wanted a better nation for all people and fought for it.

Stepping up onto a small concrete wall, I turned on the bullhorn and said to the gathering of the people, "My fellow Americans, we've shared a few moments together and now it is time for me to move on."

Immediately, loud, raucous calls rang out, "No, No, No". I tried to talk over the protest.

"Friends, we were fortunate to be able to share this time with one another. I ask that you stand up and be counted but not be disrespectful and irresponsible and listen to what I have to say."

The noise started rising again. I was afraid I would not be able to control the energy for very long.

"I am not pleased that we cannot visit longer, but we must end our meeting on a peaceful note. After all, we are the true patriots. We are the working people who made this country. We don't want the press and the city leaders to resent our being together right now and making it impossible for us to meet in the future. I will be back. I am not stopping this campaign until we either win, or we go down fighting on Election Day."

"We'll fight now….No way…Leave us be" All sorts of calls echoed from the crowd. I could feel Al and Gram very close to me. I think they were fearful that something might happen to me. Strangely, I felt very safe, almost too safe.

"Our time together is over for now, but I shall be back again as this campaign season stretches out into the spring, summer and fall. Make this a memorable day by cooperating with the police and safety services. Do not let them believe we are just a bunch of hooligans. Please. Stand up and be counted for being leaders and not followers. I ask you with all my heart."

"Leo…Leo…Leo" broke out and soon the crowd was chanting my name so loudly that there was no other sound that could be heard. I waved with both hands repeatedly, kept flashing the thumbs up sign and slowly and carefully made my way back to the bus where Big Jack and some of his people were waiting for me to get on it and leave before anything happened.

Al was already aboard. The bus was running. I climbed in and went to my normal seat in the mock living room. No sooner did Gram get on than Al shut the door and we slowly edged our way through the throngs of well-wishers who slapped the side of the bus and continued to chant my name. I felt like a coward leaving the scene of a fight and letting my friends down, but I knew that my leaving might be the best thing to curb any further actions on the part of the people. This was not a good time for things to get ugly. They still might. I hoped not.

As we headed out to the freeway and drove south on I-95, we turned on the television to see if there was any coverage of the event. Sure enough, the scenes were feeding in live from the mall. Some fighting had broken out. Police were trying to quell the disturbances.

"Jesus," I uttered aloud.

"You can't do anything about it," Gram said. "Those cops were not listening to me and so now they're getting what they deserve."

"But it didn't have to come to this," I replied disappointed in my inability to convince people to not lose self-control.

"Leo, we're not miracle workers," Al said. "We talked to those coppers until we were blue in the face. They were not going to let us hold a meeting. We tried to convince them that we were not trying to be difficult and did not want to break any laws but we did have a right to gather. They said without a permit, we were banned from such activity. So we knew we could do nothing more to convince them."

"I feel badly that we could not achieve our goal," Gram said, but maybe this will play out to our advantage.

"How can that be? Violence is not the answer," I cried out as I got up and started pacing the floor.

"The press was there. They will see what happened. They will cover it and we'll come out of this better off. We tried to do what was right but the city and its leaders were the ones who were denying the people the right to meet the person who just might be the next president of the United States."

"I just wish that it did not have to be so," I said. "I wish that I could go back there and just end this affair."

"I don't think Big Jack will let you get anywhere near that town again," Gram said.

"Nor would we," Al seconded.

I sat back down and stewed over the facts as stated. I did not like what I was hearing, but what they said was essentially true. I had no control over the people. I was not there to incite people to riot. The people could choose what to do. I just hoped they would choose to be responsible and not fall into the trap of defying authority for no good reason. After all, my not having a permit was our campaign's fault. Still, the first amendment rights were part of this equation too. So many things were all jumbled together that all I wanted to do was get as far away as I could and start over again.

We got that chance five hours later in Miami.

The crowd was gathered in a minor league baseball stadium reserved for us by Richard Johnson, and our host, Ralph Mendoza. We were excited that we would not be evicted from the space.

"Much better than Daytona," Gram said with a Cheshire cat grin on his face.

"Are you ready?" Al asked me.

"My friends, I'm always ready. We have the chance to reach a lot of people here this evening."

Ralph approached us and set the ground rules, timetable and how and when we might consider ending the speech and turning the event into a social gathering. "I think we'll have 5000 people here at least. Not bad for a day's notice. Leo, all I can say is that it's good to meet you and hopefully, we'll be able to do our part to get you elected."

"Ralph, with supportive people like you and this rambunctious crowd out there already hollering my name, how can we fail to achieve our goals?"

"Let's go do it," he said and led the way.

"We'll mill about in the crowd," Gram said, "and take the pulse of the people."

Al and Gram left me. I walked out on the stage with Ralph and psyched myself up for what was coming.

Ralph gave a glowing introduction and then turned the stage over to me. The crowd was loud and I was sure that there must be ringers sitting among them that were paid to scream loudly. This could not be for real. Or could it?

"Miamians, thank you for letting me come into your neighborhood and share a few moments of time with you. My name is Leo Pollack. I'm an unemployed American steel worker and I want to be your next president."

The crowd started chanting my name. I smiled because it came out with a distinct Spanish twang to it.

"I, like many of you, am not working. This is not because we don't want to work. It's because there is no work. America is facing a chronic problem. Corporations are consistently moving manufacturing plants off shore to save money. They eliminate jobs, and at the same time, write off the expenses they incur in the move. Americans lose in both cases because the jobs are gone and the corporation gets a tax break. This needs to stop. This is one of the first economic issues that I plan to address as your next president."

The crowd chanted "Jobs…Jobs…Jobs". Clearly, work was a major issue in Miami like it was all over the country.

"How do we bring industrial plants back to the United States? This will not be a simple plan, but first, we eliminate all tax breaks for corporations that move a plant off shore. Secondly, we set a tariff that will make imported items cost the same as if they were produced in the United States. This will take away any incentive that companies hope to achieve by moving their production overseas to save labor costs. It is time for the corporations to stop penalizing Americans. Thirdly, we immediately undertake a nationwide mission to 'Buy American'. Yes, we must and will buy those products that our neighbors make. We can and will reverse the trend that has been going on for the past thirty years."

"Buy American…Buy American…Buy American…" the chant rose and went on for a long time. I waited until it ran its course.

"We are facing a severe economic downturn that will not end until we solve the home foreclosure crisis. We bailed out banks. They got better. They banked a lot of money. Now they are reluctant to lend that money to people who want to refinance. I can fully appreciate that a bank does not want to take a loss. If Bank A can get 7% on a loan, what would possess it to refinance with a homeowner at 5%? Yes, it's bad business. You know, I agree. However, it was good business when we, yes we Americans, used our tax dollars to bail out those banks so they would not go bankrupt. We were told that if they did, the economy might crash altogether. Now, we're facing more than a million foreclosures, but the banks are unwilling to come through and help Americans. This is unacceptable. The banks are not immune from prosecution. We have not yet seen more than a half dozen financial services personnel face any charges because of this financial meltdown. It is time to hold the banks accountable and to use every means necessary to get them to renegotiate loans."

"Homes…Homes…Homes…" The chants followed a simple format.

"Now immigration has been held under the radar screen for the past three years. States have attempted to repress immigration by passing new laws that are unconstitutional. This needs to stop. We will pass comprehensive immigration reform by expecting all people who are not legal citizens to become legal ones. Yes, we cannot deny the reality of who lives in our nation. Let all who are not currently legal citizens register with the INS and face the consequences for coming here illegally. We are a nation of immigrants and there is a huge immigrant population that needs to be acknowledged and supported in becoming legal members of our community."

"Leo…Leo…Leo…" the sounds echoed across the field.

"Social Security, Medicare and Medicaid need to be protected, enhanced, expanded and protected for our children and grandchildren. There is a need for a social safety net. For those who do not need it, they can bypass it. There are 153 million people who participate fully in the two programs. There is no reason to privatize these programs any further. Look at what has happened to everything we have privatized in the past few years. Where are the savings?"

"Finally, Cuba."

A loud roar filled the skies.

"For fifty years, we have boycotted this tiny island because we don't like its communist leadership. How ironic. We don't seem to be too concerned about the communist leadership in China. In fact, we spend more money importing goods from China in one hour than we have from Cuba in fifty years. It is time to normalize relations with Cuba, and end a standoff that makes no sense. Fidel, you've proved your point. We give. You win. Now, let's make peace."

Loud laughter erupted and "Cuba" was shouted at the top of the group's voice.

"I need your support. I need your vote. I need your dollar bills to run this campaign. Please go to our Leo Pollack for President Website, donate a few bucks, and then, when it is time, vote for me. If you want someone who knows what it means to work from paycheck to paycheck, then please support me. Thank you for being here and I hope to see you all for the fall campaign."

The crowd went wild. I waved to the people and walked off the stage. For more than an hour, we made our way out of the ballpark shaking hands, signing autographs and slowly but surely exiting the place and finally getting back on the road. We eased the Liberty Bus through the dispersing crowd, listening to their cries of "Leo…Leo" and "Buy American" and "Viva Cuba" and much, much more.

"I think we were a hit here in the Deep South, what do you say?" Gram said.

"Much better than our last stop," Al said. "I'm glad to be on the road again. Where to next?"

"The Keys, then Port Charlotte, Fort Myers, St. Petersburg, Orlando, Ocala, Gainesville, and finally Tallahassee."

"Hmm. That's all the stops we're going to make?" Al asked with a smirk.

"Actually, Al, I want to go back to Daytona Beach and kick some butt. You game?" Gram asked.

"Are you kidding?" Al responded looking over his shoulder at Gram in the huge rear view mirror.

"Sure, why not. We're on a roll. Let's go back and show them who's really in charge. You dig?" Gram said with a sneer.

"I know you're kidding," Al said. "But that's okay. I can take a dig."

"South bound, hammer down," Gram said. "I've never been to Key West. Let's get there so we can do some snorkeling before we get too busy."

"Now that sounds like fun," I said. "I could use a few hours in the sunshine."

"All in favor say Aye," Gram cried out.

We all said, "Aye".

We drove to Key West and did see the coast on both sides of the highway. Crowds bombarded the bus wherever we went and so snorkeling was out. We turned back north, to Fort Myers, Port Charlotte, Bradenton, St. Petersburg, Orlando, Ocala, Gainesville, and finally Tallahassee. In each of these stops, we presented the same message. Working Americans must unite and take control of the country. Those who never faced a layoff, never lived from paycheck to paycheck, never went without healthcare insurance because the premiums were too high, never worked at minimum wage or less because the economy was so unhealthy could not relate to the message we were broadcasting. We faced opposition from the wealthy echelons of the nation, but down where the rubber meets the road, we knew that we were touching the hearts and minds of the people who would vote for us and what we all believed. Work was honorable and preferable to being unemployed. We wanted to leave our children a better world than the one we inherited. Our intolerance toward the illegal immigrants needed to be reframed into one of acceptance, tolerance and forbearance. We needed to stand up for protecting the environment from abuse just like we finally started to do for children, women and the elderly after so many years of conveniently turning a blind eye to the topic. We promoted "Buy American" at every opportunity and asked people to reject the Walmart pledge to "live better spend less" and instead spend what it takes to put your neighbor back to work. We drove over a 1000 miles through the state and on the evening of the primary sometime after 9 pm, we were rolling slowly out of Tallahassee and wondering how we would fair.

The results astounded us.

Romney beat the republican field by a large margin. Romney: 46.5% Gingrich: 32% Santorum: 13.3% Paul: 7 % Pollack: 1.2%

You could feel the bus hopping down the highway as we stomped on the floor, raised our voices and sang "Born to be Wild".

The raucous nature of our celebration started to attract attention from vehicles passing us on the highway. We chilled out. Al found a place to pull off the highway, we called Big Jack, and he came in from the cold and was as happy as we were. We called John in Ohio and he was elated. I called Basha and Janko and we talked for twenty minutes. I did not care that it was way past his bedtime. This was a day to celebrate.

On a more sober note, we realized that Romney won the primary by outspending Newt 1700 to 1 and running 12,800 negative campaign ads to Newt's 280. There was no competition in this arena. Luckily, Romney and the others left us alone. How long the major campaigns would leave us alone remained to be seen. The world was not passing us by anymore. We were catching on to the tailwind and rapidly capturing the fantasy of the nation's disenfranchised, unemployed, working poor and middle class underemployed people who were fed up with business as usual. We did not believe the president's leadership was inadequate, but we did believe he was not fulfilling his campaign promises regardless of what the obstacles facing his leadership. The republicans were clearly out of touch with working people. Their focus on a free economy was really code for a fixed economy that protected corporations and ran roughshod over working people. Reviewing the republican governors who were promoting radical "right to work" policies in their states, every working person could readily see the truth. No Republican could honestly claim to be for the working class. Indeed, they were heartily supporting the privileged class, those making in excess of $250,000 a year and living well above the median income.

We drove through the night and headed home to Ohio feeling the joy that comes from working hard and hoping that this would lead to a better future. We did not stop until we were almost back into the Buckeye. We were so full of adrenalin but we did not let that keep us from slowing down and sleeping.

Our day had arrived. We were on the playing field and we were beginning to make a statement. Our campaign boasted few tangible resources. What we possessed was the voice of the people. We continued to make a joyful noise

Our time had arrived. January 2012 was the pivotal moment in American history when the people reread the Constitution and decided to fulfill its promise by taking command of the government and leading the nation into the 21st Century with joy and enthusiasm.

29. Home Is Where the Heart Is

Early in the morning, we arrived home. Al parked the bus in front of the house and headed to his place. Gram dragged inside. Big Jack rolled past and we talked for a few minutes. He updated me on the current state of security and I thanked him for his diligence. He stared at me and did not say anything for a few minutes. I waited. Finally, he said almost in a whisper, "If anything happens to you, this country is going to be in deep trouble." He walked away to his car and drove away. I knew he would not be very far from the house, from me and my family, and this mission. I stared across the landscape of the city, smelled the fresh air, wished it were filled with sulfur scent meaning that the mills were working at full capacity, and wondered if I would ever again feel the joy of sweating and doing backbreaking labor.

Basha and I kissed for a long time. When I told her that I needed to use the bathroom, she unwrapped her arms from around me. I thought she was going to follow me. When I came back into the kitchen, we sat down at the table and talked for a while.

"When I told him that you were coming home today, Janko wanted to stay home from school. I told him no. He was not happy."

"I should walk down to the school and see him. That would be a surprise."

"Let's do it. We can go together," Basha cried out.

"We will, but first, how are you?"

"I'm fine. I'm lonely. I miss you. I need you in bed with me. I am cold at night. I don't sleep well when you are gone. Then..." she hesitated.

"Everything will be fine, Basha," I reassured her. "We are safe. Big Jack is the best man we could have on our side. Some of Jack's men are guarding our house. You and Janko are safe."

"I'm not worried about me, Leo. I don't concern myself with fear. I know that I am safe here in our home and in our small town. You are out there where the forces of evil are everywhere. We can be cautious around this place. You are out in a world where there is no real protection against those types of people who are dead set against someone like you who speaks truth to power and is not afraid to tell the story the way it needs to be told. This is something that will eventually place you right in the cross hairs of some madman or a whole group of them."

"Basha, if I were to give in to the fear that is in some people, I would never leave our home and venture into the world. No, I will be careful and do what is necessary to insure my safety, and Al's, Gram's and everyone else's. I can't be stopped by what might happen. I don't want to live in a 'what if' kind of world."

"Leo, no one is asking you to do that. You know I would not expect you to give up your hopes and dreams because of my silly worries. I just am scared at times. It's because I love you so much and would hate to lose you."

"I know. I know. Everything will be fine. We just have to pray and keep the faith."

"I pray every day for your safety, for your strength, for your voice to speak the truth and for your heart to be true to the cause you set out to lead."

"Speaking of causes, how are we fixed for money?"

"Since you are using the campaign credit card, the unemployment is keeping us above water. We don't have a lot of extra money, but the bills are paid, food is on the table, and Janko is well aware that there are no extras right now."

"I feel badly leaving you with this burden. I should be a better provider."

"You are a fine provider, my husband. You are out looking for work every day and that makes me proud and excited about our future."

"How would you feel about being the 'First Lady'?"

Basha hesitated for a few moments. "I don't know. The stage is not my world. I did not graduate from college. I do not work for a living. I am nothing but a mother, a simple housewife. How would I fit into that world of glitz and glamour?"

I smiled at her gazing at her simple, unadorned beauty. Even without makeup and a fancy hairdo, Basha was drop dead gorgeous. She did not need anything fancy to make her look glamorous. She did not know just how exceptionally lovely she was and my telling her so did not make her believe it. I still said it though because it was true. "There is no woman in Washington who is as lovely as you are, my dear Basha. You will be a first-rate First Lady, simply as beautiful and poised as any woman that ever graced that home."

"Get us there first and I'll figure out how to be 'graceful and poised' when we arrive."

"How are things here at home? Anything needing repair? Something I need to fix?"

"Oh, no, Leo. I've got everything in fine working order. You are too busy to do much of anything right now. Besides, Dan is next door. He comes over every day or so and asks if he can do anything for me. He's a fine neighbor. We are blessed to have him near us. I am sure that your campaign makes him wonder what the world is coming to because he often asks me where you are and what you are doing. When I tell him, he just shakes his head and mutters to himself, 'this younger generation'. I know he's excited for you, for us, for this adopted country of his. So, no, everything is fine. We just miss having you at home."

"I miss being there. You don't know how long some of the days are. This South Carolina – Florida run was exhausting, but very productive. I did tell you about the New York Times email didn't I. Wasn't that something?"

"When I read that, I was astounded. Right on the front page of the New York Times. How amazing is that? Leo, with that kind of publicity, there is no stopping you now. My husband, I am very, very, very proud of you."

"Kiss me then and prove it."

Five minutes later, we came up for air. Huge smiles painted both our faces.

"Now, what are we going to do?"

"Let's walk down to the school and visit Janko. It's just about lunchtime. I don't think his teacher will mind, do you?"

"No, not in the least. She's a big fan of yours, Leo. She talks about you all the time. Sometimes it makes Janko self-conscious, but he says, 'Oh well, that is the price of fame.'"

"He said that?"

"A few times, but you can tell that he is as proud of his father, as is his wife."

"You two lovers are the best."

"We are a wonderful threesome."

"Let's go see him before anyone finds out that we are at home."

How we managed to walk five blocks to Janko's school without being observed and mobbed by the press, well-wishers or even just neighbors astonished me. However, it was a treat. After weeks of intimately close contact with thousands of people, mostly strangers, it was pure joy to walk along the sidewalk holding Basha's hand and feeling the sun beating down on my face and the fresh air fill my lungs.

When we got to Janko's school, the kids were playing in the yard. We stood near the entrance and just watched him run, jump and swing. He was such a happy boy. We almost avoided breaking into his playtime, but I could not resist.

We walked in and when he saw me, he ran toward me like an Olympic sprinter and we hugged for a long time. I picked him up and whirled him around in the air. He did not speak and neither did I. Nothing needed to be said. Our closeness spoke volumes.

His teacher came up to us and said, "How good to have you home, Mr. Pollack. I know that Jon has missed you very much. He tells us every day, and proudly I have to say, where you are and what you are doing. He is amazing. Not every little fellow would be able to endure what he is facing with you out there on the campaign trail for weeks on end. You have a fine son, Mr. Pollack."

"And Mrs. Pollack," I added. "I am only half this team. Basha, Barbara, is the real saint in this family," I concluded.

"I did not mean to leave her out," Miss Mackey said. "Please forgive me, Mrs. Pollack."

"I knew what you meant. No apologies needed."

"While you are here, Mr. Pollack, would you mind talking to the class and telling them what you are doing. Give them a sense of what it means to be running for president of the United States."

"You are serious?" I asked her.

"Yes, most definitely. They need to learn as early as possible what it takes to be a good citizen of this country. Do you have time? I'm sure that you are a very busy man and I would understand if you could not do it right now."

"No. let's do it. What better time than right now!"

For the next hour, I sat with Janko's classmates and told them what I was doing, answered questions they had for me, asked them what they wanted most from their country and what did it mean to be an American, and ended the session with them by standing and pledging allegiance to the flag. I was enchanted with the entire class and when it was over, I thanked Miss Mackey for making me feel so welcome.

"Mr. Pollack, the pleasure has been all mine. You cannot imagine what it is like to be a young teacher and to have in my class the son of the next president of the United States." She smiled at me as she said that and I realized now that people were truly of the mindset that I was going to win this race. They believed there was no stopping my campaign. What I had to do was not disappoint them.

"Miss Mackey, thank you for taking good care of our son."

"You're welcome," she said.

Janko and I hugged each other. He was not embarrassed to do so. This made me more proud to see how much it meant to him to be in contact with his father. Our outward affection for one another was what created our internal bond.

Basha and I left the school. We were almost home, when the first of many groups of interested citizens met us in front of our home. They saw the bus and realized I was home again. They wanted to talk. Basha squeezed my hand and quickly departed entering the safety of our home.

I stood out on the sidewalk and entered into dialogue with a dozen or more people from nearby in the city and some from far away. Their questions, concerns and comments were similar to the ones I heard in every state that we had traveled in on the campaign trail.

"How are you going to stimulate job growth?"

"We must buy American and in so doing, we will put our neighbors to work."

"What can you do to stop the growing disparity between the wealthy and the middle class?"

"End the Bush Tax cuts and then revise the tax code so that all pay their fair share."

"How are you going to improve the education system in America?"

"Make a concerted push to limit class size, lengthen the school year, pay teachers more money, insure that public and not private, charter schools have the major share of resources and make the goal of 100% graduation for all American youth."

"What can you do to make the tax system fair?"

"Eliminate tax breaks like the 15% capital gains tax that makes investing more lucrative than working."

"When will we bring all our troops home and stop these costly wars?"

"Immediately."

"What are you going to do about the critical need to fix the decaying infrastructure in the country?"

"Designate the top 100 projects that need immediate reconstruction and authorize work to begin immediately. Then go after the next 100, and then the next and so on."

"What is the future of Social Security and Medicare?"

"We will secure their future by taking the money for Social Security out of the general operating fund and put it back into the trust, raise the cap on contributions from $106,000 to $1 million, and make sure that people participate fully in SS as well as their own 401-K."

"What can you do to improve the civility in the political arena?"

"You will not see any attack ads coming from my campaign."

"How are you holding up as a person?"

"Like a good steel worker. I can take the heat."

The last one was very personal. I thanked the woman for her concern and said, "I am doing just fine. I miss my family, but am home today and that is wonderful. My wife and I just walked down to our son's school, met with him, his teacher and his class. We spent an hour telling them about the campaign and what it means to be a good citizen. Now, we're home again and here I am meeting with you. I know that there is a movement in this country that transcends what I am doing. The movement is not left or right but American. We, all of us, citizens, want this country to work. We want our leaders to be respected. We want our systems to be efficient. We want our infrastructure to be safe. We want our schools to be effective. We want to believe in the goodness of our fellow citizens and not be suspicious of strangers and those who do not look like us. We want to know that if we get sick, we can afford the health care that will get us well again. Most of all, we want to work, make a decent living, own a home that keeps us safe, warm and protected from the elements, and now and then, have a vacation and just be happy in our own skin. If we can accomplish this in this campaign, I will feel like a billionaire because the country will be healthier and happier and I will have succeeded in my role as a catalyst for real change."

When they were finally gone, I stood in my front yard and looked around the place. Everything was peaceful. I was alone for a moment. I stared at my Grandmother's rose bushes that were sleeping now but would bloom in a month or two. I studied the garden that was lying fallow. All around me, the fecund earth was awaiting the first warm days of spring to awaken it from winter's slumber.

The black car parked on the side of the road a hundred yards away had not moved since I started talking to the group of people. It still did not move. I wondered if it were one of ours. I was almost tempted to walk over and ask, but thought twice about doing so. Instead, I pulled out my cell phone and called Big Jack.

"Yes, it's one of ours," he responded to my question.

"The car is pretty obvious," I said.

"It's supposed to be."

"How come it's not in front of the house?"

"Too obvious. Plus, it would deter groups like you just met from visiting and this is something that we don't want to stop."

"How safe was the group, Jack?"

"Safer than you think. How many people in that group were on the team?" he asked me.

"I don't know. How many?"

"That's for me to know and for you to find out. Next time, watch those who are around you and see which ones don't do any talking but are always watching the crowd and not you. Then you'll know."

"Jack, what would I do without you?"

"Find someone else to take charge of your security."

"I don't think so, Jack. This is not just a job to you. This has become a mission and I appreciate it from the bottom of my heart."

"I told you, Leo. We're relying on you to change this country. Anything less and we all lose. Now any other questions because I've got to get back to work."

"Nope. Thanks. We're on the road tomorrow, you know?"

"Already ahead of you. Lined up from here to infinity," he said.

"What?"

"Just a joke, man. Get with it. Anyway, we've got you covered across the country from Missouri, Colorado, Nevada, Arizona, New Mexico, back east to Michigan and beyond. No sweat."

"See you in the morning," I said.

"No you won't but I'll be with you. Call if you change your plans or need something really fast."

"Will do."

"I'm out of here." He hung up. No goodbye from him. He did not believe in goodbyes. He said they were too final. I agreed.

Chills raced through my body. The black car was gone. I did not see it move and I wondered what that meant. I went inside, closed the door, stood by the window and watched for fifteen minutes. Finally, it returned, parked in the same place it was before and did not move again. I was half tempted to call Jack and ask him if anything was happening, but decided to let it be.

Basha was cooking dinner. She was so happy to be making something for me that she was totally unaware of me when I walked into her kitchen. She almost dropped a pot of pasta as I kissed her on the neck.

"LEO," She screamed.

"I love you," I said.

"I almost dropped the entire pot. You are cruel. You are mean."

"But you love me anyway?"

She turned around and said, "More than you'll ever know. Now leave me alone while I try and cook this meal. Janko will be home shortly. You and he can go and play and I'll let you know when dinner will be ready."

"Lasagna! One of my favorite meals," I said, tasting the sauce simmering on a side burner.

"Hey, take your dirty fingers out of that pot," she scolded me. "I don't know where you've had your hands in the past ten minutes."

"I wasn't picking my nose, Mom," I said in a sheepish voice like a little kid being confronted.

"Leo, go and relax. Read. Watch TV. Do something."

"I'm watching you. This is such a treat. Just seeing you in the kitchen makes my heart flutter. I've missed you, Basha. That's all there is to it."

She turned around, wrapped her arms around my neck, and kissed me so hard that my heart stopped fluttering and beat like a jungle drum.

"There, now, you've had some sugar. Go and relax and let me enjoy preparing this meal for my two men."

"Will do," I said.

I left the room, went into the study, sat down and just enjoyed the silence. "Strange," I thought. "No phone calls today." I wondered what that meant.

It dawned on me then that I had not seen Gram since we came into the house. I went down to his room and there he was sound asleep on his bed. I covered him with a throw. I guess the long trip wore him out.

Somehow, I was not tired. There was no way that I could take a nap right now. I was feeling something akin to jet lag but even more intense. What it was had no name. I returned to the living room, sat down, and turned on the TV. MSNBC had coverage all day of the Florida results and the next caucuses and primaries. The Republicans were now in Colorado, Nevada, Missouri, Minnesota and Maine.

Gram came up from his room. "What did I miss?" he asked.

"Oh, let's see. Big Jack cracked a few heads of protesters out in front of the house. The Liberty Bus was towed away for being parked illegally. Janko ran away from home because we would not buy him a cell phone to carry back and forth to school. We had an earth quake and somehow you slept through it."

"Leo, I believe you about as much as I believe my ex wife who used to tell me that she was the happiest woman in the world."

"Whatever happened to you, Gram? If you want to tell me, that's fine. If not, that's fine too."

Gram looked at me and thought for a moment. "Leo, if I had going for me what you have going for you, I'd be back in Colorado and not here chasing around the country in a bus after windmills."

"What do I have that you didn't?"

"My wife didn't like my being gone all the time. She was selfish or jealous, I don't know. It eroded our relationship. We're still friends but we've been through for many years."

"You think you'll find someone else that may fulfill the void that you sometimes feel?"

"I like my aloneness. No, I'm not anxious to give that up. Besides, I make friends easily and now I have you, Basha, Janko, Al, Big Jack and the rest of America. I'm eminently happy. I mean that."

"I'm glad because we sure like having you as part of our family."

"Yes, I know that and it is greatly appreciated."

At that very moment, Janko burst into the room and seeing us both together cried out, "Daddy, Uncle Gram," and ran to me first and gave me a big hug and then scooted over to Gram and hugged him.

"What are we going to do tonight?" he asked me first and then Uncle Gram.

"What would you like to do?" Gram asked first.

"Go for a hike, Uncle Gram. Can we?"

"Leo?"

"We need to check with Mom first," I said.

Janko ran out of the room. I could hear him pleading his case. Next, I could hear him setting the table. Finally, he was back with an invitation to come to dinner.

In our family, sitting down to dinner was always a special moment, and it was even more so with the amount of time being spent away from home. We held hands and Janko led us in saying grace. We ate heartily. Basha was happy to see us gorge ourselves on the food lovingly prepared by her hands.

As we finished, Janko asked to be excused. He was and immediately he started to clear the table and prepare to wash the dishes. We sat and chatted while he ran the water and started to wash them. He was finished in no time.

"I'll dry the dishes while you fellows go for a hike. Enjoy," Basha said.

We were gone in a flash. A few miles later, we turned around and headed home. Janko was happy to be out with us and we were enjoying the freedom of walking around town without any pressing engagements.

When we got home, Janko ran up to do his homework. Gram pulled out his clipboard and studied his game plan. I made a few phone calls. Basha sat quietly in the room and mended a few of Janko's shirts. Anyone looking in would think that our home represented the typical American family relaxing at home after dinner on any given night. How inaccurate that assessment would have been.

Basha and I went up to read to Janko and then tuck him in. As I prepared to leave his room, he asked, "When are you coming back again, Daddy?"

I turned around, kneeled down next to his bed again, and said, "I'll be home as soon as we get through about a dozen states. I don't think I'll be gone for more than two weeks."

"That's a long time, Daddy. I'm going to miss you."

"I'll miss you, too. But please, Janko, I need your help. You have to look after your Mom while I am gone. You are the man in the house. You do what she asks. Keep her happy. Make her proud."

"I will Daddy."

I kissed him goodnight. "I love you, my little man."

"I love you Daddy."

Basha and I left him alone in his room. By the time we were heading downstairs, we knew he would be fast asleep. He was an exceptional sleeper.

Gram had gone to bed.

Basha and I settled down on the couch. She leaned into my shoulder and wrapped her arms around my waist. We did not talk for a long time.

"We're okay aren't we?" I asked her.

"Yes, my friend, lover and husband, we are more than okay."

"I have left you so much alone, Basha, I have to make sure."

"Leo, you are the man of my dreams. I love everything about you."

"Everything?" I challenged her.

"Yes, well almost everything."

"What is the withhold?"

"You don't kiss me enough, you silly fool."

I made up for lost time. We did not breathe for a dozen minutes.

"Let's go to bed," I offered.

"Quickly. No stops along the way!" Basha said.

Holding hands, we ran up the stairs quietly so we would not disturb Janko or Gram, slipped in silence into our dark bedroom and loved the night away.

Around the world, wars continued to be fought, children continued dying of malnutrition, banks continued to speculate on which country would next default, and governments continued to function as proxy parents for their citizens causing individual decision making to be an almost forgotten art, but in our bedroom, the only continuity was the kissing that cemented our love from now to eternity.

30. Go West Young Man

Our road trip began in the early morning the next day, and by midday, we were already in Indiana and heading west toward Nevada, the next caucus state. This was my first real trip west. I was as excited as a kid on Christmas morning. I was going to cross the Mississippi River and the Rocky Mountains. Al was all smiles because he loved an adventure. He had driven across the country numerous times and said that there was nothing more enjoyable than to cross the "Old Man" for the first time. I was enchanted with the idea.

Every time we stopped for gas, we were approached by people who had heard about our campaign, came over to meet me, talk, share their ideas, complain about the government, and now and then, tell me that I was nuts. I smiled at the critics and asked them what they wanted from their government, from their leaders and what could I do to earn their respect and win their vote. This confused them. Since I was not defensive, they did not know how to respond. When they asked me what I thought about President Obama and the other Republican candidates, I simply said, "They are all fine American men and care deeply about our country. I disagree with their policies. I am running for president because I believe that I can do a better job and better represent the 160 million working people who do not have a voice." They acknowledged my desire to be upbeat, clean and pure, not attacking my opponents, but giving them their due. I thanked them for their interest in our campaign, encouraged them to vote for me, donate a dollar or two to the effort and said my goodbyes.

Travel broadens the individual. The activity reveals the vastness of the land away from home. One's neighborhood is limited in its breath and scope. Out on the open road, the skyline extends beyond the imagination making the world appear to extend to infinity. In the fixed world of maps, there is a finite distance ahead of wherever the traveler currently is located. In the mind's eye, there is no limit to the horizon.

Horace Greeley invoked the challenge to easterners when he said, "Go West, young man." What he meant was open to interpretation. We were going west with a specific mission in mind. Greeley favored westward expansion. He saw the fertile farmland of the west as an ideal place for people willing to work hard for the opportunity to succeed. The phrase came to symbolize the idea that agriculture could solve many of the nation's problems of poverty and unemployment characteristic of the big cities of the East. It is one of the most commonly quoted sayings from the nineteenth century and may have had some influence on the course of American history. Some sources have claimed the phrase was derived from the following advice in Greeley's July 13, 1865 editorial in the New York Tribune. The article encouraged Civil War veterans to take advantage of the Homestead Act and colonize the public lands. The actual quote said, "Washington is not a place to live in. The rents are high, the food is bad, the dust is disgusting and the morals are deplorable. Go west, young man, Go West and grow up with the country." I wondered just how much we would grow up as we traversed the expanse of this great land.

Beyond Indiana, we passed through Lincoln Country. President Lincoln was born in Kentucky but his family moved to Illinois. He grew up in the state and it claimed him as its own. He was really a southerner, married one, and so his stance on slavery was an anomaly. We drifted southwest toward the great city of St. Louis.

When I saw the arch, tears welled up in my eyes. "There it is," I exclaimed. Gram said nothing. Al carefully negotiated the bus through the lines of heavy traffic. This was the point of debarking for the Lewis and Clark 1803 expedition. What were they thinking when they pushed off from the safe shores of the newly burgeoning city and disappeared northwest into the vast unknown? Their journals were difficult to read, but so informative. Ironically, they did not face any real violence on their entire journey. Three years later, they made it home safely. But three years after returning home safely, Meriwether Lewis was dead, possibly as a result of a self-inflicted gunshot wound, or possibly because he was murdered. To this day, we still do not know. Forensic science was not in vogue back in 19th century America. Their contribution to our history remains. They were the first important American explorers and their work led to the rapid development of the west. Sadly, those who followed did not go in peace as Lewis and Clark did. These two men met more than twenty indigenous tribes along the way. No record of hostilities between the tribes and the expedition exist. This was an amazing record, and one that could serve as a modern template for effective diplomacy. What did they do right? We could model their behavior and perhaps find a solution to the Arab-Israeli Conflict. Who knows what might happen if we try to do something different than we have for the past fifty years.

We stopped beneath the archway and I took pictures. Al and Gram had seen the arch before so they were not duly impressed like I was. If I passed this way every day for the rest of my life, I imagined I would feel the same way. Towering into the sky more than 630 feet, the arch symbolized the expansion of Americans into the west. I really wanted to see the arch at night.

In the small parking lot near the arch, we walked around and took pictures. Gram took one that had the arch superimposed above me as if I were holding it above my head. Al wanted one so Gram took his picture the same way. While they were fussing around, a tourist group asked if I were connected with Leo Pollack's campaign.

"I'm Leo Pollack," I said. Immediately, there was an event. The more I talked, the more people began showing up. I assumed those present were texting their friends and that was how the crowd swelled until the parking lot was a mass of people. Soon, I could see the local gendarmerie beginning to gather with them. I hoped Gram, Al and Big Jack would run interference for me.

What the people wanted to know most of all was what were we going to do to put people back to work. I introduced the newest principle in our campaign.

"Here is the principle that you and I and all Americans need to adopt. 'Americans helping Americans. What does this mean? Simply, you and I will not buy anything that is not made in America by Americans. By buying American, we are putting our neighbors back to work. If I buy a Chevrolet Cruse made at the Lordstown Assembly Plant outside my home town in Ohio, I am putting my neighbors back to work. If you buy a Cruze, you are doing the same thing even though they are not your immediate neighbors."

Someone asked what can you do when what you need is not made in America.

"Find the company that used to make the product in the United States and write or call and encourage it to move their manufacturing operations back to the USA. Recently, I wanted to buy something from LL Bean, a quintessential American company located in Freeport, Maine. Everything I looked at in its catalogue was imported. Nothing I wanted to buy was domestically manufactured. I wrote a note to the company and got a reply stating that it was sorry that I could not find what I wanted and it would do better in offering more American made goods. We won't change the conditions overnight, but we can begin to force companies to 'insource' versus 'outsource' their production capabilities."

A woman asked where could she go to donate money to the campaign. I pointed to the bus and our webpage. "You can donate by logging on to **www.ringingthelibertybell.org**. We will be glad to take your one, five, ten or twenty dollar donation."

A man asked what the reason was that we were not accepting any higher donations.

"Thank you for asking that question because it goes to the heart of this entire campaign. If a thousand people gave me a thousand dollars, I would have a million dollars in donations. I would have 1000 people supporting me. Now, if a million people give me a dollar I would have 1,000,000 supporters. I would rather have one million, one dollar donors than one thousand, thousand dollar donors. When you tally votes, a million votes will always beat a thousand votes. We are a movement of people and not money. Yes, we need money to run the campaign. Yes, we can win this election if the working people of this country, folks like all of you, donate a dollar, five, ten or twenty and vote for me. Our voice will be heard because we will represent the working people of this country. The voices of 160 million working people will drown out the few voices of that one percent of the population with lots of money but few votes."

The final question I fielded came from an elderly woman who could barely speak loudly enough for me to hear her. She wanted to know what I was going to do to make sure that she continued getting her social security check every month.

"We realize the need to secure the future for those who are already on Social Security and for those who someday hope to get their fair share. Social Security is not a Ponzi scheme as that one governor claimed. If we had privatized Social Security back in 2003, imagine what might have happened to the money that was invested in the stock market. No, we will raise the cap on contributions to social security, take the money out of the general operating budget and place it back into the trust, and most of all, revise the retirement age over the next 45 years to increase from 67 to 70 years of age."

I stopped taking questions because I was getting the sign from Gram and Al to end it. For the next half hour, I shook hands with people, had my picture taken with hosts of well-wishers, signed autographs, handed out campaign flyers, laughed, listened learned just how excited Americans were to have one of their own running for the highest office in the land. I said my goodbyes and encouraged everyone to get actively involved in the campaign to insure a better future.

Easing our way onto the freeway, we headed west on I-70. Gram navigated us that way because he would be able to see his kids for a few hours. Al wanted to take the central route because we would be able to pass through Colorado twice. . I was just happy to be heading west. After all, what did I know? I was just along for the ride.

"That was a very productive stop," I said to the team. "The people were really receptive. I just hope this continues all across the country as we head west."

Al wheeled into the passing lane and headed the bus toward I-70 west of St. Louis. We were in the "Show Me" state that was going to be holding its primary in a week or so. We were creating waves. Hopefully as we passed through the state on the way back east, we could spend more time here.

Gram was playing around on the internet. He asked me if I had seen our Facebook page. I said, "No, I didn't even know we had one."

"Three-hundred and fifty thousand likes," Gram said. "Not bad. You're a popular fellow, Leo. Come and look."

I got up and went to see the site. Given that I had never seen it before, it was truly amazing.

"Judy Bream and Fritz were the promoters. Fritz did the technical work and Judy did the entries. Nice, huh?" Gram asked.

"Sure is. Now what good is it?"

"Leo, 700 million people worldwide are on Facebook. If you are not on the site, you don't count. That's as simple as I can make it."

"You don't have to be demeaning," I said. "I didn't know."

"There are Facebook, Twitter, YouTube, Yahoo Messenger, Netmeeting, chats, a whole host of social networking sites that are increasingly becoming the go to places for anyone who wants to get out his or her message."

"I'm glad someone thought to put up a page then because I am sure that I would not have done so. I only carry a cell phone because I have to and not because I want to."

"What makes you anti-technology?" Gram asked.

"Nothing. I see the value in the technology. I appreciate its power. I acknowledge the importance of being able to connect anywhere in time and space. I just don't think that the world is that much better off because I can instantly communicate to anyone who wants to know that I just belched and it feels good to no longer have a belly full of gas."

Al laughed and said, "I agree with you, Leo. My kids are always after me to get this or that new gadget. I tell them you earn the money and then go buy it. I don't want any part of it. No way. Give me a simple flip phone and I'm happy. I'm intimidated by the 'smart phones' cause they're smarter than I am and I don't like that."

We rode along for miles watching the Missouri countryside pass by. When we crossed the Missouri River again, I was so excited that I wanted Al to stop so I could take pictures.

"Can't stop, Leo, no turn outs. Illegal," he said as he rolled over the bridge and kept on driving.

"This is what's wrong with America today," I said. "This is my first time seeing the Missouri River, the river of Lewis and Clark Expedition fame, and I can't stop and take a picture of it because the freeway doesn't have a turnout. What is wrong with this picture? I'm going to change this when we get to Washington," I concluded.

"What are you going to do, Leo? Put turnouts on every bridge on every river in the country so people can stop to take pictures?"

"No, but we're going to slow progress down to the point of its being manageable."

"What do you mean?"

"What I mean is this. Don't text me. Call me. Better yet, don't call me. Come and see me. There is nothing so important that you can't stop what you're doing and walk over to where I am and say, 'I was thinking about something'. We need to learn to be more social. This is what I mean."

"So you don't believe that Facebook makes us more connected?"

"No, not at all. The medium is one dimensional, two dimensional at most. Meeting with a person in real time is three-dimensional. This is much preferred and though more time consuming, more human as well."

"You're an anachronism, Leo. When you're president, you'll be working 22 hours a day and will need every device known to man and then some to get the job done," Gram said.

"All those devices have not solved the Arab-Israeli Conflict and you know why?"

"Why, tell me."

"Because the Arabs and Israelis will not sit down at the table in Jerusalem, a city they both covet, and decide, once and for all, how to get along with one another. We talk to Abbas on the phone. We talk to Netanyahu on the phone. We don't talk to them face to face in the same room at the same time. One of the reasons that the Camp David Accords succeeded was that then President Carter, whom so many people did not like, was willing to talk to people face to face. He forced Begin and Sadat to face each other and make peace. They finally did. This was real diplomacy because there were three dimensions, not just two."

"I agree that it is better to do face to face," Gram said, "but sometimes it is just not possible."

"Where it is not possible, do what is possible. Otherwise, strive for the ideal," I concluded.

"You're not getting away from technology, Leo. Let's face it. As time progresses, we will see even greater uses of tech gadgets and that's just the way it is."

"I don't mind technology and would not want to go back in time one minute. However, a text message is not the same as a call. A call is not the same as a face to face discussion. Yes, the technology saves time. I don't know if it achieves the ultimate goal and that is to improve communication."

Gram dropped the subject because he realized I was a 'Neanderthal' when it came to laptops, phones, pads, pods and anything that was smaller than a sledge hammer or a spud bar.

I was curious. I rarely got phone calls. This realization caused me to pull out my phone and check to see if it were on. Yes, it was. I wondered. Dialling John Gallagher's number, I waited as the phone rang. He answered promptly.

"Leo here, John. How are you?"

"Great! Great! How are you doing today or should I ask, where in the world are you right now?"

"You don't know?" I asked him.

"Should I?" John reacted to my inquiry.

"I would think that you'd have a GPS unit on this bus and would be in constant contact with us. Does that make sense?" I asked.

"Actually, Leo, we do know where you are. You know Big Jack. He doesn't like to have you worry that we are worried about you. Yes, I do know where you are and do all the time. Your signal is pinged to my cell and I can find you any time I have a signal which is all the time."

"How come I don't get phone calls? We were talking about phones, text messaging and the internet, Facebook and other media formats, and I was just wondering why I do not get many calls?"

"You really want to know?" John asked.

"Yes, is that a fair request?" I asked him in return.

"Sure, Leo, I was just being facetious. Let me make this as simple as I can. You don't get a lot of calls because we filter everything. People can call Gram, Jack, Judy, Carol, Richard, even Al, but not you directly. We take the brunt of the business calls. We thought this would free you from hassles. If you want us to stop, we can do that, but it's up to you."

I thought about what he was telling me and I said, "No, no, I think the current arrangement is working fine. I was just curious. That's all."

"We probably should have said something to you. You know, asked your opinion. We were trying to streamline the communication process as much as possible. There is so much going on that we sometimes need to make spontaneous decisions. I think you can appreciate this."

"I agree. No, I don't mind. Listen to this, John. This is really nothing major. However, when something related to our overall platform is on the table, I absolutely must be in on the decision. For instance, there can be no change to our donation policy. I mean it. Ones, fives, tens and twenties are all we are taking. Nothing more than a twenty. This must be inviolate. I don't want to be explaining to the national press a few months from now why we're accepting donations from major corporate donors. This would end our relationship immediately."

"Done," John said. "That will not happen. I don't want that to happen any more than you do. I believe in what we're doing and that is what makes these twenty hour days tolerable."

"You are crazy, John," I said. "Nothing is worth that kind of effort."

"America is, Leo."

"You don't have a life," I said.

"I have more of a life now than I did a few months ago. Before this campaign started, I was getting ready to box up this union hall and move on to greener pastures. Now we have a cause to believe in and it's all because of you and your campaign."

"Our campaign. Now I'm glad to hear that, so we're clear?"

"Clear as mud!" John said.

"John?"

"Just kidding, Leo."

"Now, one more thing. How are we doing on organizing the state-wide campaigns? I know that we talked about this months ago, but I haven't asked about it since that time."

"We are doing exceptionally well," John said. "Right now, we have at least one volunteer at the hall coordinating with someone in each of the states. These are direct connections. They interface with each other and then report to regional leaders who then report to me. You see, Leo, we have things in control and we are making extraordinary headway. You would be proud to see the war board down in the cellar. We have converted that space into what we call the 'war room' and from there we can monitor and evaluate every move across the nation. This is one high tech operation. You'd be proud."

"I'm proud and in awe and grateful that you are in charge of it and I am out on the road doing face to face meetings."

"Leo, you'll catch on eventually."

"I don't want to, John. Really, I enjoy this part of the process. To take on what you're doing would drive me nuts. Thanks for being you and doing all you do for the people."

"Leo, it is my pleasure."

"Next time we're in town for more than a minute, I want to stop by, meet all the volunteers and thank them personally for their devotion and hard work."

"They would appreciate that immensely, Leo," John said.

"John, if we can do it legally, can we compensate the volunteers for their work, mileage, just anything to take the pressure off them?"

"I'll look into it. This would be a nice gesture. I agree."

"You guys take care and yes, we'll keep monitoring you to insure that you are okay."

"I'm sure you will," I said. We hung up.

"Strange," I said to myself. "There are many things I'm not being told." Rather than asking any more questions, I just dropped the subject.

Missou signs greeted us as we got closer to Columbia, Missouri, home of the University of Missouri Tigers. We decided to pull in and get some fuel. While we were near the campus, I told the fellows I wanted to see the place. Al drove near the center of the commons. Before long, we had a string of vehicles following us around the small college town. Finally, to keep things from becoming too chaotic, Al stopped in a small parking lot. We got out and spent the next two hours talking to people, answering questions, doing what politicians do. I was impressed with the level of enthusiasm that was present in the heartland of America. Missouri was and still is the state that most reflects the Independent voter in America. If we could win the hearts and minds of the Independents in Missouri, we would be in good shape with Independents all across the country. I was careful to address the hopes and fears of all those who came over to meet me. I was elated that there was not a naysayer in the crowd. Since I presented only a positive message, this might have accounted for the lack of negativity in the people. After some time, I thanked everyone for their support, encouraged them to visit our home page, donate a dollar or two, and most of all, asked them to give me their vote in the general election.

As we drove out of town, I was waiting for the call.

I answered the phone and listened. "I got it. Thanks."

Gram said, "Big Jack kicked your ass again, didn't he? You're a hard head, Leo. When you change plans, tell Jack."

"How come you don't call him then?"

"I did, but you'd already made the decision. He is always scurrying to keep up with your whims. Leo, we have already taken a shotgun blast. We are heading into the west. Out here, folks carry guns on their hips like you carry your wallet."

"I got it, Gram."

We headed toward Kansas City, Kansas and nearby, Independence, Missouri, home of one of my favorite presidents, Harry S. Truman. His role modelling is what made me get up and take a "constitutional walk" every day. Though I missed many days hiking now that we were on the road most of the time, when I could, nothing beat a brisk walk to restore the creative juices. What made Truman interesting was he would do press conferences while he walked along the sidewalks. A story about him is told that when he left Washington, he put the pen he had used as president back on the desk and said, "This belongs to the American people." Amazing guy. Truman was a classic American character.

Riding across the Kansas City inner belt, we passed the Kansas City Chief's and Royal's stadiums. I gawked at them out the window. "Will you check these out?" I said to my teammates. I got no response because Al was busy concentrating on the traffic and Gram was surfing the web.

George Brett played baseball in Royal stadium. He was one of the greatest hit men to play the game. Probably the most famous Kansas City Chief to play in the past thirty years was the aging, Joe Montana, who came from the San Francisco Forty-Niners to the Chiefs and ended his career with them. The stadiums were off the freeway. I could imagine what the traffic must be like on game days.

The cattle pens were gone, but the railroad yards were extensive and indicated just how important Kansas City was in the West-East commerce grid. We continued west and headed into the great breadbasket of America.

Our days were getting longer and longer. About ten o'clock, we decided it was time to end this day so we found a quiet rest area, pulled off into the shadows and shut down for the night. Al had been driving for 14 hours. He was tired. He would not let me drive even when I offered to do so. He said that it was his responsibility to make sure that wherever we were going that we arrived safely.

As the day ended, Gram and I walked around the rest area to get some exercise. I called Jack. He knew we were mobile. We did not see him or his people. The cool night air felt exceptionally brisk and clean.

As we slept, we dreamed of the world as it could be, not as it was, and that promoted wonderful, fulfilling and complete rest.

31. Rocky Mountain High

Our morning routine was simple. Al checked the vehicle. Gram read the email and made phone calls. Jack would stop by and insure that he had our itinerary locked down. I cooked breakfast. We ate with gusto. We talked with passion. We were a team and enjoyed each other immensely.

When the road opened up in front of us and I could see forever, I was amazed at the vastness of the American land mass. I could not keep my eyes off the horizon.

The skies were an azure blue. Though it was January, I could see where wheat farmers had planted winter wheat for harvest in the spring. Some of the green shoots were sprouting a half foot out of the frozen earth. Life cannot be stopped from seeking sunlight. I marveled at the expansive stretches of wheat fields stretching as far as my eyes could see.

"Look at the massive cloud bank ahead of us there on the horizon. I wonder if that means we're heading into some kind of storm front," I said to the guys.

They both laughed.

"What's so funny?"

"Those aren't clouds," Gram said.

"What are they?" I asked.

Together, Gram and Al cried out, "The Rocky Mountains!"

"No, really? According to the highway sign, we're still 110 miles from Denver. They can't be the mountains, can they?"

"Trust me, Leo. Those are the Rocky Mountains," Gram said.

"Wow!" was all that I could say and stared at them for the next twenty minutes almost without blinking. They were magnificent. Each mile that we drove, we got closer to them and soon, I could distinctly make out peak after peak covered in snow rising up out of the horizon and pointing to the heavens. In my entire lifetime, I had never seen such a picture of awesome grandeur.

"The Rocky Mountains!" I uttered a number of times.

"You would think that someone just gave you a new toy to play with," Gram said to me while he surfed the internet on the laptop.

"It is almost like that," I replied. "You live here. This is nothing new. For me, this is a once in a lifetime experience. Can you still remember when you first gazed on the mountains?"

"No, can't say that I do," Gram said.

"How about you, Al?"

He thought for a moment. "Must've been 1998, the year we took the RV and traveled across the country with the five youngest kids. What an adventure that was. We didn't hit the Rockies in Colorado. We were in Wyoming, and crossed the Bighorns first and then saw the Rockies when we got to Yellowstone Park. We were all impressed."

"See, I'm not the only one."

"This might impress you even more," Gram said staring at his computer screen. "There is a company in Colorado called Denver Casting. They heard about our campaign. They want to make replicas of the Liberty Bell and sell them. But, there is a rub. The company is non-unionized and they pay very poorly. The real tension is the company has threatened to move offshore unless the workers take a pay cut and drop any idea about organizing. Thus far, everything has been calm but get this. Finally, the workers are preparing to strike today. We are right in the glide path to be there on the grounds of Denver Casting sometime around 2 pm."

"No way," I said. "This is amazing. What are the issues causing the strike?"

"The company pays less than ten dollars an hour and no benefits. The employees want a fair, living wage."

"We need to help. What a choice to make. On one hand, the company wants to make liberty bells to support our campaign. On the other hand, they are paying their employees poorly. No easy choice here. Let's do it. We have to support the workers."

"Call Jack and give him the low down. This may get ugly."

"Ugly or not, we need to be there."

I called Jack and told him what we wanted to do. He gave me explicit instructions as to when and how to get out if the situation became overheated. I accepted his guidelines.

"Jack says it's a go."

"Now, there is more to this story," Gram said.

"How can it get any better? This is what we stand for: working people making a fair wage."

"Another company is aware of the plight of the workers and has made tee shirts and flags at cost and is selling them to the striking workers. The tees are bright yellow with a blue liberty bell on them."

"Unbelievable," Al chortled from behind the wheel. "This is a made to order movie scene. We will be stars in this production when we drive the Liberty Bus onto the set."

"Oh, it gets even better. Judy says that the New York Times counter on the front page of the paper is drawing such attention that it is being enlarged and an article is being written to explain the significance of the counter. More free publicity. She said that people are calling and asking for something to put on their cars so Fritz designed a Liberty Bell Logo with your name on it that can be put on a car window and it is being distributed on the web site right now. Bumper stickers are being printed too."

"Judy's a ball of fire," I cried out. "What an awesome idea."

"There's more. She said the Face book page is being hit exponentially every day. It crashed twice this past week. Fritz had to get more bandwidth to keep it up and running. Anyway, the people are asking for your itinerary and so don't be surprised if the crowds start to get larger as we move back and forth across the country. I emailed her and said to put the Denver Casting stop on the page. We may have a massive amount of people there when we arrive."

"Holy Smoke!" was all that I could utter.

"Now, Leo, isn't modern technology wonderful?" Gram asked jibbing me a little for my comments from the day before.

"Will wonders never cease," I exclaimed.

"Leo, there is more."

"Unbelievable," Al said, laughing heartily. "This is what we were waiting for. See, Leo, we just needed to reach critical mass. Go ahead, Gram, lay it on us."

"If that hasn't tripped your trigger, then this one will definitely make your day," Gram said. "Judy got a request from a movie theatre chain to live stream your speeches. They want to be able to charge something for the service, but she was not sure what to tell them. What are your thoughts on this one?"

I sat back stunned. All this was coming at me too fast. "Gram, Al, this is beyond belief. I can't imagine what this will mean to the overall campaign. I am dumbfounded."

"Well, get yourself together. Judy needs an answer. What do you think, Leo, Al?"

"I think that people should just make a donation. Half goes to the theatre and the other half to the campaign," Al said.

"Great idea, Al," I said. "I like that. Simple. If someone can't pay, they still can get inside. If they can, the theatre makes money and so does the campaign. Al, you're a genius."

"Thank ya, thank ya very much," Al said doing his best Elvis impersonation.

"I'll call Judy and tell her our decision."

"You like that, too, Gram?" I asked.

"Sure. Simple and takes care of everyone."

Gram called Judy and was on the line with her for about twenty minutes. In the mean time, I stared at the mountains and tried to digest all that I had heard in the last half hour. We were roaring ahead like a runaway locomotive. Our limited resources would no longer be a limiting factor. We would be tapping into the mass media in a number of ways and this would enhance our ability to reach out and spread our message. No, I did not fully comprehend Face book, Twitter, and the "smart phone technology", but they were certainly creating magic in our world.

"Done," Gram, reported. "Judy is making it happen right now. We will be using our own videotaping capabilities to upload mp3 files to the web and then the theatre will take it from there. Given the amount of speeches that you will be making, the theatres will be showing you every day. Couple this with YouTube video and Twitter feeds, Leo, you will be a household name in less than a few days. You will be as famous as Andy Warhol."

"Who?" I asked.

"You don't know who Andy Warhol is?" Gram asked.

"I've heard the name but what did he do?"

"He was an avante garde artist from Pittsburgh who became famous for painting a replica of a Campbell Soup can."

"A what?" I asked.

"You heard me, a Campbell Soup can," Gram replied.

"He should have become infamous," Al said. "If he were from Pittsburgh, he should have painted a Heinz ketchup bottle."

"What is this world coming to," I uttered. "Painting soup cans."

"Big money was paid for that painting," Gram said. "Anyway, this movement is rapidly coming alive."

"And where it will stop, nobody knows," Al chuckled.

"Here, check it out," Gram said. "This is the New York Times front page. See the counter on the bottom. In real time, we are watching as the money flows into the campaign account."

Gram and I stared at the screen. We were well over $10 million and counting.

"That is more money than all of the guys down in the mill will make in a lifetime," I said.

"Sad too, because we'll burn it up in no time, once we start running real campaign ads during the general campaign," Gram said. "Romney spent $17 million in Florida alone trying to win the primary. Imagine what it will cost in the general election with three of us flooding the airways with our own ads."

"I can't," I said. "This kind of stuff is mindboggling. Are we going to be ready for that?"

"Question is can you get ready?" Gram asked me directly.

"I feel like I'm running on a speeding treadmill and I can't get off."

"Do you want to get off?"

"No. I just feel like I'm speeding and can't get off even if I wanted to do so."

"I hope you don't," Al said. "We've just started to make the big time and this is when it will start to get really fun."

"And dangerous," Gram said. "We can't make any mistakes like these fools on the Republican side. Every day one or the other opens his mouth and inserts foot. It is amazing. Romney commented that he was not worried about the rich people because they can take care of themselves or the poor people because they have a safety net, but he was worried about the middle class because they were struggling. The outcry could be heard all over the country. Poor people have a safety net. What was he smoking? Poor people don't have a safety net any more than middle class people do."

"What did he mean then?" Al asked.

"I don't know," Gram cried out. "Who knows what he's thinking half the time. Here's a guy that makes $57,000 a day from his investments and pretends he really knows what is going on with the majority of Americans. No wonder his favorability ratings are dropping dramatically. He has piles of money to smear his competitors, but what he is lacking is human decency and a sense of the needs of the common man and woman."

"Hell, I've never made more than $57,000 in a year," Al said.

"You and me, Al. We slave for an honest buck or two. Somehow, there is something wrong with this picture."

"Sure is," Gram said. "He made his money by buying and selling companies. He didn't make anything. When a company he bought made money, so did he. When a company he purchased lost money and was sold or went bankrupt, people lost their jobs, but he and his company made money anyway. His business was a win-lose proposition."

"No wonder we're in financial trouble today. We don't make the things we need to live our lives and we wonder why we can't make ends meet. This has naturally got to change," I proclaimed.

"Let's win this election and fix this situation. Now, how far are we out from Denver? Let me see." Gram studied the streets and trips program on his laptop and gave us an ETA.

"I'm going to do a little research on this Denver Cast Company so you'll have some ammunition to use when you get ready to let the ball drop, okay?" Gram asked.

"That will be helpful."

We sat and digested what we had just learned. I was amazed that so much had happened in such a short amount of time. Judy was really cooking on all four burners. She and Gram were developing a great working relationship. I wished, for his sake, that he would find more than that with her. He said it could not be, but who could tell what time might bring to both of them.

Riding up over a ridge, we could see the entire city of Denver stretched out before us. As we descended down into the bowl that cradled the "Mile High City" we started to watch for the exit we needed to take us to Denver Casting. Gram filled my ears with facts about the company and I did my best to absorb as much as I could.

Exiting the outer belt, we drove along Arapaho Boulevard for quite a while heading southwest toward the factory. Outside the window, we started to notice the traffic increasing.

"Look behind us fellows," Al said, pointing at his passenger side mirror. We did and our eyes bugged.

As far back as we could see a steady stream of traffic was following us. My initial impression was a funeral procession, but we were not the hearse and we were coming to bring life not death to the working people at Denver Casting.

"This will be one heck of a day to remember," I said.

"Let's hope so," Gram replied. "We've got a chance to get this one on the live video feed, YouTube and Face book all in one day."

"We're almost there," Al said. "I can see the factory from here."

We pulled around a slight bend in the road. There was Denver Casting. Right in front of the building, the people were already assembled to strike. Al carefully weaved through the dense traffic. A fleet of police cars was pulled off the side just past the main entrance to the factory.

"Do we have a contact here?" I asked Gram.

"Let me call Judy and find out what she knows." He did. In thirty seconds, Gram said, "Jim Young is the leader of sorts. She says he's been the main spokesperson thus far."

"We'll look for him," I said.

"What the hell!" Al exclaimed. We all looked out the window.

Police cars with lights flashing and sirens blaring secured the area.

"Here we go!" Gram cried out. "Welcome to the Revolution!"

"Let's get the camera ready, and get out there with the people," I said.

I stepped off the bus, I heard a loud cry, and then my name was being chanted. I waved to everyone as I walked back to the rear of the bus where the police were starting to pile out of a half dozen cars.

Walking up to the first car, I asked the officer who was standing in front of it, "What seems to be the problem, officer?"

"Who are you?" he asked me rather gruffly.

"My name is Leo Pollack, officer. And you are?"

"You can read can't you?" I looked at his badge.

"Officer Clanahan, nice to meet you. What seems to be the problem?"

"You coming into town is the problem," he said.

"My coming into town? I'm confused, sir. I don't understand."

"We heard you were coming and that you were here to do some speechmaking and that is against the law here in Denver."

"Officer, I'm not sure what you mean? Speechmaking is a guaranteed first amendment right and I haven't even said a word yet, so what I'm doing here is just coming into town to see some people that have mutual interests. That's all."

"We got the word you were coming. Look at that caravan backed up down the road," he said pointing at more than a hundred cars lined up behind the cop cars. If the black and whites would want to move, they could not. All the cars and people piling out of them boxed them in. A massive crowd was forming in front of the main gate to Denver Casting.

"Officer, may I help you, I'm Jim Young and I'm here to meet with Mr. Pollack. In fact, I invited him. No, better yet," he said, waving his hand across the vast expanse of the crowd, "We invited him to come and meet with us today."

"You got a permit to have this gathering right here, blocking traffic and making a nuisance of yourselves?"

"Officer, last time I checked, coming to my workplace and meeting with my friends and colleagues was not making a nuisance. What do you think Leo?"

I smiled broadly and asked Clanahan, "What would you like us to do?"

He stared at me and did not respond immediately. Finally, he said, "Pack up and go home. But I know you aren't going to do that. So what I want is that you clear this street, make it passable and then you 'visit' if that's what you're about."

"I think that can be arranged," I said quietly. "What do you think, Jim?"

"Done." He broke away and in ten minutes, the road was cleared for one lane of traffic. The crowd had increased in size while we had been negotiating with the police and now there was a sea of faces facing us.

"Now what?" I asked Jim Young when he came back.

"Let's meet some of your new friends," he said winking at me.

"Gram, you ready?" I asked him as he followed me.'

"Camera is charged and ready. Wow'em Leo," he encouraged me.

"I'll do my best."

"I know you will."

"Where's Al?" I asked.

"Look," Gram said.

Al was sporting a new yellow Liberty Bell tee shirt and waving a flag standing behind the bus, signing autographs and beaming like a rock star.

"I hope he's still with us at the end of the day and doesn't run off with some groupies," Gram said.

"Al will be fine," I said. "He's a mill rat. He knows his place."

Jim Young led me to the middle of the vast crowd and up on to the back of a pickup truck where a makeshift sound system was set up. He took a microphone, tapped it a few times to make sure it was working and then said, "Denver, the man has arrived."

A thunderous applause exploded.

"We are here today because we want a fair wage for the work we do. We have asked the company to give us what we think is a living wage. Our requests have been ignored. We want this company to succeed, but we do not want to be wage slaves any longer. We want to be able to live on what we make and not have to supplement our wages with food stamps and welfare. This is what we want. This is our simple request."

The crowd cheered. Jim Young was an eloquent young man.

"Hearing about our plight, we are fortunate to have the next president of the United States, Leo Pollack, with us today. Let's let Leo hear a hearty Denver, Colorado welcome."

The sound was ear piercing. I was humbled and hopeful that what I would share with them would make a difference.

"Working people are no longer willing to be taken advantage of, no longer willing to be threatened with job losses, no longer willing to accept second class citizenship. We are what makes America great. We work so that democracy thrives."

Young had captured the essence of our campaign motto.

"Folks, I give you, Leo Pollack," Jim Young finished and handed the microphone to me.

The crowd roared as I raised my hand and said, "Hi Ho Denver. Thank you for the warm welcome."

I waited for the noise to quiet down to a mild rumble. Gram was standing below me videotaping. We were going live now. The red light was on. I was in the zone.

"Yes Denver, when America works, democracy thrives."

"Yes," the crowd roared.

"For too many years, corporations have been unwilling to share the profits with their employees and this has created the greatest economic disparity since the Great Depression."

"Yes," the crowd roared.

"What people are asking for is a fair wage for a fair day's work and to share in the bounty of what we produce. Nothing less and nothing more."

"Yes," the crowd roared.

"Denver Casting is a good company and can become a great company if it respects its workers and takes care of them."

"Yes," the crowd roared.

"However, threatening them with shutting down and moving jobs offshore will not encourage any worker to want to be loyal to the company. It's time to end this type of strife and work together and make the company thrive so that everyone wins: employer and employees."

"Yes," the crowd roared.

"We see the same struggle everywhere across the country and it is not class warfare, but a need to realign resources. No one wants to see a company fail, but at the same time, the company must want the employees to succeed right along with it."

"Yes," the crowd roared.

"Now we all have a choice. Do we stand alone or do we band together, company and workers and make up or go our separate ways?"

"Yes," the crowd roared.

"We succeed when everyone with a vested interest in the system wins. A company makes a profit. The employees make a living wage. The consumers get a quality product. This is the real and fair form of capitalism that we are advocating."

"Yes," the crowd roared.

"In the past three decades, corporations have become unwilling or unable to see the light. They think that protecting their bottom line is all they have to do to be successful. They are tragically wrong. The people who make the products and offer the services are the reason companies make a profit, not in lieu of them. Without a quality work force, no corporation can sustain a profitable business. In the end, this flawed type of capitalism will fail."

"Yes," the crowd roared.

"I believe it is not too late to reverse our diverging goals and reunite in a common mission to make everyone successful. Realize this. When I insure that the least of my brethren has a good job and is no longer unemployed or living on welfare, he or she will be the best consumer I will ever find."

"Yes," the crowd roared.

"I heard that Denver Casting wants to make a liberty bell and market it because its management realizes that our movement, this so called 'Liberty Bell Campaign', is truly reaching out to all Americans who want to make America shine once again. I am excited they want to do this. They must understand that they need to produce this product with the willing hands, hearts and minds of their employees in collaboration with management. Otherwise, they will not be promoting what we are truly advocating and that is a sustainable financial climate with employers and employees working closely to insure that everyone wins."

"Yes," the crowd roared.

"I ask Denver Casting's leadership to meet with the employees, with John Young and his cohorts and to iron out the differences, to end this strike today by mutually respecting each side's need to succeed and to do so in such a way that its consensus building becomes a model for the entire country."

"Yes," the crowd roared.

"The days of distrust and disrespect must end. Corporate leaders must view their employees, not as human resources, but as valuable partners in the complex and sometimes turbulent world of business. Employees must reciprocate and stop forming adversarial relationships with their employers. When we think win-win, we will all win."

"Yes," the crowd roared.

"We believe in the dignity of work. The sooner we get all people who can and are willing back to work, we will be a healthier nation. The quicker we get companies to stop forming negative opinions about the needs and wants of their employees, the quicker we will return to economic prosperity where all benefit and none suffer."

"Yes," the crowd roared.

"None of us is as smart as all of us, a learned man once said. Let us take this admonition and use it to solve our nation's problems and stop discounting others who don't look like us, think like us, believe as we do. Within the body politic of this nation all answers are available to us. We just need to seek them."

"Yes," the crowd roared.

"This is the way to kindle an American renaissance. When each person contributes to his or her ability, level, or capacity, the sum total melded together forms the whole."

"Yes," the crowd roared.

"My name is Leo Pollack. I am an unemployed steel worker and I am running to be your next president. I ask for your vote. I ask that you donate a dollar or two to our campaign. I ask that you leave here today and spread the word that working people all over America, more than 160 million of us, are taking this country back from the privileged group that does not know how or does not want to share in the nation's bounty. We are the majority and as we move rapidly and inevitably toward the election in November 2012, we are no longer willing to be silent. We are speaking up because this is our right and our responsibility."

"Yes," the crowd roared.

"Thank you, Denver, for making us feel welcome today. This is America. Never leave it. Always love it. Strive to make it better every day. Keep the faith. Believe in hope. Spread the love."

"Yes," the crowd roared.

The noise was deafening. The police were gone. The crowd swallowed me and for the next few hours, I felt the magic of a thousand hands, hearts and voices infusing me with their energy producing a real Rocky Mountain High.

32. A Tour de Force Begins

We sped across Colorado and Utah and entered Nevada at the eastern border where the great deserts spread out to meet those who follow the Interstate 80 corridor. Gram suggested that we resist going only to large cities. "We'll get a reputation of being elitists if we go only to state capitals and major metropolitan areas." We did not argue with his thesis. After all, he was our "Chief of Staff". The problem was that we had limited time and money during this early primary campaign season. We would have to figure out a way to accomplish the small town tour during the general election.

Al did not care one way or the other. He was in his element. After his RV burned and we got this new and improved vehicle, he was as happy as a lottery winner. Driving came naturally to him. Rarely did I see him waver in his concentration. He did not talk to us much, but I knew he was always listening. Now and then, he would pipe up and share a few ideas. Al was salt of the earth and that is what made him such a wonderful traveling companion except he did snore louder than Gram and me. I rarely heard my snoring because I was fast asleep, but the fellows told me that I was a regular sawyer.

I continued to cook every meal. Given my prowess, my team elected me the chief cook and bottle washer. I accepted my role with humility. After all, they were doing other harder and more important work than I was. Al's driving is what made our journey possible.

Gram navigated, handled all the technology like the email, Face book, Twitter, YouTube, and conference calls with Judy, Carol, John, interfacing constantly with Big Jack, and I don't know what else. If he ever got away from the phone, computer or digital pad he was always fussing with, it was only to go to the bathroom. I wondered how he did it.

Big Jack was always nearby but I rarely knew where he was and only Gram had constant contact with him. They shielded me from much of their conversation. I accepted this because they were looking out for me. If Gram and Jack talked for more than a few minutes, I would start to get suspicious and wonder. Curiosity would burn in me like a magnesium fire, but I would not ask them what was going on even if I thought I would be consumed by my wonder.

Reno was a tour de force. We made five stops in the city and everywhere the crowds got larger and louder. Now I knew why John and Judy put the tracker on the bus. Just like Deadheads, our following started to gain momentum every time we slowed the bus and got out to get gas, supplies or just stretch our legs.

We were beginning to collect a following like a ship does barnacles. In some ways, this made our lives more difficult. I had to be aware that someone might be looking into the bus's windows. When we left town and headed toward Las Vegas, we lost some of our less ardent followers, but the string of cars behind us made me wonder if many of these folks were unemployed and just wanted to be a part of the movement.

Nevada was suffering the most because of the recession. The state led the nation in foreclosures and the unemployment rate was the highest. This concerned me because there was no way to easily fix the problem. We could not force people to travel to Nevada and gamble. Tourism was a major factor in Nevada's success and now it was the main reason it was suffering. Without a lot of discretionary spending money, most people could not afford to travel all the way to Las Vegas and gamble.

Founded in 1911, Las Vegas was a stopover place for westward travelers making the trek to California. At that time, the population was 800. In 2010, the population had exploded to more than a half million people and this number only included the city limits. In the 1950s, mobsters infiltrated Las Vegas and made it an oasis for gamblers and other types of excitement seekers. Big name celebrities drew millions of people each year to this desert watering hole. In the Twentieth Century, Las Vegas was the fastest growing city and held that honor as the century closed. The Las Vegas Strip, 4.2 miles of non-stop entertainment and gaming establishments, is the most visibly lit space on the entire planet.

We entertained ourselves with meeting people who followed us wherever we went. Our venues were mostly mall parking lots and city parks. We did not enter any gaming houses. "Not a good idea," Gram said to us. Al was disappointed but he took advantage of the numerous stops to catch up on needed rest. The weather was warm for this time of year. Highs in the 60s made being outdoors unbelievably pleasant. Everywhere we went, people were excited about our message. Even the police were rather cooperative. Sin City did give us a lot of freedom. After all, we were not trying to stop their lucrative business. I had mixed emotions about gambling, or "gaming" as they called it here to give it a less pejorative tone. In the mill, I saw guys flip quarters for their paychecks.

Our crowds were mostly minority people. We were sure that there was a major illegal immigrant population in the city. This fact was rarely discussed because the immigrants would work for less than minimum wage making them important contributors to the economy. We did attract a segment of the "gaming" crowd. However, they were not about to waste time listening to speeches being made by a politician when there was money to be made, or lost, on the craps table.

I kept looking around to see if I could find someone who's right or left arm was significantly larger than the other one, but I had no luck. Those who played the "one armed bandits" were a special breed of gambler. They could sit and pull the lever for hours and not get bored. The intense sunlight made close observation next to impossible. In my entire life, I never saw such brilliant light. All day long, we were flooded with it. We did not want to leave but we knew that there were many stops ahead of us as we continued this tour de force across the American southwest.

We stopped at dusk to rest. We were up at dawn and back on the road heading south toward our next city.

Gram kept us on task and on time. Big Jack was more visible than ever. I was not sure why, but I did not ask. We did our last gig at the south side of town before we headed back out into the desert and drove toward Phoenix. We knew that the Arizona primary was coming in a month and we wanted to make an appearance in "Sun City".

Along the way, we managed to stop for a few minutes at Lake Meade and see the Hoover Dam, pass the Grand Canyon and ogle the deep gorge carved by a million years of rushing water. We raced on to Kingman, Arizona. We made a stop in this desert city and were well received by the people who were a hardy bunch living on the edge of the Mohave Desert.

We drove east and up into the mountains near Flagstaff, and had another wonderful and exciting meeting with some of its citizenry. I expressed the need to find a solution to immigration that protected America and its current citizens and still gave people who wanted to come to our land hope that they were welcome. We did not need to fear strangers. We needed to get to know them and embrace their differences as they contributed to the greater good of our society. Some of the people on the perimeter of the crowd were not impressed with my message of tolerance. Rather than outright booing me, they just moved on.

Racing south, we made it to Phoenix in the heat of the day, but were not prepared for the vast city that lay in front of us in the "Valley of the Sun". Phoenix is the sixth largest city in the United States, the largest state capital and the fourteenth largest metropolitan area. Completely surrounded by desert, the city's survival is dependent upon the Salt River for its water, the lifeblood of any city in a desert climate where summer temperatures can reach as high as 120 degrees.

We called back east, got some guidance from John and Judy and headed to some impromptu venues in the downtown area. We were going to spend just one afternoon in Phoenix so we were not too concerned that the events were small. However, the tracking system and, what appeared to be a flash mob, greeted us at the center city park where Al pulled the Liberty Bus to a stop.

Big Jack was immediately with us and said we were going to face some "scrutiny" by the "Man". He said not to worry, though, because there were "forces" taking care of any "overly excited" security personnel. All this was code for do your thing and the rest will follow. I thanked him for his running interference for us.

"It's my job," he quickly said and disappeared into the crowd that surrounded us. I entertained them with the message that "Every American's duty is to make his or her family healthier, his or her community safer and the nation as a whole the beacon for the world. Democracy works because we, as one people, can and do care about each other even if we are don't look, sound, think, act nor pray like others." The message was fairly well received. I was sure that some in the crowd wondered what I was really trying to sell them. I knew that Arizona was one of the most rigid states regarding immigration. Its recent history was laden with repressive laws to stop illegal immigrants from continuing to use Arizona as an entry point into the country. What it had achieved in its fight against illegal immigration was a reputation as a wholly intolerant place in which to live. Tourism was adversely affected by the governor's stance and the legislature's passing the restrictive bill that gave police the right to stop anyone they thought was an illegal immigrant. The courts were still deciding on the constitutionality of the law, but in the mean time, the police departments were making it difficult for illegal immigrants to move freely around the state. The short term outcome was that many illegal persons left the state and moved north and east to New Mexico, Utah and Colorado where the laws were less stringent.

A week or so ago, Governor Jan Brewer created quite a scene when President Barack Obama flew into Phoenix on a visit and she was photographed by the press standing in front of the President and pointing her finger in his face. She later said she felt intimidated by him but did not clarify what he had done to "intimidate" her. The president did not elaborate on her claim. At least he was a gentleman about the whole affair.

When it was time to move on, we waved goodbye to those who so warmly greeted us. We headed out of the city and southeast toward Tucson, the home of Gabrielle Giffords, the Congresswoman who, just a year ago, was shot in the head and nearly killed. She was resigning her office to focus all her energy on recovering from the wound.

Vast stands of Saguaro Cactuses stood guard along the highway. We stopped at one particularly beautiful stand and photographed them. They live a very long time and can take more than 75 years to grow an arm. A cactus without arms is called a "spear". When it rains, the cactus absorbs water and stores it for later use. The trunk can actually be recorded swelling as the water inside expands. The largest saguaro cactus lives in Maricopa County and is forty-five feet tall and ten feet in diameter. Harming a cactus in any way is a crime in Arizona. We were impressed with their beauty and wished that we could grow one in our yards back home. They symbolized the true west and we were pleased to see so many of them standing tall and gracing the landscape.

For more than a hundred years, Tucson existed because the city was able to draw water from the Santa Cruz River that flowed year round. Slowly, the water disappeared and there was a major project started to fill subterranean aquifers with water pumped from wells. Water is life everywhere and in the desert, it is liquid gold. As we drove across the city and over a bridge spanning the Santa Cruz River, what we saw beneath us was nothing but sand.

"Hard to get a cool drink from that river," Gram commented.

"What river?" Al responded.

"How do people live in this bone dry climate?" I wondered aloud.

"What do you want to do now?" Al asked.

"What's on our itinerary?" I asked Gram.

"Nothing. We could post that we are headed to the University of Arizona and see what that creates for us."

"Do it," I said. "What do we have to lose?"

Ten minutes later, as we headed toward the school, we saw the telltale signs of a response to Gram's posting. Cars were lining up behind us and we knew what this meant.

"I hope Jack is somewhere nearby," I said.

"You know he is," Al replied. "In fact, just ahead of us in the left hand lane."

"Eagle eyes," Gram said. "How did you see him in this traffic?"

"I don't have my head buried in the computer screen like you do. I'm watching the road and everything else gliding past us. Like that sexy seniorita there on the sidewalk. Now that is one good looking woman."

A tall, statuesque woman dressed in a very short skirt, wearing high heels and strutting her stuff filled our eyes.

"She is quite the lady," Gram said.

"Holler out and get her number, Gram," Al encouraged him. "She might be free tonight."

"But I'm not, Al. Sadly."

"You could be free. We'll drop you off and you can catch up with us later," Al teased.

"You're not funny, Al. But the offer is tempting."

"Do it," Al said and pulled the bus over to the curb.

"Hey, watch what you're doing," Gram said, "you just about cut off that taxi in the right lane."

"He was watching her and not paying attention to me. Fool," Al cried.

We moved on. The beauty disappeared in the crowd, and with her, Gram's hope for a night on the town.

"Sorry about that, Gram," I said.

"You had your chance," Al said.

"Hush up fellows, and leave me alone," Gram said and went back to the bathroom. We could hear the water running. We figured it was the cold.

The campus was modern southwestern style architecture. The University of Arizona Wildcats men's basketball team had made the NCAA tournament 25 years in a row. The women's softball team was NCAA national champions seven times in the last twenty years. "To discover, educate, serve and inspire" is the school's motto. The only medical school granting degrees in Arizona is located at the University of Arizona.

Gram was checking the map and said, "Head to the UA mall. That is the best place for us to stop and 'meet and greet'. I'll call Jack and tell him what we are doing."

Al followed his directions, and a few minutes later, we were parked beside a vast grassy mall lined with huge palm trees. I got out and immediately was swarmed with people.

While baking in the sun for the next hour, I shared with the crowd what our vision was for the future. Given that this was a college campus, one of the themes I touched on was student loans and student debt.

"As a nation, we have short changed your generation. When I went to college, education was still reasonably inexpensive. Not any more. Many of you are graduating and facing a mountain of debt. This makes the future look very bleak. I am not sure what has stopped this administration and the last one from providing some economic relief to you, but there is one way to do that and it requires us to make a commitment to every young person who wants to earn a college degree. If you commit to serve your country for five years, we commit to provide you with a good, public university education. There is such a need in our society today for teachers, social workers, civil engineers, craftspeople, that we must and will make this investment. This is not a complicated mission to fulfill. What it requires is political will. For too many years, private sector lending agencies were making a killing from the interest they were charging college students. The current president ended this practice and I applaud him for that. He did not go far enough. I pledge to you to make college affordable again. Period."

We spent time talking to students, walking around the immediate campus, feeling the heat of the day and the warmth of the young people who wanted to believe in something greater than themselves.

As we hiked back to the bus and prepared to depart, one young lady came up to me and said, "Someday, I'll be doing what you are doing, Mr. Pollack and I'll be the first woman, third party candidate to win the presidency." She said it with such fire that I asked her what her name was."

"Daniella Montezuma. Yes, I come from an ancient family and I'm proud of my heritage.

I hugged her and said, "When you're ready to run, call me and I'll campaign along side of you, not for the office, but as your number one supporter."

Waving goodbye, we slowly exited the campus and just a few hours later, left the "Grand Canyon State and entered the "Land of Enchantment".

We planned only one stop in New Mexico. Our time was limited. We realized that to make this western swing meaningful, we needed to hit the states that were holding primaries or caucuses first and then come back later on a 48 state tour de force when the general election was in full swing.

Unlike Tucson and its pitiful Santa Cruz River, Albuquerque contained the Rio Grande River that was a major waterway providing much needed liquid to the sixth fastest growing city in the country. Boasting a population of almost a million people within its city limits, Albuquerque was alive and well and growing with the times. We drove into the city and headed toward Roosevelt Park where Gram said a "huge crowd was already gathering."

"How do you know that?" I asked him.

"If you could turn on your smart phone, you would know. But since you only carry a dumb phone, you can't see or hear what is happening."

"So what is happening? Enlighten us, O Wobekenobe," I barked at him.

"Jack says that a 'flash mob message' went out and to expect a really large crowd."

"How large?" I asked.

"He did not say, but what he did report is that the park was already full, and yes, our boys in blue were in attendance."

"So what do we do about them?"

"Tell them jokes. See if they laugh."

"What?"

"I don't know. Humor them I guess. Perhaps Jack has it all worked out."

"Let's hope so."

He did and he did not. We were accosted by the police as soon as we drove into the park. When we stopped in a spot big enough for the bus, Gram said, "Let me handle this, okay. It's time I earned more of my keep."

I did not argue with him. He got off first, met with the police and moved them off to the side. I could see him looking back at the window. This was my sign from him to make a break. I did.

As soon as the people saw me, pandemonium broke out. With Jack next to me, I pushed into the crowd and headed toward a bandstand that was located in the center of the park. All along the way, people were talking to me, saying what a wonderful thing I was doing, encouraging me to never give up, asking me what was it like to be a candidate and on the road every day and never be at home. The questions flew at me like confetti. I tried to answer as many as I could. I was in the midst of a flash mob and the pressure was intense.

On the bandstand, I was greeted by a host of well wishers, some who claimed to be representatives of the Liberty Bell Party of Albuquerque. I asked them again who they were and they laughed. "We're forming our own Liberty Bell Party affiliate here in our city. We are the antidote to the Tea Party." I liked that and told them so.

I spoke to the crowd for more than twenty minutes and concluded with these remarks.

"Today, we stand on the precipice. We can move one way and realize the American dream of a full employment economy, justice and fairness for all, and a world without war. Or we can revert back to the past decade where fear dominated our conversation, the radicals in the world were out to get us, and we were the target of every crazy that lived. I refuse to believe in this negative scenario. We are a nation of people which values diversity, religious freedom, creativity, and the hard work of its people. We just lost our way in the wilderness for awhile. We fell victim to weapons of mass deception and now we are recovering. We can see the future clearly."

We did not leave for another two hours. There was no escaping the masses. I did not see Al, Gram nor Jack after I left the bandstand. Slowly, I moved slower than a snail toward the bus parked three hundred yards away. Nobody wanted the event to end. Sunset came and went. By the time I finally arrived at the bus, it was nearly 9 pm and I was drenched in sweat, thirsty, tired and just a little irritable.

Thanking the last few well-wishers, I crawled into the bus and met Al, Jack and Gram. They were sitting around the table drinking cold beer.

"You sure took your time," Gram said. "We've been waiting for dinner for almost two hours now."

"Where's my beer?" I asked with parched lips

"You can't drink beer in front of your constituents."

"You are!" I cried out.

"We're not running for office. You are," Jack said.

"The price of fame and glory," Al said.

"Sobriety is a virtue in a president," Gram said.

"Let me have some water. I can barely talk I'm so dry."

They laughed at me as I guzzled the entire half gallon of water in the refrigerator.

"Now that you have slaked your thirst, how about our dinner?" Gram asked again.

"I'm starving, Leo," Al said.

"Me too," Jack added pressing the point.

"How about you get this bus moving, turn on the air, drive us out of town and I'll think about feeding you school boys?" I coughed at them.

"Let's do it," Al said. Jack jumped off the bus and disappeared. Gram assumed his navigator's seat. Al hopped behind the wheel and soon we were rolling out of town. Along the way, cars and trucks honked their horns at us, flashed their lights and made our exit noteworthy.

"I'm going to miss Albuquerque," I said sadly.

"We'll be back," Gram said. "We'll be back."

"Next time, it will be during the general election and then it'll be for all the marbles," Al said.

We drove on into the desert night, our tour de force continuing as we headed east again toward more states, more venues, more crowds of screaming people and the ever tightening race that was leading us to the White House and the presidency of the United States of America in the year of the Lord, 2012.

33. Going for the Gopher

Our tour de force continued as we headed east again across the vast bread basket of America, cutting through the panhandle of Texas and then Oklahoma on US 54 toward Wichita, Kansas. Gram navigated the Liberty Bus on this pathway so we could stop in some small towns along the way before we got onto I-35 and headed toward Minnesota, the next major primary state on the schedule. Given that we were now being tracked by GPS on Facebook and Twitter and people were posting videos of our stops on YouTube, the campaign was really picking up a real head of steam. The excitement was building exponentially. As a team, we could not be happier. However, with this added visibility came the increased attention we received wherever we went. We could no longer stop in a rest area without people coming up to us and talking. What used to be a quick in and out, now was an hour stop and sometimes even more. Such was the price of fame, or so Gram told us as we traveled across the heartland.

"What did you expect, Leo? This is the way it is going to be now, and probably the rest of your life."

"I hadn't figured on this," I said soberly.

"It's not too late to quit," he offered.

"That would be a cowardly way out of this," I replied.

"And I'd kick your behind if you did," Al added. "I didn't come along for just the ride, Leo. This is something I've come to believe in and we just have to finish it one way or another."

"When he gets elected, what kind of job do you want in the White House?" Gram asked Al.

"I don't want a job. I just want the satisfaction of knowing that we put one of our own in the White House. That will be enough for me."

"You know, Al, I'd want you to be my driver as long as this public lifestyle continues. No more eating graphite and sucking sulfur."

"Nah. Not for me. Besides, I can slip back into obscurity. You can't."

"You think so?" Gram commented. "Al, next time we stop, let me show you who's posted on YouTube just like Leo. You're called the man in front of the man, the leader of the pack. There are a dozen pictures of you taken from the front of the bus showing you behind the wheel, swarthy mustache shining in the sun light, sunglasses on, and your big hands gripping the wheel. People will know you as Leo's driver as long as you live."

"Who posted those shots? You?"

"No way. There are people all over America who want to know who we are, what we look like, and all the rest. I imagine it won't be long before the brand of jeans that you wear is posted on the site and the company that makes them will be approaching you to do commercials for them."

"Huh! Imagine me a clothes model. I'll have to lose some of this gut if that's going to happen."

"No way," Gram said. "That's what makes you so real. They will want the gut, too. You'll appeal to every schmuck that wears jeans and wants to think he looks sexy to all the ladies he meets."

"You saying I'm not sexy?" Al shot back.

"I'm saying it's what they want to think. Whether you're sexy or not is not for me to decide. You get any offers to get off this caravan and spend the night with a woman anywhere along the way?"

"I ain't telling you anything," Al said. "My sweetie would not like to see that on Face Book or Twitter."

"See what I mean. It's just a matter of time," Gram said.

"What about you, Gram? What are you going to do with your new notoriety?" I asked him while we rolled through the Sooner state.

"Me?" Gram thought for a few moments before answering. "I think that whatever happens, I'll be glad that I was along for the ride. I know you're going to win. The question is what happens next. How do we govern effectively? How do we make this country live up to its responsibilities as the greatest democracy in history? This is the challenge. Governing is the issue, not winning."

"So you know we're going to win," I asked. "How do you know?"

"We're going to split the vote three ways. I'm serious. Look at the republicans right now. They can't get it together. Now Santorum is starting to rise in the polls. What's up with that? He couldn't even win his re-election in semi-conservative Pennsylvania a few years ago. He was just a number in Florida. Now his poll numbers are rising rapidly. He might win some states this week and that will put him right back in the hunt. Gingrich won one state so far. He may win in Georgia. He's so flawed that the comedians can't stop blasting him. Listen to this one. Newt's against same marriage sex not same sex marriage. Think that might be a Jimmy Fallon or Letterman joke. How do you like that one?"

"Gross," Al said. "But from what we've seen of him, sounds pretty true. He sure does have a nice trophy wife just like McCain."

"Amen to that," Gram said. "So then there's Paul. He's 76 years old. No spring chicken. He has the most rabid followers. He will be a spoiler at the convention. My notion is that he is running now so that his son, Rand Paul, can make a strong bid for the presidency in 2016."

"Really?" I commented.

"Sure. What's his motivation? He says he's not going rogue and doing a third party thing. This is a sure indication that he's the set up man, the opening rock band for his son who is the real star, he hopes. We shall see but he won't break out and do a third party thing this time around and this helps us immensely."

We rode along in silence for a while digesting all that Gram said.

"This is going to be a strange year. The Tea Party upset the apple cart a few years ago by challenging the status quo on the conservative side of the ledger. Now we're coming along and moving the world to the progressive side. We are 'leaning far forward' to steal MSNBC's motto. What we are doing is making the president have to do things he was not ready to do. Did you see that he's now starting to talk about bringing manufacturing back to the United States? He wasn't saying a word about this until you laid this out as a campaign platform, Leo. Even Santorum noticed this theme and now he's pretending like he's all in favor of bringing manufacturing back to America. They are keying off what you are saying. Pretty soon, whatever we are doing will be setting the standard for the entire campaign."

"We aren't doing anything unique and special," I said. "If you want to improve the economy, you've got to make things and put people back to work. To put people back to work, you have to have factories, businesses and industries flourishing. This isn't rocket science," I concluded.

"To guys who don't even understand this like Romney and Gingrich and to some extent, the president, they were not getting it until you brought in the 'Americans Buying American' principle. It dawned on them that this was something they could co-opt and use themselves. That's okay. However we get people back to work is what matters."

"I agree. That was one of your ideas, Gram." I said.

"Yes, it was, but it came from listening to you rant and rave about how this country was always doing what was in the best interest of the corporation and not the people. Simple analysis would tell anyone what the problem is. We've sold out to the multi-nationals who don't give a damn about the workers in this country. All they are concerned about is sales and those must be done internationally now in order to compete with all the other multi-national corporations that is engaged in this destructive global economy."

There was a lull. We discussed so many of the needs that faced America that, sometimes, our conversations started to tire us. Al, Gram and I were almost constantly talking politics, economics, social issues, even now and then religion as we spent countless hours motoring along through the country from one venue to another. I was enchanted with the way we were able to morph our dialogue from one major issue to another. We used these skull sessions to form policies, our game plan for the future. In so doing, we made valuable use of the time. Our conference calls with the headquarters further added to the grist that went into our mill. We used the prompts we got from John, Judy, Carol, Fritz, Richard and Big Jack to move the process forward toward a meaningful and rich set of platform issues that would resonate across the entire country. We were not after the fringe elements in our society, the government hating groups on either side of the fence. We wanted the 160 million working people to join our campaign and wrestle the power away from special interest and privileged people who could buy and sell their way into office and control the message and, thereby, policies and the laws. This was our goal.

Our Wichita stop was exhilarating. Big Jack was ahead of us and said a large crowd was massed at the bus station and so we went there and were astounded to find thousands of people waiting for the Liberty bus to pull into the parking lot. Given that we were now becoming more accepted across the country as a movement and not some kind of fringe, hippy element, police departments and local authorities were not as apt to come to us and make an issue with our impromptu gatherings.

In fact, they were discovering that whenever the Liberty bus was scheduled to stop somewhere, the city or town or village experienced a major spike in tourism activity and money started to flow in with the onslaught of the people.

The home office alerted us to this fact when Judy Bream called Gram and said there were small towns along our itinerary who were requesting that we stop and enjoy their hospitality. Gram told her that he would begin to navigate this way. He would notify her whenever we were planning to stop so that she could do her thing and alert the locals to what we were doing. This would make every stop count. We all agreed this was a better way to manage our time. Given the vastness of the country and our inability to move any faster than 65 mph most of the time, we needed to be ready to adjust, adapt and overcome as much as we could.

Judy did suggest that we start making tapes of my talking to Gram about different things while we were driving along so that she could post them on YouTube. We liked that idea.

After we finished our session in Wichita with thousands of supporters chanting "Liberty and Leo," Gram quickly got the video set up and we were able to use it from that time forward.

"What do you think of that?" I asked the guys as we rode along. "The cops are asking me for an autograph? Have we arrived or what? I mean it, what a strange turn of events."

"This is the way we are going to make it to the White House. The police are generally a conservative group of people and when they are starting to buy into what we are doing, we are moving forward at warp speed," Gram said.

"Feels good to me because I don't have to stress whenever we park the bus," Al said. "It's always good to have the 'man' on our side."

"What's our next stop, Gram?" I asked.

"Topeka," he replied. "You know what that town is famous for don't you besides being the state capital of Kansas?"

"Of course. Brown versus Board of Education. Amazing how a little town in Kansas was the site of this Supreme Court Decision. The Supreme Court is one of those government entities that really makes you wonder. In 1954, the court proved to be above the fray and decided to make it possible for all children to get a quality public school education. This conservative court now wants all corporations to have the right to spend all the money they want to influence an election. How far we have come and yet how backward the decision making appears when we place this decision in context with other court decisions throughout our history."

"To reverse Citizens United will take an amendment to the Constitution. This is not good," Gram said, "but it is the way it is now. We will be fighting a real battle in the summer and fall with the superpacs that will come after us with 'tooth and nail' to destroy us."

"We'll fight back with the simple truth," Al said. "Working people will know what side of their bread is being buttered and by whom."

"I sure hope so," Gram said.

"I know so," Al emphatically responded and said, "fifteen minutes to Topeka. Get ready."

Gram called Big Jack. He got the alert. "We've got a large crowd gathering at the court house. Not as big as Wichita, but there will be a number of local politicians like the mayor there to greet us. We're in the loop now."

"Great!" I exclaimed. "I'm ready for them.

Education was the theme for the day. I elaborated on the need for public education to be totally revamped and concluded by saying to those who came to hear me.

"We cannot let our public school system continue to decline. This movement away from universal free education toward a voucher system and charter schools is just a new way to segregate our children. It must end immediately. We must re-allocate funding to insure that schools everywhere are receiving what they need to make a difference in young people's lives. We need to raise the age to 19 before a student can drop out of high school. We need to end this notion that teachers are the problem. NO, they are the solution. We need to pay them well, expect them to work hard to be the educators that they can be and make a difference in the lives of their students. Yes, we need to be able to remove teachers who do not perform up to standard. Yes, we also need to stop blaming teachers for the problems that our school systems face. We need to revamp the system so that our children attend school year around and do not fall behind by being away from a learning environment for a three-month period. This antiquated system denies the reality of our times. We are no longer an agrarian society. We don't need to be off for three months in the summer time to 'work on the farm'. We need to learn year around and that will be our focus when we take over and lead this nation in an American Educational Renaissance. I thank you for being here today, for your continued support, and most of all, for your vote in the fall election when we will overcome and working people united will take the White House back from special interest groups and privileged people. Thank you, Topeka, for making me feel welcome. Thank you."

An hour later, we were back on the road and heading north on I-35 across Iowa and heading toward Minnesota. The sun was setting across the Hawkeye state.

"Seems like forever since we were in Des Moines," I said.

"It was," Gram said. "In this political world, forever is yesterday. Look at all that has happened since then."

"I'm amazed that we are where we are today. Yes, so much has happened."

"By the way, we will be in Minnesota on the right day to make an impact. Though it is a caucus state, we can ruffle more feathers and this will make the establishment even more hyper-vigilant," Gram said.

"What do you guys think about calling it a day?" Al asked from the pilot's seat.

"Fine by me," Gram said. "I'll call Jack and let him know what we are doing."

After eating, we crawled into bed, rested well and were back on the road by daybreak. The Gopher State was just ahead.

Upon entering Minnesota, what we first noticed was the rich, black earth that stretched for miles in every direction. I had never seen such soil. The ebony color was stark against the white snow. This had been a mild winter. There was as much black showing as white. The sun beat down upon the earth making the winter scenes picture perfect.

"Let's stop in Albert Lea," I said.

"We had not thought about doing that," Gram replied.

"I know, but it is a small town and you said we ought to make them as important as the bigger cities."

"You're making me eat my words. Okay, let me get on it."

Fifteen minutes later, Gram said, "We're set. Jack is there now and the town is just waking up. Albert Lea is primarily a farming community that just happens to be on the interstate. Some tourist trade affects it. Crowd size may be small. This is spur of the moment."

"You okay with this, Al?" I asked.

"Leo, I'm game for anything. Every stop is a rest stop for me. I don't mind at all. I get to meet my fans and that makes it all the more enjoyable," he replied laughing out loud adding to his aforementioned aura.

We exited the freeway and headed to downtown Albert Lea, Minnesota.

"What do we know about Albert Lea?" I asked Gram.

Gram said, "Albert Lea was named after a topographer who surveyed southern Minnesota in the late 19th century. It is primarily an agricultural center. Cargill, the international food production conglomerate once had its national headquarters. The town received national attention in 1959 after Local 6 of the United Packinghouse Workers of America went on strike against Wilson & Company, one of the big four meatpacking plants at the time, over issues involving mandatory overtime requirements. When Wilson & Co. attempted to operate the plant with replacement workers, violence erupted and split the town. During the 109-day strike, Governor Orville Freeman acted to quell the violence by closing the plant, calling in the Minnesota National Guard and, on December 11, declaring martial law. A Federal district court in Minneapolis ruled against the Governor on December 23, and the plant was turned back to Wilson & Co. just days later. Get this. Albert Lea is located in 'Freeborn' County. Now how is that for a great county name?"

"Right up our alley," I said.

"We are almost downtown. Where did you say to head, Gram?" Al asked.

"To the county park just north of town."

We could see the crowd before we got to the park. Cars were lined up on both sides of the road. County Mounties were directing traffic. All 18,000 citizens must have come out to see us today because the place was bedlam. Al had a difficult time negotiating the extremely tight path through the parked vehicles. Finally, we safely pulled to a stop and I exited the bus. Jack was right there to escort me to a makeshift stage area where I met the Mayor, Vern Rasmussen and the city manager, Chad Adams. Both welcomed me to their great city and wasted no time taking charge by addressing the crowd. I could not tell by their comments if they were Republicans, Democrats or Independents. Today, they just sounded like Americans.

"We are privileged today to have in our midst, third party candidate for president of the United States, Mr. Leo Pollack. A man who comes from humble roots, much like many of us do, Mr. Pollack's campaign has caught the attention of Americans all over the country and he is here with us to share some of his thoughts. Mr. Pollack, it is with great pleasure that we welcome you to Albert Lea," Mayor Rasmussen finished shaking my hand and turning the podium over to me.

"Thank you, Mayor, for your kind words and your hospitality. What makes this campaign so special is the gracious way Americans all over this nation have received our campaign and our message. I believe it is because we are speaking to the heart and soul of America and not attacking it. We believe in the innate goodness of all Americans. We hope to inspire all Americans to participate in running their own country. Voting is only a small part of being a citizen. Being active, first in your own family, then your school, then your community, your state, and finally your country, is what it takes to make Democracy thrive, not just survive. We have been in survival mode for the past thirty years. We have abdicated our responsibility. We've permitted special interest groups and privileged people to rule. Now it is our time to take command and fix what ails this country."

A loud applause echoed across the grounds.

"We know that when America works, democracy thrives. Take your town. You are still tied to the land. You know that a crop will not grow itself. You plant seed in the spring, work the land until the crop matures, harvest it and hope that you can make a profit. The reality is your control over what you're paid for your crop is so limited that it is almost like gambling. Futures traders have more power than you do in pricing a bushel of wheat or soybeans. That is unacceptable. Companies like Cargill that used to have its national headquarters here manipulate the market and make the small farmer's life difficult. If we don't change the current pattern, the family farm will, not in the too distant future, be extinct."

A louder applause arose.

"I believe we need to end farm subsidies to large farms, conglomerates and any person or persons whose land does not produce a crop. How crazy are we? We actually pay people not to grow something and this is in a world where starvation kills thousands of people every day."

"I know that economics is a dismal science. I realize that there are times when it is practical to let the economy overshadow the needs of people. I said practical, not moral, ethical or acceptable. We need to stop this practice of letting companies dictate what we as a nation are doing because it makes good business sense. We have to do what is right, moral, and ethical, in the best interest of people all over this nation as well as the world."

More applause.

"The black earth is ready to serve humankind. We need to let it. We need to feed those who need to be fed. We may make less money but feed more people. We may have to stifle our greed so that those in need are satisfied."

A loud cry erupted as the people voted with their voices for a new way of doing business.

"I am no economist nor am I an agronomist. I don't understand the nuances of everything that needs to be done. I do know there are people who do and I will challenge them to serve America by developing policies that insure that farmers make a realistic profit for the risk they undertake in producing a crop and that the crop they produce does good in the world, feeds the hungry."

"Amen, Amen, Amen" chants went rippling through the crowd.

"We can do this together. I am Leo Pollack, an unemployed steel worker running for president of the United States. I am asking you for your vote, for your support, for your permission to proceed and lead the nation forward into a renaissance. We are entering a new era. The 160 million Americans who work hard every day want this nation to shine like a brilliant beacon once again so that all the world looks up to our democracy as an ideal. Let us make that happen. Thank you for being here today, for your hospitality and your support."

I jumped down from the stage and worked the crowd not worrying about the time or the security issues. I was an American among Americans and that was what mattered.

We finally left Albert Lea about 3 pm and were scheduled to be in the Twin Cities for a gathering at 7 pm. We had plenty of time to make it. I knew what the guys would want first, so I got up and did my thing. For once, I made a casserole and they loved it. Sausage, potatoes and corn. I had to call Basha four times to get the recipe right. She was so patient with me. I talked to Janko and he was happy to hear that I might actually be home in a day or two. I made him no promises. I did say it was "highly likely" that I would. He took that to mean I would be there. I did not mind. He wanted his Dad and I wanted him.

We selected St. Paul as the city where we would meet the people. Being considered the lesser of the twin cities even though it was the state capital, we wanted to play for the underdog. Separated by the magnificent Mississippi River from its twin city, Minneapolis, St. Paul was a wonderful place to stop and meet the people.

"Where are we headed?" Al asked Gram.

"Concordia University Commons," Gram said. "Hey, Leo, you don't mind doing a gig at a Lutheran college, do you? I know you were once a Catholic. This won't conflict with any of your beliefs, will it?"

"No, not at all. What would make you think that I might?"

"You said you were once Catholic but now you are not practicing. I thought the closeness to a holy place might affect you in some way."

I knew he was just joshing me, but I played along with him. "You know, Gram. Maybe we ought to change the venue. Can we find a good atheist college somewhere nearby instead?"

He looked at me. I gazed back at him, not grinning.

"You're not serious?"

"No, are you?"

"You had me going for about two seconds," Gram said.

"I don't care where we meet, with whom, or what time. All I want to know is what do you fellows think is the major issue in Minnesota."

"Jobs," Al and Gram cried out simultaneously.

"Got it. Jobs it will be."

"Minnesota is a strange state. It has a lot of farming, industry, manufacturing and cold weather. Hardy people live up here where the winters can get downright brutal. Most of the immigrants came from Germany and the Scandinavian countries. Climate change is dramatically affecting Minnesota as you can see today. There is bare ground in February. This was unheard of a generation ago."

"What I know about Minnesota is that the Mesabi Range, a major source of iron ore in the United States, is located. We got most of our iron ore from this source," I said.

"The range is just north of the cities. Interesting. I've always wanted to see the Boundary Waters Canoe Area," Gram said.

"You can canoe from there all the way to James Bay in Canada," Al said. "This is truly the land of 10,000 lakes and myriad rivers. I wish I had more time. I'd love to canoe all the way north," Al said.

"I didn't know you liked to canoe," I commented.

"I'll bet you didn't know that I ride a Harley, too."

"Didn't know that," I said.

"I don't. I just wanted to see if you were paying attention."

"What?" I said.

"Leo, you are slow. Gram, tell me which way to go."

We got to Concordia in fifteen minutes. We could tell we were getting close because the traffic was very congested and there was a steady stream of cars and trucks heading toward the school. Local police who knew we were coming escorted us to a parking lot. Nice. Special treatment never hurts when it is connected to driving and parking in a busy city.

We got out of the bus and I asked Gram, "Do we have a contact person?"

"A few of them and here they come. Five young men and women walked up and introduced themselves to us welcoming us to Concordia. "My name is Samuel Wallace. I'm a student here and president of the student body. We are so excited that you've chosen to use our campus as a campaign stop. We all have been looking forward to meeting you, Mr. Pollack."

"Please, call me Leo," I said. "So what's the game plan?"

"Well, Leo, we have set up some sound equipment on the library steps and so I'll just introduce you and turn the mic over to you. That's it."

"Simple. I love it," I said. "Sam, guys and gals, this is Gram, my chief of staff. That fellow over there signing autographs and looking cool is our campaign manager, Al Caruso. He's our main man. He takes us wherever we need to go."

"Welcome to all of you," Samuel said. "Now, let's get this show on the road."

While I was waiting, I tried to count in my head the number of towns, cities and places I had given speeches since we started this campaign. I could not do it. There was too much to remember. I committed that, after today, I would keep a journal and then I would be able to reflect back upon the day's events and keep track of what we were doing.

I asked Gram if he had any idea and he said, "Since I came on board, you've been in 27 cities, towns or villages. You have made 63 speeches, met with the press 22 times and shaken the hands of 137,000 people, held 78 babies, kissed 92 elderly women and cooked macaroni and cheese 37 out of 49 days we've been on the road."

Staring at him, I did not know what to say.

"Leo, how the hell would I know that?"

"You don't journal or blog?"

"Of course, I do. However, not about your statistics. I log your speeches and the themes."

"Who keeps the other stats?"

"Carol. She knows it all. After all, she's an accountant."

"Great!"

Samuel's voice interrupted us. I stopped talking and listened to his introduction.

"Ladies and gentlemen, Fellow Minnesotans, we are privileged tonight to have with us the next president of the United States, Mr. Leo Pollack. He has stopped tonight to share with us his special message for America so let's give him a warm St. Paul welcome."

I arose and walked to the center of the steps where Samuel relinquished the microphone to me, shook my hand and walked away.

"Well, I've heard it has been a quiet week in St. Paul, out here on the edge of the prairie," I said, mimicking Minnesota native son and resident treasure, Garrison Keillor.

An appreciative loud clapping round took place. I waited until they stopped.

"Yes, I do listen to NPR and love the show."

More applause.

"America is facing a dilemma and it is simply this. We live way beyond our means and right now, we just have to face the fact. We have spent too much fighting two wars that we paid for by using a credit card. We continue to use social security designated funds to finance the general operating budget of the country. We budget nearly three-quarters of a trillion dollars to operate a military that is larger than the militaries of all the industrialized nations in the world and we cannot account for how this money is actually spent. America's dilemma is that it is living beyond its means and this needs to stop now or we will never recover."

Some applause. This was not a popular theme, but one that needed to be discussed. I was setting the stage for what would come later in the general campaign.

"We cannot continue cutting taxes and cutting budgets and think we can maintain our current standard of living. This will not happen. We have difficulty decisions to make."

No applause.

"I can tell by your reaction that you realize that what I am saying is not going to win a lot of friends and influence people. I did not decide to run for president so I could win a popularity contest. We do need to make cuts. We do need to raise taxes. We do need to hold the military and all governmental agencies accountable for their spending tax dollars. We do need to stand together and make equal sacrifices to solve this problem."

Silence.

"We can do what the previous president did and continue to spend money we don't have. We can do what this president is doing and spend money we don't have. We can do what the current crop of Republicans advocates: cut spending and taxes even further. We can be sure that in a decade the government will not recover and will be bankrupt."

Silence.

"I refuse to do any of these things. We can end the Bush tax cuts and this alone will reduce the national debt by 4 trillion dollars in the next decade. We can fully fund social security and Medicare by raising the cap from $106 thousand to $200 thousand and this will insure the solvency of both programs in perpetuity. We can withdraw a quarter of our military from countries all over the world and save a trillion dollars in a half decade. We can legalize marijuana and other drugs, end the war on drugs forever and save billions fighting a war we can never win. We can provide treatment instead of incarceration for those hopelessly addicted to chemicals. Currently, we imprison one out of every one hundred men in this country."

Some applause.

"Corporations must pay their fair share of taxes. GE paid no taxes last year. Google hid funds in offshore accounts. More than 50 of the top 100 corporations did not pay their fair share of taxes and this will end."

Louder applause.

"Millionaires pay fewer taxes than you and I do because they are able to lobby congress and get tax laws fixed to benefit them and no one else. All income must be taxed as income. Capital gains is income. Dividends are income. There is a need to make this system fair and equitable. Making only the people who earn a salary or are paid hourly cannot sustain this country's future. We all need to share the expense."

Loud cheering.

"America's future is tied to America's ability to educate its children. From the moment I take office, kindergarten through twelfth grade will get more of my attention than the military will. There is nothing more important than all children getting the highest quality education possible. To that end, we will do whatever it takes to insure that this happens, and not in ten or twenty years. Right now. Right here. Today."

An eruption echoed off the walls of the nearby buildings.

"When push comes to shove, we have demonstrated our greatness because we can work together to accomplish tasks. We are faced with that now. Working together, we can make this a great time in America. If we fail to work together, we will be fighting demons the rest of this century. The answers are not simple, nor easy and pleasant. They are however, necessary, doable and imminent. I want to lead us into the future with the commitment of all Americans to do their part to make this work. I don't want to pay more taxes or sacrifice any more than I already have, but if I don't my son's future is bleak. I am unwilling to let that happen. Now I ask, how about you? What are you willing to do to make this another American century like the last one?"

Loud clapping and chants of "America" broke out.

"We are on the cusp of a renaissance. We can do it together. We can make this a glorious decade and century. I believe we can and we will."

"America...America...America..."

"Let us commit here and now to be counted as part of the solution and not part of the problem. Let us share our collective genius to solve every problem that we face. Let us pray that we remain healthy so we can persevere through any barriers we encounter."

"Leo...Leo...Leo..."

"My name is Leo Pollack. I am an unemployed steel worker running for president of the United States and I ask for your support. With your help, we will make America healthy again. Let's do it. Thank you."

Pandemonium broke out. My speech was over, but the event was not because we were surrounded by crowds for hours.

When we finally returned to the bus, Al carefully drove out of the parking lot and Gram helped him navigate back to the interstate. We got on I-94 and headed into Wisconsin and the long road home. We were exhausted but elated. Our tour de force was nearly ending for this round, but we knew there was much more to come.

The sight of the twin cities faded from our view and we descended into the rural darkness and drove for an hour before we decided it was time to pull off the highway for the evening.

"What a day, huh?" I exclaimed as we were getting into our beds.

"Amazing," was all Al could say.

"I believe we wowed them," Gram added.

"I hope that what we did today makes some small difference in the lives of the people we met."

"We did," Gram and Al pledged.

"I hope so. Good night"

We slept peacefully. We were headed into a future with a clear vision and a willingness to do whatever it took to make sure we succeeded. Anything less would be un-American. We knew that and were committed not to fail.

34. Eureka

On Sunday morning when we woke up, the results from Nevada flashed across the screen and Gram shouted, "Eureka! We hit six percent in write in votes in Nevada."

I was cooking breakfast and stopped to ponder what this meant. In each contested state, we were slowly increasing our percentage. Most likely, we were sucking away independents from both the Republicans and the Democrats. I really did not care as long as we were making progress.

"Sounds to me like the people in Nevada are not willing to gamble anymore," I said flipping an egg omelet over in the small frying pan. I made great ones and the guys enjoyed them.

Pouring some coffee for Gram and Al, I served them in the front of the bus.

"What do you make of all this? " Al asked. "Are we on a roll or what?"

"I'd say that voters in Nevada have had enough of both parties," Gram said. "They know that neither party is going to really represent them in the future. We are challenging the status quo and that is what people are beginning to accept and vote for in each of these contests."

"Now, we'll have to wait for Tuesday to roll around and see just how well we do in Michigan, Missouri and Colorado."

"We'll knock this one out," Gram said. "I predict we take all three."

"What are you smoking, my friend," Al chuckled. "Romney is spending money like water in these states and he's not going to be outdone."

"His conservative credentials are under attack. Mitt better watch out. Newt and Rick are on the warpath. They want a piece of his butt," Gram said.

"We'll see on Tuesday night what the verdict is, but I think they will split the pot. But who knows? This is one strange political year. Mitt has the greatest amount of money, but the billionaires are starting to line up for their particular horse. Even Santorum has his own billionaire backer now. So the money will determine who wins," Gram concluded.

"What a sad commentary on our democracy," I replied. "We're seeing the advent of real brokered politics. Some of these candidates would not make it past 'go' without the buckets of cash that their backers are dumping on top of them. This is the strongest argument ever for public funding of campaigns."

"We won't see that happen in our lifetime unless you get elected and make it a priority," Gram said.

"I agree with Gram," Al added. "Who can compete with the likes of Romney when he has his own millions and billions being dumped into his superpac?"

"Yet, there is Santorum giving him a run to the convention," I said. "Santorum would have been out of the race by now, but his backer, Foster Friess, put his money on him and now he's competitive."

"Kind of funny isn't it," Gram added. "Gingrich did not have much money in the first two states and got thumped. He got a backer and in South Carolina, won. Then he went to Florida, was thumped again and his backer did not give him more money so he was out of the running in Nevada. We shall see what happens in the trifecta on Tuesday."

"Let's hope that this gets resolved quickly. The longer they drag this out the more difficult it will be to focus on one contender from that party," I said.

"No, Leo, this plays right into our hands," Gram said. "The longer they beat on each other, the less time they will have to beat on Obama and you. Trust me. If they go at it until September, they will be scarred like old military ponies at the end of a war. Obama will be their primary target all the way through and we can continue to take our message of real change for real people right to the people and not have to deal with their mean spirited messages."

"I guess you're right, Gram. I just like things to be clear cut, that's all."

"They are clear cut. You're going to be in competition with one of them and Obama. He's having an easy time of it now. Wait until the general election starts and we shall see what he has in store for one of them and for us."

"I can hardly wait to get on the debate stage with them. I mean it."

"I'm sure you do," Gram said.

"Really. The way the process goes these guys never answer a question. I think the American voter deserves a simple, clear and precise answer. Give the voter that and you win his or her vote."

"I fully agree. I know you can deliver that to them. It's just a matter of time before the truth will filter out across the country and people will know who is really supporting them."

My phone rang. I answered it and listened intently. When I hung up, I said to the guys, "Expect a real busy homecoming. Big Jack just got a message from John saying that the media is camped in front of my place. This has been going on non-stop since the results from Nevada came in and they want to be ready for us when we get in sometime later today. How far are we out, Al?"

"About 300 miles. We ought to be there about 6 pm."

"More free press," Gram cried out. "Great! We can take this kind of action all the way to the bank."

"I was hoping that we might have a quiet moment or two before we head off for Maine."

"Leo, wake up and smell the roses. The days of quiet are over. You are not going to have a day to yourself unless you lose the election. Since that is not an option, your 'quiet and alone' days are over, pal. Just get used to it," Gram ended with a flourish.

"I guess this is one of the side effects I did not bank on," I said. "Oh well, if this is the price I have to pay for making a difference, then so be it."

"You can't back out now," Al said. "We're depending upon you to make this happen, today, tomorrow and for the next four plus years."

"After that, I'm done. One term and out," I blurted.

"Get the first one and then see how you feel," Gram said.

"No, Gram. I mean it. I'm only doing one term. You had better get that clear right now. This is not a career move. This is my service to my country and that's it. Get that straight, both of you," I exclaimed.

"We got it," they both replied.

For the next hour, we drove along without anyone speaking. The sounds of the highway rushing past were the only noises that filled my ears. Inside though, my thoughts were raging wildly. What was really happening in the world? Too much was coming at me and it was very sudden. I was aware that my privacy was no longer going to be mine, but I did not have to like what it meant. I was sure some day I might be able to just take a walk and not be "under guard", but with each passing day, this dream of an unimpeded future was being slowly taken away from me. I could stop now and end the folly. However, this was not an option. I was committed to the end game. I was fully responsible for making a difference and I was not willing to let anything get in the way, least of all my own selfishness. Perhaps, those other fellows were running because they had everything else they could ever want in life. After all, they were wealthy men. Senators, congressional representatives, business tycoons and lawyers who now sought the plum of all positions: president of the United States, leader of the Free World. I was in their field now. I was vying for the same title. I, Leo Pollack, an unemployed steel worker who never held any elected office in my lifetime. I was never even a shop steward for the union. I was a political virgin. I knew it and that was just fine. What difference did it make if there were a hundred vehicles in front of my house? I could always go inside and close the door. I did not have to look out and stare at them while they were out there staring in at me. I could shut the drapes and kiss my wife and hold my son on my lap and read to him and be just plain happy.

I could hardly wait to get home.

We were there in four and a half hours because Al was anxious to see all the media trucks lined up in front of my place.

What a line up there was.

We had a hard time making it through the throng of media trucks, vans, cars, light poles and camera crews standing everywhere from Wirt to Griffith Streets. The block was lit up like a Friday night football game. Every national news team was present. I even saw FOX news. Interesting.

Al, Gram and I looked at each other.

"Fellows, this is it!" Gram said. "Welcome home to the Big Time."

"How do I look?" Al asked pretending to adjust his rumpled tee shirt and blue jeans. "Well?"

"You look marvelous," I said. "Now, what do we do?"

"Go and meet our entourage," Gram said. "Keep things simple. Remember, Leo, every word you say now can and will be used against you in the court of public opinion. Choose your words carefully. Be positive. Be honest. Be a good sport."

"Be me is what you're saying," I commented.

"Was I saying all that?" Gram asked Al.

"Leo's all that and then some, but if these folks could just hear him for a minute down in the mill. Oh, Boy, would they catch an earful," Al replied.

"I'm sure that before long, someone will interview some mill rats and they will give them the lowdown on you," Gram added. "I just hope they don't have pictures of you smoking dope or sleeping on the job." He laughed heartily. Al joined him. I did not find the imagery funny.

"Let's go," I said and exited the bus.

Into the day-lit night we plunged.

A battery of microphones was thrust into my face and immediately questions were flying at me.

"How does it feel to be home again after a very productive road trip where you've taken a good percentage of the independent vote in Nevada?"

"Great. I am happy to be back home and looking forward to seeing my wife and son. As for the percentage, I am elated. We will continue to cut into the independent vote until we are viable contenders."

"How do you think you will do in the three other states holding their primaries and caucuses on Tuesday?"

"Hopefully, we'll do even better than we did in Nevada. However, the caucuses are difficult to predict because we are not as organized as the Republicans are. The general election will be easier to plan for because we won't be dealing with the confusing state systems of caucuses and primaries that are all different."

"Fund raising is an issue. You seem to be holding your own with the others. According to today's New York Times, you have now raised more than 11 million dollars. To what do you attribute your successful fund raising effort?"

"First and foremost, the generosity and goodness of the American people. The people realize that this year, for the first time in American political history, billionaires can buy and sell candidates without having to defend or hide their behavior. This election is open to the highest bidder. There is only one candidate that can't be bought and you're looking at him. This is the reason our campaign fund drive is growing and we will be competitive."

"What do you make of the battle among the Republican candidates? Whom do you think will win?"

"I believe the four men are all good Americans. Their battle is none of my concern. They will do and say whatever they choose and that will result in one of them finally emerging as the candidate for their party. So be it. I wish them well."

"If you had to campaign against any one of them, do you have a preference?"

"No."

"That's it?"

"That's it."

"Would you care to elaborate?"

"No. But I will." I stopped and waited for them to respond. They waited for me to respond. "Just kidding. I'm not going to pull a Gingrich." They caught the reference to what the former speaker had done in South Carolina during one of the debates.

"You've just traveled across the country. What kinds of things are you hearing from the people?"

"What I hear most of all from the people is this. Stop letting the partisan politics slow down governing this country. We're in the middle of a recession and the congress and the president have dragged their feet to get things done. Yes, the president has proposed countless programs to get Americans back to work, but these programs do cost money. The Republicans are unwilling or incapable of changing their focus from cutting spending to stimulating the economy. So we have a standoff. I aim to end that when I am elected."

"How will you do that, sir?"

"By taking my case directly to the people. Once I am in the White House that will be where I sleep now and then. What I have realized as I traveled across the country is that the president needs to be out in the country. No, not on Air Force One, but on a bus, in a car, meeting with people, listening to them, watching them work. He must be willing to get the story. What else does he have to do? I would park the plane and take a bus. This will save money and give more people access to their elected leader."

"Sir, just a few weeks ago, your own bus was shot at. Wouldn't traveling about in a bus be unsafe?"

"My bus does not have bullet proof glass. No, it is not safe. What is? What can any person do to protect himself from the lunatic that possesses a death wish and will do whatever it takes to destroy faith, hope and love? Nothing. So don't worry about it. Live as if this moment is your last and make the best of it."

"You are serious about parking the plane and traveling via a bus or car?"

"Serious as a heart attack. I think that the president needs to role model everything he expects his countrymen and women to do. I know I can't drive the bus. However, I can ride in it. Like today. We are here because my friend, colleague and team member, Al Caruso, has committed his time and energy to be a part of this campaign. I thank him for his devotion to this duty. I feel as safe riding with him as I did when flying in the plane a few weeks ago to New York. In fact, I feel safer in the bus. Plus, I can go to the bathroom whenever I want."

They all laughed.

"What kind of platform are you going to run on that will address President Obama's time in office? What are the issues you will need to focus on to defeat him? The economy is improving. The war on terror is being fought successfully. The unemployment rate is dropping. Home foreclosures are slowing down. What can you do to stop this president from winning a second term?"

"I can't stop him. I can only tell people what I will do differently from what he has done for the first three years. He has done his best. More power to him. I think he could have done better, not waited so long to make some policy decisions. I'll point these out as I go forward."

"Give me one example."

"Okay. The foreclosure crisis is now, at least, three years old, and if we really are honest about it, the crisis started in 2007 when banks saw people getting loans and missing their very first payments. Now, it's 2012 and millions of people all over the country are facing foreclosure. Millions of homeowners are underwater with their loans. Their homes are worth less now than when they bought them. Recently, the president proposed another round of refinancing plans. Too little too late. First, any bank that is getting federal money at .25 percent must reinvest at least 50% of that money in refinancing home loans. Second, if they do not meet this standard, they will pay double the current finance rate they are charging homeowners to borrow money. Third, if they fail this time, we will systematically take them apart, sell off their assets, and send them packing. Years ago, this needed to be done. I will do it. These megabanks are not going to hold this country hostage ever again."

"We've heard you mention college loans and the indebtedness that many young men and women are facing as they graduate and enter a job market that is wholly inadequate. What can you do to provide them some relief?"

"Currently, they are borrowing most of their money from the government and not from private lending agencies. I will free up more money so that they can get money at just a percent or two above prime rate. If Wells Fargo is getting money at .25%, then a college student will get a loan at 1.25 or 2.25% and no more. This is providing real relief because even though the principal may be $20,000, they won't be paying $30,000 by the time they pay off the loan ten years from now. Secondly, we will design programs where students can be in service to America and work off their loans. This should have been done a long time ago."

"Have you thought about a running mate?"

I laughed. "Jumping the gun, aren't we?"

"No, sir, we would like to know if you have thought about it."

"I would like to have a woman as a vice presidential candidate. However, given that there are no women running for office and that is not okay with me, I would ask the person who is second in the vote tally in the general election to be my vice president. This may seem strange to you, but I think the way we pick our vice presidential candidates is antiquated. The people should pick the person, not me."

"So you would, say, work with Rick Santorum, Mitt Romney, New Gingrich, Ron Paul, or even, Barack Obama if any one of these were the second leading vote getter?"

"Why not? After all, they are Americans as I am. They want what is best for America. What we want and how we get there may be points where we differ, but I don't think they are men who want the worst for people. I can work with anyone. You ever work in a steel mill. You soon come to realize that you're going to have to work with a lot of different folks on any given day. Some are shirkers. Some are go-getters. Some have bad breath and some smoke too much and all they want to do is kick back and take a break. You learn to work with them all. Get along or else."

"What's next for you? Where are you headed?"

"Inside to kiss my wife, hug my boy, eat some dinner, take a shower and relax in my own home. How about that for a novel idea?"

"Then what is next?"

"We're off to Maine tomorrow and then Michigan."

"What do you think your chances in Maine and Michigan will be?"

"I think my chances are as good as anyone's. I am not running for a spot on my party's ticket. I am the ticket. I am the party. I have an advantage in this way. I may even be better positioned than President Obama because he has a base to satisfy, corporate donors to appease, and the American public breathing down his neck. While I have a much less cumbersome path to follow, I do realize mine is steeper than theirs. I am anxious to keep on climbing. Things will level out."

"Any reservations?"

"Yes, I miss my family and I miss taking a hike without having to answer a ton of questions. But hey, this is the pathway I've chosen, so be it."

"What time are you leaving tomorrow?"

"O dark thirty," I replied and they laughed. "Want to come along?"

"Is there room on the Liberty Bus for a press corps?"

"I'd say not really. This is not Air Force One."

"Who does the cooking for your team?"

"I do. Who else?"

"Really?"

"Al, Gram, tell these folks who does the cooking," I cried out and waited until Gram answered them with a wise crack.

"See, what did I tell you? I'm learning to deal with adversity right now as I travel with these characters day in and out. One more question and then I'd really like to go and see my wife."

"When do you think you will know that you're in this for the long haul, that you won't drop out because your numbers are low, money is tight and you just can't make it?"

"Never. Thanks folks for the welcome party. If you have any more questions, I'm sure that Gram will be glad to answer them," I finished and pointed to him standing off to the side. He gritted at me.

I waved to the crowd and then walked over to Al, gave him a hug, thanked him for getting us home safely, and left them all and went inside to find my Basha and Janko waiting with open arms and tearful eyes. My homecoming was the sweetest moment of my life. I did not realize just how much I had missed my two favorite people on earth.

After we ate dinner, sans Gram because he was still outside meeting with the press, we settled down to watch the election returns from Minnesota, Missouri and Colorado.

Eureka! We hit pay dirt again.

In all three states, Santorum took the win upsetting Romney in two that he won in 2008. We increased our percentage in each of them by a few points and were now hovering around 9-10 %. How exciting it was to see the national press comment repeatedly on our performance in such diverse places as these three different areas of the country.

Gram walked in just as the commentary focused on our performance in Missouri where we registered the same percentage as Congressman Ron Paul. We were really in the hunt.

"Amazing Grace," Gram said. "How about those numbers?"

"What are you talking about, Uncle Gram?" Janko asked his surrogate.

"What it means, Jan, is your father is well on his way to becoming the next president of the United States."

Janko looked at Gram, his mother and then me. He replied, "The kids at school tell me that Daddy will never be president because he's not old enough and smart enough."

"The kids at your school don't know what they are talking about," Gram said. "Your Daddy is old enough and smart enough. The real issue will be can he raise enough money and compete across the country in every state where people will be voting for the president."

"Can you do it, Daddy?" Janko asked.

"I can do it, Janko. I need to keep focused. Most of all, your taking care of Mommy is what makes it possible for me to go on the road and campaign across the country. You are the most important man behind me and I thank you for doing such a good job. Mommy tells me what a big man you are when I am not here to take care of her."

Basha smiled at me and we held each other's hands. Janko held my other one.

"We are hitting the trifecta," Gram said. "Feels so good."

"Sure does. I guess those stops in St. Louis, the twin cities and Denver paid off."

"Now we'll need to get to Maine and Michigan," I said.

"No planning tonight," Basha said. "Let this day just be us together and that's all."

"Okay, I hear you," I sheepishly replied.

"Gram, go get something to eat," Basha directed him.

"I will. These results take away my appetite. I'm just wondering when we will finally crack into double digits."

"Hopefully, in Maine, Michigan and Arizona. We'll make it," I said enthusiastically.

"I hope so," Gram said.

"Me too, Daddy," Janko exclaimed. "Daddy's going to be the president."

"I hope so, son. I hope so."

"I think it's time for bed," Basha said.

Janko did not argue because he knew tonight I would be there to read with him and then we would pray together. An hour later, he was fast asleep and Gram, Basha and I were watching the final returns.

TV Commentator: "The final results are in from Missouri, and third party candidate, Leo Pollack, has take 9 % of the Republican and independent vote and is now what many consider to be a viable candidate for president in 2012. Whether or not he proves to be a 'spoiler' or 'winner' remains to be seen. In each race thus far, Pollack, an unemployed steel worker who started his campaign in an unemployment office in Youngstown, Ohio, has continued to improve his numbers. This next week, with Maine the lone state on the docket, will be a test we will have to watch to see how he does in a state known for its individualistic tendencies."

"Listen to that," Gram said. "Now that guy knows his stuff."

"You would say that about anyone who gives Leo the benefit of the doubt," Basha said.

"You're right. That's why I'm Leo's chief of staff. I accentuate the positive and minimize the negative."

"Let's do this now," Basha said. "Go to bed. I've had enough politics for one night and I don't have my man next to me enough now so I'm being selfish. Come on Leo, tuck me in. Gram can give you a blow by blow report tomorrow."

I looked at Gram. He looked at me. "You see, Gram, I live in tyranny and so I must go or else pay a dear price."

"Good night kids," Gram said. "Don't do anything I wouldn't do."

"Thanks for permission to proceed to do anything," we both offered over our shoulders as we hustled upstairs holding hands and giggling.

Gram sat alone, drinking wine and watching the late news shows.

Basha and I kissed, hugged and loved the night away.

35. Maine and Mainers

In the 2012 presidential campaign season, nobody knew anything. The pundits were having a field day. Who could predict that no one would be the leader throughout the months of intense contests in nine caucuses and primaries? From the very beginning, Romney was the front-runner only because he never stopped campaigning after his loss in 2008. He continued to promote his electability from the very first gathering of the presidential field. In the mean time, faces emerged and were quickly eliminated. By late February, Romney and Santorum were exchanging blows as they fought for the nomination. Paul and Gingrich were on the sidelines. However, each of the major Republican candidates now had a "sugar daddy" billionaire supporting his candidacy and this was making all the difference. Romney had more than one billionaire and so he had more money than the rest. He was still not the favorite of the Tea Party faithful. Santorum took that spot with the disappearance of Michelle Bachman, Rick Perry and Herman Cain. Now, he was facing media scrutiny as all the others had and some were crying foul. His supporters were upset that his record as far back as a decade ago was front-page news. We watched and wondered what the outcome would be. Along with Obama, whom would we be facing in the fall campaign? One advantage that we had was we were not running against anyone for a spot on our party's ticket. We were the ticket. This was a real bonus because we did not have to fight against someone we respected. Personally, I would not attack anyone who was challenging me for the slot. I did not see any advantage in attacking another person. Yes, we might get more votes, but that was not the way to win the hearts and minds of Americans. The current Republican campaign was an example of dirty politics that turned off American voters. Attack ads flooded the states before each event. In Florida, the Romney superpac ran 12,800 to Gingrich's 280. Santorum and Paul did not even compete in the state because it was too expensive to do so. This was the direct result of the Citizen's United Supreme Court Decision that ruled corporations, unions and other organizations were free to spend any amount of money on a campaign as long as they did not coordinate their efforts directly with the candidate. This was a "wink-wink" decision. Everyone knew it. Some said the system was broken, but they would play by the rules and do what they had to do to get their candidate elected. Even Obama consented to let superpacs supporting him do what they had to do to get him elected. He said he was not going to tie one hand behind his back giving his competitors the advantage. I wondered how he would handle my challenging him. This mystery masked our campaign.

Basha, Janko and I had a tearful morning. We left early, but I was not going to slip out into the dark before kissing my loved ones goodbye. I told them I loved them dearly and appreciated their sacrifice to make this adventure in American politics possible and encouraged them to support one another in my absence. Basha told me to be careful. Janko asked me to bring him back a moose from Maine. I said it might be a stuffed one but I would.

Maine was another caucus state. We did not have a strong presence, but what we did have going for us was our grass roots effort to spread the word across this northern most state via the internet, Facebook, Twitter and YouTube. Gram made a dozen clips of my speeches and they were going viral. He enjoyed watching them repeatedly and counting the hits they were getting. I did not fully comprehend just how powerful the medium was, but I had him taking care of it and reporting to me constantly. We would make our mark in Maine because our "Get Out and Caucus" campaign was being run on the internet and our supporters were going to both Democratic and Republican caucus sites and expressing their preference. We were elated that we could be so influential in such a low cost, low brow way.

"Get this," Gram said as we drove along through western Massachusetts on our way to I-95, the major eastern north-south highway connecting Maine to Florida, "Pollack descends on Maine like a Tornado."

"What's that?" I asked.

"Yahoo news," Gram said. "Listen to the story." He read how I was being a real spoiler in a state that always respected independence and outsiders. Mainers were a hardy people and did not like machine politics. My candidacy was tickling their fancy and they liked the idea that some blue-collar steel worker was challenging the establishment. Many were lining up to support me. Some pundits were even wondering if I might not take the state by storm and win it.

"Could you even fathom that?" Gram asked aloud.

"I can," Al replied. "We've shown these people that we are a force to be reckoned with now and in the future. These are exciting times to be alive and on the road."

"We've got a busy schedule in Maine," Gram commented. "Portland, Brunswick, Lewiston, Augusta, Waterville, Pittsfield, Bangor, Millinocket, Presque Isle and Caribou. How about that for a run?"

"Caribou? Isn't that the place where the weather is always so cold?" Al asked.

"Sure is," Gram said. "January normal lows are zero, coldest in the eastern United States. This place is cold for another reason."

"What's that?" Al asked.

"The current Governor, Paul LePage, is rabidly anti-union. In the spring of last year, he told the Department of Labor to take down the mural in the labor department's lobby that depicted organized labor's fight for justice and fairness. This caused a great deal of consternation with labor personnel across the state, but he won out. The mural was hung in a labor museum. Organized labor vowed to fight the governor's anti-labor stance. The battle has calmed down but there simmers below the surface a real resentment toward this current administration."

"What does this mean for us?" I asked.

"Mainers are an independent sort of people and do not like to be told what to do by the federal government. They lean to the right. Both senators are Republican but both congressional representatives are Democrats. They are split in the state house, but they still lean to the conservative side on most issues. What plays well here is freedom. Thoreau spent a lot of time in Maine and he was the precursor to the Tea Party, to Libertarians, to anyone who does not like big government, taxes and being told what or what not to do by others."

"I'm wondering what themes will play best."

"Stick to jobs, tax cuts, smaller government and forget about health care reform. These folks are not keen on Obama's health care plan even though I believe one of their two women senators was a deciding vote on the bill in the Senate."

"Got it."

"What are the venues we will be using?"

"Unemployment offices mostly. This continues to be our best arena."

"I agree. We sure have met a lot of people who, like me, are unsure about the future," I said.

"Your future is secure," Gram said.

"I agree," Al seconded.

"What are you guys talking about?"

"Next year at this time you'll be living in Washington, D.C. and running the country," Gram said.

"And with any luck, we'll be back to work and I'll be telling all my friends that I was there when the new president won the hearts and minds of the people," Al added.

"You guys are too much," I replied. "We have a long way to go yet before that happens. We still haven't hit double digits yet."

"We will in Maine," Gram said. "These folks are going to love you."

"We shall see," I concluded and started out the window watching the landscape slide past like a speeding videotape being fast-forwarded. This was what my life was like now: fast forward all the time. Tomorrow this and tomorrow that. Every day was a race toward another goal, another city and it would not stop until November 6, 2012 when the election would put me either in the White House or back in my own house. What was interesting was their take on it. They talked as if it was a done deal. I still had many doubts. Perhaps I was more realistic. I was not sure. However, I did believe in destiny and fate and these twins would see me through to the very end of the campaign and to Election Day.

Jobs, smaller government, and freedom it would be.

We were surprised when we entered Portland that the city was so much smaller than we had imagined. We found the unemployment office and pulled into the parking lot and there to greet us were two camps of people. Leo Pollack for President posters were flashing brightly in the sunny morning light and opposite were other signs that were not as supportive. "Leo Who for What?" caught my eye. I liked that one. Others were less flattering.

"Looks like this will be a fun venue," Gram joked, realizing that we were going to face a divided audience. "What do you make of this?"

"I don't know but we didn't plan on it, did we?"

"I'm calling Big Jack to get his take," Gram said. He was on the phone for a few minutes before hanging up.

"Seems like we got some bad press from a conservative rag that called our campaign a 'communist unionist movement aimed at taking America even further to the left than Obama had already done'. We were lumped in with the communist party from the old days when populist candidates were trying to make America more responsive to the working class people."

"These Mainers have a long memory," I commented.

"Yes, and low tolerance for anything that smacks of anything un-American like European socialism," Gram replied.

"We'll win them over. Watch," I said enthusiastically.

"Let's do it."

Boos, cheers, jeers and loud clapping greeted me when I exited the bus. I met some people who claimed to be our supporters but said there was no one person in charge. I asked them what they meant by this and they simply said, "We couldn't get anyone to take the lead. Everyone was afraid because your campaign was so new and so different."

"Al, give me that bull horn and let's get this show on the road." I waited until he handed it to me and then I walked over to a place where a bunch of wooden pallets were piled high, climbed up onto them, turned to the crowd and started.

"The American Spirit of Liberty is alive and well and living in the great state of Maine," I shouted over the bullhorn. The immediate response was a lot of cheering.

"Only strong, independent, hardy people can live in Maine where winter time takes its toll on the weak."

Loud clapping erupted.

"In a countryside where ninety percent of the land mass is covered with trees, the people who inhabit the great northern woods know a thing or two about survival, living off the land and making do with what they have."

The crowd started warming up to my message.

"America faced a crisis and it was not an external one. We started to live way beyond our means and now we are paying the price for our excesses."

Grumbling comments flooded the air.

"You and I did not make the decisions to fight two wars on a credit card or to let banks make risky loans that resulted in the entire economy hovering on a razor's edge as steep and treacherous as the one on Mt. Katahdin."

My reference to the most famous mountain in Maine garnered many cheers.

"No. We did not do any of this and yet, we are being forced to pay for it. I don't exactly agree with the way it was handled, but now we are faced with what to do. We can't cry over spilt milk. That's not an American or a Mainer way to do things. We must move on and do what is in the best interest of the country as a whole."

I could hear the people beginning to change their breathing. The sighs were audible.

"My name is Leo Pollack. I'm an unemployed steel worker and I am running for president because I believe it is time for America to be led by someone who works for a living, usually from paycheck to paycheck, does not come from a privileged family where being a national leader is part of my heritage, and like you, believe in the goodness of the working people who really make this country what it is."

Cheers and some boos persisted.

"Work is the bedrock of all life. If we do not work, we do not survive. Where else in America but in a great state like Maine is this more evident and more important. No one survives in this state without working hard because the environment is tough and unforgiving even while it is beautiful and serene."

Loud cheers rang out.

"Your state, like so many others, was thrust into the Great Recession because of the inadequate leadership of the past administration and the continuing misadventures of this one. You might hear that the current crop of Republican candidates all claim to have the fix. They are all wrong. Their solutions are throwbacks to the past. They will only make our situation worse, not better."

Confused mumblings rumbled out.

"Cutting spending will not end this recession. Nor will continued spending that is not funded by some sort of taxes. We must end the Bush tax cuts to raise more revenue again and we must cut spending and stop this negative spiral that is creating a national debt that makes all our heads dizzy when we try and wrap our minds around fifteen trillion dollars."

When I heard the applause, I sensed the shift in the people. I plunged forward.

"We all need to make sacrifices. We cannot live without a federal government. Those who want to eliminate it are foolish. Those who want to expand it are equally foolhardy. We need to find a balance. We need to share the burden of eliminating the debt and we need to share the bounty. I don't know about you, but I think there is something wrong when I pay more in taxes on my 2011 earnings of $42,000 than General Electric did on profits of 5 billion."

This fact resonated with the crowd.

"GE created 200,000 new jobs last year. The sad part was they were in countries overseas. We did not benefit by its growth. Nor did we get any of their taxes. This inequity exists and it is destroying this country. We need to end the corporate loopholes that make it possible for multi-national, global companies to hide money off shore and then wait around for their bought and paid for senators and congressman to vote for a 'tax holiday' so they can bring their money back into the US and pay minimal tax on it."

Now the crowd understood what I was saying and was with me.

"America is the most diverse nation in the world. What makes us so great is that we are a tossed salad of people who have learned to live with one another to promote the common good. We need not fear our diversity. We need to embrace it, cherish it and promote it. My grandfather came to this country from his farm in Poland to work in the steel mills and make a new life for himself and his family. My grandmother did not come to America for eight years until he saved up enough money to send for her. He wanted her to travel first class. She traveled third class to save the money. Their life together in America was an example of hard work, sacrifice and perseverance. They did not live beyond their means. They paid cash for everything. My parents were raised to believe in the same hopes and dreams my grandparents had. I am a product of these dreamers. I have not lost the dream, but I know it is being threatened by corporations who place profits over people and leaders in our government who are more concerned with re-election than with governing."

A loud cry erupted and people started to chant. "No More Years" instead of the traditional "Four More Years".

"I do not believe the current president or the Republican candidates are in tune with the vast majority of Americans who are barely making ends meet. The median income in the country is a paltry $26,433 dollars. What this number means is that 153 million Americans make less than that a year and the same make more. It is the one percent, though, who make so much more that their net worth is greater than the bottom fifty percent of all working Americans. How did this inequity develop? Special interest groups lobby congress all the time. Legislation protecting the privileged class is rampant. We fought to form unions. With one decision, a former president destroyed not only one union, but damaged the entire union movement for three decades."

"What corporations fear from unions is not that the union will overtake their company and harm it, but that the union will request a fair share of the bounty of production? How can a company justify paying its CEO ten million dollars a year in salary and bonuses and then wrangle with the union over paying a dollar more an hour to the very people who actually produce the goods and services that make a company competitive and thereby, rich? This makes no sense. The sickness in our economic system is only getting worse. The inequity is mind boggling and if we don't fix it, our economy will die from this cancer."

I did not stop to wait for applause or boos or anything. I plunged forward with the mindless energy of a speeding locomotive traveling on tracks heading into the night.

"All Americans, rich or poor, white or black, brown, red or yellow, each gender, every religion, yes, all Americans must come together and demand a fair and equitable system in which to live, work and compete. What is at stake is the very American Dream that prompted me to want to be your next president. Being unemployed, not working, not being productive is not the American way. I want to work. I want to be productive. I want to earn a living and be proud that I contribute to the greater good. I cannot because the system is stacked against working people, the very people who make this country the greatest democracy ever created by humankind."

Loud roars of approval shattered the night sky. Maine and Mainers were coming to life.

"These are not radical ideas. I am neither a communist nor a socialist. I am an American asking to be treated fairly. I am an American wanting the best for my people, you and all those who work every day. The big decision makers are not the only ones who have a stake in this nation. They are not the only risk takers. They are not the only ones who put their life's blood into their work. They are just like you and me, no better, no worse. Yes, some get ahead in the pack because of breaks, luck, brains, and brawn. This does not make them better. We are all equal in the eyes of the Almighty. Let all accept that belief and stop acting like there is something wrong with asking for a fair share."

I waited for a moment to catch my breath and to capture the momentum of a nation coming to life once again.

"Mainers, my name is Leo Pollack and I'm running for president. I am asking for your support. I am asking you to vote for me because I am the most qualified person running that can speak for 160 million working people across America. I am asking you to support our campaign by donating a dollar, five, ten or twenty, no more, for the effort. I am telling you now that I will run for one term only and my entire four years will be devoted to improving the lives of working people all over America. I will not rest until there is full employment meaning that every person who can and wants to work is doing so. I will not stop until all underemployed people, meaning those who have special skills, degrees, training and knowledge are being utilized fully. I am committed to being your voice declaring that America's greatness does not come from only the board rooms of corporations, the halls of Congress, or the White House, but also from the main streets of America where you and I live, work and play."

Chants of Leo rose up and I waved to the crowd, handed the bullhorn to Gram who was standing nearby and walked into the crowd. Enough said. Maine was on notice now that a new, vibrant, people's movement was present and the other parties were not going to take this state for granted.

We did not leave Portsmouth for hours. People kept us from moving. There was so much energy in the crowd. We wanted to harness all of it. Eventually, we made our way back to the bus and headed north.

Every day in Maine introduced us to the rugged people who call this landmass "home". They were usually standoffish at first, but once they realized that we were not foreigners, were not socialists, communists, unionists, but real Americans with real concerns about real problems, they embraced us and we were welcomed into their rugged world. Every mile up and down the long I-95 corridor made us appreciate the vast beauty of the state. To preserve the pristine quality of the landscape, state laws prohibited road signs anywhere within sight of the freeway. The result was hundreds of miles of pine trees and hardwoods lining a wonderfully contoured roadway snaking its way north to Canada.

Caribou, our last stop, enchanted us and we did not want to leave. As in most of the stops along the way, we faced heckling and even some downright disrespectful comments. This did not stop us from stating our position and engaging those who were of other political persuasions to hear our message before discounting it. Some rabid Tea Party regulars accused us of stealing their message. I rebutted their complaint by stating emphatically that we believed in enlightened government and the need for the commons to be protected by it.

We were not foolish enough to want to regress, to throw away centuries of progress because of a few decades of failed leadership. We believed the government was not the problem, but those who chose to lead it. We believed that the masses of Americans wanted to do well. There were times when a central government was essential to insure that the course of the nation was kept neither intact and pointing forward, neither straying left nor right. We believed there was a need for all people to benefit from the health care system even if they could not pay for it. After all, we lived in a civilized nation and it was our duty to look out for the "least of our brothers and sisters" even if this did not sound like something that everyone wanted to do. We were a Christian nation, and a Jewish nation, and a Muslim nation, and a Hindu, Buddhist and Atheist nation. We were not necessarily monotheistic, but we surely were a spiritual land and that was what needed to be protected from the extreme elements of any party. We stood by and watched entrepreneurs create new products, services and applauded their efforts. We stopped them when they went too far, did not act in the best interest of all people, and cut them off at the knee caps when they tried to monopolize the markets. We believed in fair, not free, trade where all who wanted to play could do so within the guidelines that favored no one person, party, company or ideological persuasion. We would not attack those who disagreed with us. We would listen to them, thank them for sharing their discontent and then move on and continue to broadcast our own simple but poignant message.

America was rising up and preparing itself to be led by the people who were simple folks that wanted the best for the greatest amount of citizens and not just the privileged few who misinterpreted the founding fathers message.

This is what we shared with Maine and Mainers and when we exhausted our time, we turned around and slowly made our way back west across New England wondering how our words would be received.

Maine did not disappoint us. As the results started to come in, we realized a new high. We received 11 % of the combined total of independent, Republican and Democratic caucus votes. We were in Maine heaven as we crossed over Lake Champlain and headed through New York State.

"Can you imagine that?" Gram cried out. "We finally made it into double digits."

"This is a red letter day," Al hollered as he drove through the night. "I feel so good I could hug and kiss you guys."

"Let's not get too exuberant," Gram cautioned. "We need to maintain a healthy respect for propriety and gender neutrality."

"Yah sure, tell that to your mother," Al chuckled.

"We made our mark in the most interesting of all the New England states," I offered. "Mainers are a special breed. No other group is as independent as they are."

"You can say that again," Al said. "We got our fair share of heckling all the way through to Caribou and back again."

"In the end, they listened to us and that made the difference," Gram responded to Al's comment.

"We kept the message focused on what they could believe in and that is the need for government to be responsive to the people and not vice versa. Government is not the problem. The people in the government are the problem. Just like a gun does not kill people, people using a gun kill people," I said.

"Nice analogy, Leo. We need to get that out on the Facebook page and on Twitter," Gram said.

We watched the results come in for a few hours and then decided that we were pushing the limit of endurance. Al offered to drive all the way home but we vetoed that idea. Big Jack responded to our call and we found a Walmart parking lot outside of Binghamton, New York and shut the Liberty bus down for the night.

When we stopped, no one approached us. We were alone with a hundred other trucks quietly idling in the vast parking lot. We were able to just peacefully relax in our little haven, drink a few beers, wait for the final commentary on the election to end and then crawl into bed to rest our weary bodies and minds realizing that our spirits did not need such creature comforts and would remain awake caring for us while we were unconscious.

36. Minute by Minute Madness

What does it take to mount a third party campaign with little money, few paid employees, a political system stacked against such a challenge and a country skeptical about change?

Every day we discovered new and interesting tidbits that added to the accumulating madness. This fact was not an indictment of any members of the team. What created the madness were the minute-by-minute decision-making adjustments we had to devise.

John Gallagher was the prince of patience. Every no to him was just another interesting challenge, another chess move trying to check us from being able to compete on the national stage. He would move his rooks or knights or even his queen and uncheck the move. There was no way he was going to let the system defeat our movement.

Judy Bream was the princess of passion. Watching her work made me realize how easy my role in this saga really was. She was connected with 50 state representatives who were coordinating their efforts with her 24/7. I wondered if she ever slept. I was afraid to ask her because I did not want to interrupt the continual flow of interfacing she was doing with her connections. I admired her tireless efforts on our behalf and told her many times.

"Leo, we're doing this for America, not just for you. Just keep on being our face. We'll do the rest." Back to the phone she went.

Fritz channeled the power of the internet and made everything techno easy to use. Our Face book page was a killer. Our Twitter feeds kept Americans tuned in to our every move. YouTube productions with Judy's help streamed constantly on the screens and repeatedly reinforced our commitment to make this a four horse race.

We heard that former Republican Congressman and Governor Buddy Roemer were mounting a third party campaign because he could not get any traction in the GOP primaries. Once, he was a Democrat, switched parties, became a Republican and was elected Governor. Now he was going to run as an independent representing the Reform Party. Gram said we needed to study his positions carefully because he was the one person who most closely aligned with us.

Fund raising was becoming a mystery to behold. Every day the New York Times listed our campaign totals. The amount was staggering. We crested $20 million at the beginning of February and were heading toward $30 million by Valentine's Day. The actual amount was growing so fast that Jim Kilpatrick said he did not realize what a popular guy I was when he called while I was in the office. He said there were no problems with access. Reporters and others were monitoring the on-line tally and he was giving everyone access to the numbers just as I had requested. "Leo, when I first met you, I was somewhat suspect. I did not think that you could pull this off. Frankly, this has been one of the most interesting experiences in my dull banker's life and so I thank you for the stimulation." I said, "You're welcome" and then asked him if he would consider a position in my administration overseeing the treasury next year? He was flabbergasted. I said, "Think about it, Jim. Government service is not all bad."

Richard Johnson, Gram, John, Big Jack and I held a number of strategy sessions planning for our eventual campaign swing through the Deep South. Richard said that he was warming up the landscape for an extended appearance by me. We knew we could pick up the Dixiecrats if we could convince them that we best represented their interests. I was excited about traveling across the south from South Carolina through Texas. Richard continued to emphasize the need to explain education and health care in very simple terms. He said anything that smacked of "universal", his southern brothers and sisters viewed as communism or socialism. "The message must be health care as a human need and a right and not some optional insurance policy that you may or may not want to buy because it is too expensive." We worked on this a lot because it was the one area that we were in the progressive column on and were unwilling to drive down the median strip as President Obama had.

My phone connected me to the world. John, Gram and the others did not filter my calls. When not in a meeting, I was talking non-stop with reporters, state leaders, interested parties who wanted to support our effort, and now and then, with Basha telling her how much I loved her and when I would, hopefully, be home. The days were long, but exciting. Nights at home helped me to keep my sanity. Sleeping in my own bed next to the woman I loved, heaven on earth.

Al kept the Liberty Bell bus always ready to go. We made short excursions to Pennsylvania, West Virginia, Maryland, New York and Indiana and were back the same day. We kept our travel light for about a week or so because we knew that once we headed off for Michigan, we would be on an extended tour. Al liked being home with his brood, too. He was a loyal trooper and never complained, but like me, he loved his family and missed them when he was out on the open road. "Now don't get me wrong, Leo. I am not complaining or telling you that I want to quit. However, I do like being home with my honey, and yes, even being in the crazy place I call my house. I didn't realize just how loud teenagers can get when they don't get their way."

We worked on campaign ads. Judy, Gram, Richard and I brainstormed many ideas and eventually came to consensus on what messages we wanted to "can" and have ready for the spring and summer. We knew that time was going to warp speed soon and we had to be ready. Carol gave us the dollar amount we could invest in the production and we hired a local company to help us produce the spots. I enjoyed being in them. We kept them simple. At first, seeing my face on screen was intimidating. After a few sessions, I started to enjoy my newfound "rock star" status. Gram cautioned me to not like it too much lest it spoil my innocence. I said to him, "You're just jealous." He retorted, "Jealousy is one of the seven deadly sins," putting me back in my place.

All of us were studying the other campaigns trying to interpret what they were doing, what they hoped to accomplish, how they were trying to overcome perceived weaknesses in the others, and lastly, how any one of them might come after us. We knew that experience would be the number one issue any of them would level against us. We accepted that and began to mount our own offense. "If experience is such an important part of a candidate's resume, then let me ask this question. When was the last time you had to balance a checkbook? When was the last time you cooked your own dinner? When was the last time you actually went to work for a full day doing heavy labor, making something, having to sweat to earn your living? When was the last time you drove your own car and did not rely on others to get you where you needed to be? When was the last time you had to make ends meet because you did not have enough money to spend lavishly on some luxury item like getting braces for your kid's teeth? We knew that these candidates functioned in another world far removed from ours. We knew that President Obama was not the simple man that he portrayed. After all, he went to Columbia and Harvard, two Ivy League colleges. This was not the normal pathway for most Americans. No, we could counter their attacks about experience by referencing other types of experience that none of them was required to master.

Where we might struggle was foreign affairs. I had never traveled outside the United States. Currently, I did not possess a passport. I asked Gram if the President needed to carry his passport when he traveled overseas and he said, "You know, Leo, that's a really good question." He did some research and discovered that the president did not need one. He was covered by presidential immunity. "Getting one might not be a bad idea," he suggested. "It would indicate that you were prepared to go overseas." We spent time discussing this issue and Gram and I decided that the best foreign policy was one that included "Listening, Learning and Leveling" with the foreign entity we were dealing with and not being afraid to tell the truth as we saw it. "You're biggest concern will be the hotspots," Gram said. They can flare up at any time and that is what drives a president nuts. Take Iran, for instance. What if they detonated a nuclear weapon? Now, what do you do? Notice that President Obama did not react when North Korea did this, or when it shot missiles in the direction of Japan. Japan would have liked us to retaliate. We did not. Prudence is part of the learning process." We spent hours discussing countries, their leaders and the possible issues these countries might present. I was excited about the learning and had my own opinions about foreign affairs, diplomacy and the building of relationships with those I did not know. No people can make peace if they do not know one another, sit across the table and stare into each other's eyes, hear each other's voices and then make a decision to stop hostilities because such behavior is in the best interest of both parties. The madness we were seeing in the world today was a result of national leaders being unwilling to sit down and make peace, break bread together. Share a meal and tell each other the truth. This was the leveling part of what Gram talked about and I fully agreed with what he believed to be essential in the process of peacemaking. I looked forward to debating the other candidates on this issue. Though I had never met a foreign leader, I worked in a steel mill with as diverse a group of men and women as could be imagined and found that I was able to find some common ground no matter what the issue was, or the task that lay in front of us. I did not want to be simplistic about this, but my notion was diplomats made diplomacy difficult so they would have something to say and do and not because they truly wanted to solve problems. Otherwise, we would have solved the Arab-Israeli conflict a generation ago.

We linked our campaign to the world through modern telecommunications grids that made it possible for me to appear on many television and radio shows and thereby minimize extensive traveling to distant sites. One of my favorites was "The Ed Show" on MSNBC. Though it was clear that Ed Shultz was a rabid supporter of President Obama, my blue-collar roots fascinated him and so he kept my campaign alive on his network by interviewing me at least once a week via satellite. I consistently explained to him and his audience that I supported the workers in every state where GOP governors were running rip shod over them, denying them collective bargaining rights and keeping working people pressed under the thumb of a relentless barrage of bum data. "It is not working people that created this nightmare recession," I told Ed on one clip, "but the lack of leadership in the White House for eight years and in Congress where special interests clouded the focus of those who were more concerned about being re-elected than governing. Government was not the problem. People were and I was determined to lead by example, take on the difficult issues, and raise workers' status, once again, to a place where all would enjoy the benefits of their hard work." Generally, Ed would end with a simple, "Good Luck, Mr. Pollack." This was enough to keep us courting his favor. Deep down, I think he was really pulling for us and not the President, but there was something that kept him from just coming out and saying so.

The topsy-turvy nature of the Republican primary was consuming a lot of airtime. We were constantly monitoring the ebb and flow of the parade of candidates. After his trifecta win on February 7 in Colorado, Minnesota and Missouri, former senator, Rick Santorum, emerged as the tentative front-runner. He was elated that his brand of conservative politics was gaining momentum.

Romney attacked him as a "Washington Insider who supported earmarks, raising the deficit five times, and supporting former Arlen Specter instead of a true conservative, Pat Toomey, in the senatorial race when he was still the junior senator. Santorum did not deny that he did do these things. He could not avoid the facts.

The others were still wallowing at the bottom of the Republican food chain. Ron Paul was a consistent 8-10% of the vote and Gingrich was languishing down at the bottom. They could not seem to gain any traction.

However, every one of them now had a billionaire "sugar daddy" that was feeding money to the separate superpacs supporting the four Republican candidates. This flood of big money was keeping Santorum, Paul and Gingrich in the hunt. Without this money, their campaigns would have folded a month ago. Everyone knew that because of the Citizens' United decision, this campaign season was going to be a long, drawn out affair.

The real winners in this political landscape were not Democracy and the American people but the ad agencies and the mass media outlets that were making hundreds of millions of dollars running these ads. The amount of money being spent was obscene. Romney spent $17 million in Florida. How much he spent in other states was sometimes difficult to calculate because there was more than one superpac backing him. Whereas, the others had a single billionaire financing their campaigns, Romney had many billionaires pushing his candidacy.

On the very day that President Obama revealed his tax reform platform, Romney released his and the contrast could not be more striking. Both proposed reducing the top corporate tax rate, but Romney's clearly rewarded the top one percent by cutting their taxes to a twenty percent flat tax that would have given every millionaire an immediate $80,000 tax cut. For some reason, he would not admit that this was true.

Gram researched the amount of money that was being spent and by whom and shared it with us during one strategy session we held just before we headed off for Michigan.

"For the past twenty years, corporations, millionaires and billionaires have followed the lead of the Godfather, Don Corleone, when donating money to campaigns. Here is what I mean by that. They don't just contribute to one party or the other. No, they contribute to both parties so that no matter who wins, they win. They have influence with either party that assumes power. Let me give you a few examples."

Gram had created a power point presentation and it was extremely revealing, informative, and in some ways, disheartening.

"Bear with me for a moment. These numbers really display what we are up against."

He pointed the projector toward the white board, and we could see many names and numbers.

"Okay. Here we go. The number one superpac and biggest bundler of campaign contributions is Act Blue. No, it is not a Republican organization but the leading Democratic fund raising machine. In the last twenty years, it has raised more than $58 million dollars. That is no chump change. Second on the list is AT&T and it plays both sides of the political fence raising more than $48 million. AFSCME, the union, is third on the list and has raised more than $47 million. Ninety-two percent of its money went to Democratic campaigns. No wonder the

Republicans are so committed to attacking public employee unions. They realize that this one union is just as powerful as AT&T. The National Association of Realtors has raised $41 million and was very patriotic donating almost equally to both parties. It wanted to make sure that its voice was heard no matter who was in power. The two unions, SEIU and the NEA, are big Democratic contributors. What comes next will surprise you. Goldman Sachs actually donated more money to Democrats than to Republicans. Go figure."

We stared at the extensive chart that Gram displayed on the wall.

"What does this all mean? This government is for sale, has been for sale for the past twenty years in a wholesale way, and we are bucking this entire system in our effort to keep the high rollers out of our campaign," Gram concluded.

We studied the groups and numbers and were amazed.

"You can see why Republicans want to destroy all unions," John said. "I didn't even know that we were so organized."

"Check out Citigroup," Carol cried out. "49-49 even for both parties. Amazing. I'd never have guessed they would do that."

"Wow, look at the United Auto Workers!" Fritz said. "They are off the scale. Ninety-eight percent to zero. Obama was right on target when he bailed out the auto industry. They are almost 100% Democratic."

We were dumbfounded.

"Notice that the first nineteen groups on this list favor the Democrats and not the Republicans. You can see that many are unions and not major banks. The numbers are fascinating. Studying the list more carefully, you will see, as I said earlier that most Fortune 500 companies do not discriminate. They contribute to both parties equally."

"What we've got going for us is we are not stuck in this paradigm," I said.

"You're right, Leo, but we are also bucking up against money and influence pedaling systems that will be harder to crack than the vaults at Fort Knox. The reasons are obvious, aren't they?"

The numbers created a buzz and for the rest of that afternoon, we tried to figure out strategies to overcome our self-imposed handicap of not accepting big dollar donations from any group or individuals.

Late in the afternoon, Carol called us together again and proposed a new idea for fundraising. "We won't ask for five, ten or twenty dollars anymore. No. We want people to contribute a dollar. No more. This will make it possible for anyone to give us money. A homeless person can donate. Millionaires won't even think about it. Everyone can kick a buck. This will lower our threshold for contributions, but boost our image of a campaign of, for and by the people."

We sat still just absorbing the idea.

"I love it," Judy exclaimed. "We'll be taking the opposite tact than the other campaigns. We'll be putting our principles where our money is. This will blow the other parties away. They won't know what hit them. If we can get this out and people flood us with dollars we'll be way ahead of the game."

"The most important thing is to be frugal on what we spend our money," Gram said. "Keep in mind that what costs campaigns the most amount of money are ads. If we limit the ads we run, we can really impact the entire process."

"So how do we get the word out? How do we compete with the other campaigns that are flooding the airways with both positive and negative ads?" John asked rhetorically.

"Simple," Gram said. "Judy and I build an entire campaign on Facebook, Twitter, YouTube, our home page, and we get as much free public relations as we can by taking the press along with us in the Liberty Bell bus. We can do it folks. We can."

"My Oh My," John said. "Will wonders never cease? What a team!"

"I agree. Folks. I've got to admit it's getting better, getting better all the time," I said.

"Nice Beatle's lyric," Gram said. "I loved that song."

"Make it happen, Carol," John said.

We dispersed again.

Gram, Al and I discussed our next trip to Michigan. We were leaving the following day. This was going to be our last trip before the beginning of March Madness, not the basketball tournament but the extensive string of primaries being held throughout the month.

"Gram, you've shared with us a number of times your 48 state tour where you try to ride your motorcycle through every state in the Union but minimize the amount of miles it takes to do it. What I want to propose is an extensive 'drive-about', a 48 state bus tour through all the states visiting as many small cities, towns and villages as we can all with the hope of taking America silently with our presence everywhere the other campaigns are unwilling to go."

Gram looked at me for a moment. Al stared at Gram. Then, they looked at each other. Finally, they said, "We like it. Let's do it."

"When do we leave?" Al asked.

"We could leave today but we're not ready for an extensive trip like this. We need to get Judy to put out the word. We want to get the most amount of press coverage out of this as we can. You and Gram need to develop the route. We want to get this out on Face book, Twitter and YouTube. We are going to be gone for a few months. I think we need to break this to our families first and get their support."

"No sweat there," Gram said.

"Don't rub it in," Al said. "You're the odd man out."

"Yes, and he doesn't have anyone waiting for him at home," I said.

"Janko looks forward to seeing me," Gram said, gritting at me.

The passing days were a blur of activity. Gram and Al had the route ready the next day. Judy and Gram worked on getting the GPS coordinates into the system. Fritz blitzed the media with the idea. As soon as the word got out, we were deluged with inquiries. Through some insiders, we discovered that the press corps was beginning to get anxious about what was happening and how to cover this phenomenon that was the "Leo Pollack for President".

Every day we were at the campaign headquarters made me appreciate just how many people were working countless hours. I would walk into the control center down in the union hall cellar and watch the hubbub of activity. More than fifty people staffed phone banks, talked, listened, laughed and coordinated activities all over the country. John was the impresario of the entire orchestra of willing minds, bodies and souls. He liked this part of the job and it showed. Hovering over his people like a male "Queen" bee, he made sure they had everything they needed to do their work. I loved to wander around, listen to the conversations, get hugs and kisses from some of the volunteers, express my absolute appreciation for their commitment to the campaign and most of all, just be close to the people who would eventually go home and remember that they were a part of making history.

Everywhere in the hall, television sets were tuned to all the news channels and they chronicled the daily shifts in the country's fickle nature. When we were on the road, we watched the tube to keep ourselves abreast of the trends that were flowing across the country. Sometimes the information was overwhelming. Most of the time, we tuned out the repetitive nature of the reports. However, there was a moment or two every day when something important rolled across the screen like when Buddy Roemer dropped out of the GOP campaign and announced he was running on the Reform Party ticket. The same day, on Hardball with Chris Matthews, Matthews and a couple of strategists said that this year, more than any time in the past, a third party candidate like Leo Pollack could really rise up and challenge the establishment. He was not endorsing me, but just mentioning my name in the same conversation with the others, made the comment pregnant with meaning.

We had arrived. This was it. There was no doubt that our campaign had gained enough traction to get the prime time news organizations to begin to promote the idea of a realistic third party candidacy. I sat still in my chair and just smiled broadly.

"What's up?" Gram said seeing me just sitting still and doing nothing at all.

"The notion of a third party candidacy this campaign year was promoted by Chris Matthews on Hardball."

"Cool beans! See, we are real trendsetters. The future is ours. Nothing can stop us now on the road to the White House."

"Only flat tires and a blown engine in our bus," Gram said.

"What?"

"Al and I have the drive-about route ready to go. We'll have it programmed into the GPS unit by tomorrow morning before we leave for Michigan. Leo, this is a great idea. We will make tons of connections along the way."

"I'm almost afraid to get too happy," I said, "because this year I lost my job and the mill seems like it will never open again. Now I'm running for president of the United States. I am amazed there are so many people working to get me elected. I'm just wondering where this will all end. What are we going to do now?"

"This is your job now, Leo. Get elected and do something to stop the negative trend toward destroying the rest of our industrial base."

"We will, but right now, let's get out of here and head home. We are not going to be able to spend much time with the family in the days, weeks and months to come."

"I hear you," Gram said. "You go on ahead. I'll walk back to the house. I've got some things to finish before I can shut down for the night."

"Be my guest," I said. I walked around and said goodbye to all those who were still working.

As I drove home, I enjoyed the quiet moments without any phone ringing. Television blaring or a reporter asking another loaded question. I was not sure how I was able to escape the union hall and not have someone tail me to my home. I knew what was waiting for me at the house and that was enough to make me drive very slowly.

A few blocks from the house, I braced myself for what lay ahead. I could see the lights. They were camped out. This was what they did. That was their job. I was their topic. I did not resent their being there. I was beginning to accept it as much as I did my own breathing. After all, they were the lifeblood of any campaign. Without them, my campaign would not even exist. As I pulled into the driveway and got out of my car, I turned around and went to talk to those firmly planted in my world.

We had a wonderful conversation and that made all the difference.

37. Great Lakes State

Michigan boasts the longest freshwater coastline of any political subdivision in the world, bounded by four of the five Great Lakes plus Lake Saint Clair. Michigan is one of the leading U.S. states for recreational boating. The state contains 64,980 inland lakes and ponds. No Michigander lives more than 6 miles from a natural water source or more than 85 miles from a Great Lakes shoreline. It is the largest state by total area east of the Mississippi River. It is the only state to consist of two peninsulas. The Lower Peninsula, to which the name Michigan was originally applied, is often noted to be shaped like a mitten. The upper peninsula, often referred to as "The U.P.", is separated from the Lower Peninsula by the Straits of Mackinaw, a five-mile-wide channel that joins Lake Huron and Lake Michigan. The Mackinaw Bridge connects the two peninsulas. The Upper Peninsula is economically important due to its status as a tourist destination. There is a variety of natural resources to be found there, including a sizable amount of iron ore.

We entered Michigan on I-75 just west of Toledo, Ohio and headed north toward Detroit. Our mission was simple. We were going to cover as much of Michigan as we could in six days. The primary was on Tuesday. We hoped to get a lot done in that time. We were making progress. Anything we did moved us ahead in the polls. We were like a slow moving tugboat gathering momentum as we continued to pile new barges in front of us the longer we pushed our campaign down the river. The race was not always won by the swiftest, but often by the one with the most perseverance and the simplest plan. Ours was very simple.

We were a half hour out of Detroit when Gram got a phone call. I was pacing the floor thinking about what we were going to say and do in this great lakes state when the phone rang. I could not hear what he was saying. He was listening more than talking.

All of a sudden he shouted, "Yes! Yes! Yes! That's great, Carol. Wow! Let me check it out and I'll email you," he said and hung up.

"What just happened?" I asked curious at his sudden outburst.

"Carol wants to take Gram out to dinner," Al said subtly. "You know, Leo, Carol and Judy are both after Gram. They want to bang his bones."

"I wish, but that's not what the call was about," Gram barked at Al and me. "Check this out," he said doing a quick search of the internet and showing us on his laptop the most recent headlines in the search column.

"Strategic Campaign Decision Nets Pollack Campaign Millions".

"What?" I cried out.

"Millions of what?" Al asked as he slowed down so he could concentrate more on what was happening and less on driving.

"Pull over Al, you've got to hear this out," Gram said. Al slowly eased the big bus to the side of the road and put the four ways on.

"Let me read," Gram said. "In an unprecedented move, the Leo Pollack for President Campaign Committee issued a statement on Thursday that it would no longer be accepting donations in excess of one dollar. A spokesman for the campaign, Carol Hawley, said, 'We are a campaign of the people and we realize that asking people for even ten or twenty dollars right now can create a burden for them. We want their voices to be heard so we are asking for donations of only a dollar. We believe that this will be a signal to all Americans that we are speaking for them, the little donors, and the ones who never have a real voice in the campaign because they don't donate millions.' In the past three days, the campaign raised a whopping $13 million dollars. This amount was greater than all the other campaigns, including President Obama's, had raised in the first month of the year. When asked what the campaign was going to use the money for, Hawley said, 'Not for millions of dollars in ads. We will find a way to use the money to get our message out and still stay within a budget that is prudent. When we win the election, all leftover money will be donated to a scholarship fund to send as many young people to community colleges as possible.'

"What do you make of that?" Al said. "I'm impressed. We are way ahead of all those other campaigns. That's so hard to fathom."

"Gram, what the hell. This is phenomenal. This is way beyond anything I could ever have imagined," I cried out.

"Carol's idea sure is paying dividends. Man, can you believe it. $13 million in four days. You know what that means don't you?" Gram exclaimed.

"What?" Al asked.

"What?" I dittoed.

"We just got 13 million votes. That's what. Think about it. No one is going to donate money to someone he or she isn't going to vote for in the election. People vote with their money as well as with their ballot. Leo, Al, we just hit the mother lode. We are well on the path to winning this election. We just have to sustain the effort."

"This is crazy," Al said. "I get the numbers but the reality just doesn't compute."

"I know, Al," I said. "It doesn't for me either, but yet it does. Dollars equal votes. One dollar from a million people means a million people are pledging their support to us. We get a dollar. It means we get a million votes. Amazing."

"It can only get better," Gram said. "Check out this headline." He read to us from the New York Times. "A month ago, the Times started documenting the growing support for Liberty Party candidate, Leo Pollack. Since then, the campaign has raised more than $13 million dollars and it accomplished this feat by lowering its campaign contribution limit not raising it. Previously, the limit was up to twenty dollars. Four days ago, the campaign lowered the limit to a dollar and fund raising exploded."

"There you go! We are in the black for the long term and no matter what happens, we will be able to make it all the way to November," Gram said.

"You know what this means now fellows," I cautioned.

"What?" Al asked.

"We are marked men. We just dope slapped the other campaigns upside the head. They aren't going to like being upstaged like this. There will be some kind of retribution. They will start to attack us in some way. I can feel it coming," I said.

"I agree, Leo. But what can they do? Check our books? Find that we are spending money for hutchie kuchie girls and entertaining them on the Liberty bus while we travel from city to city? They can't get us. We're as transparent as a naked newborn baby. Let them kiss it. That's my notion!" Gram cried out.

"I don't know how they will come after us, but they will. I need to talk with Jack," I said.

"I've got an idea. Let's contact the reporters that are already assigned to us and hold a press conference. Right on the bus. We can get them to send someone out to meet us in Detroit and we can have a powwow right here and now. While you talk to Jack, I'll arrange it."

"This is crazy, Gram," I said.

"Crazy? How about proactive? We go on the offensive. We never play defense. We hold the ball for 60 minutes of the game. We never give it up. Leo, we're in Detroit Lions country now. You've got to roar like a lion, my friend."

Gram dialed Judy's number to make the connection.

I talked to Jack. He listened to my concerns. When I was finished, he said, "Just ahead is a rest area. Stop in there and we'll talk face to face."

Al pulled over a mile ahead and stopped the bus. Big Jack stopped in front of us. He and another fellow got out and came over to the bus.

"Leo, fellows, meet Jeeves," Jack said. Jeeves was a skinny, young fellow wearing shades, a beanie cap, jacket, jeans and sneakers. He had a pencil thin mustache and a baby face. He did not say anything but he did smile wanly.

"Jeeves. Go to work." Jeeves took out some instruments and disappeared into the bowels of the bus.

"What's up Jack," I asked.

"We don't know yet. Could be bugs. We think there has been a breech somewhere. Fritz called me and said to check it out. Jeeves is the best at what he does."

"What's that?" Gram asked.

Big Jack smiled. "Plug leaks. Foil hackers. Piss off the government."

"What?" I asked. "You think we're under some sort of surveillance by the government?"

"We don't know yet, but Jeeves will find out one way or another. Could be the other campaigns. You saw the news today, I'm sure. Now that we hit the big time with raising money, the other folks are going to start to wonder what we are up to and that will lead to all sorts of things. We can't discount dirty tricks. Once Jeeves gets done with the bus, you'll be secure. However, realize this. The entire power of the federal government is an awesome force to be reckoned with so take nothing for granted."

"What do we need to hide?" I asked. "We raised a lot of money. So what?"

"That's just it, Leo," Gram said. "What Jack is trying to tell us is that money equals power. These other campaigns that are totally dependent upon raising money to continue their work can't fully understand how the money does not mean as much to us as the votes do. Just as Ron Paul is going after delegates, we are after votes. Once we get more than a $100 million in dollar bills, we'll have essentially a 100 million votes and that can take us all the way to the White House. This scares the piss out of Obama and the rest of these wannabes. We are on the fast track."

"Okay, so we have to be careful, I get it. We don't need to change our message though. We need to insure that they are not inside our underwear when we go to the bathroom, that's all," I said.

"A crude but apt image," Jack said. "Jeeves will fix the bus. I can't fix you, Leo. Realize this. We are moving into new territory. I am going to get you a flak jacket and you're going to start wearing it."

"What?" I cried out. "What the hell are we doing here?"

"Making sure that you survive. Al, in the back of the car, there's a package. How about getting it for me."

"Sure, Jack," Al said and went to the car to retrieve it.

"No one will know you're wearing it. This is the latest, greatest jacket made. I got Carol to order it last week. Navy Seals wore this kind when they took out bin Laden. It's state of the art and can stop anything short of a 50 cal.-spent uranium round. They hit you with that, well, kiss your ass goodbye. But, I'll take them out after the fact. You get my drift?"

I sat there numb and mute.

Al brought the package back and Big Jack opened it and had me try it on. I took off my shirt and slipped on the flak jacket. I put my shirt back on. I could barely tell that I was wearing it.

"I already told you this state of the art protection," Big Jack said.

"How did you get one?"

"For me to know and you to find out," Jack said seriously.

"Stand up and walk around a bit so we can see how it looks," Jack ordered.

I walked around in the bus.

"Looks good on you, Leo."

"Jack, is this really necessary?" I asked him.

"Leo, I know you want to believe in the goodness of humanity. I do, too. However, my genetic code going way back to ancient Africa does not have in it the same history. I'm suspect. I don't always believe in the goodness of people. Mine or others, if you get my historic drift? We just need to be careful. There is a lot at stake in this election and there are a lot of people who do not like the idea that someone like you is sticking it to their handpicked candidates."

Big Jack walked back to the kitchen area and said "Jeeves, you done?" Jeeves came back from the back of the bus and said, "Done."

"We're out of here. Jeeves is the master of the disaster. You want something fixed, you call him, Gram. Realize this. Your computer is not safe. We've installed a device that will protect you most of the time. However, there are some new fangled whizz-bang gizmos that the government's rolled out that we haven't figured out yet. When Jeeves gets them debugged, we'll be back."

"Thanks, Jeeves," I said shaking the young fellow's hand.

"You're welcome, Mr. Pollack," he said politely.

"Call me, Leo," I said. "We're all on the same team." Jeeves smiled but did not say another word.

"Jack, when can I take this vest off?" I asked.

"When you sleep," he said emphatically. "Inside the bus, leave it on. We don't have bulletproof windows in here. Yet." He did not elaborate on the "yet".

"Jack," I asked, "I just have to know. Is that young fellows name really Jeeves?"

Jack smiled and left without answering my question. I did not know what to make of his reluctance to tell me what I wanted to know.

When he and Jeeves were gone, I asked, "What do you make of that?"

"We're blessed to have someone like Jack on our team," Al said. "That's what I think."

"When do I get my vest," Gram asked with a disappointed look on his face.

"When you are the main target!" Al chirped. "Right now, the only thing you need is a bib to keep you from slobbering all over your shirt when you eat your lunch."

"Ha, ha, funny guy," Gram said.

"About as funny as your face," Al said. "Leo, can you do something about this guy's mug? Tell him to go shave his peach fuzz off so he looks presentable."

"Let's get going," Gram said. "We've got a date with some reporters in downtown Detroit in about an hour."

"Really?" I asked. "So soon?"

"Judy makes things happen. We're in the Big Leagues now, my friend," Gram replied.

"Jeeves. What a strange fellow!" I said. "Wasn't there a search engine once called 'Ask Jeeves'?"

"Sure was," Gram said. "I used it all the time. Ask Jeeves a question and he'd answer it for you. I don't know what happened to it, but it was very robust."

"I'll bet I know," Al said. "Microsoft killed it off because they couldn't buy it from the developers and they destroyed it with Bing and other engines that they could control."

"I didn't know you were a computer historian," Gram said.

"I'm now. My kids are the ones who burn my ears with this type of trivia," Al said. "But I do believe what they tell me."

"I can see that happening," Gram said. "Microsoft is a monopoly and the government is afraid to take it on because its tentacles are in every computer in the country. If they wanted to do so, they could shut the entire computer network down by just inserting their own 'fix' to the operating system that would destroy everything."

"You believe that?" I asked.

"I not only believe it, I know it," Gram said. "This is '1984' in real time and we are just beginning to experience some of the fallout that will eventually make the book a panacea for what really will happen to this country and the world if we don't do something to change the course of history."

"What can we do?" I asked.

"Get you elected to the presidency and then begin to fight the evil forces that exist everywhere around us," Gram said.

"Now you're starting to sound like Santorum who talks about the devil," I said.

"His devil is a religious one. The evil I'm talking about is the forces present in business and industry that want to control the entire world economy and squeeze people until we are slaves to them."

"Who are they?" I asked.

"They? I read their names off the day I did that presentation at the hall. They are all those who don't care about this country but do care about power and control. They are the ones that you will need to speak 'truth to their power'. They are the ones that Jack is trying to protect you from within his own little sphere of influence. They are invisible until they are exposed by forces like 'anonymous', the hacking crew that remains the most important non-governmental power in the world, that can take down entire countries if it, they, whomever choose to do so."

"What if they decide to go rogue? Then what?"

"Holy Hell breaks loose. What can I tell you?" Gram concluded.

We did not talk for a long time. Each of us was trying to fathom what all this grand conspiracy chatter really meant. I knew I was rather naïve. I just did not realize how much. First Big Jack, now Gram, enlightened me beyond my wildest imagination. In some ways, I was glad that I was learning what was actually happening around me, but deep down inside, my own world order was shifting. I did not like the way the internal plates were moving away from each other and causing what only could be described as an internal earthquake that dislodged some of my dearest held beliefs from their moorings.

Detroit assumed a greater than real life aura in my imagination. Though it still was the center of the American auto industry, the city was slowly dying. The new Republican governor, Rick Snyder, like many of his nearby conservative colleagues, attacked working class people with his plan to end collective bargaining for public sector employees. He followed the lead of Governor Scott Walker in Wisconsin, Mitch Daniels in Indiana and John Kasich in Ohio. Ohioans fought back and repealed the bill that Kasich had signed into law last year. Michiganders did not follow suit. What was even more insidious was a bill Snyder signed that gave him "emergency powers" to appoint a fiscal manager to any city or town in Michigan that was facing bankruptcy or that was in financial difficulty? With this authority, Snyder could eliminate the duly elected mayor, city manager or commissioners and install someone to run the government effectively undermining the democratically elected individuals. The policy was already implemented in a number of smaller cities like Pontiac, Michigan. There was a rumor that the next city to discover it was being run by a Snyder appointed city manager would be Detroit.

Into this embroiled climate, we prepared to launch our Michigan campaign in the face of the most pernicious attack waged against democracy in the last fifty years.

Big Jack met us in front of the Department of Labor where we were planning on meeting with a number of reporters from the Detroit Free Press and some national media representatives.

"We decided to meet the people here because this was convenient for them and we can hold a press conference that can be broadcast via satellites to the rest of the country," Jack said.

"Who are the contacts?" Gram asked.

"Come and meet them," Jack said and took us into the lobby. When we got inside, we were astounded to find a crowd of people gathered. As we entered the building, cheering and loud applause broke out. Looking around the main lobby area, I estimated there were four or five hundred people gathered. They ranged in age from babies in mothers' arms to the gray hair and beards set. I was elated to see so many people on this first foray into the Great Lakes State.

"Welcome to Detroit, Leo Pollack!" someone hollered over a loud speaker.

I thought I was going to a surprise birthday party. Raising my hand, I waved to the crowd and followed Big Jack toward the center of the lobby. A small group of nicely dressed young men and women came forward to greet us. They were the "Occupy Detroit" representatives. I was happy to make their acquaintance.

"We've gathered the press, supporters, interested parties and even invited the governor to come and welcome you, but he declined," a young fellow named Jimmy said to me.

"Thanks for the honor," I said. "We did not expect this kind of reception, but we never do."

"The entire state of Michigan is waiting for you," he said. "You don't know how important your candidacy is right now."

"I'm sure I don't," I said.

"This governor has made a concerted effort to attack democracy anywhere he can. We've filed a lawsuit against his most current decision to try and take over Detroit, but we are a long way from stopping his usurping power that belongs only to the people."

"How can I help?" I asked.

"Become the president and end this tyranny," Jimmy said.

"That's the plan, but first, we need to win the election."

"We'll do all we can to help you do that. Now, it's time to meet the people. Let me introduce you and then it's all yours."

Jimmy stepped up on a makeshift platform in the center of the lobby. He switched on a microphone and welcomed the people to the center for democracy.   "Michiganders, we are fortunate this evening to have with us the next president of the United States, Leo Pollack," Jimmy said and the house erupted. "Let's give a warm welcome to Mr. Leo Pollack." He walked away from the center of the stage and handed me the microphone.

I stood up and went to the center of the stage, waved my hand and waited until the crowd settled down.

A few moments later, the floor was mine.

"Thank you for the warm welcome. Let's get to work. Oh, yes, work. While the Republicans this week were debating whether women should receive birth control pills as part of their health care…" Loud boos erupted from the crowd…"Michigan is seriously suffering from the recession. Unemployment in this city is still higher than in most places in the country. What needs to happen is a radical approach to economics. We need to bring our industrial base back home again."

The crowd cheered wildly.

"Our tax codes favor wealthy corporations and people. They discriminate against working people and small business persons who try to make it against all odds. The reason we cannot change these codes is because the Democratic and Republican parties are bought and paid for by their supporters. We, Americans, must reverse this negative process and begin to protect workers from the unfair free capitalistic system that is currently operating in the country."

"We want Leo" chants started.

"There is a simple solution to this complex problem. Progressive taxation without so many loopholes in it that allows a millionaire like your native son who is running for the Republican Party's nomination to pay a lower percentage than I did last year."

The crowd went wild. I waited until they settled down.

"Now is the time to make a difference before America faces even greater attacks on working people. We've born the burden of this recession. We've taken the hit right in the gut, but we still can see because we are not blind. Our purchasing power has eroded for two decades. Many of us are facing the loss of our homes. Most of us who do own our own homes realize that the value of them is much less than when we bought them. They are sadly 'under water' as the economists say. Now is the time to stand up for our rights. We cannot wait for the Republicans or the Democrats to do it. We have waited too long. They are not listening. We're going to ring the liberty bell long and hard until they finally hear the tolling."

The crowd cheered loudly when I mentioned the bell and a "gong" chant began. I listened, smiled and waved my arm in unison with the "ringing".

"We need to begin to make American made cars again. What I mean by that is the cars we're making today are 'assembled' in America, but the parts are coming from all over the world. An American made car does not exist. The Japanese cars that are 'made in America' are really just assembled here. When we change this, we will see our economy boom again."

"Made in the USA" chants fired up.

"We are on the edge of a great movement. Your being here today is a symbol of what is coming. We are going to take over our country from the special interests groups and wealthy global corporations that care little about what they do to America. We shall overcome. We shall overcome. We shall overcome someday. Thank you."

Music started playing in the background. I immediately knew what it was. Layla by Derrick and the Dominoes. It was my favorite song. I wondered how anyone could know that and meant to ask Gram later. Pressing my way through the crowd, I met Detroit in all its glory. Men, women, children, old, young, minorities, well-to-do, down- and-out, the spectrum of a society in flux. The body heat alone was enough to warm my soul to the core, but there was another type of fire present in this crowd. There was passion, a 'fire in the hole' I called it. These folks demanded something new, something they had not tasted for a long time.

Eventually, the crowd began to disperse and Gram came and retrieved me.

"Work, my friend," Gram said.

"What?"

"Press corps is waiting in the bus like I promised," he said. "Get your game face on."

"They're invading the only refuge we have on the road," I protested.

"Leo, we've got a captive audience. Don't look gift horses in the mouth," he blurted out.

"Where did that silly expression come from?"

"I don't know. Just follow me."

Inside the Liberty Bell bus, we found six people from a host of media sites. When I entered, they all stood up out of respect. I was impressed.

"Welcome to our bus," I said and asked them to be seated. "Gram, would you mind making some coffee and get some sodas and cookies for our friends."

"Not at all, Leo," Gram said graciously.

"Normally, I do all the cooking and cleaning, but since we have guests I am fortunate to have such a wonderful surrogate as Gram," I proclaimed to the press.

"Don't get too uppity," Gram said. "As soon as the company leaves, you'll be back to chief dish and bottle washer status."

"See what tyranny I live under," I cried out.

The folks laughed along with me.

They were a mixed group. ABC, CBS, NPR, NBC, FOX, and the Free Press. I was elated that we could have them all here at one time.

"Not one to waste your time, let's get started," I said.

FOX. "What do you think your chances are of actually winning this election given you are a third party candidate in a country that has never given any such candidate more than 15 % of the vote?"

"My chances are 50-50. If I never ran, the odds would be zero. Right now, with the divisive Republican primary and the current president's low approval ratings, I would say that my chances are at least what I stated and grow better each day."

ABC. "You're campaign, this week, dropped its maximum donation from twenty dollars down to a dollar. What were you thinking and what do you hope to accomplish?"

"I'm glad you asked that question for two reasons. First, we realized that many people would like to contribute but do not have an extra ten or twenty bucks to kick in to the campaign. Hence, we lowered it so that everyone can feel like he or she is capable of making a donation. Secondly, we believe that every person who donates a dollar to a campaign does so because he or she believes in what the candidate is saying and doing. We have collected more than 13 million in four days. This is amazing, but what is more astounding is not the amount of money, but that 13 million people gave a dollar. The amount of people equals a net gain in voter support of 13 million. The numbers are astounding."

NBC. "Following up on that question, where do you see your greatest support coming from as you move forward?"

"From the 160 million working class people who are required to pay the payroll tax. This is the group that most embodies the American work ethic. As a group, they have made America what it is. Yes, there are those who make a lot of money by creating new products and ideas, but they are only successful financially. They don't make a real difference in our economy. Let's take Steve Jobs for instance, rest his soul. Nice guy. Created some nice products. However, no I phone or I pad or I pod was made in America. He outsourced all that production. Yes, he made a lot of money. Apple is a valuable stock to have. He did not raise the standard of living for many Americans. Had Jobs produced his phones, pads, and pods in America, just imagine how many jobs this would have created. I'd buy an I phone today if he had. As it is, I won't ever own one because I resent the fact that the phones are not made here."

CBS.   "You commented during your speech about the attack Governor Rick Snyder is making on the cities in Michigan that are facing bankruptcy. His plan is to provide a financial manager to oversee the return to fiscal responsibility. What is wrong with such an approach from your point of view?"

"You've got to be kidding? Wrong? Everything. Better my own elected ineffective, local leader than an appointed, disinterested political crony of some external dictator. Look, there is everything wrong with this plan. This is not democracy. This is dictatorship of the proletariat. These Republicans accuse President Obama of socialism, wanting to bring European style socialism to America. What is this? What kind of democratic process are we promoting here in the great state of Michigan? No, my friend, this is absolutely wrong, unacceptable and downright undemocratic. What the governor needs to do is meet with the leaders of the cities in trouble and solve the problems together. What he is doing is usurping his power. Putin would love a guy like this. I mean it. If I were president, I'd have the attorney general all over this governor like white on rice. He wouldn't breathe without someone asking him what the heck he is doing to the people of Michigan."

NPR.   "You're not mincing words, Mr. Pollack. You feel this strongly about this issue?"

"Wouldn't you if you lived in Pontiac, Michigan and the governor of your state told your mayor, your city council, your school board, your entire body of elected officials that they were no longer in charge and some crony of his was coming in to take over? Yes, I do feel passionately about this and I hope Michiganders do and they vote this governor out of office sooner than later. I would say right now that a recall election would not be out of the question. This is not democracy in action. What more can I say?"

Gram served coffee, sodas and cookies to the group. We stopped for a moment while he passed refreshments. "Please excuse our humble fair. We don't live high off the hog in this bus." The group did not complain.

CBS.   "What are your thoughts about the contraception issue that seems to have enflamed the Republican presidential debate leading some to conclude that President Obama is declaring war on religion?"

"First of all, this 'war on religion' position is silly. The president did not declare any war on religion. The Republicans are making this up to distract voters from really scrutinizing their policies on women's health issues and the need to let women, and their doctors decide what is in their best interest. This week, Congressman Issa held a committee hearing on this issue and there were no women testifying. The only woman the Democrats placed on the docket, Issa eliminated from the hearing. For a party that is so much against 'Big Government', the Regressives are dictating to women what to do with their bodies."

FOX. "We've heard that term before. What do you mean by regressive?"

"Yes, you will hear me say this many times during this campaign. The Republican Party is the Regressive Party. Many Republicans want to look backward fondly and claim that 'Weren't things great when Ronald Reagan was president?' Let's see. He cut taxes once and then raised them eleven times. We spent a trillion dollars bailing out savings and loans. We were engaged in the Iran-Contra fiasco. He destroyed the air traffic controllers union. What did he do for working people? Nothing much. He was a great Republican because he introduced 'trickle down economics' that really resulted in working people making less and less each year while the wealthy increased their net share of America's wealth."

Free Press.   "The auto industry bail out seems to be working. Yet, Mitt Romney and others state that a structured bankruptcy would have been more appropriate. What are your thoughts on this issue?"

"I love a back seat driver. I love a Monday morning quarterback. I love it when someone comes up with a plan that is working and the odd man out just has to claim that he had a better idea. GM still exists and is making a profit. Chrysler is making a profit. Ford is making a profit. What is wrong with that? Isn't this what capitalism is all about in the end? But no, these candidates will attack the plan no matter how well it might be working. Romney's Bain Capital might have come in, broken up GM into a bunch of parts, sold off the valuable assets, dumped the deadbeats, eliminated a quarter million jobs, made a handsome profit in the process, and then gloated all the way to the bank. I am not enamored with him and his equity firm and what they do to companies. They don't make the world a better place in which to live. They make money. They don't make the lives of people, and specifically Americans, any better by a long shot."

FOX.   "But didn't Bain Capital save Office Depot and some other companies from bankruptcy and total loss?"

"They did. How many other companies did they disassemble and reduce to a pile of assets and lost jobs? No, they are, in my estimation, more like Rick Perry said, 'vulture capitalists' and not entrepreneurs. They worked hard to make a lot of money, not to make a lot of jobs."

ABC.   "You seem to resent the financial services sector of our economy. Given that it makes up 42 % of our current economic system, what can you do to live with this reality?"

"Listen to what you just said. It makes up 42% of the current economic system. That is the problem. We don't make things. We play with money. This does not mean we don't need banks and credit card companies. What I am saying is that they should be a small part of our economic system and not the major players in it. They don't produce anything. They are just money managers and look at where this got us in 2007. We are still climbing out of the hole that they created."

NBC.   "Do you blame them for the recession?"

"Nope. Not completely. They are culpable for their part in it. So is Congress for eliminating the Glass-Steagall Act of 1933 in 1999. So much for Clinton and his legacy. So are the finance companies who sold loans to people who could not afford them. So are realtors who manipulated people into buying homes that they could not afford. So are the foolish people who bought homes they could not in a hundred years pay for on their earnings. There is a lot of blame to go around, but in the end, the government did not do its job. We needed regulation and we did not get it. The free market does not always work the way it is supposed to and this is what we get in the end: recession, pain and suffering all as a result of a failure to lead."

NPR.   "Would you advocate restating Glass-Steagall?"

"In a minute, I would. It worked to keep us out of trouble since its inception in 1933. The act kept banks from taking risks. A bank could not use depositor's money to invest in risky investments. Banks were either commercial banks meaning they took in money and then lent it back to its customers, or they were committed to financial services and prone to make riskier investments. Under this act, banks could not do both. In 1999, the act was repealed. Less than 10 years later, look at what happened? Could the act alone have prevented the Great Recession? I don't know. No one really knows. However, it might have prevented its severity. We are still in the recession because there are so many people not working. Companies, Wall Street, futures traders and a host of other economic indicators might point out that we are recovering. When we are back to a full employment economy, then I would say we are out of the recession. We are not there yet."

FOX. "Who is best positioned to lead us out of the recession as you still claim we are in? Democrats or Republicans?"

"I notice you left me out of your question. No offense. Neither party. The Republicans want to cut spending and cut taxes for the wealthy to get us out of this mess. The President wants to increase spending. Neither plan is fool proof. Neither plan alone will work. We need a combination of tax increases, spending cuts, financial and tax reform that will start us on the right path toward fiscal responsibility. Both parties are dodging the painful fixes needed to end this recession. I am not afraid to make the decisions that will end it. I am not beholding to any group of special interests, big banks, and contributors that are telling me what to do or not to do. This economy can and will be fixed but not by those who are in the back pockets of others."

Free Press.   "The housing crisis still plagues most of America. Parts of Detroit look like a ghost town. What would you do to reverse this trend in Detroit and in the major metropolitan areas where urban blight is epidemic?"

"There is no easy answer to this question. We dug a deep financial hole with all the marginal lending practices that went on for a decade. There are many people who cannot afford the homes that they own. They are in over their heads and now they are paying the price for their indiscretion. I would like to say to them, we can save you from yourself. However, that is not the truth. With refinancing, there are many who can save their homes from foreclosure. I'm appalled that the Federal Reserve can lend money to big banks at .25 % and then these banks can turn around and lend money to home owners at 4 or 5 % or higher and still not be required to refinance these loans. We have the ability to tell banks what they can and can't do. In this economic recession, leadership is essential. Laissez-faire principles do not apply. We need a fair economic system at this time, not a free one."

The hours passed like water droplets through a sieve. The questions continued to fly at me and I answered them to the best of my ability. I really enjoyed the give and take. This was fun. This was energizing. Gram hovered nearby making sure that coffee cups were full and sodas replenished. Al stood silently by, always ready to help out in any way he could. I knew that Big Jack was somewhere nearby insuring that everyone was safe and secure.

"Ladies and Gentlemen, this has been a most auspicious evening for me and my team. Hopefully, this will be the first of many sessions we have here on the Liberty Bell bus as we tour America."

FOX. "When will you begin your general campaign?"

"We already have. We don't need to win the nomination for our party. We already have it," I said with gusto.

"I mean, when will you begin traveling all over America to those states that have not held primaries yet and still are in play."

"Even before Arizona and Michigan hold their primaries, we will begin our 50 state tour of America."

"In this bus? Won't that be a slow venture?"

"Speed is not the issue. We want to visit America and Americans. We are not concerned that we make it to every major city. We want to reach out and touch those Americans who really count. The ones who live on Main Street, not Wall Street."

CBS.   "Parting thoughts, Mr. Pollack?"

"I love America and the free press. Thank you for coming by tonight and making us feel welcome in the Great Lakes State and in particular, here in Detroit. Do stop back again," I said, shaking their hands and ushering them out of the Liberty Bell bus.

After they were gone, we just sat still for a bit and did not speak. The silence was heavenly. We were unwinding. We were finished for the day and night.

"My oh my, what a day," I said.

"We made a dent in the armor tonight," Gram said.

"What do you mean?" Al asked.

"Lots of skeptics in this group, but I think you slowly moved them off center. Some of those questions were hardballs. They were not trying to give you an easy time of it. You handled them rather well, Leo," Gram concluded.

"Thanks for your vote of confidence," I replied. "Now what?"

"Let's eat," Al said.

"Can I take you fellows out and treat you to a real meal or maybe a Happy Meal?" I asked hoping they would not make me cook after this long day.

"Do you hear what the Leo's trying to do?" Gram looked at Al and raised his eyebrows and hands.

"The nerve of some fellows," Al said.

"After all we do for this guy, he wants to shirk his duties," Gram added.

"I for one am disappointed in our leader, how about you?" Al asked rhetorically.

"More than disappointed. I am disgusted that he would try and manipulate us with some foreign cooked meal just because it happens to be late at night. How dare he?" Gram railed.

"Alright. Alright already. What do you characters want?"

"Pasta!" they cried out.

38. RPGs and Other Real Issues

Gram mastered the magic of understatement and overstatement. When we were traveling anywhere, he was constantly filling our minds with trivia, humorous anecdotes, silly facts and suspicious fiction. His prompts often got Al engaged in an expose of the ludicrous and lascivious. I followed along like a willing sheep. We made travel fun because to do anything else would have been suicidal given the amount of hours we spent cocooned in the Liberty Bell bus. In our conversations, we created a future world that made all of us happy and healthy.

"The RPGs are blowing each other up again," Gram chuckled. "How do they do it? I mean, there is no end to their silliness."

"RPGs?" I asked him, wondering what he was talking about as we drove toward Flint, Michigan, our next stop on the campaign trail.

"RPGs. You know. Romney, Paul, Gingrich and Santorum. You could also call it "Republican's Pitiful Gaffs". RPGs are rocket-propelled grenades. They are a hoot. Santorum called President Obama a 'snob' because Obama said he wanted every American student to get a college education. Santorum said a lot of good, hardworking people never went to college and do good work applying their knowledge and skills in the trades and elsewhere."

"Does he not get it?" Al asked. "I hope all my kids go to college. What they do after that is their business. I just want them to have that opportunity, that's all," he concluded.

"No, Al, I don't think he gets it," Gram replied. "Even if you end up being a plumber…"

"Or a steel worker like me," I interjected.

"Yes, a steelworker like Leo," Gram continued, "the discipline a person learns from going to college is priceless."

"You got a double dose of discipline," Al said to Gram. "You went to college at the Air Force Academy. You couldn't fool around and make it. You had to wear a uniform to class and if you didn't study hard and graduate, you'd be sent out to the Marine Corps," joking with Gram who said he went to the Air Force because he didn't like pounding the ground with his feet like the Marines did all the time.

"Not exactly, but we did have an extremely high standard to live up to in school and in our personal lives."

"RPGs. What an interesting way to describe these four horses of the neoconservative apocalypse," I commented.

"Ah, you've just added another dimension to their nefarious rise in the American body politic. They are doom and gloom. According to the AP, yesterday in Georgia where the former speaker is campaigning, he said that Obama was the most radical president in the history of the United States."

"Really," Al said. "What does he mean by radical?"

"I don't know," Gram said. "Obama is anything but radical."

"If you asked me, I'd say that FDR was a 'radical' president. He was the one who started SSI, the WPA, the CCC, and so many other things including declaring war on Japan," Al said.

"You've got that right. Obama is a flyweight when it comes to taking radical stands. Even the health care act is milk toast. There is nothing radical about it. Now had he fought for and won universal health care, that might have been considered 'radical'," Gram concluded.

"This whole radical versus conservative thing is confusing as hell," I said. "Think about it. The Republicans constantly lambast the green party movement for being 'radical environmentalists'. However, what environmentalists want is a careful, scientific approach to exploring and utilizing natural resources, which, by definition, would be 'conservative'. The Republicans shout loudly, 'Drill, baby, drill'. This sounds to me like a very radical approach to environmental use. The environmentalists are labeled 'radical'. The republicans call themselves 'conservative'. The reverse is true."

"We need to protect Mother Earth," Al said. "I know I'm one to talk, given that I have, or had an RV, but I do believe that we are abusing this earth we live on and this is not sustainable."

"I agree, Al. We all can make changes in our lives to do better," Gram said. "What gets me is the foolishness of these RGPs when it comes to the entire question of oil and gas production in the US. Right now, we are producing more gas and oil in the US than we have in the last two decades. Montana, Wyoming, North Dakota, Colorado, Texas, Pennsylvania, West Virginia, Ohio and next New York are drilling right now. Alaska is on the decline. Unless we open up ANWR, it will continue to do so. There are a lot of states now adding to the gas and oil boom we are experiencing."

"Why are gas prices on the rise?" Al asked. "Right now we've seen a 40 cent increase in the past three weeks."

"Three major eastern refineries were recently taken off line because the companies said they were getting too old. The real reason was the oil companies were losing money because gas prices were too low," Gram concluded.

"Too low?" Al guffawed. "What the hell is too low about $3.75 a gallon?"

"We pay the lowest price per gallon in the world. Well, except for maybe Venezuela. In Europe, gas is usually twice, what we pay for it. Russians get no real breaks even though they have as much, if not more, oil and gas than we do. It's a matter of what a company thinks they ought to get for their product."

"So we subsidize an industry that decides how much they ought to gouge us for their product," I cried out. "We are plain foolish, and this congress and the White House are dupes of the oil and gas industry."

"No argument from me about that," Gram said. "We subsidize the oil and gas industry to the tune of two billion a year and maybe even five depending upon how you calculate it. We do the same with the agricultural-industrial complex. We spend billions privatizing prisons supporting the prison-industrial complex. Everywhere you turn, some industry is sucking the government tit."

"So this is the reason Ron Paul is against big government?" Al asked. "I'm a little confused because all the RPGs love to spout off about reducing the size of government and then they're also advocating free trade, the global economy and big business development, lower corporate taxes and a continuation of the trickle down economic platform."

"This is the reason I call them RPGs. They are blowing each other up in their fight to win the nomination and blowing up our economy by adhering to these failed policies. They don't get it. We've seen three decades of decline in the earning power of the middle class."

"We'll end all this in short order," Al said, "when Leo gets into office and finds the balance between public and private sector, business and labor and a host of other conflicts ailing America."

"I'm sure glad you have great faith in me," I said to my team members.

"We do or we would not be in this bus right now with you," Gram said. "A bus, by the way, that needs to get bullet proof glass installed in it."

"You really think so?" I asked.

"I know so," Gram said emphatically.

"Done," Al, said. "Next time we're home, I have the bus scheduled to go in and be retrofitted."

"Really? Who is paying for it?"

"The campaign, of course. You don't think I'd be paying for it, do you?"

"I didn't mean it that way. How do we justify it?" I asked.

"How do we justify letting Obama use Air Force One to go campaigning?" he cried out, almost hollering at us. "Listen to this."

"Gram read from the screen in front of him.

"President Obama and Democrats have raised $250 million dollars so far this election cycle. Who actually pays for the president's travel costs so he can get to these multimillion-dollar mansions to raise money? In part, you and I do. So far this year, President Obama has taken four trips, including 18 fundraisers outside the greater Washington, D.C. area. During each trip, he also conducted official business. That means that the White House, in other words, taxpayers, splits the cost with the Obama campaign. How do they split it? Take Obama's recent trip out west, when he travelled to three states over three days. He attended eight fundraisers, and held just two official events - a factory tour in Wisconsin and a Boeing plant visit in Seattle. According to the Air Force, the cost of operating Air Force One is $179,750 per hour. White House Pool reports show that the plane flew for nearly 12 hours for that trip, which means the plane ride alone cost more than $2 million. That doesn't even include the cost of flying advance workers and specialty vehicles ahead of time to the president's destination, not to mention the cost of setting up security. So what was the total cost of that trip to taxpayers? "We'll never know," said Brendan Doherty, who tracks presidential travel as a political scientist at the United States Naval Academy. "Even on a trip that ends up designated as 100 percent political," he added, "taxpayers end up bearing most of the cost." The campaign does not reimburse the government for the cost of flying Air Force One, but for the equivalent cost of flying the president and his staff first class on a commercial airline. Indeed, Presidents Bush, Clinton, Bush, Reagan, and on and on all used this same formula. Doherty says when it comes to presidents taking advantage of this billing technicality, each one exploits it more than his predecessor."

"That's disgusting," Al said. "Now that is what I'd call being a 'snob'."

"He's not the first to do it," Gram said. "You heard the list of abusers."

"He'll be the last, if I'm elected," I said. "No more free lunch. Air Force One will be grounded except for official, presidential business."

"What do you mean?" Gram asked.

"Just what I said," I cried out. "This kind of crap is what makes the American people get pissed off. I mean it. When I hear about this kind of special treatment, I want to go and protest myself and I'm quite a pacifist. No, when we are in control, we'll use the bus when we have to go somewhere. No junkets to Camp David. Stay at home like the rest of the people who don't have a private plane to fly around the country at the people's expense. When the plane is in the air, everyone pays for his or her drinks. There is no reason that we need to let the press and other hangers on fly free. They can pay for their flight. This way we make the plane pay for itself. $179,000 an hour? That's unacceptable. That's the real problem with people that are out of touch with reality."

"My, but that got you going," Gram said.

"Pisses me off," Al said. "We are 15 trillion in debt and we're spending almost $200,000 an hour to fly the president from Washington to California to go to dinner with people who are paying $35,000 to eat chicken and dumplings with him? This is the reason we're in such trouble."

"Yes, but he wants to get re-elected, so he'll do what he has to do to get the second term," Gram added.

"We'll see about that," I said. "He may be coasting along now, but once the RPGs are done with their internal food fight and one emerges with egg all over his face, we'll be in a three way race and then things will heat up."

"Don't forget about Buddy Roemer, the Reform Party Candidate," Gram said.

"Oh, what if Ron Paul breaks out and runs as a Libertarian Party candidate?" Al said. "The vote could be split five ways."

"Bring it on," I said. "The more, the merrier."

"Leo, stop and think about this. Splitting the Electoral College five ways will throw the election into the House of Representatives. This would not be good for us. It would probably insure that Obama gets in for a second term. Or worse. The Republican majority could throw their votes to the Republican."

"All this depends upon how many states he wins," I said.

"That's true. That's true," Gram said.

"We just have to go out and kick some butt, that's all I can say," I concluded.

"There is so much at stake right now," Gram said, "It makes one wonder how to prioritize."

"Putting people back to work is job one," I said. "How we do that is what concerns me. There is a need for a new space program. I don't mean to go to the moon and repeat what we did before. I mean real exploration. Listening to Dr. Neil Degrasse Tyson always inspires me. If I were a kid today, I'd want to be a scientist like him."

"Who is he?" Al asked.

"He's an astrophysicist who works for the Hayden Planetarium, does programs for the government, is really funny, inspirational and a role model for so many kids. By the by, he's a big, athletic looking fellow. He looks more like an NFL linebacker than a science geek. On top of all this, he's African American. He laments the fact that we are abandoning the shuttle program and have nothing to replace it with because the scientific minds that a new or continuing program would attract will go elsewhere."

"What's his biggest concern right now?" Al asked.

"Asteroids!" I said.

"Asteroids?" Al cried out curiously.

"Yes. He maintains that on April 13, 2029, we're going to get a 'blow by' as he calls it by an asteroid the size of a football field. If it hits the earth, we might have some problems. He said we should have rockets ready so that when it gets near the earth, we can send them up and use them to guide it away from earth's atmosphere. This could save us from a catastrophe."

"Just try selling that idea to the American people," Gram commented. "We'd be laughed all the way to the loony bin especially in these economically challenged times."

"We don't have mental wards anymore. Remember. Reagan emptied them in the 1980s," I said.

"You're serious about another space program?" Gram asked.

"I sure am. I think NASA was one of the best investments we made in the last forty years. We got a lot of bang for our buck. We have the international space station up there now, but we need to use Russian rockets to get us there. We are not capable now of reaching it with our own rockets."

"Many people think the space station is a waste of money."

"What is a waste of money is building sports arenas in cities to play games like baseball, football and basketball. That is a real waste of money."

"Oh, Oh, now you've done it, Leo. You're going to piss off every NFL, NBA, and MLB fan in the country. Kiss the votes goodbye."

"I don't think so. Do you think Clevelanders wanted to pay for the new Brown's Stadium? No, they didn't. Art Modell left Cleveland with his team because the city would not give him what he wanted for free. Yes, the city lost their team for a while, but the point was made. The people spoke. Let the billionaire owners pay for their own stadiums. Wherever a city coughs up the money for the stadium and taxpayers have to bear the burden through increased property taxes, the people ought to rise up in loud protest. What is wrong with Americans is that we have lost our real voice. We protest the silliest things and not those that really matter."

"I didn't think you cared that much about outer space," Gram said.

"I care about the future. We take care of the future by doing research and exploration. Space is part of this. In one year, we spent more money for the Department of Defense than we did in the entire fifty years that NASA has existed. We spend a lot of money blowing things up, but we have a hard time justifying spending money to build things that might serve humanity. I'm embarrassed when I think about how our priorities are twisted. I don't ever want to travel in space. I'm afraid of it. I don't even like to ride roller coasters so going up in a rocket ship would really make me lose all my cookies. But there is a need for the next generation, Janko's peer group, to have the challenge set before them to make space the venue of the future."

"I'm wondering what it will take for this to happen," Gram said.

"Different leadership, that's what. The former speaker talked about putting men back on the moon, colonizing it, making it the 51st state once 1500 people were living there full time. Nice idea but not very realistic and quite frankly, a little short sighted. First, we need to make Washington, D.C. a state. We already have more than 680,000 people living in the district and we don't even let them have a representative in the government."

"Funny how the district can't make this happen and no politicians will take on the cause," Gram said.

"Doesn't surprise me. If it were to become a state, D.C. would be very Democratic. What Republican wants to be seen supporting this project? I don't know what the percentage is, but I'll bet the minority percentage of the population in D.C. is more than 50%."

"Let's find out," Gram said. He did a search and found that D.C. had a population of about 680,000 people. Fifty-one percent were African-American. Nine percent were Hispanic. "There you go. The facts are stark. White folks are only 34 % of the population."

"See what I mean," I said. "No Republicans will go along with this idea. Anyway, we are not going to fix this during the campaign."

"Check out what's going on in Big Sky Country," Gram called out. "Montana's Supreme Court just shot a hole in the 'Citizens United' Supreme Court decision by invoking a 1912 Corrupt Practices Act that makes it illegal for corporations to spend money on elections in the state. This is the first real test of the Citizen's united decision at the state level. It will be interesting to see how the Republicans handle this decision by the lower state Supreme Court."

"What can they do?" Al asked.

"Challenge it in a federal district court, that's what," Gram said.

"They'd be fools to open up this can of worms," I offered.

"Hey, when did that ever stop them?" Gram laughed. "Look at what they've done with birth control and a bunch of other issues this year. The RPGs are having a field day with anything that President Obama does even though what they often say results in their shooting themselves in the foot."

"We've noticed that," Al said. "Kind of funny, don't you think?" He honked the air horn a few times to punctuate what he said.

"Where is all this heading? How is this going to affect the country? This is what we have to ask ourselves. Americans need to know that we are ahead of the curve and not following behind the RPGs or the president."

"I think we're well-positioned to propose the plan we've talked about all along. Americans Buying American. Americans Supporting Americans. Progressive taxation. Eliminating tax loopholes. Letting tax cuts expire. End the foreclosure crisis by making the Fed enforce lending practices among the big banks. There are so many things we can do right now. We just need to win and make them happen," I said.

"Speaking of winning, I just got a text from Judy," Gram said.

"Ah, the girl is still after him," Al commented.

"Funny guy," Gram barked back at him. "Listen to what she just sent me."

We sat and stared at him. For a moment, Gram did not speak letting the suspense build. We waited. He kept staring at his phone screen.

"So," Al asked impatiently after more than a minute went by.

"Fellows," Gram finally said, "you won't believe what is happening right now. You just won't believe it."

"We can't make that judgment unless you tell us what is happening," Al said.

"He's right, Gram. So what tidbit of juicy information did Judy share with you?"

"Fellows, we, the Liberty Bell Party, as many are starting to call us, are being followed in greater and greater numbers."

"What do you mean following us?" Al asked. "I don't see anyone but a few cars and trucks behind us."

"Not following us that way," Gram said. "Following us on Twitter. That's where."

"I don't get it," I said.

"Judy and I handle the tweets for the campaign. We send them out about once an hour."

"You didn't tell us that," Al said.

"You didn't ask," Gram said. "Anyway, right now we have more than 1.3 million people following us on Twitter."

"Cool," Al said. "Now what does that mean?"

"It doesn't mean anything unless you know how many people we are following."

"What do you mean by that?" I asked.

"I'll break it down for you," Gram said. "The basic premise is that someone who follows a lot of people is hoping that they will follow him or her back. They are not 'social network influential persons' or 'snips'. They are players of sorts. People who have many followers and don't follow a lot of people are snips. Currently, here are the actual numbers. Santorum is following 157 people and has 143,230 following him. Obama is following 681,879 people and has 12,706,427 people following him. Ron Paul is following 153 people and has 247,968 people following him. The ratio suggests Ron Paul is the actual leader."

"Leader in what way?" I asked. "You're speaking in riddles right now."

"Riddles, I don't think so. The ratio of following others to following him is the lowest. This makes him the leader."

"What about Romney and Gingrich?" I asked.

"There are no stats on these two that I can find now," Gram said.

"What is our ratio?" I asked.

Gram looked at me and his smile told everything.

"What is our ratio?" Al asked realizing that Gram was staring at me and then at him with a real Cheshire cat grin.

"Get this fellows. Leo's following 3 people. He has 467,387 following him. His ratio blows all the others out of the water. Amazing isn't it," Gram said enthusiastically.

I stared at him. Al stared at the road and said nothing.

"So?" I finally asked. "What does this mean?"

"This means that almost a half million people are following you and that your ratio is far better than the president's or the other candidates."

"How did it get that way?" I asked.

"Because people are following you. They are interested in your campaign, our campaign, the Liberty Party campaign. That's what it means."

"When did you start twittering for me? I mean, for the campaign?"

"Two weeks ago. We put out the first twitter after the Florida primary. Judy thought we'd better ride the wave. I agreed. In two weeks, you've picked up nearly a half million followers."

"So how important is this in the context of a presidential campaign?" I asked.

"I'll tell you," Gram said. "You may not think this is important as you are not into the Twitter thing. The Twitter Sphere is a force that many follow now for trends, for where the power is heading, and what this means is we are on the move. There are hedge funds that analyze twitter messages for number and content. I played with this for predicting stock movement through the Yahoo Message boards. It is surprisingly accurate. The number of messages means little. What matters is the positive/negative word ratio."

"What's our ratio?"

"Phenomenal," Gram said. "Our positive ratio is extremely high. Obama's is very low. The Tea Party does a LOT of spamming with obvious lies. The Republican ratio is also very low. They spend most of their time bashing each other using RPGs. Women are bashing all of them."

"How are women treating us?" I asked.

"Like you're a prince, Leo," Gram said.

"Yikes. Don't tell Basha that fact!" I said.

"She already knows because she is one of your followers," Gram said.

"She doesn't twitter? Does she?" I asked.

Gram smiled. "See how little you know about your own wife. What do you make of that, Al?"

"I think Leo's a monk, that's what I think," Al said. "After all, he only has one kid and he's how old now?"

"What does this all have to do with twitter, fellows?" I said getting irritated.

"I'll tell you what this all means. An old friend of mine is a hedge fund manager in Connecticut. I gave him a call and asked if he analyzed Twitter. He said yes he did. I asked him for an analysis of Leo Pollack's numbers. He gave me a call the next day and said 'If you were a stock, I would put all my money in you and short the others.' In other words, pal, you'd be a good buy right now. He thinks you'll be the next president of the United States if you don't RPG yourself."

I sat back and thought about what Gram was telling us. How could some simple text message become so important in the context of what we were trying to accomplish? What was the world racing toward in this information age explosion? Where would all this end? I had no clue. I was dumbfounded. I was a little scared, too, because I was behind the curve. I did not know the answers. Yet, I realized that I did not need to know all of them. I had people like Gram, Judy, John, Fritz, Richard, Carol, Big Jack, Al and others who could give me answers to the pressing questions that I asked. I did not even need to be the only one asking the questions. This was a team effort. Assemble the brightest, most passionate minds and define the problem, brainstorm for solutions, pick one from the bunch, implement the solution, evaluate it to see if it worked and then, if it worked, celebrate. If not, return to step three, pick another solution, implement it, evaluate and so on and so forth. I was the catalyst for change, the change agent, but I did not have to be the chief answer machine for all America's problems. I felt better right away, less afraid and more relaxed.

"Gram, I'm amazed that so much goes on without my knowing about it. This concerns me in a way," I said a little frustrated.

"Leo, do you know how many gallons of fuel we have burned in the Liberty Bell bus in the past week?"

"No, why?"

"Al, how many gallons?" Gram asked.

"My last total was 452 gallons. We're averaging about 4.52 miles per gallon," Al said. "Cost was $1667.32 at an average cost per gallon of $3.69."

"There. Now you know. Is this something that you need to know? Tell me. If so, we can burden you with facts, numbers, and all sorts of trivia to blow your mind away. When we get to Flint, you can tell the press and the crowd how much we spent on gas and what our mpg rate is for the Liberty Bell bus. I'm sure the voters will really be happy to hear all these numbers. Am I making myself clear? Are you getting the gist of what I'm trying to tell you, pal?"

"I think I'm getting it. I don't need to be burdened with trivia."

"That's right. What you need to focus on is the bigger picture and let us take care of the details. All you have to do is trust that we are being honest with you, are telling you all that you want and need to know and that we are doing what is in the best interest of the majority of the people."

"You got it," I said. "That's about it."

"Leo, we are not schleps. We do have some common sense."

"I know. I just feel badly that I depend on so many people to do so much."

"You can't do this alone," cried Gram. "This is not a one-man show. This is a team effort. Just like in NASCAR. You are the driver. Based upon how well you drive, you may win the race. You can't win with a slow car or one that blows up, or one that loses a tire because a pit crewmember fails to put the lug nuts back on again. We are on your team. We all do different things. Al gets you safely to every racetrack by being your number one chauffeur. He is the main person who transports the team to the races. The folks back at the union hall build engines and cars to put out on the track. Your job is to drive the car we give you. This is how NASCAR teams compete. This is what you need to understand. Okay?"

"By the way, yesterday was the Daytona 500. Who won?" Al asked.

"Rained out. They are racing again today."

"We might get to watch some of it tonight then," Al said.

"Might be a life lesson for our friend, Leo," Gram said.

"I got it, Gram. No need to elaborate anymore."

"Leo, I know what you're feeling. As a pilot, I wanted to control everything that related to flying my plane. I would check the plane over every time I was supposed to go up. I was compulsive about it. Somewhere along the line, I realized that I couldn't do that anymore. There was not enough time. I needed to trust that my Air Force colleagues, the mechanics and other ground crew, were doing their jobs. Once I believed they were, I flew much easier, freer and happier."

"So what else should I know that I don't know right now?" I asked holding my breath.

Gram physically shook when I asked him this question. I was not prepared for what he shared with Al and me.

"Okay, here you go. In the last month, John's team back home, working with coordinators in the fifty states, have registered hundreds of thousands of people. Voter registrations are soaring around the country in every state. Even in the Dixiecrat South. The rolls are growing even faster than the campaign donations. People are registering as independent. We can talk about this some more over a few beers tonight when we finally are done for the day but this is amazing. Given that there are as many self-declared independents now as there are Republicans and Democrats combined, we are well on our way to taking the lion's share of the independent vote right here and now."

"This is fact?" I asked. "Not John's estimation of the facts."

"Leo, this is fact. We're plunging into the bowels of the political machines and cutting out the voters who are not committed to the RPGs or the President and siphoning them away faster than a Dyson sweeper can pick up sawdust."

"Amazing!" Al said. "I'm psyched. We are going to win this thing after all."

"Now, just like in NASCAR, let's not start celebrating until we cross the finish line on the last lap and that won't happen until November. That's quite a few months ahead of us right now," Gram said. "But we can sure enjoy the moment, fellows. This is what comes with having a candidate you can believe in today, tomorrow and always."

"Can't we just have a little fun though," Al chuckled. "I mean, all work and no play make Al, Leo and Gram dull boys."

"We'll drink a few beers tonight," I said. "We'll invite Big Jack in for one, too. By the way, where is the mystery man today?"

"Haven't talked to him this morning yet," Gram said. "Let me give him a jingle."

While Gram talked to Jack and Al focused on the road in front of us, I sat back in my easy chair and looked around the bus. Sometimes we just do not see the forest for the trees. Our bus was plush. Al did not skimp when he picked out this model. The front seats were air cushioned with wide armrests that pivoted 360 when not locked into place. Two similar chairs were behind the front ones, but there was enough space to set up a small table among the four when not traveling. The living room area was fully ten feet long and a couch and two additional chairs completed the décor. Our kitchen was located right next to this living space and all the appliances were on one side for convenience. The dining room and kitchen table combination was large enough to seat six people comfortably. A side door separated the kitchen from the bathroom. Two large bedrooms and one small one completed the rest of the living quarters. Each of us had his own closet. I slept in the big room with Gram. Al had his own room. He was bigger than we were and he was the one who was usually the most exhausted at the end of each day. We figured he deserved his own room. He did not argue with us. The bus was forty-five feet long and easily twelve feet high and ten feet wide. Its footprint was amazing. I did not know how Al drove the behemoth around so easily in the city where some streets appeared too narrow for it to navigate, but somehow he managed and there was not a scratch on it yet. What amazed me was all the storage beneath the floors in the outside compartments. We did not lack for space. We did not need it all, but we sure possessed it. I loved the kitchen. There was ample room to do any type of cooking. Given that I was a simple chef, and some might actually call me primitive, I found the facilities elaborate. I was sure that most women would not, but in general, all I was cooking was simple fair: casseroles, teriyaki noodles and salad; macaroni, cheese and tuna fish; toasted cheese sandwiches and soup; popcorn, my favorite snack; hotdogs and pork and beans. Nothing fancy. Staple foods. Just what the hungry team ordered. They did not complain. Every time I offered to let them take over, Al said he did not know how and Gram said he did not want to cook. I was unanimously re-elected every time a dispute surfaced. What I cooked was based upon how the spirit moved me on any particular day. I would think of some food sometime during the day and that would be it. I would make it. For breakfasts, we drank coffee, ate toast and sometimes cereal. For lunch, I rarely fixed anything. Now and then, I would make some egg tortillas. We liked them. Therefore, the kitchen was mine and I kept it neat and clean. Basha would have approved. We shared the bathroom. I cleaned that, too. I was the chief cook, bottle washer and shower room attendant. I did not mind. I enjoyed taking care of my team mates. After all, they were taking good care of me. I guess this was reciprocity and I realized that I was doing for them what Gram said the team was doing for me. Yes, this was a team effort.

Gram got off the phone and said, "Big Jack's already in Flint. A huge crowd is waiting for us. Many police are on the scene. Governor Snyder appointed an emergency manager to run this city. I'm sure that he is not very popular in this neighborhood. We can use that, but be careful how you approach it. This could be one of those topics that could incite a riot."

"Are things that hot in this town right now?" I asked.

"If I lived here and the governor of my state enforced this type of autocratic policy on my city, I'd be up in arms, too," Gram said.

"Me, too," Al said. "I'd be out demonstrating 24/7 until the policy changed."

"How are the people responding?" I asked.

"Not very well, but there is no violence yet," Gram said. "We just don't want to be the spark that makes the powder in the pan flash, Leo."

"Why not?" I asked.

"You don't need that kind of publicity. You can get more mileage if you encourage a peaceful, non-violent, non-cooperation strategy like Thoreau, Gandhi and Dr. King advocated."

"You think so?" I asked again.

"I know so. We're being watched. We are on a list already and you can be sure that the minute one of our events results in violence, we will be called a 'mob' as that congressman from Virginia called the 'occupy' movement. We don't need that kind of publicity. We can continue to be the voice of reason, of pragmatism, of a new way of leading that is not like the RPGs or like the president who says one thing and does something else."

"Like?" I asked.

"Like deporting more people in the past three years than his predecessor but claiming he wants comprehensive immigration reform. He is not reforming anything. The long arm of the federal government has reached into every community in America and plucked out more than 400,000 illegal immigrants and deported them in the past two years."

"Okay, we cool it," I said.

"Be prudent, but be persuasive."

"Got it."

Flint was the birthplace of General Motors Corporation and the site of the famous Flint Sit-Down Strike of 1936-37 that led to the formation of the United Auto Workers. In 2002, the city faced its first financial crisis and was placed under an emergency city manager. The first crisis was resolved with a new election of leaders. In 2011, Flint faced a second financial crisis. Governor Snyder appointed Michael Brown to be the emergency city manager. Flint reeled under this double whammy. Population numbers continued to drop from a high of nearly 200,000 in 1960 to just about 100,000 residents in 2010. Flint was the quintessential rust belt urban area. It was the home of Michael Moore, the documentary filmmaker who started his career by making his famous first film, "Roger and Me". It chronicled the city's descent into recession after General Motors closed a number of plants back in the 1980s.

Into this complex socio-economic maelstrom, we descended. Our hope was that we could influence people to join our cause and return America back to Americans. We wanted to accomplish this peacefully through the power of organizing voter turnout. When all the votes were counted on November 6, 2012, there would be no doubt who was going to be the next president of the United States.

On the front page of every newspaper in the country on November 7, 2012, a picture of the new president would appear, and none of the RPGs or the incumbent would be in it.

39. Fire in the Hole

We left Flint fired up but not in flames. The experience reminded me of entering into the confessional as a kid and having to confess my sins. Where had America and Democracy gone wrong? How could we let a city slowly die? What kind of governor saw his role as usurping the elected officials of a city and appointing a hand selected city manager to run the "business" of the government. The people looked depressed. Their visages reminded me of the Ezra Pound haiku poem: "Look at the people's faces, petals on a wet, black bough." I was extremely careful to keep the governor's name out of anything I said, but I did comment on the need for people to resist being disenfranchised. I did not know how this statement would be interpreted. I wanted to make sure that people knew that I was in favor of resisting the governor in non-violent, non-cooperative ways.

As we traveled along the highway heading west toward Lansing, the news was streaming across the screen. Gram did not say a word. He had warned me. I took his advice. What I could not do was control the passions of the people. They would do what they believed was their right and civic responsibility. What it looked like was another Flint Sit-In Strike but this time one that involved the entire city. The message went out to every public employee to take a sick day. "Blue Flue" ruled. What the movement accomplished was a shock wave across the state.

"What do you think is going to happen now?" I asked Gram.

"Who can tell? I said be careful. We are going to face some backlash from the regressives as a result of this move."

"We didn't tell those people to call in and report off," Al said.

"Let it be," I said.

"No, we did not but the results will be linked to us. That's the rub."

"We are not going to reverse their thinking. What you said to them simply let the fire in the hole come out. Don't do anything violent. This is the way that people interpreted your words. In all the tweets from your followers in Michigan, this was the theme. By the way, you picked up another 110,456 followers in this state alone. So, yes, we can use this to our advantage. We'll just have to diffuse the bad press when it starts rolling in," Gram said.

We continued on the road toward Lansing, Michigan, our last stop on this campaign swing on the day of the primary. I tried to restrain myself from being defensive. However, Gram was partially right. We did not need this kind of press. We could have escaped the city before this exploded. What we did not know was the long-term effect of the message.

What I enjoyed most of all about campaigning was the diversity of thought and action that we considered every day we were moving forward toward November 6, 2012. There was no boring moment. We did not stop moving, thinking, wondering, laughing, crying (sometimes) and projecting.

When the news from Chardon, Ohio came on, we pulled the bus over and just watched in disbelief. This town was only a few miles away from Youngstown, Ohio. A young fellow who was supposedly bullied by students in his school showed up at the cafeteria at lunchtime with a gun and fired upon a number of students. Five were seriously wounded. Two students were reported as "brain dead". The shooter was in custody. Since he was a minor, his identity was being withheld. We drove on in silence. This kind of tragedy made no sense. I had tears in my eyes as I sat down at the table doodling on the clipboard I used to make notes and wondered how this kind of news would play in our state and across the nation.

When events like this happened, gun control advocates generally pumped up their defensive posture. They maintained that guns do not kill people. People kill people. I believed this as well, but the facts remain that handgun use contributes to the majority of gun crime, homicides and suicides. There is no easy answer to this issue. What we can do is educate people on safely and securely possessing firearms and keeping them away from children, adults with mental health issues and others who have not been trained adequately.

Our campaign would weather any storm we faced because we were not purposely advocating any kind of violence, dirty tricks nor dishonesty. Gram pointed out that the Santorum campaign superpac was making robocalls to democratic voters encouraging them to vote for Santorum because Romney had supported the idea that General Motors go into a structured bankruptcy rather than be bailed out. Romney asked Santorum to stop the calls. Santorum did not respond. His campaign was not actually in charge of the process.

Gingrich was not in the state, but was predicting that he was going to win Georgia, probably Mississippi, Tennessee, Idaho, Oklahoma and be back in the hunt after Super Tuesday, March 6, when ten states were holding primaries. Doctor Ron Paul was not in the news. This was going to be an important day for all candidates. We were not sure how we would fare. Clearly, we could not mount the type of face-to-face campaign as we were doing now, but we would be on our 48 state tour by then and so our exposure would be expanding.

John Gallagher called me and we talked about the situation in Flint. He was being deluged with press people wanting to know what we were doing and how we were going to clean up the mess.

"Leo, I tried to tell them that our message was one of non-violence. We were not advocating violent overthrow of the Snyder government. What the heck did you say to stir up the beehive?"

"All I said was you have the right and the responsibility to stand up to your government whenever you feel like you are being treated unfairly. This is the city of the famous Flint Sit-In Strike of 1936. Do what you must to let them know you are not happy. That was the essence of what I said. Nothing more," I finished my explanation.

"It sure caused a furor. We have even heard from the governor's office. They did not get specific, but they are monitoring you and know that you are on your way to Lansing and this may get sticky. Big Jack is aware. Don't be surprised if you are turned away from the city. I mean it. These guys are not playing around and this Snyder is a real piece of work. He's in ten steps ahead of our own governor when it comes to repressive beliefs."

"What do we do then?" I asked.

"Talk with Jack. Listen to what he says. You, Gram, Jack and Al need to powwow. Don't take any chances. I mean it. You don't need to get arrested right now."

"What could they arrest me for?" I asked. "Telling the people to be active in their own city, their own state? This is starting to piss me off," I hollered at John.

"Leo, I can appreciate and agree with your frustration. I'm just encouraging you to use prudence and restraint right now. That's all. Gotta run. Talk to you later."

After he hung up, I sat still and contemplated what he meant by prudence and restraint. Had I used these two traits back in the springtime, I would still be an unemployed steel worker waiting to go back to work. My imprudence and my lack of restraint created this entire movement. Now I was supposed to act totally different, back off, become like all the rest of the candidates who were being careful not to offend this block of voters or that block. The maddening part of the entire affair was that I was not even in the city when the "blue flue" started. We were long gone. I knew it would be attributed to my being there. I never said to anyone to stay home from work if you want the governor's attention. A part of me wanted to just scream out at the world. "World, don't you get it? There is injustice everywhere and we need to shout it out at the top of our lungs whenever we see it. We need to ring the liberty bell declaring our all-out challenge to the regressive policies of so many leaders in this country that are reversing the gains working people made for half a century and we're now losing. This is what we are about, my friends. Nothing more. We are about justice, fairness and rekindling a belief in the American Dream."

"What are you brooding about now?" Gram asked as he came back and poured himself a cup of stale coffee.

"Nothing," I responded.

"Liar," he said to me.

"Pretty bold aren't you," I quipped.

"Pretty accurate," Gram fired back. "I know you don't like the fact that you might have caused the city to react the way it did. You were careful enough. I know that. You know that. You can't control a mob. You can't control the gestalt of an entire city."

"You know about the gestalt?" I asked.

"I was an Air Force officer. We were required to understand the gestalt. We learned to live it. The mind set. The wave of thinking that leads to a group being in tune with one another and then functioning like one brain and ten or twelve bodies. In our case, it was airplanes. Yes, I know about gestalt."

"John says we created a crap storm in Flint. We're being bombarded with press calls, all sorts of bad vibrations are flowing and this Michigan governor is fully aware that we are heading toward Lansing right now. We're going into the lion's den so to speak."

"What will happen, will. We can't change that and perhaps we don't need to do so. Let's call Jack and we'll stop somewhere and powwow," Gram concluded.

"Huh! That's exactly what John said to do," I responded.

"Great minds think alike," Gram remarked. "Great campaigns learn to adapt and overcome." He pulled out his phone and called Big Jack.

While he was on the phone, I commandeered his seat up front with Al and watched the scenery float past as we headed toward the state capital.

Lansing is located in what Michiganders call "mid-Michigan or central Michigan". In the winter of 1835 and early 1836, two brothers from New York plotted the area known at the time as REO Town just south of downtown Lansing and named it "Biddle City." All of this land lay in a floodplain and was underwater during the majority of the year. Regardless, the brothers went back to New York, specifically Lansing, New York, to sell plots for the town that did not exist. They told the residents of Lansing, New York that this new "city" had an area of sixty-five blocks, contained a church, a public park and academic square. A group of sixteen men bought plots in the nonexistent city. Upon arriving in the area later that year, they discovered they had been scammed. Many in the group were too disappointed to stay. Others decided to remain and ended up settling around what is now Metropolitan Lansing. Those who stayed quickly renamed the area "Lansing Township" in honor of their home village in New York.

The British captured Detroit, the first capital of the region, during the War of 1812. Out of fear of future capture, Lansing became the capital. This move protected the capital from further Canadian-British threat.

Now we were heading toward this town founded by a couple of shysters more than a hundred seventy five years ago, and the outlook was tenuous.

"What do you think we ought to do, Al?" I asked him while he was focused on the traffic piling up in front of us.

"Find a better way into this city," Al responded. I could tell he was not really listening to me.

"I'll leave you alone, Al," I said.

"No, Leo, you can talk all you want. I just don't know how much I'm going to be able to respond while this traffic is filling every lane. We must be coming in right at some kind of rush hour."

We watched as the lanes of traffic merged into two and then into one. Road construction was the contributing factor. A sign on the side of the highway read: "This highway improvement project funded by the American Economic Recovery Act". President Barak Obama's name was in small letters at the bottom of the sign.

"I guess Michigan wanted the money badly enough to fix this highway. Interesting how many governors railed against the bailout, but took the money and ran with it."

"So you say," Al said. He was not paying any attention.

I left him alone. My thoughts jumbled together into an incoherent collage of images, sounds and feelings. What was happening to the campaign? John was not happy. Gram was on the phone with Jack. Al was focused on driving. I was the odd man out. I could not get off the bus and go for a walk. I called Basha. She did not answer. I wondered where she was. I looked at my clock. Janko was just getting home from school. They probably went out for a walk, to play, to be together in my absence. At that moment, I missed them more than ever. I let the phone ring until the answering machine came on. I told them where I was and that I loved them. I hung up. My heart sank a bit. I wanted to hug them both now. Not tomorrow when we would be on our way back home for a measly day and then back out again on the open road. Gram was still jawboning with Big Jack. What could they be discussing? I wanted to interrupt them. I thought better. Leave them alone. "They will tell me eventually when they think I need to know." I stared out the window and realized we could see the city skyline. Doomsday was just ahead of us. We were riding into the mouth of the beast. This was not friendly territory. We knew that when we decided to finish our campaign in the Great Lake State in the capitol. We did not know what the context would be when we got here. As always, the fog sometimes settled upon us when we least expected it. No matter, we would just deal with it as we always did.

"Al, when you get a chance, pull off the freeway so we can have a powwow with Jack and headquarters," Gram said.

"Will do," Al called back and immediately put on his turn signals. We exited in record time.

A few minutes later, Big Jack entered the bus and we gathered around the kitchen table. Gram was hooking up the conference phone. I welcomed Big Jack and asked if I could get him something to drink. He declined. He looked grim. His body was tense.

"So what's up fellows?" I asked trying to be nonchalant.

"Let's get John on first. Then we'll talk," Jack said.

John answered the phone. Judy, Fritz and Carol were with him. Richard was on the line from somewhere in Georgia.

"Okay folks. Spill it out for us, Jack," John directed.

"This is the situation. With the blowup in Flint, the governor called a special meeting of his cabinet. They are running scared. This entire state is like a keg of powder. They are watching things disintegrate in Wisconsin and they think that it won't be long until the people become outraged and start a recall movement here in Michigan. The Flint strike is fueling these fears. They blame us for the situation in that city. Whether or not we deserve the blame or credit for arousing the masses, is not the issue. We have the nod from the Republican administration. When they heard that we were heading to the state capital, alarms went off. Snyder called his attorney general and asked what he could do to stop us from entering the city. He said there was nothing that he could do to stop our campaign from coming to Lansing. The governor called in the state police captain, the head honcho, and asked him what he could do. Again, he was told there was nothing that he could do to stop us. Snyder is paranoid. He does not want to appear weak. After all, today is their primary and this is their day in the spotlight and here we are, coming into the capital and spoiling the moment for them."

"He should have thought about that when he issued the order to take over Flint, Pontiac and the other cities and place them under the control of one of his political cronies," I blurted out.

"Leo, no one on this call disagrees with you. The question is what do we do now? There is a strong possibility that, if we go into Lansing today, there might be trouble," John said laying the facts out on the table for us to discuss.

"What kind of trouble?" I asked.

"Could be nothing more than harassment," Jack said. "Could be that the state police, under orders of the governor, have you arrested?"

"Arrested for what? I didn't do anything?" I hollered.

"What you did or did not do isn't the issue. This is a regressive state right now, Leo," John said. "They're running it like a plutocracy. They don't care what others think but they are not going to let their primary election day be disrupted by your coming into their state capitol and making a scene."

"You mean, coming in and telling the people the truth about what is happening right in front of their own eyes," I said vehemently.

"We all know what is happening," Gram said. "We're trying to weigh out the pros and cons, that's all, Leo. Nothing more."

"Richard, you're down south in the land of non-violent protest. What do you think we ought to do?" I asked.

Richard was silent for a few moments. When he responded, he spoke with quiet passion that was music to my ears. "We will face similar issues all across the south. If we want Dixiecrats to become Leocrats, then we will need to make waves. I don't like the idea of pushing the system this early in the election year, but perhaps that is just what it will take for us to make a major breakthrough."

"You're saying all that to say what, Richard?" John asked.

"Go in to the city and conduct business as usual," he replied.

"Okay and what if Leo get's arrested? What then?" Jack fired back.

"He gets arrested. We blow the situation up to the greatest assault on First Amendment Rights in the history of our country. A presidential candidate being barred from entering an American city on the day of a primary election that he is possibly favored to win."

There was silence around the table.

"Who told you that I'm favored to win?" I asked.

"Nobody. I made it up. If you are arrested, Leo, you win. The publicity will destroy this state. Public opinion will go your way. Americans, Republican or Democrat, will not brook such an act on the part of their government. Imagine if Romney or Santorum were arrested today on the way to one of their last minute events. What would happen? Michiganders would be so embarrassed. The state would face the disapproval of the entire country. President Obama might even get involved and demand that you not be harassed. Up until now, we've been treated like a stepchild. Today we go in and become a full-blown member of the family. No more waiting for things to happen. Create the crisis and then let the scene play out. Let the chips fall wherever they may. Capture the moment. Seize the day. That's my take on it."

Again, there was palpable silence.

"Team, what do you think?" John asked.

There was a lot of muttering in the background. Richard had stated his position. He said no more. The rest were mulling over what he said.

After ten minutes of heated discussion, there was no real consensus. The conversation was heading toward avoiding a crisis. Finally, Al said to everyone. "Folks, I may be just the driver and that's my main role. Today, however, I think there is something we're missing. This campaign would be nothing without Leo and his American Dream Speech. This campaign would be nothing without his willingness to stand up and say that working people of America deserve more than what they are getting. This campaign is meaningless if we are afraid to take on a state government or the federal government that is so lopsided in favor of the status quo that next to nothing gets done. I think its Leo's call. What he decides, that is what we do. After all, if anyone's going to get arrested and end up in jail, it will be Leo and not us," Al laughed. "I hope they know what this is going to cost them in the long run. That's what I have to say. That's my two cents worth. Whatever you decide, Leo, I'm behind you one-hundred fifty percent."

Now there was stunned silence.

Big Jack, Gram and Al looked at me. John and the others could not see the twitching of my left cheek. None of them could see or feel the rapid twitching of my left knee, a sure sign that my vertigo was kicking up big time. The silence was deafening.

In my heart, all I could hear was the ringing of the Liberty Bell. That was enough for me.

"We go in. That's the way it's got to be. What happens happens. Judy, get the press alerted that there is a crisis about to happen. Fritz, load the home page with the pictures that Gram is about to shoot and send to you, and make them go viral. Jack, let's make sure that the flak jacket you got for me is on properly. No sense in taking any chances. Al, I love you, man. You are the main reason that we are here today. Thank you for being a true believer. Today, this one's for you, my friend."

I got up and gave him a hug. Staring into his eyes, I whispered softly so no one could hear, "Mill rats forever." He slapped me on the back and that was it.

Big Jack went out to get ready for what was coming. Al fired up the bus and headed back onto the freeway. Gram sat back in his navigation seat and stared straight ahead at the road unfolding in front of us.

I stood up and asked them, "Want some lunch?"

"How can you think about eating at a time like this?" Gram asked.

"Quite frankly, I can't think of anything better to do than eat a full meal as I get ready to do battle with the forces of evil."

"You're not Don Quixote," Gram sputtered at me.

"No, I'm Leo Pollack, an unemployed steel worker who is running for the presidency of the United States. Look out Lansing, here I come."

On the outskirts of the city, the police caravan met us and followed us all the way downtown to the state house where Big Jack told us a real flash mob was gathered.

We found a place to park. No sooner did I emerge from the Liberty Bell bus than a group of officers approached and said we could not stop in this place. If we failed to move we, or at least the leader of this movement, would be held accountable for our actions. The spokesperson was a Lieutenant and he was trying to be diplomatic.

"Officer, my name is Leo Pollack. I am a candidate for the presidency of the United States of America. I am here to campaign for the nomination to that high office. Under my rights as an American citizen, you cannot stop me from exercising my freedom of speech, freedom of assembly, and that is what I am doing here, right now, on this day of the Lord, February 28, 2012."

"Sir, I am ordering you to get back on your bus and leave this area. If you do not comply with my order, sir, you are going to face consequences for your actions. I do not want anything to happen. Please get on your bus and leave. That is what I am directing you to do."

I asked Al to get the bullhorn. He did. I repeated what I just said to the officer before but now loudly so that anyone nearby could hear my words.

"Officer, my name is Leo Pollack. I am a candidate for the presidency of the United States of America. I am here to campaign for the nomination to that high office. Under my rights as an American citizen, you cannot stop me from exercising my freedom of speech, freedom of assembly, and that is what I am doing here, right now."

A loud cheer rolled across the capital grounds. The crowd heard the message.

"Sir, for the third and last time, I am directing you to get back into your bus and leave. You are inciting a riot, sir. This is not acceptable. We don't want you here inciting people to riot. Do you understand what I am directing you to do and what the consequences are going to be?"

"They seem to want me here," I said. "They, the people of Lansing, Michigan are here to see me. These are the people that count. This is the reason I am visiting your fair city. What is wrong with that? Where is the riot? How can you deny me my constitutional rights?"

The crowd started chanting my name. "LEO...LEO...LEO..."

I knew what was coming next but I did not care. The die was cast. Life meant little if cowardice prevailed.

"Sir, you are going to have to come with me," the lieutenant said as he asked me to walk with him.

"NO. I am not going with you. The only way I'm going with you, sir, is if you arrest me and carry me off to wherever you take cold blooded criminals like me who come to an American city to exercise their constitutional rights of free speech and assembly."

The lieutenant glared at me. I knew that he was not going to back down. He knew that I was not going to either.

"You leave me no other choice," he said.

"Nor do you, I," I replied.

He called for two of his officers to handcuff me. While they were doing so, I told Gram to call John and let him know what was happening. Al was already videotaping. Big Jack was standing close just so they could not rough me up. I could see the fire in his eyes, the fire in the hole, and I was blessed that he was on my team and not on theirs. I felt the fire, too. This was going to be my first arrest. Let it be. I was ready. The time had come for a major shift in what this country was doing to its people, and I was going to take this message all the way to the White House in November and lay it on the American people. I was done with pretending everything would work out easily and with simple face to face discussion. The battle lines had been drawn. Somewhere, sitting up in his plush office the governor was calling the shots, but he did not realize just how foolish he was taking these steps to protect his fiefdom.

As I was led away and placed in a waiting police car, all I could hear was the sound of my name echoing off the cold, marble covered walls of the State House and other buildings in the environs: LEO...LEO...LEO...

40. A Ghost from the Past

Preparing to spend the night in jail, I rode along with the officers to the main Lansing precinct building. Through a side door, the police ushered me inside to minimize any contact with the press or the public. Time was suspended. I did not know how long I was in their custody. When I came into the booking area, Jack and a face that looked very familiar greeted me. I just could not place it.

"Leo, you are looking fit as a fiddle," he said, rubbing his hands together as if he was excited about something.

For a long, introspective moment, I stared at him. "Yes, it had to be," I said to myself and smiled. "Johnny Kohout, how the heck are you doing?"

Johnny walked up to me, turned to the officers and said, "Sirs, Leo Pollack is my client. I want to know what he is being charged with and I am here to insure that his rights are protected under the first and fourth amendments to the Constitution of the United States of America. You do understand that my client has rights?" he said as if he were talking to school kids. Since we had been college roommates my junior year at the State University, nothing had changed. Johnny was still the brash character he was way back then.

"What the heck are you doing here?" I asked him.

"I'm your legal counsel and right now my job is to get you out of here as soon as possible," Johnny said.

"I didn't know you were now a lawyer?" I said.

"Hey, when I went into business with my father, little did I know how important the law was going to be. I went back to law school after a few years so we didn't have to pay some mouthpiece a pile of retainer money. My father thought it was a good idea to have a lawyer in the family. He said if he couldn't trust me, he'd just close the doors and retire. I went to law school and came back into the business and was doing just fine until I heard about the crazy Pollack that was running for president and thought to myself, 'I know that guy'. I watched your initial campaign start to take off. I was excited that someone I knew might just be the next President of the US. When I knew you were coming to Michigan and Detroit, I had to come and see you. I heard that you got arrested. I called some guy named John Gallagher to offer my services. He said we sure could use help. Here I am ready to get you the hell out of here." Johnny talked a hundred miles an hour. He grew up in the suburbs of Cleveland, went into business with his father making plastic parts for automobiles and that was the last I heard of him.

"I can't believe you're here," I said.

"Touch me, I'm real," he said laughing

The lieutenant had had enough.

"Sir, you are going to have to wait until we book your client and then you can sit down and talk to him. Let's go, buddy," he said to me.

"Officer, I really would like you to consider not even booking my client. You are completely unaware of what might happen if you pursue this foolish behavior. I am not threatening you. I'm merely informing you that you, your department, the city of Lansing and the entire state of Michigan and especially your Governor, Rick Snyder, are going to face the full force and fury of the law if you do."

The lieutenant looked at him. He was not sure what to do. He stepped back for a moment and said to one of the officers who was assisting him, "Place this man in the holding cell until I make a phone call."

I was led away to a cell off to the side of the precinct's main floor. Luckily, I had the place to myself. Johnny was not allowed to talk to me. I could see him out in the lobby area talking on his cell phone.

I sat down and studied my jail cell. There was not much to it. No bed. A chair. Nice solid bars. No bathroom. No water fountain. Nothing but a chair. This was not how I pictured jail, but I was not in jail yet. I was in limbo, purgatory. I was not in heaven nor in hell. I closed my eyes for a few minutes and just listened to the sounds and deeply inhaled the scents and tried to feel the experience as viscerally as I could. This was a way of life for many people. This was the system now holding 2.1 million men or one out of every 100 adult males in the country. The United States penal system was the largest in the world and a major growth industry. The prison-industrial complex expanded because the government outsourced a significant portion of its business to the private sector. The growth of for-profit prison companies doubled in size in the past twenty years.

Now, even though I knew I was not going to prison, I was sitting inside a cell waiting for some decision about my fate. I did not have any way to contact Basha and tell her that I was okay. I thought about asking for my one phone call, but really did not want to call and worry her unnecessarily. I sat back against the wall, watched and listened to what was going on around me and hoped Johnny and now Big Jack, who showed up and was talking to Johnny, could get me out of here sometime tonight. If not, then I would learn what jail felt like and that was okay. What was there to fear? Fear, that's all. I was wondering what was going to happen next when I could see Johnny, Big Jack, the Lieutenant, and some other plain clothes personnel enter into a major powwow in the hallway. I closed my eyes, opened my mouth, and tried to hear what they were saying. There was too much noise in the precinct office to eavesdrop on their conversation.

Sitting alone in the cell, I mused on all the possibilities. What if Johnny had not come along? I would sit in this cell until they booked me. I would be photographed, "mug shots taken" and then my personal belongings would be gathered up and catalogued. I'd be issued jail clothes. My own clothing would be collected and stored. I would get my phone call. I assumed this. I would be led down to another cell. I probably would get a shower to make sure I was not infected with any kinds of bugs. I would meet my new cellmate or mates. The night would descend. I would try to sleep. I would not. I would wake up and realize I was not free. I was elated that I was not going to have to face that kind of inevitable path. I hoped for early release for good behavior. After all, I had done nothing wrong in the first place. I laughed aloud and a number of blue shirted officers looked over at me. I smiled at them. They did not smile at me.

My arrest must have caused many of them to wonder what was happening. I was not as well known as the other presidential candidates, but my name was beginning to be broadcast regularly. I knew what this would do to our campaign. In some ways, I was happy it happened just now. After all, there was no reason to arrest me for just entering the city. I did not do anything wrong. I was an American citizen traveling in my own country and had every right to be in Lansing to meet with my "friends". Their indiscretion was going to cost them dearly, not in money, but in negative public opinion.

An hour passed and still, the discussion was going on in the hallway. I could see Johnny gesturing wildly to the suits standing in front of him. I wished I could hear what he was saying. Gram showed up. He was standing right beside Johnny and now and then, contributing to the conversation. Big Jack was just standing back and watching, his arms crossed, his laser gaze focused on the people who were resisting whatever argument Johnny and Gram were making.

Voices grew louder and softer intermittently. I was happy when I could hear something. Most often, Johnny's staccato, high-pitched voice dominated the conversation.

"You guys are something else," I heard Johnny judge them and then I could not hear how he finished his line of reasoning.

Johnny Kohout to the rescue. Never in my wildest dreams would I ever think that one of my college roommates would be involved in what I was doing. Truly, he was a ghost from the past, a very pleasant one.

Johnny was a player. He always had a girlfriend or two. I remember a dozen times when I would come home and find him "entertaining" some young woman in his room. I would try to be careful not to make any noise. He did not. The sounds that roared from his love nest were loud. Many times, I would grab what I needed and leave the apartment because I did not want to be there to hear what was going on. I think I was jealous. He always said that he would fix me up if I wanted to meet some of his girl's girls. I always took a rain check. I guess I was not ready for relationships at that time in my life. He was not either because what he was doing was not forming any lifelong bonds with any of the women he brought home with him. One classy lady, Rita Boca, was the only lover that he seemed to be enchanted with and she was there more than any other woman. I liked her immensely. She was warm, friendly, bright, engaging and unbelievably sexy. Everything about her was special. Eventually, Johnny let her go because she got too serious. She wanted to marry him. He wanted to play. They were not compatible. I wondered if he were married now. I would ask him later.

Johnny and Gram were a study in contrasts. Whereas, Gram was cerebral, an organizer, slow to rise up and get going, a gentle talker unless really riled, Johnny was a firebrand. I could just imagine what he was saying to the cops and suits. He was not making their lives easy. I was hoping that someone was tape recording what was being said because I sure would love to hear the proceedings later.

The clock on the wall ticked off 10 pm. I was late calling home. Would my teammates remember to call Basha? Where was Al? Was the bus impounded? So many thoughts raced through my head that, after a while, I grew dizzy wondering who, what, where, when, how and why.

I watched the hands of the clock slowly circumscribe the face and wondered what it must be like to be facing a year in prison, or ten years or a lifetime? How could the mind conceive of the reality of not being free for a long period, or even worse, never again? The thought caused me to shiver. I did not mind facing the possibility that I would be in jail overnight or even for a few days. However, I knew that I had not "killed the pope". I was not being arrested for some felony crime. I was being singled out because my views were not mainstream in this neo-conservative landscape created by the current governor and his cronies. There was something upsetting in the entire legal system that created a plethora of "Law and Order" type shows on our television sets and flooded our society with more restrictions on our freedom. The Patriot Act was just one example. No wonder Ron Paul gained a lot of traction in his campaign by railing against the act. I did not agree with most of what the law permitted security forces to do under the guise of keeping me safe. We were living in a state of chronic fear. Our leaders sold us a bill of goods. In order to be safe, we needed new laws to protect us from "them". Whoever "they" were, we needed to be eternally vigilant. Homeland Security became the newest government department. The previous president was responsible for nearly doubling the size of government. The current president had actually reduced the size of government from 4.2 to 4.1 million in the first three years in office. So much for the lies.

The prison thing got to me. As a nation, we were spending billions of dollars every year to incarcerate a significant percentage of our population. The cost of housing one prisoner per year in a state correctional facility was estimated to be in excess of $60,000. No wonder, the Rev. Jesse Jackson once said he could take the $40,000 we spend locking up just one of his black brothers, send him to college on that money and he would turn out four years later a productive member of society. In many ways, I had to agree with him. The major flaw in his argument was not the economics of it, but the reality that most incarcerated men and women could not read. Illiteracy was endemic in the prison population with some research indicating it was as high as 73%. This was appalling. Prisoners who were not facing life needed to be educated. They were not going to make it once they were released unless they could adequately read and write. The movies "Stanley and Iris" played in my mind's eye. The stars were Robert DeNiro and Jane Fonda. DeNiro could not read, but he was a mechanical genius. She helped him learn to read, and this opened an entire world to him. The movie was a B film but very inspiring.

Sitting quietly in the cell gave me plenty of time to think. Our world was now a run and rip existence. The only time I sat still was when we were cruising down the freeway heading from one venue to the next. Even then, sometimes, the world was too much with me. The phone would ring. Gram and Al would ask for coffee. News would stream across the laptop screen and we would study it. There was food to cook, clothes to clean, beds to make and floors to mop. Our lifestyle was one of constant stimulation. This one was the antithesis. I could imagine the lack of stimulation leading to all sorts of bizarre thoughts and behaviors in the prison setting.

What was the answer? Clearly, what we were doing was insane. It was not working. We built more and more prisons because we could not keep up with the increasing population. However, if we analyzed the prison population by crime committed, we would discover that more than 50 percent of all men and women incarcerated in the United States were there for some sort of narcotics violation. Many were users as well as sellers. The addiction rate of prison inmates was off the scale. Since Reagan got "tough on crime" the nation did not see any reason to reverse the trend and provide therapy instead of incarceration for those who needed addiction treatment. Just like the military-industrial complex, the prison-industrial complex was constantly lobbying the government to continue locking up more people so it could provide "jobs", "security", and other benefits under the guise of helping society. Forget the economic and human cost of incarceration. This argument was lame, but it gained traction in the late 1980s and was now ingrained in our culture. Yes, education and treatment needed to be the focus of prison reform. This kind of investment would make a difference in just one generation.

I stood up to stretch my legs. The minute I did so, a dozen pairs of eyes stared at me. No one said a word. I smiled at the eyes. They blankly gazed back. There was no life, no feeling in them. They were doing their job. I was doing mine. I wanted to ask them if they were happy in their work. I did not. They might think I was being impertinent. If I did ask them, I probably would have been. Big Jack always said, "Let a sleeping dog lie." I heeded his advice. He was still there with Johnny, Gram, the suits, and the officers, talking away. What was going on? I was dying to know. I almost hollered over to them, but again, discretion was the better part of valor. I would just have to be patient and wait for some kind of decision about my fate to be made. After all, what else could I do? I forgot to pack a file in my sleeve on the way in to jail.

No one offered me anything to eat or drink. I found that surprising. To test the waters, I asked an officer sitting in a desk about twenty feet away if I could get something to drink. He just looked at me as if I were daft. I asked twice and did not get any response from him. I almost raised my voice and hollered at him, but decided against making a scene. He went back to his paperwork or whatever he was doing to make himself look busy.

For a short time, my mind was on empty. I thought about nothing at all. All of a sudden, I was filled again with horror, with revulsion. One point two million men and women were living just like me: behind bars. This fact made my spirit sag and my heart ache. Given this fact, something was drastically wrong with America. We were missing the essence of what it meant to be a democratic society. We were falling short of the American dream. Ah, and now my thoughts came back full circle. I smiled inside and laughed aloud. "This is not the American Dream," I said loudly and everyone in the room, including those out in the hallway stopped what they were doing and looked at me.

"Yes, you heard me. This is not the American Dream. I can imagine that as you come to work every day you wonder what is wrong with our society. Why are there so many people committing crimes? What are we doing that is not working? I'll tell you. We are not working. We are not working. We are a welfare state. We do not honor work as much as we did in years gone past. We stripped away the honor of work. We call it having a 'job'. My 'job' is. This is not work. Work is not a 'job'. Work is what I do to contribute to the greater good in the world in which I live. I make something. I serve someone. I care for my brothers and sisters. I work. I'm happy. I am blessed. Without work, I am a hollow shell of a person. This is not healthy. Long-term hollowness leads to despair, depression, illness, suicide, homicide and eventually spiritual death. Wake up Americans. Get to work. Make work work. The time has come to honor work again. Today, tomorrow and always. Honor work. Honor the dream."

I stopped, sat down and said nothing else. For a long time, I could feel the tension in the office. They heard me. They felt me. They were trying to deny what I said. They could not. My prophetic words cut to their very souls and exposed the truth for them to see, hear and, possibly embrace.

Out in the world right now, people were going about their business, working, playing, laughing, hugging, loving, but behind the walls of our prisons, the mortal combat for mental, physical and moral survival was being waged and, as a society, we were losing.

I looked up and saw Johnny, Gram, Big Jack and the others heading toward me. I stood up. I smiled. I was hopeful.

A man in a serge suit, bald headed and an intense stare came up to me and said, "Mr. Pollack, my name is James Colvin. I represent the Governor's office and am here to apologize for the way you have been treated. Officers, please release Mr. Pollack immediately." He stepped aside and let one of the men in blue open the cell. I walked out a free man.

"We are sorry that you were inconvenienced and wish that we could make up for the indiscretion of some of our public safety personnel for the over-enthusiastic manner in which they dispensed their duties."

I listened to the mouthpiece spout off the diplomatically correct words so that this city and state would not end up in court for making a false arrest. I knew that much about the law.

"We hope that you will accept our apology. You are free to go. We hope you enjoy the rest of your stay here in Michigan and will stay as long as you wish to do so."

I stared at him but did not respond.

Johnny stepped in and said, "Mr. Colvin, my client is pleased beyond words that you have seen the error in your judgment, have apologized for your officers' indiscretions and are freeing him from your care. Thank you. Now, it is time for us to leave." Johnny took my arm and led me away. I smiled at them as I walked away.

Outside, I breathed a sigh of relief.

"What was all that about?" I asked Johnny after a minute of pure exhilaration at finally being free.

"A bunch of ass kicking," Johnny said loudly, laughing like a schoolboy and rubbing his hands together like he always did when he was getting excited.

"Who was doing the kicking?" I asked.

"Neither Colvin nor his people," Gram said. "Johnny had this batch of yahoos ready to march into the Supreme Court and face the death squad for their stupidity. I might have studied law, but Johnny is the law," Gram concluded.

"Oh, I just tell it like it is," Johnny said with mirth flowing from his tone of voice.

"I like you, Johnny," Big Jack said. "You know how to cut to the chase."

"Coming from a guy like you, Jack, I cherish the compliment," Johnny said.

"Johnny always had a golden tongue," I said. "Especially with the ladies."

"Ah, Leo, you remember the days. Babes everywhere. What a world we lived in when we were younger," Johnny lamented.

"You ever get married Johnny?" I asked.

"Four times and still counting," he said. "The last one is on her way out. She's a ditz. Good in bed but no brains. I guess I was always a sucker for a good looking woman who could not think about much more than what color to polish her fingernails."

"No kids?" I continued.

"Kids? Are you kidding, Leo? No way. I never wanted anyone to be like me. I was happy to keep my seed fallow. No, but I know you're married and have a son. I can hardly wait to meet them."

"Really? Wow, that's cool. We are heading home. Where are you living right now?"

"Well, that was something I wanted to discuss with you and the team."

"Yes," I said.

"I'm considering coming along for the ride. You're going to need a mouthpiece. I'm not tied down right now. I'm between cases so to speak. I could be a real asset to your cause and Gram tells me that, even though he's been to law school, he's not a trial lawyer and I am. I'd like to be a part of your team. What do you think?" Johnny asked looking at me and the other guys.

"I think we need to get into the bus and sit down and figure out what's what," I said.

"Sounds like a plan to me," Gram echoed.

"Big Jack, you in?" I asked.

"I like this guy. He's in with me," Jack said.

"Al, where's the bus parked?"

"In the back lot. Luckily, we were not impounded. I had to convince the yokels that we were not here to stir up trouble, the bus was ours, and that I was not going to let them park it where I couldn't watch it. I was pretty convincing."

"Let's go," I said.

Once we crawled inside, Al fired up the engine, the power generator came on and we sat down at the kitchen table. I stared at Johnny and just laughed aloud.

"I can't believe that you're really here. This is great! I remember so many good times being with you when we were kids. "

"Me, too, Leo. I just had to come and help when I heard what was happening."

"Where did you come from? I mean, do you live in Lansing?"

"Nope. I live in Detroit. I heard you when you were on the news being interviewed and I said, 'Hey, I know that guy.' I told everyone around me that I knew you and they all said, 'Yah, sure. You know Leo Pollack.' I couldn't convince anyone that we were college roommates. Strange huh?"

"What is hard for me to fathom is that you're now a lawyer. What happened to your father's business and plastics?"

"Leo, it's a long story and not an important one. Suffice it to say, I screwed the pooch and now I'm working for a living. Or at least, working. I'm not making much of a living."

"You come to work for me you won't be making much of a living either," I said.

"I don't care. I want to be a part of this team. That's all there is to it."

"Team, Johnny wants in. What's the verdict?"

Everyone put his thumb up.

"You're in. Now the question is, can you cook and clean?"

"Leo, one thing I never learned was to take care of myself. You know that. How many girls did I bring over to clean my room and my clothes and my back when it got dirty? No, pal, I'm not a domesticated fellow even after all these years."

"You see, Johnny," Gram chimed in, "Leo is our chief cook and bottle washer and so he was hoping you might take over for him. He's a poor cook but he makes tolerable pasta and casseroles, now and then, and he can clean a bathroom quite well. We keep him on because he comes cheap and he doesn't complain."

"Ah, now I get it. So, you were scheming all along. You wanted to…I get it. Leo. Nothing's changed. You were always slick as a wet piece of plastic on a sidewalk."

"Johnny, I welcome you to the team because I know that you will keep us out of trouble. Now, if you can keep yourself out of trouble, that will be doubly good."

"Just keep the ladies at a distance and everything will be okay," Johnny said.

"I'll call Judy and Carol and warn them," Al said.

"What's for dinner?" Al asked.

"Hadn't thought about it, but how do egg tortillas sound to you folks?"

They voted in the affirmative. I got up to start making them.

Gram flicked on the laptop. Johnny, Al and Big Jack got out some cold beers. I watched the team as I was breaking eggs into the large Teflon skillet and was as happy as any man could be surrounded by such wonderful friends.

"Cowabunga Dudes!" Gram cried loudly making the ceiling of the bus vibrate.

"What!" we all asked at that same time.

"Romney barely beat Santorum. It was very close. Paul was third and Gingrich was fourth in both states. Romney was a bigger winner in Arizona. But get this…are you ready…? Are you really ready?" Gram cried out even louder. "We cracked ten percent in Michigan and finished with nine percent in Arizona. We took numbers from Democrats and Republicans. The news is full of coverage about our campaign. Some are calling it a win given what has been going on in this state with all the money Romney and Santorum have been spending. Our campaign released a figure that said we spent $50,000 on radio and TV ads and that was it. We're being given a big nod for next week's Super Tuesday primary elections. The independent write in vote skewed the results in both states. There is confusion as to what is going on right now on both sides of the political borderline. With us in the race, we're upsetting the applecart and it's beginning to have an effect."

Altogether, we roared our approval. Al raised a toast to the future. Everyone but Al drank a long swig of beer. Al never drank because he had quit years ago. He, Bill W. and Dr. Bob were best friends. We admired his friendship with them. Rarely did we drink around him but tonight, he did the toasting with a big draught of diet Mountain Dew, his favorite soft drink.

We ate the egg tortillas I prepared and then decided to find a place to crash for the night.

"How about right here?" Johnny said. "How much safer can we be than in the parking lot of the Lansing Police Department?"

"Do you think this is a good idea after what happened today?" I asked.

"They wouldn't dare come out and say a word to us right now. They wouldn't dare. In fact, I would dare them to do so. I'd see them all the way to the World Court, I would," Johnny bragged. He was always the man for hyperbole.

"Big Jack, we've got space for you," I said.

"I'm off to check the team," he replied.

"Where do you sleep?" Gram asked.

Big Jack just smiled.

"Men, I'll see you in the am." He left quickly, disappearing into the dark.

"What's next?" Gram said.

"I'm calling home," I said. "Basha's probably worried about me since I missed our call earlier."

"What time is it?"

"Past my bedtime," Al said.

While Gram hooked Johnny up with sheets and a pillow for the pull out couch bed, I called Basha and told her what happened today. She was crying and laughing by the end of our conversation. I told her about Johnny's coming to the rescue and being on our team now and she was elated that we would have an in-house lawyer with us at all times. We kissed each other goodbye. I missed her.

Gram was still up. Johnny and Al were in gaga land.

I walked to the front of bus where Gram was studying the returns from today.

"Leo, we are getting to the point where the other campaigns will not even be a factor anymore."

"What do you mean?"

"Remember when we were discussing votes and what we needed to accomplish to insure that we could win the popular election."

"I surely do."

"Right now, with the donations rolling in the way they are, Twitter followers growing exponentially, Face book 'likes' compounding, we are on our way to making the other campaigns irrelevant. We can win this. We can do it without having to run one negative advertisement. We can win this by keeping our message simple, clear, factual and focused on work. We are on the path, my friend."

"I believe you," I said. "I've believed it all my life. Now we just have to finish this with some real passion and then begin to lead the country toward a new way of doing business."

"Leo, do you realize what is at stake?" Gram finally said.

"The future of America. Nothing less than that," I said.

41. Family Reunion

Leaving Michigan was easy even though we leaped forward in our effort to capture a greater percentage of the independent vote. We were not sure to what extent we were picking up Republican and Democratic votes because there was no easy way to measure. What mattered was we were moving in a direction indicating we were viable in large states. This made us competitive everywhere. Heading into the Super Tuesday ten-state primary on Tuesday, we were excited about what we might be able to accomplish. Our campaign was mushrooming exponentially and this created a hopeful "Let's Go for Broke" mental attitude among all those who were intimately a part of the team. Conversations were upbeat with anyone back at headquarters. The internet blitz was paying dividends. Our Twitter followers added up into the millions now. Our Face book page continued to be "liked" by the same numbers. YouTube videos produced by Gram and Al were posted and were being hit constantly. The stage was set for a monumental effort between today and next week when we were going to face the most complex day of the campaign season.

First, we were heading home for a day of rest. I told the team that we needed to stop and collect ourselves. They did not disagree. Gram was ambivalent. Al was emphatic. Big Jack did not say anything. Johnny was excited about meeting Basha, Janko and seeing our home in Youngstown. I was anxious for the entire four hours it required us to cross the Buckeye and pull into the driveway.

The media frenzy started the minute I exited the bus. There were more vans, dishes, lights and people waiting for us than there was when we left. Our trip to Michigan, the strike, the arrest, the release and all the other things that happened while we were gone were coming home to roost. Now I was going to tell my side of the story.

"Be careful," Gram said as he saw me tuck my shirt into my jeans and start toward the bright lights, cameras and microphones.

"Got it."

"Need my guidance, support, anything," Johnny said.

"Not unless they want to arrest me," I said.

Early on in this campaign, I was anxious about talking to the press. Now I actually looked forward to it. The more I shared with them, the more exposure our message got. Given our fledgling organization, I knew that the lion's share of this task was on my shoulders. I accepted the responsibility eagerly.

As I walked up to the gathering, I smiled broadly and said, "Good day. It's great to be home again and meet with all of you. I have a few comments to make before I take any questions."

"Our campaign is gaining momentum because people across the country realize that we are speaking for them. We are not encumbered by special interest groups, lobbyists, superpacs, or any other influential groups that expect to be taken care of when we win the election. We are the people's party. We are the Liberty Party. We stand on this principle, When America works, democracy thrives. We believe in a second principle. Americans Supporting Americans. Buy American and put your neighbor to work. We are not jealous because some people are wealthier than others. However, we believe that the bounty needs to be shared equitably. We believe that a true progressive tax policy without loopholes that favor the wealthy corporations and individuals and penalizes those who are covered under a payroll tax needs to be implemented. Finally, we accept that we are our brothers' and sisters' keeper. In a civilized society, how we treat the least of our citizens is a measure of what kind of nation we are. We believe that we must and will take care of those in need, no matter what the need is."

"Now, I'll be glad to answer any questions you may have for me."

"Mr. Pollack, you were arrested in Michigan. What happened and what are your thoughts about how you were treated by the Lansing police?"

"What happened was that I was arrested and then released. I think the Lansing police were taking precautionary steps to make sure that nothing would happen in their city like what occurred in Flint. Let me go on the record today with this statement. I did not tell people to stage a sit-down strike. I said to the people to let their governor know in a peaceful, non-violent, non-cooperative way that they disagreed with his decision to eliminate the duly elected city officials and install a political crony of his to manage the city."

"Can you see how your advocacy of protest resulted in what took place in that city?"

"Sure, I can."

"You are not denying that this might be the reason the Lansing police took you out of circulation, so to speak?"

"The Lansing Police overreacted. They denied my civil rights. I don't know what they were thinking. Their behavior is all that we can measure. I was denied my rights of free speech and freedom of assembly."

"How are you going to address this issue going forward in your campaign if you face it again on the campaign trail?"

"On my team, I now have a full time lawyer to provide legal counsel to the campaign and to those security officials who do not know what the Constitution states are my rights and their responsibilities."

"His name, sir?"

"Johnny Kohout. He and I were college roommates. He's volunteered to be a part of the campaign from hence forward."

"He will be with you full time?"

"Yes," I said. "I am pleased to have him with us because he is a good lawyer and also a friend. This is a real plus for our campaign."

"Today the senate is preparing to vote on the Blunt Amendment to the Transportation Bill. What are your thoughts about this amendment and would you support or not support it?"

"First of all, this is another example of the partisan issues that result in the government not being able to get things done. The legislation being debated is a transportation bill. What is embedded in it is this amendment that has nothing to do with the major emphasis of the bill. If I were president, I'd veto the entire bill because it is promoting another social agenda that clouds the issues. We need work. We need to get people back on the job making money and providing for their families. Whether or not an employer or employee has the right to morally object to some aspect of health care is not up for debate right now."

"So you disagree with the amendment?"

"Yes."

"Care to elaborate?"

"No. Wait. Yes. I think it ironic that the Republican Party is so bent on diminishing the role of government in all our lives. This theme is the umbrella that covers most of their arguments. At the same time, across the country many state governments are passing legislation to require a woman to have ultrasound tests before receiving an abortion. The government is requiring this procedure to discourage women from pursuing their legal rights. Now this seems an overextension of government intrusion into our freedoms. You be the judge. This sure smacks of intrusive government to me. But hey, what do I know. I'm not a woman so how can I really speak to this issue. I believe this issue is one that should be resolved between a woman and her doctor and no one else."

"You'd veto the legislation if it contained this type of amendment?"

"Yes."

"Even if it would stifle job growth?"

"Yes."

"How then can you say you are for jobs and job growth?"

"Who put the amendment into the bill? This person is what is stifling job growth. You and I are not fools. We can see what is going on right in front of our very eyes. The American people are not fools. They can see what is going on in front of them. I believe that social issues have their place in our discourse. I do not believe that social issues ought to be mucking up our attempts to get people back to work. The one party says they are for jobs. What they are doing is having the opposite effect. If I were President, I'd tell them to stop the game playing and get down to business."

"What if they would not listen?"

"Then I take the message to the American people. Every day if need be. I'd hold a press conference until there was an end to this gridlock. Shedding light on the inactivity of the congress will result in its finally acting responsibly or facing the wrath of the people during the next election cycle. Yes, I do believe in the power of voters to change the system."

"Don't you think that such a tactic might actually have a reverse effect? Your bully pulpit would lose its power."

"My friends, the bully pulpit is only for those who are set on running for a second term. I said up front that I was running for president, not to make this a political career, but to serve my country, one time, one term and then come back home and go back to work. Hopefully, it will be in the steel mill, but if not, then doing some other kind of work that provides me with a decent living and the feeling that I am contributing to my country, my community and taking care of my family."

"Your campaign has gained significant momentum, but you still are not competitive with the two major parties. What is it going to take for you to perform at the next higher level?"

"Interesting question. As long as we are in this primary election cycle, the focus will remain on what the Republican Party is doing. They are bashing each other right now and this is great press. However, once they finally pick a candidate the real campaigning will begin. The President is staying out of the fray. He's no dummy. He knows that these guys are really wounding each other to his benefit. I can't concern myself with what the others do. We are running on a platform that we are the alternative to business as usual. We have no allegiance to any special interest group, billionaires, party affiliation, corporate sponsorship, or anything that would cloud our focus. We are the people's party, those 160 million working people whose voice is rarely heard because, as one, they do not contribute millions of dollars to any campaign. They do not need to contribute millions to our campaign. All we're asking for is a dollar bill. That's it. This is their way of telling us they believe in what we are doing."

"Your fundraising is way behind the other campaigns. How do you hope to compete with them down the home stretch?"

"What do you mean by 'way behind'? If you are referring to what the president has raised, yes, we are nowhere near what he will garner in big corporate and superpac money. He will need it to fight off the attacks the Republicans will wage against him like they have already started in many of these primaries. We are not immune to attacks. We just don't believe we need to spend dollar for dollar fighting their negative message. We will be attacked. Oh, it's coming. What is the worst the two parties can say about us? We don't have any experience? Has experience made any difference in the past ten years? All the experience in the world didn't keep us out of these two disastrous wars, stop the recession, halt the housing downturn, and protect us from the bank failures and the massive bail outs. These 'experts' did not do their jobs. We believe we can do better and we will."

"Super Tuesday is just ahead. How are you going to get your message out across ten states given that you have limited resources, and you are not flying from place to place but riding in a bus making your travel limited and slow?"

"How fast we travel is not the concern. Our message is speeding across the land right now. As I speak, our message is being carried live into every working person's home who wants to hear what we stand for in comparison with the other parties. We will be able to make a difference. We understand the true nature of what is necessary to make this country work again. There is no doubt that when every American who can and wants to work can do so, we will be a healthy nation again. This is our goal. This is the motivating factor in this entire campaign: the honor and decency of work."

"What are you going to do if you don't win this election?"

"We are months away from that reality. Therefore, no comment."

"How does your wife feel about your being gone so much?"

"My wife, Barbara, my soul mate, and I have discussed this many times and we realize this separation is essential for this campaign to succeed. Jon, our son, misses me dearly and I miss him. He tries to understand what is going on, but he is only seven and the real nature of my effort is somewhat hazy for him to comprehend. What concerns me more is when we win and we are living at another address, he might be very confused."

There was laughter in the crowd. A light moment always made the corps feel better toward me. I wished I were capable of being humorous. This was not one of my talents. If, for just one day I could be Robin Williams it would make all the difference in the world.

"When are you leaving again?"

"Tomorrow morning. We're embarking on a 50 state tour and will be gone for a number of weeks."

"How do you think this will play out? I mean, you're going to tour the entire country in order to do what?"

"Meet America and Americans. This is what candidates do. We will see America one day and a few towns at a time. There isn't anything magical about this process. The only difference for our campaign is that we don't have a charter plane or Air Force One to take us around the country. Quite frankly, I wouldn't want to travel by plane. You miss too much flying at 30,000 feet above the earth. Down on the ground, you can see and hear and smell America close up and personal."

"Which Republican candidate would be your toughest competitor if you had to face him in the election by himself?"

"Abraham Lincoln."

They laughed.

"If he were the nominee, I'd campaign for him."

"You won't answer this question?"

"No. Let them settle this on their own. I have no preference. I am not running against them or the current president. I am running for the people and what they want and need. This is the real difference between our campaign and the other parties. They are running against each other and not for the people. I am running for the people and not against anything or anyone. The people need a voice in Washington. I will be their voice. What we will hear out on this campaign trail in the next month or two is what the majority really wants from its government. This is what we will do. Represent them. Speak for them. Insure that the working people and the poor and those who do not have a voice are heard."

"You really believe you can win?"

"Yes."

"No doubts?"

"No doubts."

"Mr. Pollack, you've started a movement that may lead to a revolution in this country. What do you have to say about that?"

"This revolution was coming for the past thirty years. We are just giving it a voice. Working people, those without a voice, are now crying out to be heard. The Occupy Movement is a part of this. The Tea Party is a part of this. The Liberty party is the voice. We will broadcast the message across the land that we hear you, brothers and sisters."

"One more question. What is your greatest joy and your greatest fear as you proceed forward in this campaign?"

I thought about the question for a moment or two. They waited patiently.

"My greatest joy is hearing the people say, 'We want a voice in planning for our future and we want you to be our voice.' This is an honor that I will never fully deserve but I accept with utmost humility. What I fear most is the inability to achieve civility in political discourse both on this campaign trail and later, while governing. The way the candidates speak to and about one another is appalling. This disrespect hurts us all. We must have respect for one another. Yes, we will disagree. I am not in favor of a lot of things the other candidates say, but I do believe they, like me, love this country and want it and its people to prosper. The current president and all these candidates are decent men. They mean well. Sometimes they do not do what is in the best interest of the country and this is manifested in their virulent attacks on one another. I ask them now to stop it in the name of America, civility, human dignity and respect. I will not now nor ever engage in this kind of behavior. There is too much to do to get sidetracked in defending myself from someone's disrespect. This is what I fear the most."

They wanted to continue. I begged their forgiveness and said I wanted to go and see my wife, son and maybe eat a little supper at my own dining room table. They thanked me for my time and wished me well. I waved to them, walked to the back door and disappeared into the sanctuary.

Standing over the stove with her back to me, Basha looked like an apparition. I just loved her shape. She was my goddess, my Aphrodite. I stared at her for a long moment. She did not know I was behind her.

When I softly padded up to her and wrapped my arms around her slim waist, she jumped and exclaimed, "Damn you, Leo, you scared the hell out of me." So much for her goddess-like behavior.

I kissed her neck and said, "I love you, Aphrodite. You are my woman, my ideal."

"They wouldn't let you come inside this once?" she asked.

"Nope. They were doing their job. I was doing mine."

"You know how hard it is to get out of here now," Basha said. "Janko and I walk the gauntlet every time we leave the house. We get questions thrown at us all the time. I usually smile and say, not today and walk away. What am I to do? Leo, can't you make them go away?"

"No, I don't think so. After all, they want to know what the next First Lady is going to be like."

"I don't know if I want to be the next First Lady. I like being your lady."

"I love your being my lady, too, Lady Basha Pollack," I said and walked over to the sink and washed my hands. "What can I do to help you?"

"Nothing really. I'm just about finished. We'll eat in fifteen minutes."

"I guess you met Johnny already?" I was a little nervous about introducing my college chum to Basha, but I was not sure why.

"You mean Uncle Johnny? He and Janko went up to their room and probably are playing with some of his toys. What a character! You didn't tell me you were bringing another 'family' member home."

I wondered what she meant by this. "Uncle Johnny?"

"That's the way Gram introduced him to Janko and me. I was a little shocked but Janko was elated to have another uncle. The boy is starved for male companionship. After all, it's just he and I when you're gone."

"Uncle Johnny. Well, I'll be," I repeated. "Their room. What do you mean by that?"

"Janko said that Uncle Johnny could sleep in his room. Gram has that small cubby hole. Janko didn't want Uncle Johnny to have to sleep on the couch. Johnny said he didn't mind, but your son said 'no, Uncle Johnny. You can sleep on a cot in my room.' So they are upstairs fixing up 'their room'. Where do you find these people?"

"Johnny and I were college roommates. We've known each other for twenty years. I lost contact with him when we graduated."

"He is a live wire. He makes me laugh. I like him," Basha said.

"Just watch him, girl. Johnny is a player and I'm sure that he's already kissed you a half dozen times at least. He's fast and loose with women. He's been married…"

"Four times. I know. He already told me," Basha finished the thread.

"Johnny works fast. He was a godsend in Lansing. If it weren't for him, I might still be there in jail."

Basha did not say a word.

"I didn't call you because I didn't want you to be worried."

She still was silent.

"Basha, come on. I know how you worry."

Silence.

"Okay, okay. Next time I'll call. I'll call you when something happens so you don't have to worry."

"Do you realize that the minute you were arrested, it was all over the news?"

"No, really?"

"Flash: Third Party Candidate Leo Pollack Arrested in Lansing Michigan."

"No way?"

"My heart stopped the minute I heard that statement. I dropped a pot on the floor. Janko's eyes were huge as saucers. I could see his little cheeks quivering. I held him in my lap for an hour while we listened to the initial story and then waited for an update that never came."

"Damn. I didn't know any of this."

"How could you? You were locked up. We were hearing it on all the networks. I can't tell you what a hard hour that was. Finally, I called John and he told me that everything was under control. You had a lawyer and Big Jack and Gram were right there with you and there was no doubt that before long you would be out of jail and on your way home."

"I'm sorry, honey. I didn't know. Please forgive me."

"Love is never having to say that you're sorry. Next time, please call me. I can deal with knowing the bad news. What I can't and won't deal with is no news."

We kissed long and hard. I was forgiven.

"Now, run on up and get the 'boys' and tell them that dinner is served."

"Will do. We're okay?" I asked again.

"Leo, I'll love you until I die. Nothing will ever change that, but you need to stop trying to protect me. We're in this together, remember. For better or worse. Get that?"

"Got it," I said. I ran upstairs to call the "boys".

I found Johnny in Janko's room playing Legos with him.

"Uncle Johnny, you having fun?" I asked looking at my old friend playing with my son on the floor in his room.

"Loads," he said. "We're making a 747 airliner. Janko said he wants to be a jet pilot when he gets older like Uncle Gram was. I said he might want to be a lawyer like me but he said that being a pilot sounded like a whole lot more fun. When I told him I made more money than a pilot he wanted to know how much more. Now I'm stuck."

"Janko, you and Uncle Johnny need to get ready for dinner, okay?"

"Yes, Daddy. Come on Uncle Johnny. I'll show you how we wash our hands for dinner," he said grabbing Johnny by the hand and leading him down the hallway to the bathroom.

I stopped by Gram's room and invited him to dinner. He was on the phone talking rather quietly. He held up his finger to indicate he got the message. I left him alone. I wondered whom he might be calling. Perhaps he was chatting with Judy or Carol and warning them about "Uncle Johnny", the newest member of our team.

We waited to say grace until Gram arrived. He was close on Janko's and Uncle Johnny's heels.

Dinner was one of my favorites: halushki noodles, cabbage and sausage. I ate with real gusto. How nice it was to eat someone else's cooking. By the way I gulped my food, I think Basha wondered if we ate while we were on the road. She knew I was the primary cook for our little tribe.

When we were all stuffed, we sat back and just enjoyed a moment without having to think about the campaign, public relations, and issues of the day or anything else that was geo-political in nature.

"Now that was a mighty fine meal, Basha," Johnny said smiling broadly at my lovely wife. "I know why Leo settled down. He found someone who could keep him happy both at the table and in the bedroom."

I gave Johnny a dirty look. As soon as I did, Janko piped up, "What do you mean by that, Uncle Johnny?"

Now he was on the hot seat. Knowing Johnny, he was quick to reply, "Janko, what I was saying was your Mommy is a wonderful cook and she sure knows how to make a bed really well. I saw how nicely your bed was made."

"I make my own bed, Uncle Johnny. My Daddy taught me how to do it."

His face got a little red. Still, the master of disaster skated out of this one by quickly asking, "Ready to finish that jet liner, Captain Janko?"

"Sure am. Can we be excused Mommy?"

"Yes, you can but no playing on the bed. I wouldn't want it to get messed up before you get into bed tonight. You hear me, Janko, Johnny?"

"We hear you, Mom," Johnny said. He and Janko scooted out of the room.

"Is he always like that?" Basha asked.

"No, just most of the time," I answered her. "He means well. You've got to understand he never has had any kids, was an only child born to a father and mother who doted on him because he was born when they were older and so he's always been treated special."

"Johnny really needed a few sisters to teach him some conversational etiquette," Gram said.

"That's where you learned to be your svelte self?" I asked.

"Sisters and a strict mother who wouldn't let anyone disrespect a woman at any time anywhere. I got a dose of feminism at a very early age and the lessons still stick to me."

"I can tell because you're afraid to go out with a mature woman," I said with a smirk on my face.

"What are you talking about?" Gram retorted.

"Oh, I couldn't help but overhear your hushed conversation with what I assume was either Judy or Carol?" I added.

"So you were eavesdropping, huh? So much for a good friend and loyal compatriot. How do you know I was even talking to a woman? How?"

"I could just tell, that's all," I offered in defense.

"I'll have you know that it wasn't a woman but someone far more important that Judy or Carol or for that matter, you."

"Oh, really? Like who?" I asked.

"Jennifer Williamson, that's who?" he said in a haughty way.

"Ah, I knew it was a woman. Now we're getting closer to the truth."

"Who is Jennifer Williamson?" Basha asked as she started to clear the table.

"Basha, Jennifer is a New York Times reporter instrumental in getting our donation counter posted on the front page of the Times. She is one of our biggest supporters in print media. Leo should be elated that I've established an excellent working relationship with her. She wanted an exclusive interview with you and I was discussing the details with her on how she could do it without your having to go to New York."

"So I suppose you proposed, like that word, huh? You proposed she come out here and meet with me in Ohio or wherever we are on the road at the time?

"What if I did?" Gram said defensively.

"I knew it. I knew it. You're an old rake you are. She's probably 25 years old and you're what, pushing 55?"

Gram glared at me. "I'm 53 and I'll have you know that Jennifer is more like 37 and not 25."

"Oh, she's only twenty years younger than you are?"

"Sixteen to be more accurate," Gram corrected me.

"Leo, what difference does it make what age she is and whether or not Gram finds her to be a fascinating woman that he might like to get to know a little better?" Basha asked me.

"Oh, it's nothing hon," I said. "Just that Gram puts on airs like he's above the man-woman fray. He is too committed to the campaign to get involved with a woman right now. He almost wears his devotion to the cause as a badge of honor."

"I should think that would be honorable," Basha said. "You won't find many men like Gram who would drop what he was doing in Colorado, travel all the way across the country, show up at our house and volunteer to work for your campaign for the next year and not even ask for any money to do it. That's pretty special, I'd say.

"See, Basha knows when you have a really quality employee working for you," Gram said. "And this is the kind of treatment I get. Making fun of me because I was talking to a New York Times reporter about getting an exclusive interview with you so that you will get even more press coverage across the country."

"Okay. So let me ask you just one question and we'll put this entire saga to rest."

"Go ahead, ask," Gram said.

"Are you attracted to Jennifer?"

Gram was silent.

"Come on, Gram, fess up," I chided him.

"Guilty on all counts," he said sheepishly but with an air of finality.

"There. Now we're clear. Give her a call back and tell her you can't arrange an interview but when we're in New York on the tour, you'd like to take her out to dinner," I said laughing merrily and reached over and slapped him on the back.

"You're cruel," Basha said to me. "Gram has a right to some happiness in his life. I can't believe you led him on like that!"

"You ought to travel with this snake," Gram said to her. "He is a real tyrant on the bus. Ever notice how tired we always look when we get in. It's Leo. He makes us tired," Gram said pointing an evil finger at me.

"Basha, see what you've done, now? Gram will be taking the victim stance from now on because he believes you'll believe anything he says. Now we're in for some long, long road trips if this kind of surly attitude is loosed upon us."

"Gram, you're going to behave on the road, aren't you?" Basha asked seriously.

"Sure, Basha, I always do," Gram said with a smirk on his face.

"There Leo, now you two can just stop needling one another. There is too much dissension in the world as it is for you two to be going at it," Basha said finishing the dishes and starting to put them away.

"Seriously, Basha, Leo and I have this thing about the women. He's always encourages me to talk to this one or that one. I'm kind of shy and so I have a hard time approaching women I don't know very well. We just tease each other. There's no disrespect intended. I'm sorry if we gave you the wrong impression. Actually, Leo and I are getting to be like real brothers. He's like the brother I never had."

"And Gram's like the brother I never had."

"See, we're just teasing each other and making up for lost time," Gram said.

"I think I'm starting to get the picture. What do you fellows talk about all day long when you're riding along in that bus hour after hour?"

"Oh, if we recorded it, you'd probably be bored to death," I said.

"Or, if truth be told, your ears would burn and your eyes would smoke and your hair would catch on fire," Gram said.

"No, Gram, your pants would be on fire for lying to my loving but naïve wife," I cried out punching him in the arm.

"Ouch, Basha, did you see what this bully just did to me?"

She punched him in the other arm, then wrapped her arms around his neck and kissed him lovingly on the forehead, then on each cheek and then on the lips. "There, that is a thank you for being my lover's big brother. Take good care of him. I miss him dearly and the only reason I don't go crazy is because I know he is with you, Al, Big Jack and now Johnny. So please, take good care of him and yourselves and come home more often. Our family reunions are not happening often enough," she said and then came over and sat in my lap, put her arms around my neck and kissed me hard on the lips. "Now, we're even."

"I'm going up to check on the other two boys. It's awfully quiet up there. I hope they didn't do anything foolish."

Basha left us to our own devices.

"You're a lucky man, Leo," Gram said watching her walk out of the room.

"I know."

We dropped the subject.

When it was time to put Janko to bed, we all gathered in his room. What a lovely family we made. Uncle Johnny, Uncle Gram, Basha, Janko and I were all sitting on the bed together. Uncle Johnny said he wanted to read the poem for the night. We laughed as more Shel Silverstein danced off the page as Johnny brought the words to life. We said his good night prayers together. Janko got a flood of kisses. I was the last one to leave his room.

"Daddy, Uncle Johnny said you were going on the road again tomorrow and you might be gone for a long time. Is that true?"

"We are going on the road tomorrow, but we won't be gone for a long time. We will be gone for some time."

"What is the difference?" Janko asked me.

I could not tell him so I said, "I will call you every night and we will talk and I will try and let you know when we are coming back home. Janko I miss you all the time. I just have this work to do right now and I can't do it from our home."

"I know, Daddy. Being the president means you have to travel a lot. But the president now flies in a plane. Why don't you fly in a plane so you can come home every night?"

"I don't have the money the president has so I have to use a bus."

"When you become the president, will you fly?"

"I hope so."

"Good. Then you'll be home every night. "Good night, Daddy, I love you."

"I love you too, my little warrior." I kissed him on the forehead, tucked him in and left the room. Leaning against the wall for a few moments, I gathered myself together, wiped the tears away and headed downstairs.

Johnny, Gram and Basha were sitting at the kitchen table. I joined them.

We chatted for a few hours. Johnny filled us in on his life since we last saw each other and entertained us with his wild stories of law, the justice system and life in the fast lane as a corporate lawyer. Gram laughed and enjoyed the integration of another member into our family. Basha was the graceful hostess. She served some coffee and homemade cookies.

Our family reunion bound us together like a steel cable.

When midnight approached, I begged forgiveness and said I wanted to cuddle up with my lovely wife for a few hours before we had to get up very early in the morning and take a long campaign swing across this great land.

"Yah, sure, you two kids go on up there and shake the sheets a little and leave Gram and me down here to entertain each other," Johnny said. "We got it. We won't feel too hurt that you don't want us around anymore."

"Good night, Johnny," Basha said, putting him in his place.

"Good night fellows, and thanks for making this night a great family reunion," I said.

"We're lucky we have such a family," Gram said wistfully.

"Yup, I agree," Johnny added. "I'm happy that you fellows gave me the thumbs up. I needed to be connected somewhere."

"You are," Basha said to everyone. "We all are."

Basha and I slept soundly spooned against one another, my face buried in the nape of her neck and my heart wrapped in the bosom of her woman's soul. No man could be happier.

42. Another Day in Paradise

When the alarm fired off at 5 am, I turned it off and rolled back over. Basha pushed me and said, "Leo, it's time."

"I know what time it is," I whispered. "Enough's enough. One more day won't make that much of a difference. I want to spend one more day in paradise. We can leave tomorrow."

"Leo, the guys are counting on you, the campaign is backing you, and the people out there are waiting for you," Basha prodded me.

"Yes, and I will be gone for a long time so I think it is time to walk Janko to school, smell the fresh air in my own yard, stand on the porch and see the city lights and just be normal. This feeling will soon end. Once we embark on this journey, my love, nothing will ever be the same."

We were silent for a while. No one was moving anywhere.

"I know," she said. "I'm scared and excited and proud and confused all at the same time. I believe in you, what you're doing and that's the dilemma. I think we both know what is coming and are not sure if we are willing to pay the price."

"Yes, that's it. The investment is in America. The cost is our privacy and opening the window into our lives. You know that we are going to be under attack. We are already facing the vetting process. I'm sure that someone is looking into every dirty little deed I've ever done in my life. They will be into yours next. There is nothing fair about this but we have to be prepared for it. Are we?"

"I am very careful, Leo. Trust me. I don't even leave notes around the house and when I take the trash out, I burn it. I don't even shred it."

We started laughing. "Sounds like we're CIA operatives."

"Are we paranoid?" Basha asked.

"No. In fact, today, I'm going to have Jeeves come and scan this house for bugs and anything else that might be 'out of place'."

"You think that we could actually be bugged? Leo, this is creepy."

"We don't know, but we won't take any chances."

I called Big Jack and asked him if he could send Jeeves over to the house today to do a sweep. Jack said he would and then asked me when we were leaving. "Tomorrow," I said. His silence was telltale. "Yes, I know we were supposed to leave today, but I need another day at home with my wife and son. I hope you can understand. I just need this day to be with them." Silence. "Jack?" He said he would send Jeeves over later in the morning. I thanked him. "I got it, Leo. I agree. Kiss the wife and hug the kid. We can campaign tomorrow. Sometimes I wish I had a place to go home to so enjoy," he finished and hung up.

Basha kissed my forehead and said, "I'm going down to make some coffee. If you're staying home, you might want to get ready. Janko needs to be in a little while."

I looked at the clock, jumped out of bed and headed to the bathroom. Ten minutes later, I finished my morning routine. I went down the hallway and looked in on Janko and Uncle Johnny. They were both sleeping peacefully. Gram was not in his bedroom. I found him down in the living room reading a book and scanning the headline news.

"What's up?" he said. "Basha says we're staying home. Is that true?"

"Can we do it?" I asked him.

"Leo, we can do anything you want to do," he said. "It's Friday. The primaries are on Tuesday. We can't make it to every state. We can do what we want to do. I agree. You need another day at home. We have another issue that is pressing."

"And that is?"

"Remember the other day I said we were mounting a nation-wide voter registration campaign to get as many independent voters to sign up as we could."

"I sure do."

"Watch this." He played a clip from a CNN news report that indicated both parties were planning to do the very same thing.

"Interesting piece. What does it mean?" I asked.

"What would make them do something we were doing right after we started our own voter registration strategy?"

I thought about it for a moment. "Ah, I got it. Now I see the pattern. They are following our lead. However, we never announced what we were going to do."

"Right. The only time we talked about it was on the conference call we had with the team that one afternoon on the road."

"You're right," I said the light coming on. "We are being bugged. Worse, someone is not really on our team. Someone's talking to the other campaigns. We have a traitor on the inside."

I sat down and we watched the end of the clip.

"What do we do?" I asked.

"Nothing right now, but we can put out some misinformation and see where it goes. We could put out a number of different messages through as many of the team as we can and see which one gets into the political mainstream."

I said nothing for a few minutes. Watching the computer screen as it streamed the media to us, I was still amazed at the power of the technology. What we were facing was a new threat. I was not sure we wanted to go on the defense right now. This was something that we needed to discuss with the entire team.

"I don't know, Gram. This is starting to undermine the roots of what we are about and I don't like it. After all, we might put out the misinformation. We might find the mole or traitor as you said. Then what? Fire him or her. The other campaigns will not stop. The stakes are high. I think we remain transparent and share the facts with the press and let them report it. Let the public decide what to make of the tactics."

"You're being an idealist right now. This campaign is way beyond that point. We really need to be proactive when it comes to protecting our strategies and not letting the competition know what we are doing."

"No, we can let them know what we are doing because what we are doing is the opposite of what they are doing and that is what makes our campaign different from their campaign. Look, Gram, they are going to say anything they want to and we really can't stop them from doing so. That is their right, their prerogative, and if they choose to go that route, let them. We can stay above the fray. We can. I truly believe this."

"You are a true believer. I know that," Gram said. "I'm more a realist. I think we should respond affirmatively, quickly and strongly."

"Let's discuss this with the team. I don't deny that we need to do something, but what we do is less important than what we think. What I think is we are facing an ideological dilemma. If we pursue a strategy that is defensive, we will continue investing gobs of money and time in increased defensive strategies. If we don't mount any defense and just continue to move forward, take the offensive posture, continue to flood the political landscape with our ideas we can offset their attacks."

"I would like to believe that, but I'm not so sure."

"Look, we don't have to solve this now. I'm going to walk to school with Janko and then, when I get back, we can call John, assemble the team, and decide what to do. I did call Big Jack and asked him to have Jeeves come over to the house and perform his magic right here. Who knows? We might be monitored right now. I don't know that but I don't want my house to be in this campaign. Basha and Janko deserve a home without intruders lurking in the walls, floors, lights wires and toilet seats."

When I walked into his room, Janko was slowly rising. Uncle Johnny was dead to the world. I quietly rustled my son and he opened his eyes and stared at me with wonder.

"Daddy, I thought you would be gone already."

"I'm staying home for one more day. Let's get ready for school and I'll walk with you today. How does that sound to you?"

Janko cried out loudly and Uncle Johnny roused from his deep slumber and called out, "What's happening! The house on fire?"

"Go back to sleep. We're not leaving today. We're taking one more day off. Coffee's on. Janko and I are getting ready for school. You go ahead and sleep if you want to do so."

Johnny sat up in his cot. His glazed eyes stared at me. "You serious?"

"Yes. I need another day at home. We're going to be gone for a few weeks before we are back here and I just want some time with my family."

"You can always fly back from wherever we are in the country and see them," Johnny said. "There are airlines in this country that do make travel quite convenient, you know."

"Sure, I do know, Johnny, but that's not what this is about right now. We can talk about this later. Go back to sleep. I'm heading downstairs and getting ready to go to school with my boy."

"I can't sleep now. We've got work to do." He got up as I left the room. Janko was in the bathroom getting ready for school. His routine was similar to mine. The only thing he did not do was shave. Like father, like son.

Basha made oatmeal for breakfast. Gram was eating. I drank some coffee.

"No oatmeal for you?" Gram asked.

"I'm not hungry," I replied. "Coffee will do."

"Slice of toast, Leo," Basha offered.

"Now that might be better. Plain, please."

We ate in silence. Gram was reading the paper. Basha was nibbling on a small bowl of oatmeal. When Janko rushed into the kitchen, the entire family perked up. His bright spirit energized us. It was a rare day when I could take him to school so he was making the most of it.

After he ate, we loaded his daypack with his lunch and extra clothes for gym and then he kissed his mother goodbye and we left for school. The media were already posted outside the house waiting for me to emerge.

"Folks, we're off to school. We'll be here all day long. I'm sure you have more questions and I will be glad to answer all of them, but right now, I need to get my son to school."

"Doesn't your son normally go alone?" someone asked me as we started off.

"Yes, he does. I just want to go with him today. If you want to tag along, please do so, but no questions about politics. Janko and I just want to be father and son for the next twenty minutes or so. I'm sure you can appreciate and will respect that request."

They did.

Janko and I collected a few old buckeyes along the way and we talked about how big they were and how trees came from such big seeds and that all plants produced seeds of some kind so that they could reproduce themselves. We smelled the faint sulfur odor from the mill. He asked me if I wanted to go back to work in the mill and I said that I did miss the work and would not mind doing so. He did not ask me anything about what I would do if I were elected president. I think the reporters tagging along with me stifled some of his curiosity. We looked both ways at every intersection and then safely crossed the street. I let him lead the way. He was a resourceful little kid. I was proud of him. From the very first day he went to kindergarten, he walked to and from school by himself. He asked his mother to "trust me, Mommy" to make it alone. Basha had a hard time doing so, but she did honor his request. The distance was not far, just five blocks, but to Basha it was a trip around the world. I supported Janko in being free to go alone. We knew there were risks. We knew there were rewards too. I did not want my son to grow up being afraid of shadows or strangers. Thus far, he had made it on his own and that was cause for celebration. When I said goodbye to him at the school door, we hugged and kissed and I said, "I may not be here to get you at the end of the day, but you know the way home." He smiled and said, "Yes, I do, Daddy. Don't worry. I can make it on my own." He ran inside. I was proud of him.

After he disappeared into the school, I walked away and headed toward home. The entourage attracted a lot of attention. Many of the children and their parents were watching as I left the school grounds. Janko was able to handle this stressor well. He was an amazing kid. I just hoped that this attention did not start to affect his schoolwork and his ability to make friends and be as normal as possible. I knew what was coming and hoped for the best. I would deal with what happened with his best interest in mind.

As the reporters and I ambled along, I opened the door for their questions and found that this was an extraordinary way to do two things at once. Walk and talk. No wonder Harry Truman took his "morning constitutional" and invited the press along.

"What's on your minds today?" I asked as we headed east on Broadway. I was not taking the same way home. I needed a brisk walk to keep my legs moving and my heart pumping. The campaign would surely tax my strength. I needed this time to get in shape for it.

"Given that we just went to your son's school, an old one at that, what are your plans for revitalizing, for revamping education in America?"

"Old is right. Jefferson Elementary is the school where I went to kindergarten. After this school year, it's scheduled to be torn down. It is old and the repairs would cost more than actual new construction. That did not answer your question."

"Let me describe to you, in as simple terms as I can, what I think needs to happen to improve the American public school educational system."

"First, the antiquated system of nine months of school and then three months of vacation needs to end. We are losing ground each year to other countries that have discarded this agrarian based system and adopted a more realistic, twenty-first century focused process."

"What would it look like?"

"Six weeks of school. One week off. Six more weeks of school. Another week off. This pattern would run through until July when the entire month would be off for families to take vacations and be together in the middle of summer. Back to school in August for six weeks and then a week off again. Christmas week through New Years would be off. Holidays matter. Thanksgiving week would be off too. This would give us the opportunity to really educate our kid's year around and not just for a mere six months out of the entire year."

"How do you suppose parents and kids will react to this type of change?"

"We are losing this generation to the old system. It's time to change."

"What other ideas do you have to improve the system?"

"Teacher mentoring is a must. Principals who sit in offices and do not mentor their teachers are a waste of money. If a teacher enters the classroom and does not have his or her mentor observing him for the first three or four years, the teacher will not develop into a master teacher. We need feedback. We need mentors. In the mill, you can't become a first helper without learning how to be a second helper. You can't be a second helper without first being a third helper or 'slagger'. Each position is a stepping-stone to the next one. The slagger learns how to be a second helper by helping the second helper do his job. The second helper learns how to be a first helper by helping the first helper do his job. Each one, teach one. This is as old as the guilds. We are foolish to think that school can prepare people for this modern work place without mentorship."

"Who would be the mentors in the schools?"

Assistant principals. Then, master teachers who serve as nothing but mentors. Too many principals and assistants are the worst teachers that ever entered a classroom. They get their principal certificates or licenses and then disappear into 'administration' whatever that means and leave the teachers to develop on their own. There is no such thing as a 'born' teacher'. Teachers are made. Student teaching is just the beginning of the learning process. Teachers learn from others just as we all do. Doctors have a residency requirement that often lasts a year. They deal with the human body. Important stuff, I'll grant you. A teacher deals with a child's mind. Even more important stuff wouldn't you agree? It is time to elevate teachers to the highest levels of professionalism. Pay them like the professional people they are. Demand excellence. Get results that insure the future of the next generation of genius."

"These are lofty goals. How will you be able to convince principals to do this and what do you think the teachers' unions will say when you propose that their teachers undergo an intensive training period that might last years?"

"They will accept it as being best practice. What is missing in teacher education is the extensive on the job training. Theory is nice. The actual delivery of the content is what is far more important. You've all been in a boring classroom. I can think of a dozen or more that I had in college as well as in high school. Lectures suck. Poorest way to teach. In our schools today, this is still the standard. This has to change. We need to introduce the discovery method at all levels. Some schools are there. Most are not. This is part of the training. Delivery must be videotaped, studied and feedback given. Think about Peyton Manning. We're told that he spends forty or fifty hours a week watching and preparing for the next game. A football game? How much more important is it for a teacher to watch his or her performance in the classroom with his or her mentor and learn how to improve the delivery of the product?"

"This would require that teachers spend a lot of time on the job learning how to do their jobs. How would you pay for it?"

"Glad you asked. Here comes the most radical idea of all. We've funded education based upon property taxes for decades. Poor neighborhoods get less money because property taxes are low and so schools suffer. Wealthy suburbs have high taxes, schools get maximum funding and the gap between rich and poor continues to expand. Poor kids often don't get the education they need. As a result of not getting the education they need, they don't qualify for good jobs because they don't qualify and they fall behind. Wealthy kids get a better education. They go on to college or trade school and get better jobs. They make more money. They move to wealthier neighborhoods. The process repeats itself. This circular pattern dominates the system and insures that nothing will ever really change."

"So what can you do about it?"

"All property taxes will be the same percentage across the entire country. All property taxes will go into a national education fund. Money will be distributed to every school in the country equally so that every child, all children receive the same quality education, at least as far as money goes."

"This will never happen."

"No, it hasn't happened yet."

"This is socialism."

"This is Christianity. I am my brothers' and sisters' keeper."

"Just yesterday, sir, you were incensed that the other candidates were introducing religion into politics. How do you square your comments from yesterday to what you are saying today?"

"The principle I'm citing is not wholly a Christian one. It is an American one. Oh, yes, and a Judaic principle, a Muslim principle, Hindu, Buddhist, you name it. All great faith systems believe in taking care of each other. I can be an atheist and believe this. God does not need to tell me that my fate, your fate, our fate is tied to one another. Look around us. Look at us. We don't make our own clothes. We don't grow our own food. We don't do most things for ourselves anymore. We share in an economy where some of us work for money to buy the things we need to live. This exchange system requires us to accept our interdependence upon each other. The proposal I made above about sharing the wealth across the nation and spreading it out for our children is not based upon just religion but a core belief that we, as a society, are in this together. What is more important than the care and nurture of the minds and bodies of our children? They are the ones who will need to take care of us. I am committed to insuring that they are well prepared for the tasks that lay ahead of them. I think most people with common sense are so inclined to think so."

"This is a form of socialized education, wouldn't you say?"

"Yes. All education is socialization, socialism, social studies. The more we get our children to learn with, about and for one another, the healthier our society becomes. When schools were segregated, we had a cancer in our society. When they were integrated, some things changed. However, the mass exodus of wealthier white people to exclusive, or at least, different suburban areas has continued the separation of the people. Charter schools and other private schools continue to perpetuate this standard. It must be stopped, changed, improved, diversified, expanded and made universal."

"How do you fund all this without raising more taxes?"

"End wars as we know them. Stop the insane expenditure that we call military preparedness. As a nation, we spend more on our military than all the top industrialized nations in the world. How long can we sustain such an economic drain? If we don't reverse this trend, we will not make it to mid century as the world's leader in any area but national debt."

"Getting the government to buy into this idea is going to be difficult given the power of lobbyists and other special interest groups that have held up defense as the most important function of government."

"Sounds like a comment more than a question, but you are right. I don't deny we'll have a hard fight against the forces allayed against major reform. You all know that what I am saying is the truth. This is what is happening. Someone has to bring it up for discussion. The other candidates won't do it. They are wedded to a strong military and a weak educational system. If the president were truly committed to improving education, he would fire his current secretary of education and get someone in there who really can do something to make the entire country a better place for kids to learn. Look at the mess they have in Chicago right now. Who was the head of that system before he came to Washington? Need I say more?"

"This is the closest you've come to criticizing the present administration. What else do you have to say about what they are doing regarding education?"

"I just laid out my main points on how to fix the system. However, there is more. Teachers are not guaranteed a job for life. They need to perform. They need to be evaluated. Testing is one way to evaluate their performance. Their peers should have a voice in how they are rated. I think peer feedback is the most important component in developing any master teacher. Just as a master electrician gives his apprentices feedback, so must master teachers give feedback to their apprentice teachers. Sometimes that feedback is simply this: 'You are not cut out to be a teacher. Seek another profession.' Hard words to deliver. Even harder words to swallow. They are necessary and a vital part of the feedback loop to make schools the highest functioning learning environments possible."

"How long do you think it would take to engineer such a complex educational reform as you are describing?"

"One year from the date I take office, I can make this system be in full blown change mode."

"One year? Really?"

"Sure. We can't wait for a generation to pass us by. Too many kids are being lost every year to the ineptitude of principals, teachers, unions, school boards and the government that is supposed to oversee the entire system."

"That is awfully ambitious, wouldn't you say so?"

"Yes, but remember, I will only have four years to get this done, so I can't waste any time mulling over the issues. I've got to hit the ground running, pick the right change agents to make this happen, and then get out of the way and let them get down to business and fix it."

"Anything else you can think of that needs to be done in this area?"

"Oh, my friends, I'm just warming up to the task. Sure. This might surprise you, but you know that we let kids drop out of high school at age sixteen. What is wrong with this picture? How many of you at age sixteen were ready to make such an important life decision? This practice needs to change. No one can drop out of school until they are 19 years of age. If they are doing poorly in school, every resource known to education will be placed at the disposal of the student's teacher, the administration and the school to insure that we graduate 99% of all students. Our current graduation rate is unacceptable. We won't let our kids fail. We raise the bar. They will rise to meet it. At age 19, if a student is still not capable of graduating, then he or she will be required to enroll in a trade school, enlist in the military or some other type of school after they are aptitude tested and the match is found. We've been giving up too easily for the past thirty years. This needs to change and I mean now."

"That's a lot to accomplish in such a short time."

"I agree. There is one more thing I wanted to say. No GED testing until age 19. We make this process too easy. We need to teach students to have some discipline and not give in to their wants. They need an education. They may want to quit. Quitting does them no good. Finishing something is part of the learning process. That's all. I'm finished."

They laughed. We had walked an extra mile or two and were now coming back down toward the house. I was happy that I could get in a hike while we were chatting. This was so special.

"I want to thank all of you for being so considerate and not infringing on my time with my son. I appreciate it."

"What are you going to be doing the rest of the day now that you are not planning on leaving until tomorrow morning?"

"First, I'm going to check in with Basha, Barbara, my wife, and see what chores she has for me to do. Then, who knows?"

" How did she get the name, Basha?"

"Basha is the Polish form of Barbara. Her father and mother named her after a famous heroine from Polish history who fought alongside her husband when the Muslims were overrunning Poland in the seventeenth century. She is a warrior, my Basha," I said proudly.

"I'll talk to you folks later," I said as I walked up to the back door of the house and entered. I still could not get used to going in the front door even now as a grown man.

Basha did have chores for me to do. With joy in my heart, I gladly slaved on her "honey-do" list. By early afternoon, I completed it. She was grateful. I was happy to be doing things for her just because they were for her and no one else.

Gram and Johnny were on their phones, working on laptops, making notes on clipboards.

"Al called after you left for school," Basha said. "I told him what you were doing and he was so happy, he said he could give you a kiss. It seems that his wife had a list for him and he was very happy to stay home and get it done. You might give him a call and tell him what's happening."'

I called Al and we chatted for a few minutes. He thanked me for the change in plans and I said that it was pure selfishness on my part. He said he approved of being selfish now and then and hung up.

Big Jack and Jeeves showed up about three o'clock and we turned the snoop loose in the house. An hour later, he showed us what looked like a small pea with a microscopic wire sticking out of it.

Gram, Johnny, Jack and I stared at the object.

"What is it?" Johnny asked.

"Something that doesn't belong in this house," he said.

"Is it disabled?" I asked.

"Nope. We might want to play with it a bit."

"Isn't it monitoring us right now?"

"Nope. I have a shield up to stop its transmissions."

"How does it work?" I asked.

"Simple. I hold this aluminum plate near the bug and the signal can't go anywhere."

"Where did you learn all this stuff?" Johnny asked Jeeves.

"ITT," he proudly stated.

"What do we do with it?" Gram said.

"I'm going to return it to its location but now we will know where it is."

"Where did you find it?"

"It's kind of embarrassing to say but right next to your nightstand in the base of the lamp."

"How could it get there?" I asked. I was concerned.

"Don't know, but it had to be placed, that's for sure," Jeeves said.

"Basha, have we had any repairmen in the house recently?" I asked her. She came into the room and Jeeves showed her what he had found. I could see her face get white. "No, we haven't had anyone in the house recently."

"Jack, is the guard you have on this place here twenty-four hours a day?"

"Yes, they are but they are not watching the house 24/7. They are watching Basha and Janko. So if the two go out, they are with them, but not with the house. We'll change that immediately. Consider it done."

"Should we be concerned about anything?" Basha asked.

"Not now, honey. We have Jeeves on the job protecting us."

Jeeves smiled and went back to work.

"I think it's time for us to get the team together and figure out a game plan," Gram said.

"I agree," Johnny added.

"Jack, what do you think of all this?"

Jack hesitated for a moment and then said, "Leo, we're up against the most powerful government in the world and groups of people that want to take over that government, albeit through legal means, but who will do anything to accomplish that goal. We need to be careful. We need to remain vigilant. We need to stomp the hell out of the bastards who violated your house."

I smiled nervously when he uttered his last comment. "I know you're just expressing your frustration. I don't blame anyone for what happened. We caught it. That is what matters."

"I wasn't joking, Leo. This is beyond dirty tricks. This is a sacred place. This is your home, brother. I take this assault personally. We will find out who did this and make them pay."

"Just do it without killing them, Jack," Johnny joked. "I don't want to represent you in criminal court. You get my drift?"

"Like a laser beam," Jack said.

"Okay, now that we've gotten this all straightened out, Gram, can we do a conference call from here or do we need to go down to the hall?"

"I suggest we go down there and do a face to face. We haven't been down to see the people for nearly ten days. I think that would be better. Besides, no one has met Johnny yet."

"Ah yes, no one like Carol, Judy and the other ladies on the team," I said grinning at my friend.

"I'm sure they will be fascinated by Johnny's charm and grace," Gram said.

"I'm sure they will," Johnny acknowledged our teasing him.

"Do I need to sit on him?" Jack asked me.

"Nope, Jack. Johnny will be on his best behavior. Won't you my friend?"

"Swear to God, hope to die," he said. "I'll treat all the women with utmost respect and not hit on them for at least the first ten minutes after we've said hello."

We all laughed and gave Johnny a few slugs to the shoulder and back and got ready to head down to the hall. I told Basha where we were going and she said please be home by 6 pm for dinner. I said we would be.

Our meeting with the team was insightful. We discussed security issues and many wondered who might be the mole in the room. Johnny joked that maybe he should run out to the bus and get his lie detector machine and test us all. Everyone laughed. Jack said the leak was fresh and the newest member of the team was, guess who? Johnny laughed and said, "If I wanted to steal Leo's secrets, I'd go into the bathroom and hide in the toilet paper rack. He spends more time on the throne than any King I've ever known."

At my expense, everyone got a laugh.

So many things were happening.

Our registration program was in full swing and we were lining up independent voters all over the country. The push to get my name on the ballot was in high gear. Thirteen states were done. We had thirty-seven more to go. John said we were just about ready to close the deal on fifteen in the next month. "We may have trouble down south. They are really fussy and with their new laws, we're having to scramble. Richard is a big help. He couldn't be on the phone today, but he's on the ball and working 24/7 to get this done"

Donations were flowing into the campaign coffers like a raging river. There seemed to be no end to the dollar donations as they raised our current funding total to more than $36 million dollars.

"What are we going to do with all that money?" I asked foolishly.

"A general election will suck that money away faster than you can say your name, Leo," Judy said. "We could spend gobs of it right now, but we're just holding back and running just enough ads in each state to get your name out there and keep ahead of any negative trends that we see."

"I'm amazed at the amount," I said.

"So are we, Leo," John said. "You're the man they want to lead this country. Think about it. 36 million one-dollar donations equaling 36 million people give or take a million. Translating those donations into votes, that is quite a total for you, my friend."

We discussed the Twitter follower's phenomena and discovered that our number of followers was above 2 million and counting. "Getting arrested in Michigan really created a spike in your people, Leo," Fritz said. "We watched the numbers grow exponentially the longer you were in police custody."

"Damn," Johnny said, "I should not have negotiated with them so quickly. We could have pushed the number even higher."

"Sure, friend," I said. "While you were out in the hallway batting your gums, I was sitting behind bars and wondering if I were ever going to see daylight again."

"Oh, stop complaining," Johnny scoffed at me. "You knew what was coming, or so I'm told. You were the one who said, 'Let's do it', knowing you probably were going to get arrested."

"I can vouch for that," Gram said.

"Traitor," I replied.

"We have cracked into the YouTube arena as well," Judy continued with her reporting. "Gram, the videos you've uploaded are going viral. We're finding that they are having as much impact as any radio or TV advertising that we pay for in the different states where primaries are being held."

"Save the money then and don't run ads," Johnny said. "We'll need all that money later in the year."

"We know that, but there is a reason we're spending some of that money now and that is to make connections with some of the media forces. Later on, we can negotiate better prices because we'll have established a relationship with them."

"Sounds like we're really gearing up for the near future when we'll need all these forces banded together," I said.

"You got it," John said. "Now, we think the time is getting close for us to roll out our final push. We are gathering a long list of 'Leo's Stars' and we will hope to have 100 ready to go in about a month. This group of entertainers, famous people, scholars, scientists and other well-known men and women will endorse you for president. This may be a real coup that we can implement when the moment arrives and we can take Leo over the edge."

"This is beyond my imagination," I commented.

"Hey, what do you think we're doing here when you're not with us?" John said.

"There is one other thing that we need to discuss," I said. "And that's security within this team, our sites, and the campaign as a whole. "Jack?"

Big Jack rose and took the floor. "Today, we found a bug in Leo's house. We know this was not placed by us. We are facing an attack by unknown forces on this campaign and the people who work for it. Right now, I'd like all of you to let us scan your cell phones and see what we find. Jeeves!"

Jeeves got up from the back of the room and walked around the room collecting the phones on a tray. Once he had them all, he went to work carefully disassembling them and checking for implants.

"We don't know who or what is doing this. We will know in due time. However, each of you must be eternally vigilant. We know this is not a secure building. We don't want it to be. We want the people's party to be open for everyone to come in and share their time, energy, brainpower and money to make this campaign a success. Now, we must crush this threat. We will," Jack said with such intensity that a chill flowed through the room. We were sure that Jack would do what he said when he finally discovered what was happening.

"Not only will Jack crush the person or persons responsible," Johnny said, "but we'll beat the living daylights out of them in the court room as well as the court of public opinion," Johnny said. "I'm pissed off. When the bug was found today, I wanted to rip some heads off. Leo's house was illegally entered and bugged. Who does that? Who would stoop to such tactics just to get an edge? We have our suspicions. Once we get credible evidence, we'll pursue it to the letter of the law."

There was stunned silence in the room.

"We're glad to have you on the team, Johnny. Everyone who is in this room knows the importance of maintaining safety and security at work, at home and anywhere in between throughout this campaign season," John said. "What have you found, Jeeves?"

"Nothing that can be construed as a direct threat. However, I am going to make some minor tweaks in the 'simm card' so that the operating systems are less prone to attack. You won't know the difference, but we will."

"What do you mean?" Gram said.

"We'll be tracking the calls going in and out and this will give us the opportunity to monitor and evaluate, if and when there is a trace on your phone, the IP address of the attack. Then we'll be able to pinpoint the source and intercept it," Jeeves said bluntly.

"Jeeves is the best," Jack said. "We will stop this threat. Trust me."

"So we should not be making any calls to 900 numbers because you'll know we're wasting campaign time and money?" Johnny said.

"Especially you, Johnny," I piped up. "We have a special phone prepared just for you. Gram?"

Gram handed Johnny a Mattel play phone that looked like a cell phone but was just a toy.

"Ha, Ha, funny guy," Johnny said.

While Johnny pretended to make a phone call on his toy phone, everyone in the room laughed heartily going along with the practical joke.

"Now that we've had a light moment, is there anything else that we need to discuss before we break?" John asked the group.

No one said anything. Finally, I said, "My friends, there is no way to express in words how proud I am to be a part of this team. We have created the best group of minds that I've ever been privileged to work with in my life. No matter what the outcome, we have already achieved monumental results. There is no way that, as of now, we will know what the final outcome will be, but this one thing is certain, we are now and will be a force to be reckoned with throughout this campaign. I hope the bug got that statement!" All of us laughed again.

Jeeves gave everyone back his or her phone. He reported that he found nothing in any of them.

The meeting ended. I hustled everyone out and back home because we were pushing Basha's deadline.

When we got home, we found the dining room table set, candles burning, the food ready and Janko and Basha eagerly waiting for us.

"Uncle Gram, Uncle Johnny, Daddy, Mommy and I are happy to have all of you home for dinner. Would you please be seated so we can serve you?"

We sat down. Janko led us in saying grace. While we were served we chatted amiably. Basha prepared round steak, gravy, mashed potatoes and peas and later, for desert, we had pecan pie, my favorite.

We listened to Johnny tell some jokes that were childproof and Gram tell stories about flying airplanes around the world. We listened to Janko tell us about his day at school.

Basha shared anecdotes about a few of her recent shopping trips. She heard people saying things about the campaign, our platform, and me, Leo Pollack. She said it was hilarious that she was able to eavesdrop on their conversations and they did not know, yet, who she was. "Leo, I'm going to have to watch you closely because a couple of the 'ladies' were really checking you out and were openly wondering what kind of guy you were in the bedroom."

Johnny started to share something that bordered on indecent, but when Basha glared at him, he desisted. Janko asked him to finish what he was about to say and he concluded by thanking them for preparing and serving such a wonderful meal.

The pecan pie was scrumptious. I ate two pieces.

"Basha, I make a motion that you come along on the bus with us and you cook. I feel like I'm in a prison camp when Leo is cooking. I'm losing weight. My hair is starting to fall out. I'm a physical wreck. I think it's time to exchange Pollacks. I vote for you," Johnny said.

"You are so full of crap," I said to him. "You've only had to eat my cooking for less than one day."

"Right," Gram said. "I'm the one who should be complaining. I've been the one exposed to his form of torture for the past month or so. Basha, we need you. I need you."

"Yes, Mommy, let's go on the bus with Daddy, Uncle Gram and Uncle Johnny. We can have so much fun," Janko said. "Can we? Can we?"

Basha got up and gave Johnny a Dutch rub and said, "I think I'll stay at home, make sure that my son gets a good education, continue to monitor women's gossip in the aisles of the food market, and from a distance, support you guys who are out having to endure my husband's marginal cooking."

After dinner, we sat in the living room talking, laughing and enjoying another day in paradise when a family comes together and shares what is most important in every person's life: mutual respect, love and support.

43. Liberty Bell Fifty State Bus Tour

Our farewell was intense. Basha, Janko and I took a long time to say goodbye, but we did not speak. We held on to each other as if I were going on a mission to Mars. The tears flowed. The time raced. We swirled around in the vortex of sustaining our love and the desire to fulfill a dream. Wherever I was at the time, we committed to being together on Easter weekend. Once school was finished for the year, Janko asked if he could come and visit Uncles Johnny and Gram out on the road. We affirmed this request. We kissed, hugged and then said, "I love you."

Gram, Johnny, Al and Big Jack used this time to make last minute preparations for the journey.

The Ringing the Liberty Bell Tour started in the dark on a fateful March morning the day before Super Tuesday and headed west. We knew we would not be able to make it to the states holding primaries before the voting. We would do the best we could and that was to make it to all states in the near future.

We realized the other campaigns were rapidly becoming irrelevant. What they did was their business. We could not outspend them. We were facing an uphill struggle, but knew we were on the way to making the entire country aware the two-party system was becoming a detriment to true Democracy, spelled with a capital D. We were proposing the clearest alternative to the status quo.

In the last two weeks, the other two parties were broadcasting the need to increase domestic manufacturing. We had been stating this for the past eleven months. We needed educational reform. Our truly progressive tax reform package was gaining momentum in the discussion. Our plan was much more in tune with a nation that could see the unfairness of the other parties' proposals. Every major theme the parties now promoted was a variation of what we stated in our effort to change the dialogue in the nation. We were elated that our movement was catching the wave, but we would not be satisfied until we were being chased and not chasing the other candidates.

At the J.M. Smucker's Plant in Orville, Ohio, we assured the company and the workers our economic policies would restore America to industrial greatness. The audience was receptive and applauded our willingness to sit and listen to their voluminous concerns.

Our visit to Gary, Indiana was like a homecoming. Steelworkers greeted us with open arms. We were blown away by the reception. Al said he felt like he was "back home in Indiana". We spent the majority of the day with guys and gals like us who wanted nothing more than to live the American Dream.

We played Peoria, Illinois like a rock band. The crowd went wild when we pulled into the parking lot of the Block. Lights, cameras, television crews and televisions spread out around the stage area greeted us. The production was beyond my wildest dreams. I was transported into another sphere. The message was simple. When America works, democracy thrives. Working people must unite and take back America from the special interest groups that were buying and selling candidates like commodities. We were not for sale! We would not be co-opted by some Superpac. We would not let anyone donate more than a dollar to our campaign so we could insure our independence. We were the people. The people will speak. The government will listen. We were not anti-government, nor were we for big government. We wanted a government that worked to make the nation, stronger, safer, and efficient. We hoped our children would receive the best education possible. We were tired of meaningless wars that drained our blood and treasure. We found our voice and now we were proclaiming a new vision for America that promoted the middle class and stopped attacking it.

Our ride to Davenport, Iowa gave me time to think about the role of the secret service and their being assigned to protect us while we were on our bus tour. Were they here to protect me or was there some other agenda? I studied the highway as the landscape sped past outside. I wondered how many more surprises we were going to experience. Now, the issues were compounding and that was fine as long as we were able to find some way to focus on what was best for America and Americans. We spent nearly two hours touring the John Deere factory, meeting the people who ran the plant and the people who actually made the machinery that proudly carried the label, Made in the USA. Every step of the way, we could tell that the people working for John Deere loved what they were doing. The pride was obvious and infectious. As we were preparing to leave the place, the superintendent who was escorting us, James Mason, handed me a small John Deere tractor and said, "Please take this home to your son, Jon. He may enjoy playing with it."

In Madison, Wisconsin, we hosted a tailgate party at a Badger football game. It was a rousing success. I liked meeting anyone who wanted to know what we were doing and what we believed. This was the essence of our entire movement. The more I met the people and shared with them what we hoped to accomplish, the greater was our chance for success. I did not fake it. What I said, I believed and I could tell that people were catching on to that fact.

We rolled into Benson, Minnesota and were greeted by the Mayor, John Borland. He was a hearty fellow who, though a staunch Republican was more than willing to share with us his city and its history. We toured the Fribrominn biomass plant with the mayor and were impressed that such a small town was leading the way in using alternative energy. "We have an E-85 ethanol alcohol plant in town too," he said as we headed downtown to a small café where many local people gathered every day to hear the news of the town and the world. Given that it was called the Chatterbox, I wondered if we were going back in time to Lake Wobegone, a small town made famous by Garrison Keillor on his radio show, "Prairie Home Companion". "Mayor Borland assured us that this was no Lake Wobegone. "We have a lot of woe in a small town where most of our young people are leaving and most of our old people are staying put, for what seems, forever." I did not know how to take his last comment. The mayor introduced me and the team to the people gathered there for late breakfast or early lunch. "I'm not sure what brought you to our little village, but we are aware of who you are and what you're up to," he said. It sounded like an indictment and not a compliment. "Mayor, what we are 'up to' is simply this. We want to give a voice to all Americans who do not have one in the current political climate that exists today. Let me ask this question. Who in here feels like any of the candidates running for office in the Republican or Democratic Party can speak to and for you? Please raise your hand if you do." An hour later, we were receiving a standing ovation. The people believed we were the good guys and had their best interest at heart.

In Minot, North Dakota, Gram directed us to the oil field that was happening changing the prairie culture. As we drove north on ND 22 toward Manning we encountered heavy truck traffic. Out on the prairie, wherever we looked we could see the telltale signs of an oil and gas boom. This was the new North Slope, but it was not in Alaska. When we pulled off the highway and entered a vast area pock marked with drilling rigs rising up into the sky, we marveled at the amount of human activity taking place in the middle of nowhere. Parking the bus, we got out and were met by a representative of Noble Energy, a major drilling company in the country. "Welcome to North Dakota, Mr. Pollack," Jim McBride said shaking my hand. He was a gnarled Texan wearing a Gus brimmed western hat, long sleeved, pearl buttoned shirt, down vest, jeans adorned with a huge leather belt and buckle and a pair of roughed up boots that looked like they ate cactus for breakfast every morning. "Come along and I'll show you what we're up to in these here parts." Our tour was extensive. He explained every step in the process to us in fine detail. He made it all sound so simple. What was happening was anything but simple. After we met with the oil people, we visited with oil drilling crews outside a small town in the middle of the prairie. Most of them were curious about our movement, but after an hour of questions and answers, we left these wildcatters with something to think about in the future. We hoped they would support our movement. Many of them indicated they liked what they heard.

For two hours, the crowd outside a mall in Rapid City, South Dakota mobbed the bus. I stood outside and shook hands with people from all over the country and the world. The huge Liberty Bell painted on the side of the bus piqued their curiosity. What did the symbol mean? I explained repeatedly that we were ringing the Liberty Bell to signal a major shift in the democratic process in America. No longer were we going to be subjected to the false statements made by the candidates running for two major parties. We were seeking to expand the democratic process to include a viable third party candidate who represented the interests of the people whose voices were not being heard. They were fascinated by the audacity with which we believed we could compete with the major parties. We thanked them for the compliment. Al was excited about passing out literature. Gram and Johnny were working the crowds like veterans. I watched them and realized just how fortunate I was to have such wonderful teammates. Big Jack was always nearby watching me.

Inside the great log visitor center in Yellowstone Park, Wyoming, we stared at the seven by seven elk head mounting and the Bull Moose, looked up at the high ceilings, and reflected upon the number of years that Americans visited this "Great Outdoor Temple". What we knew was our national park system was being privatized and the funding reduced in every budget cycle. If some of the conservative leaders had their way, the entire national park service, like many other government programs, would not survive. Our bus attracted almost as much attention as Old Faithful. As we wandered around the visitor center and stopped to have lunch at the café, many people approached me and asked interesting and pointed questions. A few hours later as we exited this spectacular wild space, we were elated at how well the people received our message.

In the early afternoon, we headed into Missoula, Montana. There was a rally planned at the university and I was excited about being able to speak to a college crowd. The students welcomed me with gusto. They were excited about the future that I described. They wanted more. I gave it to them with all my heart and soul. When I finished my speech, the students inundated me with questions, compliments and concerns. Everything American was their focus. They wanted the country to succeed. They wanted to be a part of the change process. I asked them to join our cause by saying, "This is your country. Make it into the land that you know it can be." "What can we do?" was the constant question on their minds. "This is what you can do," I said. For the next hour I encouraged them to get involved with our campaign, but more importantly, to become active citizens year-around and not stand on the sidelines and let the system dictate to them what their society should be. We enjoyed their innate enthusiasm and were reluctant to leave such a gracious group of young men and women.

Our bus was parked near a truck stop in Idaho Falls, Idaho when the explosions followed by crashing glass and the spray of debris through the bus awakened us with horror. We pitched to the floor and did not move. The raucous sounds gave way to an eerie silence. We lay still listening intensely. I could hear my heart beating. "Is everyone okay? Al, Gram? You guys okay?" "I'm okay but pissed as hell," Al hollered at me from his room. "Gram?"   "Down here on the floor. What the hell! What the hell," he exclaimed repeatedly. A minute later, I could hear Big Jack's booming voice shouting outside. We got up, dressed rapidly and ran to the door. On the way through the bus, we saw the damage. Three side windows were plastered with bullet spray. They were bullet proof so they did not shatter. However, some bullets penetrated the side of the bus and caused the real damage. If anyone had been sitting at the kitchen table, his legs would have taken the brunt of the attack. Plunging outside into the cold Idaho morning, we found Jack and R&R already forming a response team. "What happened out here?" I asked starting to shiver in the cold. They did not answer immediately. All three were on their phones. We could hear sirens blaring in the distance. A number of dark vehicles were gathered nearby the bus and their drivers were standing outside waiting for orders. Overhead, we could hear multiple helicopters thumping in the morning light. I did not realize just how many men there were on our protection detail. From what I could count, there had to be at least ten or fifteen. How could something like this happen? As we waited for answers, Gram and Al stood next to me. "This was bound to happen," Gram said. "We're in Idaho." "What does that matter?" I asked. "Militia. This state is known for being the place where militias are a way of life." "What does that have to do with us?" I asked. "Think about it, Leo. You are running for president. Your platform is not what these radical libertarian Para-military types want. The fact that you are way up here in their territory is probably too much for them, my friend. We are rubbing our campaign in their faces." An hour later, our secret service detail recommended we move on to Spokane, Washington. They had two men in custody, but did not want to take any chances after what happened. We reluctantly left Idaho and drove westward.

We did not get much rest in Spokane. Traveling on to Seattle was different.
Al was driving differently. We could tell he was being much more vigilant. Our carefree days were over. The call from the President of the United States was a powerful message that we were in league with the forces of good, but there was evil lurking in the world that we needed to be conscious of and protected against as the campaign raced forward. Hearing the hovering of a helicopter overhead was a constant reminder of our new reality. The press was screaming at us to stop and talk. Through Judy, we scheduled a press conference in Seattle. The venue was the Seattle Space Needle. She said it was the most iconic structure in the city and symbolized our campaign. We agreed. We coordinated with Big Jack and R&R and drove into the city. Immediately, we started attracting a mass of followers. This was the new normal for us. The publicity was great. The cost was minimal. All we had to do was produce results and we would continue promoting our campaign at a grassroots level. Getting off the bus, an aggressive group of print and media journalists surrounded me. Press. "Mr. Pollack, what are your thoughts and feelings about what happened to you in Idaho?" "I am glad that no one was hurt. My team and I are blessed. We will prevail." Television. "What do you hope to accomplish on this Liberty Bus Tour of America? You are spending a lot of time in places where traditional politicians do not travel. What's the point?" They blasted me with questions for nearly two hours. I think they were impressed with our ability to withstand the pressures of a campaign that was now under close scrutiny by the left and the right. What a day.

We decided to stop in Eugene, Oregon because it was the center of anarchist activities in the west. As Gram said, "We're not anarchists, but we sure are hell bent on destroying the two party system as we know it." We descended upon Eugene with a mission to meet the people. What we found shocked us. The first thing we saw in downtown Eugene was a conclave of homeless people. Whether by choice or chance, personal calamity or self-induced tragedy because of chemical abuse or misuse of psychotropic medicines, the street people were visible and anachronistic.

We parked the bus. The press was waiting to talk to me. People hoped to capture a glimpse of me. The campaign bus and the burgeoning security detail made us more visible than ever. I knew the costs associated with the move. I realized the city leaders would be upset if we focused on the one aspect of Eugene that they did not control. I accepted the consequences. Walking over to where the people were obviously living during the daytime and waiting for darkness to forage through dumpsters and other waste recycling systems in the city, I stood watching. There was no response. Hollow eyes stared at me. I stared back, but not with the same kind of look in mine. These were the lost souls of our cities. These people lived on the fringe. They made our modern civilization cringe whenever their plight filtered into the national news. I sat down among them and did not say anything. There were video cameras rolling. The crowds were intense. The people sitting near me were frightened. Some of them were incapable of looking at me. I did not speak. The cameras rolled. There was a quintessential moment of pure humanness happening. I did not give any speeches. Finally some of the people talked to me and the discussion was recorded. We remained there for hours before we finally decided it was time to move on. The coverage was unique and special. I was aware we made a scene, but it was one needing to be revealed to the electorate.

On Interstate 5 in California, the convoy flowed behind us like a two-mile-long train. We did not encourage those who were following us. We could not stop them from exercising their freedom to travel along with us into the Golden State. In reality, we did not want to stop them. Every vehicle was another punctuation mark on our movement. We were creating a national stir. The momentum was building. The foundation of our movement was the people. Millions were following us on YouTube, Twitter, Facebook, in the news and now, in their own vehicles. Our goal in California was to meet with Hispanic leaders in Los Angeles. The Secret Service discouraged us from doing so because of security concerns. We said we were going anyway. We could feel the tension that our decision created. I wondered if this was really a security concern or something that the administration was communicating to them whether directly or subtly. Laura Lopez, regional director for La Raza, was waiting for us when we parked the bus in front of their store front offices in downtown Los Angeles. The traffic jam that we created caused a major stir, but one that would provide us with a lot of good press as the day unfolded. Exiting the bus, I was greeted by a cheering crowd of well-wishers. I was happy to be in the city with so many important issues facing the 'City of Angels'. "Buenos Dias, Mr. Pollack," Laura said as I walked up to her and shook her hand. "I can't speak Spanish so I'll just ask for your forgiveness in being culturally deprived," I said. She laughed at my comment. "I'm pleased that you aren't going to pretend to be a Chicano like some of the other candidates that have passed through here over the years." She introduced me to the crowd and I gave them my best. We were busy for hours and it was invigorating to see how many people who could not speak English kept trying to get close to me to shake my hand. I was pleased with our ability to connect with the masses.

No place in Nevada presented a greater contrast between the "haves and have nots" than Las Vegas. We passed through here a short time ago, but this trip was different because our campaign was gaining traction every day. We headed into the section of the city where home foreclosures were the highest. We spent the day talking to people who were facing the phenomena of holding a mortgage that was "under water" or "upside down" meaning their home was worth less than their mortgage. This was something that was as complicated and disheartening as the escalating cost of gasoline and there appeared to be no solution readily available. As I walked around the neighborhood with the Secret Service and the band of people and media personnel following me, I stopped and talked with anyone who was willing to tell me what he or she was experiencing regarding the home situation. People were more than willing to share their stories. In many ways, telling someone like me, a total stranger, was cathartic. We spent more time in Las Vegas than we planned, but the stop and the time invested was well worth it. Everyone believed our message was being received loud and clear by those who were not experiencing the American Dream.

With some trepidation, our second entry into the "Grand Canyon State" proved to be uneventful. The word was out that our campaign favored comprehensive immigration reform, a pathway to citizenship via the "Dream Act" as it was being called by supporters in Congress and about our recent stop at La Raza in Los Angeles. The state government was not friendly. A few weeks ago, President Obama paid a visit to the state and the Governor, Jan Brewer, was caught on video pointing her finger in his face. If she were this hostile to a sitting president, how would she act toward someone like me who was nowhere near as powerful and important as he is? We settled upon a simple strategy for making this trip productive. No controversial issues would be on the table for discussion. We wanted to neutralize the antagonist's defenses. Lull them into submission. This western bastion of

Neo-conservatism needed weaned from the influence of those who did not respect people struggling to make it into the middle class. Arizona was the last state to recognize Martin Luther King Jr. Day as a national holiday. It still did not use daylight savings time. To describe it as being reactionary is a mild description of its anti-establishment positions. Growing ever longer, our convoy now stretched at least a half mile behind the bus. R&R were not keen about the phenomena. In heated discussion with the Secret Service heads in Washington, Gram and John had to back them off from disbanding the people following our campaign from state to state. They did not want to concede. We told them these were American people expressing their freedom of speech and assembly and they would have to work around the distractions. They did not like it but we were adamant in our denial of their wish to stop the parade. When we exited Phoenix and stopped at a strip mall outside the city, the masses overwhelmed our bus. We visited for hours with thousands of people. My hand grew numb from signing so many autographs. I was shocked at the magnanimous reception.

At the Four Corners, we were surprised by how desolate and beautiful it was at the same time. When we got there, we discovered it was an artist colony of sorts. More than a 100 small booths with Native American artisans were open for business. The weather was mild. The place was busy. Our caravan added to the festive affair. For hours, we wandered around staring at the beautiful artwork. Pots, leather goods, jewelry, clothing and sundry other items were on display. Most artists were sitting with their creations. Their pride was evident in the way they spoke about their work. I bought a bone choker and some topaz earrings for Basha, and a small leather medicine bag for Janko. For Al, I invested in a four corners tee shirt that he could wear to remember this day. I bought Gram a dream catcher. We talked to the native artisans and were enchanted by their gifts of love to those of us who were merely curious about their lives and their work. New Mexico was a staunchly Democratic state, but elected a Republican governor. We hoped the state would embrace our campaign and reject the other parties.

Colorado is called the Rocky Mountain State, but a third of its landscape is prairie land. We drove across it, stopped in Trinidad and met with the people and then moved on into the panhandle of Texas where cotton farming, gas and oil drilling were still major industries. We wanted to visit an active cotton farm and so, the convoy, our Secret Service detail, Big Jack and his team and the Liberty Bell bus landed in Plainview, Texas on the farm of "Doc" Holladay, a third-generation cotton farmer who was willing to take us on a tour of his 1600-acre farm. "Brought your own fan club along with you, did you?" Doc Holladay said as he came out to meet us by the bus. I looked back at all the traffic piling onto his property. "I didn't invite them along, but they are what we call the 'caravan' and I guess until this tour is over, I'm stuck with them or maybe it's the other way around; they're stuck with me." "Running for president seems a might complicated to me," Doc said with a slight grin on his face. "Much more than I thought it would be," I said. Our stay on the Holladay ranch was enchanting and exciting. We made a lot of new friends, heard a lot of new complaints about the government and the two party system and left with many commitments to support our campaign no matter what happened in the next six months. This was good news considering the general conservative nature of Texas politics.

When our caravan descended upon Guymon, Oklahoma, there was a slow movement from inside the few buildings downtown to see what all the commotion was. We pulled into the community hoping to discover what made people in the panhandle of Oklahoma live in this small section of the state that was susceptible to tornadoes. What we discovered was a hardy group of folks, who, for generations, courageously faced the viscous weather. At a local eatery, we met a few rugged men who were descendents of some of the original "Oakies" who came west to settle this land back in the days of the land rush that created the nickname "Sooners" for those who rushed out before the official starting time to stake a claim to the free land. Ma was cooking in "Ma's Café" so we were treated to bacon and eggs and a side of pancakes with coffee to wash down the rich food. Ma was interested in what we were doing in town, the campaign, and so she asked a few questions from over her shoulder while she cooked for us. The old fellows who were hanging out in the café were paying attention to her while drinking their morning coffee. Ma was an attractive seventy-year- old woman. Even though these fellows were way past their prime, they were not dead yet. The dynamic in the group was a treat to behold. We stayed until there were no more questions being asked, no more autographs to be signed and no more pie to be eaten.

When Dorothy and Toto followed the yellow brick road, it did not lead them to Greensburg, Kansas, but ours did. In 2007, this small village was destroyed by a tornado. Eleven townspeople were killed. The tragedy captured the hearts of America. When plans for rebuilding were considered, the leaders decided they would make

Greensburg a "green" town. We drove into the center of the "new" Greensburg and marveled at all the work being done to revitalize this small Kansas community. The spirit of pioneer America was evident everywhere we looked. Gram arranged to meet with the former city manager, Steve Hewitt. He met us at the municipal building downtown. Hewitt was a tall, rugged looking, westerner with a deep tan and a heavy mustache decorating his upper lip. "Welcome to Greensburg," he said eyeballing all the vehicles parked behind the bus. "Got yourself a real party going?" he asked staring at all the people who were getting out and beginning to mill about town. "We brought along some of our friends hoping they would spend a few dollars in town and support the effort," I said. "I'm Leo Pollack and this is my team." I introduced Gram and Al to Steve. "Didn't know you'd have so many folks with you, but I guess that's what a presidential campaign is all about, isn't it? Lots of people and lots of travel." "This is quite new, Steve," I said. "We started picking up this caravan in Oregon and it just keeps getting bigger and bigger." We toured Greensburg and enjoyed a barbecue on the town square with thousands of locals and our caravan mixing together in a real down home kind of gathering. What a wonderful day to be alive!

In Omaha, Nebraska we headed toward the state bureau of employment services office and met the head of the local teacher's union, Jane Finster. She was a lively soul and welcomed us to her great state. We were impressed with the huge crowd that was gathered and when it was time, I ascended the steps of the building and addressed the gathering. The applause was deafening. The wave of energy created by the crowd transported me. "Thank you for your warm welcome to Nebraska. I'm Leo Pollack and I am running for President of the United States. America is facing a crisis and the two parties are stuck in a schoolyard battle over who is going to rule. In the mean time, working people are languishing because no comprehensive legislation addressing the creation of jobs has been passed. Here's the rub. We can grow corn and soybeans in Nebraska, because we can't move the farm fields of this great state to another country and grow crops over there. We can move factories overseas and thereby eliminate good paying industrial jobs from our shores." I finished my speech and spent a few hours shaking hands, signing autographs and being hailed as the next "Commander in Chief".

In 2011, a category four tornado hit Joplin, Missouri. The devastation was horrendous. More than 40 people were killed. Billions of dollars in property damages occurred. The tragedy profoundly altered the town's psyche. Rarely does a tornado directly hit a major metropolitan area. Racing down the main street of town, it created an impact that will never be forgotten by those who survived. We decided to make a difference. We passed the word through the caravan that we were headed for Joplin and were going to spend two days doing volunteer work in whatever capacity we could to help the city rebuild. Everyone liked the idea. Chatter on CBs, cell phones, Facebook, Twitter and text messages were swift and extensive. The word rapidly spread throughout cyberspace and before we knew what was happening, the city filled with people who wanted to be a part of the volunteer effort. Gram, Judy, the Missouri state campaign coordinator, Jess Walker and his team were already on site the minute we proposed the idea. They were coordinating with the local authorities responsible for organizing volunteers coming in to assist in the ongoing recovery effort. The news media teams were heading into town waiting for us. This was a mass movement blowing into town almost as big as the tornado itself. "You know, Leo," Gram said, "it's almost scary the way these things happen now. We put out the word and a thousand people show up to do what is being asked." "Nothing wrong with that is there?" Johnny commented. "Nope. Not in the least," I said. "We are making a difference just by being out here and drawing attention to the needs of the people." For the next few hours, we made a difference in Joplin. The people received us like were family coming home for a holiday celebration.

Phones kept ringing. Every one of us was engaged in conversations related to the last few days. Our campaign stop in Joplin captured the nation's spirit and the outpouring of support amounted to a tidal wave of praise. We were being labeled the "Random Act of Kindness" Caravan. Pictures of the circled caravan in the destroyed field were trending on all the search engines. Judy and Gram were making as much hay as they could from this. Fritz peppered the home page with a rolling commentary that let people read the messages coming in from all over the country and the world about what we did for Joplin and what we were doing for Democracy in America. The Joplin stop seemed natural. This was the neighborly thing to do. The current political environment was so unhealthy anything that projected kind-spiritedness was applauded. We did not mind the publicity. Fund raising was becoming easier than ever. Another three million dollars flowed in the next day as the videos of "Leo's People" went viral on the internet.

In 1950, the U.S. Atomic Energy Commission selected Paducah, Kentucky as the site for a new uranium enrichment plant. Construction began in 1951 and operations started in 1952. The plant was originally operated by Union Carbide, but has changed hands several times. Currently the operator is the United States Enrichment Corporation. The U.S. Department of Energy, successor to the Atomic Energy Commission, remains the owner. We headed to the plant because we wanted to understand the nature of atomic energy enrichment and what it meant to the industry that was trying to resurrect itself as an alternative to coal or gas fired generating plants. Given the push for alternative sources of energy, the promise of nuclear power was still one that some advocates said was the only way we could meet America's 2050 and beyond energy needs. While we were visiting the plant, Al was going to lead the caravan down to the confluence of the Tennessee and Ohio Rivers and the entire gathering was going fishing. Al loved to fish. He figured this was his best chance to go after river catfish. Johnny was interfacing with state coordinators and so he begged off from the meeting. Gram and I went into the plant's main offices. A receptionist greeted us. She said that James Fallon would soon be with us. While we waited, we wandered around in the lobby and studied the photographs that depicted the uranium enrichment process. I did not know much about it. Gram possessed a working knowledge but not much more than that. We wanted to learn more so we could make an educated decision on whether nuclear energy was really a viable option or were there too many risks involved in its long-range development. The press followed us throughout the tour and whenever there was a break they asked questions. I answered them as best I could and they appreciated the time and energy I expended working along with them. We made some real inroads in the Commonwealth and hoped this would translate into votes in the fall. When we exited the plant, we found Al was sitting on the bank with a pole in his hand, drinking iced tea and telling kids that had gathered around him what it was like to be the driver for the next president of the United States. He did not see us come up behind him, so we eavesdropped for about five minutes while he continued spinning his tale. He was in character and had the young people mesmerized. We did not want to rain on his parade so we left him with the kids and spent a few hours visiting with the caravan people.

When our caravan flooded Memphis, Tennessee and descended on Beale Street, the city was in shock. Every available parking spot was taken. One minute, Beale Street was sleeping and the next, March in Memphis was born. Some caravan members called it March Madness to synchronize with the NCAA basketball tournament that was being played not too many miles away in Kentucky. We had no real agenda. I had never been to Memphis. I was not a blues person, but the historical nature of this city and this famous street drew us like iron to a magnet. We had to see it. We passed the word encouraging caravaners, a new term we coined to refer to our colleagues, to enjoy the day, fill their hearts, minds and ears with music, enjoy the moment and be ready to leave town about 5 pm. The caravaners were ecstatic. Gram, Johnny, Al and I with the "SS" (Secret Service) behind us and Big Jack watching them and everything else made our way slowly up and down the street. We stopped along the way to listen to music, drink something, and nibble on the foods offered by so many of our caravaners who were eating in outside restaurants. "Come on Leo, sit down and rest a spell," one caravaner encouraged me. "It's nice to just mosey along," I said, "but thanks for the invite." A hundred times that day, I was invited to sit a spell. Now and then, I did. When there was a small family with children, I would make it a point to join them. I think it was because I was missing Basha and Janko. There were many Elvis mementoes. He got his real start in Memphis. What a special talent he was. I hoped some of his talent would rub off on me as we raced toward the election a few months away.

Outside Fayetteville, Arkansas, Al found a safe spot and we dismounted. The caravaners gathered in an open field where we could speak to them as one group. Using the bullhorn, I thanked them for being on the campaign with us. I alerted them to what was ahead. We were going into Bentonville, Arkansas, the home of Wal-Mart to participate in a demonstration taking place near the corporate headquarters. I shared with them a brief description of the Wal-Mart vs. Duke Lawsuit. Loud boos erupted when the result was explained. I could hear the higher pitched voices of the women above the men indicating to me the disfavor they felt about the decision. "We may face some discontent with our presence. Please, whatever you do, follow the law. Respect the police. They will probably not let us stay there for very long. We don't know what will happen. Obey the law. Hopefully, we won't need to use any legal authority, but Johnny is with us again and so he is our attorney of record." Everyone cheered when they saw Johnny standing next to me. He loved the praise and waved like a rock star at his loving fans. "Okay, let's head into town and see if we can make a difference in the lives of women who have taken a stand against this powerful corporation." Gram called R&R to let them know what we were planning to do. They were not pleased with our mission. Gram listened to what they said and then replied, "Mr. Pollack is adamant. We are going into town. If you want to come along, be our guest." He hung up and shook his head. "They must own stock in Wal-Mart. What a couple of slugs. They said we didn't have any reason interfering in the business operations of a major corporation just because we didn't like the Supreme Court's decision." We were met by the local sheriff and nominally arrested, but we didn't learn about this until ten hours later when we were gone and our words were still ringing across town like the Liberty Bell in Philadelphia on the day independence was declared. We let the city know we were ready to take on the corporations and make a difference in the lives of working men and women.

Getting into New Orleans was a chore but we made it. In the middle of Lent, it was a rather stoic place to visit. The caravan spread out across the ward. For the rest of the day, we did not see many people. We found a place to park the bus and looked for work. This was an easy task. In every nook and cranny, there was something to do. Gram and Johnny met an elderly man and woman who were raking their yard and planting some perennials. They got right to work with them. Al and I searched for action that did not require a green thumb. Buzz Coltrane, a lifelong native of the quarter was working on a new treated lumber deck. We asked if we could help and he said, "Shore can, but I can't pay you none." We said we were here just to help and did not want to be paid. "Well, then the price is right. Come on up and grab yourself a hammer and we'll make some noise." We spent the rest of the day measuring, cutting and nailing the deck together under the watchful eye of Buzz, who just couldn't believe that a couple of Yankees would come all the way down to his neighborhood and volunteer to work on his house. "Oh, after the big flooding, lots of folks were running around wanting to help. But they all wanted big money. My Lord, they were a lot of scam artists here with their hands out and their cars warmed up and ready to fly the minute they got the cash in their hand." "What did you do, Buzz?" Al asked. "I laid low. Pretended like I had no money. I'm alone now. My wife left me after the flood. She said she was done with living by the water and moved up to Texas with one of our kids. Ain't been back since. I miss her but I can't live in Texas. That ain't my home. This here is my home. This is where I'm going to die. Lord willing, I'll live long enough to see this here home fixed up again." The heat and humidity rose considerably as the day progressed. We stopped many times for cold glasses of lemonade proudly served by our host. "Nothing better than lemonade on a hot day. Even better than cold beer. Can't drink it now. It's Lent, you know?" Our volunteer work garnered us a lot of press coverage and added to our mystique of being a campaign of the people and not moneyed interests.

Into Mississippi, the land of lowest incomes and highest infant mortality rates, we descended. We parked the bus, got out and before we could start to tour the city, we attracted the attention of the local police. Johnny made the introductions. He jawed with the Chief of Police, cajoled him, made him feel in charge and slowly convinced the man we were not here to cause him any trouble. When the mayor, Jimmy Cockloft, heard that our campaign tour was in town, he immediately came out to welcome us. I thought it interesting that he did not meet us until after the Chief met us, but I accepted his gracious welcome at face value. "What would you like to see while you're in town with us, Mr. Pollack," the mayor asked. "I think we want to go to Red Bud Park and see the Kosciusko Monument. Since I'm Polish, I'd like to honor one of my countrymen who fought alongside George Washington and helped free America from British tyranny." "Be our guest, sir. I'd join you but there is so much to do right now. You make yourself right at home," he said, shook my hand and left us to our own devices. As we walked the short distance to the park with many of the caravaners following us, I mused on his quick withdrawal. His behavior was apolitical. Here I was, a national political figure, visiting his town and he seemed to want nothing to do with me. I filed the behavior away for future reference. As we walked around the town, it was evident that Kosciusko was not a wealthy place. There were some opulent residences, probably a throwback to slave days, but the majority of dwellings small and poor looking. I wondered if Oprah ever visited the place of her birth. What did she think? What could she do with her great wealth to make a difference in this small town? Few townspeople came to talk to us. The local paper did not send anyone out to meet with us. There was nothing normal about this stop on our tour. We were aliens in a foreign land. "I think we've worn out our welcome."

We missed the Reverend Al Sharpton's symbolic march from Selma to Montgomery, Alabama held a few weeks ago to protest the new, restrictive voter ID law enacted by the State of Alabama and signed into law by the new governor. Rather than making it easier to vote, the new law required all citizens to present a picture ID. Some forms of ID like college identification from predominantly black colleges were not good enough but those from mostly white schools were. The march attracted national attention, but the state was still not willing to change its restrictive law. In support of the movement, we decided to commemorate Dr. Martin Luther King Jr.'s symbolic walk from the Brown Chapel A.M.E. Church to the Edmund Pettus Bridge where the Alabama state police met the marchers and violently attacked them. Selma was the epicenter of the civil rights movement and remained so throughout the 1960s. Today, it is eighty percent African American. We entered the city limits and were not surprised that we were met by the local police who did not escort us anywhere. We were stopped and Johnny got to meet with the authorities. I could see R&R engaged with the local police. I did not get out. Johnny said to me, "Let me handle this one." I started to protest, but Gram added, "Leo, let Johnny handle it." We watched through the front bus window as the dialogue continued. "What do you think they are saying?" I asked. "They're asking Johnny how many kilos of marijuana and cocaine we're moving and when can they get their share," Gram replied. I looked at him. "Johnny's assuring them that they'll get all they want when we are done. We'll be happy to accommodate them." "Gram, that's not funny!" I exclaimed. "I didn't say it to be funny. I said it to be ridiculous. Here we are, a national presidential campaign, traveling around in the United States of America where, unless I missed the memo, we do not need a passport to enter a city. These people are buffoons. No wonder they get a bad rap from people all over the country. This is no way to be treated in America." Outside the city, we noticed the people were lining the road with placards of all kinds stating unequivocally Alabamans could not be judged by the way law enforcement received such an honorable guest as the future President of the United States. We honked our horn all the way out of the state in protest and acknowledgment. Everyone was pissed when we realized we were being kept from exercising our First Amendment Rights. I told Al to turn around and we went back into Selma, stopped the bus and got out and began our march across the bridge. Our march was solemn. This was a famous pathway. We did not speak. A hush surrounded us. The great souls could be heard speaking to us, "Welcome Brothers and Sisters, Welcome to Selma and the march seen round the world." We filled both sides of the Edmund Pettus Bridge. We stared into the Alabama River and wondered how much blood flowed in its waters. What made men hate one another just because their skin color was different? What caused men to hate for any reason? We marched to experience a sense of history, but the history was being rewritten as we stood there watching the water flow past. Eliminate the poll tax and institute the voter ID. What was the difference? Where was the progress? Who was so blind that he or she could not fathom what was happening? How could any justice ever exist in a world where the resistance to change was perennial? Deep down inside all of our souls is a core element that transcends all other aspects of our humanness. The soul is the temple of the spirit that elevates us above animals. This soul is universal. There is no black or white soul. There is no man or woman soul. There is no Asian, African, European nor North American soul. There is only soul. When would we finally believe in the goodness of the soul in every man, woman and child? When would we permit every soul to live in peace and harmony? When would we quarantine the hate and let it die slowly. When would we release the faith, hope and charity that were the Lord's promise to all? Standing on the bridge, we held hands and sang, "We shall overcome." The voices echoed melodiously. Few dry eyes stared at the blue skies and the green carpet spreading across the land.

Our original plan was to stop in Georgia, but when we heard there was a rally planned to bring pressure on the City of Sanford, Florida to investigate the murder of a seventeen-year-old African-American youth named Trayvon Martin, we decided to attend it. Big Jack and the SS were not keen on the idea. I asked them what was going to happen when there were thousands of people waiting for us at some sites. We discussed the security parameters and then I made the final decision. "We are going." Gram coordinated with members of the caravan. He found a place where we could park our vehicles and walk to the rally sight in a Sanford city park. This would eliminate many problems for the security people. Since figures like Reverend Al Sharpton were going to be there, the national media was covering the event. Gram, Johnny, Al, John and the home team discussed whether our appearance at the rally would be a plus or minus. The discussion hinged on whether we would be perceived as capitalizing on the incident to make political gains. This was a legitimate point and no one denied it. After some tense words, I finally said, "Look folks. This kid is gunned down in an American city. He is not packing any heat. He's carrying Skittles and a soda. The shooter, a neighborhood watch vigilante, walks away scot-free. His gun is not impounded to see if it were the actual murder weapon. This happened three weeks ago and we're wondering if we should go. I have a son. He walks back and forth to school on his own. He is at risk just as this young man was walking home in his neighborhood. We're going. Saddle up. There is nothing else to discuss." We parked a mile from the park and gathered all the caravaners together. I encouraged them to be vigilant, respectful but disgusted with the way the city and state handled this tragedy. We marched together all the way to the rally site and flowed into the vast crowd gathered to pay tribute to this young man, his parent's loss, the absurdity of the crime and the ever-growing chorus for justice. Months later, the man who shot him to death would be acquitted of the murder charges adding insult to injury. We promised the people we would be back.

Our mission in Albany, Georgia was simple: visit a state of the art school featuring the Kahn Academy model. Sal Kahn, a former hedge fund manager, gave up his lucrative financial career and started designing education programs. He offered them free of charge on the internet. His goal was to educate the world using a simple model of interactive video, audio and practice sessions that would appeal to 21st century students. Bill Gates, Microsoft's founder, discovered the project when working with his own children. He helped finance Kahn's work making it possible for him to expand his creative capabilities, hire employees, and expand the concept. All over the world, schools began interfacing with the Kahn Academy and now it was fast becoming a model for highly integrated learning using the latest technology. What made Kahn's educational model successful was the ability to measure the learning taking place. He wanted to ensure that the students were actually learning. The entire model integrated skills testing and measurement so a teacher could monitor, evaluate and intervene when necessary. What made the Kahn program interactive was the ability of students and the teacher to work together when necessary and to work separately when there was no need to provide one on one instruction. After what we had experienced in Sanborn, Florida, this stop inspired us to focus more attention on education and less on the tragedy of poor law enforcement practices.

Emanuel's Church sat on the only high spot west of Greenville, South Carolina and was nearly an acre in size. Given its octagon shape, there were openings at each of the sides making it possible for people to park anywhere around the perimeter of the building and enter conveniently into the vast interior. The sanctuary was open to all eyes and the large tele-screens with images of worshippers, music lyrics, inspirational messages and calls for mission work played continuously during the gathering. Pastor Charles Hubbard and his wife, Mary, greeted us at the door. They glowed. Their spiritual happiness was visible in the way they described their work as pastors. Founded just twelve years ago, the church grew exponentially. A dozen original members now expanded to more than 10,000. Services on Sunday began at 7 am and ran hourly from that time until 2 pm in the afternoon. "Sunday is a long day, but one that fills our hearts with utmost joy," Mary said as she led us into the main hall. "We are happy that you are here. Please make yourself at home. We must go now because we have work to do," Pastor Charles said, shaking my hand, smiling at the grand group of participants we were leading into his church and headed down to the sanctuary where the services were ongoing. Praise and worship filled the hearts, minds and souls of those gathered. We sang, prayed, and listened to two sermons, one delivered by Pastor Charles and another by his wife, Mary. We received Holy Communion served by the church's youth ministers. We witnessed an altar call where more than 100 people went forward and declared they were ready to receive "Jesus Christ as their Lord and Savior". Finally, we stood and sang a favorite hymn of many evangelical souls, "Onward Christian Soldiers". There was no politicking on this hallowed day, but we watched the news later and discovered how important it was for us to be perceived as Christian worshippers. We did not mind the good press.

Our caravan journeyed to Glencoe Textile Mill Museum and Mill Village in North Carolina where we spent half a day touring. We looked at how the industry developed. More importantly, we viewed how people lived in those days. Mill towns were the bane of working people. Living under the thumb of the company, working people could never get ahead. They could work their entire life and still owe the company store more than what they made. As we toured the village, conversations centered on the austere living quarters and the hardships that working people endured just to make a living. After the Civil War, northern industrialists realized the south was ready to be extorted. They went into the decimated land with eyes wide open and raped the people and their economy. When unions tried to gain a foothold in the south, the companies fought back with everything and left people feeling betrayed by the organizations that claimed to represent them. Even into the 21st Century, working people in the Deep South are suspect of union organizations. Most old or new industries south of the Mason-Dixon Line are to this day unorganized. Some museums inspire people to see the world in a new and unique kind of way. The learning experience raises the spirit. A vision for the future becomes clearer. This museum depressed the team. The caravan packed up and we rolled north into Virginia. There was little exuberance shown. We knew the world was not better. With the new attack on labor in so many conservative state governments, we knew the prospects for the future were grim. We vowed we would make a difference when we were in office.

The opportunity arose to meet citizens from three states at one time in the old river town of Harper's Ferry, West Virginia. Judy and Gram organized a "Get to Know Leo Pollack" gathering in the river park. We were excited about visiting Harper's Ferry because of its historic reputation and being near to the nation's capital. We decided our campaign did not need to pass through Washington, D.C. There was enough time for us to enter the capital under more formal circumstances. We continued our discussion of the goal for the day's gathering. We parked and exited the bus near the park. As we walked to through the crowd of people, those who wanted an autograph or a picture mobbed us. This really slowed us down. Twenty minutes later, we were finally on the small stage erected in the center of a large, grassy playing field. What a day! The crowd was enthusiastic and my message was well received. We were making hay while the sun shined brilliantly and it felt especially good to be doing so close the nation's capital.

In Newark, Delaware, we stopped at a closed Chrysler assembly plant to see what had happened. Originally built in 1951, through six decades the plant produced a variety of cars and SUVs. The final vehicles produced were the Dodge Durango and the Aspen. Company executives pointed to an aging infrastructure as the reason for closing the plant. The models were not top selling brands in the Chrysler lineup. We met Scott Barton, a former autoworker and union steward, at a small parking lot outside the plant's main gate. It was shuttered so we could not take a tour of the place. The caravan lined up behind our parked bus, people got out, and soon we had a huge gathering ready to listen to what Scott had to say. He was animated in his concern for America's industrial demise and hoped my candidacy and ultimate victory would restore the country to manufacturing dominance in the world. I told him we would do our best to insure this happened in the first 100 days of my presidency. The crowd cheered. No other candidate had come out as strongly for the working people as I had.

In New Jersey, Gram arranged for me to speak to a large crowd near Trenton, the state capital. I got on the radio, talked to the caravaners and let them know what we were doing. I encouraged them to be peaceful. "We're not out to make a scene. We want to challenge the leaders who think that the silent majority is just going to continue to take it on the chin. Be polite. Be diplomatic. Oh, yes, and be noisy too." The crowd was awesome. The moment was totally ours. We made the most of the opportunity. Given that the governor failed to give us an audience, we took our grievances directly to the people. For the next hour, I was in the zone. Everything that was wrong with conservative politics was slashed by the sharp words flying off my tongue. I cut away the notion trickledown economics was working. I slammed the idea that spending cuts would balance the budget, while tax cuts were not even being considered as part of the equation. I stomped on the mission of the legislature to strip public services employees from having the right to collectively bargain as if they were second-class citizens and had no power over their own lives. I challenged the belief that social security and Medicare needed to be sacrificed in the name of austerity and balancing the budget. I jumped on the rancid idea that universal health care was some virulent form of communism or socialism. I lambasted the use of public money to support big businesses. When I finished with my diatribe, the crowd was roaring and there was only one way to dissipate the energy. We marched around the state house, called for the governor to come out, meet with the people and answer some questions. There was a light on in his office but he failed to show. The press had a field day with the event. Cameras were rolling everywhere. National media teams were alerted to what we were doing. We knew that the rally would make the evening news. Evening came and there was no end in sight. Too much energy remained in the people. We kept marching like automatons. This was the safest way to expend the energy. I did not want any trouble. Everywhere, we could see the security forces just waiting for us to do something that would justify their using force to stop our activity. After four hours, we finally accepted that he was not going to come out and talk. We left our calling card at the door: a large poster that read, "When the People speak, a prudent leader will listen." We hoped he would listen. We knew better.

When we got into New York City, I said to Al, "Park in the middle of the road until the police ask you to move on. We may be able to get away with stopping traffic for ten minutes. Who knows? We can always try it," I said. "Will do," Al said. He stopped the bus. I grabbed the bullhorn and jumped out into the crowds of people scurrying up and down the sidewalk in front of the New York Stock Exchange. "Leo, this is crazy!" Gram said. "We're going to get arrested again." "I don't think so but I don't care today. It's time for a stand." "Okay. Here goes nothing," Gram said and started to clear a space in front of the exchange for me to stand. Caravaners were crowding around me, filling the sidewalk and blocking the road. This did not look good. I had to get to it because it would not be long before the police would flood the area. I could feel the tension rising in my body. Al was staring out the window. He gave me thumbs up. I smiled and flashed him back with my thumb. This was our moment. We were on the national stage. This was NY2. This was the big time. This was Wall Street. This was the capitalist's center of the Universe. "Americans," I shouted out on the bullhorn. "Today we stand here not occupying Wall Street but alerting Wall Street and all the companies that trade at this exchange that their world is hurting more people than it is helping. Profits are not the only force in nature that matter. As a nation, we have lost our way. We do not take care of each other anymore. We are an uncivilized society. Just listen to our discourse on television, radio and among people and we can see and hear the malady. Kindness has been replaced by viciousness. Disagreements often result in virulent attacks. Today, we are calling on American corporations to stop abusing working people and those in the world who are incapable of fending for themselves against the power and authority of multi-national businesses. Most companies are not worth the paper their incorporation documents are printed. They do not produce goods and services in the countries where they hope to market them. Apple makes I phones in China and sells them to Americans. The Chinese workers who make the I-phones can't buy them. Americans are making Ford F-150 trucks, but the average worker cannot afford to buy the very truck he is building. The entire system is under water. Wealthy people do not work. They do not produce anything but more money. They believe they are entitled to their bounty because they took the 'big risks'. Behind every wealthy person's fortune are hundreds of thousands of people who struggled to make the profit that one person totes to the bank and calls his or her own. Listen to the economists who study the financial sector and what do you hear? The economy is crumbling because there is no equitable distribution of wealth. Those who make four or five hundred times what the average person makes do not see anything wrong with the picture. Their selfishness and greed is eroding the belief we have in the American Dream." Everyone could hear the sirens blaring. Lights were flashing down the street. It was only a matter of time before they descended upon us. We waited but they never came. They were afraid to tackle the crowd numbered in the tens of thousands enthusiastically supporting what we were saying and doing. New York was humbled by our movement.

The next two days created a furor in American politics. We made the big stage. The other campaigns noticed we were dominating press coverage. Our appearance in New Jersey lit the fire and the protest in New York poured gasoline on it. The Fox network criticized us, but the others tempered their commentary. MSNBC was the most supportive. Ed Schultz, Rachel Maddow, the Reverend Al Sharpton and Lawrence O'Donnell commented that our challenge was gaining real momentum and that we were going to be a factor in the fall election. Chris Matthews was not sure. He hedged his comments. Gram laughed and said that was because he was Catholic and did not want to disrespect Santorum. Chuck Todd compared us to H. Ross Perot's third party candidacy, but he pointed out that this was a disservice to our campaign since we were not starting out as billionaires on a personal mission. We appreciated his insight and hoped to be interviewed by him some day. Judy was working on getting David Gregory to invite me to appear on "Meet the Press", but he was still not sure if he wanted to give us such a stage. She assured us that he was weakening. Gram said, "Make it now while the primaries are still in full swing." We could create a real explosion if I appeared now and was contrasted with Romney, Santorum and the others including the President.

We traveled to Providence, Rhode Island and made it there in time to participate in the Gay Pride Parade. The people were elated a presidential candidate would actually come and march with them. I assured them that I believed people were people. Their sexual orientation did not make them any less important in my eyes, or for that matter, the eyes of the Lord. They found this to be a fresh point of view. One fellow said to me that he rarely heard churched people use the Lord in any conversation about gay or lesbian people. I said to him, "If Jesus were here today, what would he do?" Some of the caravaners were a little uncomfortable with the openly gay demonstration, but they were good sports, came along, and did not judge the people. We were teaching tolerance. We were role-modeling inclusiveness. We were doing it not preaching it.

In Massachusetts, we stopped at Boston Common, the famous park in the center of Boston and the oldest city park in the United States, and took a walk around this historic area. The caravaners were ready to move after a long day. We needed a walkabout to stretch our legs. Gram thought it a great idea to inhale some American history. Big Jack said we needed to be careful because there were alerts out for us. New York was not happy with us. Boston, though much more liberal, was still a city and did not want trouble. I asked him if we wore Paul Revere costumes, would they be happier. He gritted at me. Johnny thought it grand to be able to see the city where it all started. He had never been to Boston. Neither had I so it was a first for both of us. The first of the "Ride to Meet Leo" cyclists met us and were satisfied just to stay put with their bikes and visit with the others who were not walking around the commons. The ubiquitous press people were with us and it was a treat to tease them as we strolled along in the early evening hours. We still had sunlight, but the gas powered street lamps were already glowing. We stopped along the way to read historic placards that explained what we were seeing. I did not bring my camera along but Gram said he would ask the press to take some pictures for us and email them to the campaign.

Our one scheduled stop in Maine was the Yankee Nuclear Power Plant in Wiscasset. Originally designed to operate for forty years, it was decommissioned in 1996 when Maine Yankee Power Company decided it was too expensive to keep repairing the structure. Its decommissioning ran from 1997 until 2005 when the last of the plant was disassembled. As of the date of our visit, the final disposal of the nuclear waste was never clearly resolved because the national waste depository was never opened. What we hoped to see was what the decommissioned site looked like. The barren land was not an inspiration. We did not have a Geiger counter, but wished we had so that we could measure the residual radioactivity of the site. We walked around the fenced in area and wondered just what might have happened if the plant had been permitted to operate for its full forty year license instead of cutting it short at twenty-five years. Members of the press asked me what I thought about nuclear power and I said, "We can use it if three things happen. One, we standardize plants, make them small and all the same and build them with integrity. Two, we find a place suitable for disposing nuclear waste. Three, we continuously work to improve the safety of nuclear plants so they do not cause the kinds of problems we saw in Japan." The press printed every word I said.

The caravan traveled into New Hampshire, the "Granite State", and headed to the city of Manchester. We had a meeting with the editor of the New England Union Leader, the main conservative paper in the entire state. This was going to be our opportunity to relay our message to the people. I was surprised they wanted to interview me. Surely, they knew that any press I got was good press because I did not have to pay for it and they were giving me exposure to their conservative readership.

In Burlington, Vermont, we descended upon a maple sugar festival. We ate maple sugar a hundred different ways and all were scrumptious. There is nothing like pure maple syrup to make the palate pucker with joy. My favorite way of using maple syrup is on waffles, oozing with butter and the sweet nectar on a cool morning. The caravaners added another dimension to the rather staid Vermonters who welcomed us with their Yankee reserve until we started to spend money. After that, we were family. Fortunately, the Green Mountain National Forest was outside of town so the caravan was able to move a few miles and we settled in for the night in the safety of a natural setting that was just springing once again into life.

44. Taking the 3 AM in the Morning Phone Call

"Hello. Who is it?" I answered groggily.

"Leo, its Basha. I'm taking Janko to the hospital. His fever's spiked at 105 and I can't wait any longer.

"Call the ambulance, Basha. Let them take him."

"I don't want to wait," she cried.

"Get Janko ready, I'll call."

"Oh, Leo, he is so hot…"

"Get him ready. I'll call you right back."

"I love you, Leo."

"I love you, too, now go."

I called 911 in my hometown. It took a minute to connect. Luckily, Gram thought ahead and had a satellite phone installed for times when we did not have cell phone coverage. They kept me on the line until they got all the information they needed.

I called Basha back. She did not answer until the seventh ring. "How is he?"

"He's awake but his eyes look so puny, Leo. I shouldn't have waited so long but morning his temperature was down to 100. I thought he was going to break the fever."

"The EMTs are on the way. I'm up now. We're about 50 miles from Albany, New York. I'll have Big Jack drive me down to the airport and I'll be home in about three hours. I'll meet you at the hospital."

"Leo…I don't know what I would do if…"

"Hush up, my love. Janko will make it through this and be a tougher kid. Now get ready and I'll see you in about 6 hours."

"I love you."

"I love you."

I was dressed in a minute and ready to pull out in five. The guys heard me rustling around and were up in no time.

"What's wrong, Leo?" Gram asked.

"Janko's temperature spiked at 105. Basha is taking him to the hospital now. I'm going to get Big Jack to take me to the Albany airport and we'll fly home. You guys will have to lead the caravan back to Youngstown."

"How bad is he?" Johnny asked.

"Bad enough to go to the hospital in the middle of the night in an ambulance. Listen, fellows, we almost made it back without any trouble. Luckily, this was going to be our last day on the tour. Something tells me Janko was holding off just so I wouldn't be called home early. Who knows? I need to call Jack."

Big Jack was fifteen minutes away. I was outside and waiting for him when he pulled up. Gram called the SS and they were following us to Albany. I wanted some of them to stay with the caravan, but their mission was to protect me, not a bunch of strangers riding in RVs, vans, cars, motorcycles and scooters.

We made record time getting to Albany. The airport was open but no flights were scheduled for an hour. The closest connection we could make was to Buffalo. From there we could fly into Youngstown. ETA was 11 am. I called Basha but couldn't get her on the phone. I left a message. Big Jack booked two seats for us. The SS team got two more. They sat and waited. I paced the floor like an expectant father. Filled with nervous energy, I could not hold still.

The plane was on time. I gritted my teeth while we waited to take off. The taxi time was interminable. Staring out the small window into the gray clouds filled me with misgivings. Would my son be okay? Nothing else in the world mattered. We touched down about 9:15 am. Our next flight left at 10. We waited again. I paced again. We took off again. I stared at the gray clouds again.

Arriving in Youngstown, Big Jack took command. Before we got out to the sidewalk, we had people waiting for us. I jumped into the car and stared blankly at the side of the road as the car sped into town.

St. Elizabeth's Hospital, the birthplace of every member of my family, was now caring for my only son. Racing up to the front entrance, I leaped out before the cab came to a full stop and raced into the building. Janko was in the children's ward on the third floor I was told. Taking the steps, I was there in less than a minute.

Janko's room was dark, warm and exceptionally quiet. When I walked in, Basha got up from the chair by the side of his bed and came to me. We embraced as if we had been separated for a lifetime. I could feel her heart pounding against my chest and her rapid breathing told me that she was frightened.

"How is he?"

"Not good. He's still at 105 but soon they are going to take him in and do a cold bath treatment. Oh, Leo, Janko doesn't deserve any of this. If only I'd taken him to…"

"Basha, be still, love. He will be fine. Give the doctors time to do their work and we'll look after each other. Now, let's just hold his hand until they come to get him."

Basha held his left and I held his right hand. We could feel our son fighting the fever. His body was roasting. Luckily, he was sleeping, but even so, now and then he would moan loudly as if to tell us that he was still struggling. We prayed together over him as he lay between us. My eyes were moist most of the time.

The doctor and several nurses came a few minutes later and wheeled Janko out of the room and down the hallway. Like shadows, we followed them. They moved quickly and disappeared into another room. One nurse came out and informed us that they were going to use an alcohol bath to help break the fever.

We walked up and down the hallway holding hands, praying now and then, mostly being quiet and just hoping that Janko would be okay. The time dragged. We did not keep track. Moments hung like hours and hours a lifetime.

A few times, we could hear the soft chatter of the professionals working inside the room. We could not tell what they were saying. The only thing we wanted to hear was that he would be okay.

Sometime later, they wheeled him back out to his room. The doctor was the last one out and he said to us, "Your son is a very sick little boy, but hopefully, the bath we just gave him and the medicine will have some effect. Now we must wait and see."

"What is wrong with him, Doctor?" I asked.

"He is fighting some kind of virus. We could do some tests, but what good would that do? A virus is not treatable. When a virus attacks the body, the battle is on between it and the human being. Janko is a healthy boy. He will make it. He's just very sick right now. Let's wait and see. I'll check back with him in an hour or so."

We went back to Janko's room. He was soaking wet, sweating, and moaning, his eyes, when he opened them briefly, were bloodshot. We resumed our places, holding his hands and praying for him.

Our vigil lasted for nearly a day. Big Jack, Johnny, Al and Gram were all waiting outside in the lobby for us. They did not want to come in and upset us. Time was suspended. There was only Janko on the bed fighting for his life.

We must have both fallen asleep in our chairs holding on to him because when he asked what we were doing, we both looked up and saw Janko staring at us.

"Oh my God," Basha cried and smothered the little fellow with kisses.

"Mommy, what's the matter?"

"I love you is what's the matter," she said.

"That makes no sense," he said.

"My turn," I cried out, hugging Janko as I never did before.

"Ouch, Daddy, you're hurting me," he said.

"I love you, Janko."

"When did you get home, Daddy?"

"Yesterday morning," I said.

"You mean I've been sleeping that long?"

"You've been a sick little fellow," I replied.

"Where are Uncle Johnny and Uncle Gram?" Janko asked.

"Waiting out in the hallway."

"Can I see them? I missed them when you were all gone on your bus trip."

"They can hardly wait to see you, Janko." I ran out and got them.

When they entered the room, Janko's eyes lit up. "Uncle Johnny, Uncle Gram, I'm better. I'm not sick anymore. Now we can have some fun together," Janko cried out.

We had a family hug and the mood in the room lightened by a million pounds. Gram threw open the drapes and let the sun shine in on all of us. A half hour later, Al waltzed in with Marie and we decided it was time to order some food for this army.

When Big Jack came into the room, Janko gave him a big hug and kissed him and said, "Now everybody I love in the whole wide world is right here with me."

We ate pizza, drank soda, held hands, talked, laughed, teased and loved one another more than ever because we knew that our son was going to be well again and all we had to do right now was celebrate.

45. Random Acts of Kindness

Taking Janko home from the hospital two days later was one of the most exhilarating days of our lives. Our son was living. His fever was gone. As parents, our worst fears disappeared and we could breathe deeply again. The doctors attributed his illness to some unknown type of virus. "Could be a new flu strain," one concluded. We did not care what it was. He fought the battle and won. Now, he would be stronger and healthier than ever.

At home, what we found made all of us realize just how small the world was becoming. Boxes and bags of gifts and cards filled the living room. The random acts of kindness expressed by so many people that we would never meet overwhelmed us.

"Mommy, Daddy, look at all this stuff," Janko said with a smile on his face and eyes as wide as saucers. "Can I open up the packages now? Are these all for me?"

"They sure are," Basha said.

"You go for it, champ," I said. "We'll watch."

"Oh, goody," he cried and went to work.

We watched in awe as he opened one after another. There were so many that we would never be able to respond to all the cards and gifts.

"This stuff started rolling in the minute we got home," Gram said. "We just piled it in the living room because we didn't know what else to do."

"I'm amazed!" I replied.

"Where's Johnny?" I asked.

"He's down at the hall meeting with John, Judy and the crew."

"Anything I need to know?" I asked as we continued observing a boy at work trying to move a mountain.

"Oh, nothing much except Romney won the three events this week."

"I completely lost track that they were taking place," I responded. "Amazing what a little illness will do to someone's focus. Do you think Obama has lapses in concentration when his daughters are sick?"

"What kind of father would he be if he were not concerned?" Gram said.

"Maybe they don't get sick?"

"Maybe the earth isn't round either," Gram cracked. "They get sick. We just don't hear anything about it."

"Romney won the Maryland, Wisconsin and D.C. primaries. There is renewed talk now about a VP running mate. Rubio is coming up a lot. While in Wisconsin, Romney and Paul Ryan were inseparable. They were acting a whole lot like a gay couple," Gram joked.

"What?" I asked.

"Just joking, but Romney did say that he was going to keep his wife and not replace her with Ryan," Gram said. "The comment was picked up by the media and there were some snarky comments made about it."

"He sure is prone to making dumb remarks," I said.

"The Ryan Budget is at the core of the support. The Republicans are getting behind this newest version. When you look at in closely, it is even more anti-middle class and working people than his first one. He is slick and makes it sound like the best thing since Hitler died, but after Hitler, we got the Soviet Union. You get my drift. There is no stopping Ryan. He's going to continue this attack until we all bow down and praise Ayn Rand as the greatest mind to ever live."

"What makes people who want to teach intelligent design in schools propose such Darwinian economic plans? I just don't get it. Ryan is a Catholic. I wonder if he ever read the Sermon on the Mount. I wonder if it is possible for anyone to actually believe in the principle that we are to love our neighbors as we love ourselves and then create a policy that takes from the poor and gives more to those with the most?"

"I don't think so," Gram concluded. "We're in the twenty first century and look at what we've accomplished thus far?"

"I can't give up hope, Gram. Look at what we have in front of us: bags of cards and boxes of gifts for a little boy whom these people have never met but who are concerned for his health and well-being. I believe. I hope. I can't ever give in to despair."

"You're a better man than me, Leo," Gram said.

"No, you and I complement one another. When I'm down, you lift me up and vice versa. We are a team, my friend, and this is what keeps us running forward."

We watched Janko make an absolute mess tearing into the packages. Most contained nothing more than a card and some small token of affection that a seven year old could appreciate. However, the volume was amazing. An hour later, he looked like he was getting tired.

"Would you like to take a break?" Basha asked Janko.

"Oh, no, Mommy, but I might like a drink of water."

I went and got it for him. He continued to work on the rest of the packages. When he finished with them, Basha and I sat on the couch and read the cards to him. Even he was in awe at the volume and the kindness of so many people he had never met.

"Do I have to send thank you cards to all these people?" he wondered.

"No, no. I think most of them will understand that you can't respond," Basha said.

"What we are going to do," I said, "is make a video with you and me and Mommy and post it on our home page thanking all the people for their kindness. What do you think about that idea?"

"Oh, boy, when can we do it?" Janko asked.

"Today. The sooner the better," I said.

"Do I have to be in it?" Basha asked.

"Of course, Mommy. You are part of this family and a lot of these cards were sent to all of us."

"See how well you have raised your son," I commented. "He knows protocols better than most adults."

Janko looked very proud when he heard me say this.

We got Gram to assist us with a camera and we made a one-minute video thanking the world for responding to our family in such a loving manner. We compared our good fortune to winning the mega-million lottery. We did not get 640 million in cash. We got a whole lot more; the love of people expressed in a way that meant the world to our family.

46. Back to Work

When Janko recovered, we got back to work with even more fervor. One unnerving thing was that so much happened in just a few days. Romney took three more primaries leaving Santorum babbling that it was intermission and there was another half of the campaign left to play. He was down in the delegate count and could not mathematically make up the difference. Pennsylvania was going to be the make or break state for him. Romney was leading in the Commonwealth and that did not bode well for the one-time Pennsylvania senator. After Gingrich suspended his campaign, he disappeared from the political radar screen. Ron Paul followed him into the abyss. They could not gain any traction. They were like kids on a playground who nobody wants on the team. Gingrich's bright ideas could not woo the voters to embrace him. Ron Paul's libertarian views fascinated fringe voters, but mainstream, middle of the road Americans were not keen on some of his ant-government positions. According to Republican super-delegates who were not bound to vote for any particular candidate, the favorite now was Romney. Like him or not, he was going to be the standard-bearer for the Republicans against President Obama and us.

We knew he would be coming after us when we got an 18% independent vote in Wisconsin. We outpolled Paul and Gingrich and were only a few percentage points down from Santorum. By far, Romney spent the most money in Wisconsin. He was careful not to be seen with Republican governor, Scott Walker, who was facing a nasty recall election in June. Wisconsin voters were after the governor's blood for the draconian cuts he made to education and other social services programs. He was instrumental in eliminating collective bargaining rights for public sector employees and that galvanized Wisconsin voters to such an extent that more than 1 million signatures were collected to authorize a recall election. The political climate in Wisconsin, Ohio, Indiana, and Michigan and to some extent, Pennsylvania, was getting ugly.

Romney's superpac, "Restoring our Future", started running ads against our campaign in Ohio. They were mild, not too incendiary. I was portrayed as somebody who had the audacity to think I could govern a country when I had never so much as been the President of the local PTA. We knew this would be their angle. Judy and Gram went to work on introducing me as a pragmatic citizen who aspired to lead because I was not tainted by any political record. The contention was that anyone who had already held public office and sought it again, was an insider and could not understand the people's point of view. They touched on Romney's daily investment earnings and asked, "If you had $57,000 to spend every day for the rest of your life, what would be your reason for wanting to become president of the United States?" I asked what they were attempting to promote with this question and Gram simply said, "Doubt about his sincerity and his ability to relate to middle class and working poor people." I told them that was the last time they would make any comments about Romney. "We don't need to win this way. We can stand on issues and that is all there is to it."

At the hall, the pace of work was frenetic. There was never a dull moment. We were shooting ads, writing speeches, working on campaign messages, making calls to every supporter we met along the Liberty Bus Tour to make sure they were still on board with our campaign, doing phone interviews and getting ready for the next extensive campaign effort. We were not sure how we would spend the summer, but it was not going to be at home. There were too many people to meet and they were not going to come and look us up.

Campaign finances were amazingly flush. We were hovering well over a 100 million in donations. There was some concern that, in the near future, we were going to face some severe scrutiny for the vast sums of money we claimed to have in our coffers. Carol and Jim Kilpatrick at Mahoning Bank were exceptionally careful to keep all our funds posted in plain sight of any journalist or campaign operative who wanted to study the amount of money we had raised and where it came from dollar by dollar. All of us were confident that our accounting methods would pass the most rigid examination. Let them look and judge for themselves. We were not hiding anything. Only fools tried to hide things in the day and age of internet hacks and eavesdroppers.

Big Jack was at loose ends because we were relatively safe at home. He hovered in the background like a friendly ghost. R&R were always within sight. They were more obvious. We decided to keep them on the job. "Keep your friends close and your enemies closer" was Jack's analysis. He did not trust them. "Leo, they work for the President. They don't work for us. I know my men and women and they will do whatever it takes to make sure that you are safe." I did not know any of "Jack's people". He did not want me to know them. They were even more "ghost-like" than he was.

Richard Johnson, our southern state liaison, called me regularly to give me an update about the work he was doing in Texas, Louisiana, Mississippi, Alabama, Georgia, Florida, North and South Carolina. The task was monumental. Winning back the Dixiecrats from the Republicans after nearly thirty years of domination by the conservatives was proving difficult. He was undeterred. "We'll get them back in this election," Richard said. "They don't trust Obama and they don't like Romney. You are the best alternative and that is how we are pitching it. You will have to spend a lot of time here in the summer and fall, Leo. These folks like a candidate who presses the flesh. I hope you don't mind." I assured him that I would do whatever it took to get the south in our corner. He guaranteed me that we would if we kept after the people and educated them in voting in such a way that they protected their own interests.

The invitations to appear on television shows were interesting and overwhelming. When the producers of "The View" contacted us, I asked what it was. "A woman's program hosted by Whoopi Goldberg and Barbara Walters," Gram informed me. "It's one of the most popular woman's programs on television now that Oprah has left the daytime lineup and is promoting her "OWN" cable television channel.

A date was set and I appeared on "The View". Whoopi liked the fact that I was dressed casually and that made her like me just a little bit. She said she was partial to "President Obama for obvious reasons. But Leo, you are one of us and that makes this choice tough for folks like me." Elizabeth, Sherry and Joy were cordial but non-committal. Barbara Walters, a woman who interviewed almost every notable figure in the second half of the Twentieth Century, was cool and careful. Her questions were probing and challenging. She was throwing hardballs and I even commented at one point that I enjoyed her giving me her best "heater". This made the crowd laugh and after that, Barbara asked me a few personal questions about my family and my beliefs and then the interview was over.

Afterwards, our web page was overwhelmed with kind comments from myriad women who appreciated my keeping my wife off the stage and not using her to promote my candidacy. I had mixed emotions about their opinions. I would have loved to have Basha along with me like the other candidates did, but they did not have a seven year old son who needed to be in school every day and have his mother take care of him.

Judy put out feelers to Leno, Letterman and Jon Stewart, but they did not reply. We were making some progress, but there were skeptics who were just waiting to see if our efforts would fizzle out over the next few months. We knew better.

Al was enjoying the time at home with the family. He stopped in every day to see when his "services" would be needed. We figured we would be moving out any day, but were just not sure what the strategy would be now that we had to focus on just one wealthy Republican candidate with hundreds of millions of superpac money backing him and a president with a half a billion dollars supporting him. Money was not our issue. We needed more name recognition. Our tour opened the eyes of many people across the country, but we were still not a household name like the other two. We would have to continue working on this facet of the campaign.

Johnny was at loose ends. He and John Gallagher were making headway with the voter registration issues across the country. A few states wanted to block our efforts. He was ready to file suit in court, but thought we might first take a "wait and see" attitude. "We don't want to piss off these folks right now. We have enough leeway to make it on the ballot in every state if we just give it some time and grease the squeaky states a little with some smoozing." I liked the way Johnny was approaching this issue. A more confrontational approach would turn off some of the state election coordinators. It was better to make them our friends and not enemies. No doubt, if the election were close, there would be recounts and we needed to be on the right side of the law. "Some of these people get my goat," he complained one day. "They claim to be a part of America, but they function like they are living in the Soviet Union. They can't make a decision to save their lives." He enjoyed the challenge. Nothing made him happier than to face an insurmountable obstacle and find a slick way around it.

Every day, Gram and I did our mental gymnastics. "You've got to be ready to debate anyone, anywhere at any time," he challenged me. "These guys are playing for keeps," he said. "You've got to get a hard edge and hone it until you're razor sharp."

We studied the state of affairs and every time we faced something that we were not sure about, we did research. Gram was an avid reader and loved trivia. He proposed we create our own financial planning service as part of the campaign effort.

"Can't hurt, can it? I mean, tax time comes around and everyone scurries about trying to fill out his or her forms. We could incorporate financial planning with tax preparation and really win the hearts and minds of the people."

"Are you really serious about this idea?" I asked him casually.

"Sure, why not? Remember Andy Dufrain in the movie, 'Shawshank Redemption'. He made many friends by doing taxes and providing financial planning for the guards. They protected him because he was so valuable."

"What's the essence of what you're thinking?"

"There is so much bum data out there, Leo, it makes me sick. The other day some woman splashed her dribble over the internet. She called it five ways to financial security or something like that. Here is what she said. Live by a budget, prioritize your debt repayment, have 6 months of emergency savings on hand, start saving for retirement now, and negotiate your salary.

"Sounds like good advice to me," I commented.

"Leo, it's all tripe. This only works if a person is getting a fair salary. Let's see what kind of advice she gives to someone making close to minimum wage with no health insurance. Then let's give her some hospital bills, etc. Just when she starts to get ahead, the car or something will break. When she tries negotiating her salary, her employer fires her. This writer is living in a dream world, Leo."

"What do you propose?" I asked.

"Financial security is different than financial success. Romney is financially successful and because of it, he is secure. What security provides is something vastly different. Financial security means free of fear of financial ruin."

"How do you achieve that?" I asked.

"One. Never take on any debt, even to buy a house. Two. Buy 'loss leaders' for cars. Keep them 15 or 20 years. You can always rent a car for a vacation. Three. Never buy a house. Many people are tied to a poor job market because of their house. They can't sell their house and move on to greener pastures where the work is better. Four. Have a large vegetable garden. Grow your own food. Save a bundle and eat better and healthier. Five. Have inexpensive hobbies. Walking is the best, cheapest and most readily available hobby and it's healthy for you."

"Gram, all I can say is 'go for it'. Perhaps some of our supporters will find this service just what they need to get ahead. It sounds a little austere for my taste, but when the chips are down, I guess we will all need to change our lifestyles."

"Will do," he concluded and headed off to find an open screen where he could play with his ideas.

Fritz called me over to his workstation and gave me some insight into the power of social media. I was flabbergasted when he showed me the number of "hits" we were getting on our homepage www.ringingthelibertybell.org everyday. "We crashed a few weeks ago. I'm not sure what was happening. Maybe it was when you were in New York and were being treated rather shabbily. Anyway, the outpouring of care and concern when Janko was sick was another spike."

"What does this all mean?" I asked a little overwhelmed.

"We are influencing millions of people we would not have reached before if it weren't for this medium. Think about the power of the message. We post your daily activities, what you're saying, who's covering you, what they are saying, and anything else that makes sense to us to promote the campaign. People view the page and then share it with their friends. Like wildfire, it spreads across the cyber sphere and you become a household name."

"How amazing is that?"

"More amazing than anything I could have imagined when I was a little kid."

"You are no spring chicken," I commented teasing Fritz who was quite a few years older than me.

"Go ahead, rub it in, Leo. However, all kidding aside, when I started to do this kind of work, I just couldn't get enough of it. My mind always was number oriented. Now I'm doing what I love and there is no end to the possibilities of where this technology will take us."

"I just hope we always make steel the old fashioned way. I mean it. Too much technology is not healthy. I don't know what I mean by that, but there is a point of diminishing returns. You can only do so much with a keyboard, mouse, screen and software."

"We shall see," Fritz said enthusiastically. "We shall see."

John Gallagher was flying about the place like always, but later in the afternoon, he called me over and asked if we could have a private session.

"Sure, John, what's up?"

"How does it feel to be off the campaign trail for a few days?"

"It's been nearly a week, John. I like being home, but the campaign is out there, not here in Youngstown. We've got to make some tracks, some contacts, get moving or I fear the others will pass us by."

"The bus tour was worth $50 million in donations. I mean it, Leo, the more miles you racked up, the faster the money poured into the bank. We got a little scared that there would be too much money coming in and the press would get some strange idea that we were being backed my some robo-billionaire. Anyway, it slowed down when we told people we had enough money. We told people to start posting the Leo Pollack for President Posters in their windows instead. Try and find a house in Youngstown that does not have one."

"Everything about this entire campaign is amazing," I exclaimed.

"To think it started more than a year ago. This is what is amazing," John said.

"What do we do to keep the spirit alive?" I asked.

"Thought you would never ask!" John said. "We need some big production. I don't know. We need something to shock the country and get them to take notice. The bus tour was good. No, Great! Now we need to step up the pressure on the other candidates. You know it is probably going to be Romney, Obama and you," John concluded.

"Sure. I'm looking forward to it."

"What do you think? We're open to anything," John said.

"While riding in the bus for more than a month, I thought about a lot of things, but the one notion that continues to take front stage is the idea of debating my competitors. I think that the current debate format is silly and unproductive. My vision is a town hall format with the people asking the questions, not some moderator, and the candidates answering them. This would require the participation of the people in a way that they have never been included before and I am all for it. We invite the others to come to the town hall debates. Of course, initially, they won't show up. But when the people demand that they come and show their faces, they will have to make a decision. They will either show up or face the wrath of the people."

John was silent for a time. I could feel the wheels turning but could not hear them. Finally, he said, "I like it. I really like it. Let's gather the team together and flesh out this idea. Leo, you are the man!"

For the next hour, the team brainstormed my idea. Pros and cons were raised. The debate was lively, energetic and productive. Everybody was ready to make the town hall debates a success.

"We put out a schedule for the next six months. One town hall debate per week until we get as many in as we can all over the country, in big and small cities with just the three candidates," Gram said.

"That's the gist of it," John said.

"What happens if they don't participate at all?" Johnny asked.

"You don't show, you blow," John said. "We can't make them come and debate."

"Obama may not want to take that much time away from his major job," Gram said. "We have to consider this."

"We are not going to beg them to come," Judy said. "They won't see this as an opportunity right now. They will see it as a trap. They would rather let their superpacs do their talking for them. We have a better idea. We want the candidates to speak for themselves."

"Travel will be the issue. We may need to fly," Carol said. "We sure have the money for it."

"We'll fly coach, same airlines as regular folks. No charters, okay?" I exclaimed.

"Got it," John said.

"Al, how do you feel about that?"

Al laughed and said, "A little flying is okay by me. I don't mind sitting back and just seeing the sights."

"When do we start?" Gram asked.

"Next week. The sooner the better," John said. " Judy, can you and Gram work on contacting the other campaigns and tell them what we are proposing. Johnny, contact the state coordinators and have them pick a city for us to meet in but make sure it is not the same one we visited before and not just state capitals."

"Will do."

"Fritz, get a blurb out on the homepage and list it as what?"

"Fifty State Challenge," I said. "We'll go to every state and meet more people and let them know who we are and what we stand for and how we are different from the other parties and their candidates."

"There you go," John said. "Now we're cooking."

Thirty minutes later, the plan was in motion. I called Basha and told her what time we would be home for dinner.

"If you hurry, you can meet Janko at school," she told me.

"Got it. I love you."

Janko and I walked home from Jefferson Elementary School. Gram drove the car home. We took our time. There was no rush. He was pleased that I was able to come and meet him. When we got home, supper was not ready yet so he and I played catch in the backyard. For a little kid, he had a strong arm. A couple of times, his throws stung the palm of my hand. When I cried, "Ouch," Janko thought I was just being funny and laughed at me.

We ate dinner together, something that would end when the new town hall debate schedule went into effect. For today, we could be a simple family sharing food and being as close as anyone can ever be in this adventure we call life.

47. Town Hall Debate – Zanesville, Ohio

We wasted no time getting on the move. Gram and Judy made the arrangements and we were off to Zanesville, Ohio for our first town hall debate. Of course, Romney and Obama did not respond to our request to appear before a gathering of the people.

Prior to leaving, Gram inquired if Mayor Jeff Tilton would mind serving as the host and he readily accepted. I asked Gram what made him pick Zanesville, and he said bluntly, "I don't know. Maybe I just liked the sound of its name. Anyway, it's in Ohio, we haven't been there yet, the working is class well represented in its constituency, and Mayor Tilton invited us to come. How's that for a rationale? Besides, Tilton worked in a foundry for 39 years before becoming the mayor so he knows about hard work and making a living by the sweat of his brow."

"Sounds good, but that isn't the only reason you picked Zanesville," I said.

"Nope. The major reason is that Zanesville has a median income that is the same as the national average: $26,640. This makes it the quintessential American city. Once, Zanesville had a booming pottery trade because of the fine clays that were available in the area. This is all gone now. It is a city in transition much like Youngstown."

"Where are we holding the town hall meeting?"

"At the court house," Al replied. He was feeling good about being on the road again. He was even happier because it was not an overnight adventure.

"Where's Johnny?" I asked as we were preparing to leave.

"I think he's got other things to do?" Al said evasively.

"Johnny didn't want to come on this first town hall debate. Strange," Gram said.

"I think he had a hot date with some woman he met last week," Al continued. "He didn't say much more than that."

"Hot woman? Where? In Youngstown?" Gram joked.

"Watch it, pal!" Al said. "Mill town women are the hottest of all. They have to be to meet the demands of their male counterparts who are a discriminating group of guys."

"Buffaloes," Gram replied. "Al, as Sarah Palin said, 'a pig is still a pig even if you put lipstick on it.'"

"Did she really say that?" Al asked.

"I don't know, but it sounds like something she would say."

"She was kind of witty," I added. "I always liked that line about the difference between a hockey mom and a grizzly bear."

"What is the difference?" Al asked.

"Lipstick," I said.

"She must have a lipstick fetish," Gram said. "Notice how many comments she makes that references it."

"She isn't bad looking," Al said. "It's just when she talks that you want to put a bag over her head."

"Al, that's not a kind thing to say," I corrected him.

"I wasn't trying to be kind, Leo. I was being blunt."

"Hey, isn't Zanesville the place where that fellow turned loose all those exotic animals a while back?" Al asked. "I hope they caught them all."

"You're right," Gram said. "On October 19, 2011, Terry Thompson, the owner of Muskingum County Exotic Animal Farm opened all the cages of the animals he kept there and then committed suicide without leaving a note or explanation of any kind. Prior to that day, he had been released from jail after serving a year's time on an illegal firearms conviction. Fifty-six exotic and dangerous animals were set loose into the surrounding countryside. The animals included wolves, black bears, grizzly bears, full-grown male lions, lionesses, baboons, mountain lions, and 18 full-grown tigers, authorities said. Local police enlisted the help of professional zookeeper and animal tracker, Jack Hanna, to assist in the effort to control the animals. Local schools were closed. One grizzly bear, three leopards, and two monkeys were captured unharmed and transported to the Columbus Zoo. The rest of the animals were killed. All the slain animals were buried on the Thompson farm."

"Amazing," Al said.

"What a waste," I commented.

"No one will ever know what caused him to do it," Gram said, "but a lot of beautiful animals lost their lives because of him."

"Wild animals should be left alone," I concluded. "They are not meant to live in cages any more than people are."

We rode along in silence pondering the significant loss of animal life.

When we got into Zanesville, we found the county court house in the center of the town on Maple Street. Mayor Tilton met us in the lobby. The place was filling rapidly and we were told that there was going to be standing room only.

"We are very excited that you are here, Mr. Pollack. This is one novel idea of yours. A town hall debate! Who would ever think one of our native sons would be coming to Zanesville and using our old and famous town for his first debate. We are honored, sir," Tilton concluded.

"Mayor, please call me Leo. Secondly, Zanesville is an all-American town. Once upon a time, this was a major pottery center. The industry was killed by globalization and this is one of the reasons that I am running for president. I want to restore some sanity to the entire global economic system."

"Good luck," Mayor Tilton responded. "Many politicians and economists have tried to do that."

"I beg to differ, Mayor. They really don't have a vested interest in solving the crisis. They want it to appear like they do care. What they really want is to kick the can down the road in front of them and not face the difficult choices that need to be made. I don't mind making those choices."

"I'm getting the impression that you don't. Let's get inside and start the debate. We're sorry to see that the two other candidates have chosen not to attend."

"Isn't it ironic," I said. "In the past, the candidate with the lowest percentage was excluded from all the debates. Now, the candidate with the lowest percentage is the only one showing up to debate."

"Does that surprise you?" the Mayor said. "They don't want to stand on the stage with you and get their butts spanked. They know what time it is. The president is avoiding many issues because there are so many that can sink his re-election bid. The other candidate is avoiding middle class America because he's out of touch with it."

"Now I know why you picked Zanesville," I said to Gram.

"Oh, you mean because Mayor Tilton is running forward as fast as you are, Leo? Hey, I do my homework. He's one of us. He's committed to working people and their hopes and dreams."

"I like to think so," the mayor said. "Now let's get to work."

Mayor Tilton escorted us into the vast conclave of the courthouse. This ancient structure made you feel insignificant by its very loftiness. We walked into the crowded room and a resounding applause erupted. I waved to everyone and took a seat. He wasted no time in opening the debate.

"My fellow citizens, it is a great honor and privilege to host the first town hall debate of the 2012 campaign season. We were chosen because we are a city that knows how to work. As a city, we are facing the effects of the last thirty years of misguided leadership. Today, we are honored to have our native son, Leo Pollack, a third party candidate running on the Liberty Bell ticket, with us. Mr. Pollack is a steel worker. Like us, he knows what hard work is. He knows what it means to live from pay check to pay check. He knows that this country can do better. I'm sorry to say that the other two candidates are not here. They were invited. Both declined. They don't believe that the people of Zanesville are important enough to come and participate in a debate about the future of America. Enough of them. Their unwillingness to participate is a strong message that we don't count, that working people, middle class people, the working poor, don't count. This debate will go on anyway. We are fortunate to have Mr. Pollack with us and he will be taking your questions until, as he said, there are no more questions. Yes, there is no time limit. We are here to do America's business. Let's get to it. Please, use one of the many wireless microphones that are available around the room to ask your question. Mr. Pollack, the floor is yours."

I stood up in front of what appeared to be three or four hundred people. Later, Gram informed me that more than 500 had gathered for this historical debate with no one on stage but me.

The applause continued as I waved at the people. Finally, they stopped clapping and I said, "My name is Leo Pollack and I am running for president of the United States. I am an unemployed steel worker who has spent his life pursuing the American Dream and now it is beginning to fade away. I want to stop this, for me, for my child, and for generations to come. With your support, we can make a difference. Now what questions do you have for me?"

A hundred hands shot into the air. I knew this was going to be a long day.

Woman. "What do you make of these politicians saying that they are going to do away with planned parenthood and that there will be no contraception coverage for women through their health care plans?"

"I say they are wrong, mean spirited and misinformed. How can men make decisions about women's reproductive rights? We have made so much progress in this area that this is not the time to reverse direction and return to the dark ages of the 1950s when women were truly second class citizens in so many ways."

Man. "I think this president is against guns. I want to know what you think about gun control and the right to keep and bear arms."

"The supreme court ruled on this a few years ago. It is the right of any citizen to keep and bear an arm. I will tell you that I do not think that carrying a shotgun, rifle or even a handgun is an issue. I do think that assault rifles are not something that we should permit people to carry in public anytime. America is a violent nation because we have too many people who are disgruntled with the way things are going. Every now and then, the most disgruntled among us rises up and needlessly shoots others. We've seen this in the past month. We need to plant faith, hope and charity everywhere, with everyone, every day until the seed takes root and we have a more peaceful nation. Eliminating guns is not the answer."

Man. "Why do you want to be president and what makes you think you can do a better job than the current one or the guy who wants to be the next president from the Republican party?"

"I believe that all men and women are given the inalienable right to pursue life, liberty and happiness. In my pursuit of the presidency, what I want to accomplish is re-instilling in all Americans the belief that we can change the world one person at a time. I have watched professional politicians for years sell out the minute they get nominated or elected. I can't be bought. This is what qualifies me the most. I don't want to be president for eight years. I want to serve one term, do the best job I can and then go back to making steel for a living."

Woman. "We've heard that your campaign has raised a lot of money but doing it one dollar at a time. What do you suppose made so many people contribute their money to your effort?"

"I hope it is because they believe in what I'm doing and what we can do together once we get special interests out of the system and start to do what is best for the majority of Americans. Both my fellow competitors are raising hundreds of millions of dollars to finance their campaigns. One of them is already famous for 'carpet bombing' his competitors with negative ads. Our campaign will not do that. We were getting an ad ready the other day and it poked fun at the one candidate that makes a lot of money strictly from his investments. I said that was enough. We don't need to do that kind of advertising. We can win on the issues alone."

Man. "Gingrich tried that and look at what it got him. What makes you think the carpet bombing, as you call it, won't affect your campaign?"

"It won't because people like you, sir, will not give it much credence."

Man. "You really believe that?"

"I do or else I would not be running for the office. How do you suppose we raised over a 100 million dollars in one-dollar denominations? The answer is simple. Americans, like you, know what the facts are. The current president has not provided us with the 'change we can believe in' and the other candidate is so flexible that, from day to day, we can't tell what he believes in because he changes his point of view so often. With Leo Pollack, what you see is what you get. I will be the same tomorrow as I am today. Now listen to me carefully. I will change what I think is best for America if there are compelling facts to indicate we need to take a different course."

Woman. "Can you give us an example of what you mean by that?"

"Sure. Let's use Iraq for example. We were told that there were weapons of mass destruction in the country and their leader might use them against them or somewhere else in the world. We went to war with Iraq. Sometime later, we learned there were no weapons of mass destruction, but we continued to fight in that country for another five years. Given the new information, I would have pulled our troops out that moment. We were finished. The old regime was toppled. An elected Iraqi government was in power. Our work was done. We needed to exit."

Man. "But they are an unstable democracy. They need our ongoing support, don't you think?"

"No. They are doing just fine. Yes, they have a long way to go, but they accomplished something in their very first national election that we Americans did not in our first 146 years of existence. Iraqi women were able to vote. American women were not eligible to vote for almost a century and a half after our founding. You see, the Iraqis are light years ahead of us. Forget about the violence in their country. We have just as much as they do. We don't want to talk about it, that's all."

Man. "What about the violence in our country. What can you do about it?"

"There is nothing I can do about it. There is something that we can do about it. You hear what I am saying? This is a 'we' thing, not an 'I' thing. What has prompted so many people to believe that they need to carry a gun to protect them? I don't know. I don't carry a gun and never will. I am not afraid of my brother or sister. I am not willing to sacrifice what little sense of security I possess by putting a gun in my pocket and walking down to the convenience store. The gun doesn't make me any safer. What makes me feel safe is my own sense of connection to you, and you and you (pointing to those in the crowd) and that is what makes all the difference."

Woman. "I'm a teacher and I am concerned that each year children come to school less prepared to learn. They are not being pushed by their parents to do their best in school. They are full of themselves. They sometimes want to run the classroom when they know very little. What is the answer? We teachers need lots of help."

"First of all, thank you for your service. Yes, you serve America just like a soldier does. You are the first line of defense against ignorance. This is a debilitating condition that results in our losing our competitive edge in the world. What can we do? I've said it many times we need to keep kids in school longer each day and more days per year. We need to pay teachers better and then demand they perform like the professionals they are. We need to fund education adequately and demand we get our money's worth. We need to hold teachers accountable for their performance and reward them for stellar results. We have a lot of work to do in this area, but it is not impossible. I look forward to making education the centerpiece of our new vision for America. Our children are our future. Let's not just say the words. Let's demonstrate this in our actions."

The questions kept coming for hours. Now and then, I took a drink of water to wet my whistle, and then I kept on tooting. The people were not ready to walk away and so I was going to remain on the stage until every question was answered. The heat began to rise. The Mayor had the air-conditioning turned on. People started getting up and down to use the restroom facilities. I called for a 20-minute break so they could do so without disrupting the gathering. We reconvened and continued as before. There was no limit to the depth of their questions. I could not remember the number of follow up questions they asked. I was grilled and that was fine with me. There was no sense in shirking any question when I was sure I would hear the same one asked repeatedly across the nation. I was thankful for Gram's skull sessions where we practiced doing just what I was today: namely, answering volumes of questions with as much sincerity and integrity as I could.

When it appeared that there were no more questions, or at least, the enthusiasm of the participants was waning, Mayor Tilton got up and thanked everyone for his or her commitment to making democracy work. "You folks are the essence of our government. Mr. Pollack has said it repeatedly in speeches that I've heard him make. 'When America works, democracy thrives.' This is democracy in action. I thank you for being willing to sit and listen to what Mr. Pollack has to say and I'm sure that he knows Zanesvillians are a hearty bunch of folks. After all, look at how long we have sat still and listened intently so that we might learn who this man is and whether or not we want to support his becoming our next president. Mr. Pollack, thank you for your patience, hard work and now, as mayor of this humble city, I declare this debate over."

The mayor and I got a standing ovation. I was not sure whom it was for, but I accepted it graciously. Mayor Tilton shook my hand and then raised it in front of everyone in a gesture of solidarity. I was greatly honored by the symbolic behavior on his part and told him so.

"Mayor Tilton, thank you for inviting us to your city and the wonderful way you hosted this event in this beautiful old court house."

"Leo, the pleasure was mine. It is rare in life when a person gets to be the first to host a general debate during a campaign season. This was my singular honor."

"Too bad the others didn't show up," Gram said walking over to us.

"Mayor, this is Gram Tashjan, my chief of staff," I said introducing him.

"We met on the phone," the Mayor said. "Good to meet you face to face. Thanks for selecting us from all the other cities in this state. Tell me, how did you pick us?"

"You really want to know?" Gram asked rhetorically.

"I sure do."

"You were a foundry worker for 39 years. This told me you know what hard work is and could relate to Leo and what he is trying to do. Secondly, Zanesville has a median income almost exactly that of the United States as a whole making it an all-American city. Third, Zane Grey was from here."

"He sure was and what an amazing author," Mayor Tilton said.

"Three out of three. Pretty good, I'd say," Gram concluded.

We laughed and walked outside and were greeted by a balmy spring afternoon in central Ohio.

"Where are you off to next on your debate schedule?" the Mayor asked.

"I think it's Johnstown, Pennsylvania," I said. "We are doing one or more a week until the election."

"Leo, this is a great idea. I think that the people got a clearer picture of your beliefs. Many folks will vote for you regardless of what the odds are. Trust me. I know my people," the mayor concluded.

"I sure hope so, Mayor," I responded.

"If this means anything, you've got my vote. I believe in the power of working people to unite and carry the real message everywhere. Don't let anything stop you, young fellow. Nothing, you hear me?"

"I do, sir, and I thank you for your vote of confidence."

"Be safe in your journey and come back and visit us again when you're the president. It would be good for business," he said giving me a slap on the shoulder and a wink.

We packed up and headed back toward home, but there was ebullience present in the bus as we drove along and I cooked dinner for the team. We were feeling the joy of public acceptance. We chattered like magpies on a cedar fence. We stopped and ate with gusto. We worried about nothing and hoped for everything. Our spirits were filled with the power of the people who wanted America to be healthy and happy once again. Our commitment to that elusive goal fired our spirits and made us staunch men.

48. An Outdoor Adventure

While we were eating breakfast the next morning, Gram stated bluntly that our town hall debate was an extraordinary success.

"What makes you say that?" I asked.

"Here are the facts. Unknown to you, Judy went ahead and live streamed the debate all across the country. Remember those movie theaters that were running your speeches on closed circuit? The theatres were packed for the debate. Estimated attendance was over 923,000. Many places added a second screen because of the demand. For the day, it was more popular than the movie, Hunger Games."

"You're kidding me, Gram?"

"No. On top of that, at least two hundred and fifty beautiful women emailed the home page asking who the stud was talking to you at the event," Gram added.

"Mayor Tilton, right?" I said.

"Wrong. Who else was there that they knew was available?" Gram asked.

"You!"

"Right on," Gram said.

This woke Johnny up. He had been very quiet this morning as we discussed the previous day's events. I think he was feeling guilty but would not admit it.

"If I would have been there, the number would be double that," Johnny said.

"But you weren't," Gram cracked at him, "and we were and I got the nods. How do you like that, pal?"

"Alright, go ahead, rub it in. I was wrong and you were right. I've learned my lesson," Johnny said. "It wasn't worth it. Now I know better to chase a woman who is after only one thing."

"What is that?"

"Marriage," he replied with a yucky look on his face.

We laughed at him and continued our discussion now that he was contrite.

"What else did you and Judy cook up behind my back?" I asked, impressed that they were so busy while I was talking to the people in Zanesville.

"Many of the networks asked if we could go on in prime time. This might be hard in some cities where we hold debates, but we're working on it. It would be hard to hit the whole country. Judy said that we should broadcast from the RV while Al is driving. That way people could see how you travel and compare that to Obama on Air Force One and Romney on his chartered jet plane."

"I like that idea," Johnny said. "We create a contrast between us and the other guys. The people are savvy. They'll get it right off. A picture is worth a thousand words."

"We thought of a new ad campaign. You would be answering the hardball questions other candidates avoid. These will come from the debates. At the end, the ad will ask, 'What do you think?' People will be encouraged to post their ideas on the homepage so we can use these in our ads."

"Right on. I love the idea," I said.

"There's more. We are putting a complete debate transcript on the website. It will have a like/dislike button and a place for comments. It is very important to get the right-wingers to voice their opinions so people can see what jerks they are. Over the past three months or so, they have pretty much disappeared from the internet. The right wing is all for war as long as they aren't in it. They are like school bullies that disappear when their friends walk away."

"You two are not missing anything," Johnny said. "I feel like I haven't been holding up my end of the work load."

"We noticed that," Gram said sideways at him.

"Okay, I got it. No more fooling around for this guy."

"We'll believe it when we see it," Gram said.

Janko was ready for school so Basha and I decided we would both walk with him. We could not remember the last time the three of us took a stroll together. The boy loved the idea. We let Big Jack and R&R know what we were doing. They were right on our tail all the way to and from the school. We were able to be a family but only within the boundaries of our security patrol. I could tell that Basha was not enjoying this part of our new lifestyle. I was not enjoying it much, but the only thing I could do about it was quit the race or press on and seize the moment. The choice was obvious.

We had a meeting at the hall scheduled later in the day. In the mean time, we were free for a few minutes. It did not last very long.

"Check this out," Johnny said, pointing to an article in the Vindicator. "Here's a family: father, mother, son and daughter, hiking on the Buckeye Trail south of here. It is part of the American Discovery Trail that stretches from San Francisco to Washington, D.C. Anyway, they sold their home at a loss because they could not afford to make the payments anymore. With the money, they decided to start hiking. Now get this, Leo. They are big supporters of yours. They wrote in one of their trail journal entries that the paper printed they would not stop hiking until you become the president. The father lost his job and this started the negative snowball rolling. Their story is tragic and inspiring at the same time. Wow!"

Johnny read the rest of the story to us. Their struggles were heartbreaking. However, they had a goal.

"We need to respond and support these people getting back on track," I said.

"What are you driving at?" Gram asked.

"Oh, Oh, Leo is ready for an outdoor adventure," Johnny cried out. "I can feel it coming right now. Leo Nesmunk's come to live in the body of Leo Pollack."

"What's he talking about, Leo?" Gram asked.

"These people need help. They are out there making a statement hiking on the trail. The father will not find work out there. If we were to show up and draw attention to their plight, he might have a better chance to get work and they could get off the trail and find a new life somewhere."

We stared at each other. Basha walked in at that moment and knew that we were up to something.

"Spill it fellows. I've seen that look before. Where are you heading?"

Johnny quickly told Basha the story. Their misfortunes saddened her. The resiliency of the father and mother and what they hoped to do while on the trail impressed her.

"Whenever we think things are bad, a million other people have it a whole lot worse," Basha said. "So when are you leaving?"

"How far away are they?" Gram inquired.

"Just south of East Liverpool," Johnny said. "They are heading slowly west."

"Too bad school isn't out. Janko would love to camp out."

"Better get the SS and Big Jack primed for this one," Gram said.

"Let's call the Vindicator and let them know they can have the scoop," Johnny said. "This will be worth some excellent PR."

"What we want to do is draw attention to this family's plight and help them get back on track," I said. "Let's be careful and not overstep the boundaries of decency."

"I agree with Leo," Gram said. "These folks have essentially lost everything."

"How do we get there?" Johnny asked.

"We take the bus, and then we hike," I said. "We've got some ratty gear in the RV that we can use."

"Let's do it!" Gram cried out.

"All for one and one for all," we shouted like musketeers.

Basha rolled her eyes in disbelief. "You guys!"

Al thought we were crazy, but he said he would drive us to the scene of the crime and drop us off. "You can't expect me to go camping at my age," he cried out. "I'll be close by in case you get scared and want to come inside for the night," he teased.

Johnny and Gram thought it best I was the only one to hike along with the family.

"Too many of us will spoil the effect," Johnny said. "Besides, they are supporting you, not us."

"For once, I agree with Johnny. Leo. I think you ought to meet these people and camp out with them yourself."

"Let's go."

Big Jack thought I was crazy, but he said, "For the good of all, let's make sure that you are safe out there. You know, I'll be nearby, but not with you. I've got younger folks who can tramp around on trails."

R&R said nothing. They were consummate professionals.

Luckily, the Vindicator reporter had the approximate location where the Faller family was last seen crossing the road. When we got close to the area, it was easy to get information because the Fallers were big news in this small town.

We found them near the outskirts of East Liverpool heading down a highway. When we stopped and I got out and introduced myself to them, tears welled up in Jerry's eyes. His wife, Meg, squeezed my hand hard and thanked me for coming. Their children, Matt and Julie, stood quietly beside their parents.

"You were the last person we ever expected to come out and meet us," Jerry said, "but this is a real honor."

"When I read about your family, there was only one thing I could do and that was to come and meet you folks. Here I am. Where are we headed today?"

"Forward is all we say at the beginning of each day," Meg replied.

"I hope you don't mind my tagging along with you," I asked.

"We'd be honored," Jerry said, replying for the family.

"Let's go hiking," I said.

For the rest of the day, we walked and talked. Meg and Jerry told me their life story. They grew up in Western Pennsylvania. Both were college graduates. Their careers rose and fell with the economy, but the Great Recession zapped both of them. First, Jerry lost his job as a consulting engineer, and then Meg's real estate business fell to pieces when the home market dried up. They used up their savings, their IRAs, their children's college funds and the last of their unemployment compensation. When they realized they had nothing left but some equity in their home, they sold it, took the money they received from the sale less expenses, and set out on the America Discovery Trail and vowed to hike until Jerry and/or Meg got a job or until I became president.

"You must be true believers if you were committed to hike until I became president," I said, honored by their goal.

"We are, Leo. We believe in what you are doing. We believe that you can understand what is really happening to people like us. We are not unique in any way. We are just a couple of middle class kids who grew up believing in the American Dream and this is what we have discovered. The dream exists only as myth."

"This is what we need to change," I said. "The time for a renaissance in America is right now. We need to protect working people from the unregulated markets that care very little whether or not a family makes it in today's economy. The bottom line has replaced any sense of social responsibility."

"We agree with you wholeheartedly," Meg said. "We don't want handouts. We don't want charity. We want to work. We want to be productive members of society."

The day passed swiftly as we hiked along and they told me more about themselves, their hopes and dreams, their likes and dislikes. The two children, Matt and Julie, expressed their hope to eventually return to high school, graduate and then go to college. "We know the odds are stacked against us," Matt said, "but we're willing to work hard and make a go of it."

"I sure hope and pray that you both get that opportunity."

We camped near a small creek along an old strip mine where the trail went off into a state park. Our evening was full of joy. We did not build a fire because of a burn ban in the area. However, we did sit outside and ogle the stars and wonder just how many there were in the vast firmament that spread beyond our comprehension.

In the morning, I explained to the family that I had other commitments, but I wanted them to know that I would be hiking with them in spirit. They fully understood.

"I want you to understand one thing. I am not forgetting about what you are enduring. There will be justice. There will be a future for your family. I cannot guarantee it, but I can tell you that I will be working on making your dreams become reality."

We hugged each other and said tearful goodbyes. They were kind, wonderful, simple people. There was no reason they should be facing this type of travail.

As I hiked back to the highway where Al was parked, I refrained from turning around until the last moment. When I looked, there they were. They were hoisting their packs onto their backs. I could see the smiles on their faces. Jerry was adjusting his daughter's pack. His wife was struggling to get hers up from the ground and her son helped her. They were ready to attack the day. When they felt my eyes on them, they looked my way. We waved to each other and then we each turned and went our separate ways.

"Enjoy your night out under the stars?" Al asked when I got into the bus.

"More than you'll ever know," I said.

"They seem like a nice family," Gram said. "I wouldn't have minded tagging along with you. It's been a while since I slept outside."

"It does wonders for your health," Johnny said facetiously.

"I feel great," I said. "You couldn't spend an evening with a nicer family. The Fallers are very special people. I mean it. Happy, on one hand, and tragic in the same breath."

"What's their story?" Gram asked.

I told them.

"Amazing. Two college educated people and they can't find work. What is wrong with America?" Johnny said.

"Contact Fritz. Get their story on the home page. Get them a job. Pronto!" I said.

"Will do," Gram said.

"Let's take this even further," I said, an idea bubbling up inside me. "Get Fritz to set up a jobs clearing house. You know. Employers seeking employees. People seeking work. Just one thing. No 'human resources' language. Call it what it is. Workers Clearing House. What have you? Anything but 'human resources'. People are more than resources. People are the essence of every industry. People are what make every enterprise successful and I'm not talking about the CEO of the company. I'm referring to the workers, the people who actually do the work. "

"I hear you, Leo," Gram said and got right on it.

"Johnny, what legally can we do to make sure we can broker jobs between people and employers? I don't want to run afoul of the law. We don't need to have our competitors clawing at our throats over this one down the road."

"Nothing is illegal about offering this kind of service. You just can't charge any kind of 'finder's fee' or any other fees for making the connections."

"Work out the details with Fritz, Johnny, and make sure we are up and running today. Whom do you know that can get Jerry Faller a job? You must have some connections."

"I've got plenty. I'll work on it right now," Johnny said.

"Good. Now I want to make some lunch for you barbarians. I know you must be hungry because I sure am."

While I was cooking, the phone rang a half dozen times. John called and wanted to know how the night went. I told him. The Vindicator reporter who first broke the story wanted to do a follow up with me. We did it over the phone. WFMJ called and wondered if a film crew could stop by and get me on tape for the evening news. I said okay. Finally, our Congressman, Tim Ryan, called and asked what he could do to help this family. I said, "Find them both a job." He said he was going to look into it immediately and thanked me for bringing their plight to the country's attention.

Before we finished with our Spartan lunch, Fritz called and said that he was being overwhelmed with employers who wanted to hire Jerry Faller and his wife.

"Yes!" we burst out in celebration. Fritz gave the facts to Gram. He and Johnny would work out the details.

"I guess we turn around and head back down to East Liverpool," Al said. "I don't mind. I'd love to see the look on those people's faces when you tell them they have job offers on the table."

"What do you think, Gram? Do we go back now, or let the system catch up with them?"

"What do you think, Johnny?"

"What the hell. Let's turn around and make their day.

We did. Their joy overwhelmed us.

"What can we do to thank you, Leo?" Jerry asked as he and his family rode with us to Youngstown where they were meeting a representative from one of the companies interested in hiring him and his wife.

"Pass it on," I said. "When you are back on your feet, there will be others who need your help. Take care of them."

"We will do that," he said. "That is the least we can do."

"I hope you don't mind but we're titling the job search engine on our home page, the 'Faller Work Connection'," Gram said.

Jerry, Meg, Matt and Julie looked at him. "What are you talking about?"

"Meeting you folks made us realize that our home page could be used as a clearing house for employers seeking qualified workers, like you two, seeking gainful employment. Our man, Fritz, got it up and running in an hour and now we're making connections."

"You folks are amazing!" Meg said.

"You didn't answer the question," Johnny said. "Do you mind if we use your name on our webpage? Legally, we have to get your permission. You understand."

"We would consider it an honor," Jerry and Meg said at once.

"Done," Johnny said.

On the ride to Youngstown, I showed our guests the Liberty Bell Bus's interior and they were duly impressed.

"No wonder you don't mind being on the road when you can sleep in a nice unit like this," Jerry said.

"Yes, but it is still not home," Meg added.

"We do the best we can," I said. "I do miss my wife and son."

"I'm sure you do," Meg said. "We were fortunate to have this trail time together even though the circumstances were not ideal."

We took them to the front of the Vindicator building where Gram made arrangements for the prospective employer to meet the Fallers. They connected with one another as planned. We said goodbye again and asked them to keep us posted on how they were doing.

I called Basha and said we would be home for dinner one more night. "Do you mind?"

"Never," she replied. "Hurry home, lover."

"See you shortly. I love you."

That night, everyone slept well. We had done our good deed for the day. We made a difference in the lives of one American family. Now, our goal was to expand the effort to include every American family across the land where hope was in short supply and charity was absolutely needed.

The next morning, Gram immediately checked and in the first eighteen hours of operation the "Faller Work Connection" hosted on the Ringing the Liberty Bell homepage connected 475 workers with employers.

Would wonders never cease?

49. Running Forward With the Wind

When it rains, it pours, and when the sun shines, everyone is happy. The mission to win a national election can inspire one to rise to the heights of engagement, or drop into the slough of despond. The mercurial nature of any movement is controlled less by the people in it than by the forces outside that want to kill it off or push it along. There is a yin and yang to the process. People inside the activist group wonder what is really going on at times as the forces push and pull at the hearts and minds of the people. No person who truly believes in the future wants the movement to fail so each works his or her hardest to make everything a success. Sometimes, the rain washes away the chalk on the sidewalk where the great formula for saving the world was last written down for posterity to behold. Poor choice of location, but there is a hidden meaning in the method. There are many who face the crowded world of disbelievers and are incapable of overcoming their disbelief. They do not see this as the supreme challenge to the movement. How committed are you to your mission? How much of a true believer are you? What keeps the fire burning down inside your soul, brother? These wonders never cease to amaze the party person who smiles and runs forward letting the wind blow at his or her back and sees the lamp of the future being lit by the Gods of Change.

Gram laughed aloud when he read that Romney said that 93.7% of the people who lost their jobs in the recession were women and it was all President Obama's fault. "Yes, it's all Obama's fault that women lost their jobs. This guy must be smoking some really good weed. Where does he get these figures? Doesn't he know that the more outrageous a statistic is the less apt people are to believe what he is saying? Roland's law says made up statistics are more believable if they are stated very accurately. Damn, what a fool"

Johnny spent the morning making the Faller Work Connection legal. Fritz, Judy and Johnny came up with a new way to connect employers and employees. Based upon a Match.com type of algorithm where the assets of a one person are matched with another person for the "perfect match", they decided to do the same with companies and prospective employees. "We have the company list all its assets and then the employee does the same. This is much better than the current method of throwing a dart at a target and hoping you hit a bull's-eye. Imagine how many employers hire people to fill a position only to find out a few months later that they are not good matches. Leaving the 'match making' up to an interviewer who asks a number of simple questions and then makes a decision to hire or not is Neanderthal."

"Sounds like a great plan," I said. "Will it work?"

Johnny looked at me as if I were a dunce. "Work? Get this. Jennifer Williamson ran a story on FWC, you know, the Faller Work Connection, in the New York Times this morning. Almost immediately, our site crashed due to so many hits. While you slept in, Fritz and I were working on the web page. Will it work? Give me a break!"

"Great!" I said, acknowledging his accomplishment.

"Oh yah, I copyrighted the process already because I can just see the Obama team coming along and trying to steal it. The Republicans don't care about jobs. They want to say they do, but what they really are about is creating a system of wage slavery in America. We've got their number on that one."

Al was busy with some of the kids who were volunteering their time with us. They were working on bumper stickers. When they came up with a doozy, they let everyone see it. "Get this one," Al said. "The Left Sucks. The Right Sucks More. Vote for Leo Pollack."

We stared at him and the kids. "Are you serious about that one?" I asked.

Al looked sheepishly at us. "Sure. Don't you get it?"

"I get it, but we want to keep this upbeat, clean, you know, not negative," I said.

"Okay. Okay, but we liked it, didn't we, team?" All the kids agreed wholeheartedly. They went back to work.

An hour later, they came back with "Running Forward with the Wind – Leo Pollack for President".

"Well?" Al asked, waiting for us to digest the message.

"I love it," Gram said. "The word 'with' is what makes it work. What you are doing is equating us to the wind, having the power of the wind, being with the wind. Cool beans!"

"We thought the letter colors for the first part would be red and the Leo Pollack part would be blue and the background white. Get it?"

"Duh! Al, we get it," Johnny said.

"I was seeing if you were awake. After you spent all those hours last night on the home page, you must be tired. We all know you spent most of your time surfing porn sites," Al laughed at him.

"Hey, that's not funny," I said. "We would give our competitors a hundred mile wide bulls-eye to hit if there were stuff like that going on. Tell me that's not true, Johnny?"

"See what you've started, Al. No, Leo, none of that is true. Damn, brother, I'm a lawyer. Give me some credit for being discrete," Johnny pleaded his case to conclusion.

An hour later, Al and the kids had a half-dozen more that we approved and his team went to see how quickly we could get them printed and available on the home page for sale. They were going for a $1.00. The proceeds were not for the campaign but for a college scholarship fund Al and the kids decided was needed. They worked with Carol and Jim Kilpatrick to set up a separate fund for the sales. Fritz restructured the home page to include this new wrinkle in our campaign.

I saw John Gallagher standing alone staring out the window. He looked a thousand miles away. I watched him for ten minutes. He did not move. There was something troubling him. I wandered over but did not say anything.

Finally, he turned to me and said, "Oh, hi, Leo."

"You okay, John?" I asked.

"Leo, we've come so far in such a short period of time. Do you ever wonder what the reason is for our success? I mean it. Sometimes it is scary to think that we are pressing the two major political parties to change the way they view us as a party. We have raised more money legally than they have from less wealthy people meaning we are not in some billionaire's back pocket. We are tallying double-digit vote counts in these primaries and we are not even on the ballot in some of them. Does this make you wonder?"

"Sure, John, I have to dope slap myself every now and then just to make sure I am awake and not dreaming."

"Leo, I have a concern. Call me a conspiracy nut, whatever. However, this campaign is going along too smoothly. We've faced little opposition. Yes, you've been shot at a couple of times, but those acts seemed more random than organized."

John stopped talking and gathered his thoughts.

"What if this is all part of a Republican plan to lose this election?" he said.

"What are you talking about, John?"

"What if you get so far ahead the Republicans pull out? They essentially have anyway. It almost seems as if there is a conspiracy by the Republicans to get Obama re-elected. When I was a kid, many of those who went through the Depression said they would never vote Republican because of Hoover. Maybe the Republicans are giving up this election to avoid a similar fate over the next 30 or 40 years."

"That's sounds crazy to me," I said. "What would they spend all that money for if they didn't want to win?"

"Who cares about the money? It's all play money to them anyway. They have so much money they don't know what else to do with it. Think about what would happen if Romney pulled out and the Republicans endorsed you. They would be trying to co-opt you as a Republican candidate hoping to use you while you're in office."

"I'd refuse to let them endorse me," I cried out.

"How can you refuse an endorsement? Huh! They are the masters of the message. They lie so much they make us think they are the only ones telling the truth. Frank Luntz and Karl Rove are two masters of this method. We are in for a rough ride in the next few months. With Santorum 'suspending' his campaign and Gingrich not campaigning but vowing to continue until the convention, their world is in turmoil."

"We are benefitting by their disgruntled electorate," I commented.

"Yes, we are but consider this. They do not like losing. If they can't control you they'd rather let Obama win."

"What? Are you serious?"

"Think about it, Leo. They can control Obama. They have their teeth into his thin skin fang deep. His campaign manager, Jim Messina, is a corporate player. He's lining up the biggest donors ever to finance his campaign. He knows Romney is a moneyman and so they are going to outspend the big spenders. In the process, the real power brokers, the donors who want to win, one way or another, are going to recognize the warning sign and put their money behind Obama. They can control him. They can control Romney. They can't control YOU."

"I'm happy to hear you say that, and it is true. What about the rest of this? Do you really think this could happen?"

John stared at me intensely. "Leo, in this political world, I think anything can happen. You're the first serious third party candidate since H. Ross Perot. He was a flyweight in comparison to you. He was a billionaire who ran the first superpac funded by him. He had enough money to spend to win the election outright."

"What stopped him?" I asked.

"I don't know this as fact, but I think he did a cost-benefit analysis and said to himself that it wasn't worth the investment of his time or money. He could have won if he wanted to do so. He got 15% of the vote as it was and that was after he essentially discontinued his campaign."

"I remember that," I said. "I wonder if what we're doing now is a result of what he did to set the stage for our effort."

"Who can tell? I am concerned that these Republican backers, when they realize that Obama is going to kick their butts, will drop Romney and back Obama and do everything they can to get him re-elected and defeat you. They don't like to lose. This is the crux of the matter."

"What do we do?"

"I don't know right now, but we need to watch for the telltale signs that there is chicanery afoot. Leo, these people love power more than anything else. Money is just a means to the end. They want to control the world. They don't care how they do it. They are not concerned about who they chew up and spit out in their quest for world domination."

"This all sounds kind of sick to me," I said.

"It is sick. There is no real reason for anyone to want to control the world. Look at all the great emperors of all time. They were in power for a while and then they all lost it. History records every one of their stories and they all end the same way. Still, these people are engaged in the same type of megalomaniac pursuits. I don't get it any more than you do, but they are dangerous. They may shroud themselves in "Tea Party" garb, but deep down inside, they are wolves and we are the sheep they want to consume."

"I think what we need to do is stay above board, keep presenting the message that we have been all along and don't let anyone deter us from running with the wind like Al's newest bumper sticker says."

"I didn't see it," John said. "I must have been encapsulated."

"Running Forward with the Wind – Leo Pollack for President".

"I like that. I really like that. What are they going to do with it?"

"Already done. Al and the kids are getting them printed and the stickers will be up on the home page in a few days. Get this. All the money raised from the sales will go toward a college scholarship fund."

"Wow! What a team!" John cried out. "Whenever I start feeling gloomy, deep, dark, November in my soul, I just have to wake up and look around and see and hear the genius at work all around me."

"I heartily agree," I said.

"See what you started, Leo. See!"

"I see and hear and am humbled by everyone's efforts."

Now I was the one staring out the window when Carol Hawley came up to me to ask a question.

"Penny for your thoughts?" she said.

"John and I were just discussing the big picture and what he thought might happen now that Romney is the likely GOP candidate. I just don't know, Carol. How does a guy like that make it in this world where so few people like him, but he's got money up the Yazoo and can buy just about anything he wants?"

"Tell me about it. You heard that he was building a new home near San Diego and that he is having elevators installed in the garage so that he can get his cars up and down inside the house."

"No way?" I cried out.

"I'm not kidding. Sounds crazy to me. I guess that is what you do with your money when you have so much that you could not spend it in a hundred lifetimes."

"I can't fathom that kind of wealth," I said. "Give me a simple life, happiness, good friends, a healthy, loving family and I'm flush as any man."

"Same for me, but some people need more to make them happy. Anyway, what I wanted to ask you was this. We are starting to make a pile of money from interest on the donations we've collected. What do you want to do with it?"

"How much are we talking about, Carol?"

She laughed. "Talk about piles of cash. We're going to make more than $600 thousand in interest for this quarter."

"What?" I exclaimed.

"Yes, I know it sounds like a lot, but I've been working with Jim at the bank and we've made some shrewd investments. Now, what do we do with it?"

"What does the rest of the team think?" I asked.

"Some think we need to hold on to it until the end of the election just so we are never short and don't end in debt. Others would like to spend it on campaign ads. I don't know. Mixed bag of ideas."

I thought for a moment and then said, "Figure out how to do it with Gram, Judy and Fritz. We can use this money to serve homeless shelters across the country. Poverty is not a choice. People don't choose to be poor. I can't speak from experience, but I don't believe that anyone really chooses to be homeless. Let's make a difference in people's lives. What do you think?"

"I like that very much," Carol said.

"How soon can you make it happen?" I asked.

"We'll get it done by the end of the week. Let's see, today is Thursday. I'd better get to work," she laughed realizing the time constraint she put herself under.

"How can we set it up so it becomes a sustainable fund?"

"I don't know, but let me work with Jim on that. Leo, when we started this campaign, I thought all we would be doing was trying to get you elected president, but this has turned out to be so much more of an adventure than I ever imagined. I don't know what it must be like for you, everyday, living out your dream. Let me tell you, I have never been so excited to come to work in all my life. This is more than just a campaign. This is a mission to change the world and I'm proud to be part of it."

Carol gave me a hearty hug and then scooted off to get the ball rolling on spending more than a half-million dollars to serve the needy.

"What wonderful people," I thought. "We're more than a NASCAR team. We're one for the ages because our effort is so much more important."

John's thoughts unnerved me. I did not want to believe there were people so concerned about power and control they would do anything to acquire it and keep it. Karl Rove was one such person who came to mind. Once, he was called "Bush's brain" referring to our last president who pretended not to be very bright. What a fox he was. He was so dumb he was elected twice as president. Yet, the theory still was floating out there that he was a "Manchurian Candidate", a programmed person groomed to become our nation's leader, but just a patsy in reality. We will never know. Mystery surrounds so much of what goes on behind Washington's closed doors. We needed to keep the clouds from hanging over us. Our mission was to become a party of the people and not the special interests groups funded by billionaires and managed by professional politicians who were their water boys. We were special. We were working people who knew how to make something with our hands. We would win. Yes, there was no doubt about it.

Was this what John was afraid of for us? Would we get co-opted somehow, bought out and then manipulated by some unknown forces that wanted national domination first, and then world domination as a collateral investment? Perhaps we would find out eventually. Today, as far as I could tell, we were still independent of those types of external forces making decisions for us. I could not remember any campaign in American, or perhaps even world history, where the candidate and his party were investing money donated by its backers to serve homeless shelters.

The day whisked us along and before any of us knew it, we were turning on the lights. We had not eaten lunch or dinner. Someone finally said, "Hey, I'm hungry."

Without a moment's hesitation, I cried out, "Let's party. Al, do we still have the grills stored in the bus?"

"Leo, Leo, what kind of party animal do you think I am? Of course we do."

"Everyone. Listen up. We'll get the meat, buns, beans and all the fixings. Let's have a barbecue right here and now. Call your families. Tell them to come on down. Call your friends. Call anyone you think needs some cheer in their life. Call the Fallers and invite them. Call the Mayor. Call our Congressman, Tim Ryan. Call Mitt Romney and President Obama. They probably could use a little break right about now. It's always time for some barbecue. What do you say? Let's have one hell of a party."

Someone shouted out, "What are we celebrating, Leo?"

"Life, Liberty and the Pursuit of Happiness!" I cried.

A loud cheer echoed throughout the building. Gram and Johnny raced up to the nearest supermarket and purchased all the food we needed. Al, his kids and I set up the grills. Other volunteers carried out tables and chairs so we could eat out under the stars. The evening was brisk but not cold. We could endure. Music blasted out from a loud speaker that Fritz rigged up. In my honor, he played a polka to get everyone in the mood to party. Families started pulling in less than fifteen minutes later. I was happy to see Basha and Janko driving up in our old jalopy. I raced over to hug them both and show them off to all my friends. Basha's beauty was radiant tonight. I was a proud man. Johnny, Gram and Al did most of the cooking. Everyone ate until he or she could not stuff one more mouthful down his or her throat. Some called for a speech from me and all I was able to say was "Thank you for all your hard work."

Later that evening, when we were finally home and Basha and I were lying in bed half-awake, she said to me, "Leo, you made a lot of people happy, you know that, but you make me the very happiest woman in the world."

"Ditto that," I whispered into her ear feeling her jerk away."

"You know what that does to me?" she said.

"I do," I confessed.

"So, what are you going to do?"

"This…"

50. The Party is Over

John's intuition proved to be prophetic. The next day, Restoring Our Future, the superpac supporting Romney, attacked us. We were accused of being paperweights in a world where a proven leader like their man was needed. The ad spoke plainly. They showed me coming out of the mill dressed in my work clothes and the narrator asked, "Is this what a President looks like?" The ad made fun of my state university education. The creators did not leave any part of my life untouched. We watched the ad a number of times so we could decide how best to address the attacks. I was not concerned about the intent. We knew this was coming. The timing was what was interesting. The moment Romney locked up the nomination, his people went to work getting down and dirty. We knew there was a whole lot more where this was coming from and we braced for an ongoing siege.

The President's campaign committee was still leaving us alone. Even though he knew our efforts would siphon votes away from him, he was playing it cool. Gram, John, Johnny and Judy wondered what was keeping him from going on the offensive. I thought it was simply that he was a decent person and did not like dirty politics. They disagreed and said eventually he would take the gloves off and we would get just as much dirt from his side of the fence as from the Republicans. Actually, they had more to lose than Romney and his people. They were already in power. The race was theirs to lose. I said it was ours to win.

The bombshell came the following day. Working People United, a superpac funded by unknown wealthy people, started to run attack ads against Obama and Romney on my behalf. The superpac left nothing to the imagination. The attacks were virulent. In their world view, Romney was a cult figure and Obama was a Muslim. We were shocked by what we saw and heard.

"We've got to stop this crap," I raged in a meeting of the minds at the hall.

"What can you do, Leo?" John said. "This is America. This is post Citizens United. Now you have Working People United exercising its constitutional rights. It's ugly. It sucks, but it is what it is."

"Can't we file a law suit against them?" I asked Johnny. "There must be something we can do?"

"What we can do is get them to stop using your name. You have the right to protect the use of it anywhere and anytime. However, the intent of their ads will still be to support you and attack the others and that runs contrary to what you've wanted to do all along."

"So what else can we do?" I asked.

"We can go on the offensive and let the world know that unless you are in the ad and specifically say 'My name is Leo Pollack and I approve this message' it is counterfeit, against what we believe and we are vehemently protesting. This may do it, but the damage is being done no matter what," Judy concluded.

We sat in dismay. What a bummer! To think that just a few days ago, we were celebrating the institution of the Faller Work Connection, a college scholarship fund wholly funded by the sale of bumper stickers, and most of all, continued support from working people all across the country, this turn of events was downright disheartening.

"John, you knew something was about to break," I said. "Thanks for the forewarning. I guess I am too naïve to believe that the world is not made up of good guys and gals."

"It is, Leo," Gram said. "They are not in politics, that's all. They do social services, teach school, become nurses, therapists, and serve their fellow humans. These power brokers are a breed all their own. I used to see them when I was in the Air Force. They were the full birds, the political players who didn't really care about the service. They cared about their careers. They didn't fly planes. They flew bull crap. They were what made the Air Force less than it could be."

"Look at where these guys learn their trade," Johnny said. "The first course I took in law school was entitled 'Legal Writing' and what it entailed was how to write in vague, confusing, indirect English. I was appalled at what I was being taught. When I was foolish enough to ask the why question, I was pounced on. 'Son, you want to be a lawyer, you learn how to write, and talk and act like a lawyer. There is no room for clarity in our profession. Our world is predicated on obfuscation. You hear me, boy.' I heard him loud and clear. Most politicians in Washington are lawyers. Most of these superpac operators are lawyers. They know what they are doing. It's disgusting."

"No wonder there are so many lawyer jokes in the world," Al said. "Other than you, Johnny, I never met a lawyer that I liked. They all suck in my book."

"Suck what? Gram asked.

"You know what," Al said.

"We're getting off track," I said. "What are we going to do?"

The team sat quietly for a while and considered all that we had discussed.

"I think we find out who's behind this Working People United organization. They can't be that hard to track down," John said. "Fritz, can you and Johnny get at it from the tech and legal sides?"

"We can do our best," Fritz said. "You know me. If there is a crack, I'll slide through it and see what's hiding on the other side."

"Johnny, what legal options do we have?"

"Thinking," Johnny said.

"Don't think too hard. You might bust a gasket," Al chortled.

"This is serious, Al," I said. "We've got a major fight on our hands and it is with people who are invisible except when what they are promoting can be seen on the boob tube and can be heard on the radio and it is affecting what we are trying to do."

"Sorry, Leo," Al said graciously.

"No problem, but from now on we've got to know when to play and when to get serious. Folks. I'm concerned. Really concerned we are in over our heads. I know what you said the other day, John, and now I'm feeling the pinch. Are we up to the task? Can we take on these billionaire polo players and their cohorts and make a run for the goal? I'm serious. Can we?"

There was dead silence in the room. I could tell that my words had had a profound effect on the thinking of everyone intimately involved with the campaign. I let the pregnant pause run its course.

Big Jack broke the silence. Generally, he attended our team meetings, but said very little. He was a profound active listener. Jack did not miss anything. His eyes were focused, but his ears were fine-tuned to the nuances of everything being said. "Folks, I'm not one to mince words. These bastards are pissing me off. We try and do good and they come along and want to steal our thunder. I don't like it. Crush them. Find out who they are and make their lives miserable. There is too much at stake to let these fools come along and mess up what we've worked so hard to build. I mean it. Smash them. Squash them like the cockroaches they are."

Everyone sat stunned after listening to the intensity of Jack's message. His eyes glared and his body was rigid. We knew he was serious. Rarely, did we experience this side of him. Time was trapped like a mouse under the spring-loaded bail.

"Jack, if you could bust their chops, how would you do it?" Gram asked.

"Find out who they are and make their lives miserable, that's how," he retorted. "Look, there is playing nice and then there is playing for keeps. I grew up in the streets. These punks don't know what grab ass really is. They are your upper north side kind of dudes that think this is just a game. We're dealing in reality here. This campaign isn't about winning or losing an election. This is about the hopes, dreams and fears of a whole nation of real working people. Working People United, my ass. I'll bet they are being funded by guys like the Koch Brothers just to stir up crap for us. They want to win so badly, they'll lie, cheat and steal our good intent to serve their sick vision."

"You didn't answer my question, Gram continued. "What would you do? Make their lives miserable?"

"That's for me to know and you to find out," Jack said scornfully.

"Jack, we can't go rogue, man," I said. "We can't do things that are illegal. This would defeat everything we believe in and have tried to create since the beginning of this campaign."

"Leo, I've been with you since the beginning I know what we're trying to do. I'm not a fool, man. I know what time of day it is. These guys hit a nerve when they equated themselves to us: Working People United. What a kick in the balls. I mean it."

"What would you do?" I asked.

"I know you don't want to go negative. I realize you don't want me to go find out who these punks are and kick their asses. What we need to do is get their identities and expose them for who and what they are. They aren't working people. They are the vermin who play on the fears of true working people. They are the very same scum that made the Affordable Care Act into Obamacare and something to be reviled. I mean it, Leo. I won't sleep until they are so naked in the eyes of the public that their little dicks are flapping in the wind."

Everybody started laughing at the image Jack was describing.

"Can we make this happen?" I asked the team in general. "Everything but the flapping that is."

Discussion went back and forth on who was going to do what, how we would coordinate the effort and when we would launch an assault on the superpac.

"I think we get Jennifer Williamson from the New York Times involved," Gram said. "The weight of that paper investigating the activities of this organization will go a long way to discredit what they are doing."

"I agree," John said. "We need to step up our own ads, Judy, and get Leo's face out there every hour on the hour wherever we can."

"That's going to cost money, lots of money," Carol said.

"We don't have a choice, do we? What did we raise all that money for but to run an effective campaign? We have to do what we have to do," John said.

"Please, Carol, can we make sure that this effort does not affect any of the initiatives we've undertaken? I know we've raised a lot of money for the campaign and we are doing well in so many ways. I'd hate to see that end."

"Leo, we'll make it all happen. Trust me," she said.

"I do, and thanks, Carol and all of you for being willing to be rational and not go the way the other campaigns most assuredly will. Politics do not have to be dirty. We can be better. We must be or we have done nothing to make America and its electoral process something we can take pride in and hold our heads high in doing so."

"One thing about you, Leo, that will never change," Johnny said, "and that is your idealism. Maybe I should have gone to work in a steel mill. Maybe I'd see the world differently. Maybe."

"You would. Trust me. Right, Al?"

"You bet, Leo. You'd see the business end of a shovel, a full blown assault on your lungs by graphite and ore dust, and sore muscles and joints that never quit aching."

"Not to mention the joy of working with a bunch of great guys who come to your aid when you walk up to them and say, 'Hey fellows, I'm running for president. Want to help out?' and they show up without even asking what the job pays and are there any benefits."

We laughed together for the first time in hours.

"Jack, can I trust you won't go rogue on me?" I asked him in front of the others.

He stared at me. The whites glittered like diamonds in sunlight. The black irises were holes in the cosmos. "You have my word on it, Leo. I have to let things out now and then. I'm not going to go and bust any kneecaps nor smash a few heads against locker walls now or in the near future. You can count on that. I sure would like to do so, but that's out."

"Thanks, you know what we are about and can't violate it for any reason," I added.

"Done," Jack said emphatically.

Our discussion continued for another hour or two and then it was time to get down to the real business of running a campaign.

"Hey, Leo, no party, now?" Gram cracked at me.

"Sure, Gram, let's party. You get the lowdown on these guys and then we can invite them to a block party where we expose them to the entire world and make them look like the chumps they are," I said.

"Let's all do what we can to make this situation a learning experience for us as we move forward," John said. "We're going to face more and more curve balls as the game goes on."

"Let them keep pitching, because I think Leo's ready to hit whatever they give us out of the park," Al said.

"That ball is going, going, going, gone. It's a home run, and Leo Pollack is taking his good old time rounding the bases and heading toward home, 1700 Pennsylvania Avenue, Washington, D.C.," Gram called out.

We stood up and high fived one another as I crossed the plate.

51. This Little Light of Mine, I'm going to Let It Shine

We decided to let the Superpac continue to run its ads without any commentary on our part. The next day, Snopes.com editor, Jim Pritchett, emailed us and said that their group was investigating the Superpac's claims and would have some definitive word for us on who was responsible for their enterprise.

"See," Gram said, "goodness does exist in the world."

"How did they know we were concerned about what "Working People United" was doing?"

Gram just smiled.

"You," I said.

"Who else?"

"Amazing."

"Actually, Judy got a call from Snopes. They wanted to know what we knew. She told them that we were not responsible for any of their claims. They said they would check it out. They did. I told you we didn't have to do anything. Others would expose this superpac's activities for us."

"I'm surprised that it was handled so quickly."

"Leo, there is something phony about these candidates and I'm sure that it is 'shachor'," Gram said.

"What is that?" I asked.

"Let me share a little of my Jewish history with you. You know my history after my Catholic upbringing."

"Be my guest," I said.

"This might shine a little light on what we are experiencing right now."

"You mean the beginning of attacks against us?"

"That and much more. Anyway, a few years ago, my Rabbi told me a story. He was asked 'What do you think about the Messianic Rabbi? He said he told the person the guy wasn't a Rabbi. He was a fake. Messianic Judaism is actually Christianity. They use Jewish customs to actively try to lure Jewish youth away from Judaism and to trick Christians into thinking they are Jewish. Anyway, that's the Jewish viewpoint. Mine is a little different. I recognized most converts came through Messianic Judaism to Judaism. I considered it a stepping-stone. Any path to God is a good one. The bottom line is how people behave towards other people. Customs can provide learning, but they are a path, not the ending. When my Rabbi asked me what I thought, I answered, 'I don't.' All the things my Rabbi said only made my Rabbi smaller in my eyes and I told him so. We don't fight falsehood. Falsehood contains its own demise. The word for falsehood in Hebrew is 'Shachor.' It means a crack in the pottery covered over with wet clay and then sold before firing. When it is fired, it breaks. Once a potter is known to produce pottery with cracks, the people learn and then never buy anything from that potter. They won't even buy good pottery if he changes his ways. The people recognize Romney is shachor or false. We do not need to do a thing. Pay no more attention to him than you pay to horse crap on the trail. Just walk around it. Trying to stamp it out or clean it up just makes it worse."

"This sounds like sage advice," I commented.

"Take it for what it is worth. We don't want any more light to shine on Romney or Obama than there already is. Their superpac spotlight machines will be illuminating them 24/7 from now until November 6."

Johnny told me, "I called a very quiet private investigator. She is somewhat mentally challenged, but she is a savant in digging up people's backgrounds from public sources. She has numerous tattoos and rings in all the loose flesh I can see and probably more where I can't see. Once she finds the group behind this, she will figuratively taser their balls with their own secrets and you won't hear from them again. The sudden stop of the ads will send a very clear message that something happened and everyone will be on notice not to mess with us."

"I don't know if I like this kind of stuff going on in the background," I said to Johnny. "The way you're describing what she is doing sounds a whole lot like 'dirty tricks'. This kind of behavior can really backfire on us, you know."

"Yah, yah, I know, Leo, but sometimes we have to fight fire with fire. These rats get over because they hide in the dark. The only way to get them exposed is to shine light on them and that is what she is going to do once she finds out who they are."

"Johnny, let's not get carried away. I mean it. We might win this battle but then we lose the war in the face of public opinion. We will overcome this crap just by letting it wither on the vine. Give it no moisture and it will die."

"I hear you, pal, but sometimes you have to be a little proactive when it comes to making sure that things do die."

"Johnny, are you listening to me?"

"I got it, Leo."

Every day brought new challenges. Big Jack continued to expand his sphere of protection to include all the families of those who worked for the campaign. "We can't be too safe," he said to me. "My concern is that someone gets co-opted by the enemies and we start to see internal documents and other valuable information begins to drift out from the confines of our campaign and end up in the hands of the Republicans or Democrats."

"Any inkling that this has happened?" I asked.

"No, and I'm happy to report that all the vetting we've done on our people has paid off. In fact, most of those working down in the cellar welcomed our inquiries. They did not want to be perceived as being a liability to the campaign. You can't believe, Leo, how loyal these people are to you. I mean it. They'd give their lives for this effort to succeed."

"I sure hope they don't have to do anything like that," I proclaimed.

"I don't either, but we will give them all the support that they need as long as we are in the business of electioneering," Jack said.

"Jack, how safe are we really? Be blunt, will you?"

Big Jack stared at me. He was assessing me to determine how much I could handle. I could see the wheels spinning.

"Jack, I can handle it."

His coal black eyes burned a hole right through me. "Leo, we are always one step away from a tragedy. These guys are playing for keeps. They won't be obvious. They will try something soon to stifle our forward progress. I don't know what it will be. Maybe they'll resort to more violence, but I think that would be counterproductive. These superpacs are just getting wound up. Soon, we'll be hearing how we're worse than Osama bin Laden. I mean it. They will compare you to a terrorist because you're undermining the 'good ole boy' network the Republicans and Democrats have created in the past 50 years. We'll be ready. This I promise you," Jack concluded.

"I know you will, Jack. What happens, happens. We can't be prepared for the sky falling in."

"Oh yes, we can," he cried out and finished by saying, "when it does, we'll use a sky hook to lift it back up again and clean up the mess quickly."

We laughed at his reference to the mythical tool that we used to wish we had in the mill whenever a heavy lift needed to be made.

Al told me the bus was ready for Johnstown. "We should have a good trip over there," he said. "Johnstown is a really friendly blue-collar place. They've been flooded out three times and they still keep rebuilding. Kind of tells you something about the people, the place. They don't know what the word quit means."

"How are things at home with you, Al? I know we've been gone a lot and it must be a little rough on Marie."

"We're doing fine," Al said. "I think they like me out of the house. You know, when I'm not working I'm a bear to live with and my being gone just makes their lives easier."

"You really are like that?" I asked him seriously.

"You bet. I don't like being out of harness. I guess I'm just an old draft horse that needs to work all the time. Leo, what would I do now if I didn't have the campaign? I'd weigh 300 pounds in six months. No, you're running for president makes my life interesting, productive and busy and that's the way I like it. You see what I mean?"

"I sure do, Al, and I'm happy that what we're doing makes everything in your life just a little brighter."

Basha enjoyed making lunch for the crew. We stopped most every afternoon and ate whatever she prepared for us. Johnny and Gram were always appreciative of whatever she made because they were not used to steady home cooking. The way they fussed over her, you would think she was the Queen of America. I know they secretly admired her beauty. Johnny fawned over her like a teenage boy. She went along with his program because he was so respectful toward her. He was never ignorant nor inappropriate. I think she really enjoyed the fact she was the object of more than my admiration. I had told her for many years that any man who could get his hands on her would consider her a 'fine catch'. I never thought she believed me. Now, with Gram and Johnny around, she was beginning to realize that I had always told her the truth, from a man's point of view.

These days, when we were not anticipating another long journey, were a treasure to all of us. The road wore anyone down. There was a need to recharge the batteries so that they could power the campaign and light the way through the darkness. I was not sure how others did it. Perhaps, they were tougher than I was, but I could not see how. After all, I worked swing shifts and learned how to be productive at any time of the day or night. I knew the hardest times were coming. We were almost through the primary campaign season. Romney was taking the lead in the Republican Party. Obama came out swinging a number of times when the attacks became too virulent to ignore. The time was ripe for the real struggle to begin.

The lull in the action only spurred us to be eternally vigilant lest we were broadsided by some information that would throw us into a tailspin and make us scurry around and do damage control. Gram and Johnny could sense my restlessness and assured me they had everything under control.

"How can you say that when none of us knows what the Higher Power has in store for any of us?" I asked them.

"We know you, pal. Sit still and take a load off your feet. Play some cards with Basha. Read a book. Do something to relax," they each encouraged me in their own way.

I did not listen to them. I was hard headed. I needed to be, like Al said, in harness. I was a worker bee not a queen.

These quiet moments gave me time to ponder things. I wondered what happened to most of the caravaners. By the end of our extensive road trip, we had more than a 1000 people following us. Their loyalty was amazing. Disbanding happened as quickly as forming. One day they were behind the Liberty Bell Bus. The next day they were gone. If we announced a new tour, would they return? I hoped so because they were a classy group of people. They were the true believers. They carried the torch and held it high wherever we traveled. Sometimes, I missed the road, the daily movement, the running forward. Though I missed the road, I missed the caravaners even more. They were the light at the end of the tunnel. I could always see because they were pointing the way for me. Even though the bus was often in the lead, they were the tail on Pollack's Comet that shone like a beacon.

We cherished the quiet moments. We knew they would not last. They would disappear like Snickers bars on Halloween Night when kids traveled around and cried out, "Trick or Treat!" and we would opt to treat them kindly.

52. The VEEP Stakes

As we traveled to Johnstown, Pennsylvania for our second town hall debate, we discussed the current Republican VEEP stakes. Gram was concerned that Romney might actually pick a winning ticket and we would have to match our choice with theirs for strengthening our chances. Johnny's opinion was we needed to hit a home run with our VEEP selection. Al said the VP nominee had better be as clean as a whistle or we would pay a dear price for nominating him or her. I understood the importance of selecting someone who exceeded expectations. However, with the Republican presidential nominee almost guaranteed to be Romney, his campaign picked a woman to head his VP vetting committee.

"A presidential candidate has two political priorities for his second-in-command: That the candidate helps and does not hurt the campaign," Gram said. "For Romney, this breaks down as follows: A candidate can help by providing the former Massachusetts governor cover from the right, recruiting some votes from the center or left, or by helping capture the candidate's home state or region. A candidate can hurt Romney by overshadowing the campaign, either with questions about his or her fitness for the top office."

"Like Quayle and Palin did in their respective campaigns," Johnny added.

"Reaching a bit farther back, you recall Thomas Eagleton of Missouri throwing the 1972 McGovern ticket into total chaos when it was revealed he was treated with shock therapy for depression and possible alcoholism."

"That leaves me out for a VP nominee," Al said jokingly.

"Romney has a lot of folks from which to choose," I said. "I wonder if he will go outside his ideological boundaries and pick someone who will clearly align him with the party's conservative base."

"He has to do that or he's done," Johnny said.

"I think he should pick Rick Santorum," Al said. "The former senator was his strongest competitor, and clearly, the party regulars liked him. What keeps the nominee from choosing his strongest rival to be his running mate?"

"You know what I think," I said. "Romney doesn't really like Santorum. My intuition tells me that deep down inside, Romney resents Santorum's attacks on him and Santorum's making it harder for Romney to win the nomination. As for Gingrich, they were ideological foes from the start. I think Romney doesn't like Gingrich either because the former speaker is such a blowhard."

"That leaves Ron Paul," Al said. "Anyone can tell he won't pick him because Paul is already 76 years old. He would definitely be a liability."

"Right on," I said.

"Let's look at who leads in the race and their individual potential for helping or harming Romney's chances," Gram said.

"According to some recent polls, Marco Rubio is 23 percent likely to gain the nod from Romney, an extremely high likelihood for a race categorized by uncertainty. He would provide cover for Romney from the right and he could possibly draw Latino supporters from the center or left," Gram concluded.

"That's right, he's Cuban-American," Johnny said. "On the other hand, he does not have much experience in the public spotlight and arguably has a few small skeletons in his closet that have come to light as the media has begun to scrutinize him more closely."

"There is a big potential upside and a medium potential downside," Gram added.

"I don't like the guy," I said. "He comes off as holier than thou. Guys like him make me want to go wash my hands and face because there is slime dripping from them."

"Pretty strong words, Leo," Johnny said. "What gives you such a visceral reaction to him?"

"What caused me to question him was his confusing story about his parent's flight to America. He made it sound like he was a Castro refugee. The fact is his family came to the US a few years before the Cuban Revolution. He is not a refugee."

"Interesting," Gram said. "I didn't know that."

"Now you do," Johnny commented.

"Rob Portman, a freshman senator from another big swing state, Ohio, follows Rubio with a 13 percent likelihood of being selected. Of the people listed in Romney's medium list, he is probably the least known. In endorsing Portman for the job, the Ohio Dispatch refers to him as 'safe and sensible'. Their argument is that he is a reliable conservative, but does not scare moderates and liberals. He would provide cover for Romney from archconservatives and his longer record of accomplishment of solid, non-confrontational public service should make him safe and not embarrass the campaign. Portman provides medium upside potential and low potential downside."

"In other words, blah," Johnny concluded. "I've listened to this guy. He's a blank. Romney needs someone to put some juice into his campaign. Portman is a duller version of Romney, in my opinion."

"I don't like him," Al said. "He's not for working men and women."

"Then he's an ideal Republican candidate, Al," Gram added.

"Next we have the lollapalooza candidate, Chris Christie, governor of New Jersey. He is rated at about 11 percent likelihood. As a moderate Republican, Christie could help Romney with moderate voters, but he will provide no cover from the right. Further, his combative style will be risky when the media film him daily. Attacks on constituents may play well at times with constituents, but is not what a presidential campaign wants dominating its nightly coverage. Christie presents medium potential upside with a medium potential downside."

"The guy needs to lose about 200 pounds. He's a disgrace," Al said. "He's a heart attack waiting to happen."

"I agree," Johnny said. "Do you remember the flack he got into over the use of the new emergency helicopter paid for by Homeland Security monies to fly to one of his son's baseball games?"

"Oh, yah, I remember that story," Gram said. "What a fiasco!"

"Sure was. He flew to the game. Landed near the ball field and then had a state limo pick him up and drive him, get this, 100 yards to the bleachers."

"No way," Al cried out. "He's lazier than I am."

"So what happened?" Johnny asked.

"Citizens made a big stink about it and he got all surly with the people and the press. He said he was a busy person and needed to get around quickly. The rest of the story is this. He left the game early and went back to the Governor's mansion to meet with a number of influential Arkansas business people who were pushing him to run for president," Gram said.

"Really," Johnny cried out. "Now isn't that special. Fly to and from your son's game in a government helicopter and get outraged when the people hold you accountable. What a hypocrite!"

"Eventually, he paid for the use of the helicopter and the limo, but only after the people held his feet to the fire," Gram said. "Christie is not someone that will play well with conservatives. He is a moderate through and through with some right wing leaning."

"Who's next on their short list?" Johnny asked.

"Old Bob McDonnell had a farm, the governor of Virginia, is in fourth place with 7 percent likelihood based upon the polling. Prior to mid-February, McDonnell looked like a better-known Portman in a similarly large swing state. He backed, and then ultimately withdrew his support, for a bill that would require all women seeking an abortion in an early stage to receive an ultrasound requiring a vaginal probe. If Romney chooses him as his running mate, this debate will become central to the campaign and, due to his sinking poll numbers among educated women, it is a fight that the Romney campaign does not want to wage."

"That guy looks like he spends $400 on his haircuts," Al said. "He's a cutey pie, he is. I'll bet he spends more money grooming his hair than his wife does."

"Sounds like you don't like the guy," Gram said.

"I don't like the guy's looks. He reminds me of Romney. He's a pretty boy. I'll bet he wouldn't last one day in the mill," Al concluded.

"What do we know about him?" Johnny asked.

"Not much. He's a social, fiscal and religious conservative that rode the 2010 wave into power. He's been slapped around a few times over some of his plans. The most recent was support and subsequent withdrawal of his backing for the ultrasound amendment. Women were all over him on this one. He backed down. Romney will think twice about this governor who actually was a part of what the press is calling the 'war on women.'"

"I don't like him," Al said. "He's squirrelly."

"Who's left?" I asked.

"None other than Mr. Paul Ryan. He is in fifth place with 6 percent likelihood. In one sense, the congressman from Wisconsin is already running with Romney, as the media ties Romney to Ryan's polarizing budget proposals. They consistently call for massive tax and spending cuts, with deficit reduction to come from unnamed closes in tax loopholes. Ryan provides Romney cover from the right and possibility some centrist support. Ryan risks massive alienation from the left and would overshadow Romney, as the media might defer to him as the more consistent ideas guy."

"If Romney wants an ideas guy, he ought to pick Gingrich. After all, 'by the end of my second term as president, we'll have a state on the moon,' Gingrich said. Remember that malarkey?" Johnny recalled.

"I don't think Romney will pick Ryan. He would place Romney at risk with independent and progressive voters."

"That's only five candidates? Amazing isn't it. Out of the entire United States, these are the only people that are available to Mitt Romney as VEEP candidates," I said.

"There are more. Anyone else represents nearly a 50 percent likelihood of being selected. Recent nominations such as Palin were hard to anticipate a few months away, and we should not discount that possibility again this year," Gram said.

"Who might be the wild cards?" Johnny asked.

"I don't really know," Gram said. "The woman governor from South Carolina, Nikki Haley, might be one of them."

"No way?" Al said. "She's a lightweight."

"What makes you say that?"

"I just don't like her," Al said.

"Actually Al, she's a heavyweight. She's the first woman to become the governor of South Carolina. On top of that, she is a minority woman, an Indian. I'd say she was more than a lightweight," Gram concluded.

"She won't get the bid for VEEP," Johnny said. "She's too controversial. She's a Tea Party favorite. This would move Romney off to the fringe again."

For a while, we rode along and enjoyed the tapestry of the rich Pennsylvania farmland. Being in the central tier of the Commonwealth, the land was almost equally divided between forested plots and picturesque farms. The highway we followed was a roller coaster ride, and around each bend, we were treated to another spectacular vista.

"I can understand why people like living in Pennsylvania," Gram said. "The natural beauty is inspirational. Many of these scenes could be on picture postcards."

"Yes, but then you have to deal with the people," Johnny said. "They are very parochial. I don't find this appealing."

"Parochial in what way?" Gram asked.

"If you aren't from here, then you're condemned to be an outsider the rest of your life. Your grandparents have to have been born here for you to be accepted into the group. Places like this I don't find appealing."

"Neither would I," I said. "What difference does it make where you were born? If you're an American, you ought to be accepted for who and what you are."

"Don't judge me by the color of my skin, but by the content of my character," Gram said. "I agree. People who are like that are ignorant."

"What will we find in Johnstown, today?" Johnny said.

"I'm hoping a very supportive, jubilant and excited crowd," Gram offered.

We did.

As in our first town hall debate, Gram and Judy arranged with the mayor to serve as the host.

Mayor Tom Trigona met us at the Cambria County War Memorial Arena, a 4000 seat multi-purpose venue. We were ushered into a side entrance and given time to prepare. The mayor made us feel very welcome by saying, "I think you're going to have one heck of a time with Johnstownians. Too bad the other two fellows didn't see fit to come along, but that is their loss and our gain."

Fifteen minutes later, I was on stage before a packed house. What a remarkable sight that was.

Questions came at me fast and furiously. I was happy to be doing another public appearance because this was the essence of campaigning. The seriousness of the questions indicated to me that these folks were sophisticated voters. They were not going to accept the okey-doke. They were discriminating people given to asking the tough questions and expecting complete answers, not just sound bites. I could not tell what the predominant age, gender or race was. The audience was definitely mixed and this added to the complexity of the questions. The Trayvon Martin story prompted a few questions and these were difficult to field without making someone upset.

"The question was what is my opinion of the entire Trayvon Martin case? First of all, a young man is dead and this is a tragedy. He was only seventeen years old. Was he the aggressor or the antagonist in this situation, hopefully, the trial will clarify? What right does anyone have to use lethal force to protect life and property? In this matter, it is not clear that lethal force was necessary. Again, the trial will present us with more of the facts. I do not believe that we need to carry arms to be safe in our towns and cities. When we get to this point, there is a need to revise the way we are living our lives. I hope I don't ever have to carry a firearm to feel safe. If you feel the need to do so, then do it. As for me, I want to live differently and that means without the need to carry."

On and on, the questions came flowing like widgets on a conveyor belt. I was not upset that we would be here for hours. This was the juice. I was ready for a long afternoon. We were guaranteed to have it.

"Regarding Medicare and Medicaid, yes, they need to be revised. There is no doubt in my mind that the long-term solvency of each program is being questioned. However, the Republicans are bent on eviscerating the programs. I am for saving and improving them. Too many people are dependent upon their life-sustaining support. Those who cannot afford health care need these two safety nets to catch them. After all, my fellow citizens, we are not talking about strangers. We're talking about Americans who, for whatever reason, may have fallen on hard times. I believe we owe it to our friends and neighbors to look out for them when they are in need. This is what Christians do, is it not?"

The time passed like water flowing down the Juniata River. I was enchanted with the questions referring to the environment.

"Yes, the Army Corps of Engineers needs to continue working on making Johnstown as flood-proof as possible. There is no doubt in my mind that another major flood will come again. Mother Nature is predictable. Where she floods once, you can rest assured she will flood again."

The toughest question came near the end and I could not answer it.

"No, I have not decided upon a vice-presidential running mate. Yes, I am very much aware that Governor Romney is vetting possible running mates as we speak. We were discussing this issue on the way here today and did not come up with any answers. I would like to ask you, as a group, who would be someone you could support as my running mate. You see, the candidate picks someone based upon political considerations. I would like to have a running mate who was more than competent to take over in the event that something happens to me. I believe this is the most important criteria for selecting a running mate. Now, with that said, I believe that the people should be more involved in the selection process. I would not mind having a running mate that was not necessarily tied to me by the hip, if that image makes sense to you. Sometimes differing points of view are healthy in leaders. Anyway, we would appreciate your input. Go to **www.ringingthelibertybell.org** and give us your point of view."

Once the formal debate was over, I milled around in the crowd for another hour or two and answered more questions. These were as intense as the formal ones, some even more so. People wanted their leader to be prepared to handle all contingencies. I did my best to convince them I was up to the task. I think they saw and heard that I was.

Mayor Trigona invited us to have dinner with him and the members of the city council. We readily accepted. He took us to a local diner that served, what he said, was the "finest home cooking in the county." He was not joking. The food was excellent and the company illustrative. We paid for our own meals even though the Mayor wanted to treat the team.

"You have to understand," I said. "We are trying to do everything on the up and up and it starts in simple situations like this."

"Mr. Pollack, I am pleased that you are walking the straight and narrow. We are not offended at all. Too bad more politicians are not like you. We see the opposite all too often. We experience people walking around with their hands out and expecting that we grease their palms before they get any work done. Thank you for being above the fray," Mayor Trigona concluded, "and thank you for choosing Johnstown as your debate venue and on the way to a great victory in November."

"You're sentiment is most appreciated," I said, shaking his hand.

Leaving Johnstown on US 219, we crossed the famous Juniata River that flooded the city three times, and headed for the PA Turnpike. Our day was nearly completed. I made coffee for the team while we chatted about the time spent in this central Pennsylvania city.

"We impressed the people," Gram said. "There were more people, for us than against us."

"What I noticed was their acceptance of the need for a government that works for the people," Johnny said. "They were not into stripping government down to its skivvies."

"I liked that baked apple pie," Al said. "It's been a long time since I had any pie that delicious."

"You would mention that now, wouldn't you," Johnny said. "I wanted a second piece but Leo wouldn't hear of it."

"What? Johnny, what are you mumbling about?" I asked.

"You seemed in a hurry to get on home," he said.

"I am. I want to be sleeping in my own bed tonight. How about you? You want to spend the night on the fold-out couch?"

"No, funny guy."

"Hush up. We'll be home by midnight and then we can sleep like normal people. God knows these close to home engagements are going to end sooner than later. Let's enjoy them while we can, shall we?"

By midnight, the Liberty Bell Bus was parked in front of the house. We were dreaming of the day when the American people would vote for the next president of the United States and my name would be on the ballot in every state in the nation.

53. The Path to Heaven is Full of Sinners and Believers

No matter how virulent the campaigns would become, we vowed to stay above the fray and continue to spread a message that working people could believe. When Santorum dropped out of the race, Gingrich curtailed his campaign activities and Paul disappeared from the radar screen, Romney went immediately on the attack. He started to sound a lot like Gingrich in the way he characterized President Obama as having failed to do anything of substance he starting governing in 2009. According to Romney, Obama failed to produce results with the economy, the wars, the jobs programs, and in foreign and in domestic affairs. Listening to him, an alien arriving in America would wonder what President Obama has been doing the past three and half years. Wherever President Obama went in the country to make a speech or raise money, Romney's political machine would show up the same day or the next and try to upstage him. In Ohio, Romney sent his campaign bus to circle the building where the president was giving a speech. The move was tacky, but they did it anyway.

We moved on to what we believed were the important matters of the day: the economy, work, education, ending the war, housing, infrastructure and trust in government. There was no end to the work needing done. We accepted the mission with joy and enthusiasm. We knew we had a short time to win the hearts and minds of the people who were still uncommitted. These Americans would make or break our campaign. We were unwilling to give up on anyone.

Our mailing campaign was top notch. Every American household received a copy of our message. We sent them a free window poster and bumper sticker. "Running Forward with the Wind – Leo Pollack for President". "When America Works, Democracy Thrives. Leo Pollack for President". Our campaign coffers were brimming with cash so we were willing to take the excess and send to all Americans whom we believed our constituents, these simple messages.

A day later, the unthinkable happened.

We were gearing up for a town hall debate in Utica, New York when we received a message from the Romney campaign stating they were willing to appear on stage with us. Gram and Judy were in shock. They negotiated with the Romney surrogates for nearly two hours before they came to some agreement about what the debate would look like. They called everyone to the powwow room and let us know what was happening.

All of us were in shock.

"What does this mean?" I finally asked.

"Romney realizes that he has to take votes back from you. He can't continue to let you go on 'debating' across the country and not participate and get in his two cents worth," Gram said.

"He's running scared now. He beat up his party pals, but now he's got to go against the real heavyweights: Obama and Pollack," Judy said.

"What do we do?" I asked.

"Invite him. But listen to this, team," Gram said. "We don't change the rules. The people are still in charge of the debate. We'll get the mayor to be the host like in the others. We don't change for him. He has to change for us."

"Will he accept these ground rules?" Johnny asked.

"He'll accept them or he won't be able to participate," Gram said.

"Their campaign people argued long and hard to have the questions pre-screened," Judy said. "We adamantly said no. This was a people's debate, not some dog and pony show. They didn't like it, they can lump it. We set the stage for the people to lead the way, not some moderator or the press that is disconnected from the people."

"Unbelievable," Al said. "We got them to double down. How cool is that?"

"Now we've got to prepare for the hardball questions," Gram said. "Leo, when do you want to get to work?"

"As soon as possible," I said.

"Give Judy and me some time to tie up the loose ends with the Romney people, and we can get right to it."

"Sounds good to me," I said.

"Folks, I always knew they would come around," John Gallagher said. "The path to heaven is full of sinners and believers. Once I was a sinner, and now I'm a true believer. All good things come to those who wait."

Rainbows always appear after the storm. Some claim they are God's message to mankind that there will always be another day to fix what was broken, to be kind where unkindness once ruled and to ask forgiveness for wrongs committed.

If it was unthinkable that the Romney political machine would contact us, the call from the Obama camp blew our socks off. John fielded the call because Gram and Judy were still haggling with the Romney people about the ground rules, the date of the event and other trivial matters that were merely their way to try to assert their authority.

We did not hear about the Obama call until John was able to calm down and gather us together again. For a few moments, he was coy. We knew he had something to tell us, but we just accepted his recalcitrance as a little abnormal. Finally he said, "While you folks were dickering with those Romney small fry, I was handling the big Enchilada."

"The what?" Al asked.

"Speak English, John," Gram cried out.

"Oh, you want English, okay. How about this? The word is out that Romney has accepted the invitation to debate. Not to be outdone, who else do you think wants a piece of the action?"

"No way! No fricking way?" Gram cried out.

"You mean…"Johnny asked.

"Right on," Al said. "I knew it would happen sooner or later."

"Who?" I asked.

"Who do you think?" John said.

"The President," Big Jack chimed in. "He had to take the bait sooner or later. He's being left behind. He knows it and he's got to come out of hiding and face Romney and us. Now we have him and that other punk where we want them. They'll be exposed. They can run but they can't hide from the truth. Leo, this is the best thing that could happen. We're going to make the world see just what fakes they both are."

We sat in utter disbelief. Who would ever have thought that in one day the entire political landscape would shift in our favor?

"Folks, this is a red letter day," I said. "Utica, here we come."

"I always knew this would happen," Al said again. "I could feel it in my bones."

"I thought you might feel arthritis first," Gram joked.

"No, really. I mean it. I felt all along that our campaign would make the others change to fit what we are doing. We've been calling the shots for quite a while now and they've just gotten the message. I love it. Leo, this is what makes this whole effort worthwhile," Al concluded.

"Al, you were the first person to show up and give me your vote of approval. We've come a long way, baby," I said shaking his hand.

"We sure have," Al replied.

"We've got a lot of coordination to do," John said. "Let's divide up the labor and get to it. Strike while the iron is hot."

"One thing to make sure we do is contact the New York Times and give Jennifer Williamson the scoop," Gram said. "She will lead the field with this story. We owe her a lot and this may earn her the Pulitzer. I'll handle it."

Silence caught us again. We sat and looked at one another. Then, spontaneously, we all busted out laughing, a deep, belly jiggling kind of laughter that brought tears to our eyes. All over the building, people could hear us and came up to see what was happening. When one of us was sane enough to tell them, they joined in with us. Soon, the entire building was electric with unbounded joy. The hard work was paying off. Loud chatter echoed from every nook and cranny. The enthusiasm went viral. The phones were ringing off the hook. The campaigns reluctantly agreed to abide by the guidelines we set and this added to the gaiety. We knew neither limits nor boundaries. We were changing the political paradigm and it felt exhilarating. We captured the moment. We were seizing the day. No amount of money could buy the joy we felt in our hearts, minds and souls. What was once just a dream was now a profound reality. We carried the banner that read, "We, the People" into the battle for the hearts and minds of the citizens who were not yet convinced there was any faith, hope and charity left in the DNA of the American political scene. We smiled and reached out with both hands to engage everyone in the magic of the moment. We encouraged involvement by being willing to keep our focus on the light that burned brightly from atop the highest mountain.

We were sinners and believers speaking out.

We were running swiftly with the wind.

We were ringing the Liberty Bell and the sound was echoing off every hill and dale, this land is your land and my land, this land was made for you and me.

54. The Great Romney, Obama, Pollack Debate

Everybody on the team wanted to attend the Utica Town Hall Debate so John chartered several tour buses to make the journey to central New York. Given the time of the event, Judy and Carol made motel reservations for everyone. Gram joked saying we had plenty of room on the Liberty Bell Bus to accommodate those who did not mind "pressing the flesh". No one took him up on the offer. Johnny was excited because he was getting a chance to visit with people we met during the bus tour. Al was elated that we were going on the road again. "I've had enough fun at home for a while." When we said this was going to be just a two-day adventure, he said, "That will do for now."

I wanted Basha and Janko to come, but she said she was not ready for the limelight. Janko said he was and implored her to go. She vetoed his request. "We'll be on the road all summer long with Daddy," she said. "You'll get sick and tired of riding all day long from town to town."

"I'll bet I don't," Janko rebutted. I think he accurately estimated his abilities.

Big Jack was concerned we would be overwhelmed with security. Given that President Obama and Mitt Romney would be in attendance, all their security people would dwarf our small force. He did not like the way this was working out, but said, "I'll make the best of it. These guys better stay out of my way and not gum up the works."

The team got on the road very early in the morning so we could be in Utica by late afternoon. The debate was not until 7 pm. Once we arrived, we would have ample time to get settled and relax just a bit. John, Gram and Judy thought it best that we not arrive the day before because this would create the impression that we had nothing else to do but wait for the other candidates to show up. In fact, Johnny suggested that we actually come in late to demonstrate that we were in charge. I vetoed the idea. I did not want to waste anyone's time, least of all, the President's. After all, he was the President of the United States and demanded that much respect.

Located in central New York, Utica was once a major manufacturing city, but was now finding new ways to transition from "Rust to Green". Mayor David Roefaro was leading a movement to create a renaissance in the city and was doing a remarkably good job in encouraging businesses and industries to relocate. The fact we were holding our first town hall debate with the three major candidates made him exceptionally proud and excited.

"You can't tell what this will do for us," he expressed to Gram and Judy when they asked him to be the host. "Words cannot express what I'm thinking and feeling."

We got to Utica about 4 pm, three hours early. The Liberty Bell bus went right to the Utica Memorial Auditorium where the event was scheduled to take place. As we pulled into the parking lot, every major news network was already setting up equipment. The place was a beehive of activity. I was a little intimidated by it all. Gram could sense my nervousness.

"Hey, Leo, these guys put their pants on one leg at a time, and yah, they pee and poop just like you and me," Gram said to reassure me that I was not out of my league. I realized we were entering into the real campaign. Until now, everything was warm-up and practice. This was the big show.

Mayor Roefaro met us as we were disembarking. He was a lively person with a concern for his city and its future and this showed in everything he said and did.

"Welcome to Utica, Mr. Pollack. I'm Mayor David Roefaro."

"Hi, and make that Leo," I said shaking his hand. I introduced the team to him and he welcomed all of us warmly.

"I'm sure you want to get inside and rest a bit. We have some rooms reserved for each of you. I think the media teams will want some time to do their makeup routines. I can't thank you enough for picking Utica and giving us all this free publicity. You know we were once a dying city and now are just beginning to come back to life."

"We hope this event will give you the boost that you need to really take off and go from 'rust to green'," I said to the mayor.

"Oh, so you know about our initiative?" he asked.

"Yes. You are leading the way on the east coast," I said. "Yes, we are very much aware of progressive mayors like you who are not afraid to take risks, look into the future and run forward toward it."

"I'm extremely pleased that you are aware of what we are doing in Utica. Thank you for making my job easier. Now, if you will excuse me, I need to go and meet the president and the other candidate," he said and walked away with a definite bounce in his step.

"He would make a good vice president," Gram commented.

"You think so?" Johnny asked.

"Sure, he knows how to run a small city," Gram said, "and he's hospitable, down to earth, and doing progressive things in an area that sure needs it."

We found our waiting rooms. No sooner did I sit down than a makeup person from NBC showed up and asked if she could "do me?"

"I hope you mean put make-up on," I said.

Everyone laughed at my small joke. There was tension in the room and it was good that she was there to lighten things up a bit. As she "made my face" as she called it, she asked me a number of questions about what I hoped to accomplish in the campaign and beyond. She was very insightful.

"You know, Mr. Pollack, working people all over America are rooting for you tonight. We've had enough people with silver spoons in their mouths telling us what to do. You give us real hope, not the kind we were sold three years ago."

"I'm happy to hear that," I said. "We know how high the stakes are right now and want to make sure that folks like you have a voice."

"In you, we do. Get them tonight. Take no prisoners," she said finishing my face.

"Now that you've made me look like a movie star, I'll do that," I said lightly.

"Would it be too much to ask if I could get your autograph?" she said.

I smiled and thanked her. I signed the back of her pass and then she left.

"How cool was that?" I asked.

"See, Leo, there's nothing to worry about now. The people know who is on their side," Gram said. "Don't be surprised if you hear a lot of booing tonight. Romney's going to get it from the working people who are going to be in the audience. The president may hear some of it as well. He's only taken on this working people theme in the past few months. Three years of nothing and now it is election time and he's all about jobs."

At 6:45 pm, I was escorted to the stage alcove. Gram and Johnny left me waiting in the semi-darkness.

"We're with you all the way, Leo. Give them a dose of reality like only you can do," Johnny said.

"Answer the questions in short, simple phrases. Don't beat a dead horse. Know when to say 'Nuf said'. Got it?" Gram asked.

"Got it. Thanks fellows for all your support. This is one hell of a team to be on."

"You've got it, Leo. Sock it to them," Johnny said to encourage me.

A moment later, the mayor walked up and said, "We're right on time. Mr. Romney and President Obama will be out shortly. I guess you are ready to take the field first. Well, Leo, that doesn't surprise me. You're leading the field in my book."

His smile made me feel totally at ease. "I thank you for those kind words," I said.

The President walked in with his security detail surrounding him.

I smiled at him.

He walked up to me and said, "Mr. Pollack, it is good to meet you."

"I am honored and privileged to meet you, Mr. President," I said. "Thank you for accepting this invitation to debate."

"I guess it's 'game on' from hence forward," he said. I was not sure what he meant.

"Yes, I would say so," was how I responded.

Mitt Romney entered with a flourish. He was a good-looking man, with exceptionally thick hair and a clean face. His eyes were sparkling. He walked up and greeted the president first and then, what almost seemed reluctantly, introduced himself to me.

To fence with him, I said, "It was good of you to finally accept the invitation to come to one of these town hall debates."

He did not respond.

The mayor said we were ready to go. He would give us the call when we were to enter the stage. He walked out into the bright lights and the show began.

"My Fellow Americans, welcome to the third town hall debate being promoted by the Liberty Bell Party and tonight hosted by the City of Utica, New York. I am Mayor David Roefaro and I am excited that our city is hosting the first debate of the 2012 presidential campaign with all three major candidates on stage with us tonight. Let me introduce them. First, the President of the United States, Barack Obama."

President Obama walked onto the stage, waving his hand and taking a seat in the center. Loud cheers filled the room.

"The Republican candidate for President of the United States, Mr. Mitt Romney."

Romney walked out waving and took his seat to the right of the President. His supporters clapped loudly trying to outdo the President's people.

"Finally, the people's candidate, representing the Liberty Bell Party, Mr. Leo Pollack."

I walked out into the light and all I could see was black and white. The faces of the people were gone. The bright lights were overwhelming. I waved and made my way to the seat left of the president. I could hear the eruption as I sat down and realized that I had as great a following in the room as the other men. This buoyed my spirit and gave me a boost of energy.

"Ladies and Gentleman, this town hall debate has only a few simple ground rules. There are no prepared questions. All the questions will come from you, the audience. There are a number of wireless microphones around the room. When you want to ask a question, please raise your hand, get a microphone and ask your question. There is no time limit. We will go until we exhaust the candidates or you, whichever comes first," he said and the people applauded wildly because they liked the idea that they were in control.

"Please be respectful. Please permit the candidate to answer the question. Please express your approval or disapproval in an appropriate manner. When it appears that we are beginning to repeat ourselves, I, and I alone as host, will declare the debate over. Without any further ado, let us begin."

Woman. "Mr. Pollack, you are taking on the two major political parties and I want to know how you hope to compete with them on a national scale given that you are not a well-known person and don't have their name recognition?"

Pollack. "Ma'am, I would like you to consider this. Tonight, we are here debating because our party invited the President and Mr. Romney to come and debate with us. We have invited them twice before and got no response. I think their being here is ample evidence that we can and will compete with these two fine gentlemen."

Man. Mr. Romney, you keep talking about the economy and how bad it is and yet, the jobs numbers keep going up, more people are working now, the stock market is soaring and consumer confidence is almost back to normal. Don't you think that your doom and gloom message is just to make the President look bad and you look good?"

Romney. "Sir, this economy is in a shambles and it is the President's fault. Things might be getting better, but they would be a whole lot better if I were the president. I know how the economy works. I was a businessman for twenty-five years. I ran a company and was very successful at it. I turned around the Olympic Games. I was an effective governor of the great state of Massachusetts. I can lead this country into a better future."

Woman. "President Obama, what do you say to all these claims that you are a Muslim? What makes people continue to think that you are?"

Obama. "Madam. I think the press keeps this myth alive. My father was a Muslim. My mother, grandmother and grandfather raised me to be a Christian. I've been a Christian all my life. If I had used 'Barry Obama' as my name, maybe folks would have thought I was an Irishman. The fact is I do have some Irish ancestry…on my mother's side."

The people laughed at the president's joke.

Man. "This is a question for all three of you. What can you do to put Americans back to work?"

Romney. "My 59 point plan has an extensive agenda for putting Americans back to work. We need to get government out of the way. We need to end regulations that stifle job growth. We need to cut taxes on the 'job creators' and then we'll see the unemployment figures go down. President Obama has not made the right steps to ease this burden on working people. His policies have failed. I can fix them and I will."

Obama. "For more than 23 months, we've had positive job growth in the United States. It is not as fast as I would like it, but it is moving forward steadily. We're still coming out of the worst recession in two generations. We have a way to go, but we are making progress month by month."

Pollack. "Buy American. Put your neighbor to work. End every tax loophole that lets a corporation move its operations offshore. My campaign team wears American made clothes. We drive American made cars. We buy American made products and this is what puts Americans back to work. You can talk about the government being the problem, blame excessive regulation and all that other stuff, but in the end, when the choice is to buy American or buy foreign, and you choose to buy American, you create jobs. Neither Mr. Romney, the President nor I can truly create jobs. We can all create the climate for large and small companies to create jobs by buying their American made products."

I received a resounding applause on this answer.

Woman. "Gentleman, there is what is called a 'war on women' taking place right now. How are you going to end it?"

Romney. "First of all, I didn't start it. President Obama's Obamacare health plan required women's contraceptive prescriptions to be covered by companies and some of these found this to be unacceptable on moral grounds. Still, the president forced the issue. Only after strong opposition to the measures, did the president back down. My wife, Ann, is a woman and my biggest backer and she knows that I am a big supporter of women's rights."

Obama. "I never declared war on women. This is something that the press made up and tried to shove down our throats. One of the first bills I signed was the Lilly Leadbetter Law that made it illegal to pay a woman less for doing the same job a man was doing. The Republicans opposed the bill, but we were able to pass it. I fought hard to keep Planned Parenthood Clinics open. I have two daughters and want them to be able to have the same rights as boys do in the society we live."

Pollack. "The war on women is real, but it wasn't Mr. Romney or the President who started it. Around the country, in conservative states there are repressive measures being passed that are making it harder for women to receive the reproductive care they need. This is what is at the core of this struggle. I don't know what makes men think that they know what is best for women. I applaud those congresswomen in numerous states that are making it mandatory for men to receive counseling if they want to get Viagra or Cialis. Let men feel the same kind of disrespect that women are made to feel and then see how quickly this furor over women's reproductive rights ends."

Man. "Mr. Romney, many people think you are out of touch with reality and that you can't relate to the average, working person. Sir, is it true that you are building a home in San Diego and there is going to be an elevator in it to bring your car from the road up to the garage? Oh yes, and when was the last time you pumped gas for yourself?"

There was some laughter after this question.

Romney. "The answer is yes, I am building a house in San Diego that has a very unique problem and that is my car is down on the road and I can't drive it into the garage because the hill is so steep and the only solution is to install what you might call an elevator. It's just a simple way to raise the car up to the garage and be able to park it. That's all. As for pumping my own gas, I do that regularly when I'm not flying from one campaign stop to another. I don't drive much right now, you know."

Woman. "Gentlemen, this question is for all three of you.
What is the current price of milk, bread, sliced bologna, a bag of Fuji Apples and single ply toilet tissue?"

A roar broke out when the woman finished.

Obama. "Madam, I'm really not sure because the people in the White House do all the shopping, and before we moved to Washington, Michelle took care of that end of our domestic affairs."

Romney. "I would like to take a guess, but that would be all that it is. I don't know."

Pollack. "You hit almost all the essentials. For me, I would include popcorn on the list. I'd rather eat popcorn than steak. Okay. The prices vary, but in Safeway, the store nearest my home where Basha and I shop, milk is averaging about $4.29 a gallon for whole. The kind of bread we eat is made in my hometown. Schwebel's Rye costs $3.29 for a one pound loaf. I love it. Sliced bologna, the generic kind I eat, costs $1.89 regular price and on sale, I can sometimes get four packs for $5.00. We stock up when it gets that cheap. Fuji apples the other day were $4.89 for a four-pound bag. Toilet tissue is important stuff. We get the generic four-pack for $2.29, single sheet variety. It's easier on the sewer system than the two-ply version. Oh, and popcorn is $1.49 for a two pound bag at Walmart. Yes, that is one thing I do buy at Wallyworld."

The people applauded my answer. I heard many women shouting comments acknowledging my awareness of the cost of household goods.

Man. "President Obama, what difference would it make if we left Afghanistan this week rather than waiting for another two years and pulling our troops out in 2014?"

Obama. "I think we need to give Afghanistan time to finish preparing its military and police forces to take over security tasks by the date set in the SOFA we agreed to with the leaders of that country. To leave before then might undermine their overall successful transition to self-protection."

Man. "Mr. Romney, how would you answer the question?"

Romney. "I think we leave all decisions to the generals, to the leaders on the ground. Let them decide. Telling the enemy when we are pulling out just plays into its hands. They can just wait us out. I think this is poor leadership, and when I'm president, I will do things differently. One thing I will do is expand our military by at least 100,000 troops and increase military spending to make us the best military in the world.

Man. "Mr. Pollack?"

Pollack. "First of all, we have the best military in the world. We spend more on our armed forces than all the other industrialized nations combined. Secondly, I'd pull out now. No nation throughout history that has ever invaded Afghanistan has been able to change that country. To believe we have really changed it is ludicrous. We have done nothing to end the heroin trafficking. We have not changed the way we are perceived by most Afghanis. We are still perceived as an occupying force. No, we can pull out tomorrow, no, how about today, and bring all our troops home and spend our treasure here rather than abroad."

Two hours into the debate, the Mayor called for a twenty-minute intermission. People acknowledged the gesture with a loud round of applause. The break gave me time to go to the bathroom. The hot lights made me a little queasy. We started back on time.

Woman. "President Obama, we know who your candidate for Vice President is, but we don't know who Mr. Romney or Mr. Pollack is going to choose. Would you gentlemen wish to elaborate on this decision?"

Romney. "Right now, my campaign staff is vetting a host of the most qualified people in the country. I have not made a decision yet. I know that whomever I pick, he, or she, yes, I'm considering some women too, you know, women make up 52% of the voting public, will be an asset to my ticket and serve well as vice president in a Romney administration."

Pollack. "To return to post- revolutionary war times, the vice president was the person who got the second most votes after the president in the general election. I think that was a much better system than what we have today. I am not disparaging President Obama's choice of former Senator Joseph Biden to be his Vice President. Frankly, I voted for them. I would be honored to have either President Obama or Mr. Romney as my vice-president. Being realistic, I know this is not going to happen. I would like to open the field to anyone who wants to apply for the job. If you are a man or woman who is eligible, is willing to work long hours, knows how to see both sides of an issue, then I encourage you to apply for the job on our home page, **www.ringingthelibertybell.org**. If you are the lucky candidate chosen, realize this; the job is for four years only. After that, you'll have to go back into private life. I don't plan on serving more than four years as president."

The audience liked my answer so well they gave me a standing ovation.

Man. "Given the uncertain times we live in, what does it take to be successful in this world? Do you think that working hard will provide you or anyone else with a secure living?"

Obama. "I believe that if you get a good education you can and will get a good job. A good job is what insures that you will have a secure lifestyle. While nothing is certain in this life, this is the best way to make sure that it happens for you.

Romney. "I bought and sold companies at Bain Capital. I was very successful at it. I worked hard and made a lot of money because I was not afraid to take risks. Our society rewards risk takers. I believe the risk takers, the entrepreneurs, are the foundation of a health economy. Yes, a secure lifestyle is possible if you are willing to be a risk taker."

Pollack. "While I would like to believe in the simplistic answers that my two competitors have presented, the answer is no. It's simple math. There aren't enough jobs out there to give everyone a secure lifestyle. No matter how hard everyone works, someone will still fill the low paying jobs because there aren't enough high paying jobs to go around. Given the continued attack by the conservatives in this country on working people's wages and benefits, even the most secure jobs like teaching, police and fire protection, the rock bed middle class jobs for the past half century, are losing their security. The only people who are secure are the multi-millionaires who really are immune to any fluctuations in the job market because they got theirs and they don't need anymore."

Man. "Mr. Romney, your healthcare plan that you signed into law in Massachusetts is really working well. Polls indicate the people really like it. Why do you keep saying that on the first day you are in office you will repeal Obamacare? Obamacare was based on your own program?"

Romney. "I'll repeal Obamacare because it gives too much power to the federal government. We need to leave health care reform up to the states, not the federal government. The federal government is getting too big. We need to cut it down to size."

Man. "Mr. Obama?"

Obama. "Mr. Romney has a difficult time accepting credit for doing something good. I applauded his efforts on health care reform when he was governor. I liked his plan so well we made it the template for our own plan. What we did was expand it to include many uninsured people that would not qualify because of pre-existing conditions. We are very thankful that Mr. Romney set the stage for what we accomplished."

Romney. "May I respond to the Mr. Obama's comments?"

Mayor. "No. That is not in the rules. There is no rebuttal."

Man. "Mr. Pollack.

Pollack. "I think former Governor Romney did a fine job in Massachusetts developing the template for the health care reform act. President Obama fought long and hard with the Republicans and his own party to make some healthcare reforms. I don't think either plan went far enough. In the end, the profit motive in health care is driving the cost up. Health care is not an option. It is not something that you can avoid. If you are alive today, some day, during your lifetime, you will need to seek health care. Unless you are worth millions, you will need health care insurance. Therefore, the sooner we make single payer health care available to all Americans, the better off we will all be. Regardless of what lobbyists and special interest groups say and do, most Americans would rather see this kind of system in effect right now."

Man. "What is wrong with the American economy?"

Obama. "We inherited a mess. We've worked diligently for three and a half years to keep us from falling into a serious depression. We've turned the corner on the recession. We still have a way to go before we are completely recovered. The fact of the matter is this; Democrats have tried a host of ideas to make things better and at each step along this pathway, the Republicans have been the party of 'No'."

Romney. "Yes, I will acknowledge that President Obama inherited a tough economy. However, he made it worse by not acting decisively and by pursuing policies that added to and did not solve the problems. I know economics. I know how to run a business. I know how to make the tough decisions that will fix this economy. I think our government is too big. I'll shrink it. I think our budget is too lopsided in favor of discretionary spending. I'll end that. I think we have too many people waiting for the government to give them a handout. I'll stop the welfare state from growing."

Pollack. "We're experiencing some of the worst financial problems in 75 years because we let big banks and other lending institutions gamble with other people's money. I would re-institute the Glass-Steagall Act. Secondly, the ability of every working person to collectively bargain for his or her labor is a civil right. These so called, 'Right to Work' laws are a sham. How does it profit a company to pay its employees poorly hoping to make a little more money, only to find out that because its employees can't afford to buy the products it produces, it is forced to lay off the employees who make the very products it wants to sell? The American corporations' hostility to working people needs to end. We are in this together: CEOs, managers, labor leaders and workers. The sooner we accept this fact, the better off we will be."

Working people in the room applauded loudly when I finished my statement.

Woman. "What would each of you do to fix the economy?"

Obama. "I've been working on this for the past three and a half years and I think we've made a lot of progress. I hope to see us end the recession and move into a full employment economy. I think our stimulus plan kept us out of a deeper recession. We can see that saving the auto companies bolstered our economy, saved many jobs and is paying dividends in consumer confidence. While I could talk more about what we have done, I know we have a whole lot more to do and I'm up to the task of making the tough decisions that will insure a better future for America and Americans."

Romney. "The president is wrong. He's failed this country. He's made the worse decisions possible. He has extended the pain we feel as Americans. The unemployment numbers are still too high. We need to lower corporate taxes as an incentive to get them to begin reinvesting in America again. We need to institute a flat tax. We need to give incentives to entrepreneurs to create the businesses of the future. Lastly, we need to end the glut of government regulations that make running a business more expensive in America than anywhere in the world."

Pollack. "President Obama has done a fair job in making the economy work better. I don't agree with anything that Mr. Romney says he would do to improve the economy. He is pro-business and not pro-people. Corporations are not people. They are legal entities created by people to make business more efficient. In the creation of them, we forgot to put one thing into the corporate charter: a soul. Of course, we are in financial trouble. Our government checkbook is in disarray. We keep issuing new debt to pay old debt. It's like a family paying off their Visa bill with their MasterCard. In the long term, it doesn't work. Printing more money is devaluing the dollar. This country's massive debt must be paid. If not, we are going to be consumed by our mounting interest payments. Americans are going to have to pay more in taxes. Some economists have been telling us for 40 years debt doesn't matter and what we have discovered is that they lied. It does matter, and we need to address the issue now. It will be hard. We will have to pay more taxes. The only way we can do this is if we have higher paying jobs. The government must learn your money is not its money. At every level, money can only be spent to benefit you, not the government. Sorry, big parties are out. I won't have an expensive victory party at your expense. Nor will the campaign donations pay for one. We can celebrate just as well by getting down to business and ending this credit card economy, once and for all."

A roar went up in the audience. I hit a nerve that made the citizens really feel the impact of what needed to be done.

Man. "Mr. Pollack, which are you? A socialist, a communist, a Nazi or fascist?"

Pollack. E. None of the above. I'm an American who believes in a government of, for and by the people. We haven't seen this type of government for a long time. With your help, I aim to bring it back again."

Woman. "Mr. Romney, most people consider you irrelevant in this election. What do you say about that?"

Romney. "Well, I don't know who most people are and what they think. I don't think I'm irrelevant. My wife, Ann, doesn't think I'm irrelevant. My five sons, whom I'm very proud of, don't think I'm irrelevant. I think I'm very relevant. That's my answer."

Man. "President Obama, why should we think you will do anything different in the next four years when you didn't get it done in the first four years?"

Obama. "We started to do a lot of good things. We need more time to finish. This is what I want to do in my last four years: finish what we've started. I'm asking you to give me the chance to do it."

Man. "Mr. Pollack, what do you think of your opponents?"

Pollack. I respect and admire President Obama for his accomplishments, his honesty, integrity and his being a good family man. I respect Mr. Romney for his success as a business man and for being a good family man."

Man. "What do you think about them as president or president to be?"

Pollack. "I think the American people will judge who they think will best serve the majority of Americans in 2012 and beyond. What I think of President Obama or Mr. Romney is not important. I'm not running for office to please them but to serve the people."

Man. "That's it?"

Pollack. "That's it."

Woman. "Mr. Pollack, is it true that you cook for everyone who travels with you on the Liberty Bell Bus?" Laughter broke out in the crowd.

Pollack. "Yes, it is true. They won't let me drive, answer the phone or do anything but cook. I don't mind because it keeps me busy and out of trouble. I'm no gourmet cook, mind you. My specialty is macaroni, cheese and tuna fish casserole. Note the emphasis is on casserole. Usually, my version of this dish comes straight out of the four quart pot."

More laughter. Even Romney and Obama smiled. I waved to all those who found my effort humorous.

Man. "President Obama, you've struggled to get people to accept your health care plan. What do you hope to do in another term to insure that the plan, as designed, actually gets implemented?"

Obama. "That's a tough one. Almost every day, you see and hear the Republicans trying to undermine the plan in one way or another. Twenty-three Republican state attorney general's filed law suits against the health care plan and now it is before the Supreme Court. If the court upholds the bill, I will be happy. If it does not, then I think most Americans will lose the benefits of the health care reform we crafted. I wish people were less mean spirited and more open minded about what we can do to make the lives of those who do not have health care better."

Man. "Mr. Romney?"

Romney. "I think if we let the private sector and the free market economy work, the health care issue will get resolved in a most satisfactory way. Too much government intervention is what makes the system bog down."

Man. "Mr. Pollack?"

Pollack. "Let's keep it really simple. Three hundred and seven million Americans all have one plan that is negotiated by Medicare. The risk is spread across the entire population and all pay for it equally. We accept that we are our brother's and sister's keeper. We eliminate the fear of getting sick, of getting old and not being able to cover insurance costs. We pay for it by sharing the expense across all people that work. After all, we spend the most amount of money in the entire world per person on health care. We ought to get a lot more bang for our buck."

Woman. "Mr. Romney, I heard you on television talking about Planned Parenthood and this is what you said. "We'll just get rid of it?" What did you mean by that and aren't you one of the people that has declared war on women?"

Romney. I may have said something about getting rid of Planned Parenthood as we know it, but I would not get rid of Planned Parenthood because it does provide services to women. You can ask my wife, Ann, if I respect women. She'll tell you. I'm her biggest supporter and she's one heck of a woman."

Man. "Mr. Pollack, don't you think that never having held political office in your life you've bitten off more than you can chew?"

Pollack. No. I'm not a professional politician, but I am a very practical person. I know how to work hard. I know how to work easy, too. I know how to ask questions and learn from others. I know how to ask for help. I am able to inspire people to do good work. I think I'm eminently qualified to lead this country having never held office before because I don't owe anyone, anything. Isn't this the one major complaint that we and I include myself in this equation, complain about politicians? We think they are more concerned about being re-elected than serving the people. We believe they are unduly influenced by special interest groups. I am not going to seek two terms. Secondly, we've raised our money completely through small donations. I am beholden to know one except the people who vote for me. This makes me unique and the one candidate in your lifetime and mine who cannot be bought and sold."

Man.   "Mr. Romney, why can't you seem to connect with the average voter? You can talk to the rich people easily enough. You've said many times that your friends own race car teams. Yet, when it comes to simple folks, you act like a fish out of water."

Romney. "I think I connect well with all Americans. There is a perception that I'm above everyone else. Just because I have a lot of money doesn't mean that I'm not a regular guy. After all, I put my pants and shirt on like any other person."

Woman. "President Obama, what are you going to do to end the debate about whether or not you were born in the United States and if you are really an American citizen?"

Laughter erupted. The President let it die down.

Obama. "I don't know. Can you help me? Just when I think this issue has been buried forever, someone like Donald Trump will come along and ask the same question all over again. Can you help me?"

The people laughed.

Man. "Mr. Pollack, you are an unemployed steel worker, right?"

Pollack. "Yes sir."

Man. "You've been getting unemployment benefits for about a year now, right?"

Pollack. "Yes sir."

Man. "When are your benefits going to run out?"

Pollack. "When the states stops paying them."

Man.   "Don't you feel guilty living off unemployment benefits and running around the country trying to become president?"

Pollack. "No, not at all. I am really looking for a job and it pays better than the one I have."

The crowd roared.

Pollack. "Seriously, sir. I understand what you're getting at so let me be candid. I did not want to get laid off. I want to work every day. I want to be productive. I love making steel. However, for whatever reason, I was laid off. I was eligible, by law, for unemployment benefits. My company paid for this insurance. It costs them quite a bit of money to provide this benefit. I don't take the money and think, 'Oh, this is the best of all possible worlds getting paid for doing nothing.' In the end, sir, I think it is not healthy to not work and be paid. However, as long as the benefit is there and I am legally entitled to receive it, I will take it. Once the benefits run out, I will be using my savings to get by and that time will come very soon."

Man. "You don't feel guilty about living on the dole?"

Pollack. "I'm not living on the dole, sir. I'm living off unemployment compensation benefits that are a part of my company's benefits plan. If it were illegal to get the money, I wouldn't take it. I am eligible for it so I accept it as part of my condition of employment at the steel mill."

Romney. "It's unemployment benefits and all those other government subsidies and entitlements that make the cost of doing business in America so great that corporations are forced to move off shore to save money."

There was silence in the auditorium. I was not sure what to say, so I let the pregnant pause hang. Before anyone could respond, Romney went on.

Romney. "Americans have gotten used to reaching out for the government to do too many things for them. Once government is cut down to size, then Americans will once again do things for themselves."

Still, more silence.

The mayor said, "Mr. Romney…" but Romney continued his rampage.

Romney. "When I'm president, we'll create incentives to work hard and penalties for shirking personal responsibility. This is the American way. We know what works and what does not work and paying people not to work just doesn't cut it. It makes people lazy and unproductive and, in the long run, hurts the economy and America in general."

Someone in the crowd started booing and it caught on. Romney tried to play it off, but the look on his face told the entire story.

Obama. "Folks. Folks. We don't need this now. Mr. Romney is stating his opinion. Let it be, folks. Booing won't get us anywhere. This is what makes for bad feelings. I don't agree with Mr. Romney, but I'm not going to boo him."

Pollack. "Thanks, Mr. President."

Romney. "You see, this is what is the matter with America today. A man can't say what he believes and be disrespected. This is not the way America is supposed to be. I tell you, this is going to change."

Mayor. "Gentlemen, we have been at this for almost four hours. I think we may be running out of questions. To end this town hall debate, each of you can make a closing statement. There is no time limit. You are on your own. President Obama, as our sitting president and leader, you may go first."

Obama. "My fellow Americans. You entrusted me with the honor of being your president three and a half years ago. We've faced some hard times together. We've made tough decisions. We've accomplished a lot in this short period. However, there is more to do. I'm asking you to re-elect me so that together, we can finish the important work we set out to do four years ago. Thank you, God bless you, and God Bless America."

For an extended period of time, the crowd applauded wildly.

Mayor. "Mr. Romney, you may go next."

Romney. "Thank you, my fellow Americans, for giving me this opportunity to be your president. I will not disappoint you. I promise you that I will use all my God given talents, wisdom, abilities to lead this country into a new era of total prosperity. America's greatest days are ahead of us, not behind us. America needs a proven leader, a savvy businessman, to take it into this century as the true leader of the free world. I am the person to lead this nation forward. By voting for me, you are voting to insure that America's future remains great. Thank you. God bless you, and God bless America."

There was muted cheering.

Mayor. "Mr. Pollack, it is your turn."

Pollack. "Only in America, can a young person grow up and aspire to become the leader of this great nation. President Obama has fulfilled that dream, and because of it, I admire him immensely. Only in America, can a young person grow up and aspire to be successful in business and industry. Mr. Romney has accomplished this and for it, he is to be commended. I am that young person who is fulfilling his own dream. A year ago, I became distraught when I saw my fellow workers facing an uncertain future because the mills were closing and the recession was tightening its grip on the working people of this nation. I realized this was not the American dream. I wanted to champion its return to the American experience. As president, I believe I can lead this nation into an era when people will see themselves as a part of the whole with a share in its purpose. Together, we can return this country to a government of, for and by the people. I am a simple man with a simple vision, but it is no different than Thomas Jefferson's was when he penned the Declaration of Independence. Come, join me in Ringing the Liberty Bell once again and make America fulfill its promise. Let's pray that God blesses us each and every day even though we sometimes don't deserve it. Thank you."

Everyone in the auditorium stood up and gave us a standing ovation. The debate was over. I shook the President's hand and thanked him again for accepting the invitation. He smiled but it was strained. Romney came over and congratulated me on a fine job. I said, "You're welcome." He moved on quickly to the press corps that was waiting nearby to ask him more questions. President Obama was deluged with those who wanted his autograph and to wish him well. I meandered out into the crowd where the people were and there I spent the next hour and a half answering more questions, getting my picture taken with babies, brothers and sisters, and hearing the plight of the people who mattered.

By midnight, the crowd was disappearing, President Obama and Romney were long gone and I was closing down the auditorium with the Mayor and some of his people. Gram, Johnny and the team were busy with logistics.

"Wonderful night, wouldn't you say?" the mayor said.

"Extraordinary would describe it better," I replied.

"Leo, you must feel like a million bucks right now. I mean, you've brought the debate to the people. Imagine that? Tonight, the people were doing the asking, and the candidates the talking. No stuffy moderator. No prepared scripts. No time limits. What an amazing process. What a way to do politics. I would like to adopt this method the next time we hold mayoral races. I mean it. Get the people involved."

"I agree, mayor, and all I can say is do it."

"What's next for you?"

"Get something to eat, drive home, sleep," I said.

The mayor laughed and said, "You really are a simple guy, aren't you?"

"What you see is what you get."

"I thought Mr. Romney was going to lose it tonight," the mayor said. "That's the reason I cut the debate off at that moment."

"You saved him, that's for sure," I said. "That was very diplomatic of you."

"You know I'm a Republican," the mayor said.

"I didn't know that," I replied.

"I'm disappointed in my party. We've lost our way. We pander to those who have an axe to grind. I'm losing my intent. I can't brook the chronic mean-spiritedness."

"Neither can I," I said.

"What is a man to do?"

"Come and join me," I said. "The VP job is open. You could apply. I'm serious. Think about it."

We laughed, shook hands again and thanked one another for the memories. I exited the auditorium and headed back to the bus. The team was gathered together and waiting for me.

"Well?" I asked.

They slapped me on the back, hugged me, clapped, hooted and hollered.

"Leo, Leo, Leo," they chanted.

"Folks, let's not get carried away."

"Carried away! Leo, we just made American history! Do you realize our kids will be reading about tonight in history books in the not too distant future?" John said.

"Amazing Grace!" Al said. Amazing Grace."

"I feel honored and privileged to shake the hand of the next president of the United States," Johnny said shaking my hand sideways and giving me a hug. "I'll never forget the end when Romney stuck his foot in his mouth and Obama bailed him out. What a man! He deserves a medal for that gesture."

"Obama is a class act. He could have left Romney dangling slowly in the wind, but he saved him," Gram said.

"Fellows, thanks for all your support. I couldn't have done it without your backing me all the way. I mean it," I said.

"If you really mean it, will you make us something other than Mac and cheese and tuna fish on the way home?" Johnny asked.

"I'll do my best," I said.

My phone rang. I looked at the screen. Basha was calling.

"Oh, Leo," I heard her say when I answered, "my love, you were wonderful. I watched every moment of it with Janko. He wants to say something."

Janko said, "Daddy, that was you and the president sitting side by side. How cool! Now the kids at school won't make fun of me anymore. They'll know that my Daddy knows the president. I love you, Daddy. Here's Mommy."

"Will you be home tonight?" Basha asked.

"Yes, so please leave the light on for me," I requested.

"I'll leave more than that on for you tonight," she added.

"On or off?" I asked.

"Silly goose, I love you."

"I love you."

As a team, we made a decision to head home instead of staying in a motel. We did not need to spend the money. Most members of the team wanted to sleep in their own beds. As we headed west across Interstate 90, our buses formed a caravan. I cooked teriyaki noodles for the fellows. They sang my praises for almost five minutes after they finished eating. Al said he was not hungry. "Too excited," he maintained.

A little after five AM, we rolled into town. We invited all to come in for a celebration coffee, but everyone asked for a rain check.

When I crawled into bed, I found my two lovers sleeping peacefully. Basha woke up and held my hand.

"He was so excited tonight that he couldn't sleep and asked if he could stay with me until you got home," she whispered to me.

We hugged him and one another. A sleepy Janko woke up, kissed us both and fell back asleep. We did not have the heart to move him.

We fell asleep happily in one another's arms, one happy, simple family together once again.

Some dreams will never end. Others will never be fulfilled. Who can tell the difference? Who would want to anyway?

55. Miles to Go Before I Sleep

I was sleeping like a dead one so I did not hear or see anything.

The crowd started to arrive early in the day. Someone passed the message via Twitter that we were holding a big block party. Caravaners from all over the country rolled into town. The police closed the roads leading to my home on Oxford, and that made it safe for everyone to set up their tail gate parties on the streets.

Fritz came over with a huge 60" flat screen TV and set it up on the front porch for everyone to be able to see. Inside the house, he installed another one that covered the wall in the dining room. We were amazed by its size. "Sure beats your 19" box doesn't it?" Fritz said as he made the final connections.

"Leo's Friends" as we called everyone who helped us in any way in our frenetic march across America were invited. Seth Rogan, Erin Kennedy, Matt Laner, Jesse Sepulveda, Bill Reilly, Jason Witt, Hollie Stram, Chris Tye and many other state coordinators arrived in the early afternoon. I was excited to see all of them. We shared treasured moments with one another. They were ready for a great night's entertainment.

Jennifer Williamson flew in from New York. Johnny went and picked her up at the airport. He showed her every consideration. She was a lovely young woman and I could see what made Johnny so excited to be her escort for the day. She was nominated for the Pulitzer Prize for her coverage of our campaign. She thanked me repeatedly for being so available to her and giving her all the copy she could handle. "Oh, I think it was Johnny who made that possible. He was always saying to the team that we needed to contact Jennifer and give her the scoop." Johnny winked at me but I didn't wink back.

Gram and Judy were comparing notes, calling state coordinators who were staffing the polls across the country, maintaining a huge white board set up in the kitchen to Basha's discontent, laughing and chatting and clearly enjoying one another's company. They were prepared to keep us posted throughout the night with the latest election results.

Al brought Marie and his eight kids to the house early in the day. Marie helped Basha with the snacks. They reinforced their friendship even though they met just a few times during the campaign. Being mothers bonded them intimately. Basha was amazed at Marie's ability to care for so many little ones. The Caruso children ranged in age from four to fourteen. Watching them together made me wonder if Basha would have enjoyed having more than one child. We made it just in time. We created our diamond.

John, Carol and the phone bank teams showed up in the middle of the afternoon. John took over the barbecuing in the front yard. I think we counted more than a dozen grills lined up down the sidewalk. Krafchik's Meat and Poultry donated a ton of hamburger and hot dogs, and of course, Polish sausage. Coolers were filled to the brim with meat. Schwebel's Bakery provided the hamburger and hot dog buns. Carol spread good cheer throughout the crowd by distributing Leo Pollack for President Buttons, tee shirts, hats, and other memorabilia. We wanted our supporters to have everything they needed to celebrate.

Jim Kilpatrick brought his family and wandered around the festivities. He was amazed at the number of people from all over the country. I really liked him. He defied the banker stereotype. He was warm, friendly, pragmatic and a wonderful man. His support made our finances so easy to manage. We did not face one discrepancy throughout the campaign and that was due to his impeccable attention to detail.

Richard Johnson surprised us when he walked into the living room and said, "I heard there was a party here today." His tireless work for us in the Deep South made our campaign a viable contender in what was for thirty years solidly Republican country. We hoped to steal the thunder down below the Mason-Dixon Line and this was because of his efforts.

Big Jack was omnipresent and invisible. He never stopped. I could not have had a closer friend, brother, bodyguard, protector, human shield and pair of infrared eyes that never slept. Today, he introduced me to most of his crew. I met each one with joy. I shook each one's hand and gave him or her a hug. I thought I might have seen them before but could not remember. Jack made them invisible but omnipresent. I had tears in my eyes when I realized many of these men and women were actually my work colleagues from the steel mill. No wonder I was so well protected. They were steel workers. The best.

R&R were enjoying themselves. Kind of. They were still on duty. They did not like the confusion of a block party. It complicated the task of providing for my security. I assured them we would be safe. We were among friends. I encouraged them to eat and drink as much as they wanted and enjoy the moment. Ron Jeffords thanked me and then disappeared into the crowd. Ray Hood took my offer to heart and ate heartily and then decided to take over and do some barbecuing for the crowd. We got a picture of him with an apron on and a beer in his hand and threatened to send it to his boss. "When you win, you'll be my new boss and you can cover my ass," he said, while he went about flipping burgers and turning hot dogs.

The 60" wide screen TV on the front porch was streaming election coverage from all over the country. There was a sense of surrealism about the display and that was because my picture and name continued to flash across the screen as the commentators tried to factor in the "Pollack Effect" on the election. "What will Pollack's strong showing in so many swing states mean to the president's re-election chances? How will Pollack destroy Romney's efforts to unseat an incumbent president? Stay tuned as we continue to interpret every nuance of this unique 2012 Presidential Election," Wolf Blitzer concluded on CNN. Somehow, Fritz created a program that would let the programming move from channel to channel and avoid any commercials. We received nothing but news coverage. How cool!

Jeeves rode his bicycle to the party. He was a strange bird, but his charisma was infectious. For some reason, he was a hit with Al's kids and Janko. He showed them a number of magic tricks. Before we knew it, he was doing a Penn and Teller show on the street corner for all the children. He was the hit of the party.

My body was filled with adrenalin. I could not sit still. As the day progressed, I wandered through the crowds, met with caravaners, rekindled relationships, laughed, cried, hugged, kissed and hoped that everyone was having a wonderful time. As far as I could see, there were people milling around and the scene could only be called a zeitgeist. What an honor to have so many people show up who believed in what we were doing. I thanked everyone who came to be a part of our celebration. No matter what the results were tomorrow morning, we had won.

Every now and then, I would catch sight of Janko and his Caruso chums. They were running around everywhere, sodas in hand, eating hotdogs, laughing and having the time of their lives. I was excited for them. What a way for children to be introduced to politics.

Whenever I passed through the house, I would seek out Basha, put my arms around her, and tell her I loved her. "You don't have to work all day. We have more than enough to eat." She looked at me and said, "Leo, this is my party, too. Let me do my thing. You've had your fun. Now it's my turn." I kissed her neck and left her to her own devices. She was such a treasure.

Now and then, I could hear booing erupt in the crowd. When I would ask what was going on, someone in the group would say something like, "They're minimizing your chances. They think this is still a two-man race. Where have they been for the past six months? Don't they know that this race is wide open and you are going to take more states than they can count?" I hoped so. My true believers were adamant in their support.

Johnny and Jennifer were really hitting it off. I watched them from the shadows and wondered if something would emerge from their close encounter of the most important kind. I wondered the same about Gram and Judy. They were a couple of mature people. Judy was a class act. Gram was an officer and a gentleman. I wished the best for them. For everyone! Happiness was a real treasure and everyone deserved to find his or her share.

The weather was glorious with brilliant sunshine and crystal blue skies and an Indian Summer-feel that made everyone burst with joy. We did not pray for it, but received it anyway. We were getting our last tan of the season and everyone appreciated this fringe benefit.

I was so excited I did not remember eating or drinking all day long. I must have indulged in some of the delights present everywhere. The caravaners were tailgating and the plethora of food, the scents and smells wafted into the air. The neighborhood was filled with the odor of culinary America. Every known ethnic dish was represented. This made our celebration a United Nations event.

My hand grew weary with the number of autographs I signed. Flashes going off as I posed for pictures with my supporters glazed my eyes. Thankfully, the only questions I had to answer were "How do you feel, Leo?" and "What do you think?". I felt great and what I thought was the election was in the hands of Americans and that they would decide in our favor.

Our house was completely open and there were people milling about in every room upstairs and down. The lights were blaring. The television set in the dining room was tuned to MSNBC. The smaller set in the living room was displaying the NPR coverage from Washington with Jim Lehrer hosting with Judy Woodruff and Bill Moyers, my favorite journalist, assisting.

The polls were scheduled to close in Ohio at 8 pm. We decided to gather in time to catch the first results. I demanded that Basha and Janko come and sit with me on the couch and watch the show. She reluctantly took off her apron and came and sat down beside me. Janko was lassoed by Johnny and Jennifer and dragged into the room. Surrounding us were the rest of the team: John, Judy, Carol, Gram, Johnny, Al and Marie, Big Jack, yes, he came inside, Richard, Jim Kilpatrick, Jeeves, and as many of the phone bank team that could fit. There was not an inch of space open, but it felt wonderfully close and personal.

It was time.

A year and a half of work was on the line.

The faces of the people revealed the joy and enthusiasm that they felt now that the work was done and the results were about to flow.

I gripped Basha's hand and wrapped my arm around Janko's shoulder. We were pressed together on the couch because Johnny and Jennifer, Gram and Judy, joined us.

We stared at the wide screen television as Rachel Maddow, the hostess for the MSNBC reporting team, welcomed all of us to the 2012 Presidential Campaign.

"With the polls closing in a number of states across the country," Rachel Maddow said, "the races are too close to call. Yes, there is no clear winner in any state thus far. But, in a surprising turn of events, NBC news is prepared to call the race in Ohio. With 17% of the polling stations reporting, NBC is declaring…"

"Leo, Leo, wake up…Leo, you've got to get moving. Remember where you're going today. Leo…"

My eyes opened and a vision of pure loveliness greeted me.

"What?" I whispered.

"The campaign!" Basha cried out. "You've got to get up and run, my love."

"Yes, yes, so many miles to go…"

THE END

for 2012 A.D.